The Origins of Modern Mexico

Laurens Ballard Perry, General Editor
Universidad Veracruzana

Juárez and Díaz
Machine Politics
in Mexico

Laurens Ballard Perry

Northern Illinois University Press   DeKalb 1978

About the artist: The scenes depicted on the jacket, frontispiece, and in the details throughout the book are from original artwork created by Mario Pérez Orona especially for the Origins of Modern Mexico series. Mario Pérez has exhibited his paintings, collages, and drawings in more than twenty-five exhibitions throughout Mexico in the past fifteen years.

Library of Congress Cataloging in Publication Data

Perry, Laurens Ballard   1934–
    Juárez and Díaz.

    (The Origins of modern Mexico)
    Bibliography: p.
    Includes index.
    1. Mexico—Politics and government—1867–1910.
2. Díaz, Porfirio, Pres. Mexico, 1830–1915.
3. Juárez, Benito Pablo, Pres. Mexico, 1806–1872.
I. Title. II. Series.
F1233.5.P44   320.9'71'081   76–14671
ISBN 0–87580–058–0

Copyright © 1978 by Northern Illinois University Press
Published by the Northern Illinois University Press
DeKalb, Illinois 60115
Manufactured in the United States of America

DEDICATED TO
Dorothy C. Perry
who demonstrated to me
the pleasures of being
a teacher and a historian;
and to
Dolores, David, Vico, and Stephen—
beautiful young people

Contents

List of Appendixes

List of Maps

Preface

Traditional periodization of nineteenth-century Mexican history marks the Independence Period from the first decade of the century to 1821 or 1824, the Early Republic to 1854, the Reform and Intervention to 1867, the Restored Republic to 1876, and the Porfirian Period to 1910 or 1911. The latter dates refer respectively to the commencement of the Great Revolution of the twentieth century and the resignation of Porfirio Díaz from power. This periodization has all the conveniences and inconveniences and gives rise to the disputes among historians characteristic of periodization elsewhere; it is honored, modified, or disregarded according to the politics, interpretations, and purposes of each historian. One of the implications of this study is that 1876 was less a watershed in Mexican history than traditional periodization affirms.

In its narrowest sense the scope of the present study is limited to the politics and militarism of the period of the Restored Republic from 1867 to 1876. It commences with the optimism of the stunning liberal victory against the Maximilian empire and the vindication of the republican ideals of the Constitution of 1857, and it terminates with the nation in full civil war and beginning of the establishment of the dictatorship of Porfirio Díaz. One principal concern is to explain how the optimism of 1867 was misplaced and in what ways the liberal republic failed. The study, however, does not merely narrate the political and military events of the decade. It also attempts to examine the governmental system, the liberal model upon which it was based, and the tragic flaw in the Mexican political character. Thus the study, both narrower than a comprehensive history of the Restored Republic and broader than the immediate tragedy of the decade, aspires to explain the failure of liberalism, the origins of modern machine politics in Mexico, and to some degree the Latin American condition in general.

The study is divided into two parts. The first demonstrates how the liberal model failed to respond to the concrete conditions of Mexico and in what ways the real political practice deviated from the model. The issues and their implications are presented in an introductory chapter. Then studied in detail in the following chapters are several of the component parts of the political system as practiced: the origins of opposition factions, the conduct and consequences of elections, the importance of political rivalry in the states, the manifestations of federalism and its fate, and the significance of congressional factionalism. The Benito Juárez administration from 1867 to 1872 and the administration of Sebastián Lerdo de Tejada from 1872 to 1876 are analyzed for the opposition they created. One theme continually emphasized throughout this first part is how the political practices contributed to the establishment of a monolithic political machine that tended to monopolize political office. Another theme is the manner in which the political system alienated individuals and groups who turned to insurrection as a means of seeking redress to what they considered to be mounting tyranny. Of particular interest are those individuals and groups that gravitated to the political circle that looked to the leadership of Porfirio Díaz. This analysis of machine politics in the Restored Republic explains the motives for the war of 1876 and demonstrates that the centralized political system characteristic of the Porfirian dictatorship was prepared in advance of the dictator.

The second part of the study examines the civil war of 1876, which raged widely over the nation for a full twelve months. It examines how an insurrectionary army is raised, supplied, and deployed. It discusses both the tactics and the strategy of the insurgents and examines the nature and importance of guerrilla war, which is here appraised as a major contributing factor for the collapse of the government of Lerdo de Tejada. The scope then widens to analyze the political and military movement of José María Iglesias as it turned the politics of 1876 into a three-cornered war. The Iglesias movement is here found vital but flawed as the belligerent factions of Díaz and Iglesias confronted one another to fill the power vacuum after the fall of Lerdo. An analysis of the relations between the two factions within the concept of political machines offers a new appraisal of the final Porfirian victory.

The concluding chapter places Mexican political norms within the total flow of Mexican history and discusses the importance of the experience of the Restored Republic for political developments within machine politics to the present time.

The undertone of fatalism that has crept into this study during its slow incubation is not intended to imply that the political tragedy has been inevitable, but rather that the results were consistent with the failure to solve the real social and economic problems that, although alluded to, are necessarily the subjects of other studies.

A note about terms: The Spanish words *Juarismo, Lerdismo, Porfirismo,* and *Iglesismo* come naturally from the movements, plans, and governments of Benito Juárez, Sebastián Lerdo de Tejada, Porfirio Díaz, and José María Iglesias. From these terms emerge their derivations, *Juarista, Lerdista, Porfirista,* and *Iglesista,* used in Spanish (and herein) as adjectives (*Lerdista* military forces, etc.) and as nouns to donote partisans ("Generals González and Toledo were *Porfiristas*"). *Tuxtepecano* was used synonymously with *Porfirista* in 1876, meaning a rebel of the insurrection of Tuxtepec. The personalism implied in the terms has led many historians to think exclusively of charismatic leadership; herein the concept is one of factionalism for the creation of political machines. These terms are retained in the Spanish language for convenience and fidelity to the documentation. Although they are not capitalized in Spanish, it seems desirable to do so as they appear in English text.

Acknowledgments

I wish to express my gratitude to the numerous persons who aided me during the course of researching and writing this book. Courteous and helpful were the directors and employees of the *Archivo de Correspondencia e Historia de la Secretaría de le Defensa Nacional, Archivo General de la Nación, Archivo General del Estado de Nuevo León, La Biblioteca del Congreso Nacional de México, La Biblioteca del Museo de Antropología e Historia, La Biblioteca Nacional, El Centro de Estudios de la Historia de México, La Hemeroteca de la Universidad Autónoma de México, La Universidad de las Américas,* the William Clements Library, the Graduate Library and the Law Library of the University of Michigan, and the Newberry Library in Chicago. Particular thanks are extended to my colleagues who read and criticized parts of this work, Stephen Niblo, Errol Jones, James Hamon, and Nancy Gurrola. I also wish to thank Dr. Charles Gibson for his contribution to my training and intellectual growth and for his personal friendship. None of these people is responsible for the interpretations herein, for the ineloquence of the prose, or for the errors; quite to the contrary, their aid assures that the manuscript contains fewer blemishes than it otherwise would have had.

Jalapa
1977
L.B.P.

Abbreviations of Archival Sources

This study relies primarily upon archival sources and minimally upon newspapers and secondary works. To facilitate the notes the following abbreviations are employed.

ADN   *Departamento de Archivo Correspondencia e Historia de la Secretaría de la Defensa Nacional.* Mexico City.

AFIC   *Archivo de don Francisco Iglesias Calderón,* in *El Archivo General de la Nación.* Mexico City.

AJ   *Archivo de Benito Juárez, Gabinete de Manuscritos de la Biblioteca Nacional de México.* Mexico City.

AJB   *Archivo de Lic. Justo Benítez; Correspondencia del Archivo del Ejército de Oriente,* in *El Museo Nacional de Antropología e Historia.* Mexico City.

AGN   *Archivo General de la Nación.* Mexico City.

AGNL   *Archivo General del Estado de Nuevo León, Sección Histórica.* Monterrey, Nuevo León.

APD   *Archivo del General Porfirio Díaz, Memorias y Documentos,* ed. Alberto María Carreño. 30 vols. Mexico: Editorial Elede, 1949–61.

ASP   *Archivo de la Dependencia de Asuntos Terminados de la Secretaría de la Presidencia.* Mexico City.

CPD   *Collección General Porfirio Díaz.* University
          of the Americas. Cholula, Puebla.

DDC   *Benito Juárez: Documentos, Discursos y
          Correspondencia,* ed. Jorge L.
          Tamaño. 16 vols. Mexico: Secretaría
          del Patrimonio Nacional, 1964–72.

PDP   The Porfirio Díaz Papers. William
          Clements Library, Ann Arbor,
          Michigan.

Part 1

Chapter 1
The State of the Union— An Introduction

The most common and patriotic interpretation of politics during the Restored Republic is that Benito Juárez, Sebastián Lerdo de Tejada, and a small group of determined liberals surrounding them were given the reins of power by a grateful nation to create a united democratic republic. The grand plan was to establish nineteenth-century liberalism in Mexico. Liberals of the period believed they were on the right road, and twentieth-century Mexicans, if present official ceremony is a measure, believe that Juárez was the right leader. The program of those men is hailed by Mexicans who believe that it saved Mexico from European monarchy, from ecclesiastic aristocracy, from United States expansion, or from regional dissolution—and it may have. Nevertheless, the grand plan could not be implemented because it did not coincide with Mexican reality.

The liberal program grew out of a complex historical heritage: the reaction against the Spanish colonial experience; the influence of the European Enlightenment, the French Revolution, the Spanish constitutional experience, and Anglo-American federalism; the wars for independence and the struggles of the constituents of 1824, of the Reformers of 1833, of the revolutionaries of Ayutla; the reaction to the war with the United States, to the Santa Anna dictatorship, to the Three Years War, and to the French Intervention. All of those traumatic experiences contributed to Mexican nineteenth-century liberalism.

Liberalism was written into the Constitution of 1857 and the laws of the Restored Republic. The liberal faith in the goodness of the common man was translated into popular sovereignty (article 39). Fear of tyrannous centralism was hopefully avoided by the sovereignty of states in federal union (articles 40 and 117). Dictatorship was guarded against by separation and balance of power in a strong legislature, an independent judiciary, and a weak executive (articles 50, 72, 85, 88, 92). Liberal concern for individual liberty was guaranteed by a panoply of civil rights ("Rights of Man," articles 1–29). The belief in popular participation in the political process was promoted by public education and expressed in universal manhood suffrage (articles 3 and 34). The liberal's dogmatic belief in private property and his suspicions of communal and corporate land tenure are reflected in the protections of the former and the attack against the latter (articles 16 and 27). The development of the economy through individual initiative, promoted by governmental investment in infrastructure, was voiced by the Reformers *ad infinitum* as an article of faith. Clerical influence upon society and government was guarded against by a number of constitutional and legislative measures (articles 3 and 7 and the *Leyes de Reforma* of 1859 and 1860).

In summary, nineteenth-century liberalism was composed of republican political institutions, democratic social values, a panoply of civil rights to protect individualism, the economic principles of laissez-faire free enterprise, and a strong component of anticlericalism. This was the program that the liberals of the Restored Republic tried to impose upon Mexico after 1867, but Mexican reality contradicted several basic elements of it.

Because the theory of liberal republicanism was contradicted by Mexican reality, politicians of that day were forced to modify liberal republicanism in political practice. The real practice of politics alienated a growing body of men from the political class, many of whom, withdrawing support from the government and gravitating to the position of armed insurrection, became followers of Porfirio Díaz by 1876. Some of the important areas of such contradiction between liberal republicanism and Mexican reality are described below.

Federalism and *Caudillismo*

A major contradiction between liberalism and reality existed in the complex relationship between federalism, regionalism and *caudillismo*. Liberalism in nineteenth-century Mexico was founded upon federalism as the most certain means of safeguarding individual guarantees from centralist dictatorship. Federalism was basic to the liberal Reform and was written into article 40 of the Constitution of

1857, which declared that the various states of the republic were sovereign in their internal affairs. The solemn assurances given about the sovereignty of states by Juárez and Lerdo were perhaps only exceeded in frequency by the promises of rebel chieftains to save the sovereignty of the state from the centralism of the same Juárez and Lerdo.[1]

Even as liberals applauded federalism, they abhorred regionalism as an obstacle to national unity. Mexico was a collection of regions, as all Mexicans, liberal or not, were well aware. Juárez and Lerdo sought to create a national union from those regions, but regionalism was the real base for federalism. Subordinating regionalism to nationalism without destroying federalism with centralism was one of the greatest problems of the age.[2]

Caudillismo made the task more difficult. Liberals detested *caudillismo* as local dictatorship, the antithesis of republicanism. Nothing was more basic to the governing of Mexico, however, than *caudillismo*. Many regions of Mexico in 1867 were more or less dominated by the *caudillo*-generals who supplied the resistance to the French Intervention, and numerous *caudillo*-generals were more or less allied with the Liberal party. The *caudillo*-generals then became the governors of the several states or commanders of federal or state military units in the areas in which they had created followings. Upon that base they proceeded to exercise their political influence.[3]

1. Examples are legion: for example, Plan de San Luis Potosí, 30 December 1869, in Benito Juárez, *Documentos, discursos y correspondencia,* selection and notes by Jorge L. Tamayo, 16 vols. (Mexico: Secretaría del Patrimonio Nacional, 1964–72), 14:196–200 (hereafter cited as DDC; when the words of Tamayo are cited, the note will be Tamayo, *Juárez,* followed by volume and page). In contrast see the closing speech of Juárez to the third session of the Fifth Congress, 15 December 1870, reprinted in ibid., pp. 773–74.

2. The problem as exemplified in congressional debate is described in Chapter 6.

3. Generals who had acquired personal military followings during the Republican Resistance, with political consequences during the Restored Republic, included Mariano Escobedo in San Luis Potosí, Ramón Corona in Jalisco and Durango, Porfirio Díaz in parts of Veracruz, Puebla, and Oaxaca, and Diego Alvarez in Guerrero. *Caudillos* of more limited scope but effective control included Gerónimo Treviño and Francisco Naranjo in Nuevo León, Servando Canales and Juan N. Cortina in Tamaulipas, Fidencio Hernández and

To one degree or another every *caudillo* had the power to limit or compromise the efforts of the federal government in his area. The local population frequently saw him as the man who protected the region from outside influence, including the influence of the central government. He frequently had the power to name and replace local political chiefs (*jefes políticos*), who characteristically ruled county (*municipio*) or village (*pueblo*) with an iron hand. The *caudillo* and his political chiefs monopolized the ability to recruit armed followers in the area of their influence. Moreover, the *caudillo* sometimes exercised economic influence through personal holdings, legal favors, and oligarchic alliances with wealthy families. He generally combined charismatic leadership, personal or family prestige, and brute strength with his military, political, and economic position. The tradition of caudillistic control was at least as old as the independent nation, but the *caudillos* of the Restored Republic had on their side the federalist theory of resisting centralist dictatorship. The point is that *caudillismo* was an integral part of the political system, a part which compromised republicanism, militarized factionalism, and heightened rivalry by the monopolization of power in each of the states—a rivalry that had much to do with the manner in which the liberal government of the Restored Republic modified liberalism.

Rivalry for caudillistic power was the first reality of regional politics, which was continually agitated by strenuous factional struggles. Furthermore, since local republicanism was no match for *caudillismo,* political liberalism was threatened. Yet when liberals used the power of the national government against *caudillos,* federalism was threatened by centralism. Moreover, since *caudillos* could raise private armies, any attempt by the central government to eliminate individual *caudillos* threatened war. The liberal program was thus endangered either by the local violence inherent in *caudillismo* or by the national warfare inherent in attacking it. Juárez and Lerdo had to deal with this dilemma. We shall see in chapters 4 through 8 that Juárez and then Lerdo alternately replaced *caudillos* with loyal subordinates or

---

Francisco Meijueiro in the Sierra de Ixtláz, Juan N. Méndez, Juan Francisco Lucas, and Juan C. Bonilla in the Sierra de Puebla, Florencio Antillón in Guanajuato, Ignacio Pesqueira in Sonora, Luis Terrazas in Chihuahua, and Manuel Lozada in Tepic.

made alliances with *caudillos* against local rival factions. That in turn alienated rival factions and forced them into the camp of Porfirio Díaz.

Executive Centralism

A second area of contradiction that led to modifications of liberalism and to political alienation existed in the separation and balance of powers between the executive and legislative branches of government. Liberal theory at the constitutional convention in 1856–57 favored a weak executive and a strong legislature. The dominant idea was that the government should be a parliamentary system in which the cabinet should reflect the majority party in Congress.[4] The constitutional framers attempted to assure legislative supremacy and ministerial responsibility.[5] "The constitution of '57 does not state it," observed Francisco Bulnes, "but it compels it."[6] Later deputies in the Congresses of 1861–63, like José María Mata, Joaquín Ruiz, Francisco Zarco, Ignacio Ramírez, Manuel María de Zamacona, and León Guzmán, spoke and acted as though the legislature controlled the cabinet and through it executive policies.[7]

After 1867 there remained a parliamentary bloc in Congress that believed in ministerial responsibility to Congress. That congressional group included some of the earlier framers and advocates of parliamentarianism of the first Congresses, such as Manuel María de Zamacona and José María Mata. Ezequiel Montes, a constitutional lawyer of importance in the Fifth Congress, raised the theory of parliamentary government in a debate on an administration tax bill: "In our system," he said, "only the president is necessary. The ministers who surround him are obliged to abandon their posts when they do

4. Frank Averill Knapp argues this thesis convincingly in "Parliamentary Government and the Mexican Constitution of 1857: A Forgotten Phase of Mexican Political History," *Hispanic American Historical Review* 33 (1953):65–87.

5. Ibid., pp. 67–71.

6. Francisco Bulnes, *Juárez y las revoluciones de Ayutla y de la Reforma* (Mexico, 1904), p. 209, cited in ibid., p. 67.

7. Knapp, "Parliamentary Government," pp. 73–80.

not enjoy the favor of public opinion."[8] By "public opinion" Montes, and all congressional liberals, meant the majority of Congress.

Francisco Zarco and Guillermo Prieto, early advocates of ministerial responsibility, largely dropped the issue after 1867 and usually voted with Juárez in Congress, even though on other matters they were strongly independent. Zarco died in 1869, but Prieto lived to join the revolutionary government of José María Iglesias in 1876 in opposition to Lerdo's use of executive power in the elections of 1876. Joaquín Ruiz opposed Lerdo from the court of the state of Puebla and attempted to unite the anti-Lerdo forces in 1876.[9] Similarly, León Guzmán opposed Juárez and Lerdo from the Supreme Court. In 1876 he tried to unite the *Porfiristas* and *Iglesistas* and, failing that, joined Iglesias.[10] Others of the old parliamentarians, however, gravitated to *Porfirismo*. Ignacio Ramírez was a *Porfirista* from the Supreme Court. Zamacona, Mata, and Montes were congressional *Porfiristas* from 1867 forward. Delegates of the constituent assembly of 1856–57 who were members of the Fifth Congress, 1869–71, and who regularly voted with the *Porfiristas,* included José Eligio Muñoz, Justino Fernández, Antonio Lemus, Espiridión Moreno, and Francisco Fernández de Alfaro.

Juárez and Lerdo acted as though Mexican reality demanded a strong executive.[11] They increased executive powers when they could, thus modifying liberal principles and creating opposition. Many congressmen during the Restored Republic who opposed the executive

8. Mexico, Congreso, *Diario de los debates, quinto congreso constitucional de la unión,* 4 vols. (Mexico: Imprenta del Gobierno, 1871–73), 6 December 1869, 1:585.

9. José María Iglesias, *La cuestión presidencial en 1876* (Mexico: Tipografía Literaria de Filomena Mata, 1892), pp. 255, 395–99; Alberto María Carreño, ed., *Archivo del General Porfirio Díaz: memorias y documentos,* 30 vols. (Mexico: Editorial Elede, 1947–61), 14:304–5; 15:18, 29 (hereafter cited as APD; when Carreño's comments are cited, the note will read APD, vol., *notas:* page.)

10. Daniel Cosío Villegas, *Historia moderna de México, el porfiriato, vida política interna,* 2 vols. (Mexico: Editorial Hermes, 1970–72), 1:41, 51–54.

11. Mexican authors usually have held that the Constitution of 1857 gave too much power to the legislature and too little to the executive: Ricardo García Granados, *La constitución de 1857 y las leyes de reforma en México* (Mexico: Tipografía Económica, 1906), pp. 44–45; Emilio Rabasa, *La organización política de México, la constitución y la dictadura* (Madrid: Editorial América, n.d.), pp. 200–219; Daniel Cosío Villegas, *La constitución de 1857 y sus críticos* (Mexico: Editorial Hermes, 1957), p. 153.

concentration of power voted with the opposition and eventually became *Porfiristas* by 1876. Opponents to presidential centralism, therefore, merged with the general opposition to Juárez and Lerdo.

Economic Liberalism

A third area of contradiction between the liberal creed and Mexican reality was economic and fiscal. Laissez-faire, free-enterprise liberalism in Europe was the voice of the Industrial Revolution. It assumed the existence of investment capital, a domestic market, and efficient and cheap transportation and communication. It assumed a modernizing agricultural sector, an industrializing sector, an active, educated, urban middle class, a banking system, and international trade based on an assortment of efficiently produced goods for exportation. Finally, it assumed a solvent, inexpensive government able to maintain internal order.

Mexico was characterized by none of these. She suffered massive poverty, economic stagnation, and fiscal penury. Years of warfare had left mines and fields in ruin. Commerce was depressed because of lack of markets and deplorable roads and was harrassed by banditry. Investment capital was destroyed, confiscated, hidden away, or taken out of the country. No banking system existed. The rural population was mired in traditional subsistence agriculture and widespread peonage. The cities were precariously supplied. Employment was unavailable for urban poor and migrant labor. The urban middle class was small, weak, and politically divided. No sector of the economy was modernized and capitalized for efficient exportation. Mexico had no merchant marine, and only after 1873 did a railroad operate from Veracruz to Mexico City. The possibility of applying a political and social theory of the European Industrial Revolution to Mexico in the mid-nineteenth century was doomed to failure.[12]

12 The economic stagnation is described and quantified in Francisco R. Calderón, *Historia moderna de México, la república restaurada, la vida económica* (Mexico: Editorial Hermes, 1955). The failures of liberal remedies are discussed in the essays found in Luis González, ed., *La economía mexicana en la época de Juárez* (Mexico: Secretaría de Industria y Comercio, 1972), especially the introduction by Luis González and the chapter "Política económica, antecedentes y consequencias," pp. 57–102.

The federal tax base was miserably depressed. Governmental income did not allow for expenditures on social services or even for regular payment of salaries to bureaucrats and soldiers. Francisco Mejía, Juárez's last minister of the treasury, wrote in his memoirs of the despair he felt during those years, of the many sleepless nights, knowing there was not a cent in the treasury for the next day. He recorded that in the four years and four months that he was the minister of *hacienda* "there was a deficit of five to seven million pesos between the budget and expenditures paid."[13]

Fiscal insolvency and economic dislocation created severe luxation. The level of economic discontent was dangerously high and could at any time be translated into political opposition. Banditry was the most obvious of the maladies stemming from economic dislocation, and highwaymen carried political manifestos in their pockets in order to be treated as political opponents upon capture, rather than be shot as bandits or kidnappers.[14] José María Gálvez was such a bandit leader in the state of Mexico, who periodically issued manifestos for the restoration of the empire.[15] The case of Miguel Negrete in the Sierra de Puebla was complex and enduring. The part of his checkered career of interest here is that he was able to find a group of followers in Tlaxcala, who called themselves *los plateados,* whom Negrete led into the depressed Sierra de Puebla. He offered them a degree of leadership and received support from them for his political ambitions, which were never clear.[16] The depressed economy, political discontent in the Sierra de Puebla, and banditry were interrelated

13. Francisco Mejía, *Memorias de Francisco Mejía* (Mexico: Secretaría de Hacienda y Crédito Público, 1958), pp. 136–38.

14. The Constitution of 1857, article 23, prohibited the death sentence for political prisoners; the law of 12 April 1869 authorized capital punishment to *salteadores y plagiarios.*

15. In this case the protective precaution proved useless; Gálvez was shot by a government officer, Pedro Bernal, "while trying to escape." Tamayo, *Juárez,* 13:383–84; Gálvez's manifesto is reprinted in DDC, 13:400–402.

16. Negrete offered his services to Díaz in 1867 but was rebuffed; he rebelled in 1868 for Jesús Gonzlez Ortega, joined the Martínez-Aguirre rebellion of San Luis Potosí in 1869, threw his support to Díaz in the rebellion of La Noria in 1871, accepted Lerdo's amnesty in 1872, and joined the insurrection of Tuxtepec in 1876.

phenomena that offered the opportunity to a man like Negrete to harass the government for years.[17]

Legal opposition blended economic and fiscal issues with political and military resistance. Even as the government was seeking new taxes and recruiting soldiers to contend with the serious rebellion of San Luis Potosí in 1869, an opposition *Porfirista* congressman, Manuel Mendiolea, argued that military expenses were not necessary: "We have an army because the government has to hold down the people. . . . we have 12,000 men, half of whom suffice [without further taxation] to sustain the public tranquillity and the unpopularity of the ministry."[18] The rebellion was not a popular insurrection but rather an intraliberal struggle, emerging from local factional struggles and electoral irregularities in the state of San Luis Potosí.[19] Nevertheless, Mendiolea used it to discredit the administration.

Other implications of fiscal instability and economic dislocation were unmet social and economic expenditures, problems which tended to discredit the administrations of Juárez and Lerdo. Failure to meet governmental obligations gave a ready weapon to opposition leaders, who cried corruption and incompetence. When pensions were not paid, the government was accused of callousness, when payrolls could not be met in one area or another, the cry was favoritism, and when taxes mounted to meet deficiencies, the cry was tyranny. Congressman Manuel Mendiolea in 1869 proposed that the minister of finance be summoned to inform the congressmen "if wages in the offices of the treasury and of the finance ministry are as far behind in payment as those for the congressmen and magistrates of the Supreme Court . . . , designating, in case of the absence of

17. The meanderings of Miguel Negrete can be appreciated if not fully detailed by following correspondence about him in APD, vols. 4–6, and DDC, vols. 12–14; it becomes clear, however, that there was more guesswork than certainty in governmental circles about Negrete's movements and motives. For an interpretation of his overall career as a social revolutionary, see John M. Hart, "Miguel Negrete: la epopeya de un revolucionario," *Historia Mexicana* 24, no. 1 (July–September 1974): 70–93.

18. 6 December 1869, *Debates, quinto congreso,* 1:575.

19. Francisco Antonio Aquirre to Juárez, 15 December 1869, DDC, 14:188; Plan de San Luis Potosí, 30 December 1869, ibid., pp. 196–200; Gustavo López Gutiérrez, *Escobedo, republicano demócrata* (Mexico: n.p., 1968), p. 431.

uniformity, the privileged offices."[20] The object of the resolution was to embarrass the administration, and the opportunity arose from fiscal penury.

All liberal governments in the nineteenth century were involved in infrastructural development; Mexico was no exception, principally in the erection of a telegraph network and in debate on railroads, roads, and riverworks. Developmental projects were undertaken as fast as fiscal conditions permitted, but not fast enough to head off militant discontent.

The failure to transform Mexico by rapid economic development and the rivalry for scarce funds heightened political opposition; the governmental reaction was further to centralize political power. That in turn fed the opposition charges of exclusiveness and dictatorship and even the charge that the administration used developmental expenditures to corrupt bureaucrats and to suborn officials.[21] Throughout the decade the opposition accused Juárez and Lerdo of splitting the liberal party by policies of exclusiveness and favoritism, much of which was born of fiscal penury. The anguished cry for domestic stability that should have been based on economic development and sound fiscal conditions prodded the administration to political centralism, which in turn became the expressed justification for insurrection.

Empleomanía

A fourth and related characteristic of Mexico which clashed with liberal convictions was the condition of *empleomanía*. Liberals everywhere

20. 1 October 1869, *Debates, quinto congreso*, 1:93.

21. Vicente Riva Palacio sums up these charges in *Historia de la administración de don Sebastián Lerdo de Tejada* (Mexico: El Padre Cobos, 1875), pp. 152–60. He cites a resolution presented to Congress by the budget committee, composed of opposition congressmen in 1873, which in part reads as follows: "With the budget we are presenting, the administration will find itself empowered with all the means of action that are truly necessary, and only deprived of the major part of the expedients which frequently have been placed in play to squander the public wealth and to feed the corruption which so often forms the base of an official party."

assume that men prefer their private lives and personal interests, but that patriotic men will serve their country when called upon by the people. They assume that after a public servant has met his civic responsibility, he will gladly return to his private affairs. This is probably a false assumption for most individuals on governmental payrolls everywhere, but in Mexico the absence of opportunity in business and professional occupations compelled capable men to clamor for governmental positions. Juan José Baz, appointed political chief of the area around Mexico City after the seige of Mexico in 1867, wrote these prophetic words to Juárez: "The major difficulty that you are going to have is that of choosing among so many talented men and so many patriots of eminent services for public positions."[22] One wonders if Baz or Juárez knew how many there would be.

The intense competition for public positions caused incumbent bureaucrats to give unconditional political loyalty to their bosses in order to safeguard their employment. Conversely, those people who wanted public jobs were ready partisans of opposition leaders who called for bureaucratic turnover. The call was sufficiently threatening to incumbent politicians that they demanded yet more obedience and subservience from subordinates. Thus the employment interest of bureaucrats drew them together around the executive figure at state and national levels into effective political parties. Subsequently, the bureaucracy constituted the most effective tool in the strengthening of the governmental party in electoral activity. This build-up explains why the governmental opposition in 1871, when for a few weeks they controlled Congress, tried to limit the role of officeholders in elections. Probably the most effective promise Porfirio Díaz made during the insurrection of Tuxtepec was to turn out all individuals who held public office under Lerdo de Tejada: the positions would be open to the "outs."[23] Many disappointed office-seekers, alienated from the government, became allies of the Porfirian opposition. The United States consul in Tampico, Veracruz, wrote to the State Department in 1876 during the Porfirian insurrection of Tuxtepec that "the strife is between the Out's and the In's. The Out's are those that have held previous positions, and are now poor, very poor and des-

22. Baz to Juárez, 1 June 1867, DDC, 12:47.
23. Plan of Tuxtepec, article 3, 10 January 1876, APD, 12:99–100.

perate, and will try and gain, or lose their lives. The In's are to the contrary."[24]

Minority Republicanism

A basic contradiction between the liberal creed and Mexican reality was the liberals' assumption that the Mexican people were able and willing to support republican institutions and to participate in the public life of the nation. The population of Mexico had been kept overwhelmingly illiterate, politically inert, traditionally subservient to local authority, and incredibly poor. They were in no way trained to the responsibilities of republican institutions. Men are capable of holding beliefs and simultaneously being skeptical of those beliefs; they can alternately subscribe to an ideal and with equal sincerity contradict the ideal in respect to real conditions. In practice, the liberal politicians knew that the masses could not participate in and could not support republican institutions; that is why elections were made indirect.

Liberals were not facetious when they directed their manifestos to "the inhabitants of the sovereign state of . . ." or when they decreed that "public opinion demands that. . . ." All references to "public opinion" and "popular will" and even to "popular sovereignty," which stood behind every political act of the period, were expressions of the liberal dream. When it was pointed out that the masses stood outside of the system, the acceptable retort was that the conservatives had not educated them. True or not, the political acts of the day did not emanate from the majority, which was as true when Juárez was "popularly elected" in 1867 or 1871 as it was when any general assumed the command of a "despoiled people" who "called upon him" to redress their wrongs.

The basic truth was that liberals were a numerical minority, holding power on a theory of majority rule. Conservatives were also a minor-

24. United States, Department of State, *Despatches from United States Consuls in Tampico, Mexico, 1824–1906*, (hereafter *Despatches From Tampico*) Microcopy, no. M–304, roll no. 6, E. Johnson to W. Hunter, Second Assistant Secretary of State, 4 April 1876, doc. 111.

ity, but they included classes—especially the clergy—that could potentially influence the masses more effectively than could the liberals. After the fall of the empire many liberals believed that the conservatives, if given the opportunity, would utilize the republican institutions to place in office men who would expunge the anticlerical laws of the Reform and cancel the liberal victories. Since the liberals were convinced that conservative political power was not in the interests of the masses or of the nation, they became as guilty of paternalistic attitudes and exclusivist practices as were the conservatives, but they professed to believe that their own paternalism would eventually train the masses to protect the republican institutions through participation.

Contemporary records demonstrate an almost paranoiac fear of a conservative revival and reaction, and therefore an apologetic tone toward exclusivist political methods as a necessary evil against such a possibility. Jesús Camarena, a Jalisco liberal, wrote to Juárez that the conservatives in his state disguised themselves among the liberal factions "and when [the liberals] are well-divided and weakened, [the conservatives] will take off their masks and jump into the arena. . . . It is taking on colossal proportions, and at the least expected moment they will give us a scare and put liberty in danger."[25]

The question of returning rights to the ex-imperialists was highly political. Some men opposed amnesty because it would increase the competition for public jobs. Other men recognized the factional advantage of incorporating them into one or another faction. Juárez in 1867 practiced a moderate policy toward those who had cooperated with the French intervention. He faced, however, strong opposition on the issue. Thirty-four congressmen of the preparatory session of Congress presented a resolution that no one who had served the empire could sit in Congress even if rehabilitated, and several individuals' credentials were rejected by the Fourth Congress for that

25. 13 June 1869, DDC, 13:947. The liberal newsman Francisco Zarco wrote after the election of 1869: ". . . the reactionary party, immersed in their pretended inertia, applaud and promise themselves that the divisions in the liberal party are irreconcilable and hope to contemplate the suicide of the great political communion that triumphed over the intervention and empire." Francisco Zarco, *Textos políticos* (Mexico: Universidad Nacional Autónoma de México, 1957), p. 21.

reason.[26] In his opening speech to Congress in December 1867, Juárez spoke in favor of leniency.[27] A few days later the opposition in Congress sponsored a bill granting extensive amnesty, which failed to pass.[28] Then in November 1868, Fransisco Zarco and a group of *Juarista* congressmen presented an amnesty bill, but the committee broadened it to include rebels then in arms against the government.[29] The ministry then opposed the bill, and it failed to pass. A more moderate bill passed in May 1869 after Zarco added that "no individual who served the intervention or the so-called empire may be elected to the federal Congress."[30]

The next year the politics of amnesty became more intense. The general law of amnesty of 14 October 1870 only passed through Congress when *Lerdistas* cooperated with *Porfiristas* to outvote the *Juaristas*. It still excluded regents and generals of the empire, but it granted amnesty to the greatest number of "imperialists" as well as to all men who had borne arms against the government between 1867 and September 1870. The Juárez ministry at that point opposed the bill because of the amnesty offered to rebels.[31] A number of those rebels were able to lead the "out" factions against the "in" factions in important states. The bill became law, and new elements were added to the political classes. In Veracruz in 1871 a *Juarista* wrote to the president's secretary that "the amnesty opens the doors of Congress and public posts to many men who were compromised with the empire. Among them are useful and talented people, men of arms as well as letters."

26. Pantaleón Tovar, ed., *Historia parlamentaria del cuarto congreso constitucional*, 4 vols. (Mexico: 1872–74), 28 November 1867, 1:23–25.

27. Ibid., 8 December 1867, 1:56.

28. Proposing amnesty in December of 1867 were J. M. Mata, M. M. Zamacona, and J. Benítez—all *Porfiristas*—and Guillermo Prieto; Tovar, *Cuarto congreso*, 1:65–66.

29. Proposing the bill in November were Zarco, R. Palacios, Barragán and Vega: ibid., 3:611.

30. *Ley de 5 de Mayo de 1869*, Manuel Dublán and José María Lozano, *Legislación mexicana o colección completa de las disposiciones legislativas*, 30 vols. (Mexico: Imprenta del Comercio, 1876–99), 10:588–89; Raymond C. Wheat, *Francisco Zarco, el portavoz liberal de la reforma*, trans. Antonio Castro Leal (Mexico: Editorial Porrúa, 1957), p. 309.

31. Dublán ad Lozano, *Legislación mexicana*, 11:184; Walter V. Scholes, *Mexican Politics during the Juárez Regime* (Columbia: University of Missouri Press, 1969), pp. 130–31.

He reported that the "Catholic party of the state" favored Lerdo, the bureaucracy would support Juárez, and most liberals would follow Díaz.[32] And so it was: in 1871 Lerdo won the conservative vote, and the earlier rebels, many of whom had been eliminated in state factional struggles, drifted into the ranks of *Porfirismo*.

In practice, minority republicanism could not be true republicanism. Politics in the Restored Republic was conducted by a tiny minority in whose interests it lay to exert pressure on the political machinery. Not everyone who could do so did, but that merely left open an easier path to public power for those who would. Monopolization of power was the easier in a system of minority republicanism, and exclusivist minority republicanism alienated other groups—who turned their energies against the regime.

Elections

A more covert contradiction between liberalism and reality related to elections. The politically inert mass, the liberal minority, the fear of a conservative revival, the bureaucratic involvement, the caudillistic control of local politics, the centralist tendency of the executive—all of these factors compromised elections. Elections in a republic theoretically determine which set of men establish policy and administer law. Mexican politicians considered those questions too important to leave to electoral fate. Inasmuch as liberals in the Constitutional Congress of 1857 had written universal manhood suffrage into the fundamental code of the land, voters existed in large numbers to be taken to the polls by whoever exerted authority. If one party did not do so, it was thought, another would. Ricardo García Granados later wrote that "one cannot reprove our presidents for having erected a dictatorship and for influencing the elections, for had they completely abstained, the governors would have made the elections. And if the governors had abstained also, the clergy would have obtained the triumph, putting an end to the Constitution and to our dreams of liberty."[33]

32. Gonzalo A. Esteva to Pedro Santacilia, 26 September 1870, DDC, 14:780–81.

33. García Granados, *La constitución de 1857*, p. 125.

In Oaxaca in 1867 a *Porfirista* wrote that a certain military leader, López Rascón, ". . . threatened the miserable Indians that if they did not name *don* M. Castro for governor . . . the troops would burn down their villages. Those miserable creatures . . . are so timid [that] they become frightened not only by the presence of armed forces, but even by [political] authorities, whom they submissively obey."

The same observer reported that "in the neighborhood of [General] Rincón all the dependents of the *hacienda* of Santa Gertrudis went out . . ." to vote for the incumbent governor.[34] "We won't win the election in Tuxtla," wrote another man to an opposition leader in 1871, "because we cannot count on the Indian element, which is powerful and which the authorities always utilize."[35] In Veracruz in 1875 Rafael Zayas Enríquez and Teodoro Dehesa contested a seat to Congress. According to one observer, Zayas was the popular candidate, and Dehesa was the one favored by the party in office. "Unfortunately," the observer wrote, "the villagers generally obey . . . the orders of the political chief, and as the one here has exhausted the resources of every kind in order to favor Dehesa, we cannot yet know what will result from the counting."[36]

Such use of the illiterate masses as voters was not the rule; abstention was the rule. Most Mexicans simply did not vote. Hubert Howe Bancroft wrote in the 1880s that "to assume that one tenth of the qualified voters participated in the most popular of late presidential elections is a generous estimate, hence the ease with which officials can influence or decide the result. . . ."[37]

Because the masses overwhelmingly abstained from voting, a small amount of corruption or force could determine election results, and this in turn discouraged the literate class from voting. And so the abstention spread from the lower classes to all classes. "There is no popular suffrage in this country," the German ambassador in the 1870s once explained to the ambassador from the United States, "and there cannot be in this generation for two reasons: first, the want of intelligence on the part of the masses; second, the general conviction

34. Antonio P. García to Díaz, 15 November 1867, APD, 5:318.
35. P. L. León to Díaz, 1 April 1871, ibid, 9:129–30.
36. *El Monitor Republicano*, 10 July 1875, p. 3.
37. Hubert Howe Bancroft, *History of Mexico*, 6 vols. (San Francisco: The History Company, 1888), 6:482.

that the votes cast are so manipulated by the authorities that there is no assurance that the results will be according to the wishes of the voters. . . . The intelligent people as a rule do not vote for the same reason—the want of confidence in the ballot being properly returned."[38]

The United States ambassador noted that "during my seven years residence in Mexico I often visited the polling places on election days, but I never saw a citizen deposit a ballot, and rarely did I find any person at the polls besides the election officers. Everybody understood that the elections were a farce. . . ."[39]

A routine news item in a large Mexican daily reported that in Guanajuato not all the elections were verified because "some of the voting places were not open or were installed in the afternoon due to the absence of voters or because the number of voters were less than seven [as the law stipulated] for opening the booth."[40]

We will never know to what extent elections in the Restored Republic were fraudulent. It is clear, however, that many Mexicans believed that politicians worked essentially to stay in power and that once in office and in control of the electoral machinery, a politician could not be dislodged without force. Mexicans simply did not believe in their elections. The following examples are grouped here to demonstrate that basic belief.

In the congressional elections of 1869 a politician wrote to Porfirio Díaz that "the government has authorization to spend a million and a half in 'reserved affairs' under the title of 'amortization of the debt' and is employing it well in the elections."[41] In a speech on the floor of Congress Manuel María Zamacona told of a person who was asked if the support of armed force would be necessary to secure the triumph of a given canditate. The person answered that "two or four years ago maybe such support would have been needed; since the last elections those villages are domesticated. A few men with sharp sticks will suffice in order that they vote conveniently."[42] An observer in Chiapas

38. John W. Foster, *Diplomatic Memoirs,* 2 vols. (Boston: Houghton Mifflin Co., 1909), 1:54

39. Ibid., p. 53.

40. *El Siglo XIX,* 8 July 1869, p. 1.

41. "Teococuilco" to Díaz, 9 June 1869, APD, 8:29.

42. 16 March 1871, *Debates, quinto congreso,* 4:61.

noted in private correspondence that "the *Juaristas* here work desperately, not missing a trick, no matter how ruinous and underhanded it may be to secure their ends."[43]

Manuel María de Zamacona, as president of Congress, read into the record that because of his journalistic experience ". . . an infinity of documented complaints about attacks upon the popular vote has come to my hands. They fill a box—and this is not hyperbole—of two cubic feet, which I keep as material for the political history of the present presidential administration."[44]

An election observer in 1871 wrote that "we know the government has a fund of two or three thousand pesos to buy congressmen."[45] Manuel Mendiolea, a congressman through much of the Restored Republic, wrote that "Sánchez Mármol . . . will be elected congressman for Tabasco, according to the postulation which can be seen in the newspaper of San Juan Bautista; and that postulation will triumph, because it is official."[46] A Mexico City newspaper in 1875 commented that there was no electoral contest in the state of Puebla because Governor ". . . Romero creates [electoral] credentials as he sees fit. . . ."[47]

Ignacio Ramírez wrote that "men stand as congressional candidates not because the people know them, but because the ministers know them; and some are passed over for the grave reason that the people want them."[48] Some years later, Ricardo García Granados wrote that "it would lack historical veracity if we were to say that the majority of the people had gone with full confidence to the urns in order to designate their representatives, and that the elections were verified strictly in conformity to the dispositions of the law." The system, he explained, was that "the local governments . . . arranged affairs to their own liking and . . . they were the more free to do so as the distance was greater from the capital."[49] "At the bottom of it," he said,

43. Manuel Iturbe to Díaz, 14 April 1871, APD, 9:131.

44. 16 March 1871, *Debates, quinto congreso,* 4:63.

45. Anon. to Díaz, 23 August 1871, APD, 9:262.

46. Mendiolea to Díaz, 24 May 1875, ibid., 11:266.

47. *El Monitor Republicano,* 6 July 1875, p. 3.

48. Ignacio Ramírez, "La apelación al pueblo," *Obras,* 2 vols. (Mexico: Editora Nacional, 1966), 2:297.

49. García Granados, *La Constitución de 1857,* pp. 22–23.

"politics was no other than a wholecloth of intrigues and conspiracies, with armed rebellion as its result. . . . *It is a falsehood when it is assured to us that in those good times there were really popular elections.*"[50]

Foreigners made observations, too: John Foster, the American ambassador to Mexico, wrote that "there was a conviction among the voters that the party in power would control the results of the election in favor of its candidate, without regard to the ballots cast." The electoral procedure, he wrote, was that "the officers 'to be elected' were fixed upon by the Governor and a special group, and the list was generally known before the election was held."[51]

Clearly, large numbers of Mexicans did not believe in the rectitude and legitimacy of their electoral process. Such lack of faith added to the widespread abstinence from participation, which doubtless aided the task of willful men who sought to influence election returns. In turn, the lack of faith and widespread corruption led to semiautomatic cries of fraud by those who reportedly lost elections. The losers in any given election may have exaggerated the degree of corruption and may have joined other losers in generalizing the irregularities, thereby contributing to a paranoiac belief in a conspiracy on the national level. Moreover, the violence and corruption of purely local officials was always seen as part of national policy, ordered by the president. Finally, men who were removed from office or who thought they were barred from office cited irregular electoral procedure, which they claimed was tyrannical, as justification for armed rebellion. The newspaperman José María Vigil, editorializing about the absence of public confidence in elections, wrote that "in Mexico the elections are not considered as the ultimate exercise of popular sovereignty, but rather as the result of intrigue and abuse of power. Consequently, he who loses the race does not attribute it to lack of favor in public opinion, but to the fraudulent practice of his adversary, who violating a right, commits the crime of usurpation."[52]

The connections between elections and insurrections stand out sharply in the very *pronunciamientos* of the rebels, although it may be expected that they exaggerated their grievances. In his pronounce-

50. Ibid., p. 123; italics in original.
51. Foster, *Memoirs*, 1:52–53.
52. *El Siglo XIX*, 29 June 1871.

ment of May 1868, Gen. Aureliano Rivera claimed that "Juárez directly and criminally intervened in the elections and corrupted them to his advantage. He deprived the people of their franchise to select the officers . . . of their choice."[53]

Prominent in the *pronunciamiento* of Donato Guerra in 1871 was his "surprise" at "their infamous machinations to falsify the popular vote in order to perpetuate themselves in power. . . ."[54] When Gerónimo Treviño, then governor of Nuevo León, rebelled in 1871, he declared to his legislature that "*don* Benito Juárez, determined to perpetuate himself in power against the will of the nation, has not omitted any method, nor is there any abuse of power he has not employed in order to limit freedom in the recent elections and to falsify the free vote of the people."[55]

Díaz's pronouncement of La Noria carried the same message—the relationship between electoral abuse and rebellion: "When violence usurps the rights of liberty . . . [and] falsification usurps the place of truth, then the inequality of campaigning . . . inflames passion and obliges the losers to reject the [electoral] results. . . ."[56] Again the connection was made in the pronouncement of Tuxtepec in 1876: "Political suffrage has been converted into a farce, because the president and his friends, by means wholly reproachable, arrange that 'official candidates' become public officials, overriding all independent candidates. . . . Lerdo de Tejada . . . [has utilized] the extraordinary faculties and the suspension of guarantees to turn elections into a criminal farce."[57]

Even had those rebels not believed their own propaganda, and although the *Porfiristas* were also guilty of electoral irregularities, their accusations demonstrate that their fellow citizens at least harbored suspicions that governmental officials abused their power to affect election results.

53. Ciro B. Ceballos, *Aurora y ocaso*, 2 vols. (Mexico, 1907–12), 2:324–27.

54. Donato Guerra, *proclamación*, 29 October 1871, APD, 10:15.

55. Francisco G. Cosmes, *Historia general de Méjico, continuación a la de don Niceto de Zamacois, parte contemporanea, los últimos 33 años*, 4 vols.,19–22 (Barcelona, 1900–1903) 22:48–49.

56. Plan of La Noria, APD, 9:44–45.

57. Plan of Tuxtepec, ibid., 12:96–100.

Rural Policy

Yet another contradiction between liberal theory and Mexican reality was manifested by the totally unsuccessful social and economic policy toward rural Mexico. The nineteenth-century liberal position toward social and economic problems was to restrain government from any activity beyond education, public health, and public works, to leave the problems to individual initiative, and devil-take-the-hindmost. The hindmost was without doubt rural Mexico, where the vast majority of Mexicans lived in poverty, illiteracy, exploitation, and disease.

Liberals dedicated scant attention to rural misery. They believed that the institutional changes of the Reform guaranteed that Mexico would become a modern nation, and that if peasants did not prosper, it was because they lacked the spirit of individual enterprise. Liberals looked upon villagers as obstacles to progress, for which European migration was the longed-for solution.[58] State budgets in the center of Mexico during the Restored Republic, although derived from the countryside, were used almost exclusively to pay bureaucrats and to police the rural areas. The state governments made almost no expenditures for education, public health, or public works. No federal funds were available to the states except military aid to repress the reaction to rural misery.[59]

The major concern in rural Mexico was land. Before the Reform a number of forms of ownership and usufruct of land existed side by side. Chief among them were the secular *haciendas,* the church estates (frequently rented to small farmers and peasants), free farms (*ranchos*), communal village lands, and public lands (*terrenos baldíos*). The liberal reformers idealized private property and abhorred corporate ownership. Although a political and social theory designed to free men from servitude, Mexican liberalism in the name of private property and freedom abetted the growth of aristocratic *latifundia.* Liberals attacked church land while protecting and promoting *hacienda,* which was the most exploitative form of organization of rural population in

58. González, *La economía mexicana,* pp. 47–48.
59. T. G. Powell, *El liberalismo y el campesinado en el centro de México, 1850 a 1876* (Mexico: SepSetentas, 1974), pp. 136, 139–40.

Mexico. *Ley Lerdo* of 1856 and Juárez's decree of 1859 stripped the church of its wealth in real estate, which largely found its way into the ownership of the *hacendado* class.[60]

Other liberal laws also benefitted the *hacendados* at the expense of peons.[61] The case of the *hacendado* of Las Bocas in San Luis Potosí illustrates how a proprietor was able to reorganize his labor force within laws promulgated by Benito Juárez in 1871 and adopted by the state of San Luis Potosí, a reorganization greatly prejudicial to the peons of that *hacienda*.[62] When Congressman Julio Zárate proposed a bill in 1868 to prohibit *hacendados* from maintaining private jails, inflicting corporal punishment, or passing on debts of peons to their sons, and to demand that *hacendados* erect and support schools for the children of peons, the congressional committee returned the bill to the floor with a negative recommendation, saying it was not in the competence of Congress but rather of local judges to protect civil rights and of local governments to provide schools.[63] While liberals

60. Jan Bazant describes *hacienda* labor organization and the plight of peons in "Peones, arrendatarios y aparceros en México, 1851–1853," *Historia Mexicana* 23, no. 2 (October–December 1973):330–57 and in "Peones, arrendatarios y aparceros, 1868–1904," *Historia Mexicana* 24, no. 1 (July–September 1974):94–121, as well as in *Cinco haciendas mexicanas, tres siglos de vida rural en San Luis Potosí, 1600–1910* (Mexico: Colegio de México, 1975). See also González, *La economía mexicana*, p. 49; and for the consequences of *Ley Lerdo:* Jan Bazant, *Alienation of Church Wealth in Mexico, Social and Economic Aspects of the Liberal Revolution, 1856–1875*, ed. and trans. Michael P. Costeloe (Cambridge: University Press, 1971); Robert J. Knowlton, *Church Property and the Mexican Reform, 1856–1910* (DeKalb, Ill.: Northern Illinois University Press, 1976). Liberal politicians also picked up choice pieces of alienated church land: Powell found that among prominent liberals who bought alienated church lands were Ignacio Comonfort, José María Iglesias, Francisco M. Olaguíbel, José María del Rio, Juan A. de la Fuente, Manuel Payno, Ignacio Mejía and even Benito Juárez: *Liberalismo y campesinado*, pp. 74–75.

61. For convenience one can speak of peons (the term covers a number of groups attached to the *haciendas*) as distinct from peasants (communal villagers, renters, small farmers, day laborers).

62. Bazant, *Cinco haciendas*, pp. 162–63.

63. Powell, *Liberalismo y campesinado*, pp. 134–35. Powell describes other attempts of congressmen to alleviate rural misery, frustrated by congressional adherence to liberal theory, pp. 135–36. Luis González mentions a few liberal attempts to protect peons in *La economía mexicana*, p. 50.

continually spoke of the horrible consequences of peonage, they could not bring themselves to interfere with the internal organization of private property.[64] Congress chose to ignore the reality that *hacendados* frequently controlled local judges and local governments, prejudicial to the interests of peons and peasants. Furthermore, the *hacendado* class was a major ally of Mexican liberalism, and many liberals owned *haciendas*.

Ley Lerdo of 1856 not only alienated church land but also mandated that village communal land be divided among the village peasants in fee simple. The traditional land pattern of Mexican villages was communal, and peasants everywhere resisted the divisions. Liberals assumed, however, that if private property predominated in the countryside, progress would follow. Throughout the decade of the Restored Republic the national government urged the states and municipalities to quicken the pace of distribution. If the process should cause villagers to resist, private owners should be protected and the law enforced by all the power of the state. The peasants complained, however, that communal lands were alienated to people outside the villages, absorbed by adjacent *haciendas*, or sold by political authorities as "unoccupied" public land.[65]

The unoccupied public lands, or *terrenos baldíos*, were legally those which had been crown land in the colony and state or national land during the various periods since independence, but they came to be those lands for which peasants could not produce a title. The Reform liberals dealt with them as assets to be set into production within the framework of private property. The Law of *Terrenos Baldíos* of 1863 became a legal mechanism during the Restored Republic and later in the *Porfiriato* enabling those with access to the courts to despoil villages of their traditional lands, a widely utilized procedure that hastened the alienation of land from the peasants, the growth of *latifundia*, and deeper divisions between wealth and poverty in rural Mexico.[66]

64. Jean Meyer cites the exhortations of prominent liberals in Congress and the press against peonage in *Problemas campesinos y revueltas agrarias, 1821–1910* (Mexico: SepSetentas, 1973), pp. 71–86.

65. Powell, *Liberalismo y campesinado*, pp. 134, 140.

66. James L. Hamon and Stephen R. Niblo, *Presursores de la revolución agraria en México* (Mexico: SepSetentas, 1975), pp. 35–36, 47–50.

Peasants did not submit passively to the alienation of their land. They petitioned at every level of government but were told to seek redress in local courts. There, they complained, they were not protected. Frustrated and alienated peasants then turned to social banditry, which became endemic in rural Mexico. It endured in spite of local and state militias, in spite of suspension of constitutional guarantees, in spite of the creation of rural police, in spite of the law allowing pursuing officers to execute bandits without trial. Several thousand executions every year did not eliminate banditry.[67]

Liberal reaction to rural banditry was repression rather than rural reform, and peasant reaction was rebellion. Peasants rebelled against local governments; they rebelled against state governments; they rebelled against the national government. Peasant rebellions during the Restored Republic were widespread and continuous. When isolated villagers rebelled, governors sent in militias. When whole areas rebelled, their protest was called "caste war" and they were labeled "barbarous Indians" to be dealt with by the federal army. Juárez stated to Congress in 1871 that violence in the countryside was due to "a few perverse Mexicans who . . . provoke disorders and rebellions in order to obtain their personal criminal designs."[68] The liberal solution was always more repression.[69]

67. Powell, *Liberalismo y campesinado*, pp. 29–31, 132.

68. Ibid., pp. 131–33.

69. Moisés González Navarro (*Historia moderna de México, el porfiriato, vida social* [Mexico: Editorial Hermes, 1957] and *Raza y tierra, la guerra de castas y el henequén* [Mexico: Colegio de México, 1970]) places rural rebellion within the context of loss of village land. Jean Meyer (*Problemas campesinos*) catalogues a series of peasant rebellions and associates them directly with changes in land tenure. Other studies do the same: John H. Coatsworth, "Railroads and the Concentration of Land Ownership in the Early Porfiriato," *Hispanic American Historical Review* (1974):48–71; John M. Hart, *Los anarquistas mexicanos, 1860–1900* (Mexico: SepSetentas, 1974); Gastón García Cantú, *El socialsimo en México, siglo xix* (Mexico: Ediciones Era, 1969); María Galaviz de Capdevielle, "Descripción y pacificación de la Sierra Gorda," *Estudios de Historia Novohispana* 4 (1971): 113–49; Donald J. Frazier, "La política de desamortización en las comunidades indígenas, 1856–1872," *Historia Mexicana* 21, no. 4 (April–June 1972): 615–52; Powell, *Liberalismo y campesinado*, pp. 141–48; Paul J. Vanderwood, "Los rurales: producto de una necesidad social," *Historia Mexicana* 22, no. 1 (July–September 1972):34–51. The literature of this phase of the liberal failure is vast and growing: Stephen R. Niblo and Laurens B. Perry, "Recent

Liberal policies toward rural Mexico frequently influenced political and military developments. In 1872 during the insurrection of La Noria, while many functionaries in the state of Hidalgo favored Porfirio Díaz, Juárez used a large scale peasant rebellion in that state as an excuse to declare martial law (*estado de sitio*) and to remove the functionaries. The *Porfirista* political chiefs and municipal authorities conspired to sustain the rebellion against Juárez, arming "bandit" chiefs who supported Díaz.[70] The governmental policy toward rural Mexico in that case added to the strength of the political rebellion and the instability of the liberal government. Thus, in addition to the essential injustice—not merely neglect but positive assault—of Mexican liberalism upon the largest and poorest class, it turned rural Mexico into recruiting grounds for political insurrection.

Extraordinary Faculties

Yet one more contradiction between theory and reality added strain to the period of the Restored Republic. It is clear that the many problems were interrelated, some of them both cause and result of the contradictions. Such was the practice of suspending the individual freedoms guaranteed by the Constitution and congressional awarding of "extraordinary faculties" to the president to decree at will in the departments of war and treasury without further congressional approval of individual acts. These were major modifications of liberalism, born in an atmosphere of unsettled times and contributive to further opposition to the government.

The facts are that the president requested and Congress approved the suspension of constitutional guarantees nine times in nine years, for a total of 49 of the 112 months of the Restored Republic. Furthermore, the president held extraordinary faculties for all but 57 days of the same period, awarded eight separate times by Congress.[71]

Additions to Nineteenth-Century Mexican Historiography," a paper presented to the American Historical Association, 1975.

70. Powell, *Liberalismo y campesinado*, p. 147.

71. Richard N. Sinkin, "Modernization and Reform in Mexico, 1855–1876," (Ph.D. diss., University of Michigan, 1971), pp. 167–71.

The suspension of constitutional guarantees and the granting of extraordinary faculties constituted major modifications of liberalism and fed the fires of the opposition, but had their origins in real problems. The lack of faith in the electoral process, the rivalry of factional politics, the thirst for public office, the economic discontent and rural misery were increasingly manifested in insurrections. The frequency of insurrection is a measure of the size of the problem. More than two score of them kept the nation in a state of insecurity and anxiety during the Restored Republic. Some of them were not serious as events transpired, but all of them had to be dealt with. Several were serious; those were troubled times.[72]

Related to insurrection, but in their purest form less political in content, were banditry and kidnapping. Those armed acts of violence, widespread and incessant over great areas of the republic, kept the countryside and even the city streets in perpetual insecurity. No one has ever attempted to count the incredible number of acts of banditry, assault, and kidnapping. Perpetuated by bands of all sizes and victimizing all levels of society, including governmental depots and convoys, such acts were related directly to the depressed economy and indirectly to politics. Bands frequently joined the banners of rebellion, even as rebels frequently resorted to banditry. One activity blended into the other. So extensive was the activity that it seriously discredited the government, which had to maintain expensive garrisons and armed forces, even as the banditry consumed revenues.

In addition to the instabilizing effects of insurrection and disturbances to the peace, rumors of secession, dissolution of the Union and foreign encroachment further unsettled the times and seemed to demand greater centralization of power. The nation had suffered traumatic experiences. In the 1820s Guatemala and Central America had seceded from Mexico. In the 1830s Texas followed suit. In the 1840s Mexico lost California and New Mexico, and Yucatan declared its independence. During the decade of the 1850s a Mexican faction favored a new Spanish connection, while another considered a quasi-dependency upon the United States, and another piece of territory was transferred to that country. In the 1860s the French Intervention almost extinguished independence. Talk ran rampant

72. A list of insurrections appears as appendix 1.

throughout the decade after 1867 of a Republic of the Sierra Gorda and Republic of the Sierra Madre torn from Mexico. Tepic tried to secede. Many men feared a new expansion from the United States, sometimes substantiated by real threats and plots.[73]

However necessary were the suspensions of constitutional guarantees and awarding of extraordinary faculties, the opposition regularly argued that they made a mockery of constitutional government, were used for political ends, and caused popular discontent.[74] The manifestos of the rebels reflected the same arguments, that rebels turned to insurrections as the only means of changing the personnel of gov-

73. A Sinaloa politician wrote of a plot to erect a "Republic of the West" in 1870: Eustaquio Buelna, *Apuntes para la historia de Sinaloa, 1821–1882* (Mexico: Departamento Editorial de la Secretaría de Educación, 1924), p. 108; Pablo M. Castro warned Juárez of a plot to establish a republic of the northern states and territory of Baja California: Castro to Juárez, 7 May 1869, DDC, 13:875; a United States consul in Monterrey, Nuevo León, reported to Washington that important men in Mexico were preparing for six northern states to secede from the Mexican Republic and that "the United States should be ready to pick up the pieces which would be integrated rapidly due to small northern population and to the benefits of U.S. rule to them": J. Ulrich to Department of State, 12 February 1874, United States, Department of State, Despatches from U.S. Consuls in Monterrey, 1849–1906 (hereafter *Despatches from Monterrey*), M–165, roll 3, doc. 202; the same consul reported rumors of a "Sierra Madre Republic": ibid., 6 October 1874, doc. 211, and 13 October 1874, doc. 214. For the Mexican fear of new territorial expansion from the United States, see *Correspondencia diplomática relativa a las invasiones del territorio mexicano por fuerzas de los Estados Unidos, 1873 a 1877* (Mexico: Imprenta Ignacio Cumplido, 1878); issues of *Periódico Oficial de . . . Nuevo León*, 7 October 1874 and 17 February 1875, carry articles indicative of Mexican fears of U.S. expansion. Some were real; see Michael G. Webster, "Intrigue on the Rio Grande: the Rio Bravo Affair of 1875," *Southwestern Historical Quarterly* 74, no. 2 (October 1970):149–64; Michael G. Webster, "Texan Manifest Destiny and the Republic of the Sierra Madre, A Chronicle of an Expansionist Concept," (paper delivered at the Western History Conference, Fort Worth, Texas, 1973); Paul Horgan, *Great River, the Rio Grande in North American History*, 2 vols. (New York: Rinehart and Co., 1954), 2:857; Luis G. Zorrilla, *Historia de las relaciones entre México y los Estados Unidos de América, 1800–1958*, 2 vols. (Mexico: Editorial Porrúa, 1965), 2:510–26; Walter Prescott Webb, *The Texas Rangers, A Century of Frontier Defense*, 2d ed. (Austin: University of Texas Press, 1965), pp. 238–80.

74. Such is a major thesis of Cosmes, *Historia general de Méjico* and Riva Palacio, *Lerdo*, pp. 134–42.

ernment and of "saving the nation from tyranny." That theme was constantly reiterated in the opposition press of the period. "Today's law-breakers," one newspaper insisted, "are found in the national palace, not in the villages of the highland plateau nor in the columns of the opposition press."[75]

In contrast, one prominent Mexican historian correlates the suspension of constitutional guarantees with the important insurrections to demonstrate his thesis that the rebellions caused the concentrations of power. He judges that the extraordinary faculties were not used harshly, were softened in their rigor over the decade, and were not abused; they were publicly debated and openly enforced; they were never used against opposition congressmen and only three times against newspapermen who would have been found guilty in any court.[76] When authors argue, however, whether rebellions caused increased presidential power, or if concentration and abuse of power caused rebellions, the major point is obscured: the contradictions within the Restored Republic bred a massive confluence of problems, of which rebellions and concentration of presidential power were two interrelated aspects.

The Constitution of 1857 describes how the political system ought to have worked. It also describes the idealism of a generation of great men. The contradictions between the liberal theory and Mexican reality, however, did not allow politicians to behave according to the theory. Practicing politicians therefore turned to the techniques of party centralism. Whether to effect a program or simply to reap the rewards of office, politicians had to have an eye on elections. To assure bills through a factional congress, a parliamentary majority had to be organized. To enforce the presidential program, the cooperation of governors and political chiefs was necessary. To police the system, the loyalty of the federal army and, equally important, the national guard of the several states was mandatory. Only governors could make them available to the president. In effect, a president needed to work closely with governors, because they potentially con-

75. *El Monitor Republicano,* 14 July 1875, p. 1.

76. Daniel Cosío Villegas, *Historia moderna de México, la república restaurada, vida política* (Mexico: Editorial Hermes, 1955), pp. 347–49.

trolled local legislatures, recruitment of soldiers, and selection of congressmen.

Juárez worked well with most of the governors. Indeed, many of them were his appointees from the war years when he held extraordinary powers. They remained his political allies. In other states, however, the governors did not accept his political leadership. Other governors during the following administration resisted the leadership of Sebastián Lerdo de Tejada. Within the reality of Mexican politics, the threat always existed that unfriendly governors would use their enormous power in their states for the benefit of an opposition party or for insurrection against the national government.

Since the cooperation of governors was essential to the presidency, it was natural that the president should aid cooperating governors. This is normal in the political process; however, presidential manipulation for the replacement of uncooperative and even independent governors with partisans and presidential aid to partisan governors against rival groups in state elections border on illegal use of office for party monopolization of power. That such happened during the two administrations of the Restored Republic has long been part of the political lore of the *Juarista* opposition.[77]

To one degree or another the presidents of the Restored Republic used the power of the national government to insure the continuation in power of cooperative governors, replacing opposition and independent governors with factional allies. They augmented executive power at the expense of an increasingly captive legislature; they overlooked, even contributed to, the electoral irregularities that amplified the strength of the presidential party; and the party was used to capture an increasing number of political positions in the statehouses, the municipal palaces, the legislative chambers, and the courthouses of Mexico.

Concomitantly, the use of party techniques removed from or locked out of office an increasing number of men. Some of those men were idealists who interpreted the march of events as a betrayal of the fruits of the Reform; others were factional politicians who had motives of

77. See, for example, Ignacio M. Altamirano, *Historia y política de México,* series "El liberalismo mexicano en pensamiento y en acción" (Mexico: Empresas Editoriales, 1958), pp. 180–81.

self-interest but who could pose as the defenders of freedom and liberalism. Because of the combination of idealism and self-interest of the "outs," the "ins" continually had to strengthen the party monopoly; that in turn augmented the numbers of the alienated "outs." It was but a matter of time, a decade as it happened, that the "outs" organized and turned out the "ins." The benefits of that alienation and organization redounded to Porfirio Díaz.

Increasingly more men arrived at the conclusion that insurrection was the single means of stopping the march of centralistic and monopolistic control of politics through political machines. Old federalists drifted away from *Juarismo* and *Lerdismo*. Many gravitated to *Porfirismo*. Influential and powerful *caudillos* were courted by all factions. Men of caudillistic powers, alienated by Juárez and Lerdo, gravitated to opposition leaders. When the government succeeded in removing a *caudillo* from public office, he stood as a potential enemy of the regime and a focal point for rebellion. Such men included Trinidad García de la Cadena in Zacatecas, Hipólito Charles in Saltillo, Luis Mier y Terán in Veracruz, Juan Haro in Tampico, Juan N. Méndez in Puebla, Vicente Jiménez in Guerrero, Carlos Díaz Gutiérrez in San Luis Potosí, and Juan N. Cortina in Matamoros. Juárez and Lerdo opposed all of them, and all of them eventually became *Porfiristas*. Juárez, we shall see, kept those disgruntled individuals isolated. Lerdo managed to bring them together. That they slowly gathered around Porfirio Díaz is the story of the rise of Porfirian Mexico.

Chapter 2
The Origins of Opposition

A struggle for power characterized the years after the liberal government of Benito Juárez occupied the capital city in mid-July 1867. Old issues between the liberals and conservatives still excited some men in both factions, but conservatism was broken: clerical wealth had been confiscated; conservative party strength had been destroyed; and monarchy—tied to foreign intervention in the public mind—was discredited. In spite of warnings against a conservative revival during the Restored Republic, the liberal-conservative antagonism did not constitute the primary struggle for power.[1]

The real struggle took place among the liberals. The alliance that had turned out the French in 1867 was much broader than the alliance that had won the Three Years' War ending in 1860. The Three Years' War had been a civil war, but the liberal leadership of the Republican Resistance had successfully turned the more recent war into a nationalist revival. The victors in 1860 were the old *puros*—radical, anticlerical republicans. The victors in 1867 were Mexican patriots—a larger, more heterogeneous group. There would necessarily be a struggle for power after the common enemy of the wartime coalition was beaten. The origins of the splintering of the liberal alliance and the first encounters in the struggle for power are the subjects of this chapter.

Juárez undoubtedly enjoyed more political support than any other Mexican leader in 1867. His contribution to the national resistance was rightfully honored, and his services to his nation were almost universally recognized. It was argued that he deserved a peacetime administration to effect his program of reconstruction, and it was frequently observed that if he did not use his wide support, it would divide among various contenders, endangering the Liberal party and

1. Cosmes, *Historia general de Méjico*, 19:3–7; Cosmes, pp. 7–8, argues that the Liberal party was united in 1867 and should have been able to achieve national reorganization, but the government committed grave errors; such is not the thesis here.

the Republic. Furthermore, the argument was widespread that Mexico could best refute conservative and French propaganda—that Maximilian and monarchy had been called to Mexico by a free vote of the people—by overwhelmingly voting in 1867 to retain in the presidency the man who led the Republican Resistance.[2]

Nevertheless, by August 1867 some former supporters were dissatisfied with Juárez's continuation in the presidency. Some thought him too intransigent to work the task of reconciliation and reconstruction; others believed that nine years in the presidency, although only four of them as constitutionally elected president, were more than enough for one man and that four more years would be dangerous to the spirit of republicanism. Others feared, or claimed to fear, the centralist tendencies of the *Juarista* government. Still others claimed to see dictatorial tendencies. More importantly, a number of political issues took shape immediately upon the return of the republican government to Mexico City. Collectively they caused the republican alliance to splinter.

The military reorganization of 27 July and demobilization, according to some accounts, were among the causes of disturbance.[3] In July 1867 Juárez reorganized the army into five divisions of 4,000 men each, reduced from some 80,000 men.[4] While the reorganization doubtless upset the plans of some officers to keep their personally

2. *Correo de México,* 12 September 1867; *El Siglo XIX,* 22 December 1867; Justo Sierra, *The Political Evolution of the Mexican People,* trans. Charles Ramsdell (Austin: University of Texas Press, 1969), pp. 426–27; and, for example, Francisco Zarco to Juárez, 25 July 1867, DDC, 12:260; Matías Romero to Juárez, 21 July 1867, DDC, 12:314; Antonio M. Zamacona to anon., 12 September 1867, DDC, 12:433; Rafael Zayas Enríquez, *Los Estados Unidos Mexicanos, sus progresos en veinte años de paz, 1877–1897* (New York: H.A. Rost Co., n.d.), p. 23; Cosmes, *Historia general de Méjico,* 19:70.

3. Bancroft, *History of Mexico,* 6:352–53; Francisco Bulnes, *Rectificaciones y aclaraciones a las memorias del general Porfirio Díaz* (México: Biblioteca Histórica de "El Universal," 1922), p. 262.

4. The First Division was placed under the command of Gen. Nicolás Régulas with headquarters in Mexico City, the Second Division under Díaz at Tehuacán, the Third under Mariano Escobedo in San Luis Potosí, the Fourth under Ramón Corona at Guadalajara, and the Fifth, composed only of the garrison of Acapulco, under Juan Alvarez. See Porfirio Díaz, *Las memorias de Porfirio Díaz, 1830–1867,* 2d ed., 2 vols. (Mexico: El Libro Francés, 1923), 2:197.

raised forces under their personal command, the troops as well as many officers were clamoring for demobilization. Within the year, however, the government was again forced to use the levy to raise troops for national needs.[5] Both the government and the opposition acknowledged the problem of paying for the oversized military establishment, and both Díaz and Gen. Mariano Escobedo were demobilizing units before they were ordered to do so.[6] The demobilization threw veteran soldiers out of work, many of whom thereafter turned to banditry and even lent their experience to factional warfare, but the liberal leaders in 1867 did not oppose the demobilization. Although the decision about which officers would remain in governmental service and which would be separated may sometimes have been influenced by politics, it may be concluded that military reform was not a divisive issue among liberal leaders. Three other issues, more important than the military reorganization, account for the breakdown of the liberal alliance.

One issue that divided liberals was what to do with the men who had accepted employment with the empire. For a short time the government adopted a policy of persecution, which by the law of 16 August 1863 included the confiscation of estates of all men who had served the empire. Some imperialists were tried and shot, some were sentenced to prison, twelve prominent imperial adherents were exiled, and a larger number were paroled under official surveillance. Confiscations were soon commuted by presidential order and replaced by a system of fines. While the rigors of persecution lessened, some liberals demanded full compliance with the law. Simultaneously, many liberals condemned the prosecutions as unconstitutional and pressed for a law of amnesty. The government tended to a middle course, which appeared to yet others as an off-and-on procedure, characterized by political favoritism. The issue was necessarily emotional, from which no government could have emerged unscathed. It had the net effect of agitating the heterogeneous Liberal party.[7]

5. Cosío Villegas, *República restaurada,* pp. 124–35.
6. Díaz, *Memorias,* 2:190; Juárez to Díaz, 3 July 1867, Porfirio Díaz Papers (hereafter PDP), box 9, William Clements Library, Ann Arbor, Mich.
7. Bancroft, *History of Mexico,* 6:350–51; Dublán and Lozano, *Legislación mexicana,* 10:32, 42–43, 109–10, 112; Tovar, *Cuarto congreso,* 1:iv–vi, 65–400 *passim; El Monitor Republicano, La Orquesta, El Siglo XIX,* August–September,

A second issue dividing the republican alliance related to the popular Zacatecan general, Jesús González Ortega.[8] In 1862 González Ortega was elected to the presidency of the Supreme Court, a position which placed him first in line of succession to the presidency.[9] When Juárez's constitutional presidency, by the widest interpretation of his legal term of office, should have terminated on 30 November 1865, it was openly known that Ortega was planning in New York to claim the presidency.[10] Furthermore, by the summer of that year it was also clear that not all republican leaders would accept an extension of Juárez's term of office without elections.

What some men called the Juárez coup d'état involved three steps. It began with Lerdo's circular of 28 October 1865 to the state governors: high governmental or military personnel who had left Mexico during the Intervention were to be apprehended by the first military or political authority having the opportunity and held for trial. The second step transpired on 8 November 1865: Juárez decreed the extension of his own presidential term and that of the president of the Supreme Court until elections could be held. Third, Juárez then decreed that Ortega had voluntarily abandoned his post with the Su-

---

1867; Cosmes, *Historia general de Méjico*, 1:8–10, 13–20. Cosmes's theme is that liberals deplored the vengeful measures of the government, which were a reflection of Lerdo's harsh policy, whereas the natural inclination of Juárez was to be lenient and conciliatory whenever the presidential chair was not in contest.

8. Except where noted, the following sketch of the González Ortega affair is taken from Ivie E. Cadenhead, "González Ortega and the Presidency of Mexico," *Hispanic American Historical Review* 32, no. 3 (August 1952):331–46. González Ortega was known to his contemporaries as Ortega, not González.

9. The Constitution of 1857, article seventy-nine, says "In the temporary absences of the president of the Republic, and in the absolute [absence] until the president-elect is inaugurated, the president of the supreme court will exercise the executive power." Men of the Restored Republic frequently referred to the president of the Supreme Court as "vice-president."

10. Juárez suspected as much as early as March 1865, when he gave Ortega license to leave Mexico in order to reenter at another point to fight the French: "It seems that what he wants is to rest and only when the presidency is cooked and served will he return to claim it." Juárez to Pedro Santacilia, 30 March 1865, in José Manuel Puig Casauranc, ed., *Archivos privados de D. Benito Juárez y D. Pedro Santacilia* (Mexico: Publicaciones de la Secretaría de Educación Pública, 1928), p. xiii.

preme Court by remaining in a foreign country "without permission or commission of the government." The decree meant that Ortega should be arrested and tried for desertion.

Juárez thereafter destroyed Ortega's public career. After Ortega and other republican leaders issued a series of protests and a flurry of pamphlets, partially legalistic and partially propagandistic, Ortega reentered Mexico in December 1866. Arrested and held without trial, Ortega was in prison during the election of 1867. He was released in July 1868 with the understanding that the government reserved the right to prosecute him.[11] The apparent governmental clemency diminished the chances for an *Orteguista* attempt to revive his claims to either public post which he had held, while the government's reservation of rights to prosecute him was a real threat to do so if Ortega reentered politics. Upon his release, he dramatically resigned from the presidency of the Court and interim presidency of the nation and promised to retire from all politics.[12] He remained loyal to his promise to his death.

The object here in raising the case of González Ortega is not to question the legality, wisdom, or motives of Juárez's decision between 1865 and 1868—one can hardly imagine a happier termination of the French Intervention under the leadership of González Ortega.[13] The case is raised because it was a point of controversy throughout the

11. See Cadenhead, "González Ortega," footnotes, for extensive bibliography.

12. *Manifiesto,* 19 August 1868, reprinted in Ceballos, *Aurora y ocaso,* 1:328–32; Tamayo, *Juárez,* 12:459–62, and documents, DDC, 12:463–76; José González Ortega, *El golpe de estado de Juárez* (Mexico, 1941).

13. The imagination soars with the implication of the following note from the Mexican minister in Washington: "Among the correspondence of Mr. Campbell [Louis Campbell was sent to Mexico with ministerial credentials by Secretary of State William Seward in the summer of 1866] which was recently released . . . is a document that *don* Jesús González Ortega was in connivance with the French. The document consists of a memorandum of a conversation between Mr. Seward and the French Minister, in which the latter proposed to the former that the United States and France set you and Maximilian aside to advance and favor the candidacy of Ortega. I believe it is certain that Napoleon would not have taken this step without having made a previous arrangement with Ortega." Matías Romero to Juárez, 17 August 1867, DDC, 12:393.

election of 1867, when opposition to the Juárez government was forming.

The *Orteguista* affair had important political consequences for some men. Some *Orteguistas* left politics altogether. Miguel Ruiz retired from politics, and José María Patoni, who returned to Mexico with Ortega and was imprisoned with him, was shot upon release. Some other liberals lost much of their political significance during the Restored Republic by having joined *Orteguismo*. Guillermo Prieto and Felipe Berriozábal fell from high positions and joined the movement of José María Iglesias in 1876. Other *Orteguistas* returned to Juárez, such as Gaspar Sánchez Ochoa, José Montesinos, and Juan José Baz. Yet others remained alienated from Juárez, and in the absence of Ortega in 1867 gravitated to and supported Porfirio Díaz: Servando Canales, Miguel Negrete, and Manuel María de Zamacona all became important in the rise of the "Porfirian Circle."[14]

A third issue dividing the liberal alliance was the *convocatoria* of 1867. On 14 August, when Sebastián Lerdo do Tejada, as secretary of *gobernación*, published the decree, or *convocatoria*, calling for the election of president, justices of the Supreme Court, and congressmen to the Fourth Congress, a controversy developed that became the principal cause of the division of the Liberal party.[15] The *convocatoria* of 1867 is unique in Mexican history in that attached to it was an order that at the time of choosing electors the people should signal their approval of or displeasure with a proposition authorizing Congress to consider and enact five constitutional amendments without having to proceed in accordance with the constitutional amendment process.[16]

14. For a discussion of the careers of these men see appendix 2.

15. The *convocatoria* is discussed in the following: José Fuentes Mares, "La convocatoria de 1867," *Historia Mexicana*, 14, no. 3 (January 1965):423–44; Frank Averill Knapp, Jr., *The Life of Sebastian Lerdo de Tejada: A Study in Influence and Obscurity* (Austin: University of Texas Press, 1951), pp. 122–28; Ceballos, *Aurora y ocaso*, 1:27–33; Cosmes, *Historia general de Méjico*, 19:21–45, 53–66, 84–86; Sierra, *Political Evolution*, pp. 517–18; Bancroft, *History of Mexico*, 6:367–68; Cosío Villegas, *República restaurada*, pp. 81–82, 189–95, 220–21; Tamayo, *Juárez*, 12:319–24, 407–12, 517–20. The Second Congress, 1863–65, was elected but could not conduct sessions due to the French Intervention. The Third Congress, 1865–67, was never elected. The Congress of 1867–69 was called the Fourth Congress.

16. Dublán and Lozano, *Legislación Mexicana*, 10:44–49, and Tovar, *Cuarto*

The probable object of the so-called plebiscite within the *convocatoria* was to rush through the amendments while Juárez's prestige was high by authorizing Congress to legislate them without reference to the ratification process, which required the approbation of a majority of the state legislatures.

A cursory glance at the proposed amendments indicates that Juárez was attempting to bolster executive strength at the expense of the legislature within the federal government. The first amendment would have created a senate within Congress to share the legislative function, thus diluting the legislative power between two chambers and creating congressional rivalry useful to the executive. The second amendment would give the president a veto over legislative bills, which could only be overridden by a two-thirds vote of Congress. The third amendment would authorize ministers to respond to congressional inquiries in written communications, replacing the verbal reports which had enabled the First Congress (1861–63) to cross-examine cabinet ministers in Congress, frequently to the embarrassment and generally to the harassment of the administration. The fourth amendment would limit the power of the "permanent commission" (a body of congressmen who represented the legislature when Congress was recessed) in its authority to call special sessions of the whole Congress. The fifth amendment would allow Congress to stipulate the line of succession to the presidency beyond the president of the Supreme Court. The probable object of the last amendment in 1867 was to give Juárez, after he had declared González Ortega ineligible to succeed to the presidency in 1865, an apparent claim to the argument that he would have surrendered the presidency to an eligible successor had there been one stipulated by the Constitution.[17]

---

congreso, 1:3–7; reprinted in APD, 4:327–34, and DDC, 12:325–32; the "plebiscite," or *apelación al pueblo* is ordered in article 9.

17. The fifth amendment proposed in the *convocatoria* of 1867 may also have been calculated to take the edge off the objection that the amendments were centralistic, or simply to disarm the opposition of the argument that the administration was personally interested in the amendments. Attached to the *convocatoria* when sent to the governors of the states was a circular written by the secretary of *gobernación,* Sebastián Lerdo de Tejada, explaining the urgency and wisdom of the amendments. Included in the circular were these words: "According to the constitutional organization, the legislature is every-

The protest against the *convocatoria* was immediate and furious. A few men questioned the urgency and merits of the proposed amendments; more men attacked the rehabilitation of the "imperialists" and clergy, as stipulated in articles 22 through 26 of the *convocatoria;* and yet other opposition was aimed at the presidential initiative of constitutional reform by plebiscite in disregard of the ratification by state legislatures. Manuel María de Zamacona led the fight from his newspaper *El Globo,* in which he held that the procedure was an attack upon the constitution and recommended a boycott of the plebiscite.[18] Pantaleón Tovar, speaking from the prestigious *El Siglo XIX,* said, "We do not speak now of whether the amendments are convenient; we speak of the danger to our constitutional rights because of the manner and form with which they are introduced."[19] On 20 August a protest against the *convocatoria* was published and signed by the editorial staffs of ten capital city newspapers, including some of the most outstanding men of journalism—and of the Liberal party.[20] Many of those men thereafter opposed the election of Juárez, and some of them became and remained *Porfiristas.*

So loud was the protest that Juárez felt obliged to issue his own circular to justify the administration's position, in which he pressed the urgency of the reforms and the legality of appealing to the sover-

---

thing, and the executive lacks proper authority. . . . This could occasion grave difficulties for the normal function of both branches." The circular is reprinted in Tovar, *Cuarto congreso,* 9–13, APD, 4:339–47, and DDC, 12:332–41. The best explanation of the circular is Knapp, *Lerdo,* pp. 126–28.

18. *El Globo,* 19 August 1867.

19. *El Siglo XIX,* reproduced in APD, 4:358–60.

20. For *El Siglo XIX,* Pantaleón Tovar, Joaquín M. Alcalde, Alfredo Chavero; *El Globo,* Manuel M. de Zamacona and Juan Bustamante y Chico; *El Monitor Republicano,* José María Castillo Velasco, Gabino F. Bustamante, José M. Villa; *El Boletín Republicano,* Lorenzo Elizaga, Juan Abadiano, Basilio Pérez Gallardo; *El Constitutional,* Gregorio Pérez Jardón, Juan N. Mirafuentes, Manuel Gordillo Reynosa, Carlos de Gagern; *El Defensor del Pueblo,* Luis Picazo and Braulio Picazo; *La Consciencia Pública,* Manuel Morales Puente; *La Sombra,* Juan de Dios Arias; *El Diablo Amarillo,* Luis Iza; *La Orquesta,* Vicente Riva Palacio and Constantino Escalante. It will be noted that the first collective protest of these same newspapers was against article 4 of the law of 14 August 1867 on freedom of the press, but the issue was drowned out by the *convocatoria.*

eignty of the people.[21] José Díaz Covarrubias, editor of the *Diario Oficial*, acknowledged the protests in order to maintain that they only concerned the mode of presenting the reforms and to justify the procedure; nevertheless, the tone of his writing indicates that not even he had his heart in his work.[22] When he attempted to leave the impression that only the capital city press was objecting, *El Correo de Mexico*, edited by Ignacio M. Altamirano, published editorials for six weeks from all over Mexico that were hostile to the *convocatoria*.

The Juárez archive is filled with correspondence relating to the *convocatoria*, and the overwhelming majority of it is adverse. Esteban Castillo wrote from Tlaxcala that the *convocatoria* was disliked in the country and ought to be revoked, and that should Juárez not do so he would "run to his ruin like wretched Comonfort."[23] Interim governor of Puebla, Gen. Juan N. Méndez, wrote Juárez that the publication of the *convocatoria* "has produced a strong and disfavorable sensation among all classes, and that the city council has drawn up a manifesto against it." The military commander in the port city of Veracruz, who analyzed and criticized the document at length, told Juárez that "the reprobation is general, almost unanimous." Clemente López, long-time liberal and friend of Juárez, wrote that although the intentions of the *convocatoria* were sincere and the reforms necessary, nevertheless the timing was wholly wrong and the method so badly considered that civil war might yet result. Indeed, López thought the *convocatoria* would not be published in Puebla and that, if it were not withdrawn, some persons would resort to arms. In his private correspondence, Juárez admitted that "the press in this city has almost totally declared itself against the government because of the *convocatoria*."[24]

21. 22 August 1867, reprinted in Tovar, *Cuarto congreso*, 1:13–14; APD, 4:356–57; DDC, 12:341–42; Ceballos, *Aurora y Ocaso*, 1:309–11.

22. Reprinted in APD, 4:349–55. *Diario Oficial* has led several authors to conclude that the major opposition to the *convocatoria* was based not on the substance of the reforms but on the mode of presenting them. A large sampling of *La Orquesta, El Globo, El Correo de México*, and *La Conciencia Pública* indicates that the clerical vote, the presidential veto, the creation of a senate, and the written ministerial reports received as much criticism as the "plebiscite."

23. Castillo to Juárez, 21 August 1867, DDC, 12:413.

24. Méndez to Juárez, 22 August 1867, ibid., p. 415; Luis Mier y Terán to Juárez, 24 August 1867, ibid., pp. 416–19; López to Juárez, 21 August 1867,

The storm continued unabated. Gen. Pedro de Baranda spoke "with frankness, that had it been presented in other terms, free of all ideas that could be considered at battle with the Constitution . . ." no one would have objected. Gen. Miguel Auza, governor of Zacatecas, swore his loyalty but also spoke "with all frankness" that the *convocatoria* and the proposed reforms "have displeased everyone, who do not believe them necessary, but on the contrary believe they falsify the principles for which the nation has fought so many years" and recommended that the reforms be withdrawn from the election. The loyal *Juarista* governor of Sinaloa, Gen. Domingo Rubí, acknowledged the good intentions of the government but thought the *convocatoria* constituted "a bad example which could have imitators." Juárez's friend and *compadre* in Chihuahua and later orator at Juárez's funeral, Rogue J. Morón, wrote "with profound sentiment that . . . the *convocatoria* . . . has been badly received here and the opinion of the press in general is unanimous and explicit against the decree." During the independence celebration on the evening of 15 September Juárez shouted the traditional words from the national balcony "long live independence, long live liberty, long live Hidalgo," to which a man in the crowd added "long live the constitution." According to *El Correo de México,* "his shout was picked up by the crowd with tumultuous applause." When the electoral college for Mexico City met in October, the electors unanimously approved a declaration of protest against calling upon the people in a general election to initiate amendment procedures.[25]

Finally, when Juárez opened the Fourth Congress on 8 December, he capitulated on the constitutional reforms. Although a great many people voted in favor of setting aside the constitutional amendment process, he said, Congress might better discuss the reforms than count the votes. The administration would propose the amendments at a later time in the prescribed manner.[26] Less nobly, Juárez wrote to

---

ibid., pp. 422–23; Juárez to Matíaz Romero, 28 August 1867, *Epistolario de Benito Juárez,* ed. Jorge L. Tamayo (Mexico: Fondo de Cultura Económico, 1957, 1972), 1st ed., p. 408.

25. Baranda to Juárez, 2 September 1867, DDC, 12:428: Auza to Juárez, 2 September 1867, ibid., p. 429; Rubí to Juárez, 18 September 1867, ibid., p. 437; Morón to Juárez, 18 September 1867, ibid., p. 438; *El Correo de México,* 16 September 1867, p. 3; Declaration, 6 October 1867, DDC, 12:589.

26. Tovar, *Cuarto congreso,* 8 December 1867, 1:58.

the governor of Chihuahua that most of the protesters were "those people who by the same *convocatoria* had to rehabilitate themselves in order to enjoy certain political rights"—that is, those who had worked for the empire.[27] In fact, the principal opposition to the *convocatoria* emerged from within the liberal alliance.

The more probable reasons why Juárez recommended that Congress not count the vote on the amendments were that the issue had raised much more opposition than he had supposed and that the count might have been adverse.[28] Moreover, since the elections of 1867 had safely returned a majority of *Juarista* governors, Juárez had nothing to fear by a normal constitutional amendment process, even in the face of a dissolution of the wartime coalition and a hostile press.

The attitudes of the press of the capital city during the summer and autumn of 1867 provide an indicator of the dissolution of the wartime coalition. Virtually all the Mexico City press at midsummer of 1867 stood squarely behind the newly arrived republican government of Benito Juárez. Even though a plethora of newspapers had commenced publication in the larger cities of Mexico, Vicente Riva Palacio wrote on 3 July that "there is still lacking an opposition press." After writing an eulogistic encomium of Juárez and his ministers upon their arrival in Mexico City on 15 July, Riva Palacio moved his own paper, the semi-weekly *La Orquesta,* into a position of mild opposition to the cabinet by late July.[29] *El Globo,* edited by Manuel María de Zamacona, sang the praises of the ministry until the first week of August, when it too began urging faster action toward a *convocatoria* and a return to constitutional government. Its first broadside attacks were against the amendments and the plebiscite in the *convocatoria.* Becoming a bitter enemy of the administration by mid-September, it urged the candidacy of Porfirio Díaz. *La Conciencia Pública,* edited by Manuel Morales Puente, who shortly became a *Porfirista* congressman, entered opposition in strong fashion against the amendments and the plebiscite in the *convocatoria.* By September Altamirano's *Correo de México* was printing arguments against the reelection of Juárez, saying that it was

27. Juárez to Tarrazas, 10 October 1867, *Epistolario,* 1st ed., p. 415.

28. *El Correo de México,* 28 September 1867, p. 2, reported that the Mexico City popular vote had registered only 897 votes in favor of the amendments, 2,352 against, and 6,500 "not recognizing the administration's right to reform the Constitution."

29. *La Orquesta,* 17 August 1867, p. 1.

not Juárez who had won the war and that Juárez should not have abandoned the capital in 1863. A September editorial in *La Orquesta* deplored the fact that Díaz's division in Tehuacán was being cited as a threat of Caesarism and dictatorship: "Why does the present dictatorship, which is real and positive," it asked, "terrify us less than the problematical and conjectural one . . ." of Díaz.[30] *Correo*'s 1 October issue included a thirty-inch article by José María Mata, who cited the *convocatoria* as the reason why the "Democratic Constitutional Party" was withdrawing its electoral endorsement of Juárez and supporting Porfirio Díaz.

Wartime alliances frequently collapse upon victory, sometimes because the allies subordinate their real differences in the face of a common enemy, only later having to deal with those differences. At other times the warfare itself turns merely competent men into exceptional leaders who later compete for supreme leadership. In Mexico in 1867 some elements of both of those conditions existed. The issues were authentic. The problem of what to do with the adherents of the Maximilian regime was a thorny one that was bound to cause various profoundly emotional reactions. The case of González Ortega was also disturbing. The Juárez argument was widely accepted in 1865 in favor of unity against the invading army, but to retain Ortega in prison during the peacetime elections of late 1867 upset some men and seemed to indicate that Juárez coveted power more than he courted legal process. The issue of the *convocatoria* was the major factor. At the least, the inclusion of the amendments in the *convocatoria* was an enormous political mistake. At most, Juárez attempted a coup d'état in the march to the supreme executive. The *convocatoria*, above all other issues, was the impetus for the creation of an anti-Juárez party, which variously called itself the Constitutionalist party or the Progressivist party, and which chose Gen. Porfirio Díaz to be its presidential candidate.

Historians have traditionally interpreted the estrangement of Porfirio Díaz and Benito Juárez during the summer of 1867 as one of the most significant political developments in nineteenth-century Mexico. The change in the relationship between them from friends and allies to political adversaries and ultimately to leaders of warring

---

30. *El Correo de México*, 12 September 1867, p. 1; *La Orquesta*, 14 September 1867; José María Mata to Díaz, 22 September 1867, DDC, 12:512.

parties surprised contemporaries and was later seen as the tragedy of the Restored Republic. Such historians attribute the estrangement and ultimately the replacement of "Juárez democracy" with "Díaz dictatorship" to trivial personal affronts, related repeatedly in historical anecdote, rather than to the frequent dissolution of wartime alliances and to the impossibility of reconciling the theory and the practice of the age.

One series of events later seen as the origin of opposition was the competition for manpower and materiel of war between Díaz and Gen. Mariano Escobedo during the simultaneous sieges of Mexico City and Querétaro. The real needs of the two generals were necessarily competitive. In retrospect, their cooperation and gestures of abnegation are incredible, although some historians would like to believe that Juárez favored Escobedo and thus laid the groundwork for a future rupture with Díaz.[31]

Another issue frequently cited as the reason for the estrangement of Juárez and Díaz related to prisoners of war. That Díaz is generally considered to have been more lenient to captured enemies than Juárez has been singled out as a mutual irritant.[32] Neither man, however, was shooting all prisoners. Upon the fall of Puebla, Díaz shot twenty high-ranking imperialists and then ordered the release of all prisoners taken in the battles of Miahuatlán, la Carbonera, Oaxaca, and Puebla—doing so reluctantly, according to anecdote, saying he did not wish to give Juárez reason to believe he was competing with him for public esteem.[33] In his memoirs, however, Díaz said that the number of prisoners was too large to shoot and that the order specifi-

31. See Carleton Beals, *Porfirio Díaz, Dictator of Mexico* (Philadelphia: J. B. Lippincott, 1932), pp. 158, 170–73; David Lynn Miller, "Porfirio Díaz and the Army of the East," (Ph.D. diss., University of Michigan, 1960), p. 283; cf. Díaz, *Memorias,* 2:107, 147, 155–56, 163, 173, 323.

32. Salvador Quevedo y Zubieta, *El Caudillo, continuación de Porfirio Díaz, ensayo de psicología histórica* (Mexico: Libería de la viuda de C. Bouret, 1909), p. 175; Angel Taracena, *Porfirio Díaz* (Mexico: Editorial Jus, *"Figuras y episodios de la historia de México,"* 1960), p. 81; Nemesio García Naranjo, *Porfirio Díaz* (San Antonio: Editorial Lozano, 1930), p. 178; Carreño, APD, 4:*notas,* 6–7.

33. Miguel Galindo y Galindo, *La gran década nacional,* 3 vols. (Mexico: Imprenta y Fototipía de la Secretaría de Fomento, 1904–1906), 3:556; Bancroft, *History of Mexico,* 6:340; see also Juárez to Díaz, 27 April 1867, *Epistolario,* 2d ed., pp. 672, 674; Díaz, *Memorias,* 2:123.

cally stated that all prisoners were thereafter "at the disposition of the Supreme Government"—that is, at the call and final judgment of Juárez. Thus Díaz was not even making a final disposition. When Díaz later asked the minister of war, a Juárez appointee, for instructions on treatment of prisoners upon the fall of Mexico, he received a general outline and was told to proceed as he wished.[34] Taken together, the events seem to indicate that Juárez did not disapprove of Díaz's policy and that the two men were not far apart in their thinking.

Díaz later dictated into his memoirs two incidents—his refusal to arrest the French minister in Mexico City as Juárez had ordered him to do and his appointment of Juan José Baz as political chief of Mexico City—which others have emphasized as irritants to Juárez.[35] Díaz's supposed reluctance or refusal to keep Juárez informed during the siege of Mexico and Juárez's supposed coolness in his congratulations upon the assault of Puebla and his lack of recognition of Díaz when Juárez returned to Mexico City in July are alternately made the basis of future antipathy.[36] Those incidents, however, were initially seized upon by contemporaries who had not seen the private correspondence between the two men.[37] Both men were tired and busy in mid-year 1867. Juárez had reasons of state for lauding the people's resistance to the French rather than citing individual generals on all occasions, but the generals were not slighted in private correspondence, public ceremony, or personal considerations. This was not the basis of the later estrangement between Juárez and Díaz.

34. Díaz, *Memorias*, 2:133–35; telegrams, Díaz to Ignacio Mejía and answer, both 21 June 1867, DDC, 12:195.

35. Beals, *Porfirio Díaz*, pp. 170–73; Quevedo y Zubieta, *El Caudillo*, p. 175; Taracena, *Porfirio Díaz*, p. 82; Miller, "The Army of the East," pp. 283, 321; Díaz, *Memorias*, 2:194–95; Díaz to Justo Benítes, 7 June 1867, DDC, 12:50.

36. For example, Henry Bamford Parkes, *A History of Mexico*, 3d ed. (Boston: Houghton Mifflin Company, 1970), p. 281; Quevedo y Zubieta, *El caudillo*, p. 174; Taracena, *Porfirio Díaz, p. 81;* García Naranjo, *Porfirio Díaz*, p. 177; cf. the friendly correspondence between Juárez and Baz, DDC, 12:193.

37. See APD, 1:174, and various letters in APD, 4; especially see DDC, 12:187, 193. Cosío Villegas (*República restaurada*, pp. 212–18) argues compellingly that Díaz was regularly praised by his superiors for his victories, that Díaz regularly mentioned his gratitude toward them, and that historians have produced no evidence to support the thesis of cooling relations between Díaz and Juárez.

Díaz's resignation has also been offered as a point of friction between him and Juárez. Díaz submitted his first resignation on 21 June, the day of the capitulation of Mexico City. It went unanswered. On 11 July Díaz sent a circular to the various governors of the states in his command "worded in such a way as to suggest that it was a farewell message from a retiring commander."[38] Two days later Díaz tendered his resignation to the minister of war, citing the end of the emergency, since the government had returned to the Federal District.[39] Supposedly, Juárez was piqued by the resignation, or Díaz was irritated that the resignation was not accepted.[40] It is unlikely, however, that the resignation was a factor in the estrangement of the two leaders.[41]

Another tale honored in anecdote is that Juárez snubbed Díaz as the presidential carriage rolled into Mexico City on 15 July, passing by the great general who had captured the city from the "imperialists," organized the festivities, and ordered the flag not to be raised above the national palace until Juárez arrived.[42] In fact, Juárez had met with Díaz in Tlalnepantla, where, according to Díaz, Juárez asked Díaz to arrange payments for Juárez's escort and ministers.[43] The protocol of the ceremony had doubtless been carefully worked out so that the second carriage, in which Lerdo was riding, would stop for General Díaz.

One final event singled out as the breaking point between the president and his general was a dinner reception given for Juárez in August by some outstanding liberals in the name of Díaz, who publicly denied his sponsorship of the reception in an open letter to the *Diario Oficial*. The denial was interpreted then and later as an insult to the president.[44]

38. Circular, 11 July 1867, PDP, cited by Miller, "The Army of the East," p. 279; the resignation is reprinted in Díaz, *Memorias*, 2:190.

39. *El Siglo XIX*, 15 July 1867.

40. Quevedo y Zubieta, *El Caudillo*, p. 178; Carreño (APD, 4:*notas*, 6) has Juárez remove Díaz, "possibly with the idea of weakening him," having noted that Díaz was more popular than himself.

41. The case is discussed in appendix 3.

42. Parkes, *A History of Mexico*, p. 281; Carreño, APD, 4:*notas*, 7; Quevedo y Zubieta, *El Caudillo*, p. 176.

43. Díaz, *Memorias*, 2:193–94.

44. *Diario Oficial*, 27 August 1867, reprinted in DDC, 12:377–78; Quevedo y Zubieta, *El Caudillo*, p. 180; Taracena, *Porfirio Díaz*, pp. 82–83.

Díaz, thereafter, included disparaging remarks about Juárez in his correspondence. To requests for recommendations to the government he frequently answered that he no longer had the favor of the government and had less power than a corporal in his own division.[45] For a time after mid-August Díaz used the *convocatoria* as his major complaint. Later Díaz complained of his lack of authority to care for the military units in his command, the unconstitutional acts of the government, and the removal of his appointees in areas he had formerly controlled.[46]

Nevertheless, Juárez did not press for the rupture. Díaz sometimes sent recommendations for individuals and for military administration, which Juárez assiduously answered until his separation from the army in early 1868. In January 1868 Díaz sought and received a four-month leave from military service. In May 1868 Díaz sought a two-year extension of his separation without pay, and Juárez insisted that Díaz accept two-thirds of the salary as the law provided. Furthermore, Juárez extended to Díaz through their mutual friend, Matías Romero, the appointment to the important embassy in Washington, which Díaz refused, and Romero suggested to Díaz the presidency of a railroad company, complete with governmental contracts.[47]

The key to the Juárez-Díaz relationship in 1867 resides not in fears, jealousies, snubs, or affronts, but rather in the natural dissolution of

45. This response took various forms; for example, Díaz to J. Robles, 1 August 1867, APD, 4:143–44; Díaz to Juan N. Méndez, 26 September 1867, ibid., 5:70; Díaz to Eufemio Rojas, 9 October 1867, ibid., p. 139.

46. Undated answer to letter from Vicente Jiménez to Díaz, 8 August 1867, ibid., 4:168, and DDC, 12:375; I. Robledo to Díaz, 1 August 1867, and answer, APD, 4:141–43; Miguel Arechavaleta to Díaz, 21 August 1867, and answer, APD, 4:215–16; Juan Bustamante to Díaz, 16 August 1867, and answer, APD, 4:197–99; Julian Díaz Ordaz, 22 September 1867, and answer, APD, 5:59; Díaz to Fidencio Hernández, 21 October 1867, DDC, 12:504.

47. In one, Díaz recommended someone to Juárez, 23 October 1867, DDC, 12:691: see also another in which Juárez responded courteously and affirmatively, October 1867, ibid., p. 691; Díaz to Juárez, 20 May 1868; Juárez to Díaz, 26 May 1868, *Epistolario*, 1st ed., p. 464; DDC, 13:337–39; Carreño, APD, 4 *notas*:9; Romero to Díaz, 18 December 1867, ibid., 5:413. Romero later suggested that Díaz join him as a partner in a sugar hacienda in Cuernavaca: Romero to Díaz, 2 April 1869, *Colección General Porfirio Díaz*, University of the Americas, Cholula, Mexico, *legajo* 42, doc. 1188 (hereafter CPD).

the wartime coalition and the emergence of an opposition to Benito Juárez. We do not know when Díaz made his decision to enter national politics as a challenger for the presidency of Mexico, but it would be an unimportant decision to history if Juárez had not acquired an opposition. At that time, Díaz did not commence to put together an opposition party. Rather, a group of individuals, mostly lawyers and newspapermen who opposed Juárez, looked about for a leader and seized upon Díaz. Once having accepted, Díaz broke with Juárez; his public denial of the honorary dinner and his complaints about and attacks upon the administration all follow his acceptance of the leadership of the opposition as a candidate for the presidency in the elections of 1867. The sometimes offensive way in which Díaz attacked Juárez was designed to disassociate himself from the government and to demonstrate his commitment to the opposition role.[48] The real question, then, is not what Juárez did to alienate Díaz, but why Juárez's opponents chose Díaz to lead them.

It has never been satisfactorily explained why so many individuals over the decade gravitated to Porfirio Díaz of all the great men of the Restored Republic. In 1867 he had a magnificent military reputation and projected himself as an obedient servant of the nation. He seemed in 1867 a likely candidate to obtain the military vote and curried the favor of those elements over the years. Although he did not have long years of administrative experience, what experience he had was untarnished by scandal. He respectfully observed legality and constitutionality. He had a simple republican bearing and came to be regarded as a Cincinnatus. His great ambition was obscured by an appearance of modesty and abnegation, and he enjoyed a reputation for impeccable honesty. He was not a man of intellectual or philosophic interests, but he had a consistent and quick ability to judge and to motivate others. A leader with an aptitude for obtaining loyal adherents who made continuous efforts at his request, he could call for a personal sacrifice as well as make one. As Juárez withdrew from public view to give eminence to the presidential office, Díaz retained his image of popular appeal. While the intellectuals attacked

48. Díaz's brother Félix simultaneously did the same thing. By accusing the minister of war of selling supplies to the enemy five years earlier, *don* Félix was announcing his withdrawal from the president's circle a month before he initiated his candidacy for the governorship of Oaxaca. See DDC, 12:378–84.

Juárez on constitutional grounds and philosophical levels, seemingly without effect, Díaz remained for many men the man of action.[49]

It is probable that Díaz had yet another appeal to many worldly men of affairs: ironically, even as Díaz became the fixed point of opposition, many men seem to have regarded him as pliable. Over the years a good many men seem to have thought that support of Díaz would rebound to their own advantage. Few men joined Juárez after 1867, and probably no one ever joined Lerdo, thinking to impose a program or to extract an advantage. Díaz gave many men the impression that he would support their causes. The author of Lerdo's "memoirs" had Lerdo say that "Señores Justo Benítez, Ignacio Luis Vallarta and Protasio Tagle formed the brain of the Revolution of Tuxtepec. . . ." In the *Memorias* Tagle says to Lerdo, "Don Porfirio does not belong to himself; he belongs to the *Porfirista* Circle. He takes not a step without consulting us, and we do not permit him to take a step without our consent."[50] Apocryphal as the conversation was, Díaz seems to have allowed some men to think they would always have his support for their ambitions, which is perhaps the reason that *Porfirismo* during the Restored Republic contained such disparate figures as Ignacio Altamirano and Servando Canales, Ignacio Ramírez and Gerónimo Treviño, Manuel María de Zamacona and Juan N. Cortina, Joaquín Ruiz and Trinidad García de la Cadena.

Finally, Díaz may have inspired some men to support him in 1867 because even then he seemed to enjoy the basis for a political party. At the collapse of the monarchy, General Díaz, as general of division and commander of the Army of the East, had in his control an area of some eight states in eastern and southern Mexico. Some of the governors of those states and a large number of political chiefs and members of municipal governments, as well as the military commanders, were Díaz's appointees. Such was the base upon which careers in national politics were made, a circumstance which may not have been lost upon some men who chose Díaz as the most probable candidate to challenge the reelection of Benito Juárez in 1867.

49. Cosmes, *Historia general de Méjico*, 19:66–67, contains a good passage paralleling this on Díaz's popular appeal.

50. (Adolfo Carrillo), *Memorias inéditas de don Sebastián Lerdo de Tejada* (Puebla: Imprenta Guadalupana, n.d.), p. 56; Frank Averill Knapp, Jr., "The Apocryphal Memorias of Sebastian Lerdo de Tejada," *Hispanic American Historical Review* 31, no. 1 (February 1951):145–51.

We do not know if Díaz made his appointments with an eye to his own political future: some of those men did later support Díaz, but many did not. Many of the liberal leaders in the later congressional opposition to Juárez did in fact go to Congress in 1867 from the area of Díaz's early command, but this probably sprang from his natural political support in that area rather than from foresight and planning. Díaz says in his memoirs that he left the political administration of his area of command to Justo Benítez, who was highly politicized, while he himself concentrated on the military command.[51] But if Díaz's goal was political, he missed numerous opportunities for self-advancement. Replacing Rafael García with Juan N. Méndez in the governorship of Puebla may have been a political decision, but it was an isolated one: Méndez was the only governor from the area of Díaz's command who later supported him. Díaz appointed his brother Félix to the military command of Oaxaca in March 1867, where he would have later been useful, but in June he called Félix to the siege of Mexico, leaving Oaxaca to Gen. Miguel Castro, who supported the Juárez candidacy in 1867.[52] On the whole, it would seem that Díaz did not use his military command to support his later political career. That is, Díaz apparently did not envision a political career until sometime after the fall of Mexico City.

General Díaz's electoral campaign took shape slowly. As commander of the Second Division he was obliged to reside at Tehuacán, Puebla. He was the object of a reception in the Hotel Iturbide in Mexico City on 9 September. He left two days later for Apizaco, the railroad center of the Mexico-Veracruz line, but was back in the capital on 15 September at another theater function for a public celebration on his birthday. He then went straight to Puebla, where, as the object of public gatherings of frankly political significance, he was careful neither to accept nor to reject overt offers of the presidential candidacy. At the same time eighty-nine delegates of the "Convention of the Progressive Party" met in Mexico City to nominate Díaz as a presidential candidate.[53] Neither then nor later did Díaz speak in public on political matters. In that respect he accepted the advice of his political mentor and advisor, Justo Benítez: "I implore you to

51. Díaz, *Memorias*, 2:57.
52. Ibid., pp. 173, 323.
53. Tamayo, *Juárez*, 12:477; Cosío Villegas, *República restaurada*, pp. 173–80; *El Correo de México*, 12 September 1867, p. 3 and 21 September 1867, p. 3.

assume systematically a character of reserve, complete reserve, and to everyone who speaks to you . . . remember to answer that the nation has the right to entrust its destiny to whomever it wishes. Moreover, better than to enter discussion is to keep silent. . . ."[54]

Neither Juárez nor Díaz campaigned in 1867, in terms of addressing public gatherings for the purpose of gaining votes. Indeed, no Mexican presidential candidate did so until Francisco I. Madero in 1909. It was not in the nature of either man to seek popular support, and both men were public officials during the campaign. In 1867 Juárez counted upon his grand prestige, and Díaz assumed the air of a disciplined professional military officer who would serve his nation in any capacity to which he might be called. When Francisco Ossage, who was soliciting funds to launch a Porfirian press, urged Díaz in July to campaign for the presidency, Díaz answered, "I have never denied my services to the nation, but I have always accepted them with the fear that one accepts an onerous task. For the present I desire nothing; indeed, I would fear to mislead the public, whom I want to leave in liberty, so that if I were to err, they could only complain of their bad judgment."[55] Díaz never publicly circulated a list of officials to be elected, as did Divisional Gen. Ramón Corona in Jalisco in 1867. Díaz noted these words on his copy of Corona's list: "A general who commands a division should not in these cases thrust himself upon his subordinates in this manner."[56]

Both Juárez and Díaz let their subordinates promote their candidacy in 1867 and quietly used their personal influence by means of correspondence and agents to promote their partisans for governorships and congressional seats. Nevertheless, both men covertly used what official power they had for the campaign. When it became clear that certain governors opposed Juárez's reelection, Juárez turned upon them.

The course of events in 1867 proceeded in this manner: Querétaro surrendered on 15 May. Maximilian and the Mexican collaborationist generals, Mejía and Miramón, were executed on 19 June. Mexico City

54. Benítez to Díaz, 23 November 1867, APD, 5:338.
55. Minute of letter, Díaz to Ossage, 24 July 1867, PDP, box 8; Díaz was proud of never having sought an election: Díaz to Toribio Montiel, 24 February 1871, APD, 9:120.
56. APD, 4:137.

capitulated on 21 June, and Juárez entered Mexico City on 15 July. The military reorganization was decreed on 27 July, and extraordinary powers of governors were terminated by the decree of 16 August.[57] The *convocatoria* for new elections was issued 14 August, calling for popular elections on 22 September and college elections on 6 through 8 October. The Supreme Court was reconstituted by the decree of 21 August, and Juárez made interim appointments pending elections. Congress was installed in early December, and the president-elect was inaugurated on 25 December. On 8 December Juárez surrendered his extraordinary faculties to Congress, and constitutional law was reestablished in the republic. Although some idealists were anxious along the way because of the slowness of the return to constitutional government and some ambitious men were hurt in the eliminations, all in all the process was orderly, incredibly rapid, and just in recognition of individual roles, abilities, and sacrifices. It would be objectively difficult to claim that Díaz was slighted in any way. Furthermore, there is no evidence in either the Díaz correspondence or the correspondence of Juárez that Díaz objected to the pace of reconstruction.

On the other hand, it can now be seen that the order of events favored Juárez's retention of power. The most powerful generals lost their authority to govern by decree and were relegated to the provinces by the military reform in July. The extraordinary powers of governors were terminated in August. The only man in the republic to enjoy extraordinary powers during the elections of 1867 was Benito Juárez, who was then a candidate and who made strategic use of those powers against governors who opposed his reelection.

Juárez first purged Gen. León Guzmán from the governorship of Guanajuato. He had appointed Guzmán as governor and military commander of Guanajuato during the Intervention. But in 1867 Gen. Mariano Escobedo asked Juárez to replace Guzmán with Gen. Floren-

57. The decree limited the power of appointed governors to the executive function; they thereafter could not decree law or suspend constitutional guarantees. Governors could arrest but not punish and were obliged to recognize the federal guideline on freedom of press. The governors lost their powers in the areas of public finance and military administration to the federal government. Dublán and Lozano, *Legislación Mexicana*, 10:56–57; APD, 4:347–49.

cio Antillón because Guzmán caused "irregularities," was a "sick man," and "has offended me." Guzmán complained bitterly to Juárez of Escobedo's attacks upon him and offered his resignation. Then in September Guzmán informed Juárez that the *convocatoria* was unacceptable in Guanajuato and that he had published it with the ninth article omitted. Within the week, still wielding extraordinary wartime powers, Juárez replaced Guzmán with General Antillón and wrote to prominent men in the state to support the new regime.[58]

The appointment of General Antillón to the interim-governorship of Guanajuato in time to conduct the elections of 1867 is a case in point against the argument that Juárez supported true liberals who believed in the march of constitutional law against men of caudillistic ambition. León Guzmán was an old liberal and an important member of the Constitutional Convention of 1857, while Antillón had long sought power in Guanajuato and had a personalistic faction within the military organization. Antillón looked to Escobedo, who looked to Lerdo as secretary of *gobernación;* and Lerdo made the appointment.[59]

The replacement of Guzmán also serves as an example of the alienation that characterized the political policy of replacing independent men with loyal partisans. Antillón, after giving Guzmán three days to flee the state, settled down to work for the electoral victory of Juárez, Lerdo, and Antillón. "I have news of the results of seven districts," he wrote to Juárez in late October, "and in those you and Sr. Lerdo have won. I hope that the rest of them give the same results."[60] Antillón won the gobernatorial election, and in December the state gave its delegation vote to Lerdo in the national congressional run-off election for president of the Supreme Court. Guzmán thereafter joined the anti-Juárez opposition. Until 1876 Antillón supported the *Lerdistas,* when he joined Iglesias to save himself from Díaz.

58. Mariano Escobedo to Juárez, 7 June 1867, DDC, 12:25; León Guzmán to Juárez, 12 June 1867, ibid., pp. 201–2; Guzmán to Juárez, 4 September 1867, ibid., p. 430; *Correo de México,* 20 September 1867, p. 3 and 21 September 1867, pp. 2–3; Juárez to Jesús Garibay, 11 September 1867, *Epistolario,* 1st ed., pp. 410–11.

59. Cosío Villegas argues that Juárez had to replace Guzmán, because by refusing to publish the *convocatoria* in complete form Guzmán was in rebellion. See appendix 4 for a refutation.

60. Florencio Antillón to Juárez, 21 October 1867, *Epistolario,* 1st ed., p. 422.

Juárez replaced another governor who was even more closely related to Díaz—Gen. Juan N. Méndez of Puebla. During the Republican Resistance Juárez named Gen. Rafael J. García as governor and military commander of Puebla. Rafael García established his government in Zacapoaxtla in the Sierra de Puebla where Gen. Juan Méndez operated as commander of the Line of the North. Méndez accepted his subordination to García, and they apparently worked in harmony.[61] When Díaz commenced the Puebla campaign, leading the Army of the East from Oaxaca to Puebla, he relied upon the aid of García and Méndez. After Díaz assaulted the city of Puebla on 2 April, the García government naturally and without incident moved to the state capital of Puebla, and Díaz sent General Méndez to aid Gen. Mariano Escobedo at the siege of Querétaro. Then during the siege of Mexico, apparently dissatisfied with Rafael García as governor of Puebla, Díaz replaced him with Méndez on 25 April.[62] In August Méndez refused to publish the *convocatoria* with the plebiscite intact.[63]

García's attitude toward the *convocatoria* and the state of Puebla underwent a rapid evolutionary course. In late August García registered a mild disapproval of the *convocatoria* with Juárez.[64] In early September García informed a friend in the ministry of foreign relations that he would neither publish the document nor take charge of the state.[65] By mid-September García feigned shock that Governor Méndez had published the *convocatoria* in "mutilated form," that is, that four articles had been omitted. He then informed Juárez of conditions which must have hung heavy on the President's mind; "Méndez . . . has officials who are his creatures in all the districts. Thus if elections finally take place here, even if the *convocatoria* were published as the Supreme Government decreed, the [public] vote would be falsified." García suggested that "everything would be different by changing the personnel of the state government and, of course, the defenders they have in the districts, who can exercise a direct influ-

61. Galindo, *Década nacional,* 3:440.

62. Miller, "The Army of the East," p. 314.

63. Méndez to Juárez, 30 August 1867, DDC, 12:426–27; *Correo de México,* 21 September 1867, p. 3 and 27 September 1867, p. 3.

64. García to Juárez, 24 August 1867, DDC, 12:408.

65. Cosío Villegas, *República restaurada,* p. 169; *El Correo de México,* 4 October 1867, p. 2.

ence. Otherwise, Sr. Méndez will name himself governor [and] all the authorities will be as he desires. . . ."[66] Besides that point of view, which Juárez would have appreciated, García could have been piqued with General Díaz, who had removed him from the governorship in April. That might have influenced the president also. Juárez removed Méndez from office and named Rafael García as governor of Puebla on 19 September.

After a few tense days during which Juan Méndez hesitated to transfer the state government to Rafael García and failed to respond to a military summons to Mexico, he finally surrendered the office to García on 25 September.[67] Juárez wrote to the governor of Oaxaca that "the little scandals in Guanajuato and Puebla terminated happily. . . ."[68] Juárez, therefore, having stripped governors and military commanders of the authority to rule by decree, used that same authority, enjoyed at that point only by himself, to be rid of governors who could be expected to oppose his reelection. And as will be seen below, Méndez used his important caudillistic influence in the Sierra de Puebla to harass Juárez, and then Lerdo, for a full decade.

So the lines were drawn between *Juáristas* and *Porfiristas* by the fall of 1867. Juárez held the power and made the important decisions. In making them, within the political framework in which the ruler of Mexico had to establish political alliances in the state government, Juárez made both allies and enemies. The enemies of *Juarismo,* and later of *Lerdismo,* gravitated to the opposition that recognized Porfirio Díaz as their standard-bearer.

66. García to Juárez, 17 September 1867, DDC, 12:451; Lerdo to García, 24 September 1867, PDP, box 9.

67. The interchange of telegrams between Lerdo, García, Ignacio Mejía, and Méndez were published in *Correo de México,* 30 September 1867, pp. 1–3.

68. Juárez to Miguel Castro, 3 October 1867, *Epistolario,* 1st ed., p. 411.

Chapter 3
The Selection of Leaders

No one will ever know to what extent the elections during the Restored Republic were honest or fraudulent. Many abuses were certainly committed and it was widely believed that there was little relation between popular suffrage and the selection of the men who occupied public office. It is equally certain that electoral fraud was the declared motive for insurrection. The social and economic realities of Mexico doubtless demanded some modifications in the legal prescription. And doubtless the modifications that were practiced helped to perpetuate the centralization of power toward dictatorship, even as they contributed to the insurrections of the period. This chapter describes some of the electoral mechanisms and some of the reactions they inspired; it also traces one of the most interesting elections of the period, one which defined the rivalry between Juárez and Díaz at the outset of the Restored Republic.

Elections during the Restored Republic, and later during the *Porfiriato,* were conducted according to the election law of 12 February 1857.[1] The state governors were responsible for dividing their states into electoral districts of 40,000 inhabitants and for designating a city in each one to serve as the seat of the district electoral college. The municipal government *(ayuntamiento)* of the electoral seat was to divide each electoral district into sections of 500 inhabitants. A national primary election was held every two years by decree *(convocatoria)* of Congress. On the final Sunday of June the appropriately registered voters (within the principle of universal manhood suffrage) selected an elector to represent the section at the district electoral college.

In the district electoral colleges, commencing on the second Sunday in July, the electors cast their votes in the "secondary elections" for a congressman and an alternate to represent the district in the unicameral Congress and for one or more of the magistrates of the Supreme Court. Every other secondary election—that is, every fourth year—

1. Dublán and Lozano, *Legislación mexicana,* 8:409–18.

the electors also cast votes to select the national president, and every sixth year to determine the president of the Supreme Court.

State laws varied for the election of congressmen to the state legislatures, of judges to the state courts, and of governors, but generally the same electors selected them according to the *convocatorias* of state legislatures at the same time as the secondary elections.

The highest ranking political authority of the district seat, as well as the governor, published the results of the college balloting, while the president of each electoral college issued credentials to the national congressman and sent the electoral results of the balloting for president and magistrates to Congress. Congress in turn checked the credentials of each incoming congressman and counted the electoral votes for the national president and national magistrates. In case no candidate won a clear majority for president or justice, Congress transformed itself into an electoral college and cast votes by state delegation to select a final victor between the two candidates with the most electoral votes. Then Congress declared the winners by resolution.

The electoral procedure at the local level was closely prescribed by the same electoral law. Every municipal government named for each section a registrar (*empadronador*), who composed a list of voters as they registered with him. The final and official list was to be posted in a public place eight days before each election so that any individual could protest the absence of his name. If not satisfied by the registrar, one could still protest at the polling table on the day of the election to the booth officials, who made the final decision whether the individual could vote. Three days before a primary election the registrar was to give a ballot to each voter. The ballot bore on one side the name and signature of the voter, and on the other side the name of the person whom the voter was selecting to be the section elector. The voter placed his ballot in an urn or box at the polling table.

The electoral law of 1857 comprised sixty-three detailed articles, representing the best intentions of idealistic and consciencious legislators to do everything within their power to make elections fair and honest. Nevertheless, many articles of the law were violated in one manner or another.

Infringements of the spirit of the law were abetted by the composition and prerogatives of the official personnel at the voting place. The law required that the municipal government name a person from every section to open the voting station. He was to empower the first seven citizens appearing at the station to select five individuals from their number to serve as the election officials, or *mesa*. One person served as the *mesa* president, two as secretaries, and two as "poll-watchers" (*escrutadores*). Among the powers of the *mesa* officials were those of making final decisions on who could vote, of counting the votes at day's end, and of writing the official report that would be forwarded to the municipal authorities and then to the electoral college.

One interesting aspect of *mesa* powers was that of recording irregularities. Any citizen could complain ". . . of bribery, subornation, trickery or violence to the ends of influencing the election in favor of a particular person."[2] The complaint was to be included as part of the official record. A vote would immediately be taken among the five *mesa* officials; should the majority agree with the complainant, the person charged with the irregularity would lose his vote. If that person belonged to the *mesa*, he would thus have no more voice in the writing or adoption of the official report. On the other hand, if the complainant should be outvoted, his vote would be suspended. In 1867 a group of voters complained that at their voting place the president of the *mesa*, Mariano Botello, applied to himself thirty-five votes that were cast for José L. Botello. Having lost their appeal to the *mesa*, they directed their complaint to the governor.[3] It is doubtful that any redress, or even investigation, was made, for no appeal existed above the decision of a *mesa*. In this case, the powers of the president of the *mesa* allowed him to elect himself to the electoral college.

Elections were frequently won or lost by the partisan establishment of the polling *mesa*. In the 1867 election both the *Juaristas* and the *Porfiristas* in the state of Oaxaca circulated lists of persons who were to install the *mesas*, and a good deal of politicking was done among agents of both parties with municipal and village officials to insure that the right persons were named to install them.[4]

2. Law of 12 February 1857, article 10.

3. *Vecinos de la sección números 119 y 78, El Correo de México,* 30 September 1867, p. 3.

4. José F. Valverde to Díaz, 25 September 1867, APD, 5:76–80.

The object of requiring the voter to use his registration card as a ballot was to discourage double voting, particularly the practice of sending groups of men—peons and soldiers, for example—from one booth to another. The signed ballot made box-stuffing more difficult. Those safeguards must have seemed to the lawmakers more important than the secret ballot. There were ways, however, for corrupt officials to circumvent the safeguards: In an effort to stop a popular elector the ballots were simply lost.[5] More blatantly, the ballots could be tampered with before the election, as happened in a village in Puebla in 1875. According to one observer, "in Chalchicomula the ballots were handed out for the election with the names of the electors already written on the backs . . . leaving the voter who opposed the official choice with no recourse but to keep his ballot. The result was that which the authorities wanted."[6] Or the ballots could be altered after they were cast. In 1867 a witness in Acatlán, Puebla, claimed that "the names of the candidates of our party were erased from our ballots and supplanted with the names of those favored by the authorities."[7]

According to a witness in Tehuacán, virtually all the safeguards were overridden there in 1875. "The elections were conducted with a multitude of abuses," he said. "They started by registering no one. They continued by not distributing ballots. And they terminated by installing the *mesas*—some by soldiers of the rural police and others by [governmental] employees with jurisdiction, that is, by everyone whom the law prohibits from taking part in the elections." Not only had such activity not been seen before in Tehuacán, he said, "but we did not even think it could happen. But it happened throughout the district."[8]

Since the legislators knew that officials would perpetuate their party in power if they could work their way into the electoral colleges, article 16 made all public officials ineligible for candidacy as electors in the section of their political jurisdiction. This restriction may have

5. This seems to have happened in Coalcoman, Apatzingan, and Tancítaro, state of Michoacán, in 1875. The government answered that the ballots were delayed in the mail. *El Monitor Republicano*, 8 July 1875, p. 3.

6. Ibid., 10 July 1875, p. 3.

7. Rafael Mejía to Díaz, 9 December 1867, APD, 5:396.

8. *Monitor Republicano*, 3 July 1875, p. 4.

been partially effective in keeping public officials out of the electoral colleges, but it did not keep them from determining the composition of those bodies. Agustín O'Horán, a gubernatorial candidate in Yucatan in 1869, claimed that electors favorable to his candidacy were chosen by a plurality of 23,000 votes in the popular election, but that Vice-Governor Manuel Cirerol sent forces to a number of pueblos to replace the political chiefs, who then sent an alternate set of electors to the colleges in order to elect himself to the governorship.[9]

Despite article 16 of the electoral law, many complaints were registered in the newspapers, in the electoral colleges, and in Congress against electors who exercised political power in the areas of their residence. The mere expediency of belonging to the majority faction at the electoral college sufficed to control the credentials committee and to carry that committee's resolution by a majority vote on the college floor. The *Monitor Republicano*, an anti-Lerdo paper in 1875, claimed that in Atzcapozalco in the Federal District, the voting booths, once established, were commandeered by the commander of the armed forces, and electoral credentials were handed out to partisans in official positions, such as "the secretary of the prefecture, a schoolteacher and others employed [by the government]—to the degree that the village councilmen and even the president of the municipal government obtained credentials" as electors. The newspaper added that those who complained were jailed.[10] In the same election the six electoral colleges of the Federal District choose six well-known *Lerdista* partisans as presidents of the six colleges. Nearly all of them were on the federal payroll and exercised jurisdiction in the Federal District.[11]

In Campeche in 1871 the outgoing governor of the state, Alejandro García, served as the president of one of the two electoral colleges in the state and even emerged from it as the elected representative to Congress. In Alamos, Sonora, in 1871 Bartolomé E. Almada was the president of the municipal government who installed the electoral college of his district. He emerged from the voting as the district

9. O'Horán to Juárez, 23 November 1869; DDC, 14:155–57.
10. *Monitor Republicano*, 7 July 1875, p. 3.
11. They were Manuel Romero Rubio in the first district, Francisco de P. Gochicoa in the second, Juan Pinal in the third, Ramón Guzmán in the fourth, Luis Valle in the fifth, and Mariano Zúñiga in the sixth. Ibid., 12 July 1875.

representative to Congress, and his son was elected to the state legislature.[12]

Article 34 of the election law prohibited any public official from running as a candidate in the area of his incumbent jurisdiction. Again the restriction could be overcome if the individual belonged to the dominant party of the electoral college and of Congress. Porfirian Congressman Eleuterio Avila took the floor on 11 September 1869 to object to the election of Francisco Clavería to Congress from the district of Toluca on the grounds that he exercised federal jurisdiction as a district judge at the time of the elections. Avila's motion was overridden by a *Juarista* Congress.[13]

Article 34 of the electoral law of 1857 stipulated that the district electoral colleges needed a quorum of a simple majority of the legal number of electors in order to conduct its sessions. In the absence of a quorum the election results of a given district could not be computed or sent to Congress. This gave rise to two types of fraudulent practice. First, because party lines reached down to the section level, where popular elections took place two weeks before the final selections in the electoral colleges, the composition of the electoral college could be known, and therefore the results of its balloting could be predicted before the district college convened. Therefore, the minority could boycott the college in hopes of forestalling the quorum and force the entire district election to be declared void. If, of course, the majority party could urge their electors to the college, the strategy of the boycotters (*faltistas*) would be foiled, and a larger plurality would be recorded. When the plurality was small, however, a small amount of money for bribes, spent on men who could be persuaded to be absent but who could not be brought to change their votes, would suffice to invalidate a district election due to the lack of a quorum.

It was this phenomenon, if not the outright buying of electors' votes at the colleges, that influenced one correspondent to write of an important congressional race in Veracruz: "The independents have a majority of electors, but the government has a majority of favors and of money to offer. You calculate who will be the winners." Nevertheless, the outright purchase of electoral votes was also believed to be a

12. García to Juárez, 11 July 1871, DDC, 15:210; Almada to Juárez, 11 July 1871, ibid., pp. 210–11.

13. *Debates, quinto congreso,* 1:9–11.

part of every election. One observer in Mexico City wrote in 1867 that "the government has won the election by . . . openly buying electors, some of whom have sold themselves for 200 pesos."[14]

In a three-way race the electors of the two minority parties could withdraw when their numbers would deprive a quorum from the plurality party. This happened in the district of Tepeaca, state of Puebla, in 1871. The *Lerdistas* and *Juaristas*, according to a correspondent to Díaz, withdrew from an electoral college when they saw that the *Porfiristas* outnumbered each of the other two parties.[15]

A second fraud was simply to overlook the quorum requirement and conduct the secondary election without reference to it. When this was done, the minority would petition Congress for a resolution declaring the election void. A group of electors in Huamantla, Tlaxcala, so petitioned in 1871, declaring that the business of the college was conducted by only thirty-three of the seventy-four electors. They also sought annulment of the election because the primary elections had not taken place in the six sections of the municipality of Ixtenco in the district of Huamantla; one elector was underage; the credential committee carried a resolution against a *Porfirista* elector for representing a section not of his residence without applying the same rule to a *Juarista* elector in the same circumstance, who was serving as president of the college; and armed soldiers had voted in formation in one section, raising their commander to elector.[16]

It is not certain what then happened. The twenty Porfirian electors may have withdrawn from the college, leaving the thirty-three *Juarista* electors without a quorum, which did not stop them from continuing in session. Or, as described in a letter to Díaz from a partisan witness, they were driven out by a contingent of 150 dragoons under orders of Colonel Campillo, the military elector at the college, in complicity with the prefect of the town. At any rate, the *Porfiristas* retired to a theater,

14. "Our correspondent from Veracruz" to *Monitor Republicano*, 10 July 1875, p. 3; Juan Espinosa Gorostiza to Díaz, 9 (*sic*, 29?) September 1867, APD, 5:28.

15. J. R. Hernández to Porfirio Díaz, 8 August 1871, ibid., 9:236. In this case a district judge at the time of the letter was arraigning the *faltistas*.

16. Petition from a delegation of electors to the permanent deputation of Congress, 9 July 1871, ibid., pp. 185–86; Club Porfirio Díaz of Huamantla to Díaz, 12 July 1871, ibid., pp. 197–99.

"shouted *vivas* and *mueras*," and drew up their protest. One commented to Díaz that "the whole village is ready to pronounce [against the government] but your partisans here will not let them. . . . We await new elections; and if they are not held we are ready to pronounce, that is to join the first one to shout out."[17]

Article 35 of the electoral law of 1857 stipulated that the district deputy to Congress should be selected in the electoral college by secret ballot. Article 43 stipulated the same procedure for the national president, and article 45 for the president of the Supreme Court. Nevertheless, the secret ballot did not seem to be universally respected. The governor presided at an electoral college in the state of Tabasco. The electors cast their ballots by voice vote for deputies to Congress, the members of the state legislature, and the governor.[18] The governor in this case, in addition to calling for voice vote instead of secret ballot, conducted the sessions in contravention to article 16, that no elector could be a public official; article 24, that the president of the college would be chosen from the electors; and article 25, that the local political authority would retire from the hall once the officials of the electoral college were impaneled.

Another electoral fraud common to the period was the "double election" that took place on both the primary and the secondary levels. At the primary level, a second balloting place was opened by persons who claimed that the first one was illegal. Municipal authorities merely recognized the results of the poll that convenienced them. This was said to have happened in Guadalajara in 1875, where the anti-Lerdo forces controlled the offices of the state. According to one correspondent, the opposition to the state party appointed *empadronadores* to make up alternate voting lists and set up alternate voting booths, and printed circulars that citizens could vote without ballots. Whether or not violence occurred is unclear—the literature is partisan. At any rate, federal troops moved into the city. The state governor and the commander of the federal troops exchanged hostile notes. In the end, both men authorized credentials for the winners of the double elections to go to the electoral college.[19]

17. P. Junco to Díaz, 13 July 1871, ibid., pp. 203–4.
18. Scholes, *Mexican Politics*, p. 133.
19. Anonymous letter to Vicente García Torres, editor of *Monitor Republicano*, 9 July 1875, p. 3; "El corresponsal" to Torres, ibid., 10 July 1875, p. 2.

Double elections on the secondary level proceeded from a group of electors who recognized that the results of the electoral college would not favor them. The minority electors merely established a second college and sent a different set of returns to Congress. If their party in Congress controlled the credential committee and floor vote, the procedure could be successful for the minority electoral college.

A double electoral college occurred in Veracruz in 1875. According to an observer there, some of the electors who had arrived in Veracruz to participate in an electoral college were summoned to the municipal governmental building two days before they were to meet, "without previous announcement to the majority of the electors." There the political chief of Veracruz formed them into an electoral college, with an officer of the garrison and the chief accountant of the customs house serving as officers. The antigovernment electors soon became aware that they were authorizing illegal procedures by their presence and withdrew from the building, leaving the college without a quorum. The next night the same group formed another electoral college and sought official installation from the political chief, which was refused. The result was two sets of returns for senators and magistrates.[20]

In that same year a double electoral college occurred in the electoral district of Orizaba, where Rafael Herrera opposed the *Lerdista* candidate Amado Talavera. According to one of the electors, Talavera recognized that a majority of the electors would favor Herrera and withdrew his partisans to Naranjal to establish a second college. A pro-Herrera elector claimed to have information that a federal force of eighty men from the twentieth infantry regiment left Orizaba "with the object of assuring the election of Talavera in Naranjal."[21]

That double elections had become a recognized pattern is seen in the *convocatoria* decree of Governor Carvajal of the state of Tlaxcala in

---

In these accounts the entire transgression lies with Gen. José Ceballos, sent to Guadalajara to win the elections for the *Lerdista* candidate. Documentation for this election is abundant, highly contradictory, and thoroughly partisan. See Knapp, *Lerdo* pp. 183–84; and Luis Pérez Verdía, *Historia particular del estado de Jalisco.* . . , 2d ed., 3 vols. (Guadalajara: Gráfica Editorial, 1951–54), 3:511–14.

20. "X. y Z." to Vicente García Torres, *Monitor Republicano*, 13 July 1875.

21. Luis M. Hernández to Tomás de Rojas; Tomás de Rojas to Vicente García Torres, ibid., 10 July 1875, p. 3.

1875, which stated that the returns from a college composed of illegal electors or from one not installed by the competent authorities were invalid.[22]

Other important articles designed to stem irregularities were 13 and 14. The first indicated that soldiers should vote as private citizens in the sections of their residence, and the other forbade soldiers from voting if they presented themselves at the polls in formation or if their superior officers led them to the polls.

One *Porfirista* would have used his national guardsmen as voters in the Veracruz elections in 1870 had not the *Juarista* governor, Hernández y Hernández, dissolved the unit. The officer had received instructions from Díaz to work for the electoral victory of Justo Benítez and Juan Torres. Had the unit not been dissolved, reported the officer, he would have had 3,000 secure votes.[23] In 1867 a commanding officer in Mexico City, according to one observer, took his whole batallion to the booths to vote for an elector pledged to Juárez. Nevertheless, "more than sixty men," wrote a partisan to Díaz, "gave their votes to you for elector, believing that they were voting for the presidency."[24]

Blatant disregard of articles 13 and 14 was not necessary. After the elections of 1867 one newspaper told how "at five o'clock Sunday morning [22 September, election day] some soldiers at the order of their officer went to the home of the authority who was to establish a voting booth, with the object of taking control of the *mesa* and obtaining [a victory for] the elector consigned to them." Another use of soldiers in the primary elections was to have them appear at a voting place of a section in which a military officer lived. "They ask for a great number of ballots from the *mesa* for the soldiers, saying they live in the house of the officer—all with the purpose of assuring [the victory of] the elector consigned to them." Yet another electoral deployment of federal troops, according to the opposition, was to station military units on election day in districts where their votes could overcome opposition pluralities in the primary elections. One Porfirian

22. *Archivo General de la Nación* (AGN, Mexico City), *Ramo de Gobernación, legajo* 383, doc. 11, 30 July 1875.

23. José M. Pérez Milícua to Díaz, 24 August 1870, APD, 9:13–14.

24. F. Mejía to Díaz, 27 September 1867, ibid., 5:89.

partisan claimed that it happened in his district in Veracruz in 1871.[25]
Local authorities often perpetuated another kind of fraud to thwart
unfavorable results in an electoral district. They could switch the location of the college to an area where force could be applied without
witnesses or relocate the college without advising the electors of the
opposition party. One *Porfirista* advised Díaz that the state authorities
in Puebla changed the district seat of an electoral college in 1871 from
Acatlán to Chinantla "at the final hour and under the cunning pretext
of insecurity in this town." Some of the electors then sought a stay of
executive order (*amparo*) from a district judge. The case, however, was
shifted to a court in the city of Puebla; the judge there was a *compadre*
of the governor. When the stay was denied, the electors moved to
Chinantla, where the local political chief sent in cavalry to disperse the
college. Manuel Espinosa claimed in a letter to Díaz that the military
orders came from the *Lerdista* governor, Ignacio Romero Vargas.[26]

As a last resort, a governor could aid his faction in Congress by
delaying the credentials of an opposition winner. That gave the governor's party an advantage during the initial meetings of Congress
when officers were selected and the credential committee was chosen.
Justo Benítez complained on 4 November 1867, and Juan Torres
complained a week later, that the *Juarista* governor of Oaxaca had not
sent them their credentials.[27]

Local authorities could also delay credentials; political chiefs might
fail to issue them to the elector in time for him to participate at the
electoral college, or they might not send the sectional results at all.

25. *Defensor del Pueblo,* reprinted in *El Correo de México,* 28 September 1867,
p. 3; Vicente Llorente y Alegre to Díaz, 11 July 1871, CPD, 42:1784.

26. Espinosa to Díaz, 18 July 1871, APD, 9:212. Another witness claimed
that the object was to obtain the electoral victory for the *Lerdista* congressional
candidate and that the person in charge of the political maneuver was Pedro
Contreras: Manuel Arias to Díaz, 18 July 1871, CPD, 42:1790.

27. Benítez to Díaz, 4 November 1867, APD, 5:302; Torres to Díaz, 11
November 1867, ibid., p. 313. Benítez suffered the same fate in 1869: Francisco Mena to Díaz, 28 December 1869, ibid., 8:109. Gov. Gerónimo Treviño
delayed the credentials of his rival, Simón de la Garza y Melo, in 1867: Garza to
Treviño, 30 December 1867, *Archivo General del Estado de Nuevo Leon, Sección
Histórica* (hereafter AGNL), *Ramo Gerónimo Treviño,* (hereafter RGT), *Caja Garza,
expediente Simón Garza Melo,* 2037.

According to one witness in Oaxaca, the latter happened in a municipal election in 1870.[28]

Political authorities did have abundant means to influence elections.
According to the *Monitor Republicano*, the governor of the Federal
District reversed the choice of an electoral college in 1875: of 126
electors only 92 were present, the majority of whom chose Pablo
Zayas. Gov. Othon Pérez then sent in police agents. The "more honorable" electors left the college, reducing it to 49 electors, who then
did not form a quorum. "Sr. Gallardo was then illegally named."[29]

Where governors had close control over the local political chiefs,
there was no need to change election results. Everyone recognized
that political chiefs were the basic electors. A *Porfirista* wrote in 1867
that the opposition was working for Juárez in Silacayoapan, Tlaxiaco,
Teposcolula, Nochistlan, and Huajuapan, state of Oaxaca, "but the
political chiefs are in agreement with us and I do not believe we will
suffer a reverse." The *Lerdista* governor of Morelos in 1870, Francisco
Leyva, refused to publish a law passed by the *Porfirista* state legislature
that would have empowered the legislature to name the political
chiefs of the villages. A *Juarista* observer noted that the law gave the
Porfiristas the opportunity to falsify the public vote and recommended
to Juárez that he support Leyva on the issue, since the present political chiefs were *Juarista* and "would deliver the villages of the state" to
Juárez. In 1869 Miguel Castro, governor of Oaxaca, advised Juárez
that Félix Díaz was running for the governorship and had good relations with the political chiefs, "who, as you know, control the elections,
and the rest of the people do as the political chiefs command."[30]

The *Juarista* Marcos Andrade wrote to Juárez in 1869 that "the
governor of Veracruz, Hernández, is ... recommending in all the
cantons of the state and is notifying all the political chiefs that congressmen in the next elections should be agreeable to you. ...." In
1871 an informant wrote to Díaz that the political chief "Antonio
Ortega rounded up thirty-three Indians, who signed [their names]
with a cross." The commander of a unit of rural police in Otumba,

28. Laureano Sánchez to Díaz, 23 December 1870, APD, 9:74.
29. *Monitor Republicano*, 13 July 1875.
30. J. Segura y G. to Díaz, 6 November 1867, APD, 5:305; Antonio Arriaga
to Juárez, 15 January 1870, DDC, 14:248; Castro to Juárez, 25 September
1867, ibid., 12:492.

state of Mexico, asked Juárez "to indicate to me what person it would be convenient to support for governor. I know that the government needs people in these posts who cooperate and who are in agreement with your thinking. The political chief of this district is very well disposed. . . ."[31]

In 1871 the *Juaristas* sent José María Alatorre to work for the reelection of Juárez in Guanajuato, Aguascalientes, and Jalisco. He regularly reported by mail to Castillo Velasco, minister of *gobernación*. From Lagos he wrote that he had spoken with the political chief, "who is a relative of mine, and with various other persons 'of representation,' and although I had to overcome some inconveniences and difficulties with which they opposed me, finally we agreed that Sr. Juárez and good congressmen will be elected there."[32]

In the same letter Alatorre offers an excellent example of how governmental troops were used to aid local authorities to win an arranged election when other influences, in this case an *hacendado*, planned a different outcome: He told how in a municipal election earlier in the month a number of armed men from the *hacienda* of Rincón Gallardo had commandeered the electoral *mesas*. The local authorities, he wrote, rightly feared that the same activity would be repeated in the gubernatorial elections, as well as in the general elections for president and congressmen. "Although the political chief has absolutely promised me to work and to win the election in favor of Sr. Juárez," Alatorre wrote, "he insists that a military force be in Lagos during those days of at least two hundred men, who without taking part in the contest will serve to cause respect for authority—because the Rincón men, who work openly for *señor* Lerdo, abusing their wealth, want to impose themselves."[33]

31. Andrade to Juárez, 21 June 1869, Archivo Juárez, Biblioteca Nacional de México, Mexico City (hereafter AJ), doc. 6940; P. Junco to Díaz, 13 July 1867, APD, 9:203–4; José María Kampfner to Juárez, 23 October 1871, AJ, 10311.

32. Alatorre to José María Castillo Velasco, 18 May 1871, ibid., 9091.

33. Ibid. This letter, passed over by Tamayo in his publication of the Juárez correspondence, is a gold mine for the study of electoral manipulation. In one case Alatorre obliged the minister of *gobernación* to send a *título de escriba nacional* to Lic. Jesús Briseño as the price of his cooperation in Cocula, where "they are partisans of General Díaz." Elsewhere, "in Tepatitlan, Salos and Zapotlanejo I did the same, and everywhere they have given me their word to

In all these examples relating to the local political chiefs, when the report was not one of actual fraudulent practice, the assumption made by working politicians was that electoral results were determined by the political chiefs.

Military commanders also had the power to influence elections. A *Porfirista* general, B. Zárate, military commander in Teposcolula, Oaxaca, wrote to Porfirio Díaz that his brother Félix "was unanimously elected for governor in this district of my command, by which I believe I have delivered all your wishes and orders." That same year Díaz wrote that "some indigenous electors whom I have asked the reason for their vote have given me this explanation": the commander of the national guard of Puebla brought together the electors of indigenous villages and "harshly admonished them that if they did not vote according to his indications, he would burn their villages and recruit them as soldiers. As they have seen him execute the threat, they believe him, and fear fastens them to his dictates."[34]

Even more fraught with violence was the use of federal troops in states controlled by governors of the opposition. The governor's party in Jalisco in 1875 claimed that federal forces disturbed the electoral procedures to prevent the candidates of the state party from winning and to secure the election of the candidates of the presidential party. The governor made pointed reference to federal forces sent by General Escobedo from Zacatecas to the canton of Colotlán and those sent by General Caballos into Colula.[35]

In similar fashion the interim governor of Nuevo León in 1875,

work in good faith; of course, in order to accomplish this, I had to make some propositions to various of them who wield influence, as you and I agreed."

34. B. Zárate to Díaz, 12 November 1867, APD, 5:315; Díaz to Juan N. Méndez, December 1867, ibid., p. 364.

35. *Monitor Republicano*, 6 July 1875, p. 3; the same Gen. José Ceballos was earlier accused in Congress of impeding the election of Manuel M. Zamacona in Cholula, Puebla, in 1871 with a battalion at his command: *Debates, quinto congreso*, 22 March 1871, 4:118. Earlier yet, in 1869, *El Siglo XIX* carried an item in which the same officer denied using armed forces in Cholula that year, saying that the charge was a slander against him: 10 July 1869, p. 3. Existing documentation on a single incident is frequently contradictory, as each party accuses the other of scandals and frauds; cf., for example, José Francisco Valverde to Díaz, 25 September 1867, APD, 5:76, and José V. Silva to Juárez, 25 September 1867, DDC, 12:490, for the 1869 election in Oaxaca.

Francisco González Doria, claimed that Gen. Carlos Fuero of the federal garrison in Monterrey disturbed the elections in that city. The official state newspaper printed the reports of three different *mesas* which had closed because the pro-Lerdo party terrorized the area around the polls while the federal forces looked on, protecting the rioters, according to the state newspaper. The governor reported to Congress that "this act on the part of the federal force . . . [is] a flagrant abuse to the sovereignty of the state of Nuevo León and a predatory attack against the liberty of suffrage." The legislature then nullified the elections, set a new date, and authorized a letter of protest to President Lerdo.[36]

The use of illegal influence and outright violence in the electoral process was sufficiently overt to distress thinking men. Records from the period suggest, however, that even worse conditions prevailed in some areas, that virtual terror was employed as a means to thwart the opposition of local regimes. Juan Bustamante, ex-governor of San Luis Potosí, claimed in an open letter to the press in 1869 that after electors pledged to his candidacy were known to be in a majority following the popular election, he "was a victim of all kinds of abuses and violations of my constitutional guarantees." Imprisoned and held six days incommunicado, Bustamante accused agents of the administration of murdering three of his servants, ransacking his home, and stealing his correspondence and valuables.[37]

According to one observer in Oaxaca in 1875, Governor Esperón was terrorizing his opposition. One lawyer, Carlos Ballesteros, a doctor, Manuel Bustamante, and the editor of *Azote*, Gregorio Chávez, were in jail for opposing Esperón's reelection. A Dr. Gómez had been heavily fined. One Francisco Peña had left the state to escape arrest, while another lawyer, José J. Cañas, was in hiding. A local official, Marcial Salinas, had been dragged from his home after a political chief had knocked down his doors. Troops stood guard in all the

36. *Periódico Oficial . . . de Nuevo León*, 9, 12, 16 June 1875. Some evidence appears in the official newspaper that the presidential party denied that the federal forces did more than keep the peace—issues of their paper, *El Mosquetefe*, are not available—and that the state party was rigging the election for its own candidate. Nevertheless, the *mesa* reports and the legislative protest are graphic in the incidents of federal interference which they cite.

37. Bustamante, open letter, *El Siglo XIX*, 4 July 1869.

district towns, according to the correspondent, to intimidate the voters. "In such a way are elections conducted, and it supplants the public suffrage."[38]

A political worker in Acatlán in 1867 testified to a terroristic policy of a newly appointed political chief, who prohibited the carrying of arms without a license from him, ordered the arrest of those who protested, persecuted one family out of the district, sacking their home and that of a partisan, and finally ordered the arrest of opposition party workers.[39]

According to Agustín O'Horán, gubernatorial candidate in Yucatan in 1869, Interim Governor Manuel Cirerol inaugurated a terroristic policy to assure his own election. O'Horán accused Cirerol of setting loose a band of armed and mounted thugs in Mérida to chase off the *mesa* officials on election day; the *mesas* were then occupied by partisans of Cirerol, resulting in a number of injured persons and others who were dragged off to jail. The local police who interfered were disarmed and jailed. In other areas of the state the political chiefs and military commanders falsified electoral documents on orders of Cirerol or were forcefully replaced. During the next few days, according to O'Horán, the homes of electoral officials who refused to cooperate with the interim governor were ransacked on the pretext of recovering stolen electoral documents. During the whole time, the press was threatened not to report the violence, and a pro-O'Horán press, *Los Pueblos,* was closed. In this way, although O'Horán thought the popular vote was 23,000 in his favor to 4,000, Manuel Cirerol became the new governor.[40]

In the face of widespread absence of confidence in electoral freedom, reaction varied from resignation to insurrection. Some men tended to be philosphical. In answer to an editorial deploring the lack of public interest in the ongoing elections of 1875, Carlos de Olaguibel y Arista wrote in *El Monitor Republicano* that "no one believes any more in public suffrage. The more candid believe—and know—that there are no elections, but rather appointments made by means a little more indirect and complicated than those used to hire a

38. "El Corresponsal" to editor of *Monitor Republicano,* 6 July 1875, p. 3.
39. Rafael Mejía to Díaz, 9 December 1867, APD, 5:396–97.
40. O'Horán to Juárez, 23 November 1869, DDC, 14:155–57.

clerk or secretary." This, he said, was the cause of the "complete indifference to the elections." Olaguibel thought Juárez had been a great patriot, but believed that he had falsified elections in order to save the institutions from a Catholic revival. He recognized that the *Porfiristas*, "blinded by the republican ideal . . . , justly condemn it" and want the government "overthrown with bullets." Olaguibel, however, did not blame the government, but rather the church, for maintaining the masses in ignorance. He saw a dilemma in the situation. It was painful, he pondered, for the patriot and honest statesman to see official interference in elections to such an extent that it created general disrespect for the institutions. Yet it was equally painful to watch "the sovereignty of ignorance" destroy the institutions by abstaining from the polls. Olaguibel thought governmental violence against the suffrage would last for many years before the people would learn to treasure its suffrage; meanwhile, Mexico needed time, not revolution.[41]

Other men were less philosophical, more confused and distraught. One Laureano Sánchez assured Díaz that "our institutions, day in and day out, are in worse condition with the evil acts of our officials." In Oaxaca, he said, "the court, the judges, the political chiefs, all are one and they work together and cover each other. . . . Where shall we seek the remedy?"[42]

Still others arrived at the conclusion that the only remedy was force. Ignacio Ramírez wrote that the constitutional system had to be sacrificed and an appeal made to the people. "Revolutions do not frighten us. We accept the revolution, with the condition that it signifies an appeal to the people and the will of the people." Violence would be effected in one of two ways, he said; either the government would work violence in the elections, or the people would work violence upon the government.[43]

41. *Monitor Republicano,* 9 July 1875, p. 1. Francisco Zarco agreed: "Electoral abuses, falsification of the public vote, incapable or perverse functionaries, arbitrary acts, despoilment of public funds, all this can exist within a republican system; but . . . the great problem is finding a pacific and legal remedy against the abuses . . . not armed rebellion." *El Siglo XIX,* 9 July 1869, reprinted in Zarco, *Textos políticos,* pp. 22–23.

42. Sánchez to Díaz, 23 December 1870, APD, 10:74.

43. Ramírez, *"La Apelación al Pueblo," El Correo de México,* 26 September 1867, p. 1.

If present historians overlook the connection between machine elections and insurrections during the Restored Republic, it is not the fault of the rebels, who left a public record easily uncovered. One of Díaz's supporters wrote to him in 1871 that "the electoral question in its colossal proportions is a monster, whose frightening howls from all corners of the Republic terrify us and presage a battle of blood and bitterness." The war, he said, "is indefectible. We must enter it and flatten with a blow the monopolizers of national power."[44]

Plácido Vega wrote in May 1871 of the "highly undignified and criminal conduct of the party of *señor* Juárez in Guadalajara." He wrote of forced elections and governors of western states removed from office by the federal army. He presumed that the people wanted Díaz for president and hoped that elections would be honest. Supposing, however, that the men in office continued to falsify elections, he asked, "what recourse remains?" Answering his own question, he proposed that "no other recourse remains but the road of force. For God's sake, what else can we do?"[45]

Another *Porfirista,* deploring the state of public affairs, came to the same conclusion. The future of the republic was sad, he wrote, "if these evils are not remedied, and if for some blind respect for the principles of order the remedy is only sought in the so-called electoral urns, although everyone recognizes there is no electoral freedom." Thinking men, he believed, were sensing that in order to make the laws respected in the face of attacks upon them to win elections, "no recourse remains but that of arms."[46]

Yet another correspondent of Díaz wrote that "money was not lacking on the part of the government to make allies for the reelection. The Revolution is waiting, and is already justified."[47]

Genaro Olguín thought that the men in power "will respect nothing which detracts from their triumph in the reelection." He concluded "that all independent men must appeal to the final recourse in order to have justice." Manuel Márquez believed that "our enemies do not

44. Vicente Llorente y Alegre to Díaz, 29 April 1871, APD, 9:133.
45. Vega to Díaz, 24 May 1871, ibid., pp. 138–39.
46. Ignacio de la Peña to Díaz, 6 June 1871, ibid., pp. 163–64.
47. José Montesinos to Díaz, 30 July 1871, ibid., pp. 222–23.

cease to invent ways to falsify the public vote . . . and I must jump into the arena. . . ."[48]

In this way elections led directly to insurrections. It was finally the election of 1875 which triggered the insurrection that ended the Restored Republic and commenced the age of Porfirian Mexico.[49]

One of the most interesting ways to gauge the level of electoral morality and practice and to comprehend the interrelation of local and national interests in them is to trace a single state election from inception to conclusion. Although any state for any of the several elections of the Restored Republic might be chosen, the elections of 1867 in the state of Puebla are especially interesting and reveal some unexpected sidelights of that fascinating year.

Throughout the campaign season of 1867 Porfirio Díaz was in the state of Puebla at the headquarters of the Second Division at Tehuacán. There he easily sent and received political envoys to and from every part of the state, as well as from Veracruz, Oaxaca, Mexico City, and other points. Gen. Juan N. Méndez remained in close contact with Díaz from Huamantla, where he fled after turning over the state government to Rafael García. Huamantla is across the state line in Tlaxcala and close to the mountain villages of northern Puebla (*la Sierra de Puebla*), which Méndez knew well and from whence he drew his support. From Huamantla Méndez advanced the interests of all Porfirian candidates and directed his own gubernatorial campaign. From there he also proposed to foil García's plans to substitute the political chiefs, who were Méndez's appointees and friends, in the towns of Puebla. He was determined to use arms if necessary.[50]

García had indeed planned to appoint his own political chiefs. He had recommended such action to Juárez before his appointment and received euphemistic written confirmation that he was "in complete liberty . . . to change the employees, who in your judgment do not

48. Olaguín to Díaz, 13 August 1871, ibid., p. 242; Márquez to Díaz, 7 May 1871, ibid., p. 134.

49. Some historical accounts by Mexican and American authors about the ways elections were conducted during the Restored Republic are compared in appendix 5.

50. Méndez to Díaz, 26 September 1867, APD, 5:82–84.

merit confidence and can in the least [way] alter the peace of the state." On the following day García was able to write that he had "changed all the political chiefs who do not inspire my entire confidence and those whom I supposed were working under the inspiration of Sr. Méndez. . . ."[51] The political chiefs of Tepeji, Acatlán, and Tecamachalco were immediately replaced.[52] In the latter town the *Porfirista* political chief, mistakenly replaced by another *Porfirista* who secretly worked for Díaz in the elections, told Díaz that "many [*Juarista*] agents are coming with money to cut down" his candidacy.[53] In Teziutlán Rafael Avila had great difficulty taking over the office of political chief from the *Mendista*. García asked the minister of *gobernación*, Lerdo de Tejada, for permission to delay the elections. "Although [the *convocatoria*] will be published in two or three days, there will not be time to arrange the electoral work. . . ." Lerdo granted the extension "for the time strictly necessary."[54] In Zacatlán the political chief replaced on García's orders was one of Mexico's minor *caudillos*, Gen. Juan C. Bonilla, who refused to turn over the office, and the new appointee was obliged to commence his duties without a formal transfer.[55] Bonilla recruited his neighbors in the following months and years; in 1871 he fought for Porfirio Díaz in the rebellion of La Noria.

Gubernatorial changing of political chiefs violated the Puebla law of municipalities, which called for popularly elected political chiefs, but during the electoral period of 1867 all constitutional procedure was still suspended from the war years. To argue that replacing political chiefs nevertheless violated the spirit of the law overlooks the fact that those officers had been appointed anyway: The real violation was that the political chiefs were chosen by one party or the other in order to return desirable election results. This was understood by everyone, by Juárez, Lerdo, and García, as well as by Díaz and Méndez. No one, even in that first election of the Restored Republic, misunderstood how elections were made, and all of them dealt in the same coin.

51. Juárez to Rafael J. García, 2 October 1867, DDC, 12:558; García to Juárez, 3 October 1867, ibid., p. 559.

52. M. González Fernández to Díaz, 12 October 1867, APD, 5:188–89; Rafael Mejía to Díaz, 9 December 1867, ibid., p. 396.

53. Jesús Arenas to Díaz, 1 October 1867, ibid., pp. 104–5.

54. García to Lerdo, 8 October 1867, PDP, box 9; García to Lerdo, 7 October 1867, ibid.; Lerdo to García, 11 October 1867, ibid.

55. García to Lerdo, 7 October 1867, ibid.

The greatest political activity took place in the capital city of Puebla. Gov. Rafael García twice postponed the elections, "because the agents of don Benito," claimed a *Porfirista*, "have not captured [enough] terrain in the districts . . . of the state." Another *Porfirista* reported that there was a veritable "cloud" of *Juarista* agents in the city, and Méndez had word that Carvajal was the chief of them, "passing out money, letters, and I know not what else, all in favor of the candidacy of *don* Benito."[56] García gave the state military command to General Figueroa, who—according to a Porfirian observer—immediately commenced to establish his own faction. The informant was José R. Cuevas, who refused to arm Figueroa's volunteers from the federal armory and feared for his position as commander of artillery in Puebla. The new state regime had obliged him to sign several releases of personnel. "It seems that everything that pertains to [the old Army of] the East smells bad," he wrote to Díaz. Díaz advised him "to proceed with prudence in order to conserve your position, which is very important." Holding a military command was important, for Cuevas was running for elector. He won a seat to the electoral college in Puebla, which was illegal in itself, but was ordered to Mexico City by the minister of war to report on the state of the artillery. "To me it is pretext," he wrote to Díaz, to keep him from the electoral college.[57]

The developments in Izúcar de Matamoros in southern Puebla exemplify the factional struggle. At war's end the political chief and military commander of Izúcar de Matamoros was Gen. Román Márquez Galindo, who had fought at the battle of Puebla in April 1867 under Méndez.[58] Galindo became one of the *Mendista-Porfirista* political chiefs to be replaced by Governor García in the fall of 1867. The position was given to Col. Jesús M. Vizoso, who had earlier secured his military position from Díaz, and for a period of time the *Porfiristas* did not know whom Vizoso would favor. Galindo, who remained in Matamoros to form the "Club Pavón" for the promotion of Díaz's presidential candidacy, asked Díaz to persuade Vizoso not to serve "as

56. M. González Fernández to Díaz, 12 October 1867, APD, 5:188; Agustín León to Díaz, 14 October 1867, ibid., pp. 207–8; Méndez to Díaz, 4 October 1867, ibid., p. 138.

57. José R. Cuevas to Díaz, 1 October 1867, ibid., p. 107, and answer, p. 108; Cuevas to Díaz, 17 October 1867, ibid., p. 230.

58. Galindo, *Década nacional*, 3:539.

an instrument for García in the electoral struggle." Díaz wrote to Vizoso and received an assuring reply. Nevertheless, Galindo reported that Vizoso "clandestinely" posted warnings that to abstain from voting on the amendments would invalidate the whole ballot. The strategy of the governmental opposition was to encourage popular abstention.[59]

The elections went badly in Izúcar de Matamoros for the *Porfiristas.* Márquez Galindo reported that the town was crowded with conservatives and men who had served the empire, working for various candidates, and that a rumor had circulated that the *Juaristas* would defend religion. He said that the popular balloting had selected *Porfirista* electors and had voted down the constitutional reforms, but that thereafter the Matamoros electoral college chose *Juarista* candidates. Galindo blamed the Juárez victory following a Porfirian lead on corruption, threats upon the electors (one of whom was himself), and the perfidy of Vizoso. "I will soon remit to you a newspaper, in which the dirty story of the elections in Matamoros will appear, and which justifies [petitioning Congress to decree] that the elections are absolutely null."[60] García apparently served Juárez well in Izúcar de Matamoros, and Vizoso complied with the responsibility that García had entrusted to him.

Chalchicomula was another town in Puebla where the factions clashed. Early in the campaign Méndez suggested to Díaz that "it would not be a bad idea" on the day of elections in Chalchicomula "to send some troops under intelligent officers, with whatever pretext, who can work in accord with our agents in the elections, because if not we will lose that district." Díaz assured Méndez that he had "sufficient

59. Ramón Márquez Galindo to Díaz, 1 October 1867, APD, 5:108–10; Vizoso to Díaz, 1 October 1867, and answer, 3 October 1867, ibid., p. 111; Vizoso to Díaz, 4 October 1867, and answer, 8 October 1867, ibid., pp. 139–40; Galindo to Díaz, 13 October 1867, ibid., pp. 199–200. Vizoso's action was illegal: Lerdo had written that "the citizens, according to the law, may vote in favor of or against the proposed amendments, or may abstain from voting on them." Open letter, Lerdo to Guzmán, reprinted in Cosmes, *Historia general de Méjico,* 19:60.

60. Galindo to Díaz, 15 October 1867, APD, 5:212–13; Galindo to Díaz, 13 October 1867, ibid., pp. 199–200; Galindo to Díaz, 26 October 1867, ibid., pp. 274–75.

activity working in Chalchicomula."[61] Gen. Eufemio M. Rojas, a *Porfirista* officer of cavalry who had fought at the battle of Puebla in 1867 under Gen. Manuel Toro, was in regular communication with Díaz about the elections. Rojas wrote, "I hope you will make use of your influence . . . in Chalchicomula, where we are in the minority. . . ." Díaz answered that Rojas should "not doubt that he would attend to your indications" and asked Rojas who in Chalchicomula wielded the most influence. Rojas informed Díaz that José María de Borbolla was the man but that he was working for Juárez. Rojas named three other men with whom the *Porfiristas* might work[62] Gen. Manuel Toro soon quartered the First Infantry Brigade of the Second Division in Chalchicomula, where he sent election news to Díaz. Díaz wrote to a confidant in Puebla that General González Paez, an officer subordinate to Toro, "will direct the election" in Chalchicomula in accord with instructions from Zamacona.[63]

The presence of a military unit in Chalchicomula caused some scandal. The Mexico City newspaper *Continental* asked the editors of the Porfirian *El Globo* to explain the presence of a Second Division brigade there. Toro saw the article reprinted in *El Amigo de Puebla* and wrote to the editors that the lack of pasturage in Tehuacán necessitated units of the Second Division to be posted in various localities within the command and that its presence there should cause no alarm to the peace of the area. Díaz was disturbed at the appearance of the notice and told Toro that the simplest answer would have been to consult the minister of war, who had given the order.[64] The *Porfiristas* apparently overcame their "minority" in the town of Chalchicomula, for the elector chosen there was Juan G. Ibarra, who had wished to represent the district in Congress, but settled for casting his ballot for Díaz in the electoral college both for president of the Su-

61. Méndez to Díaz, 26 September 1867, ibid., pp. 82–84; Díaz to Méndez, 20 October 1867, ibid., p. 151.

62. Eufemio M. Rojas to Díaz, 28 September 1867, ibid., p. 94; Rojas to Díaz, 2 October 1867, ibid., pp. 116–17; Rojas to Díaz, 7 October 1867, and answer, ibid., pp. 151–52.

63. Manuel Toro to Díaz, 10 October 1867, ibid., p. 176; Díaz to Agustín León, 14 October 1867, ibid., p. 208.

64. Manuel Toro to Díaz, 27 October 1867, and answer, ibid., pp. 281–83.

preme Court and president of the nation.[65] Nevertheless, the Porfirian manipulation in the town was insufficient to carry the entire district of Chalchicomula, which went *Juarista* and sent Borbolla, "the most influential man in Chalchicomula," to Congress.[66]

The intensity of politicking continued to mount. Manuel M. Zamacona, who arrived in Puebla on the eve of the elections to attend to his own candidacy as congressman from Puebla's Second District, counted some ten *Juarista* agents from Mexico a week preceding the elections. He immediately contacted General Díaz, to whom he complained that "the government has its whole battery aimed at frustrating my campaign."[67] Well the government might! Zamacona had been *Orteguista* and had led the fight against the *convocatoria* from *El Globo*.

On 18 October the college for the district of Puebla City met to cast its votes for governor: Méndez received thirty-two, one *Bautista* received twenty-two, and García twelve. Zamacona reported the same day that he had contacted the *Bautistas* to swing their votes to Méndez for the runoff to be held in the state legislature.[68] Since the Puebla elections had been postponed and electoral college voting had already taken place in most other states, the *Juarista* lead across the nation was well known in Puebla. Zamacona noted that men from all factions in Puebla were rushing to the *Juaristas* for accommodation. Rumor had it that money was being employed: "Even the friends of *don* Juan Méndez are getting fewer, because of the generous largesse employed today."[69] On the next day the electoral colleges in Puebla cast votes for president: Juárez won both colleges by a combined vote of seventy-seven to forty-three for Díaz.

A brother of General Méndez attributed the vote in the two districts of Puebla to "the presence of Carvajal in the electoral colleges and the lack of dignity, patriotism, and honesty of the electors in this city." Rumor had it that Carvajal "had visited the majority of the electors, buying votes and threatening them in case they broke their promise." The informant would not vouch for that, but "later they told me that

65. Agustín León to Díaz, 14 October 1867, ibid., p. 207.
66. Tovar, *Cuarto congreso*, 1:xxii.
67. Zamacona to Díaz, 14 October 1867, APD, 5:211.
68. Zamacona to Díaz, 18 October 1867, ibid., pp. 240–41.
69. Zamacona to Díaz, 19 October 1867, ibid., p. 247.

there was one elector who held out for fifty pesos for his vote." Governor García, however, was quite satisfied with Carvajal; he earlier thanked Juárez for sending Carvajal, adding, "I will take advantage of his influence and services."[70]

The college balloting on the following day was for the deputies to Congress. Zamacona claimed that orders came by telegraph from Mexico to offer the Porfirian electors a gambit for abandoning Zamacona in the Second District. The García-*Juaristas* apparently were planning to file nullification procedures if Méndez won the gubernatorial elections but would not do so if the *Profiristas* in the Puebla college would dump Zamacona, probably on the strategy that the Méndez vote in the Puebla college would be overbalanced by García votes in the other colleges of the state. Zamacona claimed that he worked through various "loyal friends" to crush the intrigue and won one of the two congressional seats in the city.[71]

On the final day of balloting, the electoral college cast votes for the president of the Supreme Court. Either *Juaristas* were not championing Lerdo in Puebla, or the elections were freer than the opposition was claiming: Díaz won the tally in both colleges of Puebla City for the presidency of the Court by wider margins than Juárez had for the presidency of the republic.

Díaz had asked Zamacona to watch over election activity in western Puebla. Nevertheless, the *Porfiristas* lost San Andrés, Cholula, Huejotzingo, and San Martín de Texmelucan. Zamacona insisted that in Cholula "the election . . . is null, because there was verified bribery." Galindo, in Texmelucan during the election, reported that the balloting was conducted "in the most scandalous manner by *señor* García." Rojas reported that in Tepeaca, where he was candidate for congressman, Lt. Col. Rafael Bueno "is balancing our work . . ." and recommended that Díaz, "using your military character, call him [to Tehuacán] and keep him there with some pretext. . . ." Díaz answered that he could not do so, "because he is not at my orders; but I am sure

70. A. Méndez to Díaz, 22 October 1867, ibid., pp. 257–58; Juan Arenas to Díaz, 22 October 1867, ibid., p. 254; García to Juárez, 3 October 1867, DDC, 12:560.

71. Zamacona to Díaz, 21 October 1867, APD, 5:253, and Zamacona to Díaz, 19 October 1867, ibid., p. 247.

and confident of our friends, who are working in that district."[72] Rojas finished better than Díaz in Tepeaca, winning a seat in Congress, while Díaz lost the college presidential balloting by two votes.[73] From wherever the winning influence came in these elections, clearly everyone involved assumed that elections were not determined by the popular vote.

Porfiristas also lost in Tehuacán. Díaz credited the *Juarista* victory to the "treason" of the political chief, Carlos Andrade Párraga, whom Díaz had trusted to deliver the election "on the recommendation of his brother and various other friends who work with us in good faith." García earlier asked Juárez to recall Andrade Párraga from Tehuacán because he was a *Mendista*. Two years later a *Juarista*, recalling the elections of 1867 in Tehuacán, claimed that "of the thirteen sections in which this city is divided we only won the *mesa* which I installed, because the rest were illegally taken over by soldiers." The political chief (Andrade Párraga), he said, worked in accord with Díaz to impede the installation of the electoral college. On the morning of the election the political chief gave orders to the soldiers to round up all the electors, who were held for the day in the home of Colonel Ceballos. There the political chief declared the college in session. The voting took place without the electors being able to communicate among themselves or to see the ballots, and the results were anti-*Juarista*, contrary, according to the informant, to the will of the people.[74]

The probable explanation of the contradictions about which side Andrade Párraga was favoring is that they refer to different balloting

72. Zamacona to Díaz, 21 October 1867, ibid., p. 253; Galindo to Díaz, 26 October 1867, ibid., p. 274; Rojas to Díaz, 22 October 1867, and answer, 31 October 1867, ibid., p. 258.

73. Méndez to Díaz, 30 October 1867, ibid., pp. 294–95; Tovar, *Cuarto congreso*, 1:xxii.

74. Díaz to A. Méndez, 26 October 1867, APD, 5:258; García to Juárez, 3 October 1867, DDC, 12:559–61; Joaquín G. Cuevas to Juárez, 16 June 1869, AJ, 41:7490. The local constitution of Tehuacán called for popular election of the political chief; the election was held 30 October by Carlos Andrade between Joaquín García Heras and Francisco Villaseñor, the latter of whom had occupied Tehuacán for the republican government upon the withdrawal of the French garrison on 14 February. The rugged, intense election was won by García Heras, but Andrade worked a reform into the constitution by which he remained in office. Joaquín Paredes Colín, *Apuntes históricos de Tehuacán*, 2d ed. (n.p., 1953), p. 313.

in that confused year of annulments and reelections. Two things are clear, however: first, Andrade changed sides along the way from *Porfirista* to *Juarista;* and, second, Andrade did have the electoral power, which in those days was attributed to political chiefs.

From Huamantla, Méndez managed the Porfirian agents in the northern Sierra de Puebla. Méndez had more influence there than Díaz had in Tehuacán, or than Márquez Galindo had in Izúcar de Matamoros, or than Zamacona had in Puebla. Méndez was a true *caudillo,* working in home territory. Teziutlán went for Díaz by a vote of 42 to 36 for Juárez, even though Romero Vargas, who became Puebla's next governor, was there working for his personal faction. In Zacatlán the vote was for Díaz, 82 to 8. In Libres, Díaz received 47 to Juárez's 7 electoral votes for president, and 49 to Lerdo's 5 for the Court presidency. The college at Ixcaquistla gave 104 votes to Díaz for both top positions in the nation and sent the *Porfirista* and later historian of the Fourth Congress, Pantaleón Tovar, to Congress.[75] The Sierra de Puebla remained *Mendista* and *Porfirista* throughout the Restored Republic.

The strong-man of Zacapoaxtla, another Sierra village, was Gen. Juan Francisco Lucas, a minor but effective *caudillo* and Indian guerrilla soldier, who had fought under Méndez and remained during the Restored Republic an influential man in the Sierra de Puebla. Zacapoaxtla formed an electoral district with Tetela, where, according to Méndez, "the reactionaries joined Juárez." Governor García asked Juárez to direct a letter to General Lucas in order "to obligate him," which Juárez apparently did, for Lucas promised Juárez to work for García "in the removal of Sr. Méndez."[76] Lucas probably promised falsely, for Díaz won Zacapoaxtla ninety-two to seven, and Lucas rebelled against García a few months later and joined Díaz in the rebellion of La Noria.

Of all the towns in the Sierra, the *Juaristas* won only Huauchinango. Méndez claimed that the government had given 20,000 pesos to the Cravioto brothers, payable from the receipts of the customshouse in

75. Méndez to Díaz, 25 October 1867, APD, 5:268–69; Méndez to Díaz, 30 October 1867, ibid., pp. 294–95; José Antonio Camarillo to Díaz, 29 October 1867, ibid., p. 286.
76. Méndez to Díaz, 25 October 1867, ibid., pp. 268–69; García to Juárez, 3 October 1867, DDC, 12:560; Lucas to Juárez, 10 October 1867, ibid., p. 640.

Tuxpan, to spend on the elections. García wrote to Juárez before the elections that Huauchinango "gives me the best guarantee, because of the influence of General Cravioto." "You already know," wrote Justo Benítez from Mexico to Díaz, "that Cravioto and [Pedro] Santacilia understand each other perfectly, and that the latter was elected congressman for Huauchinango."[77] Pedro Santacilia was Juárez's son-in-law.

The final electoral activity of the year in Puebla was to select the governor. New popular elections were held in November. The votes were divided among four candidates, but remaining in contest was a block of votes which the *Mendistas* claimed and which would have given Méndez a clear majority.[78] At that point, the elections were referred to the state legislature, which voted ten to five to annul the elections altogether, to remove García from the governorship, and to name Juan Gómez as interim governor, pending new elections, which were announced for 19 January. This maneuver was arranged on a Méndez-Romero alliance in the legislature against García, who protested vigorously and asked Juárez to intervene. Díaz's only role was to counsel the *Méndez-Porfiristas* to insist that the newly elected political chiefs be allowed to assume their positions in order to avoid the election irregularities that were attributed to the García appointees.[79] That would place *Méndez-Porfirista* political chiefs in all the towns of the Sierra for the new election.

The January elections were held under tense conditions with the reported results divided among four candidates. The election was therefore again thrown to the state legislature, where Romero Vargas withdrew his minority candidacy for the right to vote upon the electoral returns. His vote broke an eight-to-eight tie on the contested college votes from Tehuacán, which according to Porfirian sources

77. Méndez to Díaz, 23 October 1867, APD, 5:262; García to Juárez, 3 October 1867, DDC, 12:560; Benítez to Díaz, 26 October 1867, APD, 5:277.

78. Congressman Antonio Esperón claimed the popular vote was 64,204 for Méndez, 22,862 for García, 20,681 for Romero Vargas, and 6,582 for Ortega: Tovar, *Cuarto congreso*, 1:543.

79. Agustín León to Díaz, 1 December 1867, APD, 5:366–67; Eufemio M. Rojas to Díaz, 21 December 1867, ibid., pp. 442–43; García to Juárez, 29 November 1867, DDC, 12:711; undated minute of letter, Díaz to Agustín León, APD, 5:367; undated minute of letter, Díaz to Méndez, ibid., pp. 364–65; minute of letter, Díaz to Rojas, 5 December 1867, ibid., p. 368.

were returned to the capital with a number greater than the number of electors in Tehuacán. Furthermore, a new García-Romero majority decreed that Méndez was ineligible for the governorship because he was a federal employee—a general of the army—and García was declared the governor of Puebla.[80]

Protests were immediately raised, and the local government of Zacatlán refused to recognize the governorship of Rafael García. Thereupon García sought federal intervention. Federal forces were sent from Tehuacán and Tulancingo to Zacatlán, where they were quartered for several months. *Mendez-Porfirista* congressmen sponsored a bill to withdraw the federal forces on the basis that the president had sent them illegally: a governor could ask for federal military aid only if the state legislature was not in session, which had not been the case. Furthermore, they argued, federal troops in the Sierra of Puebla could only serve to antagonize the people; Gen. Miguel Negrete was used in the congressional debate as an example of local force that would feel threatened. The bill to remove the federal forces was defeated sixty-seven to thirty-six, and several months later Negrete was in full revolt.[81]

Throughout the unfolding of those events, all participants believed, or wished others to believe, that they were the victims of vicious machinations. García called the legislative annulment of the November elections "highly immoral and scandalous," causing "grave injuries to the state and a blow to democracy." Méndez claimed that "García had opened the election returns for governor and had supplanted more than 20,000 votes in his favor, which he took from me." Congressman Antonio Esperón called the nullification of Méndez's candidacy "the most flagrant extortion of the popular will." Antonio Gamboa wrote to Díaz that the Puebla legislature "put aside

80. *Manifestación que hace al Estado de Puebla el ciudadano Ignacio Romero Vargas, diputado por el primer distrito de la capital, de los hechos ocurridos con motivo de la elección de gobernador constitucional* (Puebla: Impreso por José María Osorio, 1868), written in reply to *Mendistas* who had declared the election of García illegal. *Colección de folletos, Recinto de Juárez, Palacio Nacional*, Mexico, *Segundo Emperio, tomo* 3. The pamphlet includes a denial by the political chief of Tehuacán of having falsified the vote and copies of letters sent between the political chiefs of Chiautla and Jicotlán as evidence of their manipulations of voting in those districts in favor of Méndez.

81. Tovar, *Cuarto congreso*, 1:509, 519, 522, 541–45, 567.

the free and spontaneous vote . . . in favor of *señor* Méndez." He added that "here [in Ixcaquistla] . . . one can detect a deep discontent."[82]

One final grievance, this one held by the *Porfiristas*, concerned the ineligibility of Méndez because of his military rank. As early as 14 October Zamacona told Díaz that the anti-*Porfiristas* in Puebla planned to nullify the candidacy of Méndez. The honorable jurist Joaquín Ruiz wrote personally to Juárez, imploring the government to accept Méndez's resignation from the army so that he could figure as a gubernatorial candidate. Juárez answered that Méndez had not solicited a separation from the military and was in open rebellion by having failed to publish the *convocatoria* and by having refused to present himself to the minister of war on orders to do so. Méndez finally went to Mexico to press "the question of the generalship, the resignation of which they have not admitted." Méndez was in Mexico in December; the state legislature decreed the nullification of Méndez's candidacy on 8 February.[83]

Gen. Juan Méndez never became reconciled to the Juárez and Lerdo administrations. He joined the rebellion of La Noria in 1871, acted as second in command to Díaz during the insurrection of Tuxtepec in 1876, and assumed the interim presidency of Mexico after the overthrow of Lerdo while Díaz campaigned against José María Iglesias.

Another aspect of the Puebla elections of 1867 may provide a key to the irregularities of that year. Even as Méndez was turning over the state government to García on 25 September and as the minister of war was ordering Méndez to the capital, Porfirio Díaz was closeted with José de Jesús Islas. Upon leaving Tehuacán, Islas wrote to Mén-

82. García to Juárez, 29 November 1867, DDC, 12:711–12; Méndez to Díaz, 1 December 1867, APD, 5:363–64; Tovar, *Cuarto congreso,* 1:543; Gamboa to Díaz, 6 March 1868, APD, 6:164–65.

83. Zamacona to Díaz, 14 October 1867, ibid., 5:207–8; Juárez to Ruíz, 23 November 1867, DDC, 12:710; Méndez to Díaz, 1 December 1867, APD, 5:363–64. Juárez wrote to Gen. Juan Francisco Lucas that the federal government "has remained neutral in the electoral campaign of Puebla, and conceded the license [of separation from the army] that Sr. Méndez asked for in order that he could figure as a candidate in the election." Juárez to Lucas, 18 February 1868, *Epistolario,* 1st ed., p. 443.

dez that "General Díaz . . . charged me to tell you without losing a moment that for no reason should you turn over the government, even if the President orders it. However, if you finally resolve to do so, go immediately to the Sierra to await his orders . . . [and] for no reason should you go to Mexico. . . ." The letter in some manner reached García, who sent it on to Juárez. Juárez acknowledged receipt and added, "I have read the letters from Islas and Gamboa, which are of very great importance, for they reveal the plans which are being brought into play to support Méndez in his attempt to pronounce against [*desconocer*] the National Government."[84]

The significance of this intelligence can only be speculated about. Neither Díaz nor Méndez ultimately offered armed resistance to the events that unfolded, even though they claimed they had been deprived of electoral victory. *Porfirista* correspondence clearly demonstrates that most *Porfiristas* believed that elections would have favored them without *Juarista* interference, even as that same correspondence demonstrates their own interference. For example, Zamacona stated that the elections throughout the state were characterized by governmental "corruption and abuse of force." Such was the only way he could account for the results: "Only that explains it, our part having all the influential men in the state."[85] Perhaps Díaz and Méndez talked a bolder game than they planned to play, each to assure the other of the depth of his commitment. Other *Porfiristas* were probably not aware of the depths of the commitment that their candidates had made. All that many of them could see was a sizable governmental influence on the events transpiring around them, and we may assume that they saw all of the events that did not end favorably to them as being results of governmental influence.

Furthermore, Díaz may have revolted in 1867 had not Juárez won so overwhelmingly that year, and perhaps part of the Juárez landslide was a result of well-spent funds, which *Juarista* advisors may have

84. Islas to Méndez, 25 September 1867, DDC, 12:488; minute of letter, Juárez to García, early November 1867, ibid., p. 709; "Gamboa" was probably Antonio Gamboa, who had been replaced as political chief of Tepeji in the Sierra de Puebla in early October by Cristobal Palacios on the order of Governor García; see M. González Fernández to Díaz, 12 October 1867, APD, 5:188–89.

85. Zamacona to Díaz, 21 October 1867, APD, 5:253.

justified in order to avoid the Porfirian rebellion implied in the intercepted letters. The point is that both parties escalated their campaigns beyond legal practice in the knowledge that the other was doing the same thing. Méndez, as governor, probably opposed the *convocatoria* in order to embarrass Juárez, and Juárez doubtless removed Méndez from the governorship as the first step in removing opposition political chiefs and winning the elections. The Díaz-Méndez plan to oppose Juárez by force was the natural result, but it justified Juárez's involvement in the elections, which in turn seemed to justify all Porfirian attempts to win the elections by any means left to them. The most hypocritical part of the entire sordid atmosphere is that both Juárez and Díaz maintained then and later a popular reputation of having held themselves neutral and aloof from electoral politics.[86]

Before the final voting in Puebla, the national officials had been chosen. Congress constituted itself into an electoral college on 19 December to count the electoral returns from the district colleges. A short debate centered on the question of waiting for the remainder of the returns, since only 180 of the 208 colleges had rendered reports, but the proposition carried to proceed with the counting. Of the 10,380 electoral votes cast for president, Juárez received 7,422, Díaz 2,709. For the presidency of the Supreme Court, Lerdo received 3,874, Díaz 2,841, Ezequiel Montes 1,238, Vicente Riva Palacio 750, Juárez 721, and León Guzmán 140. Congress voted 117 to 3 to declare Juárez president and to select the president of the Court from the two candidates with the greatest votes by state delegation. Lerdo then won the presidency of the Court by 17 state delegations to Díaz's 6.[87] Díaz's comment was that "Benito Juárez was elected president of the republic and Sebastián Lerdo of the Supreme Court; this is a fact, above which is the vote of the citizens."[88]

86. Even Cosío Villegas *(República restaurada,* p. 87) says that Díaz always intoned that he would serve in whatever position to which he might be elected, but "never would he make any effort to obtain it."
87. Tovar, *Cuarto congreso,* 19 December 1867, 1:91–92.
88. Undated minute of letter, Díaz to Eufemio M. Rojas, APD, 5:443.

Chapter 4
Rivalry in the Provinces

One of the major problems of the Benito Juárez administration after the fall of the Maximilian Empire in 1867 was a series of factional rivalries for the control of state governments. Much of the political struggle and most of the insurrections of the period originated from those state rivalries, which frequently threatened civil war on the state level—and even at the national level. The fundamental reality of Mexican politics was that the years of warfare had generated more leaders than there were positions for them, while war had militarized politics. Opportunity was limited, and rivalry was intense. Forced to employ strong tactics for political stability, governors tended to establish bureaucratic machine factions loyal to themselves, which animated rival factions to cries of tyranny and further opposition to those governors.

Dedication to liberal republicanism was tenuous and everywhere tempered by factional rivalry for the control of office. Employment of fraud and force became the political norm. Republican election was merely the stage on which fraud and force played their roles: office was used to secure given election results, not to secure honest elections. Because Mexicans were skeptical of the fairness of the elections, an insurrection of the "losers" against the "winners" was normal post-election activity, and violation of the electoral procedure inevitably justified it. No matter who the winner, employment of such tactics caused the losers to revolt or to threaten revolt. The deplorable social conditions in the countryside added to the discontent and facilitated recruitment to factional insurrections.

Juárez, as a party leader, tended to support local allies, in great part to deny local positions of strength to his opposition. Inasmuch as governors usually tried to monopolize all political opportunity in the states, any president would have had to support governors whose state factions supported presidential policies and politics. That dire need for the president to work with cooperative governors, in addition to the potential for local civil war if the president did not intervene, led to frequent presidential involvement in factional rivalry in the states. The losers in the local rivalry always charged their loss to official violence, frequently blamed presidential interference, and sometimes gravitated to the national opposition faction.

In fact Juárez did allow, or could not prevent, the electoral victory of some governors who were not of his circle of allies, such as Félix Díaz in Oaxaca and Gerónimo Treviño in Nuevo León, both of whom later used their official positions to marshal the resources of their respective states in rebellion against Juárez. Juárez might later have deplored the degree of liberalism and local freedom which he had allowed in those cases and which cost his administration so dearly. His successors, therefore, became even more involved in state politics for reasons that had become the common property of working politicians.

An examination of rivalries and presidential involvement in three states demonstrates the variety of experiences on these themes and explains how utterly hopeless was the expectation that the model of liberal republicanism could have been followed. Although case studies could be chosen from states almost at random, so universal was the phenomenon, in the early Restored Republic the states of Guerrero, Sinaloa, and Yucatán graphically exemplify how the president secured governors favorable to his alliance, how local rivalries became interrelated with national factionalism, now elections resulted in insurrections, and how the losers in the local rivalry ultimately allied themselves with the Porfirian opposition.

Guerrero

All of the dangers to Mexican republicanism and political stability are demonstrated in the case of the southern state of Guerrero. For three decades before the Reform its mighty *caudillo* was Gen. Juan Alvarez, who had initiated the insurrection of Ayutla by which Santa Anna was overthrown in 1855.[1] As president of Mexico, Alvarez formed the government in which Juárez figured prominently as minister of justice. He assumed the military direction of the liberal army in the south during the Three Years' War and again during the French Intervention. Besides Alvarez, Guerrero produced other leading mili-

1. See Fernando Díaz y Díaz, *Caudillos y Caciques* (Mexico: El Colegio de México, 1972); Mgisés González Navarro, "Venganza del sur," *Historia Mexicana 21*, no. 4 (April–June 1972):667–92.

tary figures, two of whom served as governors of the state in the decade from 1857 to 1867. One was Juan Alvarez's son Diego, and another was the *caudillo*'s loyal lieutenant, Vicente Jiménez. Diego Alvarez and Vicente Jimémez became generals and fought both wars with brigades at their command.[2]

Early in 1866 state republican armies forced Maximilian's military and civil authorities from the state and pushed northward. The brigade of Diego Alvarez served with Porfirio Díaz at Puebla and in the seige of Mexico, while the brigade of Vicente Jiménez joined General Escobedo at Querétaro. Thereupon General Jiménez marched his brigade back to Iguala in Guerrero and on 7 June 1867 pronounced against the governor of the state, Diego Alvarez. Both generals recognized the national government, both pledged support to Benito Juárez, and both had caudillistic powers, Alvarez in the southern coastal districts and Jiménez in the northern mountain districts. Jiménez claimed that he was supporting the democratic aspirations of the villages, which were suffering feudalistic bondage established by the Alvarez family.[3] Diego Alvarez pointed to his legal titles, which in lieu of elections during the war years Juárez had extended by decree in August 1866. While the dispute raged, Juan Alvarez died in August 1867.[4]

In mid-June Jiménez defeated the forces of Alvarez; in August he occupied the state capital, and in November he overran the district of Tlapa. Everyone knew that Guerrero was on the verge of a civil war that could well spill into other areas and perhaps involve the entire nation. Various persons and even a congressional committee implored Juárez to name an interim governor to conduct the scheduled elections of 1867 and turn over the office to the winner. Ignacio M. Altamirano, outstanding Reform figure and citizen of Guerrero, urged Juárez to that kind of solution. Díaz also interceded with Juárez in favor of a pacific solution. Jiménez insisted that that was all he wanted. One would-be meditator informed Juárez that Alvarez would turn over the state to anyone except Jiménez or Altamirano. "Jiménez

2. Moisés Ochoa Campos, *Historia del Estado de Guerrero* (Mexico: Porrúa Hnos., 1969), pp. 196–204.
3. Jiménez to Juárez, 30 September 1867, DDC, 12:547–49; the Plan de Iguala, 1867, is printed in *El Siglo XIX,* 1 August 1867.
4. Ochoa Campos, *Guerrero,* pp. 205–37.

does not want the command of the south," Altamirano wrote to Juárez, "but neither does he want to be proscribed."[5]

Juárez's solution, however, was to uphold "the principle of authority." Diego Alvarez should remain in the governorship until replaced by his legally elected successor, and Jiménez should publicly disclaim the Plan of Iguala and present himself to the minister of war to explain his conduct.[6] To compromise was to invite factions out of power across the nation to demand changes in the governorships. Furthermore, discharging Alvarez was not even a compromise, but rather a concession to the full demands of Jiménez. Jiménez answered Juárez that he could not deny the Plan of Iguala, which was supported against the tyranny of Alvarez, he said, by many villages that would fly to arms were the Plan withdrawn. Besides, Jiménez candidly admitted, "that is to ask me to commit political suicide." "Where would we be," he asked Juárez, "if in 1854 and 1855 that respect for the principle of authority had been proffered to Santa Anna . . . ?"[7]

From beginning to end, even as observers insisted that the "Guerrero business" was a local affair, regional factionalism was immediately and thoroughly related to the national divisions. Jiménez was a recognized *Porfirista,* and Díaz in Guerrero was a *Jimenista.* Late in the Three Years' War the then Col. Porfirio Díaz fought under General Jiménez to defeat Leonardo Márquez and Félix Zuloaga in Jalatlaco, Guerrero. During the French Intervention, Jiménez and Díaz joined forces in Chilaca in November 1863, and Jiménez accompanied Díaz in the Oaxacan campaign. When Díaz escaped from his French captors in Puebla, he presented himself to Jiménez in Tixtla in October 1865 with only a servant. Jiménez put two batallions at his orders which became the nucleus of the later great Division of the East.[8] Díaz liked Jiménez and, furthermore, disliked Alvarez. After the assault on Puebla, Díaz ordered Alvarez to garrison Puebla, while Díaz pursued

5. Altamirano to Juárez, 9 June 1867, DDC, 12:197–200; Jiménez to Díaz, 8 August 1867, ibid., p. 374, and undated reply, p. 375; Jiménez to Juárez, 30 September 1867, ibid., p. 548; Ignacio C. Ocádez to Juárez, 2 October 1867, ibid., p. 551.

6. Ochoa Campos, *Guerrero,* p. 240; José V. Hernández to Díaz, 25 October 1867, APD, 5:267.

7. Jiménez to Juárez, 30 September 1867, DDC, 12:547–49.

8. Ochoa Campos, *Guerrero,* pp. 211–27; Díaz has a slightly different version, *Memorias,* 1:427.

Márquez.[9] To a friend in Guerrero Díaz wrote about Alvarez that "I look upon him as a child and as such I tolerate him."[10]

The frequent correspondence between Díaz and Jiménez in the final quarter of 1867 in part concerned the desired influence Díaz might have on Juárez for a pacific solution in Guerrero, and in part it concerned the influence Jiménez might have on the elections for a *Porfirista* victory in Guerrero. Indeed, the Díaz electoral campaign contained a "southern strategy." "I think that with Guanajuato, Puebla, and Guerrero," wrote Justo Benítez in mid-October, "we will have enough to make the election terribly questionable and dependent upon congressional resolution." Furthermore, Guerrero was a convenient state in which to run *Porfirista* congressional candidates who had already lost in other districts because of the seven certain seats from the districts under Jiménez's control. "Send [Genaro] Olguín to Tlapa or to whatever other district of Guerrero," wrote Benítez to Díaz, "to supervise the election of congressman for [Felipe] Buenrostro and for Olguín as alternate."[11] Jiménez's earlier envoy to Juárez wrote to Díaz that "our good Zenteno will represent Tlapa." Jiménez doubtless recognized that his electoral work for Díaz in Guerrero assured important out-of-state support for his precarious in-state position; he was working for Díaz's candidacy, he assured the general. The good news reached Díaz in early December: "In the State of Guerrero you were elected unanimously for president of the republic in seven electoral colleges."[12]

The other alliance was not as happy. Juárez could not have been completely satisfied with Alvarez, who represented the older caudillistic class and who was not as submissive as, for example, Gov. Domingo Rubí of Sinaloa, Gov. Miguel Auza of Zacatecas, or Gov. Manuel Cepeda Peraza of Yucatán. Alvarez was also pressing for a solution to the "Guerrero business," by requesting Juárez to send federal troops to crush Jiménez. Juárez asked Alvarez to wait until certain other

9. Miller, "Army of the East," p. 114.

10. Díaz's note on a letter from Manuel López y Osario, 6 December 1867, APD, 5:385.

11. Benítez to Díaz, 14 October 1867, DDC, 12:506; Benítez to Díaz, 26 October 1867, APD, 5:277.

12. José V. Hernández to Díaz, 22 November 1867, ibid., p. 336; Jiménez to Díaz, 22 November 1867, ibid., p. 336; Juan Torres to Díaz, 10 December 1867, ibid., p. 401.

reports arrived in Mexico City. Indignant, Alvarez replied that "that means the reports I sent you are not sufficient, [although I am] Governor and Military Commander of the State, and have never given any motive to the Supreme Government to [make you] doubt my word of honor."[13] Alvarez, however, although guilty of offenses against the federation more severe than failure to publish a questionable *convocatoria,* could not be dumped like León Guzmán in Guanajuato or Juan N. Méndez in Puebla: Juárez needed Alvarez to offset the Porfirian Jiménez. Nevertheless, federal troops could not be sent into Guerrero during a national election. National politics were unsettled, and Juárez waited.

Meanwhile elections were conducted across the nation. Jiménez published the *convocatoria* in his region and sent the returns to Congress.[14] Alvarez did not receive the order in time, held elections late, and decreed the Jiménez elections void. The national legislature was convoked without the Guerrero delegation present, and the whole issue was thrown to Congress.

When Congress commenced its sessions in early December it had to face the "Guerrero business" and so established its own temporary committee on Guerrero. A month later the permanent Committee on Constitutional Points (*Comisión de Puntos Constitucionales*) presented a bill to annul the Jiménez returns. The issue on the first day of debate revolved around whether Congress should sit as a legislative body on a political question, or as an electoral college on an election issue. The discussion remained in legal clothing, but speakers for the political solution were *Porfiristas* (Mata, Zamacona, Barrón); the other view was supported by *Juarista* (Cendejas, Dondé, Inda). Days later Zamacona unmasked the issue, saying that on every piece of business before Congress two factions had faced each other. He called for unity, but threw more fuel on the fire by claiming that the administration was guilty of having produced a profound discontent in the country. He claimed that the movement of Iguala was legal and pacific, that numerous persons in the press and in both camps, as well as the special congressional committee on Guerrero, had asked the president to send an impartial authority to conduct elections, but that the government had turned a deaf ear. As in Guanajuato and Puebla

13. Alvarez to Juárez, 14 August 1867, ibid., p. 397.
14. Tovar, *Cuarto congresso,* 24 January 1868, 1:275.

(the Guzmán and Méndez cases) the administration policy had been "to pull from the scene one of the counterweights in order to leave the one which has the executive favor in possession." In short, he said, by factional politics the executive had deepened the problem and hindered a solution. The bill that became law by a vote of a seventy-four to forty called for a count of all votes from Guerrero, declaring them neither valid nor void until the state should be pacified.[15]

Juárez became deeply involved as the "Guerrero business" complicated during 1868. In March he quietly sent Gen. Francisco O. Arce to Guerrero as "mediator." Arce had sufficient federal troops under his command to defeat Jiménez, who surrendered in April. By the terms of submission Jiménez was to report to Mexico without loss of rank, the *Jimenista* brigade was to be demobilized, and Alvarez was not to persecute *Jimenistas*.[16] Jiménez delayed his departure from Guerrero all summer, claiming that Alvarez was removing *Jimenistas* from office. Juárez tried to induce Alvarez to leave the state also, so that "no one . . . can argue that you are an obstacle to free elections." Alvarez refused to leave the state on the grounds that Jiménez was still actively promoting disorder. In reality, everyone was preparing the ground for gubernatorial elections, Jiménez, Alvarez, and Arce.[17] Jiménez finally went to Mexico City in August and was placed on orders without troops in the capital. Arce and Alvarez settled down to personal accusations as Arce tried to inherit the Jiménez faction. In the fall the *Alvarista* Division of the South was disbanded by orders of the minis-

15. Ibid., 23 December 1867, p. 100; 28 January 1868, p. 300; 30 January 1868, pp. 311–12.

16. Ochoa Campos, *Guerrero*, p. 240; Juárez to Arce, 16 March 1868, DDC, 13:160–61; Juárez to José María Martínez de la Concha, 19 March 1869, ibid., pp. 162–63; Arce to Juárez, 4 April 1868, p. 285; Arce to Minister of War, 6 April 1868, ibid., pp. 285–87; Minister of *gobernación*, Sebastián Lerdo de Tejada, to Congress, 11 January 1868, ibid., p. 153; Arce to Juárez, 3 May 1868, ibid., pp. 291–92.

17. Jiménez to Juárez, 10 February 1868, ibid., p. 157; Juárez to Alvarez, 26 May 1868, ibid., pp. 299–300; Juárez to Alvarez, 22 April 1868, ibid., p. 289; Juárez to Alvarez, 26 May 1868, ibid., pp. 299–300; Juárez to Alvarez, 30 May 1868, *Epistolario*, 1st ed., p. 463; Alvarez to Juárez, 4 May 1868, DDC, 13:294–96; Alvarez to Juárez, 27 July 1868, ibid., pp. 301–2; Arce to Juárez, 3 May 1868, ibid., pp. 291–92; Arce to Juárez, 30 September 1868, ibid., p. 661.

ter of war.[18] Only Arce remained with troops under arms, and gubernatorial elections raised Arce to the governorship.[19]

This review of events in Guerrero demonstrates the various contentions raised above: caudillistic rivalry, electoral violence, national involvement, and the absolute necessity of presidential interference—not to save republicanism but to save the peace. Juárez also obtained a loyal and trustworthy governor in the process.

Sinaloa

The case of the northwestern state of Sinaloa was characterized by the same complex set of factors as those that disturbed Guerrero, and the immediate resolution of the covert problems demonstrates the same powers at work. Upon the liberation of the state from the French regime, Gen. Ramón Corona had advanced all the men of power in the state. Gov. Antonio Rosales had been killed in warfare; after a period of disruptive factionalism, General Corona and some of his officers in May 1865 raised Gen. Domingo Rubí to the position of governor and military commander of the state. Rosales rebelled against Rubí, bringing civil war to the area in addition to the battles against the French and against Yaqui and Mayo Indian rebellions, in one of which Rosales was killed September 1865. Rubí, thereafter, was Corona's man in the governorship.

Other important men in Sinaloa with personal followings were Lt. Col. Jorge García Granados and Gen. Angel Martínez. García Granados was a republican general without a command in 1865 because of an earlier rebellion against Rosales. In two later attempts to suborn the "mixed brigade" (Indian and Republican) García Granados was captured and condemned to death, but he escaped on both occasions. In 1866 he was again commanding troops under Corona. At war's end Juárez named Corona commander of the Fourth Division at Guadalajara. Directly responsible to Corona for the

18. Ochoa Campos, *Guerrero*, *p. 241; Alvarez to Juárez, 22 September 1868*, DDC, 13:660; Alvarez to Juárez, 20 October 1868, ibid., pp. 662–63; Alvarez to Juárez, 1 December 1868, ibid., p. 720.

19. Tamayo, *Juárez*, 13:794.

federal forces in Sinaloa was Gen. Angel Martínez, titular leader of the Tepic faction in Sinaloa who had refused to follow Manuel Lozada of Tepic when the latter recognized the Maximilian Empire. In that set of uncertain alliances Juárez cultivated the loyalty of Gov. Domingo Rubí, calling him "one of the cooperators in the great work of regeneration."[20] Rubí became the object of Juárez's confidences.

In the elections of 1867 Rubí campaigned for constitutional governor of Sinaloa. Running against him were three others, Gen. Angel Martínez, commander of the garrision at Mazatlán; Manuel Monzón, prefect of Culiacán; and Eustaquio Buelna, district judge. Rubí removed Monzón as prefect to "guarantee the freedom of elections," and Buelna had no wide support; the contest was between Rubí and Martínez. According to Buelna, partisans for Martiínez used federal forces, threatening to rebel if they did not win, and those of Rubí for their ends used the influence of gubernatorial power. The stormy election was pitched into the state legislature, which ruled in mid-December that both Martínez and Rubí were ineligible because they held office during the elections and had abused the freedom of suffrage. Threats, riots, and violence, involving the parties of both Martínez and Rubí, spilled into the streets, agitated the legislature, and even invaded the homes of congressional members. The legislature finally withdrew its earlier decree and declared Rubí governor and Monzón vice-governor.[21]

General Corona immediately stepped into the turmoil. He sought and received orders from Juárez to go to Mazatlán "to organize the forces that garrison that state."[22] Even as Corona left Guadalajara colonels García Granados and Adolfo Palacio, with Ireneo Paz, newspaperman and publisher, and twenty-five officers of the state forces in Culiacán, pronounced against the election of General Rubí. Their charges were specific: Rubí had supported his own candidacy from his official position by replacing prefects with military men loyal to him. These men had instructions to work for his election by spending public funds for electoral work, by using the official newspapers to sustain and promote his candidacy, by forcing the state legislature to

20. Juárez to Rubí, 4 December 1866, *Epistolario*, 1st ed., p. 378.

21. Buelna, *Sinaloa*, pp. 99–101.

22. Corona to Juárez, 19 December 1867, and answer, 23 Ddcember 1867, DDC, 12:871–73.

declare his victory, and by ordering the arrest of persons who opposed his election. The rebels proposed to elevate Manuel Monzón to the interim governorship pending new elections.[23]

Rubí called upon Martínez as commander in Mazatlán to suppress the rebels. Martínez claimed he could not count on his troops but would go alone to Culiacán, if Rubí would promise to drop charges against the rebels. Rubí refused, sent for the national guard unit of Cosalá, and rushed off to Concordia to raise more soldiers. He asked Juárez to authorize his having taken 15,000 pesos from federal funds at the customshouse. Juárez told Rubí to operate in accord with Corona "and soon you will have caused all germs of disorder to disappear from that state, for now more than ever it is indispensable to conserve unalterably the public peace of the nation."[24]

New units shortly joined the rebellion by the Plan of Elote. Written by Gen. Jesús Toledo, the new plan called for the withdrawal of recognition from all elected state officials and the placement of power in General Martínez.[25] The following day the state legislature gave full powers to Governor Rubí and closed its sessions. General Corona arrived shortly; unsuccessfully attempted to influence Rubí to resign from the governorship pending new elections; unsuccessfully offered 50,000 pesos to Martínez to buy off the rebels; ended by giving military command to Martínez; and then departed for Manzanillo to raise troops and organize finances. Corona had scarcely left when Martínez, accepting the rebel command by the Plan of Elote, proclaimed himself provisional governor pending new elections, all in the name of the national government, to which he pledged his allegiance. Two more districts joined the rebels, and Governor Rubí officially asked for federal intervention.[26]

Juárez reacted quickly and completely. He ordered Corona to Sinaloa with the whole Fourth Division and commanded Martínez to come immediately to Mexico City. He then turned over the command of Mazatlán to Gen. Bibiano Dávalos, ordered Gen. Sóstenes Rocha

23. *Plan de Culiacán,* 4 January 1868, ibid., 13:59.
24. Rubí to Juárez, 4 January 1868, and minute of undated answer, ibid., pp. 61–63.
25. *Plan de Elote,* 14 January 1868, ibid., pp. 64–65.
26. Buelna, *Sinaloa,* pp. 102–3; proclamations of Gen. Angel Martínez, 28 January 1868, DDC, 13:68–71; Corona to Juárez, 1 February 1868, DDC, 13:72–73; Rubí to Juárez, 2 February 1868, ibid., p. 74.

out of San Luis Potosí to cover Guadalajara with his brigade from Escobedo's Third Division, and arranged financing from federal depots in Colima, Jalisco, and Mazatlán. Juárez then wrote to Martínez that "whatever were the reasons for launching a revolutionary movement . . . the government cannot and must not approve that step, because the approbation of such an act would soon establish a fatal precedent, which would occasion great evils in the future. It is necessary to terminate forever the uprisings and disorders of earlier times."[27] Juárez was correct, but political alignments and fraudulent elections made "revolutionary movements" inevitable.

The Fourth Division arrived piecemeal from late February to mid-April. Battles spread out across the state with the outcome inclining one way and then the other. By May Martínez was defeated and had escaped to San Francisco, California; Toledo, Granados, Palacio, and Paz were arrested in Tepic. Corona sought mercy from Juárez for Martínez and was told that Martínez did not deserve any and ought to receive the full judgment of a military court. Juárez's final remark to Rubí is strange in light of the extent of the rebellion and the effort in men and money necessary to suffocate it: "We have nothing serious to fear from these men, because they cannot count upon the support of public opinion."[28]

Porfirio Díaz was not directly involved with the Sinaloa affair; it was a local struggle for power. Nevertheless, Jesús Toledo and Jorge García Granados had earlier fought under Díaz, and Toledo was in communication with Díaz as early as January 1868. Toledo wanted Díaz to use whatever influence he had with the government to convince Juárez to let the rebels overthrow Rubí and to recognize the new rebel regime. Díaz answered that he doubted that the government would ever sanction an insurrectionary regime, "nevertheless, I will intercede my friendship with Sr. Juárez so that this affair might end well . . . in favor with your ideas." By way of a mutual friend in Mexico City, Díaz began counseling Toledo to a more prudent course of action than outright rebellion. Díaz confided to Manuel González that

27. Juárez to Corona, 12 February 1868, *Epistolario*, 1st ed., pp. 444–46, and DDC, 13:76–77; Juárez to Martínez, 12 February 1868, ibid., pp. 78–79.

28. Buelna, *Sinaloa*, p. 104; Rubí to Juárez, 2 May 1868, DDC, 13:344; Juárez to Rubí, 20 May 1868, ibid., p. 345; Juárez to Corona, 7 August 1868, ibid., p. 424; Juárez to Rubí, 22 July 1868, ibid., p. 424.

he was happy that "there is no human power to oblige me to take part in another war without flag or glory" such as putting down the Sinaloa rebels, a "scandal . . . which in my judgment is easy to conclude with a little tact instead of at the point of a bayonet."[29]

Toledo and García Granados were captured and condemned to death by a military court; however, Juárez commuted the sentence to four years imprisonment with loss of rank. Justo Benítez acted as defense for one of the captured rebels and thought Díaz might be named president of the military tribunal, a position which he urged Díaz to accept. By October Toledo was again in communication with Díaz for favors, to which Díaz responded "with joy in serving men of your kind." Granados wrote Díaz in December 1868 complaining of the government's treatment of him.[30] Jesús Toledo, García Granados, Ireneo Paz, and Adolfo Palacio rebelled again in the 1869–70 insurrection of San Luis Potosí, where they tried to convince Díaz to lead them. García Granados was killed in that rebellion, but Toledo and Paz played roles in Díaz's rebellions of La Noria and Tuxtepec.[31]

29. Toledo to Díaz, 31 January 1868, and minute of undated answer, APD, 6:67–68; Apolonio Angulo to Díaz, 21 February 1868, and answer, 2 February [sic] 1868, ibid., pp. 124–25; idem to idem, 26 March 1868, ibid., p. 199; minute of letter, Díaz to González, 2 May 1868, ibid., pp. 277–78.

30. Telegram, Escobedo to Juárez, 24 August 1868, DDC, 13:538; Mejía to Escobedo, 29 August 1868, ibid., p. 538; Benítez to Díaz, 17 August 1868, APD, 7:38; Toledo to Díaz, 10 October 1868, and minute of answer 21 October 1868, ibid., p. 64; Manuel Fernando Eduardo Vega to Díaz, 14 November 1868, and undated minute of answer, CPD, 42:1163; Jorge García Granados to Díaz, 1 December 1868, APD 7:134.

31. Angel Martínez did not become a *Porfirista* during the Restored Republic. A native of Tepic, he fought in 1865 with Corona against Manuel Lozada, the *caudillo* of Tepic who recognized Maximilian, and could not go home until Lozada was beaten and killed in 1873. From San Francisco, California, after the rebellion in Sinaloa, he joined the Prussian army in 1870 to fight the French. Returning to Mexico in 1872 he was indicted by Juárez for stealing *aduana* funds in Mazatlán in 1868, applied for amnesty from President Lerdo in late 1872, and returned the funds to the customshouse. He became an *hacendado* in Colima, representing that state as national congressman in 1873 and senator in 1875. Returning to the army in 1876 he fought for Lerdo against Díaz, occupying the governorship of San Luis Potosí for a time. He recognized the Iglesias government in 1876 and 1877, followed Iglesias into foreign exile, and joined the *Lerdista* attempt to regain power in 1878. Later he benefited by Díaz's policy of conciliation, served in Congress from Colima

The events in Sinaloa again demonstrate how local factionalism threatened the peace of the nation, how electoral violence was part of the system and a prelude to war, how the president had to become involved, and how the opposition to the state regime, in this case part of the opposition, gravitated to the national opposition.

Yucatán

Yucatán has always been an anomaly in Mexico but has always greatly affected the republic. The man to emerge from the republican campaign against the imperialist regime in Yucatán was the old liberal, ex-governor, one-time exile from Santa Anna's Mexico, Manuel Cepeda Peraza. By the spring of 1867 Cepeda had cleared Yucatán of imperialist forces and had commenced the campaign against Mérida. The siege of Mérida lasted from 21 April to 15 June. After the imperialists capitulated on condition of free passage abroad, Cepeda established the state government and put himself at the orders of Juárez.[32]

It was probably inevitable that Cepeda would be the principal man in Yucatán for some time to come, and equally probable that both Díaz and Juárez knew it. Díaz recommended Cepeda to the government for a promotion to brigadier general and sent to him an honorary membership to a "patriotic philanthropic association," which included the most important political figures in Yucatán, Chiapas, and Tabasco.[33] The association was an electoral vehicle managed by Ig-

---

from 1880 to 1904, leaving Congress only to serve Díaz in occasional military commands. As zone commander in the Yaqui War in 1885, Martínez gave the command to execute the Yaqui chief Cajeme: Francisco R. Alamada, *Diccionario de historia, geografía y biografía sonorenses* (Chihuahua: n.p., n.d.), pp. 449–52.

32. Albino Acereto, *Historia política desde el descubrimiento europeo hasta 1920*, vol. 3 of *Enciclopedia yucatanese*, ed. Carlos A. Echánove Trujillo, 8 vols. (Mexico: Gobierno de Yucatán, 1944–47), pp. 318–20. The treaty of surrender to Cepeda is found in Bernardino Mena Brito, *Reestructuración histórica de Yucatán*, 3 vols. (Mexico: Editores Mexicanos Unidos, 1965–69), 2:116–17; Manuel Cepeda P. to Juárez, 1 July 1868, DDC, 12:226.

33. Minute, Díaz to various men in the southeast, 6 September 1867, APD, 5:17.

nacio Altamirano for Díaz's presidential candidacy, but its goals seem to have been too vague to net firm commitments. Cepeda thanked Díaz for both and appealed to him to use his influence with the government for military aid to Yucatán against an Indian caste war, which the republicans inherited from the empire.[34]

Díaz's intervention with the government for military aid to Yucatán was the subject of many communications throughout the final months of 1867 between Díaz and the Yucatecan leaders, to whom Díaz consistently gave the impression that he agreed that the republic should fully deploy federal forces against the Indians.[35] Never, however, was Díaz able to convert his military support of their cause into political support for his own. Apparently, from the ignorance of Yucatecan electoral news demonstrated by all his partisans, Díaz had no agent working there. In contrast, Cepeda sent Juárez his appreciation for the military promotion, his political adhesion, and half a dozen congressmen to the national congress—two from Cepeda's hand-picked Council of Government.[36]

In November 1867 a series of events began to unfold in Yucatán. A reactionary movement commenced in the Villa de Peto, which Cepeda suffocated before the end of the month, sending more imperialists abroad.[37] On 11 December a more serious revolt broke out in the Mérida garrison. Seven Yucatecan imperialists, whom Cepeda had earlier allowed to leave Yucatán, returned from Cuba, pronounced against Cepeda, suborned the garrison, and captured the state government. The imperialist Marcelino Villafaña declared himself governor and military commander of the state. There were wild proclamations and rumors of others in favor of Yucatecan independence, for the Queen of Spain, or for Santa Anna.[38] At one point in

34. Cepeda to Díaz, 23 September 1867, and answer, ibid., p. 65.

35. J. de la Parra to Díaz, 24 September 1867 and 23 November 1867, and answers, ibid., pp. 71–72, 343–44; P. de la Parra to Díaz, 23 October 1867 and 11 December 1867, and answers, ibid., pp 262–63, 406–7; Manuel Cepeda to Díaz, 9 November 1867 and 7 December 1867, and answers, ibid., pp. 308, 387–88.

36. Manuel Cepeda to Juárez, 25 September 1867, DDC, 12:458; R. González Paez to Díaz, 29 October 1867, APD, 5:462.

37. Manuel Cepeda to Juárez, 9 November 1867, DDC, 12:717.

38. Acereto, *Enciclopedia yucatanese,* 3:323; Mena Brito, *Yucatán,* 2:118; Joaquín Baranda to *Siglo XIX,* 23 December 1867, DDC, 12:865–67.

the melee Villafaña put himself at the orders of Díaz, saying he recognized the national government and merely opposed the government of Cepeda. For a few days it was thought that Cepeda had been killed, but he showed up in Campeche. The minister of war sent orders to Díaz to ready Gen. Ignacio Alatorre's brigade of the Second Division for Yucatecan service.[39]

Díaz initially adopted the strong position that the situation in Yucatán was a serious matter of national consequence that required a full military response. He expressed that view to the Yucatecan congressional delegation, which had hoped Díaz would go to the peninsula in person with the whole Second Division. One brigade, he answered them, "I think insufficient." There was not enough transport, ammunition, or artillery, he added, but "they have not wished to listen."[40] By the end of December, however, Díaz's views reflected those of the congressional opposition. The *Porfirista* congressman from Oaxaca, Juan Torres, wrote that the affair in Yucatán was a local movement against Cepeda, "which could be suffocated with a change of governor." By that time Cepeda had demonstrated that he was a *Juarista.* Díaz agreed: It was purely local. To another *Porfirista* congressman, José María Mata, Díaz wrote that "the Yucatecan affair is purely local and relative to the person of the Governor." Then he added the concept that became his lasting personal stance as opposition leader and later as president: "In my purely private opinion, this business ought to be treated with politics, holding armed forces in reserve, but not forcing the insurrectionists to an indispensable necessity of defending themselves to the wall."[41]

The events in Yucatán unfolded rapidly. General Díaz personally accompanied the first brigade to Veracruz in January 1868 to supervise the embarkation. Villafaña died in battle on 31 January; Alatorre

39. Marcelino Villafeña to Díaz, 23 December 1867, APD, 5:448–49; Ignacio Mejía to Díaz, 18 December 1867, ibid., p. 432.

40. Yucatecan delegation to Díaz, 18 December 1867, and answer, n.d., ibid., pp. 433–34; also Ignacio R. Alatorre to Díaz, 22 December 1867, and answer, in which Díaz favored more strength, ibid., pp. 445–46; Díaz to Ignacio Mejía, minister of war ("it seems to me few forces and insufficient arms"), 18 December 1867, Mena Brito, *Yucatán,* 2:210.

41. Juan Torres to Díaz, 29 December 1867, and answer, APD, 5:464–65; undated answer to the letter from Mata to Díaz, 27 December 1867, ibid., pp. 454–55.

and Cepeda captured Mérida on 2 February. Cepeda then reassumed the gubernatorial powers, and Alatorre wrote to Juárez that Cepeda was extremely unpopular. To keep Cepeda in office, he reported, would require the conquest of the state and a continual battle against its inhabitants: "Indeed, they reject him unanimously." Alatorre recommended that Juárez send a "diplomat . . . with full powers" to Yucatán.[42]

Juárez took a direct hand in Yucatecan affairs. He wrote to Cepeda, congratulating him for the military victory and advising him to hold the governatorial elections with "full liberty for the citizens." In reference to the "diplomat" Juárez informed Alatorre that "it has seemed convenient that Congressman [Eligio] Ancona should go, because he has good relations in that state."[43] Ancona arrived and conducted the elections, which confirmed Manuel Cepeda Peraza as governor and José María Vargas as vice-governor.[44] Cepeda returned from Campeche and assumed gubernatorial command on 2 August 1868.[45]

The governorship of Manuel Cepeda Peraza bumped along from crisis to crisis for six months until insurrection erupted on 31 January 1869. The state legislature declared military law (*estado de sitio*) and turned over the government to the military commander, Col. José Ceballos. Ceballos shocked the people of Mérida and greatly disturbed the political circles of the nation when he arrested and exe-

---

42. ". . . in order to sustain democratic principles here it will be indispensable to make grand sacrifices in men and money, and even then, we would have to live as in a conquered country. . . . they consider us as sons of another country and as such they treat us." Alatorre to Juárez, 4 February 1868, DDC, 13:44; Alatorre to Juárez, 7 February 1868, ibid., pp. 44–45.

43. Juárez to Cepeda, 19 February 1868, ibid., p. 49; Juárez to Alatorre, 19 February 1868, ibid., p. 48.

44. Tovar, *Cuarto congreso*, 2:519.

45. From extant documentation it is not possible to know if Juárez convinced Cepeda to retire from Yucatán during the elections or if Cepeda did so voluntarily. According to Alatorre, Cepeda turned over his office to one Juan Cervera to hold elections and retired to Campeche (Alatorre to Juárez, 23 March 1868, DDC, 13:54). Tamayo (*Juárez*, 13:250) says that "Juárez insinuated to him the convenience of retiring from office." Cepeda to Juárez (DDC, 13:257) indicates that Cepeda asked Juárez if he could resign, for he thanks Juárez for accepting the proposal. At any rate, Juárez planned Cepeda's retirement, Cepeda withdrew, and Juárez's agent, not Cepeda's, conducted the election.

cuted eight men in early February.[46] The rebels withdrew recognition of the government and named Liborio Irigoyen as governor. Within the month Col. José A. Cepeda beat the rebels in Peto. Gov. Manuel Cepeda then died on 3 March, Vice-Governor José María Vargas resigned, and in April the state legislature decreed the interim positions to Col. José Cepeda and Manuel Cirerol.[47] José Cepeda then conducted the gubernatorial elections in November 1869. When they were concluded, an observer wrote to Juárez that Agustín O'Horán had won, but that José Cepeda and Cirerol captured the electoral *mesas* in Mérida with 300 armed men and "Sr. *don* Manuel Cirerol was elected."[48]

Cirerol and José Cepeda Peraza took office for a two-year term on 1 February 1870. Thereafter they pushed through an amendment to the state constitution which lengthened the gubernatorial term to four years. When they did not call elections for a renewal of officers for 1872, a new rebellion flared up in March 1872 in the eastern part of the state. The rebels protested their loyalty to the federal government and to the Constitution of 1857 and placed in command Col. Francisco Cantón, who crushed the state forces sent against them. José Cepeda died in battle in Quintana Roo, and the rebels occupied Mérida. Again the central government placed Yucatán under martial law and sent in federal forces. The federal general, Vicente Mariscal, established order and named Olegario Molina as the interim governor and Francisco Cantón as military commander of the eastern zone. Juárez then sent Ignacio Alatorre to Yucatán to conduct the elections for a constitutional governor; the state legislature decreed him a citizen of Yucatán and raised him to the interim governorship. The state historian Acereto maintains that the following gubernatorial elections featured fraud and violence, "official candidates" killed and wounded, and police aggression, closing with the imposition of

46. The congressional committee that studied the issue found Congress incompetent to try Ceballos on the argument that he was not a legal governor (Congress had jurisdiction over governors), because state legislatures did not have authority to declare a state of siege. The committee was composed of Zamacona, Zarco, and Montes, all of whom, as advanced liberals, preferred to lose congressional jurisdiction than to allow a proliferation of the power to declare military law. Tovar, *Cuarto congreso*, 16 April 1869, 4:168–70.

47. Tamayo, *Juárez*, 13:847–48; Acereto, *Enciclopedia yucatanese*, 3:325–26.

48. Carlos Rueda y Tusa to Juárez, 4 March 1870, AJ, 8886.

Miguel Castellanos Sánchez over "the partisans of Colonel Cantón, whose party, supported by Dr. O'Horán, had triumphed, in reality, in the real election."[49]

Yucatán remained as unstable during the Lerdo presidency as it had been under Juárez. It would be difficult to imagine an alternative to Juárez's handling of the affair within the spirit of republican institutions, for the spirit in Yucatán did not in practice recognize liberalism. At any rate, both Manuel Cepeda and Castellanos Sánchez sent cooperative congressmen to Mexico City, as Cantón probably would not have. He fought for the *Porfiristas* in the civil war of 1876.

The affairs in Guerrero, Sinaloa, and Yucatán demonstrate the factional warfare that existed in the states. Elections were manifestly fraudulent in all three cases, factionalism was painfully apparent, and all the parties patently refused to accept the legal formulas of republican liberalism. Had Juárez tried to remain aloof from the state struggles the nation would have been engulfed in civil wars.

Juárez sent agents to each of the three states, Arce to Guerrero, Corona to Sinaloa, and Azcona, later Alatorre, to Yucatán. Arce went as a "mediator" with troops and emerged as governor after destroying one faction and after Juárez ordered the army of the other faction demobilized. The action was good for Guerrero, good for the nation, and good for the *Juarista* party. Corona went to Sinaloa as a mediator also, but Rubí would not step down as did Cepeda in Yucatán, nor could Martínez be bought off. The electoral methods preceding the Sinaloan insurrection demonstrated that there was no difference between the two contenders from the point of view of liberal principles. Legal reason could have been found to support the first decree of the Sinaloan legislature, which disqualified the election of both Martínez and Rubí. That might have taken some wind from the sails of the rebellion and thus saved large expenditures from state and federal treasuries. Such an approach, however, might have encouraged yet other rebellions in states where losers contested the results of elections, such as happened in San Luis Potosí in 1869. It might also have called into question normal electoral procedures which, as has been seen, were necessary to, and an integral part of, the political process.

49. Acereto, *Enciclopedia yucatanese*, 3:326–29.

There is no evidence that Azcona favored Cepeda's reelection by illegal means, although Azcona was *Juarista,* and his not changing the *jefes políticos,* particularly with the state under military law, would have guaranteed Cepeda's reelection. Later elections in Yucatán were more violent.

The military was also involved in each of the three cases. Juárez asked for congressional authorization after sending troops to Yucatán. He sent units of the army to Sinaloa on the petition of Governor Rubí, who then held total power by the will of the state legislature. In the case of Guerrero he dispatched the troops surreptitiously. In the years to come the marching of federal troops to the areas of state factional struggle became increasingly common, smoothed the first time by the liberal fear of conservative reaction in Yucatán. Yucatán provided another first as well—the first congressional suspension of constitutional guarantees in the Restored Republic. The antigovernment congressmen desperately fought against it but thereafter found it increasingly difficult to stop later readoptions of the same suspensions.[50]

The three states remained highly volatile during the remainder of the Restored Republic, demonstrating that the opposition did not accept the results of the solutions brought about by federal intervention. Even as the winners in those episodes remained good members of the *Juarista* alliance, so the losers became *Porfiristas.* It will be apparent how ten years of such affairs, touching each year upon one or another state, created by 1876 a "Circle of *Porfiristas*" of such magnitude that the Insurrection of Tuxtepec contained the potential for overthrowing the government of Sebastián Lerdo de Tejada.

50. For the partisan debate on the Yucatecan bill see Tovar, *Cuarto congreso,* 1:88–90, 106, 117–19, 122–23, 127–29, 136–44.

Chapter 5
Federalism under Attack

This chapter focuses upon four closely interrelated characteristics of the political system of the Restored Republic that led eventually and directly to dictatorship. The first was a major constitutional problem bearing upon the relationship between the national government and the theoretically sovereign states. That problem, not solved in time to save the nation from the civil war of Tuxtepec, is discussed first.

The second characteristic of the political system was factional rivalry in the states. Since such rivalry continually threatened miniature civil wars and affected the interests of the national factions, the issue drew the attention of the federal government. The factional rivalry in four states are discussed below. The four case studies illustrate the alignment of state factions with national factionalism, and in them the congressional debate about the constitutional problem is traced.

The third characteristic was the presidential manipulation of the political system to strengthen presidential alliances with governors. How Juárez protected governors of his faction and replaced other governors is seen in the four case studies. That intervention heightened factional rivalry and alienation, drew cries of tyranny, and led to civil war.

The fourth characteristic under discussion was the factionalism within Congress that rendered impossible a solution to the constitutional problem. As Congress dealt with the various state disputes, sometimes congressional determination to guard legislative prerogatives against presidential centralism predominated; at other times congressional factionalism overrode all other considerations.

The relationship between those four characteristics of the political system was that rivalry in the states demanded a response by the national government, thus throwing a formidable constitutional problem, upon which hung not only the peace of the nation but also the longevity of the republican system, to a factional Congress for solution. The individual solutions to specific cases inevitably strengthened or weakened the presidential alliance with governors. Congressmen, wholly free to debate the constitutional issues, voted overwhelmingly for the political results of factional alignment, which in fact favored the presidential party and thus alienated the opposition and "justified" armed rebellion and civil war. The alternative was to solve the constitutional problem, strengthen the federal system, weaken the centralism of the presidency, and face resultant civil wars in the states and national dissolution. It was a Hobson's choice, above which the politicians of the day could not ascend and which ended in the Porfirian dictatorship.

The Constitution of 1857 prescribed the relationship between the national government and state governments in terms of federalism. Article 40 stated that "the will of the Mexican people is to constitute themselves in a representative, democratic, federal republic, composed of free and sovereign states in all matters concerning their internal governance but united in a federation established according to the principles of this Constitution." Article 109 then stipulated that "the states will adopt for their internal governance popular, representative republicanism," and article 114 stipulated that "the governors of the states are obliged to publish and enforce the federal laws." Thus it was clear that, although the states were "sovereign" in their internal matters, they were to be governed in a "republican" manner and that governors had to obey and enforce federal law.

Articles 40, 109, and 114 proved to be difficult to interpret and enforce. After 1867 some congressmen would accuse a governor of violation of those articles before Congress, which, sitting as a grand jury, had the authority to try the governor. If found guilty, the governor was removed from office, and his case then went to the Supreme Court for sentencing.[1] In all, seven governors were accused before congressional grand juries between 1867 and 1871.[2]

1. Constitution of 1857, article 105.
2. The seven governors were Julio Cervantes of Querétaro, Antonio Gómez Cuervo of Jalisco, Pablo García of Campeche, Florencio Antillón of Guanajuato, Bibliano Dávalos of Baja California, Diego Alvarez of Guerrero, and Manuel Monteverde of Sonora. Only the first three were tried as described. Congress dismissed the next two cases with decrees that it was not competent to investigate the internal workings of a state, and the last two governors were found innocent of the charges. The Supreme Court refused to sentence the convicted governor in one of the first three cases because Congress had not established the list of punishments; see below, n. 48.

Another aspect of the federal relationship was even more fraught with uncertainty. Article 116 stated that the federal government had "the obligation to protect the states from all exterior invasion or violence, and in case of insurrection or internal disturbance shall provide the same protection, but only when sought in writing by the legislature of the state or, if not in session, by the [state] executive." Apparently the writers of the constitution did not foresee the possibility of a state legislature appealing for federal aid against a governor accused of violating the republican form of government, with the possibility of the governor declaring that the legislature was not in regular session. That is, whom was the federal government to aid when the legislature and the governor stood at odds? Further, what was the federal government to do when there were two governments in a state, each declaring the other illegal and each seeking federal aid against the other? And finally, which branch of the federal government should deal with the problem? Events proved that article 116 needed an ordinance law to spell out the exact interpretation of and procedure for federal intervention.

In the process of sending federal aid to a state, constitutional power favored the president. The constitution authorized the president to "dispose of the permanent armed forces . . . for the internal security or external defense of the federation" (article 85, section 6), apparently making the president the ultimate arbiter of state rivalries when the federal government was petitioned for aid. Moreover, the general practice was for state authorities to communicate with the federal government through the secretary of *gobernación*, who was a presidential cabinet appointee.

Nevertheless, Congress sometimes became involved in the process of federal aid. Congress held the constitutional authority to allow the president to use the national guard (state militia) of one state for service in another state, as well as to designate the number of armed forces the president could call up (article 72, section 2). This complemented congressional control of monetary appropriations and suspension of constitutional guarantees (articles 29 and 119) which were occasionally necessary to effect federal intervention. Finally, as seen above, Congress had the jurisdiction to try governors charged of violation of federal law.

The Supreme Court was also involved in the federal relationship, having original jurisdiction in cases arising from conflict between a state and the national government (article 98), as well as the sentencing authority in judicial cases originating from congressional grand jury trials (article 105).

When Congress became officially congnizant of petitions for federal intervention in state rivalries, amid the charges that tyrannical governors were denying republican forms of government, individual congressmen could applaud national intervention to overthrow such dictatorships as the advance of republicanism or could claim to abhor national action against such governors as a blow to state sovereignty and federalism. The stance taken by a given congressman was likely to reflect his party alliance. It is to the controversy over whether such congressional factionalism ever existed that we now turn.

The official record of the Fourth Congress, published in 1872–73, is the work of Pantaleón Tovar, deputy from Ixcaquistla, Puebla. For the official history Tovar succeeded in assuming a commendable stance of factional neutrality, and in his general appraisal of the work of the Fourth Congress he insisted that the sessions always showed independent, patriotic concern for the material progress and institutionalization of the Republic. He claimed great pride in having been a member of those memorable sessions, and particularly eulogized a congressional manifesto of 8 January 1868 by which Congress dedicated itself to the protection of constitutional law and peaceful restoration. The factional spirit in that Congress, he maintained, was always subordinate to national interest, not an obstacle to it.[3] This thesis has sufficed for historians to write that the later factionalism of Congress developed slowly during the Restored Republic, as evidenced by its absence in the first of the post-Maximilian congresses.[4] The cooperative spirit of the Fourth Congress was "almost pastoral" in Cosío Villegas's term, only when compared to 1871–72, when factionalism had deteriorated into civil war and when Tovar was writing and publishing his history of the Fourth Congress.

3. Tovar, *Cuarto congreso,* 1:ii–iv. The congressional manifesto is found in 1:165–67; the congressional commission of the official history of Tovar took place in the session of 14 January 1869, 3:1055.

4. For example, Cosío Villegas, *República restaurada,* p. 85. Francisco Zarco wrote in *El Siglo XIX* (3 August 1869) that the congressional elections of that year brought new men to the Fifth Congress, "entirely foreign to the struggles that in the last Congress have divided the liberal party."

Tovar's thesis, accepted by Cosío Villegas, will be hard to test because of his exclusion of roll-call votes; he recorded final votes without the names of the congressmen for and against proposals, making it impossible to identify a consistent opposition or a hard core pro-administration party. Furthermore, every issue was complex; the vote on the withdrawal of federal troops from the Sierra de Puebla in 1868 is a case in point. One did not have to be a puppet of the administration to support military force in Puebla for the purposes of peace, overlooking the strict constitutional interpretation of how it got there. Conversely, one could vote for withdrawal of troops out of respect for constitutional precepts without being a *Porfirista* or a partisan of Juan N. Méndez, the recently defeated gubernatorial candidate.[5]

Certainly the Fourth Congress should not chiefly be characterized by factionalism. The overwhelming amount of congressional time was dedicated to concrete attempts to stabilize the national revenues, bolster the economy, and draft sound organic laws for the implementation of constitutional articles. The official record of congressional sessions is impressive for the sincerity of the efforts of the legislators.

Factionalism, nevertheless, existed in Congress from the beginning. The congressmen who tried to delay the balloting for president were *Porfiristas,* as were those who opposed the balloting for the president of the Supreme Court. Juan Torres wrote to Díaz, "The ministry put bad law into play and lured away several states that you won."[6] González Báez, congressman from Veracruz, attributed the *Lerdista* vote of the seven-man delegation from Veracruz to factional corruption:

> Among the seven of us only Mata, Hernández Carrasco, and I voted for you; the lawyer [Manuel] Herrera, who had promised to vote with us, which would have completed the majority, received a thousand pesos [from the national treasury] on overdue salary for which he has no claim, and at the last minute voted for Lerdo, which put the majority against us.[7]

Whatever role corruption may have played, one imagines that many congressmen judged that the intellectual and legal expert, Lerdo de

5. The issue is in Tovar, *Cuarto congreso,* 1:509.
6. Juan Torres to Díaz, 20 December 1867, APD, 5:439.
7. R. González Báez to Díaz, 29 December 1867, ibid., p. 463.

Tejada, would make a better president of the Supreme Court than General Díaz. Nevertheless, after only the preliminary meetings of Congress had been held, during which officials and committee chairmen were determined, Torres was able to tell Díaz that the opposition generally voted about thirty, while the administration could count upon about seventy.[8] Those proportions held rather consistently throughout the Fourth Congress.

By constitutional precept no congressman could accept a paid position in the executive branch without a license from Congress.[9] Two congressmen, Lerdo de Tejada and Blas Balcárcel, sat in Juárez's cabinet. "We will oppose the licenses," wrote Torres to Díaz, "but I do not think we will win, since until now the opposition has only received beatings one after another."[10] The question of the licenses, however, was larger than mere factions. It touched the very core of congressional predominance and the whole issue of ministerial government. "A license for Lerdo," said Zamacona to Congress, "is a vote of confidence in the ministry."

Factionalism was always tempered by a consistent jealousy of congressional prerogatives in the face of a strong executive. The Constitutional Convention of 1857 apparently wished to establish legislative supremacy with ministerial responsibility to Congress. Several later historians of the period contend that such was the intention of the Convention—to create a legislative branch stronger than the executive branch, to raise the president above the political arena, and to assure that the cabinet ministers would reflect the majority party in Congress and be responsible to it. In this manner a congressional censure of the executive or a defeat of a "ministerial bill" should have resulted in the replacement of a minister or the fall of the cabinet. It is clear that some congressmen accepted this theory of government and voted accordingly, even though Juárez refused to replace ministers upon the defeat of "ministerial bills" and refused to consider that his policies should emanate from the majority of Congress. Presidential nominations of cabinet appointees clearly required congressional approval, but Juárez maintained that he could ask for their resignations at will.

8. Torres to Díaz, 1 December 1867, ibid., pp. 369–70.
9. Constitution of 1857, article fifty-eight.
10. Juan Torres to Díaz, 10 December 1867, APD, 5:400.

The practical result of the disagreement on ministerial versus presidential government was that Juárez had a congressional opposition independent of his Porfirian opposition. Nevertheless, most "congressional" opposition melted into the general opposition to Juárez, because the opposition charge that Juárez was centralizing federal power in the executive was similar to the general opposition charge that the federal government was overriding the rightful sovereignty of states. In both cases the charge was that *Juarista* "centralism" would lead to dictatorship.

Congressional opposition seldom missed an opportunity to embarrass the administration. For example, Zamacona asked Congress to accept a resolution calling upon the minister of *hacienda* to report to Congress on the effects of the law of 17 August 1867. The law referred to the separation of state and federal funds in the maritime customshouses. The problem of securing federal contributions from state governors was a serious one, and compliance was vital for the federal treasury. Zamacona feigned an interest in helping the administration by congressional legislation based on sound information. Such requests for ministerial information made by one congressman were usually acceded to by his colleagues as a courtesy, and the resolution passed. On the following day Lerdo de Tejada, secretary of *gobernación*, appeared before the body, inasmuch as Matías Romero had only that day assumed responsibility for the treasury department (*Ministerio de Hacienda*). Lerdo reported that the law was being respected in nearly all instances, that no problems were present, and that should the executive need legislation, Congress would be notified. When pressed for details, Lerdo admitted to an infraction in Sinaloa, where the governor had ordered the administrator of the customshouse at Guaymas to proceed in a manner contrary to regulations, but the federal government had made appropriate changes in the personnel at the customshouse, and all was well.

Then Zamacona, obviously knowledgeable about the case, made his point: Why had the executive fired the administrator rather than proceeding against the governor who had given the order? The governor was the very loyal *Juarista* Domingo Rubí, whom Gen. Angel Martínez had challenged for the leadership of the state in the recent elections. Lerdo was a master debater and an accomplished sophist who was not without words on that occasion: The governor needed funds for federal expenditures, while the administrator should have refused payment. However, Lerdo went on, since the congressman wanted examples, there had been a case, which could now be mentioned, "because the governor has been pardoned and because the case is already in the public domain . . ." and he proceeded to describe a discrepancy in the state of Oaxaca: There the governor was don Porfirio's brother Félix. Not to be worsted, Zamacona summed up: "It is said that employees of the treasury are punished because they have regulations to observe. Why? Do not the other functionaries also [have to observe] federal law? The government tells us that the law has been obeyed except where it has been violated, and the first to violate it has been the party which promulgated it, in not making effective the penalty that the law establishes."[11] It was a good encounter and exemplifies an aspect of congressional opposition.

Perhaps Zamacona had thought to go further with the Rubí case until he learned that the administration was prepared to prove that the funds had been spent for federal expenses and that the governmental party could drag out the Oaxacan case. But ten months later an almost identical case arose involving a governor who enjoyed a good deal less favor with the independent congressmen. The governor was Diego Alvarez, whom a handful of liberals were determined not to leave in peace. It was well known that the Alvarez dynasty had long lived upon the receipts of the customshouse at Acapulco. It had been Santa Anna's assault upon that arrangement in 1854 that drove Juan Alvarez and his administrator of the customshouse, Ignacio Comonfort, into rebellion. The ability of the opposition to couple the Alvarez case with the issue of congressional prerogatives is indicative of the opposition strategy against the administration. The case follows.

In mid-November 1868 Congressman Barragán asked the chamber to approve a resolution to call the minister of *hacienda* to report on rumored irregularities in the customshouse of Acapulco. The report was explicit enough—Alvarez was using funds marked for the federal treasury on expenses accruing to the state—that a number of deputies filed charges that went to the Committee on Grand Jury Proceedings. Only in January 1869 did that committee report out a resolution, to

11. Tovar, *Cuarto congreso*, 15–16 January 1868, 1:215, 230–32.

the effect that Congress had no jurisdiction over a governor appointed by the executive. Because no gubernatorial elections had been held in the state since Juárez had extended the tenure of Alvarez in 1866, Alvarez was not a popularly elected governor. Congress was outraged on the grounds that *all* governors were responsible to Congress on matters of federal law, and overruled the committee by one hundred to six.

On the day of the Alvarez trial the Committee on Grand Jury Proceedings reported out a resolution of not guilty. The determining factor in the defense was a document from the executive to Alvarez, authorizing him to draw upon the customshouse at Acapulco. Congressman Barragán, who had registered with the clerk as first speaker against the resolution, could do no other than admit that "there is no doubt that by these communications *señor* Alvarez in not responsible, inasmuch as official data operates in his favor." But he went on to say that the initial indictment had originated in the administration's report to Congress. After reading the report of the minister of *hacienda* and comparing it to the document presented by the defense, he asked, "And how is it that by the report Alvarez appears not authorized to spend customs funds and by the documents he appears authorized?" Condés de la Torre, usually loyal to the administration, was indignant:

> The accuser of General Alvarez was the government, who manifested to Congress that it was not possible for the treasury to collect the revenues of the products in the customs of Acapulco because General Alvarez disposes of them. The accused does not deny that fact, but excuses himself with orders received from that same government.

The grand jury had to find Alvarez not guilty and accepted the resolution by a vote of eighty-five to twenty-one.[12] In this manner a governor allied to the president was saved from congressional indictment, even though the opposition for a while attracted a group of independents and those who voted for congressional prerogatives against executive power.

12. Ibid., 13–14 November 1868, 3:521, 526–31; 5 January 1869, pp. 948–51; 20 January 1869, 4:449–91.

The major difference between the records of the Fourth Congress and those of the Fifth Congress (1860–71) is that the latter include the names of those who voted for and against congressional resolutions and bills whenever a majority wished to vote in that manner. From the Fifth Congress, therefore, it is an easier task to measure consistent administrative voters—that is, factions.

In order to determine factional alliances, eight "test cases" are chosen from the first eight months of the Fifth Congress. All the cases are chosen as "political issues" upon which factional loyalty to the president or a sense of opposition might be measured. They are not great issues for which the period is known nor issues that test the statesmanship of individual congressmen in light of subsequent history, but simple issues embodied in bills and resolutions designed to embarrass or rein in the executive. The eight "test cases" are described in appendix 6, and the roll-call voting on them is recorded in the first eight columns of the charts in appendix 7. The statistical analysis is described later, and the conclusion is clear: A significant number of congressmen maintained a voting pattern which defies the contention that voting took place on the merits of the issues; indeed, a majority of congressmen held a political position vis-à-vis the executive. That is as it should be, for the issues were chosen for their political and factional importance. Thus the "test scores" are sufficiently reliable to use for a comparison with similar scores for each congressman on the issue of using the national army in state politics, the subject to which we now turn.

The four cases chosen for examination below are those of Querétaro in 1868–69, Jalisco and San Luis Potosí in 1870, and Guerrero in 1870–71.[13]

Querétaro

One of the most instructive cases of federal intervention in state factional rivalry concerned the state of Querétaro. The case eventually

13. In the course of the congressional debates a few important votes were recorded by roll-call procedures. Those votes are tabulated in appendix 7, columns A–J, as pro-administration votes ("o") or anti-administration votes ("x") according to the political context uncovered in the descriptions. Later,

involved all three branches of the federal government, the federal army, the local courts, a federal district court, two rival state governments, their respective governors and legislatures, and an interim military governor named by President Juárez.

The strong-man governor of Querétaro following the collapse of the Maximilian government was Col. Julio María Cervantes. In April 1869 a congressman of the Querétaro legislature, Próspero Vega, made formal accusations before the state legislature against Cervantes. Order broke down as Querétaro succumbed to factional violence. One group of persons forced some of the state congressmen to meet and vote down the accusations, and Congressman Domínguez was assaulted. Governor Cervantes gave Domínguez assurances of personal safety, but his assailants were not found.[14] On 1 May Próspero Vega formally asked the minister of *gobernación* for federal protection for the Querétaro legislature. José María Iglesias, minister of *gobernación*, informed Vega that the president had received a telegram from Cervantes, claiming that peace reigned in the state. Iglesias said that President Juárez had requested the governor to assure the legislature all the liberty that it needed in order to function but to say that the president did not wish to become involved in the affairs of the state.[15]

The national government, nevertheless, was soon drawn in. On 3 May seven of the thirteen members of the Querétaro legislature signed a formal accusation against Governor Cervantes for violation of articles 17, 41, and 109 of the federal constitution and officially petitioned the minister of *gobernación* for federal aid. Iglesias wrote to the secretary of *gobierno* of Querétaro that the president would not act on the request of the state legislature before consulting Congress.[16] In the context of political alliances the attitude of no-action aided the Cervantes faction in Querétaro, but in reference to the whole problem of federal intervention in state affairs the president's position set

---

the two scores for each congressman are statistically treated to test the hypothesis that factional rivalry in Congress influenced the question of national intervention in factional struggles in the states.

14. *El Siglo XIX*, 12 May 1869; Tamayo, *Juárez*, 14:83–84.

15. Tovar, *Cuarto congreso*, 4:811–12.

16. Tamayo, *Juárez*, 14:84; Tovar, *Cuarto congreso*, 4:809–10, 812–13; Iglesias to Secretary of *Gobierno*, 6 May 1869, Tovar, *Cuarto congreso*, 4:811.

a precedent that Congress would be consulted in cases of intrafactional struggles among the branches of state governments. Congress took immediate cognizance of the Querétaro problem. On 7 May the permanent Committee of *Gobernación* placed a resolution on the floor to deny federal aid to the legislature of Querétaro, because the petition did not represent the legislature but a mere seven members of it. The resolution was withdrawn after congressional discussion in secret session. On the same day two congressmen from the state of Querétaro, Ezequiel Montes and Gudiño y Gómez, initiated the same charges before Congress against Governor Cervantes as those Próspero Vega had made before the Querétaro legislature. The secret session must have been animated against Cervantes, for on 8 May Congress adopted the resolution that the "federal government will proffer to the state of Querétaro the protection which is referred to by article 116 of the federal constitution."[17]

Immediately thereafter the affair escalated. The seven members of the Querétaro legislature who constituted the governor's opposition formed themselves into a grand jury, declared Cervantes guilty of the charges against him, and removed him from office. Cervantes retaliated with a manifesto declaring the factional legislature illegal. In turn the seven-man opposition legislature declared itself in permanent session and named Mariano Vázquez as interim governor pending new gubernatorial elections. In a secret session of 31 May Congress passed a resolution that the executive send federal forces to Querétaro to effect the verdict of the state legislature against Governor Cervantes.[18]

Escalation continued. Cervantes obtained a stay of execution (*amparo*) from a federal district judge against the congressional resolutions of 8 May and 31 May. Continuing to act as governor, Cervantes designated Ignacio Luis Vallarta to represent him before the Supreme Court, where all *amparo* cases were heard. Opposing Cervantes in the Supreme Court was a representative of the legislature of Querétaro, who sought a reversal of the conceded *amparo*.[19]

The Querétaro case before the Supreme Court was important to the issue of congressional resolution of state factional struggle. It can

17. Ibid., pp. 810–16.
18. Tamayo, *Juárez*, 14:84; *El Siglo XIX*, 1 June 1869.
19. Tamayo, *Juárez*, 14:85; *El Siglo XIX*, 18 June 1869.

be presumed that Juárez hoped the *amparo* would be upheld, for the congressional resolutions would be struck down, and a factional ally would remain in the governorship. On 4 August however, the court revoked the *amparo*, which moved León Guzmán, the highly independent attorney general (*procurador*, who by Mexican law was a member of the Court rather than a member of the cabinet), to present a lengthy dissenting opinion.[20] Two days later Vallarta presented his brief to the Supreme Court. The major thrust of his argument was that state sovereignty must be saved from congressional resolutions such as those of 8 May and 31 May, and he asked the court to overrule them. In his personal appearance before the court on 11 August Vallarta added two new arguments. First, the congressional resolutions supporting the legislatures's governor (Vázquez), if upheld, would result in the fall of the legal governor (Cervantes), and there would be no legal power in Querétaro to appeal to the courts. Second, he argued, the congressional resolutions usurped executive power in the use of federal forces.[21] Had Vallarta won his contention, the power of the president would have increased substantially.

Before the Supreme Court rendered its judgment, the Fifth Congress convened on 16 September. The opposition legislature of Querétaro immediately complained to Congress against Governor Cervantes, and Congress set 16 October for its session as a grand jury to hear the case against him. Cervantes turned over his office to a partisan, Angel Dueñas, who was then prefect of the central district of the state (a position in Querétaro parallel to that of *jefe político* in other states), and awaited his trial.[22]

The Cervantes trial in Congress was sensational. The defense lawyer summarized events within the interpretation that the legal legislature had rejected the charges against the governor and disbanded after the sessions terminated, and that the opposition faction met illegally to call for federal aid. He spoke of rural life and its rancors and hatreds over little matters which Montes and Gudiño y Gómez had exaggerated. He argued that Cervantes had acted legally and had quickly restored order, and that the legislature had not cooperated in sending to Congress a number of petitions from towns of

20. Tamayo, *Juárez*, 14:85; *El Siglo XIX*, 5 August 1869, p. 1.
21. DDC, 14:89–96.
22. Tamayo, *Juárez*, 14:87.

Guerétaro in support of Cervantes. Finally, the defense argued that Congress did not have jurisdiction to interfere in a state matter.[23]

Congressional debate was animated. Montes's prosecution was based essentially on precedents established in the United States. Congressman Francisco Báez advocated that his colleagues find Cervantes innocent of the charges brought against him, because a conviction would be an invasion of state sovereignty. Moreover, he argued, Cervantes had violated no constitutional articles and claimed that the constitution did not allow federal authorities to try governors for their political activities in their own states. He concluded that only the state of Querétaro could try Cervantes. Sánchez Azcona, usually an opposition congressman, spoke simply and forcefully against Cervantes. The governor had declared a legislature illegal and had decreed a new election, thus overriding a legislature and usurping its power. By doing so he failed to provide a republican form of government to the state of Querétaro, which violated article 109 of the constitution. By a vote of seventy-seven to fifty Cervantes was found guilty.[24]

In the final week of October Cervantes sent letters to Juárez indicating that he had received the president's envoy who had informed him of the congressional verdict and of the continued support of Juárez. Cervantes told the president that he had no intention of surrendering the governorship to Mariano Vázquez, and he asked Juárez to declare the state under military law and appoint an interim military governor who would retain state officeholders who were loyal to Cervantes and Juárez.[25] Had the President complied with the request, the nature of federal intervention in state affairs would have taken a decidedly different course. Meanwhile, Congress took the next step.

Still in October congressmen Montes and Alcalde, two of the three members of the permanent First Committee on Constitutional Points, sponsored a resolution to oblige the president to have Cervantes arrested and brought before the Supreme Court for sentencing. The third member of the committee, the *Juarista* Rafael Dondé, registered his opposition. The *Porfirista* Eleuterio Avila asked for suspension of

23. *Debates, quinto congreso,* 1:194–200; *El Siglo XIX,* 17–19 October 1869.

24. *Debates, quinto congreso,* 1:210–13; the roll-call vote is registered in column A of the chart in appendix 7, where a negative vote is considered pro-administration.

25. Two letters, Cervantes to Juárez, 24 October 1869, DDC, 14:97–99.

procedures in order to vote on the resolution immediately. Even Joaquín Baranda, almost always *Juarista,* argued for suspension in an obvious congressional outrage over executive flouting of a congressional grand jury verdict. The suspension passed seventy-four to twenty-seven and debate commenced on the resolution. The *Juarista* congressman Manuel Rincón led the opposition to the resolution, saying that the question was out of congressional hands, as the court could call upon the executive to produce the convict for sentencing. Nevertheless, the resolution passed. Perhaps rumors were already running that Juárez was seeking a reason to declare the state under military law, for Joaquín Baranda and Manuel Macín immediately proposed to call the minister of war to inform Congress if it were true that an insurrection had broken out in the Sierra of Querétaro. That resolution also passed.

Two days later a resolution was proposed that the president name a provisional governor to oversee new gubernatorial elections in Querétaro. Unfortunately, the record does not indicate the initiation of all resolutions, but this may have been an opposition tactic by individuals who suspected an impending declaration of military law, for the resolution pointedly specified that the nomination should receive congressional approbation. Nevertheless, *Juaristas* could probably have counted on congressional approbation of the executive nominee once congressional jealousy of its jury function had been assauged by the removal of Cervantes. But the congressional officers that month were *Juaristas,* and the bill was sent to the permanent Second Committee on Constitutional Points, which was dominated by congressmen friendly to the administration, and it never reappeared on the floor. That kind of answer to state factional disputes—a federally appointed interim governor—might have developed in the Restored Republic as an effective solution. Although it ran counter to state sovereignty, would certainly have required a constitutional amendment, and would presumably have been opposed by principled federalists, advocates of central power should have supported it. Juárez, as it turned out, used an alternate procedure for naming an interim governor that did not require congressional confirmation.

A full week later Eleuterio Avila, a young and active *Porfirista* congressman, proposed that the minister of justice tell Congress why Cervantes had not been separated from his office and remitted to the court. In a request for suspension of procedures and as an obvious bid for the vote of the group who guarded congressional prerogatives, he noted that "it is scandalous the lack of respect with which the resolutions of Congress are taken, especially by the executive, who ought to be the most assiduous in attending to them." The resolution passed without discussion. The minister of justice shortly appeared and reported that he had taken no steps whatever because communications between the federal and state governments were handled by the secretary of *gobernación.* Avila immediately secured the passage of a resolution summoning the secretary of *gobernación.* When the secretary appeared, he told the congressmen that plans were afoot to name an interim governor in a manner designed to avoid public disorder, but he understood that the minister of justice was handling the case. Executive stalling was apparent. Surprisingly, no one asked how the executive was going to name an interim governor for Querétaro; certainly no constitutional power authorized the president to name interim governors, except with congressionally approved extraordinary powers used to declare military law.

Juárez's temporizing tactics were so obvious that Avila mocked the minister: "It is not strange that Colonel Cervantes, confident that the president will sustain him, continues committing abuses without abandoning his power." He then proposed a resolution that the executive telegraph orders to the federal military unit in Querétaro to publish the congressional resolution of 27 October and to remit Cervantes to the Supreme Court. The *Juarista* congressman Joaquín Baranda and the opposition congressman Juan Sánchez Azcona cosponsored the resolution, indicating the degree of congressional ire the issue had raised. Baranda said that it was not incredible that Cervantes should retain power, for the governors of Querétaro usually set themselves up as dictators: "Erected in ominous dictatorship, they govern with no more law than their will, with no more reason than their caprice." What was surprising, he said, was that the executive had not enforced the law. The *Juarista* Velasco opposed the resolution, but it passed eighty-eight to thirty-nine—an important censure of the president's policy.[26]

On 10 November the Second Committee on Constitutional Points

26. *Debates, quinto congreso,* 27 October 1869, 1:303–4, 312, 341–42; ibid., 5 November 1869, pp. 347–50; the roll-call vote is recorded in column B of the chart in appendix 7; a negative vote is considered pro-administration.

reported out a resolution that the petition of the legislature of Querétaro for federal aid should not be conceded because the concept was not comprehended within article 116 of the constitution.[27] Avila sought suspension of procedures and produced two telegrams from the opposition legislature of Querétaro that their governor (Vázquez) could not enter his office because it had been empowered by Dueñas. He terminated, "Congress must act." Emilio Velasco, a *Juarista*, argued that the major problem in Querétaro was that Congress had sent too many directives.[28] Avila lost the vote for suspension of procedures by eighty-five to forty-eight.

The resolution of 10 November only came to a vote a week later, and the constitutional arguments were pertinent to the whole problem of federal intervention. Velasco wanted a strict interpretation: There was no insurrection and no internal disturbance in the state; therefore, to send arms would effectively broaden the precedents of article 116. Furthermore, he argued, the legislature of Querétaro that sought aid had been illegal, because its sessions had by law terminated on 16 September. He hoped Congress would find a better solution to state factionalism than to send federal forces. Montes, a *Porfirista*, argued that the legislature was legal, for it had officially prolonged its sessions. The congressional obligation by article 116 was to provide aid to a legal legislature asking for it. Isidro Montiel first noted that the executive, not the legislature, commanded the army and then argued that article 116 made provision for aiding a state but not for assisting one branch against another branch within the same state government. That concept was undoubtedly accurate but failed to meet the problem. Avila argued that the constitutional framers must have foreseen the problem, for they gave the authority of seeking federal aid to the legislatures, knowing that governors had sufficient power. If Congress did not support state legislatures, he accurately noted, gubernatorial dictatorship was assured. By a close vote of fifty-eight to sixty-two the resolution was defeated.[29]

27. The Second Committee on Constitutional Points was composed of Romero Rubio and Isidro A. Montiel, *Lerdistas*, and Ramón Rodríguez, *Juarista*.

28. *Debates, quinto congreso*, 1:385.

29. Ibid., 17 November 1869, pp. 423–28; the roll-call vote is registered in column C of the chart in appendix 7, where a positive vote is considered pro-administration.

Upon the failure of the resolution *not* to send federal aid to the Querétaro legislature, the road was open to consider a resolution to send aid. Immediately the opposition congressmen Avila and Sánchez Azcona proposed a resolution that the executive telegraph orders to the federal forces in Querétaro to place Mariano Vázquez in possession of the gubernatorial powers. The resolution went to the *Juarista* Second Committee on Constitutional Points, where it was buried. Avila and Sánchez Azcona tried to bring it to the floor by a resolution of 20 November, but that resolution was also sent to committee.[30] On that same day the Supreme Court handed down its judgment on the Cervantes case. He was declared guilty of violating article 17, on evidence that the mobs which terrorized the legislature were Cervantes's agents; of violating article 41 by impeding the exercise of the legislative function; and of violating article 109 by failing to protect republican institutions. The sentence was removal from office for one year without pay.[31] Enforcing the court order became the next matter of business.

On 25 November Avila and Sánchez Azcona succeeded in having Avila's resolution of 16 November withdrawn from the unfriendly Second Committee on Constitutional Points and given to a special committee. Congress adjourned its session to establish itself as a grand commission to choose the special committee.[32]

The Special Committee presented a resolution on 27 November to extend federal aid to the legislature of Querétaro. Debate on the resolution commenced on 30 November. Francisco González spoke in opposition, ending a long constitutional argument heard before with the observation that although Cervantes was a usurper, so was the legislature, which did not have the authority to name an interim governor, and that he did not now want Congress to usurp the authority of the executive. Sánchez Axcona supported the bill with interesting arguments. Noting that Talancón had dissented from the resolution of the Special Committee on the grounds that there was no armed insurrection in Querétaro, he argued that Dueñas was supported by

30. Ibid., pp. 428, 456.
31. DDC, 14:99–101.
32. *Debates, quinto congreso*, 25 November 1869, 1:493. The Special Committee was composed of Serrano (*Juarista*), Lemus (*Lerdista*), and Talancón (*Porfirista*).

the arms of Cervantes against the legal governor, Mariano Vázquez, an act which constituted armed insurrection. Second, he addressed himself to the arguments of Francisco González, agreeing that the executive commanded the army but insisting that Congress had the faculties to order the executive to use it. Finally, he argued that the question of the legislature's legality should be reduced to whether it had legal origins, a matter which had never been doubted. Sánchez Azcona asked for adoption of the resolution. Rafael Herrera then spoke against the bill, raising again the important argument Montiel had earlier voiced, that the object of article 116 was to grant federal assistance to a state when the state government sought help against armed resistance, not to aid one element of the state government against another.[33] The session adjourned without a vote.

When Congress opened on 1 December the *Porfirista* congressman Nicolás Lemus spoke for the Special Committee with an important new argument. The Querétaro case did not involve one branch of a government against another branch, he said. The legislature was legal when it named Márquez as interim governor and when it sought federal aid. The state supreme court had recognized Márquez, and Márquez had agreed that federal assistance was necessary. Therefore, the total government of Querétaro was seeking support against an armed seizure of power: "Dueñas is a usurper on the bayonets of a deposed tyrant."[34]

Still there was no agreement. Rafael Herrera, a *Juarista*, asked for another two weeks to let a solution develop. Montes, a *Porfirista,* tied the problem directly to the executive, reminding his colleagues that the Fourth Congress had dealt with the Querétaro problem three times, the Fifth Congress three times, and the Supreme Court twice, but that the executive had failed to take action. Juan Carbó argued that the factional problem of Querétaro was one for the state court and that if the federal pact was broken, it was the business of the federal court, not of Congress. Sánchez Azcona berated Carbó severely for ignorance of the state of the argument: Cervantes had been removed by action of the courts, and now Querétaro suffered a usurper. A roll-call vote was taken, and the resolution passed

33. Ibid., 27 November 1869, p. 511, 30 November 1869, pp. 520–24.
34. Ibid., 1 December 1869, pp. 529–30.

seventy-five to forty-six.[35] Federal aid was to be extended to the Márquez government of Querétaro. The next step depended on Juárez. Juárez did nothing for two weeks. The first notice Congress received that he did not find himself bound by the congressional resolution was on 15 December when the Second Committee of *Gobernación* and the Special Committee on Querétaro reported out a bill (not a resolution) stating that: (1) the resolution of 1 December should not serve as a precedent for interpreting article 116; and (2) the executive should send the military force which had been sought by the legislature of Querétaro and by Governor Márquez.[36] Debate on the bill began two days later. Lemus argued for the committee that the executive required a law rather than a resolution and that the object of denying the precedent was to leave a way clear to write an enabling act or organic act for article 116. Congress had not previously made fine distinctions between a bill (*proyecto de ley*) and a resolution (*acuerdo económico*), and the executive had never failed to enforce a resolution. It was by a resolution that Congress had extended extraordinary powers to the president in May 1868, which he had solicited and accepted.[37] The bill passed and was sent to Juárez, who had seven days to present his observations.[38]

Eleven days later Avila presented a resolution stating that, since the president had not used his right to make observations, Congress should assume he had none and proceed to the definitive vote. The secretary of the session that day was Sánchez Azcona, who announced that the resolution passed. Immediately commotion broke out on the floor, and several men called for a motion of order. Cañedo argued that the president could not be denied his right of observation. More commotion followed. Baranda asked that the business on the floor be explained. Emilio Velasco accused Sánchez Azcona and Avila of

35. Ibid., 1 December 1869, p. 536; the roll-call vote is registered in column D of the chart in appendix 7, where a negative vote is recorded as pro-administration.

36. Ibid., p. 658.

37. Tovar, *Cuarto congreso*, 2:ix.

38. *Debates, quinto congreso*, 17 December 1869, 1:673–75. Article 70 prescribed the steps for forming a law; fraction four gave the president seven days to present his observations to Congress, and if he disapproved of the bill, it returned to the original committee for reconsideration, re-presentation to Congress, further debate, and a new vote.

steamrolling a resolution, while Montes sorely attacked Velasco and accused the president of delaying the legislative process even as the disorder in Querétaro was spreading to San Luis Potosí. Rojas defended Velasco and attacked Sánchez Azcona. At that point the minister of war entered the chamber with the president's observations on the Querétaro bill. The business on the floor, however, was Avila's resolution, upon which some men wanted a vote. Vincente Baz tried to make seven days out of the period between 17 and 28 December, which insulted Zamacona's sense of counting. Finally Avila withdrew his resolution. It had been a magnificent factional fracus.[39]

The president's observations delivered by the minister of war were mere technicalities, obviously to delay the action he was required to take. The observations attached to the bill of 17 December stated that the resolution of 1 December should have been a law, but that the law of 17 December failed to state that each branch of the federal government should be aware of its separate prerogatives in relation to article 116, and that the legislature of Querétaro should have been explicitly recognized. It was legal hair-splitting, but it served to send the bill back to committee, with a resolution added by Avila that it should reappear on the floor "with preference."[40] The bill, however, never reappeared on the floor; other events prevailed.

During all of November and December Julio Cervantes retained his executive power behind Angel Dueñas. In January 1870 the insurrection of San Luis Potosí necessitated granting extraordinary powers to the president, by which Juárez placed Querétaro under military law (*estado de sitio*). The insurrection of San Luis Potosí was crushed by February 1870, but Querétaro remained under military law into the summer months, owing to an insurrection, according to the cabinet, in the Sierra de Querétaro.

Meanwhile, the presidentially appointed military governor, Col. Margarito Mena, conducted new elections for a constitutional governor. Again the election produced a schismatic legislature, which, representing the state factions, divided and pronounced two different individuals as the winners of the elections: Francisco Zenco and Julio Cervantes. When Colonel Mena sought orders from the ministry about whom he should confer the state government to, the minister of

39. Ibid., 28 December 1869, pp. 749–56.
40. Ibid., pp. 756–57.

gobernación, Manuel Saavedra, ordered him to turn over the government to Cervantes, because, Saavedra said, he had received communication that Cervantes had been chosen by the "legal" legislature. Mena followed orders, and Gen. Julio Cervantes again became the governor of Querétaro.[41]

The particular case was thus closed. Executive policy had prevailed against the will and judgment of the Supreme Court and over congressional resolutions. The only legal precedent set by the entire affair toward a permanent solution of the problem was that national intervention in a conflict of powers in a state government required a law rather than a resolution. In the realm of politics, a Juárez ally had been saved.

Jalisco

Some of the most important ideas and developments in the controversy over federal intervention in state factional struggles took place in relation to the problems of the state of Jalisco. There in January 1867 General of Division Ramón Corona, easily one of the four or five individuals with the greatest military reputations to emerge from the French Intervention, occupied Guadalajara, capital of the state of Jalisco. He immediately proceeded to organize an administration loyal to the republic and named Gen. Antonio Gómez Cuervo as interim governor and military commander of the state with extraordinary powers pending public elections and the complete return to republican government in the nation.[42]

After the fall of Maximilian and during the election campaigns of 1867 Corona assumed a political stance. He openly supported Juárez for president and Gómez Cuervo for governor of Jalisco. Running against Gómez Cuervo was a group who called themselves the "true liberals" or "La Unión Liberal." They supported Ignacio Luis Vallarta for governor and tried to convince Juárez that they were his better

41. Margarito Mena to Juárez, 9 June 187Y, DDC, 14:510–13; Saavedra to Mena, 29 June 1870, ibid., p. 514; Mena to Saavedra, 30 June 1870, ibid., p. 515.

42. Galindo y Galindo, *Década nacional*, 3:573.

allies. Among the "true liberals" were Jesús Camarena, ex-president of the Jalisco supreme court and personal enemy of Corona, Gen. Amado A. Guadarrama of local military glory, and José María Alatorre. Alatorre advised Juárez that the only way to win the elections in Jalisco was to use presidential extraordinary powers to replace Gómez Cuervo with Vallarta or Dávila as interim governor during the elections. Vallarta thought Gómez Cuervo would win the governorship because "Corona has the elements of power, none of which he has failed to utilize to assure his truimph. But if we do not win we will make him recognize the strength of the opposition party, giving the state governor a terrible competition."[43]

Gómez Cuervo won the gubernatorial election, and the first attack of the *Vallartista* "terrible competition" was to introduce a resolution into Congress that the government of Gómez Cuervo was illegal because Gómez Cuervo had served the Maximilian empire. The attempt failed, as Congress accepted the resolution of the Committee on Constitutional Points, dominated by the *Porfiristas* Montes and Zamacona, which held that Congress had no jurisdiction over state legislation pertaining to state politics. Vallarta then led an attempt to force Gómez Cuervo to step down in favor of Emeterio Robles Gil. Vallarta kept Juárez informed of the matter, from a pro-Robles Gil point of view, with which Juárez was in accord.[44]

Then an issue arose in Jalisco that brought the matter again to Congress. To arrest spreading banditry in Jalisco, the state legislature ordered the governor to suspend personal guarantees of the constitution and to execute bandits without judicial procedure. The governor did so, and in mid-February 1868 he ordered five bandits executed, although a federal district judge had authorized a stay of execution (*amparo*). Those congressmen who had earlier attempted to remove Gómez Cuervo as an ex-imperialist then accused him before Con-

43. Camarena to Juárez, 20 September 1867, DDC, 12:439–40; Vallarta to Juárez, 27 September 1867, ibid., pp. 525–26; José María Alatorre to Juárez, 28 September 1867, ibid., pp. 529–30; Alatorre to Juárez, 4 October 1867, ibid., pp. 563–64; Vallarta to Juárez, 7 October 1867, ibid., p. 594.

44. Tovar, *Cuarto congreso,* 24 December 1867, 1:100; 30 December 1867, 1:222; 2 January 1868, 1:133; especially 1:vii, 331–32; Vallarta to Juárez, 25 January 1868, DDC, 12:923, and note of Juárez's answer, p. 924. Robles Gil had been *Cuervista* in 1867 but became his enemy by 1870.

gress, acting as a grand jury, of violating the personal guarantees of federal law.[45] The deliberations of the grand jury were important to the federal-state relationship. Francisco Zarco sought a conviction against Gómez Cuervo, proclaiming that "the day that the public sees that a governor . . . can fall legally, that day the great principles of the Republic are secured." Jesús Sánchez Román sought an acquittal because the accusation was clearly a factional maneuver to destroy a governor. Pablo Gudiño y Gómez feared that an acquittal would embolden bandits and that a conviction would make it possible for any district judge to remove a governor. The defense lawyer, Alfonso Lancaster Jones, pointed out that a governor of Jalisco was barred from failing to promulgate and enforce a legislative decree. Nevertheless, the congressional grand jury voted for conviction 114 to 25.[46]

Although Juárez's attitudes toward these events are not a matter of record, some speculation is possible. He was apparently concerned about Gómez Cuervo, whose connections with Vicente Rivas Palacio and Porfirio Díaz were known, but he was able to work well with Corona, who became Juárez's *compadre.* Juárez probably sealed his alliance with Corona very early, for Corona thereafter was explicitly

45. Tamayo, *Juárez,* 13:349–50. The congressmen who made the accusation were from Jalisco and were members of the Vallarta faction. See Pérez Verdía, *Jalisco,* 3:511.

46. Tamayo, *Juárez,* 13:351–53; Tovar, *Cuarto congreso,* 9 May 1868, 2:295ff. Unfortunately, Tovar did not record roll-call votes; it would be interesting to see if the principle of the constitutional guarantees were tempered by factional voting. Tamayo (*Juárez,* 13:353) notes that Pedro Santacilia and Pedro Contreras Elizalde, both sons-in-law of Juárez and members of the Fourth Congress, voted against each other. This issue was of great constitutional importance. The legislature of Jalisco decreed that the governor was correct in overriding the *amparo* in the execution of the bandits (Tovar, *Cuarto congreso,* 26 May 1868, 2:451). The legislature of Colima disagreed (ibid., 6 July 1868, p. 519). The minister of justice, Antonio Martínez de Castro, asked the attorney general (*procurador general*), León Guzmán, for an opinion on the responsibilities of functionaries who were obliged by legislative decrees to publish and enforce anti-constitutional law. Guzmán held that they should not do so and recommended certain reforms to the law of *amparo* of 26 November 1861 (Tamayo, *Juárez,* 13:353; Guzmán report, DDC, 13:375–76). The Fourth Congress did rewrite the law of *amparo.* The case is described in Pérez Verdía, *Jalisco,* 3:410–19.

loyal to him. We have seen that Juárez agreed with Vallarta to replace Gómez Cuervo with Robles Gil, which took place on 18 May 1868, after the grand jury trial. Furthermore, after Vallarta's electoral defeat in October 1867, Juárez named him to the cabinet as secretary of *gobernación.*[47] Vallarta, however, was hard to work with and quarreled with others in the cabinet. Wags accused him of conspiring with the Supreme Court to deny Lerdo his license to serve in the cabinet, and he resigned his ministerial post (1 September 1868) the day after the Supreme Court returned Gómez Cuervo to the governorship of Jalisco (31 August 1868), citing the court's action as one of his motives.[48] Gómez Cuervo resumed the governorship of Jalisco, and quite possibly Juárez learned that he could live better with a law-and-order governor like Gómez Cervo than with a *"puro"* liberal like Vallarta. Jesús Camarena was correct when he said that Juárez's neutrality in the state was comforting to Gómez Cuervo. "Do you not fear establishing another precedent of fatal consequences," he asked Juárez,

> leaving those Governors of the states to do as they please, who although suspended from their functions, usurp the public powers and constitute themselves as dictatorial despots . . . protected by you in fact beneath the pretext of not wanting to interfere in the internal administration of the states?[49]

One wonders whether Juárez would have been neutral if presidential neutrality had damaged his faction.

The opportunity soon arose to test those questions. In mid-January 1870 Juárez declared Jalisco under military law (*estado de sitio*) owing to the grave rebellion of the military units in San Luis Potosí and of the governor of the state of Zacatecas. Juárez named Col. Florentino Carrillo as the interim military governor to replace Antonio Gómez Cuervo. Colonel Carrillo reported to Juárez that Gómez Cuervo was

47. Robles Gil to Juárez, 21 May 1868, DDC, 13:355; Juárez to Vallarta, 16 January 1868, ibid., 12:921.

48. Vallarta to Juárez, 1 September 1868, *Epistolario*, 1st ed., pp. 470–72. The Supreme Court did not acquit Gómez Cuervo, but in the absence of a law designating punishments for official crimes, the Court ruled that his three-month separation from office should satisfy the congressional grand jury verdict. See Pérez Verdía, *Jalisco*, 3:416–19.

49. Camarena to Juárez, 20 July 1870, DDC, 14:598.

cooperating with the military government but that the legislature had refused to recognize the military government and was demanding a return to constitutional government. Many persons in the state government, including some in the legislature, he said, were aiding the rebellion. Carrillo recommended leaving the state under military law until after the administration had been revamped to exclude the "unpatriotic" persons. Juárez responded by asking Carrillo for a list of those "who are conducting themselves well" and those who "work evil." But military law had to be lifted, he added, "for very powerful considerations," meaning an increasingly vociferous press and Congress that were looking askance at the prolonged military law in several states.[50]

No sooner had Gómez Cuervo been reinstated in the governorship than the state legislature clashed with him, ordered him from office, and named Aurelio Hermoso as interim governor. During those difficulties Gómez Cuervo assumed extraordinary faculties, declared the legislature illegal, and told Juárez that the legislature's object was to prepare for the 1871 elections. Florentino Carrillo, who remained in Guadalajara as military commander of the garrisoned federal forces, kept Juárez informed from a pro-Gómez Cuervo point of view and identified the legislators with the group of traitors who favored the recent rebellion, calling their accusation of Gómez Cuervo "impassioned . . . exclusively motivated by political ambition . . . in order to secure the results of the coming elections." He assured Juárez that the federal forces remained absolutely neutral in the political question and merely kept the peace.[51] The state legislature forwarded to Juárez its version of the problem and officially sought federal intervention against Gómez Cuervo. Juárez urged both parties to seek a pacific solution and told the legislature that in the absense of armed insurrection in the state he could not intervene but that it was free to communicate with Congress.[52]

50. Carrillo to Juárez, 13 March 1870, and note of Juárez's answer, ibid., pp. 348–52; Carrillo to Juárez, 23 May 1870, ibid., pp. 588–91. The warfare was formally concluded in Jalisco on 3 March 1870, and the *sitio* was lifted only on 6 April 1870: Pérez Verdía, *Jalisco*, 3:438.

51. Gómez Cuervo to Juárez, 12 June 1870, DDC, 14:591–93; Pérez Verdía, *Jalisco*, 3:439–48; Carrillo to Juárez, 12 June 1870, DDC, 14:593–95.

52. Telegrams, legislature of Jalisco to Juárez, 12–13 June 1870, and answer, ibid., pp. 595–97; Gómez Cuervo to Juárez, 13 June 1870, ibid., p. 597;

The petition from the legislature of Jalisco for federal intervention came before Congress on 17 September 1870 and was sent to the Committee on Constitutional Points. The following day Congressman Manuel Rincón presented a resolution that offered a novel solution to the problem of federal intervention. The resolution called for the Supreme Court to decide if intervention should be sent and to decide if the federal power of sending such aid belonged to the executive or to Congress.[53] The process explicit in the resolution might have clarified a troubled area of constitutional law but might also have introduced politics into the court and thus complicated the problem. At any rate, the resolution died in committee.

The proposed solution that received consideration emerged from the Committee on Constitutional Points. The *Juarista* congressmen Dondé and Alcalde introduced a bill specifying that the case go directly to the Committee on Grand Jury Proceedings to see if there were grounds for indicting Gómez Cuervo for violation of federal law. Their reasoning for this measure was that the information about the case was contradictory, since the legislature had withdrawn recognition from the governor and the governor from the legislature. They also claimed that an examination into the legal workings of the state of Jalisco was outside the competence of Congress.[54] The implications of the procedure constituted a solution to the problem of federal aid to states wherein the governor was a part of a state conflict: If he were found guilty of violating federal law, his removal would solve the problem without armed forces, and if he were acquitted Congress would presumably deny federal aid.

Complicating the committee bill, however, was a minority bill (*voto particular*) presented by the third member of the committee, Ezequiel Montes, a *Porfirista*. His bill would have ordered the executive to

---

Secretary of *Gobernación* to the legislature of Jalisco, *Debates, quinto congreso,* 15 June 1870, 3:99; also see E. Cañedo to Juárez, 5 September 1870, DDC, 14:600–2; Pérez Verdía, *Jalisco,* 3:450.

53. *Debates, quinto congreso,* 3:12, 24. The resolution also referred to the parallel case of Campeche.

54. Ibid., 28 September 1870, pp. 97–98; Pérez Verdía (*Jalisco,* 3:451) judges that the Dondé-Alcalde bill was "equivalent to denying the aid which was sought, since the committee on grand jury proceedings would not find an infraction of federal law in the Governor's conduct."

"reestablish constitutional order in Jalisco" by remitting Gómez Cuervo to the state supreme court for trial, since the legislature of the state, acting as a grand jury, had removed him from his office, and to use federal forces if necessary. Only then, the third part of Montes's initiative, should a federal grand jury try the case.[55]

The majority bill came to the floor for discussion on 6 October 1870. Juan José Baz noted that Dondé, co-sponsor of the bill, took a different stand on the Campeche issue, where the legislature of that state also sought federal aid to oust a dictatorial governor.[56] Baz mentioned rumors that the executive or one of his ministers had offered to assist the legislature of Campeche (against the García-Aznar government), if "the interested ones" (meaning at least the Campeche congressman Rafael Dondé) would separate themselves from the Jalisco deputies, who wanted to remove Gómez Cuervo.[57]

The facts used by Baz and all others who sought to remove Gómez Cuervo were these: (1) The legislature of Jalisco could not meet in its regular first session, which should have been from 1 February to 30 April, because of the declaration of military law. (2) The legislature opened its sessions on 11 April and on 30 April decreed that its sessions would continue until 10 July; Gov. Gómez Cuervo published that decree without objection. (3) On 7 June the legislature ordered Gómez Cuervo to submit certain documents which were necessary to investigate an accusation of mishandling of public funds against the governor. (4) Gómez Cuervo refused to yield the documents, declared that the legislature was illegal because it was meeting outside of the

---

55. *Debates, quinto congreso,* 3:18.

56. The case of Campeche, although instructive, is not examined here in detail because the issue never came to a congressional vote, being solved in another manner: The state was garrisoned by federal forces while the legislature's interim governor, Salvador Dondé, held elections for constitutional governor, won by Joaquín Baranda, who left Congress to take the governorship. The *caudillo* of Campeche, Pablo García, and his interim governor, Tomas Aznar Barbachano, enjoyed little prestige in Congress even among the opposition. Aznar was probably correct when he said that "the key to the situation in Campeche is the [federal] batallion of [Col. Francisco] Castañeda. . . ." Aznar to Juárez, 16 January 1871, DDC, 14:886. See *Debates, quinto congreso,* 17 September 1870 to 8 November 1870, 3:12–401 passim, and various letters, 19 July 1870 to 16 January 1871, DDC, 14:604–886.

57. *Debates, quinto congreso,* 3:153.

constitutional period ending 30 April, and decreed extraordinary powers for himself. (5) The legislature decreed the dismissal of Gómez Cuervo from office for withdrawing recognition from the legislature, reserved its rights to try him for the earlier accusation, named Aurelio Hermoso as interim governor, and called for federal intervention.

Emilio Velasco criticized the Dondé-Alcalde bill. Besides stating his usual argument that article 116 provided for aid to a state but not to one branch of the state government against another branch, he added that automatic federal support to legislatures calling for it might in the recent Zacatecas rebellion have led to the ridiculous position of the federal government supporting the state legislature to remove Gov. Trinidad García de la Cadena in favor of Jesús González Ortega, had the governor refused to join the rebellion. This had not happened in Zacatecas, since García de la Cadena had joined the rebellion before the legislature did, but the point was excellent. Velasco maintained that congressional duty was to determine if the state legislature could extend its sessions beyond the limits set by the state constitution, and if not, then the legislature as it sat in grand jury was not legal and Gómez Cuervo was still the legal governor. His point, while well taken, was inconsistent with his usual stance that Congress was incompetent to examine the internal laws of a state.

Atilano Sánchez also opposed the bill, but for a different reason. He pointed out that making federal aid conditional upon a grand jury trial altered article 116 so significantly that a constitutional amendment would be necessary. Federal support to the Jalisco legislature, he said, must be extended or denied.

Championing the bill, Joaquín Alcalde sensibly pointed out that Congress could not send aid to every legislature that opposed its governor; such action would be unfair to the taxpayers, and the 23,000 soldiers of the federal army would not suffice.[58]

Ezequiel Montes objected to the bill for what it omitted. He wanted to send federal aid to the legislature of Jalisco for these reasons: (1) The precedents of two congresses had held that states should receive federal protection to insure that governors obeyed legislatures. (2) The governor of Jalisco raised himself above the legislature and the

58. Ibid., pp. 154–63.

court, which contravened articles 41 and 109 (states shall be governed by their respective constitutions, and states shall observe republican forms). (3) The most distinguished commentators of the United States constitution teach that the federal government not only should protect the state governments against popular insurrections but also should defend the people against the ambitions and usurpations of governors.[59] (4) The governor of Jalisco had usurped the legislature's function and had illegally assumed the authority to declare a legislative act unconstitutional. (5) The chief benefit of a federal system "consists in the ability of states, where peace and order exist, to offer aid to another state which suffers rebellion or internal disorder." Montes ended his extended examination asking for the defeat of the Dondé-Alcalde bill and the acceptance of his minority bill.

Juan José Baz took the floor again on 8 October to answer Velasco's criticism of the legislature of Jalisco holding sessions outside of its constitutional limits. He noted that Congress had held its sessions from 8 December 1867 to 7 March 1868 because of the problems following the Maximilian Empire rather than from 15 September to 15 December as stipulated in the constitution. He also noted that Dondé had approved of the bill which had set the session. In the case of Jalisco, Gómez Cuervo had accepted the resetting of the legislative sessions.

At that point the minister of justice addressed the issue. He argued that conflicts between branches of state governments were not comprehended in article 116. If they were, he correctly noted, then the beneficiary of the aid would depend upon whether or not the legislature was in session. The point was excellent, for article 116 clearly stated that the legislatures were authorized to seek federal aid, or the governor, if the legislature was not in session. He thus logically deduced that article 116 could only be used for cases of insurrection and invasion. Furthermore, he reasoned, "If legislatures could remove governors by calling for federal forces, then it would be simpler to

59. American examples were frequently used in Mexican congressional debate (and in court as well) not because Mexicans of the Restored Republic were inordinately awed by Americans but because nineteenth-century liberals believed that republicanism was universal and that precedents set in any republic were useful in all others. Montes cited John C. Calhoun, *Works* (New York, 1855), 6:211–18, 229, 234–36, but also Montesquieu, *De l'Esprit des Lois*, vol. 60, chap. 1.

change the constitution to read that governors are named and removed by legislatures." Then the minister referred to an executive initiative, which had earlier been read on the floor and which at the moment was under study in committee, whereby conflicts between branches of a state government would be considered within the terms of article 109—that state governments must be republican. He recommended that Congress adopt the presidential solution, identical in the Jalisco case to the Dondé-Alcalde bill, that when legislatures seek federal intervention, the governor should be tried by Congress as a grand jury to see if he had violated the republican form of government.[60]

After several more short speeches, none of which added new arguments, a roll-call vote defeated the Dondé-Alcalde bill by a vote of sixty-eight to seventy-three.[61]

Two days later, on 10 October 1870, debate opened on the minority report (*voto particular*) of Ezequiel Montes. This was the bill seen above, which would have obliged the executive to use federal arms, if necessary, to force Gómez Cuervo to the Jalisco supreme court for trial.[62] The Montes bill included as an addendum a resolution that the case be sent to the congressional Committee on Grand Jury Proceedings to see if Gómez Cuervo was guilty of violating the federal pact. Thus the resolution (*acuerdo económico*) was identical to the Dondé-Alcalde bill in its text. The bill was first under discussion without the resolution addendum.

Francisco W. González, a *Juarista,* argued against the bill. He contended that article 116 could not be enforced without a regulatory act, nor could Congress deploy federal troops or legislate for a particular

60. *Debates, quinto congreso,* 7 October 1870, 3:167–87. The executive initiative is in ibid., 17 September 1870, p. 9.

61. Ibid., 8 October 1870, p. 188–89. It is for the executive initiative, after which the Dondé-Alcalde bill was modeled, that a positive vote is here recorded as pro-administration. Logically, if Juárez wanted to save Antonio Gómez Cuervo, he would have preferred a negative vote on both the Dondé-Alcalde bill and the Montes bill, but he would certainly have preferred the former to the latter. The vote is recorded in column E of the chart in appendix 7.

62. Unlike Congress, which judged as a grand jury and then sent the case to the Supreme Court for sentencing, the legislature of Jalisco, when sitting as a grand jury, merely could declare cause for trial, which was heard and judged by the state supreme court.

individual. It could not legislate retroactively or approve a resolution which affected persons outside Congress. As all his arguments ran counter to many precedents, no one bothered to answer him. Avila, a *Porfirista* congressman, spoke well for the bill. Dondé argued that it would authorize the executive to meddle in Jaliscan affairs, which was accurate, and that "to approve this bill would be to destroy the federation," which was too strong. Montes took the floor a last time to point out that the question was simply whether Congress would sit back and let this governor establish a tyranny. By a roll-call vote the bill was defeated eighty-five to sixty-five.[63]

The Montes resolution then passed seventy to fifty-nine, indicating that some congressmen, who wanted Gómez Cuervo evicted as well as judged by a congressional grand jury, voted against the Dondé-Alcalde bill in order to vote for the Montes bill, and then voted for the Montes resolution as the only measure they could obtain.[64] The anomalous situation in Jalisco had lasted eight months.

The problem in Jalisco by no means terminated in October 1870. The correspondence of Benito Juárez indicates that he tried as mediator to mend the hostility existing between the governor and the legislature and between the governor and Gen. Ramón Corona. The legislature, however, insisted upon trying Gómez Cuervo for the original charge of mishandling public funds, named Jesús Camarena interim governor, and petitioned Congress for federal intervention by article 116. Finally, in March 1871 during the national presidential election and the Jaliscan gubernatorial campaign, Juárez convinced Antonio Gómez Cuervo to surrender his office to Jesús Camarena, whom the legislature of Jalisco had named as interim governor. It appears that this development was pleasing to Juárez, for by then Lerdo had left the cabinet and was running for president against him. Gómez Cuervo was identified with Lerdo by then, and Jesús Camerena with Juárez.[65] Again, constitutional procedures for federal

63. *Debates, quinto congreso*, 10 October 1870, 3:189–95. The vote is recorded in column F of the chart in appendix 7, where a negative vote is considered pro-administration.

64. Ibid., 10 October 1870, 3:197. This vote was also taken by roll-call procedures and is recorded in the chart in column G, appendix 7, where a negative vote is considered pro-administration.

65. Various letters, Juárez, *Epistolario*, 1st ed., 30 January to 7 March 1871, pp. 503–10; Pérez Verdía, *Jalisco*, 3:450–52.

intervention in states suffering factional conflict was not advanced, but the presidential alliance of governors was. Furthermore, as the later statistical analysis will show, irrespective of the constitutional arguments, congressmen voted along party lines.

San Luis Potosí

In the state of San Luis Potosí the deep factional struggle, the extreme anticlerical administration of Juan Bustamante after 1867, and the fiscal penury, the widespread banditry, and the serious insurrection of 1869–70 left the state politically unstable. There were four governors during the year. The state elections of 1870 took place under tense conditions that gave way to violence and factional discord; they resulted in two opposing legislatures and two governors.[66] On the one side was Miguel María Esparza, who had conducted the last elections for constitutional governor and belonged to the *puro* faction of Juan Bustamante, Ramón Fernández, Carlos Díez Gutiérrez, Benigno A-rriaga, Bruno García, and Manuel Muro—all *Porfiristas* in later months and years. On the other side was Gen. Mariano Escobedo, partisan of Lerdo and Juárez and hero not only of Querétaro in 1867 but also as the governmental general against the Aguirre-Martínez rebellion of San Luis earlier in the year. The legislature should legally have computed the votes and declared a winner. But the legislature divided and held different sessions, each claiming that the other was illegal.[67]

The issue was soon taken to Congress. On 20 September 1870 Ramón Fernández, congressman from San Luis Potosí and ally of Esparza, asked the minister of war and the secretary of *gobernación* to inform Congress about the situation in San Luis Potosí. He based his request on information he had that a fraction of the legislature had established itself into a "revolutionary convention" and called for their own alternates to form a quorum to name Mariano Escobedo the elected governor. The motion passed and the secretary of *gobernación* appeared. According to him the state legislature met to compute the gubernatorial electoral returns and, being unable to do so, named

66. Primo Feliciano Valázquez, *Historia de San Luis Potosí*, 4 vols. (Mexico: Sociedad Mexicana de Geografía y Estadística, 1948), 4:1–26.

67. For the two versions, see the respective telegrams from the two legislatures in *Debates, quinto congreso*, 20 September 1870, 3:39.

Miguel Esparza interim governor, pending the computation. At that point six of the thirteen members of the legislature boycotted further meetings to deny a quorum for counting the votes. The others met in a legal session and called the six to the session of a given day. When they did not return they were purged from the assembly and deprived of citizenship, and their alternates were officially called.[68] The legislature then installed itself, counted the votes, found Mariano Escobedo the winner, and declared him governor. The secretary of *gobernación* also reported that Miguel Esparza informed him that seven legislators illegally usurped power, expelled the other six members, called their own alternates, and named Escobedo governor; Esparza did not recognize the acts. The secretary added that the president had ordered the federal forces in San Luis to remain neutral.[69]

Four days later Esparza's petition for federal intervention was read in Congress. He impugned the legality of procedures by which the legislature was installed, declared his refusal to recognize its acts, and added that Gen. Sóstenes Rocha, commander of the federal forces garrisoned in the capital of the state, had explicitly recognized the legislature and its acts.[70] If Rocha had done so, it was undoubtedly upon orders from the minister of war, that is, from the cabinet or the president.

In mid-October the Escobedo legislature of San Luis Potosí advised Congress that the three branches of the state government were functioning and that there was no reason for Congress to be concerned.[71] Such was later the view of the Second Committee on Constitutional Points, which reported out a bill denying the federal aid sought by Miguel Esparza.[72]

The discussion on the bill commenced on 10 November. Speaking for the committee, Juan Sánchez Azcona argued simply that the state legislature was initially unable to compute the election returns and named an interim governor; then it did compute the returns and declared a constitutional governor, at which time the interim gover-

68. Article 112 of the state constitution allows the procedure.
69. *Debates, quinto congreso,* 20 September 1870, 3:39.
70. Ibid., 24 September 1870, p. 73.
71. Ibid., 13 October 1870, p. 213.
72. Ibid., 19 October 1870, p. 270.

nor should have ceased his functions. The interim governor, however, had declared that the legislature was illegally constituted in its second meeting and called for federal assistance. The question, Sánchez Azcona said, was whether Congress had the authority to examine the legality of a state legislature. The committee had decided that Congress did not.

Speaking against the bill, Nuños Silva, a *Porfirista*, offered yet another version of what happened in San Luis Potosí. The federal forces of the Third Division in San Luis, he said, had intervened in the elections in behalf of Escobedo; nevertheless, Sóstenes Escandón received the largest number of votes. In the absence of a majority winner, he said, the legislature correctly named an interim government and disbanded. Then a group of *Escobedista* congressmen illegally called a new session, although only the *diputación permanente* (the legally established body of congressmen who sit in representation of the legislature between sessions) could legally convoke the legislature in extraordinary session. According to this version, five *Escobedistas* then established themselves as a grand jury, purged their colleagues, called alternates, and named Escobedo governor. Esparza then correctly sought federal intervention.

Ramón Fernández also opposed the bill. He first implied that the members of the Committee on Constitutional Points were personally interested in establishing the precedent of congressional incompetence to determine the legality of legislatures because they came from states where legislatures had usurped authority. (Sánchez Azcona was from Campeche, where another such case was proceeding.) Fernández was quite willing to investigate the internal politics of the state. He claimed there had been no elections in some districts due to insurrections and no elections in the capital because 152 of 251 persons in the electoral college abstained from voting, "protesting against the threats of the federal forces . . . [and against] the irrevocable resolution [of the commander of the Third Division] to blast apart the meeting with grapeshot because a seditious shout had been heard." When the legislature met, therefore, the majority of the election committee resolved that the elections had been illegal, which was the reason several congressmen boycotted the meetings until the period for verifying elections had passed. Only then did the legislature meet to name Esparza interim governor, pending new elections. And only then did the illegal sessions of the *Escobedista* legislature commence. In short, the Esparza government was legal and had the right to seek federal intervention against Escobedo by article 116.

The discussion continued with Joaquín Alcalde, Manuel Contreras, and Rafael Martínez de la Torre supporting the bill. A roll-call vote passed the bill eighty-seven to thirty-three, meaning that no federal aid would be sent to the Esparza government.[73] Shortly thereafter, Esparza, forced by circumstances, surrendered his pretensions, and Mariano Escobedo exercised the powers of governor. Once again Congress sustained the presidential policy, and again no advance toward a federal solution to state factionalism was achieved. The statistics of the congressional vote (appendix 7) will again show a near perfect factional division.

Guerrero

Politics in Guerrero remained strife-torn in the months after the special elections that Gen. Francisco O. Arce held, and won, in 1868. Federal troops were operating in the state against bandits because, as Arce stated, the national guard was *Jimenista*. The legislature of the state also contained a group of *Jimenistas* who in May of 1870 succeeded in carrying a grand jury verdict, depriving Arce of the governorship on a charge of violating the independence of the state judiciary. Arce turned over the governorship to Francisco Domingo Catalán, a *Jimenista*, who was appointed by the legislature as interim governor. Arce then went to Mexico to consult with Juárez.[74]

Juárez committed himself to aid Arce in the Guerrero factional dispute. It was arranged for Juárez to name a partisan, Congressman José María Condés de la Torre, to a judicial position in Guerrero to hand down the verdict on the Arce case from the Guerrero grand jury. The congressman arrived in Tixtla de Guerrero in August, but the *Jimenista* legislature denied his appointment to the court. Then

73. Ibid., pp. 413–25. The roll-call vote appears on pp. 425–26 and in column H of the charts in appendix 7, where an affirmative vote is considered pro-administration.

74. Arce to Juárez, 3 May 1870, DDC 14:450; Ochoa Campos, *Guerrero*, p. 242; *Debates, quinto congreso*, 15 October 1870, 3:243.

Condés de la Torre established a court in Iguala, ruled that Arce's removal from office had been served in full, and reinstated him in the office of governor. Arce then established a new legislature at Chilpancingo and refused to recognize the *Jimenista* government at Tixtla de Guerrero.[75]

At that point Guerrero had two complete governments, with the president and the federal forces recognizing the Arce government and the national guard generally loyal to the Catalán government. Catalán named General Jiménez to protect it against the "rebel" government of Arce, and Juárez named General Alvarez to advance against the "revolutionary" forces of Jiménez. From October to December 1870 the two forces clashed repeatedly in open battle.[76]

Congress became officially cognizant of the problem in September, when a petition from the Catalán government was read asking that federal forces be removed from Guerrero.[77] A few days later the same government sought federal support against Arce. The petition advanced a legal argument based upon three points: Arce had been legally removed from office; the court of Condés de la Torre had not been constitutionally established, because the legislature could not swear him in without a license from Congress; and only the legislature could designate a place other than the capital city of the state for the establishment of a branch of government.[78] In October the Committee on Constitutional Points presented a bill ordering federal forces to "support the powers of the state that function in the city of Tixtla de Guerrero."[79]

Congress was sorely divided on the issue. The *Juarista* congressman Rafael Dondé, one of the members of the Committee, dissented from

75. Arce to Juárez and note of answer, 9 June 1870, DDC, 14:454; Tamayo says Juárez sent Condés de la Torre: *Juárez*, 14:679; official petition of the legislature of Guerrero for federal intervention, 26 September 1870, DDC, 14:685; *Debates, quinto congreso*, 15 October 1870, 3:244.

76. Arce to Juárez, 26 January 1871, DDC, 14:898; Juárez to Alvarez, 11 October 1870, ibid., pp. 691–92; various letters, ibid., pp. 698–708.

77. *Debates, quinto congreso*, 17 September 1870, 3:13.

78. Official petition for federal intervention, 26 September 1870, DDC, 14:685. The Constitution of 1857 prescribes that no officeholder in one branch of government may assume a second position in another branch without a license of permission from the first.

79. *Debates, quinto congreso*, 15 October 1870, 3:245–46.

the bill of the other two. Three times in late October different *Juarista* congressmen tried to introduce bills that would render federal aid to the Arce government, but they were blocked.[80] Congress recessed in December without taking action. By then General Alvarez had defeated Jiménez, and the Arce government occupied Tixtla de Guerrero, while the Catalán government retreated to Cuaxtlahuacan.

In April of 1871 the bill authorizing federal aid to the Catalán government came before Congress. The minister of war testified that the federal troops in Guerrero had been neutral on the question of which government was legal and were merely fighting the Jiménez forces as rebels. The debate was long and acrimonious, but the bill was eventually defeated by the close vote of eighty-five to eighty-seven.[81]

Some days later a new bill was offered by the Committee on Constitutional Points. Montes argued for the Committee that the executive essentially was waging war in Guerrero without congressional consent. He informed Congress that the president in sessions with the committee had opposed a plan to name a new interim governor to be ratified by Congress. The bill, "in order to bring peace to Guerrero," would have recognized Francisco Domingo Catalán as interim governor of the state and would have ordered the withdrawal of all federal forces. This bill was also debated at length, with *Juarista* congressmen and the minister of war speaking against it. Two days later it was defeated, ninety-five to ninety-three.[82]

The political climate of Guerrero remained turbulent in the following months. The Catalán government dispersed, and Jiménez joined the Porfirian rebellion of La Noria until July 1872, when Juárez died and Lerdo granted him amnesty.[83] Again the Juárez presidential policy predominated in Congress and again no congressional solution was found for the problem of federal reaction to state conflicts. And again congressmen voted according to their factional loyalty.

80. Ibid., 22, 27, and 28 October 1870, pp. 283ff.
81. Ibid., 5 April 1871, 4:252–55, 273–82, 296–300, 302–5, 308–21, 324–27; this vote appears in column I of the chart in appendix 7, with a negative vote registered as pro-administration.
82. Ibid., 26 April 1871, pp. 433–36; 28 April 1871, p. 464; this vote appears in column J of the chart in appendix 7, where a negative vote appears as pro-administration.
83. Ochoa Campos, *Guerrero*, p. 244.

Some conclusions emerge from this examination. First, the issue of congressional reaction to conflicts within branches of state governments was vital to the future of the nation. Not only was constitutional, republican government hanging in the balance, but so too was the peace of the nation. Inasmuch as congressional aid was difficult to mobilize, strong-handed governors were encouraged to override legislatures, particularly when they could count upon presidential support. Elsewhere, men dissatisfied with *caudillo* governors and despairing of federal remedy must have been encouraged to take up arms. The proclamations of rebels of the period contain the accusation, and so some men justified further militarism. Porfirio Díaz ultimately put together a coalition of such men, gained power by successful insurrection, and later solved the federal problem by overriding it.

A converse occurrence was the frequent, unrelentless legislative harassment of governors. That is, legislatures were not always victims. More than one governor resigned his office rather than confront continual attacks from his legislature. Juan José de la Garza, governor of Tamaulipas, resigned for such reasons.[84] Francisco Gómez Palacio, governor of Durango, was so harried by his legislature that he named himself as alternate congressman and left the state when Francisco Ortiz de Zárate, congressman for Durango, died in late 1868.[85]

Mexicans were unused, perhaps, to the patience, compromise, and cooperation required by republicanism. It is suggested above that the lack of opportunity in the professions, commerce, and industry raised the level of competition for public posts to intense rivalry. It may also be true that public authorities so routinely used their official positions to promote their personal and family businesses that rival circles, threatened by exclusion or even persecution, united politically to thrust factional members into the legislature through control of local areas to oppose the incumbent faction at the state level. This is, however, an area not yet explored.

A second conclusion is that the Fourth and Fifth Congresses achieved little toward developing a workable solution to the problem of conflict within state government. Although Congress did in fact

84. Gabriel Saldívar, *Historia compendiada de Tamaulipas* (Mexico: La Academia Nacional de Historia y Geografía, 1945), p. 247.

85. Gómez Palacio to Juárez, 13 January 1869, DDC, 13:754–55.

review the internal law and politics of the states—only because some congressmen used their freedom of debate to do so—the principle of the matter was never admitted. Articles 40, 109, and 116 certainly needed regulatory laws for their interpretation and implementation. Article 116, however, was an inadequate instrument to resolve struggles between branches of the same government or between rival governments. The suggestion of a grand jury trial for governors, based on article 109, merely threatened removal from office. Congress lacked the power to enforce its verdict, and governors could have themselves replaced by their partisans, as Cervantes did in Querétaro and García in Campeche. In this sense the Dondé-Alcalde bill in the Jalisco case was not a satisfactory solution.

A solution to the federal problem might have evolved by employing the Supreme Court in state struggles in order to obtain a juridical solution rather than a political one. Congressman Manuel Rincón proposed such a procedure in September 1870 for the cases of Campeche and Jalisco. The procedure, however, was only as viable as the willingness of the president to enforce the court judgment, and the danger of politicizing the Court was great. The Court could not enforce its judgment in the Querétaro case and lost prestige by restoring Gómez Cuervo in Jalisco.

The executive initiative of 17 September 1870 might have provided a partial solution. By article 1 the president would have had authority to use federal forces, and with congressional permission he could use national guard units outside the states of their origin, in cases of invasion of a state. Article 2 allowed the executive the same authority in case of insurrection or internal disturbance when federal intervention was sought by a state legislature or, when not in session, by a governor. That much was already in the constitution. Then to guarantee republican government in the states in conformity with articles 40 and 109, "in case of conflict between the branches" of a state government, article 3 specified that the federal executive would proceed according to the judicial decree of Congress sitting as a grand jury. And article 4 authorized the president to reduce the state to peace, pending the grand jury judgment.[86] The bill gave the president no more power than he already had but would have made

86. *Debates, quinto congreso,* 17 September 1870, 3:9.

the trial of the governor automatic. Nevertheless, the proposal contained the disadvantage that in any given case everyone would know who the next governor would be, thus reducing the grand jury trial to a gubernatorial election. The proposal was a step in the right direction, but Congress irresponsibly allowed it to die in committee, although fourteen states petitioned Congress to act on the initiative.[87]

The problem of generating a solution by precedent was that every case had its immediate political result and therefore its immediate opponents. The only workable solution was a process in which no one would know the outcome of the next step. Perhaps the best formula would have commenced with a state legislative accusation of a governor, followed automatically by a Supreme Court trial. In case of the governor's removal the president would nominate the interim replacement subject to congressional approval, as recommended in the Querétaro case and suggested by the Special Committee on Guerrero. The advantage would have been twofold. First, the impeachment of a governor might have been more impartially judged, because no one would have known who the interim governor would be. Secondly, all three branches of the federal government would have been involved in the process, with appropriate checks and balances. The process would have required a constitutional amendment, but a real solution might have emerged. As it turned out, only in 1874 upon the creation of a senate with authority to review the legal origins of local regimes, and its establishment in 1875, was the problem solved. The Senate, however, also became an instrument of executive will, and during the *Porfiriato* the Senate solution reduced all state regimes to presidential domination. It is certain that no solution to the problem emerged in time to save the Restored Republic before the tragic civil war of Tuxtepec.

A third conclusion of this examination concerns politics. By various means Juárez was instrumental in saving his best allies in the statehouses. The four cases demonstrate that the political system favored presidential power and that Juárez used that power to strengthen his political alliances. National military forces were in control of Querétaro, and military men sent by Juárez conducted the 1870 election by which Cervantes was returned to power. The decid-

87. Ibid., 3 October–14 December 1870, pp. 124–90 passim.

ing factors in 1870 in Guerrero and San Luis Potosí were that the federal army recognized the governments of Arce and Escobedo, while Congress debated the claims of Catalán and did not even review those of Francisco Zenco. Juárez skillfully used the military to neutralize the *caudillo* García in Campeche, while armed forces kept the peace in Jalisco to the benefit of Gómez Cuervo. Then Juárez deftly aided Camerena in replacing Gómez Cuervo, as he had aided Arce in replacing Alvarez and Jiménez, and aided Dondé in replacing Aznar. The Supreme Court headed by Lerdo de Tejada frustrated Congress when it tried to remove Gómez Cuervo, and Juárez simply ignored Congress when it ordered him to aid the Márquez government in Querétaro. In truth, the president held the power and Congress was ineffectual.

Two additional observations help place these events in wider dimension. First, the nation benefitted by the removal of Alvarez, Jiménez, and García. Jiménez later proved so inept as governor for Porfirio Díaz that Díaz replaced him with Alvarez. Probably the administration of Jalisco benefitted by substituting Jesús Camerena for Gómez Cuervo, and San Luis Potosí may have needed the rest and reconstruction provided by Escobedo. Apart from politics, an argument can therefore be made that Juárez served his country with vision. Second, it should be remembered that the cases examined here were not the only ones involving law, politics, and militarism during the Juárez administration; several others arose due to contentious elections. Juárez utilized armed force in Durango, Puebla, and Sinaloa without congressional approval in support of Francisco Gómez Palacio, Rafael García, and Domingo Rubí in 1868.

The final conclusion concerns the congressional debate and voting patterns of the Fifth Congress on the issue of whether units of the national army should intervene in state struggles to protect or remove a given political faction. It has been noted that a "test score" on eight political issues is calculated for each congressman to denote factional tendencies. Furthermore, the vote on ten questions of military intervention from the cases of factional struggle in the four states is recorded for each congressman vis-à-vis the presidential alliance, from which a so-called "federal score" is tabulated for each congressman. By statistical comparison of the two scores it is shown and explained in the appendixes that the positive correlation between the scores could have happened by chance in less than one time out of one hundred random samplings.[88] Therefore, although congressional debate was free and formulated into constitutional principles, and although the facts of each case allowed numerous interpretations about which state group was guilty of wrongdoing, a significant tendency existed for congressmen to cast their ballots on the issues according to which political faction on the national level would benefit from military intervention. It may be concluded that the elitist and frequently fraudulent elections, by which factions attempted to fill Congress with party loyalists, led directly to presidential domination of the state political regimes and dictatorship.

For the various reasons described in the foregoing chapters, Juárez came under severe attack during the months before his death in 1872. The nature of the attack, studied in chapter 6, is instructive for understanding the political system of the Restored Republic and the march toward national dictatorship in Mexico.

88. The descriptions of roll-call votes on the political issues are in appendix 6. The roll-call votes on all issues are recorded in appendix 7. The scores are in appendix 8, and the statistical analysis and explanation in appendix 9.

Chapter 6
Juárez under Attack

The first responsibility of every government, according to Lord Acton, is to survive. For the first three and a half decades following independence more executive figures tried to govern Mexico than there were years. Benito Juárez inherited the task in 1858 and died in office in 1872. In terms of survival, he was a successful politician. Because the ideological model of liberalism championed by his party had become by 1867 the common property of the political class, and because the model did not correspond to the realities of Mexico, survival depended upon a subtle blending of adherence to the model and violation of it. Whether Mexico needed Juárez so absolutely as to necessitate the violations can be debated, but it appears unlikely that closer adhesion to the model would have strengthened the government. The liberal model did not fit. Juárez knew that, modified the model, and survived. In the process he created enemies. He would have made enemies anyway, but the violation of the model gave ready arguments to his opposition.

This chapter concerns two major attacks upon Juárez during the last seventeen months of his life. The first one was a parliamentary combination mounted against his congressional party, and the second was a major military insurrection. An examination of them exposes a great deal about the real political practices of the day which the rhetoric of the model has confused. The same examination also explains some aspects of the rise of Porfirio Díaz.

The *Juarista* political alliance in 1871 was in disarray. Sebastián Lerdo de Tejada had served Juárez loyally since 1863, was aware of the discontent against Juárez, and apparently felt that he was the natural heir of the liberal alliance and of the liberal program and thus should succeed to the presidency in 1871. As a cabinet member after 1867, Lerdo had used much of his energies to create a faction of office holders loyal to himself, including the governors of Puebla, San Luis Potosí, Hidalgo, Morelos, Jalisco, and Guanajuato. There was also a group of about eighty *Lerdista* congressmen, some of whom expected to advance into the executive branch when Lerdo should become president. When it became clear to Lerdo that Juárez planned his own reelection, he resigned from the cabinet in January 1871 to prepare his personal electoral campaign.[1]

As it became clear that Juárez would seek reelection and that both Lerdo and Díaz would challenge him, the congressional *Lerdistas* joined the *Porfiristas* to overcome the *Juarista* plurality. Leaders of the two opposition parties confirmed the arrangement, known then and later as the *liga*, on the following bases: The two factions would cooperate upon a resolution to call extraordinary sessions of Congress in the spring of 1871, at which they would alternate the presidency of the Congress between them; they would seat the *Lerdista* municipal government (*ayuntamiento*) of Mexico City instead of a *Juarista* body, after double electoral colleges had created two separate municipal governments; they would recognize the Porfirian Vicente Jiménez government in Guerrero and vote to withdraw the federal forces supporting the Francisco Arce government; they would pass a bill for electoral liberty and another to end presidential declaration of states of seige, by which local elections were won by federal forces. The *liga* would also empower Congress to name the governor of the federal district, resolve the question of Querétaro, cut the administration's projected budget—particularly the "extraordinary funds" that the opposition always claimed were spent on elections—and name a second grand jury committee in order to handle the accusations against the members of the cabinet. Justo Benítez thought in early February that the arrangement was "probable."[2]

The *liga* was consummated, and extraordinary sessions were called which lasted from 6 March to 31 March, followed immediately by the preparatory meetings for the regular session and then the fourth and last period of the Fifth Congress. *Liga* politicians, commencing with the *Porfirista* M. M. Zamacona, chaired the sessions.[3] Juárez opened the extraordinary session on 10 March with a speech that accentuated the peace in the land—excepting Guerrero, he noted—and recom-

1. Knapp, *Lerdo*, p. 150; editorial comment of the day is recorded in Tamayo, *Juárez*, 15:7–11.
2. The *liga* is explained at length in two letters, Manuel Mendiolea to Díaz, 4 June 1871, APD, 9:159–60; and Zamacona to Díaz, June 1871, ibid., p. 146. In the latter, Zamacona claimed to be the author of the plan (p. 145). A list of *liga* priorities as of 8 April are read into a bill found in *Debates, quinto congreso*, 4:292. Benítez to Díaz, 11 February 1871, APD, 9:113–14.
3. *Debates, quinto congreso*, 4:2ff.

mended that Congress use its time to constitutionalize the Laws of the Reform of 1859–60. Zamacona interrupted Juárez's speech in less than five minutes, leaving the president in the middle of a sentence. Law and order were not the only questions of the day, Zamacona said, but also liberty. Congress was called into special session, he said, not to constitutionalize the Reform, for which there was no time, but to assure electoral liberty, which was being violated by some members of the administration.[4] It was the most insulting speech by a president of Congress to the national executive since the reestablishment of the republic, and it set the tone for the next three months.

Early on the congressional agenda was the task of examining the election returns of the rival electoral colleges for the municipal government of the capital city. The issue was important because the *ayuntamiento* of Mexico City would be in charge of registering voters and installing the officials of the polling places in the upcoming congressional and presidential elections. Zamacona turned the bill over to the First Committee on *Gobernación,* which itself had several members who had been electors in that contest.[5] *Juarista* Sánchez Azcona sponsored a bill for the creation of a new committee to study the recent *ayuntamiento* election, composed of unbiased individuals who had not been electors. Immediately, all the issues poured forth in a tangled and lively debate. Eleuterio Avila, *Porfirista,* maintained that the original committee was impartial. Juan José Baz, *Juarista,* called Avila's words sophism and called for a new committee. Agustín Fernández, *Lerdista,* noted that the object of the bill was to steal time from the *liga* freedom of suffrage bill. Baz charged that Fernández used *his* time defending *Lerdista* governors: Romero Vargas "who . . . has falsified the public vote in the elections of Puebla, . . . protecting in Jalisco the usurper Gómez Cuervo, in San Luis [Escobedo] who had assaulted power with bayonets, in Querétaro the governmental pretender . . . against the legitimate Cervantes. . . ." The Sánchez Azcona bill was eventually defeated by *liga* politicians, and the *liga* committee proposed to seat the *Lerdista ayuntamiento.*[6]

The norms of political practice and the interests of individual politicians are best revealed when politicians turn against each other. An outsider's exposé is rarely as complete or as devastating. In this

4. Ibid., pp. 4–6.
5. Ibid., p. 31.
6. Ibid., pp. 31–35, 72, 99.

case, as *Juaristas* and *Lerdistas* tore at each other over the bill to recognize the *Lerdista ayuntamiento,* they left a record of abuses of power scattered over three hundred pages of official transcript, appalling enough to make one wonder if any election was honest or any politician free from taint. Among the charges and countercharges were these: voting lists of factional adherents were drawn, and other men were denied ballots; the registration lists were not published at the time of the elections; the number of electors exceeded the legal limit from 383 to 500; some electoral credentials were not remitted to the electors in time to register at the college; credentials were given out by the secretary of *gobernación* to others than the electors; ballots were distributed to partisans at the door of the college by employees of the government; electors appeared from districts in which they had not been candidates; one group of electors bolted an electoral college to establish another, without the voting records they were to examine and count, but nevertheless announced the twenty-two winners of the municipal government. Furthermore, fifteen names on the protest of one of the colleges against the other were found duplicated, including five *Juarista* congressmen who were then present in the debates; fifteen other names were of persons without credentials—including two national congressmen (Francisco Mejía and Manuel Rojo)—and others signed for persons not present; the governor of the federal district (Otón Pérez, *Lerdista*) named employees to establish the *mesas,* did not have registration lists posted, and gave out twenty-one more credentials than the legal limit. Present in the debates were several men who figured as members of the current municipal government, others who had participated in one or the other electoral college, and yet others who were declared winners of one or the other college for the new municipal government of the capital city.[7] In short, what had apparently been an electoral free-for-all was now to be sorted out in parliamentary debate by the persons who had perpetuated the violence and who would be the beneficiaries of the decision.

On a straight *liga* vote the *Lerdista ayuntamiento* was declared the winner.[8] The resolution was sent to the president of the republic, who returned it on a technicality: he needed a law, rather than a resolu-

7. Ibid., pp. 99–382 passim, and Tiburcio Montiel to Díaz, 24 December 1870, APD, 9:76.

8. *Debates, quinto congreso,* 4:379.

tion, he claimed.[9] The *liga* majority insisted that the resolution sufficed. Some members of the old *ayuntamiento* refused to surrender their posts, even as the new government was levying fines upon them; a select group of the declared winners was called and established into a government, while the *Lerdista* governor of the federal district dissolved the old *Juarista* government.[10] Eventually, after Congress adjourned at the end of May, Juárez replaced the governor of the district with Dr. Gabino Bustamante, who suspended the *Lerdista* government with the accusation that it was preparing "to falsify the public vote in the coming elections" and ordered the old *Juarista* government to resume powers.[11] That was the body in charge of the summer presidential and congressional elections which Juárez won in 1871.

From the beginning of the extraordinary session the *Juaristas* sowed dissension and wasted time. *Juarista* congressmen claimed that the session was not legal until Congress was informed of the emergency that motivated the call, which could then have been debated and even put to a vote. The *liga* politicians opposed the ploy as a strategem of delay. The *Juaristas* nevertheless were able to place a number of time-consuming resolutions upon the floor. According to Zamacona, the administration "opposed the development of our plan with all the obstacles within the reach of their obtuse intelligence [of which] corruption was the principal [tool]. . . ." For example, the *Juaristas* shaved off a small group of *Porfiristas*, according to Zamacona, with the gambit of a ministerial post to Ignacio Ramírez.[12]

The bill that caused the greatest controversy was the Law of Free Suffrage of 8 May 1871.[13] Among its many provisions was one that required secret balloting when Congress conducted presidential, vice-presidential, or magistrational selections. The aim was to destroy the administration's influence upon congressmen. Another section of

9. Ibid., p. 382. The political crisis caused by the issue is discussed by Tamayo, *Juárez*, 15:149–51, and revealed in a letter from Castillo Velasco to Juárez of 29 April 1871, DDC, 15:168–71.

10. *Debates, quinto congreso,* 4:393.

11. Knapp, *Lerdo,* p. 155; proclamation of the *ayuntamiento* to the citizens of the district, 13 June 1871, DDC, 15:205–7.

12. Zamacona to Díaz, June 1871, APD, 9:147–50. Zamacona explains other *Juarista* maneuvers on p. 148 of the same source; the minister of *gobernación* suggests another ploy to Juárez in a letter of 20 April 1871 in DDC, 15:171.

the law drew up the scale of fines and prison sentences for electoral violations. The loss of civil rights and government employment rang down through the list of punishments for electoral abuses, including the abuses of bolting from an electoral college to establish another, failing to post lists of voters, falsifying credentials, stealing election documents, and disrupting voting booths or electoral colleges. The suspension or commutation of sentences by higher authority was specifically prohibited. An attempt was made to curb the influence of the political chiefs by giving their authority over the electoral colleges to commissions elected by the local *ayuntamientos*. The two sections of the law that came under greatest attack were those which restricted military activity on election days and which held higher public authorities responsible for electoral violations of subalterns.[14]

In a grand ploy to win the favor of the military, perhaps even to keep it active on election day, but certainly to convince military men that the administration's opposition was discriminating against them, Juárez sent the bill back to Congress, objecting to "the censure of the conduct of the army." He also objected to what he called the illegal placing of criminal responsibility on authorities for crimes committed by their subordinates, and to the states' loss of equal sovereignty occasioned by congressional secret ballot, which necessarily replaced voting by state delegation. Congress repassed the bill, which Juárez then sent to the governors with a public circular of protest, an action which was bound to cause public disrespect for Congress and perhaps even military repercussions.[15]

The specific Porfirian objective of the *liga* was to withdraw the federal forces which supported the Catalán-Arce government in Guerrero and to seat the government of Vicente Jiménez. We have seen in chapter 5 how that plan failed by one vote in Congress. Ma-

13. Mexico, *Diario Oficial, Recopilación de leyes, decretos, y providencias de los poderes legislativo y ejecutivo de la unión formada por la redacción del Diario Oficial* (Mexico: Imprenta del Gobierno en Palacio, 1873), 10:200 (hereafter *Leyes y decretos*); Dublán and Lozano, *Legislación Mexicana*, 6:495–98.

14. For those who have claimed that the *Porfiristas* never initiated a congressional reform to overcome an abuse of which they complained, note that the latter section of the law was presented as a Porfirian measure in December 1870 that never emerged from committee: *Debates, quinto congreso*, 3:631, 643–45, 661.

15. *Leyes y decretos*, 10:197–98; see also DDC, 15:173–78.

nuel Mendiolea explained the case to Díaz in a letter of early June. The *Lerdista* Núñez, he explained, voted with the *Juaristas*, nine of the eighty *Lerdista* congressmen abstained from the voting, and the Porfirian congressman García Guerra absented himself from the session. Mendiolea nevertheless praised the *Lerdista* leaders, Ramón Guzmán and Manuel Romero Rubio, for their Herculean efforts on behalf of the *liga*. He pointed out that the nine-vote *Lerdista* defection on the Guerrero vote was equal to the three defections out of twenty-seven *Porfirista* congressmen on the *ayuntamiento* vote—one-ninth in each case.[16]

Other *liga* initiatives included a bill to cease publishing the *Diario Oficial*, the executive's political mouthpiece printed at public expense. Another bill would have prohibited the president from declaring any state or part thereof in a "state of siege." Soon after, the *liga* politicians proposed a bill to empower Congress to name the governors of the federal district and the territory of Baja California, whom by existing law the president had appointed. On the following day they sponsored a constitutional amendment disallowing the immediate reelection of the president. None of these bills, however, ever came to a vote, for the *liga* ran into unexpected problems.[17]

The *Porfiristas* were internally divided in the summer of 1871. The thrust of Mendiolea's June letter to Díaz was to urge Díaz to rein in Justo Benítez, who was cooperating with *Juaristas* and attacking *Lerdista* governors in Puebla and San Luis Potosí. "We who reject the tyranny of Juárez and Lerdo," wrote Mendiolea, "cannot now accept the tyranny . . . of Benítez." Benítez, he said, by raising the issue of San Luis Potosí, aided the *Juaristas*, because insufficient time remained to examine the budget, and Congress would have to accept the executive version.

Benítez was also responsible for ruining the agreement with the *Lerdistas* for the "election" of eight or ten *Porfirista* congressmen in Puebla, two in Morelos, and five in San Luis. "Now our men in those states will have to compete with the other two parties that oppose us." Mendiolea said that the *Lerdista* leader Ramón Guzmán was even will-

16. Mendiolea to Díaz, 4 June 1871, APD, 9:159–60.
17. *Debates, quinto congreso*, 11 March 1871, 4:19; 8 April 1871, p. 284; 10 April 1871, p. 302; 11 April 1871, pp. 306, 416. Another form of the bill against the "state of siege" passed on 25 May. Tamayo, *Juárez*, 15:152.

ing to have the *Lerdistas* in Veracruz work for the *Porfirista* Luis Mier y Terán for governor and for Porfirian congressmen there in order to defeat the *Juaristas*, inasmuch as the *Lerdistas* had no candidate in that state. And "for the primary elections in this capital they [the then-installed *Lerdista ayuntamiento*] have named me as voting registrar, with the condition and conviction that in my section, which returns three electors, I would pull them from the *Porfirista* party." Mendiolea was not objecting to this criminal electoral manipulation, which he was ready to commit but which he would have condemned on the part of Juárez; rather he was angered at Benítez for scotching the arrangement by attacking *Lerdista* governors in Puebla and San Luis Potosí.[18]

Mendiolea was not alone. Zamacona, Avila, and Montes also disagreed with Benítez, and Francisco Carreón reported their "swinish conduct" to Díaz.[19] Zamacona sent his own letter to Díaz, recalling to Díaz the many services to the party that Zamacona had performed in the press and in Congress, and pointing out the differences in character and role between himself and Benítez. He told Díaz that José María Mata had organized Díaz's presidential campaign and that Benítez had opposed it. Zamacona unfortunately did not explain the details of Benítez's objections, but they were overcome and the *Porfiristas* together founded the newspaper *Mensajero* for the purposes of the election.[20]

The strategy developed by Zamcona was based on appraisals distinct from Benítez's. He foresaw that some of Lerdo's governors would fall from power after Lerdo left the ministry, as happened to Gómez Cuervo in Jalisco, pitting *Lerdistas* and *Juaristas* in the states against each other as "irreconcilable enemies." That would help the Porfirian party to pick up a larger congressional contingent for the Sixth Congress, which would be counting the presidential votes. Even then Zamacona was in contact with *Lerdistas* about places where the latter would cooperate with *Porfiristas* to defeat *Juarista* candidates.

18. Mendiolea to Díaz, 4 June 1871, APD, 9:161–62.
19. Carreón to Díaz, 8 June 1871, ibid., p. 166.
20. Zamacona to Díaz, June 1871, ibid., pp. 143–45; on *Mensajero's* support of Díaz's candidacy, see Justo Benítez to Díaz, 21 January 1871, ibid., p. 90, and DDC, 15:19–25. Walter V. Scholes wrote about the establishment of the *Mensajero* and its attacks upon Juárez in "*El Mensajero* and the Election of 1871 in Mexico," *Americas* 5, no.1 (July 1948): 61–67.

Ultimately, the *Lerdistas* in the Sixth Congress, after running third in the presidential race ("absolutely lacking a popular base"), would join the congressional *Porfiristas* to elevate Díaz to the presidency.[21] All of this depended upon a temporary alliance between *Porfiristas* and *Lerdistas*. Benítez, however, was sabotaging the *liga*.

Porfirian sabotage of the *liga* began early. The presidency of the Congress was held by a *Porfirista* in March and a *Lerdista* in April, with the vice-presidency in reverse fashion. *Porfiristas* were to receive the chair in May, but a number of *Porfiristas* voted with the *Juaristas*, elected a *Juarista* to the presidency, and received in return the vice-presidency—leaving the *Lerdistas* off the executive committee. That inspired Zamacona to call a caucus, which lasted three days. Zamacona warned that the only result of attacking *Lerdistas* in San Luis Potosí and Puebla would be to destroy the parliamentary majority, lose the question of the budget, and compromise the composition of the permanent deputation that would sit in for Congress after the recess in June. He said that *Lerdistas* were already closeted with Juan José Baz, *Juarista*, over electoral exchanges in Puebla. Zamacona warned that an attack of Governor Escobedo of San Luis Potosí could lead to a *Lerdista* rebellion, which would possibly throw the country in such turmoil that the year would end without elections, and Lerdo, as president of the Supreme Court, would step into the presidency. Zamacona said that Montes, Muñoz, Mata, Avila, Mendiolea, and Hermosillo spoke for this view at the caucus and that Tagle and Mirafuentes spoke against it. In the vote on whether to maintain the *liga*, only Pablo Herrera voted against, and Benítez abstained.[22] Benítez, apparently, had his own plan.

In order to implement his own plan Benítez held a meeting of a few *Porfirista* congressmen, at which it was decided that Benítez would approach the *Juaristas* for a joint attack upon Romero Vargas, *Lerdista* governor of Puebla. The *Juarista* congressman Juan José Baz filed the charge in Congress in mid-May. Baz explained that Romero had been accused in a Puebla court in November 1870 of having established a dictatorship, but the accuser was then in a Puebla prison for libel. Reaching out for his Porfirian allies he added that only that day the Porfirian newspaper *Padre Pastelito* was suppressed in Puebla and its

21. Zamacona to Díaz, (?) June 1871, APD, 9:146–47.
22. Ibid., pp. 151–52.

editor and pressman jailed: "This is the way Sr. Romero Vargas respects the guarantees." The *Juaristas* wanted a grand jury trial. The debate was complex and heated, with many technicalities thrust forth by a battery of experienced constitutional lawyers. Finally, on 22 May a motion to transfer the case from the Puebla court to Congress for a full grand jury trial on 27 May was defeated, eighty-four to seventy-six. *Porfiristas*, confused by the tactics and the inconsistent advice of their leaders, divided on the issue.[23] This affair must have influenced the Guerrero vote fourteen days later, in which nine *Lerdista* congressmen abstained.

After the Puebla affair not only the *liga* but the Porfirian congressional party fell apart. Zamacona resigned from the staff of *Mensajero*, and Congress bogged down on a constitutional battle over the rights of *amparo*, which was associated with the Puebla case and which devoured congressional time. The *Juaristas* won their budget and were then, according to Zamacona, "able to invest in the elections something like 700,000 pesos without having to report on its use until two years from now." Finally, in the selection of the permanent deputation, always performed on the last day of each session, León Guzmán for the *Lerdistas* offered sixteen of the twenty-nine seats to the *Porfiristas*. Benítez, however, then leading a sizable group of the *Porfiristas* and having commitments with the *Juaristas*, settled for roughly thirds from each party. The *Lerdistas* on the permanent deputation, apparently in a final bid to mend the alliance with the *Porfiristas*, offered the congressional presidency to the *Porfiristas* and a total domination of the offices for the *liga*. Benítez, however, led the Porfirian members in a combination with *Juaristas*, allowing the latter to dominate the offices, "giving important functions," Zamacona wrote to Díaz, "to the very efficient agents of reelection." "These maneuvers might have some political purpose," Zamacona lamented, "but it is so profound that I do not perceive it."[24]

23. *Debates, quinto congreso*, 4:630, 691–702.
24. Zamacona to Díaz, (?) June 1871, APD, 9:153–54; compare ibid, pp. 154–55 with Mendiolea to Díaz, 4 June 1871, ibid., p. 161. Zamacona then explained how the *Juaristas* were able to dominate the permanent deputation, "because they always have at their backs the resources of power and receive the aid and accessories that corruption makes available to them." *Porfiristas* voting to the end with the *Lerdistas* were Zamacona, Avila, Carballo, García

Mendiolea's letter of early June discloses the key to the division in the Porfirian party in the summer of 1871. In reality the party was made up of a legal element that favored an electoral victory by way of the *liga* and a military element that sought power by insurrection. Benítez belonged to the second group, an alliance which provided his motive for undermining the *liga*. Mendiolea paraphrased Benítez's thinking this way:

> accusing Escobedo [in San Luis Potosí] in whatever manner, and condemning Romero [in Puebla] however you want, we push the *Lerdistas* into rebellion, and when they find themselves thoroughly involved with the government, we blast our way in and finish off both parties.

Thus Benítez's strategy was to push the *Lerdistas* into rebellion first. The plan, as events showed, demonstrated a terrible misappraisal of Lerdo and the *Lerdistas*.

Mendiolea's criticism of Benítez's strategy was not that rebellion was wrong in itself but simply that to force the *Lerdistas* into rebellion was not a good Porfirian tactic: only one-fourth of the Porfirian party, he wrote, was loyal to Díaz; the three fourths were hangers-on. "They want to prosper, and only figure on our side because they believe it is the only party that can rebel successfully."

> But the moment they see Escobedo at the head of twelve thousand men, which *Lerdismo* can raise in San Luis, Guanajuato, Morelia, and Puebla, from then, I say, [the Porfirian hangers-on] will wait no longer; they will run to fatten the ranks and we will remain exposed, to become the victims of our own project, because once victorious they will not abandon their ranks to fight with us in search of a doubtful victory.[25]

The politics of the *liga* ran parallel to the election politics. *El Siglo XIX* led the electoral struggle for Lerdo, printing his platform in its

---

Trinidad, Garza y Garza, Hermosillo, Martínez Negrete, Mendiolea, Merino, Montes, Muñoz, Ordorica, Quintana, Rosas, Sánchez Atilano, San Román, Talancón, and Zenteno: ibid.

25. Mendiolea to Díaz, 4 June 1871, ibid., pp. 162–63. One can imagine that Benítez is talking about insurrection in his letter to Díaz of 15 May 1871, ibid., pp. 135–36. Probably the insurrectionary strategy was arranged when Díaz was in the capital during November 1870.

issue of 2 February.[26] Ignacio Altamirano in *El Correo de México* and
Manuel María Zamacona in *El Mensajero* championed Díaz. As long as
the *liga* was operative in Congress, *Porfiristas* used their newspaper
efforts to blacken Juárez rather than to attack *Lerdistas*. *El Mensajero* of
11 Janaury printed Díaz's program. It stressed the need to observe the
constitution, to respect individual guarantees, to assure freedom of
elections, and to protect the division between national and state governments. It attacked governmental corruption, swollen bureaucracy,
and military intervention in politics. It called for improving public
credit and proposed a complete amnesty for all Mexicans. Díaz accepted the *Mensajero* program and candidacy by letter, which was
published in the 28 January issue, but thereafter offered no leadership to the campaign being carried out in his name. Throughout the
spring of 1871 *El Mensajero* attacked the government in general and
Juárez and his cabinet in particular. Zamacona resigned from the
editorship on 31 May, replaced by Ignacio Ramírez, who claimed to
condemn insurrection but seemed to imply that one was merited.[27]
Meanwhile, the elections of June and July sank to lower than usual
levels of violence and fraud.

The vote in the electoral colleges was divided between the three
presidential candidates, denying any one of them the necessary
majority. The nation was therefore obliged to await the opening of
Congress, where the decision would be made between the two leading
candidates, Juárez and Díaz. Congressional returns, however, gave
the balance of power to *Lerdistas:* Ninety-eight *Juaristas,* sixty-two *Lerdistas,* and fifty-two *Porfiristas,* according to Ezequiel Montes, would sit
in the Sixth Congress to decide whether Juárez or Díaz would be the
next president. Montes calculated that Juárez would do anything to
win: "corruption and bribery will be the weapons of power, to be
wielded this fortnight to conquer the majority of Parliament." He
counseled Díaz to reconstruct a *Lerdista-Porfirista* "antireelection
league" to raise Díaz to the presidency and to establish a mixed
cabinet. Montes saw that the *Porfiristas* were divided, some wanting
electoral victory via a *liga* and others thirsting for total power by
insurrection. Montes knew that Benítez was the leader of the insurrec-

26. Knapp, *Lerdo,* p. 156.
27. Scholes, *"El Mensajero,"* pp. 61–67.

tionary strategy and claimed to believe he thought Díaz preferred the constitutional path. He urged Díaz to telegraph Benítez immediately, because the *liga* had to be formed by 1 September for the opening of Congress. "In a word," wrote Montes, "without the parliamentary league, the revolution will come, which will bring to our unfortunate country all manner of evil."[28] Montes was correct, but Díaz had decided upon insurrection.

Other politicians agreed with Montes's appraisal. Ramón Márquez Galindo wrote on 28 August that he had won a seat in Congress and was hastening to Mexico with other elected congressmen to talk with the *Lerdistas:* "By the notices I have, it seems to me that our friends in Mexico have not had the necessary tact to attract the *Lerdistas . . .*" which was imperative, for the alternative to the *liga* was *Juarismo* and revolution.[29] He was too late; the *Juarista-Lerdista* "fusion" had been consummated three days earlier.[30] Díaz was listening to the voices of war.

Porfirio Díaz had launched none of the insurrections prior to 1871, nor were any of them of *Porfirista* inspiration. Immediately after the elections of 1867 an insurrection broke out in the name of Díaz in the state of Hidalgo. The reasons given for the rebellion were Juárez's "ambition for perpetuating himself in power" and that "delirium of dictatorship [which] has occasioned an abusive atmosphere, winning the elections in various places with armed force. . . ."[31] The movement lasted seven months and spread into three states. Díaz did not figure in the revolt or communicate with the rebels, although at least three of the leaders later joined Porfirian insurrections: Jesús Betanzos, León Ugalde, and Ascensión Gómez. Another rebellion broke out in 1870 when a handful of colonels issued a *pronunciamiento* against the government of Juárez and called upon Díaz to assume the provisional presidency. One of the signers of the proclamation, Luis del Carmen Curiel, later became Díaz's private secretary; but Díaz was not behind the plan, nor did he support it.[32] A fairly extensive examination of

28. Montes to Díaz, 20 August 1871, ibid., pp. 251–54.
29. Galindo to Díaz, 28 August 1871, ibid., p. 266.
30. Unsigned letter to Díaz, 26 August 1871, ibid., p. 264.
31. *Plan de Picachos,* 7 October 1867, DDC, 13:334–35, 341–42.
32. *Plan de Jonacatepec,* 9 February 1870, ibid., 14:298.

Díaz's correspondence failed to turn up any evidence that Díaz supported any of the insurrections prior to La Noria.[33]
The insurrection of La Noria, however, was a Porfirian insurrection, and Díaz was planning it well before the presidential elections of 1871. The thesis that Díaz was "drafted" to give leadership to the numerous insurrections of the autumn of 1871 is attractive for the Porifiran interpretation of the Restored Republic: The nation was so outraged by the electoral corruption of that year that many rebellions were inevitable; Díaz was finally imposed upon to unify and lead them, and had he not done so he would simply have lost the leadership of the opposition to another general.[34] Díaz did receive much unsolicited correspondence during 1871 from men who offered their services if he would rebel.[35] The *Revista Universal* published an important letter dated 29 September, purportedly written to Díaz by gener-

33. Díaz was accused of several of them. For example, José Pantaleón Domínguez, governor of Chiapas, wrote Juárez that ex-governor Angel Albino Corzo was working for the separation of Veracruz, Oaxaca, Guerrero, Chiapas, Tabasco, and Yucatán from México to form a new Republic of the East, "whose president would be Porfirio Díaz" (15 December 1868, ibid., 13:694), but Díaz's archive demonstrates a different course of action: Corzo asked Díaz for Porfirian aid in Congress to accuse Governor Domínguez before a grand jury, to which Díaz answered that he would forward the request to Benítez, but expected no results, "because Domínguez . . . can count upon [the aid of] don Benito. . . .": Corzo to Díaz, May 1869, and answer, APD, 8:10–11. Corzo thereafter worked with Díaz for the electoral defeat of Juárez in 1871: Corzo to Díaz, 31 March 1871, CPD, 42:1661.

34. Bancroft, *History of Mexico*. 6:379; Rafael de Zayas Enríquez, *Porfirio Díaz* (New York: D. Appleton and Co., 1908), p. 103; José María Domínguez Castilla, *Ensayo crítico histórico sobre la revolución de la Noria* (Mexico: Casa Impresora el Cuadratín, 1934). p. 160, suggests that Gerónimo Treviño or Vicente Riva Palacio would have led the inevitable insurrection had Díaz not done so. Neither man, however, had either the national following or the capacity.

35. Epifanio Santomé to Díaz, 22 January 1871, APD, 9:94–95; Vicente Llorente y Alegre to Díaz, 29 April 1871, ibid., p. 133; Manuel Márquez to Díaz, 7 May 1871, ibid., p. 134; Placido Vega to Díaz, 24 May 1871, ibid., pp. 138–40; M. Gil to Díaz, 24 May 1871, ibid., p. 140; José María Díaz to P. Díaz, 7 June 1871, ibid., p. 165; Agapito García to Díaz, 18 June 1871, ibid., pp. 170–71; J. Antonio Blanco to Díaz, 3 July 1871, ibid., pp. 181–82 (see Díaz's answer to Blanco, pp. 182–83); Santiago Mauro to Díaz, 10 August 1871, ibid., pp. 236–37; Silvestre Hernández to Díaz, 12 August 1871, ibid., pp.

als Manuel Márquez, Donato Guerra, Gerónimo Treviño, Francisco Naranjo, Eulogio Parras, Luis Mier y Terán, Francisco Carrión, and Ramón Márquez Galindo, and colonels Lomelí, Borrego, Mena, and Fernando González, urging Díaz to rebel.[36] Nevertheless, we cannot know if there would have been an important insurrection without Díaz. What is certain is that the correspondence from the archives of Díaz and Gerónimo Treviño demonstrates without doubt that Díaz had been preparing insurrection since at least February.[37]

The Díaz brothers had been feeling out Treviño for some time. Once the *Juarista* machine had identified the Porfirian congressional opposition in the Fourth Congress and set out to defeat them in 1869, Díaz asked Treviño to find a safe district to return Justo Benítez from Nuevo León. Treviño answered that he could not do so, because the *pueblos* of Nuevo León "are accustomed to electing their representatives from among the citizens of their own kind, or at least among those they know. . . ." Díaz sought Treviño's support for the 1871 presidential election and Treviño told Díaz that he thought the whole north was sympathetic to Díaz but that everyone was too independent in the north to be led one way or another. Treviño then wrote to friends that, knowing they were completely independent and patriotic, he recommended Díaz to them and recommended that they

238–39; Romualdo Bervera to Díaz, 12 August 1871, ibid., p. 239; Miguel Tello to Díaz, 17 August 1871, and undated answer, ibid., p. 247.

36. *Revista Universal,* 14 December 1871, cited by Cosío Villegas, *La Noria,* pp. 89–90; he used the letter as the most probable origin of the *Plan de la Noria,* although it is unlikely that all those military men, scattered around the nation in 1871, co-authored or even universally saw the letter. Cosío argues convincingly that the letter is a more acute rendering of Mexico's problems than the plan turned out to be. The letter is reprinted in DDC, 15:358–60.

37. Documentation is abundant to demonstrate this in APD, vol. 9 and in AGNL, RGT, *caja D, expediente Porfirio Díaz, expediente Félix Díaz* and *caja N, expediente Francisco Naranjo.* Cosío Villegas uses a good sampling of it and of Paz, *Algunas campañas,* vol. 3, to prove the contention in *Porfirio Díaz en la revuelta de la Noria* (Mexico: Editorial Hermes, 1953), pp. 19–27. See also Bulnes, *Rectificaciones,* p. 261, and Carreño, APD, 10 *notas:* 8 Matías Romero pleaded with Díaz on 8 August 1871 not to revolt and hinted that Juárez might name him to a public post: APD, 9:234–35; see also Romero to Díaz, APD, 9:286–88 and 289–90, in which Romero mediates between Díaz and the government.

recommend Díaz to all the other independent and patriotic men "for the happiness of the nation."[38]

Díaz wrote again in late November of 1870 in a tone that may have referred only to the upcoming electoral battle, but the hint of military battle is also there. Díaz kept a formal distance, however; it was brother Félix who had the informal relationship with Treviño. Twice in May of 1871 Félix wrote to Treviño, first to sound him out on the subject of Juárez, and a week later this:

> Sr. Juárez has lost the little prestige that he had. . . . In spite of his . . . intrigue and money . . . no one, from the bureaucracy and the merchants to the last hobo, wants the reelection. . . . If Juárez insists on running . . . we will have to enter a "God is Christ" (a "knock-down-brawl").

Félix Díaz needed to be "entirely united with you so that the luck you and your friends run we will run too." He then explained his supply route from the United States and suggested he send a thousand rifles to Treviño: "tell me to which port to send them."[39]

Díaz was early committed to war; nevertheless, the insurrection of La Noria would have been of small account, like most of the others between 1867 and 1871, had not many of Juárez's enemies joined it. The workings of Mexican politics alienated individuals and political factions that felt locked out of office. During the insurrection of La Noria many of those individuals and factions took up arms in conjunction with the Plan of La Noria. The Porfirian newspaper *El Ferrocarril* wrote that "the victims of [governmental] power in the last four years are so numerous that it is not at all sure that they will sit back with arms folded if the revolution breaks out."[40] Díaz may have been as personally ambitious in 1871 as his detractors have always charged; but *Porfirismo* that year embraced many men who harbored their own grievances, some of which were sincere concerns for the republic, although most concerned local power. The point is that Díaz

38. Díaz to Treviño, 31 March 1869, and answer, AGNL, RGT, *caja D, expediente Porfirio Díaz*, 1144; minute, Treviño to Díaz, same to Isidro Triveño, 3 November 1870, ibid., 1145.

39. Díaz to Treviño, 25 November 1870, ibid., 1147; Félix Díaz to Treviño, 14 May 1871, RGNL, RGT, *caja D, expediente Félix Díaz*, 1138, 1139; see also 1140, 10 June 1871.

40. *El Ferrocarril*, 16 September 1871.

and the other rebels needed each other. This observation must stand out as more significant than that Díaz sought power by the sword that he failed to gain at the polls, or that Díaz was "drafted" for insurrection by the men who called themselves *Porfiristas.*

Attenuating the charge of Díaz's "ambition" is a letter from Díaz to Benítez two months earlier than the *Plan de la Noria* in which Díaz insisted that "although you will not like it" he would not issue the manifesto without specifically denying his own candidacy for at least four years. "Freedom of suffrage," he wrote, "is of great national interest that merits my entire sacrifice, but I want to do it free of all suspicion of personal advantage. . . ."[41] Thereafter the *Plan de la Noria* specifically stated that "a convention of three representatives from each state . . . will name a constitutional president, who for no reason can be the present leader of the war."[42]

Why General Treviño joined the rebels in the insurrection of La Noria is not immediately clear. He was not an "out" politician; he had been elected governor of Nuevo León in 1867 and again in 1869, and, although he and Juárez were not friends, he fought on the side of the government in the San Luis Potosí-Zacatecas rebellion of 1869–70. His complaints against Juárez's reelection in 1871 were ludicrous; he secured his own reelection in the same 1871 elections by applying pressure upon the legislature to declare his opponent ineligible after the popular vote for Treviño amounted to only 5,000 against 11,000 for his opponent.[43] It may be that the strenuous local rivalry in Nuevo León even played a part in this case, as in so many others in 1871. Sources used by Cosío Villegas indicate that opposition was mounting against Treviño's administration. Treviño may have feared that in the next general violence he would be turned out by his local rivals. Guessing that Juárez would be overthrown, Treviño "decided to be a revolutionary," "which could possibly open the way to the presidency of

41. Díaz to Benítez, 6 September 1871, APD, 9:282.
42. Ibid., 10:46. The implications here ring true to my understanding of Díaz's "ambition," which was always, I believe, combined with an overpowering desire to be considered a disinterested patriot and savior of the national institutions. That is, his ambition for a reputation as savior of Mexico was as strong as his ambition for power.
43. Santiago Roel, *Apuntes para la historia de Nuevo León*, 2 vols. (Monterrey: n.p., 1938), 2:62.

the Republic."[44] The Díaz brothers knew their man. Although Treviño held office, he never enjoyed governing. Treviño was first a
fighter, and he joined the fray.

The dynamics of the insurrection of La Noria proceeded along the
following lines. The insurrection was to commence sometime after the
congressional declaration of Juárez's victory. Félix Díaz, then governor of Oaxaca and until shortly before estranged from his brother
Porfirio, had used his office to accumulate forces and supplies. The
Plan de la Noria, however, was finally published by the state government of Oaxaca on 8 November. Apparently Díaz waited as long as
possible for the federal government to respond first to the northern
insurrections, which were declared in September and October, so that
he might take the forces of Oaxaca against the capital. That simple
plan was foiled by the government's refusal to be led astray.[45]

Díaz appealed to the federal soldiers to defect to the revolution and,
fortified by the defection from Tecamachalco of Pedro A. Galván with

44. Juan E. Guerra, cited in Cosío Villegas, *La Noria,* pp. 149–50. Juan
Guerra, brother of Donato, is a hostile source for Treviño; so is Cosío.
45. Cosío Villegas, *La Noria,* p. 168. Juárez knew at least by late March that
Félix Díaz was collecting forces and supplies (Joaquín Mauleón to Juárez, 29
March 1871, DDC, 15:122). In April the commander of rurales, Gen. Juan M.
Kampfner, warned Juárez that Negrete, Aureliano Rivera, Cosío Pontones,
and Jesús Toledo were conspiring (13 April 1871, DDC, 15:203–4), and Juárez
wrote the names of nine persons, including Negrete, whom he knew to be
communicating with Díaz, on the bottom of an intercepted letter from Plácido
Vega to Díaz (24 June 1871, DDC, 15:204–5). Rumor was rife of insurrection,
and even the newspapers spoke regularly of it all summer of 1871. Gen.
Manuel González, then commander of the palace guard, warned Díaz in July
that the government was preparing for an insurrection (22 July 1871, APD,
9:216). Carreño says that Juárez "probably" knew that Díaz was fabricating
munitions of war (APD, 10 notas: 6). Juárez did have that information (Ismael
Solares to Juárez, 9 August 1871, DDC, 15:229). The earliest good description
of Díaz's plans, complete with names and locations, that the author has found
among governmental papers, is a letter from Félix Barrón to Juárez (21
August 1871, DDC, 15:276) based on an intercepted letter from Justo Benítez
to Leonides Torres. See also Francisco Mont to Juárez, 3 October 1871, DDC,
15:280–81; Ismael Solares to Juárez, 16 October 1871, DDC, 15:363–64; Joa-
quin G. Heras to Juárez, 27 October 1871, DDC, 15:367–68; and José de Jesús
López to Juárez, 26 October 1871, DDC, 15:375, in which parts of Díaz's plans
are revealed.

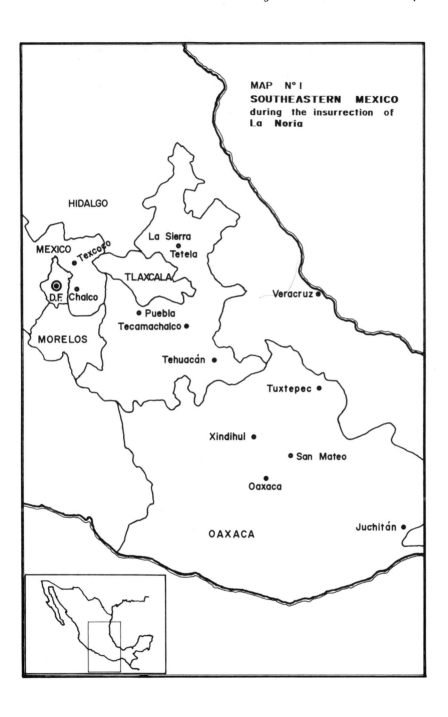

MAP N° I
SOUTHEASTERN MEXICO
during the insurrection of
La Noria

the fifteenth cavalry regiment, left Oaxaca with 1,000 cavalry to Tehuacán. There he apparently expected more defections, which were not forthcoming, and Alatorre slipped in behind him, cutting off his connection with Oaxaca. Juárez sent Gen. Sóstenes Rocha to Tehuacán, where Carlos Fuero commanded the reserves. Thus Díaz stood between Alatorre and Rocha.[46] Undaunted, Díaz led his men across southern Puebla through Morelos, entering the Valley of Mexico to Chalco and Texcoco, where he expected a general insurrection in the capital to rally to his cause. When it did not occur, he retired rapidly to the Sierra de Puebla to confer with the opposition *caudillos* Juan N. Méndez, Juan Crisótomo Bonilla, and Juan Francisco Lucas.[47] Without that opposition to Juárez in the Sierra de Puebla, Díaz might not have escaped Rocha's pursuit.

The Oaxacan campaign was a governmental success. Even as Díaz entered Tetela in the Sierra de Puebla on 22 December, the rebel forces in Oaxaca were beaten in the battle of San Mateo de Xindihuí. On 3 January 1872, Alatorre and Rocha entered Oaxaca, abandoned by Félix Díaz, who met his assassins in Juchitán near Tehuantepec.[48]

The insurrection in the north commenced earlier than in the south. Gen. Pedro Martínez pronounced in Galeana in late September; Treviño in Monterrey on 1 October; Donato Guerra three weeks later in Durango; Col. José Palacio rebelled in mid-November in Mazatlan, Sinaloa, carrying the federal garrison with him after a local rebellion failed. After a lengthy siege Saltillo fell to the rebels on 5 December. Pedro Martínez marched on San Luis Potosí; Trinidad García de la

46. Cosío Villegas, *La Noria,* pp. 126–34.

47. Domínguez Castillo claims that General Mejía ordered Rocha, then entering the Sierra de Puebla in pursuit of Díaz, to Oaxaca, where Alatorre needed no aid, in order to keep Rocha from being defeated in the Sierra; his argument is that Alatorre, who knew the Sierra as Rocha did not, had never been able to dominate the Sierra, even with Generals Cravioto and Rodríguez Bocardo. Had Rocha been beaten in the Sierra, Puebla would have fallen to the *caudillos* of the Sierra, there would have been no battle of La Bufa, Alatorre's connection with the capital would have been blocked, and the federal district would have been open to the *caudillos* of the north: Domínguez, *La Noria,* pp. 18–21, 172–79.

48. Battle report, Gen. Luis Mier y Terán to Félix Díaz, 26 December 1871, APD, 10:21–23; Bancroft, *History of Mexico,* 6:382; Domínguez, *La Noria,* pp. 27–28; Cosío Villegas, *La Noria,* pp. 134–46.

Cadena captured the capital of Zacatecas, as did Donato Guerra in Durango. As Gen. Sóstenes Rocha headed north with a new army organized in Mexico, the rebel leaders of the north gathered some seven to ten thousand soldiers in Zacatecas. At the battle of La Bufa on 2 March 1872 Rocha badly mauled and scattered the rebel concentration. The 1,000 casualties and prisoners suffered by the rebel forces, led that day by General Treviño, do not represent the total rebel losses, for the various insurrectionary leaders were only able to reorganize something like 2,000 of the former rebel army. Nevertheless, the battle of La Bufa was not decisive; it changed the nature of the northern war from massive encounters to a war of multiple centers and guerrilla tactics that harassed the government for months to come. Battles spread out across the north, leaning one way and another. Several of the most important cities of the north were occupied at least once, and some of them several times by rebel forces. We do not yet know to what extent the rebels controlled, or were supported in, the countryside.[49]

The death of Juárez in July, rather than the battle of La Bufa in March, was the decisive factor in the failure of La Noria. Juárez died of heart failure on 18 July, and Lerdo de Tejada as president of the Supreme Court became interim president on 19 July. Only a week later he called for presidential elections to be conducted on 13 and 27 October, thus destroying any fears that he might use a long interim presidency to prepare for his own election. On the same day Lerdo issued his celebrated amnesty.[50]

---

49. There is an unreal tone to the most recent and most complete account of the insurrection of La Noria, in which one rebel general after another is soundly whipped several times yet repeatedly reappears to threaten another attack or another concentration. One suspects that the interpretation suffers from the unfortunately few available sources upon which it is based, largely capital city newspapers and the official *Memoria* of the minister of war: Cosío Villegas, *La Noria*, especially chap. 5. Carreño argues that La Bufa was not definitive (APD, 10:*notas*, 28–33); Bancroft (*History of Mexico*, 6:384), Domínguez (*La Noria*, p. 35), and Riva Palacio (*Lerdo*, pp. 12–14) concur. Riva Palacio (*Lerdo*, p. 97) suggests that the political implication of the battle of La Bufa was that it ended the attempt of certain *Lerdista* agents to combine *Lerdismo* and *Porfirismo* against Juárez.

50. The amnesty, 27 July 1872, is reprinted in APD, 10:35, and in Riva Palacio, *Lerdo*, pp. 59–60.

Three basic reasons explain the failure of the rebellion of La Noria. First, the government was better supported than were the rebels. Although Díaz was widely admired and Juárez's reelection was widely regretted, relatively fewer men approved of insurrection and civil war as the method of redress. The rebel *caudillos* were able to recruit, but the government was more successful. The rebels acquired remarkable quantities of supplies, but the government, although sorely pressed, had access to more. The *Plan de la Noria* was a second rebel disadvantage: it was poorly framed and insulted the intelligence of thinking men. The complaints against the government—election irregularities, presidential coercion in the states, etc.—did not become the principal points of public debate. Rather, the proposed solutions, which were as unconstitutional as the alleged abuses of the president, were ridiculed by the governmental press and pondered apologetically by the Porfirian press.[51] Finally, there was an incredible lack of leadership in the rebel forces. Luis Mier y Terán was beaten at Xindihuí in a surprise attack. Félix Díaz abandoned Oaxaca without a fight, and the great stock of supplies there fell to the governmental forces. The northern leaders were hardly on speaking terms. Trinidad García de la Cadena and Donato Guerra were natural loners. Treviño was distrusted by everyone, particularly after the battle of La Bufa, from which the generals fled before their soldiers did. Pedro Martínez refused to work with Treviño, and Treviño distrusted Quiroga. No one supplied coordinated leadership to the score of rebel leaders in Veracruz, Puebla, Mexico, Morelos, and Michoacán. The least effective leader of all was Porfirio Díaz.

Díaz's leadership was faulty on all fronts. First, Díaz created no

51. Cosío Villegas, *La Noria,* pp. 100–112, and Riva Palacio, *Lerdo,* pp. 30–31. López-Portillo (*Porfirio Díaz,* pp. 83–84) and Domínguez (*La Noria,* p. 159) follow Paz (*Algunas campañas,* 3:55–81) in saying that the plan was written by Benítez, Zamacona, and Ignacio Ramírez. With perfect logic Cosío Villegas (*La Noria,* pp. 87–94) destroys that contention. As seen above, Zamacona disagreed with Benítez's plan of rebellion during the period when Paz claims that the plan was written, and Ramírez (Montes to Díaz, 20 August 1871, APD, 9:252) was counseling the tactic of the *liga.* Note also Zamacona's attempt in Congress to disassociate himself from armed rebellion: Mexico, Congreso, *Diario de los debates, sexto congreso constitucional de la unión,* 4 vols. (Mexico: Imprenta del Gobierno, 1872–74), 1:437 (hereafter *Debates, sexto congreso*).

system of communications.[52] For months at a time no one even knew where he was. Second, he was never at the right place. He might better have been at Xindihuí than in the Sierra de Puebla in December, but better in the Sierra in January to threaten a sally on Puebla or upon the captial to keep Rocha from heading north until the rebels had occupied more capitals than embarking at Veracruz. When he was needed at La Bufa in March, Díaz was entering Mexico from the United States on the northern Tamaulipas border. Leadership was then needed everywhere, but Díaz went to San Francisco, California. Almost anywhere would have been better than to go next to Jalisco, where Díaz had no party. Then instead of offering leadership to the forces fighting for him, such as in the Sierra de Puebla, Díaz appeared next in Tepic, at the court of Manuel Lozada, the *caudillo* most despised in all Mexico, whom Díaz unsuccessfully courted from early April to late July. All the while he communicated with virtually none of the men who could have contributed most to the insurrection if their efforts had been coordinated. It is hardly surprising that in August and September the *Porfiristas* accepted the amnesty and left Porfirio alone. It will be noticed—and was—that Porfirio Díaz participated in not one battle during the insurrection of La Noria.

Lack of leadership caused the congressional *liga* to fail in the summer of 1871, by which Díaz might have legally become president. In October, therefore, only three *Porfirista* congressmen voted for Díaz in the congressional runoff between Juárez and Díaz; three voted for Díaz, most abstained, and many of them voted for Juárez. Then again during La Noria, after having decided on military deployment for total victory, Porfirian leadership failed. The rebels then accepted amnesty, and Congress voted 150 to 3 to accept the resolution that the October 1872 elections had elevated Sebastián Lerdo de Tejada to the presidency.

The lessons of the *liga* and of La Noria were not lost on Lerdo or on Díaz. Many *Porfiristas* believed that Lerdo, after the death of Juárez, should have established a *Lerdista-Porfirista* coalition government, but the *liga* showed Lerdo that *Porfiristas* were neither united nor

52. An anonymous but acute document, written by a disgruntled *Porfirista* in June 1872, stresses this weakness of the rebellion: APD, 10:8–12.

trustworthy. La Noria demonstrated that the *Porfiristas* lacked leadership. The army had remained loyal to the government, which was everywhere controlled by *Juaristas*. Lerdo therefore chose to govern with *Juarismo*, an already established machine. On his part, Díaz heightened his distrust of Lerdo, of legislatures, and of elections, and, learning from his failures, perfected his insurrectionary strategy. Lerdo commenced a presidential term on 1 December 1872 which was to end on 30 November 1876. He came within ten days of completing it.

Chapter 7
The System of *Lerdismo*

Sebastián Lerdo de Tejada had received religious training in Puebla, where he received minor orders. Abandoning an ecclesiastical career, be began legal studies in Mexico, rising in an academic career to become rector of the College of San Ildefonso, which he directed from 1852 to 1863. He concurrently launched a career in public office, serving under President Santa Anna and joining the cabinet of President Ignacio Comonfort as minister of foreign relations. After the Three Years' War Lerdo figured in Congress, where he distinguished himself as an orator. When the French armies approached Mexico City in 1863, he left Mexico with Juárez as the "permanent delegate from Congress." Soon he joined Juárez's cabinet as minister of justice, then minister of foreign relations and minister of government *(gobernación)*. During the incredibly difficult period of the French occupation Lerdo's duties were to persuade foreign governments to recognize the Juárez government of the Republic of Mexico rather than Maximilian's Mexican Empire and to negotiate with nearly independent *caudillos* for contributions to the starved republican treasury and for armies against the French. In 1867 when the Republicans returned victoriously to Mexico City, Lerdo enjoyed a national reputation as one of the "Triumvirate of the North," Juárez, Lerdo, and José María Iglesias.

In retrospect it is surprising how universal was the belief among Mexican political classes that the ascension of Lerdo de Tejada to the presidency would signify change. Conservatives could believe that replacing the Indian president with a cultured, intellectual creole of clerical training would somehow elevate and dignify government and blunt the anticlericalism that was associated with Juárez. Men who thought Juárez had moved too slowly for economic growth could hope for more vigor and energy from the Lerdo administration. Some men claimed to believe that the death of Juárez would mean the passing of an era and the healing of old wounds. Many others anticipated the opening of governmental posts. Others were simply happy that the presidential succession transpired legally and ended a civil war rather than signaling a new one. Lerdo entered office with overwhelming good will and near universal anticipation of change.[1] That was not to be the case: The administration of Lerdo was the natural extension of that of Juárez.

The manner in which Lerdo handled the question of patronage is one measure of continuity from the Juárez administration. He announced that he was the national president, not the head of a given party, and would name men to appointive office by merit, taking into consideration the present employees.[2] Politicians of that day were astounded that Lerdo kept Juárez's administrative team. They expected Lerdo to name a new cabinet drawn from the *Lerdista* contingent in Congress, from his supporters in the presidential campaign of 1871, and from the journalists who had promoted him against Juárez and Díaz. Many of those men thought he was obliged to compose a new administration from those elements. When he did not do so during his interim presidency, it was thought he would do so after the October election or after assuming the constitutional presidency in December. Even the members of the Juárez cabinet whom he inherited expected to step down to Lerdo's new appointees and duly sent their resignations to him.[3] Lerdo, however, retained the ministers appointed by Juárez and did not even fill posts left vacant by resignation and death until seven weeks before his downfall.

Lerdo's biographer, Frank Knapp, speculates upon Lerdo's motives and collects contemporary opinions about Lerdo's patronage policy: Lerdo loved mystery; he was capricious; he harbored a misplaced

1. Knapp, *Lerdo*, pp. 159–60, 164–66; Cosío Villegas, *El porfiriato*, 1:249, and "Lerdo," p. 181; Riva Palacio, *Lerdo*, pp. 45, 55, 84–85; Emilio Ordaz, *La cuestión presidencial* (Mexico: Imprenta de Francisco Díaz de León, 1876), p. 13.

2. Knapp, *Lerdo*, p. 161.

3. Riva Palacio, *Lerdo*, pp. 47–53; Cosmes, *Historia general de Méjico*, 22:356–60, 366–67. Francisco Mejía, Juárez's final minister of treasury, wrote in his memoirs of his attempt to resign to Lerdo, telling him, "I was your political enemy, particularly during the final election of Sr. Juárez . . . when I divided the electoral college of San Ildefonso, carrying half of the electors to the Circo de Charini where the double election was made that congress approved." Lerdo answered, according to Mejía, "I know all that . . . but why did you undertake those tasks?" Mejía: "*Señor*, for my loyalty and love for Sr. Juárez. . . ." Lerdo: "Very well, I applaud those good and deserving qualities; I am sure you will have them by my side. I do not accept your resignation and implore you to stay with me" (Mejía, *Memorias*, p. 129).

sense of independence that motivated him to denigrate his ministers; he wanted to elevate the presidency by downgrading the cabinet; he wanted to destroy the governmental theory of parliamentary rule; he had worked with those men as a member of Juárez's cabinet; he knew that satisfying the political aspirations of some men would alienate other men with equal aspirations; he wished to terminate the practice of political spoils.[4] Some, perhaps all except the last of these explanations contributed to his decision, but the analysis of politics of the Restored Republic proffered in this study suggests a much more practical reason for retaining the *Juaristas:* the government of the nation was an alliance of incumbents who supported the system in return for executive support of their own political longevity. That alliance was *Juarista:* the great majority of governors, political chiefs, legislators, judges, military men, and bureaucrats had a vested interest in no change in governmental personnel. Lerdo did not need to build a *Lerdista* machine for political stability; he had inherited the *Juarista* machine.

The same political analysis should be given to Lerdo's first major act as interim president—the amnesty of 27 July 1872. Vicente Riva Palacio, a *Porfirista* who wrote an open letter to Díaz after the amnesty was published urging Díaz to lay down his arms for the peace of the nation, later wrote in 1875 that Lerdo should have constructed a coalition government of *Lerdistas* and *Porfiristas*—the two factions that had opposed Juárez's reelection in 1871.[5] Cosío Villegas asserts that Riva Palacio wanted into that coalition government, that he had written the open letter to demonstrate that he was a moderate *Porfirista,* eligible for Lerdo's coalition government, and that his disappointment explains why he turned his talented pen against Lerdo.[6] Porfirian accounts of the amnesty stress its humiliating aspects—the loss of rank, decorations, and credits upon the treasury. They note that

4. Knapp, *Lerdo,* pp. 176–78.
5. Riva Palacio, *Lerdo,* pp. 98–99; Riva Palacio argues that *Lerdistas* until the battle of La Bufa supported the war against Juárez: ibid., pp. 206–25.
6. Cosío Villegas, "Lerdo," p. 180. When Riva Palacio lost his congressional race, he expected to become the president of the Supreme Court. *El Imparcial* counted twenty-five newspapers for José María Iglesias, 9 for Porfirio Díaz, and thirty-nine for Riva Palacio: 20 February 1873. Knapp assumes that Lerdo swung his electoral machine behind Iglesias: *Lerdo,* p. 199.

Lerdo alienated the *Porfiristas* by treating them as rebels rather than embracing them as saviors of the republican institutions against *Juarista* "tyranny." In retrospect the amnesty appeared to some observers to be Lerdo's first political mistake as president—the first of a series of mistakes that by 1876 drove the *Porfiristas* to rebellion.[7]

By my analysis of politics in the Restored Republic the amnesty was a political masterpiece. Lerdo gained two objectives that were more important in national politics than was friendship in 1872 with the *Porfiristas*. He had first to bring the war to a close. The amnesty immediately divided the men who opposed Juárez's reelection from those who sought to elevate Díaz to the presidency. It isolated the latter group, contributed to their discredit, and accomplished the early pacification of the nation.[8] Second, the amnesty left public office in the possession of the incumbents, an act which, while alienating the discredited and broken *Porfiristas*, gained for Lerdo the confidence of the *Juaristas*, who in mid-1872 held the majority of the governorships, the plurality in Congress, the great majority of bureaucratic positions, and the military commands that would not have to be shared with *Porfiristas*. The amnesty thus sealed the *Lerdista-Juarista* alliance in support of Lerdo's administration until mid-1876. The amnesty makes perfect sense when the government of Mexico is viewed as a political machine.

This explanation has not been entirely overlooked. Knapp affirmed that Lerdo desired to retain the backing of the *Juaristas;* and García Granados, among guesses and contradictions, ventured that "maybe Lerdo attempted to attract the *Juaristas* who predominated in congress."[9] The most complete and accurate statement is that of Daniel Cosío Villegas, who affirmed that Lerdo kept the *Juarista* cabinet "because Lerdo upon entering the presidency found himself lacking support of his own." His analysis is that

> the dominant strength of *Juarismo* was exercised mainly in the governments of the states, the essential lever of the electoral machinery, which in grand measure decided the elections of the

7. Riva Palacio, *Lerdo,* pp. 46–47; Paz, *Algunas campañas,* 3:333; Cosmes, *Historia general de Méjico,* 22:129, 371–72; Zayas Enríquez, *Porfirio Díaz,* pp. 109–12.

8. *Porfirista* acceptance of the amnesty is described in appendix 10.

9. Knapp, *Lerdo,* p. 177; García Granados, *Historia de México,* 1:71.

federal congressmen, the justices of the [Supreme] Court and in the final instance the president of the republic.

So certain is this appraisal that Cosío Villegas is probably also correct in speculating that civil war might have erupted if Lerdo had called the *Porfiristas* to his side, because the *Juarista* governors would not have acquiesced. "But in any case, Lerdo would have remained with no support at all."[10]

The continuity of the Lerdo administration with the Juárez administration related to policy as well as personnel. This is not surprising, considering that Lerdo had been a guiding figure in Juárez's administration. Frank Knapp outlines the policies of the Lerdo administration—peace, respect for law and for the principles of the Reform, a national presidency rather than factional leadership, laissez-faire economics, and centralization of power in a strong, independent president.[11] This statement, however, contains a contradiction between "the principles of the Reform" on the one hand and the "national presidency" and "centralization of power" on the other. The politics and militarism of the Restored Republic only become clear if it is recognized that executive centralism gradually expanded and finally replaced the "principles of the Reform," that is, replaced the spirit of the liberal republican model.

The replacement of the liberal republican model with executive centralism commenced with Juárez, as has been seen, because the model did not work. Lerdo continued the policy. Frank Knapp wrote that "Lerdo, . . . centralist to the core, attempting to spread the tentacles of the national government underneath the attachment to localism, . . . managed to carry the presidency to its furthest point of

10. Cosío Villegas, "Lerdo," pp. 183–84; thereafter Cosío Villegas says that Lerdo commenced to replace *Juarista* governors with men "personally loyal to himself"; however, "he did not accomplish it, and succumbed." Lerdo's political procedure was to merge the *Juarista* and *Lerdista* elements wherever possible, removing any governor—*Juarista, Porfirista,* or independent—whom he did not trust. Whatever the shortcomings of the above statement of Cosío Villegas, it serves as a better analysis of the politics of the Restored Republic than his one-thousand page book on the subject, which unfortunately adopts the thesis that Lerdo's government succumbed in 1876 because of the bastard ambitions of Porfirio Díaz and the treacherous defections. *República restaurada,* pp. 107, 805.

11. Knapp, *Lerdo,* pp. 167–70.

advance under the Constitution of 1857."[12] "Localism" is a rather picturesque word for what Lerdo was attempting to undermine. The two most serious rebellions after 1867 had been the San Luis Potosí-Zacatecas rebellion of 1869–70 and the rebellion of La Noria of 1871–72; they had been serious precisely because they had enjoyed the support of state governors. As long as the real problems of the Restored Republic remained unsolved—economic depression and unemployment—then political realities demanded centralization of power to safeguard the resources of state governments from the hands of possible rebels. Partisans of Lerdo's faction held the governorships in Durango, Guanajuato, Hidalgo, Michoacan, State of Mexico, Morelos, Puebla, San Luis Potosí, and Veracruz. Most of the remaining governors were *Juaristas.* This explains why Lerdo, already head of the *Lerdista* faction, made important gestures to unite *Lerdismo* with *Juarismo.*

Another aspect of executive centralism was presidential control of Congress. Juárez suffered from a strong opposition faction in Congress but generally maintained his majority. Lerdo, by fusing *Juaristas* and *Lerdistas* in Congress, easily outweighed the *Porfirista* and independent minority, particularly as the Porfirian leadership during the 1871 election year placed more emphasis upon preparing for insurrection than for electoral victory—and had fewer governors returning Porfirian delegations in 1871 than in 1869. Congressional opposition was dilatory and outspoken in the Sixth and Seventh congresses but was unable to cause Lerdo serious problems. Congress accepted Lerdo's leadership in constitutionalizing the laws of the Reform in 1873 and passed the enabling acts the next year. It conferred extraordinary powers upon Lerdo when he petitioned for them and even weakened itself at his insistence by creating a Senate as a second branch of Congress. The small rebellion in Congress in April 1873 had no important repercussions: it attempted in the budget to censor his spending for political purposes.[13]

The most important step during the Lerdo administration for the creation of executive centralism was the addition of the Senate to governmental machinery. The attempt to establish a Senate had a persistent history. It was one of the five constitutional reforms postu-

12. Ibid., p. 170.
13. Riva Palacio, *Lerdo,* p. 155.

lated in the *convocatoria* of 1867, which friend and foe alike laid to Lerdo's inspiration. Juárez consistently requested Congress to consider the matter but met no success. The *Lerdistas* in Congress sponsored a Senate bill again in 1873, which finally obtained the necessary two-thirds approval in April 1874. By the fall of 1874 the necessary majority of state governments had ratified the amendment and the Senate was created by law in November 1874. Its first membership was chosen during the summer elections of 1875, and it first convened in September 1875, four months before the insurrection of Tuxtepec broke out. Interestingly, the Plan of Tuxtepec made only one small mention of the Senate, which Díaz used for the greatest centralist development yet seen in independent Mexico.

Three essential elements of the Senate contributed to executive domination of the political system. First, the Senate provided fifty well-paid sinecures to be distributed among hand-picked partisans whom the president could indicate to obedient governors "for popular election." Second and more important, the Senate would serve as a veto upon the more turbulent chamber of deputies without openly demonstrating the controlling hand of the president. The third element was the most consequential in the development of a full presidential system: the Senate was empowered to intervene in state conflicts, thus finally solving the constitutional dilemma of federalism and state sovereignty that had troubled the Restored Republic with local civil wars and uncertain federal intervention. The Senate was empowered to authorize the president to appoint a provisional governor to call new elections when in its opinion the state executive and legislative powers had "disappeared." It was further authorized to resolve those state conflicts between legislative and gubernatorial powers upon the appeal of either one of them, or without such appeal in cases of armed conflict, again by authorizing the president to install an interim governor. Such interim governors, later supported by the federal army, arranged the results of the sponsored elections.[14]

Full presidential control of the political system ultimately required executive control of the press. Governmental control of the press was an element of the executive system that did not develop during the

14. The political implications of the Senate are fully exposed in Knapp's discussion of it (*Lerdo,* pp. 189–91), and in García Granados, *Historia de México,* 1:110.

Restored Republic. This fact has led historians to two conclusions. First, an essential difference existed between the Restored Republic, which was republican as evidenced by the freedom of the press, and the later *Porfiriato,* which was a dictatorship as evidenced by the persecution of the opposition press.[15] The second conclusion drawn by historians who have used the press to study the Restored Republic is that it was a powerful force in overthrowing the Lerdo administration.[16] Juárez and Lerdo, by respecting freedom of the press, provided a convenient weapon to the opposition for attacking the incumbent administration. Freedom of the press during the Restored Republic meant the right and practice of every political faction to distort and even to invent news, to libel at will, and to promote rebellious activity against the established government in the most open manner.[17] One of the most active newsmen of the period observed later in 1882 that "the liberty of the press [in 1876] was not restricted, and proceeded to the extreme in its violences."[18]

The press in the late Restored Republic was a world of factional papers, subsidized by individuals with political careers for the promotion of those careers and by vested interests for the protection of those interests. *El Federalista* was *Lerdista* in 1876 and for the next two years. *El Siglo XIX, Lerdista* until 1873, became an anti-*Lerdista* paper that supported the rebellion of 1876 by ridiculing governmental efforts to contain the rebellion and by exaggerating rebel victories, doubting government releases, and daily predicting doom. *La Revista Universal* had been *Lerdista* since Lerdo's opposition to Juárez. In mid-1876 it was abandoned by several of its writers, including Justo Sierra, Gui-

15. For example, Beals, *Porfirio Díaz,* pp. 268–73; Ralph Roeder, *Hacia el México moderno, Porfirio Díaz,* 2 vols. (Mexico: Fondo de Cultura Económico, 1973), 1:337; the press enjoyed freedom in Díaz's first administration: Cosío Villegas, *El porfiriato,* pp. 208–9.

16. On the press of 1876 Knapp says: "Ironically, the freedom of the press, by his [Lerdo's] standards one of the brightest jewels of his presidency, transformed itself into a monster which turned upon its patron. In time the press became a potent instrument of revolution and another of the principal causes of Lerdo's eventual downfall." *Lerdo,* p. 223.

17. For the sustained press attack on Lerdo see ibid., pp. 223–33; for the press harshness against Lerdo after his fall see Cosío Villegas, *El porfiriato,* 1:194–208.

18. Altamirano, *Política de México,* p. 182.

llermo Prieto, and Francisco Bulnes, all *Iglesistas* in 1876, and went out of business three days after the battle of Tecoac. *El Bién Público,* edited by Congressman Eduardo Garay, was *Iglesista,* as was *Two Republics,* Mexico City's English newspaper. *La Legalidad* began publication in 1876 by Porfirian partisans. The *Monitor Republicano* was anti-*Lerdista* and frequently *Porfirista. El Combate,* later directed by Gen. Sóstenes Rocha and known for its aggressive anticlericalism, began in January 1876 as an anti-*Lerdista* paper. *La Voz de México* was the voice not of Mexico but of the Catholic church, which supported the *Cristero* Rebellion during 1875–76. *El Pajaro Verde* and *El Pensamiento Católico* were also conservative, and all three attacked the Lerdo government.

The official organ of government, printed in the National Palace and subsidized by law, was the *Diario Oficial.* It printed what was useful to the government, less obviously using the tactics of sneer and smear that the others regularly employed. Other government papers existed also, by virtue of having sold a favorable editorial policy for subsidies or political favors to the papers' owners. The opposition press regularly accused the government of subsidizing *El Eco de Ambos Mundos, La Tribuna, Correo del Comercio,* and *Porvenir.* [19] More blatantly in violation of truth were those papers of the satirical press.

The satirical press in 1876 was in its heyday.[20] More than twenty satirical publications began their careers in Mexico City during that year. The more famous of the *Porfirista* satirical sheets were *El Ahuizote,* published by Vicente Riva Palacio, *El Padre Cobos* by Ireneo Paz, *La Metralla, El Jicote, La Orquesta, La Hoja Eléctrica,* and from Guadalajara *Juan Panadero.* Short-lived and short in length, these papers were hostile, libelous, and frequently seditious. Their tools of trade were

19. Writing favorably for the government, according to an editorial in the opposition newspaper, *Monitor Republicano,* had its recompense in elections. It noted that Darío Balandrano, editor of *Diario Oficial,* had been elected to the Senate and that editors of *Siglo XIX,* Julio Zarate, Juan A. Mateos, and Hilarión Frías y Soto, had been elected congressmen. It also named two editors of *El Eco,* one from *Correo del Comercio,* one from *El Federalista,* and four from *Revista Universal* who were elected congressmen, while José María Vigil, editor of *Porvenir,* "will be elected" to the Supreme Court. He was. *Monitor Republicano,* 15 July 1875, p. 3.

20. B. Dean Cary, "The Role of the Satirical Press in the Downfall of Sebastián Lerdo de Tejada," (unpublished paper, University of the Americas Archive, Cholula, Puebla).

biting wit, ridicule, open insult, and character assassination. Lerdo and his cabinet were accused of gluttony, licentiousness, indolence, hypocrisy, sloth, womanishness, and stupidity. They held that opposition to his government was patriotic and that open rebellion was heroic. As evidence of hypocrisy and cynicism they compared Lerdo's antireelectionist campaign of 1871 with his reelectionism of 1876. They recommended boycotting the July election and after the election played upon the theme of fraud. They generally applauded the work of Díaz and interpreted all efforts of Lerdo to crush the rebellion as the tyrant's methods of oppressing the people. The self-appraisal of *Ahuizote*'s mission, appearing in its final issue in December, serves well to describe much of the satirical press:

> No one can dispute its merits; it was the first to combat, and combat energetically, the administration of D. Sebastián Lerdo; it carried on a fruitful propaganda of defamation of that government, covering it with ridicule [and] working for the interests of the revolution until it saw its success consummated.[21]

Opposition factions used the press to vent their rage and even to see their local problems as part of a national problem of monopolized incumbency. As such, the press worked to some degree to unite "out factions" and in 1876 helped Porfirio Díaz to formulate his alliance, a development which Lerdo apparently depreciated but which Díaz later understood and prevented by a restricted press. Nevertheless, it is believed here that the press of the Restored Republic was a symptom of the factionalism and alienation of the Restored Republic rather than a major factor causing them. The economic conditions, not the press, created the basic discontent, and the political system, not the press, created the alienated factions.

Although most of the issues raised in the press were fraudulent, being mere weapons for factional warfare, one rings through with a degree of sincerity. That issue was referred to by all as "reelectionism." The elections of 1876 were crucial to the events of that year. They were the reason and justification for both the Porfirian revolt and the Iglesias revolt. Because the *Porfiristas* revolted six months before the elections took place, the political commentators of the time and the historians since have claimed that the rebellion was entirely

21. *El Ahizote*, 29 December 1876, cited in Cary, ibid., p. 21.

personalist and without principle.[22] This may or may not be the case with Díaz himself, and that is not important. The insurrection of Tuxtepec was an alliance of local "out" factions and was intimately related to *no-reeleccionismo.*

Nineteenth-century liberals looked for various means to prevent dictatorship and convert the process of succession from insurrection to election. During the first quarter-century of independence the liberal panacea was "federalism," partially based on the Jacobin notion that human liberty was guaranteed by local government, but also based on the observation of the times that strong state government frustrated the practice of national politicians to control elections in all localities. When the radicals came to power during the period of the Reform, they wrote into the Constitution of 1857 the concepts of state sovereignty, universal suffrage, and free elections. Doing so, they overlooked two realities of Mexican life, that governors and local officials could also build machines for monopolistic control and political longevity and that liberal presidents would work alliances with such governors for mutual security in sustaining their public careers. In the decade of the Restored Republic a new panacea arose to obtain the same ends.

The new panacea of the Restored Republic was "no-reelection." It was thought that if reelection were absolutely prohibited, politicians would not use the power of office to remain in office, candidates would appeal to the people instead of to arms, suffrage would become effective, rebellions would cease, and government would become responsive. These arguments were voiced in 1867, again in 1871, and more universally in 1876. In all three elections the presidential incumbent was running for reelection, Juárez in 1867 and 1871, and Lerdo in 1876. Therefore, principle and political opposition to the

22. "The base metal of personalism of the Rebellion of Tuxtepec glittered in the eyes of everyone": Cosío Villegas, *República restaurada,* p. 805; "None with any degree of enlightenment should have been deceived that [Díaz] was other than a typical barracks leader. . . .": Knapp, *Lerdo,* p. 236; "At bottom the Plan was nothing; sympathy for the *caudillo* . . . was everything": Quevedo y Zubieta, *El caudillo,* p. 232; "The document is nothing more than a political trick, a gambit, a magnificent artifice for the attempt to vault into power. . . .": Ceballos, *Aurora y ocaso,* 2:432; the plan was a pretext, a cover for ambition: José López-Portillo y Rojas, *La elevación y caída de Porfirio Díaz* (Mexico: Librería Española, 1920), p. 110.

incumbents coincided, and many who merely sought office masked themselves behind the principle of no-reelection. Nevertheless, the principle itself grew more popular during these years[23]—so popular that Díaz, once in office, worked the formula into the constitution and duly stepped down in 1880, as did Manuel González in 1884. During the process of amending the constitution to prohibit reelection in 1878 the *Monitor Tuxtepecano* expressed the general optimism: the no-reelection principle, it declared, was a "conquest" of the *Tuxtepecanos*, a "triumph for democracy" which would make Mexico great, and "a theory that will plant the holy seed in the other republics of the world that should terminate dictatorship."[24]

The *Porfiristas* were early associated with antireelectionism. The *Porfirista* Vicente Llorente was hoping in 1871 that the congressional *liga* would legislate no-reelection. A Porfirian *liga* politician in that year proposed a constitutional amendment for no immediate reelection of the president. The *Plan de La Noria* specified no immediate reelection of the president. In Díaz's circular, written in Chihuahua in September 1872, one of his stipulations for laying down arms and accepting Lerdo's amnesty was a presidential initiative to Congress for no-reelection.[25]

The *Porfiristas* were anti-reelectionists in 1876. Article 2 of the Plan of Tuxtepec stated that "No-Reelection of the president of the Republic and governors of the States . . . will have . . . the character of supreme law." In this way Díaz was associated with the radical liberalism of his day, by promising the panacean reform in a country in which it was already believed that the elections of 1876 would be fraudulent. Díaz later changed his politics and became the major practicioner of reelectionism in Mexican history, but in 1876, whatever Díaz thought personally, *Porfirismo* was associated with antireelectionism—and was so associated long before José María Iglesias pronounced against the government of Lerdo de Tejada.

In his "Program of Government," issued in Salamanca, Guanajuato,

23. Various states adopted the no-reelection formula for governors during the Lerdo regime: Riva Palacio, *Lerdo,* pp. 284, 298.

24. 11 April 1876, cited by Cosío Villegas, *El porfiriato,* 1:193.

25. Vicente Llorente y Alegre to Díaz, 29 April 1871, APD, 9:133; *Debates, quinto congreso,* 10 April 1871, 4:302; *Plan de la Noria,* APD, 10:47; Riva Palacio, *Lerdo,* p. 75.

in late October 1876, José María Iglesias stated the same liberal belief, that "the principle of no-reelection has become an imperative necessity among us. . . . When hope for renovation is lost, revolution breaks forth as the only means of obtaining it." Iglesias therefore promised that his government would propose a constitutional amendment against reelection of the president.[26] We shall see that Iglesias had another panacea to insure free elections.

The aspect of the elections of 1876 that has attracted the most historiographic comment is Lerdo's motive for conducting them in the face of so many disadvantages and for trying to impose the results upon an incredulous Mexico. He had alternatives. He might have postponed elections to a time free from insurrection, announcing his intention to surrender his post to the legal successor as interim president upon the expiration of his term on 30 November. Or he might have imposed his chosen successor upon the nation by those elections of 1876, which presumably would have taken the anti-reelectionist winds from the sails of the rebellion.[27] Even having held those elections and seeing that they were immensely unpopular, he might have declared them void and then proceeded with the first alternative. That Lerdo chose none of these has been variously explained: Lerdo was vain, he looked about for a candidate, but "Lerdo saw no other candidate than Lerdo";[28] he wished not to step down while the country was at war;[29] his sycophants convinced him of his indispensability.[30] These explanations, however, overlook the logic of the politics of the Restored Republic.

Emilio Velasco editorialized in *El Siglo XIX* that the most popular idea in 1876 was to defer the elections to the following year, turning over the presidential office to the president of the Supreme Court, José María Iglesias, on 1 December. The historian Francisco Cosmes, himself an *Iglesista* in 1876, later wrote that the plan was superb, for Iglesias's known honesty would have guaranteed a free election in

26. *"Programa de gobierno del presidente interino constitucional de la república mexicana,"* 28 October 1876, reprinted in Iglesias, *Cuestión presidencial,* pp. 412–13.
27. García Naranjo, *Porfirio Díaz,* p. 190.
28. Cosío Villegas, "Lerdo," p. 172.
29. Knapp, *Lerdo,* pp. 235–36; Iglesias, *Cuestión presidencial,* p. 21.
30. García Granados, *Historia de México,* 1:102.

1877 and would have deflated the rebellion. Furthermore, he added, Díaz would have won that election.[31] Here is the answer to the question of why Lerdo rejected that plan: he did not want Iglesias in the interim presidency and certainly not Díaz in the presidency.

The most obvious reason for the reelection is overlooked. Lerdo had a program to develop; he had built a party machine to keep him in power; he liked the position; he thought in June and July of 1876, the period of the elections, that he would crush the Porfirian rebellion and with it the remainder of his opposition; and he full well meant to be president at least for the next four years.[32]

Lerdo also believed the conventional liberal wisdom that the prosperity of the nation required political stability rather than, for example, land reform, governmental operation of the mining industry, and some form of guaranteeing economic opportunity. He believed that political stability demanded executive centralism and a monolithic political machine. To allow power to fractionalize in an open election was to spiral Mexico into civil war, destruction, perhaps territorial division or foreign intervention. To avoid those evils, an alliance of governors, which was greatly advanced by late 1875, had been painfully constructed. Those authors who later accused Díaz of rebellion before Lerdo even announced his intention to seek reelection have ignored what all politicians of the Restored Republic knew: the *Porfiristas* had no real chance for electoral success in 1876. "In regard to the *Porfiristas*," wrote Altamirano in the 1880s, "as no other road was open to them but revolution, they prepared themselves for it at the end of 1875."[33]

That Lerdo used presidential power to subordinate regional authorities and to construct his executive alliance with governors figured prominently in the complaints of the Porfirian *pronunciamiento* in 1876. There the accusation was made "that the sovereignty of the states has been repeatedly violated; that the president and his favorites arbitrarily dismiss the governors, giving the states to their friends,

31. Cosmes, *Historia general de Méjico*, 22:772–74.

32. Cosío Villegas ("Lerdo," p. 171) ponders, but does not answer, why Lerdo, after opposing Juárez's reelection in 1871 and becoming president in 1872, did not add the no-reelection principle to the Constitution. The answer is the same: Lerdo planned to be president a long time.

33. Altamirano, *Política de México*, pp. 193–94.

as has happened in Coahuila, Oaxaca, Yucatán and Nuevo León, and as they attempted to do in Jalisco . . . with offense to the Federal Pact. . . ."[34] Essentially the charge was true. It was a carefully conceived and systematically applied procedure for the very necessary business of denying the base of power to potential rebels. An examination of three cases mentioned in the Plan of Tuxtepec demonstrates this.

The Oaxacan case to which the *Porfirista pronunciamiento* of 1876 refers is explained by the state historian Jorge Fernando Iturribarría in this manner. Upon the flight of Félix Díaz in December 1871 and the occupation of the state capital by the forces of Ignacio Alatorre and Sóstenes Rocha, Juárez named Miguel Castro as interim governor. Castro had been a friend of Juárez, and the interim administration of 1872–74 was composed entirely of *Juaristas.* However, by the time of the scheduled state elections of 1874, the *Juarista* group had divided. José Esperón led the group that was identified with Lerdo and that captured nine of the sixteen seats in the local legislature. To offset Esperón the *Castristas* absorbed old Porfirian elements. In order to remove Castro from office the Esperón group then accused him of unlawfully usurping legislative powers. Both groups stooped to legal maneuvers for political ends, involving local and federal courts until the case landed in Congress upon the petition of the *Esperonistas* for federal intervention. The *Lerdistas* in Congress sponsored a bill in favor of federal intervention on the basis of Castro's abuse of power in overriding the legislative majority in Oaxaca, while the congressional opposition, mainly *Porfirista,* argued in favor of Oaxacan sovereignty in internal matters. The bill carried in October 1873, and Lerdo ordered his minister of war to send Gen. Ignacio Alatorre of the Second Division with troops to Oaxaca. Castro was forced to resign, and after several days of political jockeying José Esperón occupied the governor's chair as interim governor. Iturribarría concludes with the observation that "General Alatorre returned to Mexico, leaving the way open to the aspirations of Esperón, President Lerdo's candidate, to neutralize the presidential pretentions of General Porfirio Díaz" in the coming elections of 1876.[35]

34. APD, 12:96–97.
35. Jorge Fernando Iturribarría, *Historia de Oaxaca,* 4 vols. (Oaxaca: Publicaciones del Gobierno del Estado, 1935–56), 4:132–37; Riva Palacio, *Lerdo,*

These were the events about which the *Porfiristas* complained in the press of the day and to which they referred in the Plan of Tuxtepec in 1876. They were correct that the *Lerdistas* on the national level used federal power to assure a friendly governor, and it is equally certain that Castro was doing everything in his power to bring about conditions favorable to his own reelection in 1876, including electioneering for General Díaz. Such was the way that politics was played during the Restored Republic and for many years thereafter. Interestingly, it became significant for all later Mexican history that two of the casualties of Castro's fall from power in 1874 were the *caciques* of Ixtlán, Fidencio Hernández and Francisco Meijueiro, who had fought against Félix Díaz in 1871 and had occupied Oaxaca with Generals Alatorre and Rocha. In Esperón's drive to bring the state under his total domination, as almost all governors tried to do, he virtually drove Hernández and Meijueiro to rebellion in January 1876; consequently Oaxaca became the base from which Díaz overthrew Lerdo's government later in the year.

Nuevo León was another of the states mentioned in the Plan of Tuxtepec where President Lerdo was accused of having interfered in state politics in order to obtain a governor amenable to his reelection. The man who emerged with the greatest military reputation from the war of the Reform and French Intervention in Nuevo León was Gen. Gerónimo Treviño. Juárez had appointed Lic. Manuel L. Gómez as governor, and Gómez conducted the elections of that year. Gómez was a fair man without ambition. He did not want the governorship himself and urged Juárez to allow Treviño to resign his military commission to run for governor because he was the most popular man in the state and to deny him access to the governorship would threaten the peace. Running against Treviño was Simón de la Garza y Melo and Gen. Lázaro Garza Ayala, both of whom led opposition factions during the decade of the Restored Republic.[36] Treviño won

pp. 420–22; Genaro Olguín in 1874 led one group of *Oaxaqueños* in a movement to elect Díaz to the governorship: *Manifiesto de Silacayoapan*, 6 December 1874, PDP, box 9.

36. Garza Melo and Garza Ayala apparently were enemies also; as president of the state legislature in 1871 Garza Melo tried to arraign Garza Ayala for a crime and thus remove him from the state supreme court: *Periódico oficial . . . de Nuevo León*, 10 June 1871, pp. 1, 4.

the election of 1867, developed a sure hold over the state, and secured his reelection in 1869 and again in 1871. In 1871 the state legislature declared Treviño reelected with 5,000 votes by nullifying the 11,000 of his opponent, who was Simón de la Garza y Melo.

Treviño took part in much of the warfare of the Restored Republic. He fought for the government in the insurrection of San Luis Potosí-Zacatecas, beating Pedro Martínez at Charco Escondido when that rebel leader appeared in Nuevo León with the insurrectionary remnants after the battle of Lo de Ovedo. Thereafter, Treviño joined the *Porfiristas* in the insurrection of La Noria. During the rebellion Treviño's interim governor, Genaro Garza García, was evicted from Monterrey by federal forces, and Juárez appointed General Garza Ayala as governor and military commander. Upon the death of Juárez, Treviño accepted Lerdo's amnesty and reentered Monterrey arm in arm with General Rocha. Lerdo then passed over both the *Juarista* Garza Ayala and the *Porfirista* Treviño, appointing a compromise governor, Narciso Dávila.[37] Dávila held the elections which left Treviño out of power.

The state was politically unstable and racked with factionalism during the Lerdo administration. There were a number of factions and a series of governors—Dr. José Eleuterio González in 1872, Lic. Ramón Treviño in 1873, Dr. González again in 1874, Ramón Treviño and Lic. Francisco González Doria in 1875. A scandal of some importance took place in June 1875 that seems to have been the prelude to the *estado de sitio* of September that year. Elections were held in June for municipal officers of Monterrey and for the state and federal legislatures. Gen. Carlos Fuero had recently become the commanding officer of the federal forces stationed in Monterrey under direct orders of General Escobedo, Lerdo's protégé. To what extent the soldiers under Fuero's command tried to influence the elections is not clear. Fuero denied political intervention, claiming that his troops were patrolling the city to maintain the peace, but three separate reports of *mesa* officials, printed in the official newspaper of the state in Monterrey on the following days, recorded concrete instances of

37. The Treviño papers indicate that Narciso Dávila was earlier a close friend and collaborator of Treviño. AGNL, RGT, *caja D, expediente Narciso Dávila-1867*, 991–94. Davila became Lerdo's man in Nuevo León by the mid 1870s, as will be seen.

intervention which resulted in their having to close their polling place. The interim governor, González Doria, protested against federal intervention, and the state legislature sent an official protest to Lerdo and declared the elections null.[38]

A lacuna exists in all the sources for September 1875. Francisco González Doria, Treviño's partisan, was interim governor. Santiago Roel's history of Nuevo León holds that Lerdo wished to take advantage of the fact that all the generals in Nuevo León were out of power and anxious to return. "Pedro Martínez," he says, "in accord with Fuero (the governmental general not being unaware of that plan) pronounced against the authority of the state, succeeding in raising guerrilla forces in Galeana, Linares, Monte-Morelos, etc., which threatened to march on Monterrey. ..."[39] At that point González Doría officially sought federal aid. General Fuero, without consulting authorities and exceeding the powers of a military officer, declared the "state of siege" and wired Mexico City. Lerdo, using his extraordinary faculties, covered up the precipitous action of his general by officially declaring Nuevo León in a "state of siege."[40] Fuero then dismissed González Doria and issued a declaration to the people of the state that if other politicians had abused their power during elections, "for my part . . . I solemnly declare that I will be the first to respect the sacred electoral right. . . ."[41] No elections, however, took place. Instead, Fuero replaced the authorities of the state, naming Treviño's enemy, Trinidad de la Garza y Melo, first to the state court and then to the position of secretary of government.[42]

The following events blended into the insurrection of Tuxtepec. Generals Treviño and Naranjo pronounced against the state authorities and recognized the Plan of Tuxtepec, fighting thereafter with Díaz. Generals Carlos Fuero, Garza Ayala, Pedro Martínez, and Julián Quiroga fought for Lerdo. Fuero in 1876 named Garza Ayala

38. *Periódico Oficial . . . de Nuevo León,* 16 June 1875, p. 2; ibid., 9 June 1875, p. 1; AGNL, *Ramo Circulares 1875,* 11 June 1875.

39. Roel, *Nuevo León,* 2:77; the parenthetical statement appears in the source.

40. Ibid.; Ceballos (*Aurora y ocaso,* 2:423) agrees. Fuero's decree is in AGNL, *Ramo Circulares 1875,* 15 September 1875.

41. Proclamation of General Fuero, 23 September 1875, Ceballos, *Aurora y ocaso,* 2:421.

42. AGNL, *Ramo Circulares 1875,* 4 October 1875, 16 October 1875.

military commander and Narciso Dávila interim governor.[43] Both men were *Lerdistas;* González Doria did not recover his governorship. With the victory of the *Tuxtepecanos* Treviño seized power in Nuevo León, and both Garza Ayala and Narciso Dávila went into exile in the United States for a number of years.

Several problems are apparent with this account of the events of 1875. We cannot know that Carlos Fuero was ordered to declare the "state of siege" in order to assure Lerdo's reelection.[44] Supposedly the immediate threat in Nuevo León was an insurrection led by Pedro Martínez, but Martínez thereafter supported Lerdo under Escobedo and Fuero. The official newspaper of Nuevo León was earlier involved in a running battle with two independent papers in Monterrey, *El Imparcial* and *El Mequetrefe,* the latter of which was apparently edited by General Garza Ayala. Those opposition papers have not survived, but the *Periódico Oficial* was definitely the organ of the state administration and was frequently anti-Lerdo; its comments to *El Mequetrefe* indicate that the latter newspaper was pro-Lerdo and decidedly opposed to the government of González Doria.[45] Roel's history, as seen above, is sketchy on these events, although he believes that Fuero was somehow involved in the insurrection that he then used as pretext for the "state of siege."

Furthermore, Fuero's first act as military governor was to replace the secretary of *gobierno* with Trinidad de los Garza y Melo, an enemy of Treviño, who commenced to change the various local *alcaldes* (Nuevo León's equivilant of the *jefe político,* although there were some *jefes políticos* also) and ordered the new *alcaldes* to form auxiliary forces.[46] There is definite room for belief that Lerdo was behind the events in Nuevo León, and it is easy to understand that the *Porfiristas* believed he was. Treviño would have seen to that. Out of power after 1872, Treviño played an important role in Díaz's climb to the

43. Decree of Carlos Fuero, 13 June 1876, ibid., *Ramo Circulares 1876.*

44. A year earlier Lerdo named Carlos Fuero to be interim governor to hold the elections in Coahuila by which the anti-*Lerdista* governor Zepeda was replaced by a *Lerdista* governor: Riva Palacio, *Lerdo,* pp. 288–403 passim.

45. *El periódico oficial . . . de Nuevo León,* especially 6, 12, 20, 27 January 1875. Available in the *Biblioteca Alfonso Reyes,* Monterrey, this paper has a lacuna from 21 July 1875 to January 1877; it apparently was not published.

46. AGNL, *Ramo de Alcaldes Primeros, caja García 1875–1885;* ibid., *caja Gral. Bravo 1873–1876;* ibid., *caja China 1873–1877.*

presidency and thereafter in the national life of Mexico for many years.

The state of Jalisco is also mentioned in the Porfirian *pronunciamiento* of Tuxtepec, but as a state where Lerdo only "attempted" to replace the public officials with *Leridstas*. The "attempt" thereafter was realized: the *pronunciamiento* was written in December 1875, it was publicly proclaimed in January 1876, and Lerdo removed the governor of Jalisco in February 1876. In brief, the events proceeded in the following manner.

After Juárez helped replace Gómez Cuervo with Jesús Camarena in time for the presidential elections of 1871, Camarena replaced all the *Cuervistas* in the state, even the employees of the public school system, who ran to San Luis Potosí for the protection of the *Lerdista* governor, Mariano Escobedo. General Corona took charge of the 1871 election for Juárez. Lerdo's earlier antagonist in the Juárez cabinet, Ignacio Luis Vallarta, was chosen as the gubernatorial candidate and supported by the Camarena government. The elections were violent, and Vallarta was proclaimed the winner.[47]

After the death of Juárez the anti-Vallarta elements in Jalisco supported Lerdo and set out to topple the Vallarta government. The *Vallartistas*, however, supported Lerdo, and the state returned to tranquillity.[48] Then in 1873 the *caudillo* of Tepic, Manuel Lozada, invaded Jalisco, and Lerdo ordered a federal military campaign against Lozada. Lerdo thereafter refused to rejoin the canton of Tepic to the state of Jalisco, and the "Tepic question" became an emotional issue in Jaliscan politics. Vallarta opposed Lerdo's policy of retaining Tepic as a federal military territory, and the enemies of the Vallarta government rallied around Alfonso Lancaster Jones, becoming a *Lerdista* party for the 1873 congressional elections. The *Vallartistas*, controlling all the *municipios* of the state, returned a large anti-Lerdo contingent to the national Seventh Congress. That was the election, according to Pérez Verdía, in which the double election made its debut in Jalisco. Congress accepted the credentials of the

---

47. This sketch of Jalisco is drawn from Pérez Verdia, *Jalisco,* 3:451–56; Lerdo and Vallarta were bitter political enemies: Knapp, *Lerdo,* p. 131.

48. Pérez Verdía, *Jalisco,* 3:476–77.

men from the *Lerdista* electoral colleges.[49] The legislature of Jalisco, dominated by *Vallartistas*, denounced three of the *Lerdista* congressmen as not representing the people of the state, but Congress did nothing about the complaint. Factionalism mounted considerably until December 1873, when Vallarta was accused before Congress of denying a republican form of government in Jalisco.[50]

The gubernatorial elections of 1874 further exacerbated local factionalism. Vallarta supported the candidacy of Jesús Camarena, who won amid widespread cries of fraudulent counting of votes. Factionalism mounted as Camarena pressed for the return of Tepic to Jalisco and entered crisis proportions in early 1875 when General José Ceballos, the *Lerdista* general who had led the federal campaign against Lozada in Tepic, took command of the Fourth Division in Guadalajara, capital of Jalisco. Ceballos aided the enemies of Camarena, and the federal forces became involved in the mid-year congressional elections. Double elections resulted in contested credentials.[51] That was the election referred to by the Porfirian *Plan de Tuxtepec*. After its issue the conditions in Jalisco became yet more fraught with danger.

Elections for the state legislature were held in December 1875, and the two parties entered the fray with determination. Double elections created two legislatures, one recognized by the Camarena government and the other sustained by the Fourth Division. Federal soldiers and state troops vied for strategic places in the state capital and clashed with arms during the days of tense crisis in early February 1876. At that point Gen. Donato Guerra rebelled on 7 February in favor of the Porfirian Plan of Tuxtepec, and Ceballos declared a "state of siege." He removed Camarena and all the state and municipal authorities, and the state entered the civil war of Tuxtepec under the command of Gen. José Ceballos, governor and military commander.[52]

49. Riva Palacio claims that Congress accepted the false credentials of Sabás Lomelí "from an electoral college in Tototlan, which was not a district seat" over the credentials of Alfonso Azco and accepted those of Alfonso L. Jones, signed in the *hacienda* of La Trasquila, over those of J. M. de Jesús Hernández, which were legally signed by the electoral college in Atotonilco: *Lerdo,* pp. 390–91.

50. Pérez Verdía, *Jalisco,* 3:501–4.

51. Ibid., pp. 506–13.

This account of the events of the 1870s in Jalisco, in which state authorities intervened in every election, demonstrates the thesis that republican liberalism did not prevail in the states and that if the president did not intervene in state elections, the faction of the governor dominated. In either case, the concept of popular sovereignty was a legal fiction. Lerdo was undoubtedly involved in the local dispute in Jalisco, as the *Porfiristas* correctly charged as justification for insurrection, but his abstention would merely have denied the resources of Jalisco to the national government in case of a grave insurrection, or even have contributed to rebellious forces, as Oaxacan resources during the governship of Félix Díaz and those of Nuevo León under Treviño entered the list against Juárez in 1871.

In none of these cases is the *Lerdista* hand in state controversies absolutely proved. But the tendency is seen in the results. Beyond those governors cooperating with Lerdo in 1872, governors favorable to the *Lerdista* machine by 1876 had emerged in Zacatecas, Coahuila, Yucatan, Oaxaca, Nuevo León, and Jalisco. Whether *Lerdista* intervention in state politics helped cause the civil war of Tuxtepec, or on the other hand his abstention would have merely aided his enemies to overthrow his government with greater ease than they did, is impossible to judge. Given the level of monopolization of power and opportunity in the states, the rivalry for that monopolization, and the importance of gubernatorial cooperation for the national executive, it is clear that a president had to centralize power and control state governments. Juárez and Lerdo attempted to do so in the 1870s, and Porfirio Díaz did so in later years.[53]

Lerdo's reactions to the insurrection of Tuxtepec were time-honored. Armies were sent to rebellious areas, arrests were made of suspicious persons, and extraordinary powers were sought and duly authorized. The "state of siege" was regularly declared in state after

52. Ibid., pp. 515–20.

53. For *Lerdista* intervention in Yucatan see Acereto, *Enciclopedia yucatanese,* 3:330–31, and Riva Palacio, *Lerdo,* pp. 399–404, 412–13, 422–23; Cosmes investigates or repeats all the accusations that Lerdo interfered in state politics to secure governors favorable to his government and inevitably finds Lerdo guilty: *Historia general de Méjico,* particularly vol. 22; Knapp finds the charges true also: *Lerdo,* pp. 181–84.

state in which rebel activities grew large or persistent, forced loans and extraordinary taxes augmented normal governmental revenues, and the ranks were filled by forced recruiting as former troop levels became inadequate. The opposition charged that official "tyranny" threatened civil rights. In retrospect, it can be seen that civil rights were no more harshly treated in 1876 than is normal in reaction to rebellion. Not even the forced loans and levy were unusual. Although a few newspaper editors were arrested early in the year, at least the arrest of Ireneo Paz was warranted by self-admitted revolutionary activity; and even he was released to exile.[54] Censorship of the press was only resorted to as late as October, after a full year of astonishing abuse.[55]

The government of Sebastián Lerdo de Tejada fell in November 1876 because the many factions and individuals in numerous local areas, which had been alienated by the monopolistic hold of a national political machine upon the public offices of the nation, were welded into a successful insurrectionary alliance by Porfirio Díaz. The emphasis must be laid, however, upon the individual motives and the individual prizes to be won in numerous local rebellions.

The conclusions for the first part of this study should now be simple and clear. The political rhetoric of the Restored Republic emerged from the liberal model, not from political practice. The practice was distinct from the model because imported liberalism did not conform to the realities of Mexico or solve the obvious economic stagnation, lack of opportunity, rural misery, unemployment, and insecurity. What opportunity was available was monopolized at local or state

54. Paz complained bitterly in his memoirs about his arrest but explained in detail his own conspiratorial efforts in the preparation for the Insurrection of Tuxtepec: *Algunas campañas,* vol. 3, chaps. 36–42.

55. Dublán and Lozano, *Legislación mexicana,* 13:86–87. The decree made this accurate statement by way of justification: "The press was serving as an organ of the revolution. It was publishing the plans, pronouncements, and illegal decrees of the enemy. . . . The press released the real or feigned movements of the military operations of the enemy; it revealed to the enemy the movements of our troops, their numbers, and their equipment; it was publishing false triumphs of the rebels and false defeats of the government troops; it was exaggerating the number of the enemy and diminishing those of the government."

levels, fanning intense local rivalry. The many local rivalries in turn threatened the liberal view, accepted by Juárez and Lerdo, that prosperity would flow from political stability. Certainly the personal positions of national politicians were threatened by the ability of opposition governors to control congressional and presidential elections in their states. Therefore, Juárez and Lerdo adopted and advanced a policy of executive centralism to control the whole political system by using presidential power to support cooperative governors and replace uncooperative ones. Presidents and governors shared the interest of staying in office, which aided the process of creating collaborative relations—a political machine by which they all retained office.

Executive centralism, however, alienated individuals and factions who attacked the incumbent government for their own economic and career interests. They cited the same political rhetoric as the power-wielders, but if they obtained office and planned to stay, they used the same successful tactics of machine politics used by former enemies. The major factor of instability was that the system could neither satisfy the aspirations of a large class of potential leaders nor solve the basic social and economic problems of the nation. Those whose aspirations were blocked could appeal to the liberal model and correctly accuse the men in power of abusing the model to remain in power. In this manner, by 1876 the men of the political class who were barred from the benefits of office were sufficiently large to challenge the incumbents. The result was the civil war of Tuxtepec, led by Porfirio Díaz, experienced rebel of La Noria, and his numerous allies of the many factions that operated in the various states against the *Lerdista* machine.

The nature of that warfare—the strategy (tactics and logistics) and the politics (militarism and finances)—are the subjects of part two of this study. Who participated and why they did so is now clear. How Díaz emerged as the sole national leader in a political arena of many potential leaders, to a leadership role which he retained and wielded for the greater part of thirty-four years, is examined in the chapters that follow.

Part 2

Chapter 8
The Call to Arms

Having lost on the political terrain, the military wing of the Porfirian alliance rebelled in January 1876 by the Plan of Tuxtepec. Like the insurrection of La Noria, that of Tuxtepec commenced in the northeast, but unlike the earlier one, Porfirio Díaz led the northern insurrection in 1876.

The usual historical analysis of those events is simply that nothing of importance happened there. That General Díaz launched his personal campaign in that region, crossing the international frontier from Brownsville to Matamoros, is well known. His strategy, however, has attracted little comment, with infrequent appraisals ranging from the hostile interpretation that Díaz removed himself from the matrix of the rebellion to observe its incubation from a safe distance to the more general belief that Díaz hoped to raise the north against the government, occupy the major northern cities, and march upon the capital from that direction.

The historical questions focusing on 1876 have concerned Díaz's morality and motives in attacking the constitutional government of President Lerdo de Tejada, the political implications, if any, of the Plan of Tuxtepec, the problems of liberty and militarism in the final year of the Restored Republic, and the constitutional, political, and military implications of the defection from the Lerdo government of the chief justice of the Supreme Court, José María Iglesias. The question of why General Díaz won the rebellion of 1876, when asked at all, has invoked the answer that Lerdo had wasted his political support, or that the Iglesias defection in October of 1876 divided the nation so irrevocably that the ambitious General Díaz was able to steal through the chasm and seize the presidential chair, or that Lerdo's opposition and Díaz's supporters created Díaz for reasons of their own. There is something to be said for each of these interpretations, but left understudied, excepting the final maneuvers which brought Generals Díaz, González, and Alatorre to the battlefield of Tecoac, is the nature of Díaz's successful military and political campaign.

The narrative accounts, as distinct from the broad interpretive histories are unsatisfactory unfortunately. Generally they go little beyond the following scheme: Matamoros was taken by treachery; Díaz was quite unsuccessful in acquiring supplies and support in the north; Monterrey was saved from rebel investiture because Gen. Carlos Fuero destroyed the rebel army at the battle of Icamole, and with it the rebel strategy for seizing power from the north; and Gen. Mariano Escobedo pacified the northeast. All attention then shifts to the south, where Díaz operated in his own setting, with friendly authors stressing Díaz's personal leadership and unfriendly authors emphasizing Lerdo's weakness, Díaz's opportunism, or Iglesias's perfidy.

The major reason for the universal depreciation of the northeastern campaign was that Díaz, once he had gained presidential power, never corrected the belief that his northeastern campaign had been a failure. Díaz practiced a policy of conciliation in an attempt to end factional politics in Mexico. An examination of his rebel tactics would have reopened old wounds, encouraging argument and investigation. The argument was to be avoided on the grounds of political stability, and the investigation was to be discouraged for the simple reason that once Díaz was in power he was not interested in having others learn the strategy of successful insurrection.

A second reason for the misappraisal of the northeastern campaign has been, until recently, the lack of understanding of guerrilla warfare. The fact that the nature of the republican resistance to the French occupation of Mexico in the 1860s—those campaigns in which Porfirio Díaz developed his tactics—was that of guerrilla warfare, has escaped the attention of historians. Of Díaz's many encounters during that period, numbering almost fifty, only the great frontal attacks, dramatic charges, and long sieges are widely known.[1] The background and preparation for them, that is, the very factors which made them successful, were the months and years of guerrilla warfare that financially, psychologically, and militarily weakened the enemy so that the more dramatic battles could be successfully waged. General Díaz was a master at guerrilla warfare, and the northeastern campaign had many characteristics of guerrilla war.[2]

1. Service record of Porfirio Díaz, CPD, 1:133.

2. One of many letters among government officials which indicate that they did not understand the nature of the guerrilla warfare they confronted is from Gen. Marcos Carrillo to President Lerdo with this comment: "A band of

If no more were written about the northeastern campaign than this, the thesis should appear suspect that Porfirio Díaz failed wherever he went in 1876, losing his battles and campaigns, being saved only by defection, but nevertheless winning the war.[3] This chapter concerns the basic questions of how an insurrection is raised, who are invited to join, who did join in 1876, how an insurrection is supplied and financed, and how its leaders expect it to survive the initial governmental response. The answers to these questions are derived from the historical documents left by the rebels and the government in 1876. The rebels, then and now, have been referred to as the *Tuxtepecanos*.

Personal influence (*personalismo*) frequently is singled out by historians as the moving factor in Hispanic American government. That may be a misappraisal of the importance of economic and traditional factors; nevertheless, personal influence certainly was a significant factor in raising insurrections. The leader of an insurrection (*caudillo en jefe*) uses his personal influence with local leaders who are then "authorized" to pronounce, raise forces, and collect resources for the movement. If they accede, they "second" the insurrectionary plan, "de-recognize" (*desconocer*) the governmental authorities, and "recognize" (*conocer*) the insurrectionary *caudillo* as the legitimate authority—as president, interim president, or simply "chief-in-arms" (*jefe en armas*).

Inasmuch as the most important elements to attract to a rebellion are the constituted military forces, both federal units and state militias, the rebels shower special attention upon the officers in com-

---

men have appeared near Medellín composed of ranchers who join together when they attempt a robbery and who cowardly disperse when the government forces approach": 6 October 1876, APD, 13:124.

3. Numerous historians have said this in one form or another. Lerdo was made to say in his apocryphal memoirs, "If the ambition to rule had not bitten *señor* Iglesias, indeed, the great rebellion would have fallen apart like a cobweb on the point of a broom." (Adolfo Carrillo), *Memorias . . . de . . . Lerdo*, p. 43. Knapp's judgment is that "Díaz himself had little if any personal credit to glean from the result, since it was the fortuitous shifting of events which spelled his triumph" (*Lerdo*, p. 236). Cosío Villegas wrote that "thus the destiny of the Republic was determined by the accident of a military victory, which Díaz obtained at Tecoac, thanks to the defection of generals Tolentino and Alonso" (*República restaurada*, p. 107).

mand of those units. In the insurrection of Tuxtepec, Díaz had little success in attracting the officers on the active list to his banner. There were, however, many military men in the north who were not on the active list in 1876, men who had separated from the army after the collapse of Maximilian's empire in 1867 or who had been purged from the army for participation in previous rebellions against the government. (Gen. Gerónimo Treviño serves as the best example.) Those men were the principal adherents of the Plan of Tuxtepec in 1876.

Another important group of men to win to the insurrectionary cause were the state governors, because of the control they exercised over state militias and financial resources. Although the governors were invited carte blanche to join the rebels in many nineteenth-century insurrections, the insurgents vigorously sought out those governors who were known to be in conflict with the central authorities. Díaz was generally unsuccessful in attracting the state governors to his cause in 1876, a fact which has been used as evidence that Díaz's call to arms in 1876 lacked all semblance of political ideology and patriotism. Better explanations of why the governors did not join Díaz can be cited, however. First, Lerdo had realized considerable success in incorporating governors into his faction and in replacing independent governors. Second, the established governors did not join the insurrection, although the Plan of Tuxtepec even offered them the right to choose the interim president upon the success of the rebellion, because the plan also promised to amend the constitution to make reelection of governors illegal. Thus the governors, primarily of Lerdo's faction anyway, would have preferred the reelectionist Lerdo to the reformist Díaz.

An important exception to Díaz's inability to attract governors was Gen. Servando Canales, governor of Tamaulipas, who had maintained his independence from the centralizing tendencies of Juárez and Lerdo. That Canales had not been replaced is indicative of his personalistic strength in Tamaulipas. He had, nevertheless, been useful to Juárez and Lerdo by opposing both the insurrection of San Luis-Zacatecas in 1869–70 and the insurrection of La Noria in 1871–72.

Wherever a governor belonged to the president's faction, the insurgents sought out a local rival. Such a rival was a person of local importance, frequently a *caudillo* with a personal following of the governor's opponents. He was perhaps a former governor or the military hero of an earlier conflict who aspired to be governor. The turbulent northeast in 1876 was replete with such men, many of them earlier partisans of Díaz or simply rival faction leaders of the local authorities who well understood the means of rebellion and the rewards of success. One of the implications of the relationship between the *caudillo en jefe* and the local *caudillos* who supported him was that the *caudillo en jefe* was subject to the recommendations of the local *caudillos* to name partisans of the latter men to positions as they arose.[4]

The call to arms as stated in the appeals to the local *caudillos* from the principal *caudillo en jefe* was never stated in terms of prizes to be won, either in wealth or in office. Such a written arrangement would have been unfavorable to the insurrectionary leaders should the correspondence be made public. Rather, the call to arms was based upon considerations of patriotism, duty, and love of liberty against a tyrannical government. It may well be, of course, that the insurrectionists wholly believed themselves. However that may be, it was universally understood in practice that the principal leaders of the successful insurrection would receive the offices of state. Even in the appeals for support, the *caudillo en jefe* might appoint a potential partisan as governor and military commander of his state upon the condition that he second the plan and immediately proceed to raise forces.[5]

When the regional rebel leader lacked personal influence in a given town, an agent, typically a lower officer of local origins, would recruit there, based on the understanding that he would command the men he raised.[6] Sometimes the local recruiter would be named *"jefe militar político,"* chief military and political officer of the town, a position that

4. See examples of Treviño recommending his followers to Díaz, 8 April 1876, APD, 12:168; 12 April 1876, ibid., p. 192, 17 April 1876, ibid., p. 212.
5. The patriotic phrases from Díaz to various military men in the north, as well as his personalist appeal to them as acquaintances and friends, are seen in Díaz to Rosalio Rubio, Francisco Guerra et al., 28 February 1876, ibid., 11:329–30; Díaz to Francisco Naranjo, 28 February 1876, ibid., pp. 327–28.
6. Exemplifying this is a letter from Díaz: "I hope you will [join us and] work with the activity which characterizes you . . . assuring you that the forces you bring will continue under your orders and that . . . you will take part in the council of war. . . ." Díaz to Juan Múñoz, 19 March 1876, ibid., 12:93.

he would have to fight to occupy.[7] The appeal of the local recruiter was essentially personalist, but it was more successful if it corresponded realistically to local grievances, if the reputation of the *caudillo en jefe* were known, and undoubtedly if the local townsmen were poor, exploited, unemployed, or adventuresome, or simply if they harbored hope for something better. Usually the recruiter carried letters from the greater *caudillo* authorizing him to recruit; he was aided by propaganda which either preceded him or which he disseminated as copies of the pronouncement of the local *caudillo* and perhaps even of the pronouncement and plan of the *caudillo en jefe*.[8]

The state government of Nuevo León, attempting to pacify the state, decreed a general amnesty in late May 1876 for all men who had joined the rebels and who wished to return to their homes. The circular announcing the amnesty reveals some of the rebel recruiting methods:

> The Governor and Military Commander of the State knows that many of those who have accompanied and who still accompany the roving bands of the revolutionaries of this frontier have [done so] because the rebel chiefs in order to attract recruits, themselves or by their agents, have tricked them with elegant promises, or even by making them believe that only for their former relations with some of the insurrectionaries or for their personal congeniality for them, they would be persecuted by the government, although they had not committed any revolutionary act; and many, many others have been obliged to join the ranks of the insurrectionaries by force, pulled from their *pueblos* and their places of work. . . .[9]

7. Col. Rómulo Cuellar was so named for the villages of San Fernando, Cruillas "and neighboring villages." Porfirio Díaz to Rómulo Cuellar, 27 March 1876, CPD, 1:342.

8. One of the many examples of this procedure is this one from the Díaz papers: "In Mier I found with great satisfaction all my good friends very willing to second the revolutionary movement. I had a conference with them, making use of the authorization you gave me. . . ." Blas M. Zamorano to Díaz, 4 March 1876, APD, 12:34. General González made special mention of having received the proclamations from Díaz while the former was recruiting in the frontier towns: Manuel González to Díaz, 17 March 1876, ibid., 12:70.

9. AGNL, *Ramo Circulares, 1876*, 29 May 1876.

One soldier who took the amnesty swore that he joined the *Tuxtepecanos* "because Eugenio González de Terán, with whom he had close relations, insisted that he do so, and he could not refuse to accompany him."[10] González de Terán was a *Tuxtepecano* who recruited in the county (*muncipio*) of China, Nuevo León. As for forced conscription, the *Tuxtepecanos* may have engaged in the practice; everyone did. Later in the year General Tolentino advised Díaz that *Porfiristas* in Nopala, Hidalgo, recruited all the men in the area by force, making the Porfirian cause unpopular there. Díaz answered, "Release some of them in order to leave the population content."[11]

In the decade of the Restored Republic tens of thousands of men from towns and *haciendas* across the land had experience from military campaigns of previous years. Nevertheless, Díaz was disappointed at the small number of men who were recruited by his supporters in the northeast in 1876.

The immediate forces that Díaz led against the town of Matamoros were recruited from ranches and towns along the Rio Grande by a handful of local *Tuxtepecanos* who united their men under the leadership of Gen. Manuel González. González, himself a native of Tamaulipas with personalist influence there, crossed the Rio Grande at a point near La Pascuala, not far above Matamoros on 11 March. On that day he reported 100 men in his force. On 13 March Col. Eugenio Loperena joined his forces with those of González. His force then numbered 160, 35 of whom were probably recruited in Texas by Sebastián Villarreal; and the arrival of one Matías with 60 or 80 more was expected momentarily. On 15 March Colonel Hinojosa incorporated his men into González's force, raising it to 190. Capt. Francisco Argüellas left for La Chapeña and Colonel Loperena for Rancho de los Olmos, both to recruit more men. Two days later Loperena returned with 20 additional men, with more to join later, and Captain Zúñiga awaited orders to recruit near Laredo. In mid-March González ordered Pedro Arreola, then in Laredo, to bring his force to the concentration point, recruiting in the towns along the river. But A-

10. Fernando Hinojosa to *Secretario del Gobierno*, 8 June 1876, AGNL, *Ramo Alcaldes Primeros, China.*

11. Francisco Tolentino to Díaz, 15 December 1876, and undated answer, APD, 14:334.

rreola never arrived; indeed, on 18 March he fought an encounter near Laredo and thence marched south to Lampazos. On the previous day Col. Miguel de la Peña, against his will, surrendered command of his forces to General González.[12]

Miguel de la Peña was a political exile residing in Brownsville.[13] Recruited by the *Porfiristas* probably in January and named "Colonel in Command of the Expeditionary Section of the Rio Grande" by General Díaz, he set himself to recruiting for the cause, crossing the river at Reynosa on 28 February at the head of 15 or 20 men. Soon he was joined by Capt. Alejo Sánchez, Praxedis Cavazos, Col. Castro Sotomayor, Capt. Alejandro Zúñiga, and Col. Santos Garza. He promised Díaz to appear before Matamoros with 600 or 1,000 cavalry, given time only to recruit in Las Cuevas and Camargo. On 3 March he admitted to having only 80 men. On 9 March he spoke again of "a little more than 1,000 men," but upon joining González on 17 March, the latter confided to Díaz that Peña "has no more than about 200 men." Even then González had in his knapsack an order he had carried from Brownsville authorizing him to take command of Peña's force, which Peña contested as contrary to Díaz's promise. To avoid strife Díaz sent him a warm congratulatory note and called him to his side. Thereafter, Peña played an important role in Brownsville as a recruiter for the force that would accompany Díaz across the border, and later as purveyor of arms and supplies to the Porfirian forces, tasks he performed with dispatch and pride.[14]

12. González to Díaz, 11 March 1876, ibid., 12:60; Díaz to González, 11 March 1876, CPD, 1:130; González to Díaz, 11 March 1876, APD, 12:60; González to Díaz, 13 March 1876, ibid., pp. 63–64; Villarreal to Díaz, 11 March 1876, ibid., p. 59; González to Díaz, 15 March 1876, ibid., p. 68; González to Díaz, 15 March 1876, ibid., p. 69; Blas Zamoramo to Díaz, 18 March 1876, ibid., p. 81; undated answer to letter from Pedro Arreola to Díaz, 19 March 1876, ibid., p. 88; González to Díaz, 18 March 1876, ibid., p. 78.

13. Elena Villarreal to Porfirio Díaz, n.d., CPD, 40:863; an undated and interesting document written years after the event, it relates among other things her employment of men as rollers of cigarettes in her home-factory in Brownsville. Recruited by Miguel de la Peña, they accompanied Díaz when he crossed the international border on 20 March. This is the only document known to this investigator that verifies the belief that Díaz crossed the frontier with any soldiers at all.

14. Miguel de la Peña to Díaz, 2 March 1876, APD, 12:26; Peña to Díaz, 2 March 1876, ibid., p. 28–30; Peña to Díaz, 3 March 1876, ibid., p. 34; Peña to

One of the officers who joined Peña near Reynosa in early March was Col. Castro G. Sotomayor. Peña could not give him a commission in his own force, although Sotomayor "conducts himself well and with much abnegation," because "the men of the frontier are very jealous of their prerogatives and do not want to be ordered except by their own." When Peña's forces were turned over to Gen. Manuel González in mid-March, Sotomayor was sent with fifty cavalry to Nuevo Laredo, where they met government forces and drove them from Güero Sánchez, an island in the Rio Grande belonging to Texas. While Sotomayor was absent from Nuevo Laredo during the next few days, General Díaz telegraphed to Laredo, Texas, what might well have been a prearranged marching order: Nicolás Sánchez was asked to inform Sotomayor upon his return that Díaz had something "of interest and importance" for him. Sotomayor's name appears on the 5 April Matamoros General Order of the Day, appointing him aide-de-camp to General Díaz. Five days later, however, Colonel Sotomayor fought against government forces led by Gen. Pablo Quintana again in Nuevo Laredo, some two hundred miles from Matamoros.[15] The distance is great and the time short, but Sotomayor's force was small and entirely composed of cavalry; he could have been present in both places, particularly if the route was familiar. The evidence of the Order of the Day of 5 April is so overwhelming that it may be taken with reasonable certitude that Sotomayor was present with his forty or fifty cavalrymen at the capture of Matamoros.

The task of arming and supplying the Army of the North was even more difficult than that of raising it. To a *Porfirista* in Mexico City,

---

Díaz, 9 March 1876, ibid., p. 45; González to Díaz, 13 March 1876, ibid., p. 63; Díaz to González, 11 March 1876, CPD, 1:130; Peña to Díaz, 17 March 1876, APD, 12:78; Díaz to Peña, 18 March 1876, ibid., p. 86; Elena Villarreal to Díaz, n.d., CPD, 40:863; various letters from Peña, APD, 13:101, 121, 123, 125, 127, 138, etc.

15. Peña to Díaz, 2 March 1876, ibid., 12:29; González to Díaz, 17 March 1876, ibid., p. 69; Doctor B. Combe to William H. Russeel (Russell?), n.d., ibid., p. 80; Nicolás Sánchez to Díaz, 19 March 1876, ibid., p. 87; Vidal Delgado to Abraham Aguirre, 17 March 1876, CPD, 1:30; Ignacio Hernández to Díaz, 20 March 1876, APD, 12:94; Díaz to Nicolás Sánchez, 24 March 1876, ibid., p. 110; T. C. Sheldon to J. J. Smith, 11 April 1876, CPD, 1:24–27, 36; Edward Dougherty to Abraham Aguirre, 11 April 1876, ibid., docs. 32–33; Castro Sotomayor to Díaz, 11 April 1876, ibid., doc. 35.

Díaz wrote that "the battle is disadvantageous to begin because, having neither weapons nor money, we cannot incorporate into our ranks the great unarmed masses who offer themselves, only accepting those who bring their own weapons, horses, ammunition, and food. . . ." Indeed, the rebel chiefs constantly appealed to Díaz for arms and supplies. González feared that eighteen men he had to leave in camp would desert for lack of horses, for ". . . they don't know how to walk." "There are people," he wrote, "but we need one or two hundred carbines." There was nothing to do but remain near the river bank to receive "opportune" news of arms from Díaz. Treviño wrote incessantly: "I need arms, above all sabers, carbines and ammunition." "I have enough soldiers [but] the greater part is unarmed. . . . Make the effort to remit arms to us, and as many as possible." General Naranjo frankly marched north to the river "because with anxiety I desire to obtain some arms and ammunition which we lack so much in these moments."[16]

Lack of arms doubtless slowed recruitment and operations. Díaz was unable to send Col. Juan de Haro into southern Tamaulipas for lack of arms and wrote to Carlos Díez Gutiérrez "with much sentiment" that the arms he asked for were unavailable, for "not a single weapon remains in the depot." Rafael Vivero could take no more men in Camargo because "many citizens lack [their own] arms and horse." "The lack of money to buy arms and ammunition," wrote Colonel Falcón from Monclova, was detaining him from pronouncing, "for the poverty in which these towns find themselves permits nothing else."[17]

In Brownsville Díaz recognized the grave financial need and its debilitating effect. To Protasio Tagle, *Porfirista* in Mexico City, he wrote, "If we had money we would now have arms, and if we had arms I would now be in the middle of the Republic." Seizing the

16. Díaz to Protasio Tagle, 7 March 1876, APD, 12:38; González to Díaz, 11 March 1876, ibid., p. 60; González to Díaz, 13 March 1876, ibid.; González to Díaz, 13 March 1876, ibid., p. 64; González to Díaz, 14 March 1876, ibid., p. 65; Gerónimo Treviño to Díaz, 7 April 1876, ibid., p. 159; Treviño to Díaz, 12 April 1876, ibid., pp. 186–87; Francisco Naranjo to Díaz, 17 April 1876, ibid., p. 215.

17. Díaz to Carlos Díez Gutiérrez, 22 April 1876, ibid., p. 237; Vivero to Díaz, 26 April 1876, ibid., p. 251; Anacleto R. Falcón to Díaz, 22 April 1876, ibid., p. 235.

initiative he added, ". . . authorize me to draw [on your name]." Then to the heart of the matter: ". . . better yet, prepare yourself, for I am going to do so in order not to lose time." To other friends, partisans, and men of wealth in Mexico City, Díaz sent an agent from Brownsville to explain terms for loans. "Thirty or forty thousand pesos, I believe, will suffice to change the face of the country," he wrote to José Ives Limantour. "It will do the country a positive service," he wrote to his Masonic brother, Juan Martínez. "If the revolution grows every day," he wrote to his old friend, Nicolás de Teresa, "it is easy to understand that with a little money it will triumph quickly." To Pedro Ogazón, Mexico City lawyer and his future minister of war, he wrote, "With money the revolution will finish quickly."[18]

Money for revolutionary ventures was scarce, and interest rates were high. The *Tuxtepecanos* approached Ismael Morales, a Matamoros businessman, on the day after occupying that town, for a loan of 100,000 pesos at 20 percent interest, payments to begin one month after the occupation of Mexico City. Morales gave them 500 pesos on short terms. Rates rose. Practice became to render receipts for twice the sums offered—100 percent interest. In mid-April 2,500 pesos were taken from contributors in Brownsville in return for receipts at face value of 8,333 pesos—an interest rate of 233 percent.[19]

The difficulty with which Díaz acquired and paid for the absolute necessities he bought while in Brownsville can be recognized. He originally had a personal account in the Texas city upon which González drew during his recruiting in Tamaulipas.[20] Once Díaz crossed the border and officially pronounced, he established a treasury department (*hacienda*) under Francisco Márquez, to which contributions were remitted and bills presented. Since few merchants would accept promissory notes, most purchases were paid for by Porfirian partisans, who then sent their bills to Díaz. He in turn notified the treasury to repay the individual. Indicative of the state of the treasury, the

18. Díaz to Protasio Tagle, 7 March 1876, ibid., p. 38; Díaz to Limantour, 17 March 1876, ibid., pp. 77–78; Díaz to Martínez, 17 March 1876, ibid., p. 77; Díaz to Teresa, 18 March 1876, ibid., p. 82; Díaz to Ogazón, 18 March 1876, ibid., p. 83.

19. Díaz to Ismael Morales, 3 April 1876, CPD, 1:454; Julio Eversmann to Díaz, 30 April 1876, APD, 12:266; Peña to Díaz, 1 May 1876, ibid., p. 269; list of contributors, 15 April 1876, ibid., pp. 205–6.

20. Antonio Tijerina to Díaz, 18 March 1876, ibid., p. 85.

orders usually stipulated a rate of payment to commence at some future date rather than total and immediate payment, or they were accompanied by the phrase "as soon as that sum is available in the office of your charge."[21] The practice of individual commanders paying for supplies and remitting bills was not encouraged. Accompanying authorization to pronounce and recruit, a phrase was frequently attached urging the commander to use economy in purchases and to send all bills to Díaz's headquarters rather than directly to *hacienda* for payment.[22]

The most usual expedient for raising money in nineteenth-century Mexico, on the part of both rebels and government, was the forced loan. Whatever group held a town or region, it customarily decreed contributions, sometimes according to a scale related to the net worth of all the inhabitants of the town or region under control. Gen. Bernabé de la Barra, Lerdo's commanding general at Matamoros after 13 March declared the town under martial law on 30 March and demanded 1,500 pesos from each of six resident American merchants. Whether Mexican citizens were similarly taxed is not a matter of record, but one presumes so. When *Porfirista* forces recaptured Nuevo Laredo from the government garrison on 11 April, they decreed a forced loan from the city merchants. The inclusion of American residents almost caused an international incident and might have resulted in United States armed intervention against the *Porfiristas*. That may explain why Díaz never resorted to forced loans in Matamoros. He had had time to do so earlier, however, and could merely have excluded foreign residents. Twice Díaz convened the Matamoros merchants to solicit financial support but, according to the United States consul, was unable to "awaken [their] enthusiasm."[23] After Díaz

21. One Antonio Guerra was to be repaid in four monthly installments after the occupation of Monterrey: undated answer to letter from Antonio Guerra to Díaz, 20 April 1876, ibid., pp. 223–24; Juan N. Treviño was to be repaid 3,146.25 pesos "for material of war" at the rate of 1,000 pesos per month commencing 1 June: Díaz to F. Márquez, 23 April 1876, ibid., p. 242; Díaz sent an order to the treasury that 570.50 pesos be paid to J. Rouede "as soon as that sum is available. . . .": Díaz to F. Márquez, 24 April 1876, ibid., p. 246.

22. Díaz to Rómulo Cuellar, 27 March 1876, CPD, 1:342.

23. Richard Blaine McCornack, "Porfirio Díaz en la frontera texana, 1876–1877," *Historia Mexicana*, 5 (January–March, 1956): 388, 392–94. No evidence has appeared during this investigation that Díaz applied forced

left Matamoros in the care of General González, the latter wrote to the former that "I find no possibility of obtaining financial resources, for the fear and lack of confidence ... among the inhabitants of this city—speaking of the wealthy ones, of course."[24] He referred to the absence not of money but rather of confidence for volunteer contributions; no forced loans are mentioned.

Financiers of frontier commerce, targets of the *Tuxtepecano* financial campaign, could justly be apprehensive of making loans to rebels. More valuable to them than promissory notes were certificates of credit redeemable at the customshouse against future import duties. It is not clear what the inducements were for merchants to take certificates. Perhaps threats of forced loans or of confiscation of goods sufficed. The rebels at Nuevo Laredo threatened to open the stores of American merchants and sell their goods if loans were not forthcoming.[25] Such merchants might have settled for certificates. Perhaps the desire to make cash available to willing but impecunious clients, such as the *Tuxtepecanos,* sufficed for them to buy certificates. Perhaps the few merchants who took certificates were sympathetic to the Porfirian cause. Perhaps the importation certificates always sold at discount. Whatever the explanation, once the insurgents controlled the customshouses of frontier towns, they were able to sell negotiable importation certificates to commercial houses. Clearly, certificates were preferred by frontier merchants and were used by the *Tuxtepecanos* as a source of income.[26]

In one way or another, arms were purchased. In March Remington Arms Company was contacted for 500 rifles, 250,000 rounds of ammunition, and 2,000,000 cartridges for recharging. A month later

loans. McCornack cites from the American consular reports that consul Wilson at Matamoros feared Díaz would levy a forced loan, and although McCornack was dealing with the matter, he never says that Díaz did so.

24. González to Díaz, 14 May 1876, CPD, 1:21.

25. McCornack, *"Frontera tejana,"* p. 394.

26. The company of José Fernández and Brother remitted 14,000 pesos to the *Tuxtepecano* treasury in return for the certificates worth 28,000 pesos: Díaz (?) to F. Márquez, 12 April 1876, APD, 12:190. Arms were bought from the company of Sánchez y Salinas with importation certificates negotiable at Nuevo Laredo: "Instructions," 19 March 1876, ibid., p. 92; the company of Julio Eversmann returned a promissory note to Díaz, reminding him that part of the debt was to be paid in importation certificates: Eversmann to Díaz, 30 April 1876, ibid., p. 266.

100 Remington carbines and 20,000 rounds of ammunition were ordered; then 100 Remington carbines and 29,000 rounds of ammunition; 100 Remington carbines and 6,000 rounds; 72,000 rounds; 50 Remington carbines and 10 Winchester rifles, with 13,000 rounds. So a small arsenal was collected; so also horses, wagons, mules, uniforms, cattle, and forage were gathered, and the suppliers were somehow paid.[27]

As long as Díaz was in the north, the financial problem and lack of arms plagued him. Two days before he crossed the border and pronounced, Díaz wrote to the man he shortly named second in command of the "Constitutional Army": "Stretching my financial resources and compromising my credit, as well as that of some friends, I have ordered armament of good quality which I will put to use shortly. If I had had arms from the first I would now be in the heart of the country, because I have more than enough men, all of the courage we need, and with more spontaneity than one could desire; but the scarcity of resources has obliged me to maintain an exasperating personal silence." Over a month later, after having captured Matamoros and during the preparation for his campaign into the interior, he wrote to a friend, "You cannot form an idea of the scarcity of my resources." At a moment when Díaz's troops were deserting for lack of arms and González was fortifying Matamoros against the approaching federal army of Mariano Escobedo, 300 carbines costing 6,600 pesos sat near but could not be bought, for this was "a sum greater than I can raise here." On 1 May González wrote that lack of credit negated any negotiation for arms; indeed "funds can hardly be secured for the relief of the garrison. . . ." Treviño, despairing, wrote that he was commencing a march "in whatever direction in order to distract the troops and divert them from the absolute lack of funds."[28]

27. Order by conduct of Francisco Iturria, 9 March 1876, ibid., p. 50; Vidal Delgado to Díaz, 9 April 1876, ibid., p. 174; receipt, J. Rouede to Díaz, 15 April 1876, ibid., p. 203; list of shells . . . , n.d., ibid., pp. 203–4; receipt (order?), Emilio C. Forto to Díaz, 17 April 1876, ibid., p. 294; various documents: for example, ibid., pp. 235, 265, 282, 283, 295, 298, 299, etc.; CPD, 1:455.

28. Díaz to Donato Guerra, 18 March 1876, APD, 12:84; Díaz to Francisco M. de Prida, 22 April 1876, ibid., p. 239; González to Díaz, 26 April 1876, ibid., pp. 257–58; González to Díaz, 1 May 1876, ibid., p. 270; Treviño to Díaz, 5 May 1876, ibid., p. 270.

The rebel forces were not alone in their need for financial and material resources. The communications in the war ministry leave no doubt that the government forces were facing the same problems. Lieutenant Colonel Cristo, second in command at Matamoros before 2 April, informed the minister of war that the troops that arrived to strengthen the garrison "are very much behind on their rations. . . . The same [is true] for the rest of the garrison, to whom is owned the major part of last month's wages. The customshouse has no income, the police force lacks funds, there are no supplies." Lieutenant Colonel Parrat, also at Matamoros, telegraphed the war ministry two days later that "there are no supplies here nor place from which to obtain them. Businessmen will not loan us money, for the customshouse cannot repay them." In addition to the total lack of supplies at Matamoros, according to Cristo, "neither foodstuffs nor pasturage is obtainable."[29] In mid-March the officials of the customshouse at Matamoros offered importation certificates at 50 percent discount in the hope of raising 10,000 pesos.[30]

General Fuero in Monterrey was doing what he could to bolster Matamoros, but, he wrote, "the lack of rations here is absolute: it is difficult to provide basic necessities." He asked that at least the officers be paid, and ten days later dramatically stated that "the treasury remits nothing. The cavalry horses are being destroyed for lack of forage—and the troops . . . also." This situation existed not only in the northeast; everywhere in the country the military was complaining of lack of supplies, overdue paydays, and the lack of food for troops and horses.[31]

29. José L. Cristo to Ignacio Mejía, 11 January 1876, *Archivo de Cancelados de la Secretaría de la Defensa Nacional* (hereafter ADN), 11:481.4:9224:18; Manuel Parrat to Mejía, 13 January 1876, ibid., doc. 25; Cristo to Mejía, 16 January 1876, ibid., doc. 28.

30. Peña to Díaz, 21 March 1876, APD, 12:101.

31. Carlos Fuero to Ignacio Mejía, 16 January 1876, ADN, 481.4:9224:28; Fuero to Mejía, 16 January 1876, ibid., doc. 25; Fuero to Ignacio Mejía, 25 January 1876, ibid., doc. 60. General Flores in Zamora complained that no rations had come to his force in two months: P. Flores to Ignacio Mejía, 7 January 1876, ibid., doc. 15; in Durango, General F. Carrillo complained that authorized funds had not been forthcoming: F. Carrillo to Mejía, 13 January 1876, ibid., doc. 25; in Chihuahua the government general complained that neither the treasury nor the *aduana* had resources for the military colonies

The government reaction to the fiscal problem was to order a troop reduction in January—even as the *Tuxtepecanos* were mobilizing. In the northeast 200 men from the garrison of Monterrey and 100 men at Tampico were released from service. Matamoros, however, was strengthened by about 190 men.[32] Thereafter, governmental units on all levels commenced to recruit.

The interaction of rebel recruiting, forced loans, and governmental reaction can be seen in an example of such activities in a small area of eastern Nuevo León, in the counties (*municipios*) of General Bravo and China. Matías Rodríguez, the *primer alcalde* (equivalent to the *jefes políticos* of the *municipios* of other states) of China, reported to the state government on 1 February 1876 that "some malcontents of insignificant number hope for some revolutionary movement." On 1 March he had information that Vicente Garza Benites from Linares would lead a "revolutionary movement" in the *municipio*. Rodríguez's problem was that he did not have forces or arms, or access to them: "What do I do in this case?" By the third week of March Rodríguez reported that the rebel Felipe Cuellar was in the area with thirty or forty men "taking corn, sweets, and other objects." Six leagues away was another party of twenty men, and the *municipio* was "without resources, arms, and ammunition to confront the situation." Rodríguez was told to raise a local militia and await orders.[33]

---

under his command: Joaquín Herrera to Mejía, 6 January 1876, ibid., doc 26; in Orizaba the troops were ready in mid-January to march against the rebels of Veracruz, but could not leave because rations had been exhausted on 1 January: Marcos Carrillo to Mejía, 16 January 1876, ibid., doc. 27; in Tula, Tamaulipas, the commanding officer said his funds in mid-January could not cover the expenses for forage for the horses: Francisco M. Ramírez to Mejía, 18 January 1876, ibid., doc. 36; two weeks later he announced that the troops had exhausted their rations and that the government treasury office at San Luis Potosí which supplied him had informed him it had no funds: Ramírez to Mejía, 2 February 1876, ibid., doc. 70; General Palacios in Saltillo informed the war ministry in mid-February that "the desertions from this garrison continue and have no other origin than the lack of rations. The situation is grave": Domingo Palacios to Mejía, 17 February 1876, ibid., doc. 86. Examples from every quarter of the land demonstrate the same condition.

32. Carlos Fuero to Ignacio Mejía, 25 January 1876, ibid., docs. 54–55; Jesús Alonso Flores, 1 February 1876, ibid., doc. 67; José L. Cristo to Mejía, 11 January 1876, ibid., doc. 19.

33. Matías Rodríguez to *Secretario de Gobierno*, 1 February 1876, AGNL, *Ramo*

According to Merced Leal, the *primer alcalde* of the *municipio* of General Bravo, the rebel leader Eugenio González entered town on 24 March with twenty-six or twenty-eight men, demanding pasturage for his horses, which Leal provided. On the next day Felipe González led a group into town and took thirty-one *pesos*, fifteen *centavos* from the state stamp office and demanded that Leal make ready three saddled horses, ten "long arms," five pounds of powder, and six pounds of lead. Leal reported the two incidents by extraordinary carrier on 26 March but the carrier joined the rebels.[34]

In China on 4 April the rebel leaders Francisco Cirlos and Pedro Cantú tried to collect a forced loan upon the town levied by Eugenio González, and as no one paid, they rounded up some volunteer recruits, stole 70 *pesos*, 50 *centavos*, and left town. On 11 April Domingo Zambrano, an officer in Cirlos's band, returned and obtained 50 *pesos* by forced loan. Then on 21 April Juan Garza Elizondo and Felipe González entered town with a small band and presented an order from General Vara for a forced loan of 1000 *pesos*. They raised 150 *pesos*.[35] The state government changed the local *primeros alcaldes;* Fernando Hinojosa was named in China and Luz Cantú in General Bravo. Hinojosa reported that according to orders he had organized twenty-five men into a national guard unit, incorporating fifteen *rurales* of the *municipio*, "although they are generally badly armed, for those who have arms do not have ammunition, and those who have the latter lack the former, for both articles are extremely scarce in this *Municipio*." The state government appointed a military commander, Antonio Dávila, over both *municipios* and ordered Dávila to raise a force for the defense of the area.[36]

Porfirio Díaz crossed the Texas-Tamaulipas border on 20 March, occupying a position named in his correspondence "Campo de San

Alcaldes Primeros, China 1873–1877; idem to idem, 1 March 1876, ibid.; idem to idem, 20 March 1876, ibid.; *Secretario de Gobierno* to Rodríguez, 23 March 1876, ibid.

34. Leal to *Secretario de Gobierno,* 31 March 1876, ibid., *General Bravo 1873–1876*.

35. Fernando Hinojosa to *Secretario de Gobierno,* 25 May 1876, ibid., *China 1873–1877;* idem to idem, 26 May 1876, ibid.

36. Leal to *Secretario de Gobierno,* 26 May 1876, ibid., *General Bravo 1873–1876*.

Matías."[37] On 2 April he captured the frontier city of Matamoros by a political defection of several important persons in that city. The arrangements took place in late February and March 1876. Díaz did charge the city in a frontal attack on 2 April, but although he commanded fewer men at the moment of attack than those nominally at the command of Gen. Bernabé de la Barra, because of the defection of the national guard units led by Gen. Jesús Toledo, the defenders were significantly outnumbered and confused.[38]

Porfirian problems of finance, armaments, and recruiting were partially alleviated by the occupation of Matamoros. Díaz gained the customshouse, the Matamoros arsenal, and some armed forces that he incorporated into his army. He immediately offered to enlist all the men of the federal garrison and of the national guard into his army, and gave the others three hours to leave Matamoros "to wherever was convenient for them." Díaz himself claimed that he left Matamoros with 2,000 men. Commander Johnson of the *USS Rio Bravo* personally observed the exit and calculated Díaz's force at 1,500.[39] Other estimates exist, but 1,500 and 2,000 form the reasonable limits. Considering that between 500 and 600 men remained in Matamoros with González[40] (more than the number of soldiers who had attacked Matamoros on 2 April), then all the men who left with Díaz on 25 April were added to his force between those dates. This included some, entering Matamoros between 2 April and 25 April, who were already recruited by Porfirian officers in adjacent areas. Nevertheless, the margin is significantly large to conclude that Matamoros proved an important point for recruitment.

The psychological value of the occupation of Matamoros was also significant. *Porfiristas* everywhere could believe that Díaz was then *en route*, and the government had more difficulty convincing the public that the rebellion was contained and would shortly collapse. The United States ambassador to Mexico, John Foster, wrote to the State

37. Díaz to Julián Quiroga, 20 March 1876, APD, 12:95; Díaz to Juan N. Méndez, 23 March 1876, ibid., p. 102.

38. The several historiographical problems of the "treason" of Matamoros are discussed in appendix 11.

39. Mauricio Gracía, report, 1902, CPD, 27:9198; Díaz to Donaciano Lara, 30 April 1876, APD, 12:262–63; McCornack, *"Frontera tejana,"* p. 397.

40. Manuel González to Díaz, 14 May 1876, CPD, 1:21.

Department that "this is the most important accomplishment of the revolutionaries . . . ," not only for arms and supplies but because it resulted in a new series of pronouncements in all parts of the country.[41] Foster wrote in his memoirs that by April Lerdo had declared almost all the important states under martial law and had imposed forced loans to combat the insurrection, that the railroad to Veracruz had been destroyed at various points, that postal communications with the port as well as into the North were "uncertain and difficult," that coaches were everywhere stopped and robbed, and that travel throughout the country suffered great interruptions and dangers.[42] Such is the nature of widespread guerrilla warfare. It is significant that Foster marked the month of April to begin his discussions of the disturbances of that year. Matamoros had fallen to Díaz on 2 April.

Historians have been oblivious to the larger tactical considerations of the northeast, in which Matamoros was a part. The assumption seems to be, when one is made at all, that the *Porfiristas* wanted to converge upon Matamoros for one grand blow. Although Matamoros was important to the rebels, they were not making a general concentration there. Both a theoretical consideration and a reconstruction of the location of the Porfirian forces will demonstrate this.

A general concentration of rebel forces in the northeast upon Matamoros would have been both a tactical and a logistical error. It would have elicited a governmental concentration, and Matamoros would have become the anvil upon which the Porfirian forces would have been crushed by governmental forces. Furthermore, until Matamoros was taken, there were not sufficient supplies in the Matamoros area to sustain the numbers required for a siege or general assault.

The chance of rebellions succeeding in Mexico until recent times has been a function of time: When the government could not stamp out a rebellion quickly, it tended to grow. The longer a rebellion lasted, the more support it attracted. That support was attracted to the local *caudillo*, whose strength was ipso facto local. Pulling him away from his source of power with the men and resources available to him in the early phase of a rebellion was generally not as advantageous as

41. McCornack, *"Frontera tejana,"* p. 396.
42. Foster, *Diplomatic Memoirs,* 1:60.

leaving him there to augment his power through the factor of time—defying governmental authority locally, and, by absorbing local resources, depriving governmental forces of them.[43] The early tactics of successful rebellion have not been concentration but rather fragmentation. Better a hundred uprisings in a hundred different places than a single large force in one region. Díaz needed forces at Matamoros, but he was not making a major concentration there.

The strategy in the Northeast at the time of the fall of Matamoros was designed to isolate that city from all succor, while arranging as many other points of diversion as possible. A consideration of the location, activities, and mission of other Porfirian chieftains in relation to General Díaz and Matamoros will demonstrate this.

The *Tuxtepecano* generals Treviño and Naranjo with "six or seven hundred men between them" were stationed midway between Matamoros and Monterrey, holding down the forces of the governmental officer, Col. Jacinto Ordóñez. The federal government released reports of victory in one skirmish between those forces, but even Ordóñez's communications indicate that the Porfirian forces were avoiding battle. On 28 March, five days before the investiture of Matamoros, Ordóñez was reported between Naranjo with 400 men and Treviño with 300 in the vicinity of Mier and Los Aldamas.[44]

General Díaz at one point did want Treviño to join him for the capture of Matamoros. In one of several expressions to this effect, Díaz wrote to Treviño after mid-March that he hoped that Treviño

43. Cosío Villegas supports this point in reference to the 1869–70 "San Luis-Zacatecas Revolt" when he attributes the failure of that movement in part to the rebels having left their natural base of operations to unite elsewhere: *República restaurada*, p. 568.

44. Juan Muñoz to Díaz, 28 March 1876, APD, 12:124. Cosío Villegas holds that Treviño and Naranjo did not help Díaz at Matamoros because Ordóñez had beaten them at Lampazos on the western border of Nuevo León on 17 March (*República restaurada*, p. 871). Naranjo had occupied that town on 9 November and had taken the reserve unit and governmental garrison as prisoners (Naranjo to Díaz, 9 March 1876, APD, 12:48; Juan C. Vara to Díaz, 12 March 1876, ibid., p. 61). It is likely that Naranjo had a skirmish with Ordóñez on 17 March and retreated. Fuero's victory report is cited in Ceballos, *Aurora y ocaso*, 2:437. Cosío's source is *Siglo XIX*, a capital city newspaper. Ordóñez's complaint that Treviño and Naranjo would not give battle is in Ceballos, *Aurora y ocaso*, 2:494.

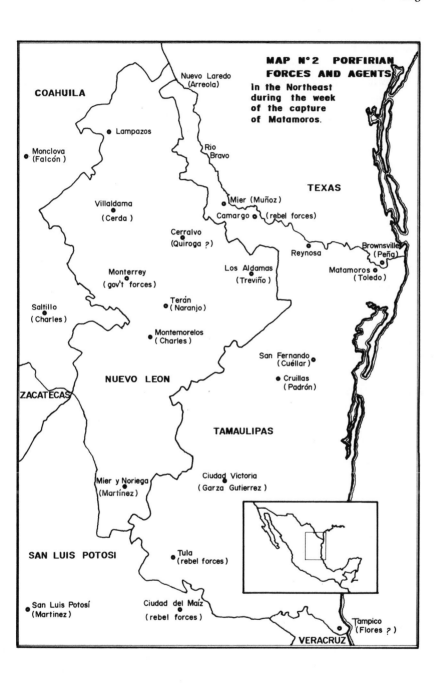

MAP N° 2   PORFIRIAN FORCES AND AGENTS in the Northeast during the week of the capture of Matamoros.

COAHUILA

Nuevo Laredo (Arreola)

● Lampazos

● Monclova (Falcón)

Rio Bravo

TEXAS

Villaldama ● (Cerda)

● Mier (Muñoz)

Camargo ● (rebel forces)

Cerralvo (Quiroga ?)

Reynosa ●

Brownsville (Peña)

Monterrey ● (gov't forces)

Los Aldamas ● (Treviño)

Matamoros ● (Toledo)

Saltillo ● (Charles)

Terán ● (Naranjo)

Montemorelos ● (Charles)

San Fernando ● (Cuéllar)

NUEVO LEON

● Cruillas (Padrón)

ZACATECAS

TAMAULIPAS

Mier y Noriega ● (Martínez)

Ciudad Victoria ● (Garza Gutierrez)

SAN LUIS POTOSI

Tula ● (rebel forces)

● San Luis Potosí (Martínez)

Ciudad del Maíz ● (rebel forces)

Tampico ● (Flores ?)

VERACRUZ

could join him with forces at Matamoros or "that you will send me some aid." Clearly, that was not a military order to march to Matamoros but only an appeal for aid if Treviño could spare his presence or some forces. There was obviously an alternative to joining Díaz at Matamoros, something to do "if you believe that you ought not come in person," a strategic plan in which the capture of Matamoros was but a part. Treviño wrote from Los Aldamas that he had information that General Fuero from Monterrey "will dispatch [a column] against the forces in your command," but he did not think it possible because the Monterrey garrison was small and "we here will impede their passage. . . ."[45]

General Treviño was perhaps presumptive of his capabilities, but the effect of his presence was clear. "They work with much activity," Fuero had telegraphed to the minister of war as early as 8 January. He could not send aid to the various points of rebellion, he said, "because I have not 500 men at hand."[46] Fuero could not send aid to Matamoros while rebel forces hovered around Monterrey. This explains why Díaz kept forces elsewhere in the northeast rather than ordering a concentration at Matamoros.

Northwest of Treviño and Naranjo was the city of Nuevo Laredo, important for supply connections with the United States. The *Tuxtepecanos* there were Sotomayor, Zamorano, Arreola, and Sánchez. Pedro Arreola and Eufemio Sánchez pronounced on 14 March with 150 men.[47] Colonel Sotomayor, as has been seen above, probably joined Díaz from there in time for the occupation of Matamoros. Zamorano had recently arrived.

Col. Blas María Zamorano was recruited into the Porfirian ranks by Francisco Naranjo in February, and soon received the complete confidence of Porfirio Díaz. Zamorano seemingly had friends and acquaintances along the whole of the frontier, for he was sent to Mier, Guerrero, and Lampazos before going to Nuevo Laredo, organizing Porfirian parties to pronounce against the government. By 18 March he was in Nuevo Laredo organizing the national guard, harmonizing

45. Undated answer to letter from Gerónimo Treviño to Díaz, 16 March 1876, APD: 12:74; Treviño to Díaz, 28 March 1876, ibid., p. 124.

46. Fuero to Mejía, 8 January 1876, ADN, 11:481.4:9224:17.

47. Vidal Delgado to Díaz, 16 March 1876, APD, 12:71.

local factional disputes, and naming individuals to positions in the *Tuxtepecano* administration. Zamorano soon received either an order or a suggestion that forces from Nuevo Laredo join Díaz near Matamoros. Zamorano urged General Díaz not to withdraw troops from Nuevo Laredo because of the importance of the city as a port of trade and supply and because it would immediately fall to federal forces in the area without the presence of Porfirian forces. Furthermore, he said, the soldiers in Nuevo Laredo were not ready to march.[48]

Díaz did not receive troops from Laredo and probably sent men to that area. Perhaps Díaz hoped to dominate the Laredo area quickly and call all the troops from there. On 20 March, however, Zamorano was called to Lampazos to aid General Naranjo. "I will comply with this order because it seems more urgent," he telegraphed to Brownsville. It would seem he had another order which he considered less urgent. On 24 March General Díaz told him to "continue organizing your force." Then no more is heard of Zamorano until 7 April, five days after the fall of Matamoros to the *Tuxtepecanos*. On that day Colonel Zamorano wrote from a *hacienda* near the city of Terán in central Nuevo León, congratulating Díaz for his triumph and excusing himself for not joining Díaz. He was occupied, he said, with operations with General Naranjo.[49]

Southwest of Nuevo Laredo in Villaldama, in late March or the first days of April, Col. Jesús María Cerda pronounced against the government, incorporating his forces into those of Gerónimo Treviño. Further west in the state of Coahuila Gen. Anacleto Falcón was in communication with General Treviño in early April, giving assurances of his loyalty to the Porfirian cause and promising to pronounce

48. Naranjo to Díaz, 20 February 1876, ibid., 11:318; Díaz to Naranjo, 28 February 1876, ibid., pp. 327–28; Díaz to various persons, 28 February 1876, ibid., pp. 329–30; Blas María Zamorano to Díaz, 4 March 1876, ibid., 12:35; Naranjo to Díaz, 9 March 1876, ibid., p. 49; Naranjo to Díaz, 16 March 1876, ibid., p. 72; Zamorano to Díaz, 18 March 1876, ibid., pp. 81, 86.

49. Nicolás Sánchez wrote on 19 March that "the 50 men you sent have not yet arrived": Sánchez to Díaz, 19 March 1876, ibid., p. 87; Zamorano to L. A. R. Aguirre, 20 March 1876, ibid., p. 94; Díaz to Zamorano, 24 March 1876, ibid., p. 108; Zamorano to Díaz, 7 April 1876, ibid., p. 161.

in Monclova after arranging some family affairs. During the first week of May Falcón pronounced, as promised.[50]

To the south of Matamoros a number of military figures were operating in southern Tamaulipas and northern San Luis Potosí. Comdr. Marcelino Padrón and Col. Rómulo Cuéllar were recruiting in Cruillas and San Fernando in late March and early April. In Ciudad Victoria the leading Porfirian officers were Carlos Díez Gutiérrez and Ignacio Martínez. In early March Carlos Díez Gutiérrez had 120 men, mostly mounted and armed, in Victoria, some 200 miles south of Matamoros. He intended to continue operating in southern Nuevo León and eastern San Luis Potosí. By mid-March he sought Díaz's permission to seek the governorship of San Luis Potosí, which Díaz gave. During the critical first week of April Díez Gutiérrez was involved in the important task of acting as liaison between Díaz and Servando Canales.[51]

Gen. Ignacio Martínez pronounced in early March in Tula, a city of 14,000 in southern Tamaulipas. By the end of the month he was preparing the local authorities to pronounce in Mier y Noriega, another town in southern Tamaulipas. During April he was operating in San Luis Potosí in connection with Díez Gutiérrez. Needing supplies, he returned to the area around Ciudad Victoria near the end of April, where Díez Gutiérrez apportioned some supplies available to him. Díaz approved of Martínez's operations to the extent that in early May he sent Colonel Juan de Haro with 300 men to aid him in San Luis Potosí.[52]

The important figures, however, in southern Tamaulipas were

50. Hipólito Charles to Díaz, 5 April 1876, ibid., p. 150; Treviño to Díaz, 12 April 1876, ibid., p. 187; Falcón to Díaz, 22 April 1876, ibid., p. 236; Treviño to Díaz, 8 May 1876, ibid., p. 305.

51. Díaz to Cuéllar, 27 April 1876, CPD, 1:342; Díaz to Padrón, 27 March 1876; ibid., doc. 132, Justo Robles to (?), 3 April 1876, APD, 12:131; Cuéllar to Díaz, 4 April 1876, ibid., p. 139; Díez Gutiérrez to Díaz, 1 March 1876, ibid., p. 26; Blas M. Zamorano to Díaz, 18 March 1876, ibid., p. 82; Díaz to Zamorano, 24 March 1876, ibid., p. 190; Díaz to Canales, 9 April 1876, ibid., p. 174.

52. Anon. to Díaz, 8 March 1876, ibid., p. 43; Martínez to Díaz, 28 March 1876, ibid., p. 123; Díaz to Haro, 19 April 1876, CPD, 1:461; Carlos Díez Gutiérrez to Díaz, 26 April 1876, APD, 12:254; Díaz to Haro, 8 May 1876, ibid., p. 304; Díaz to Martínez, 8 May 1876, ibid., p. 308.

Generals Jesús Alonso Flores in Tampico and Servando Canales in Ciudad Victoria, governor of the state of Tamaulipas. General Flores, although he ultimately chose to support the government, had given General Díaz some reason to believe that he would join the cause of Tuxtepec and carry the garrison and important customshouse at Tampico into the Porfirian camp. Ten days before the fall of Matamoros, Díaz had sufficient confidence to inform his co-religionist in Oaxaca that Tampico was about to fall to the *Tuxtepecanos*. General Flores, however, did not take the final step to join the rebels. Garza Gutiérrez, *Porfirista* agent between Tampico and Ciudad Victoria, wrote Díaz that "although [Flores] writes us in almost every dispatch, he has maintained a reserve." A month after Lerdo resigned the presidency Flores finally accepted the Plan of Tuxtepec.[53]

Affairs in the state capital were no more certain in March and April, yet in the long run they were more helpful to the rebels. When Matamoros fell in April, Gov. Servando Canales had not yet pronounced. He was in communication with Díaz and was telling Díaz's agents in Ciudad Victoria that he wanted to take "a more direct part" later in the year. In late February Díaz urged Canales to join soon and thereby save Tamaulipas needless suffering, for "with your powerful help a bloody and ruinous revolution [could be made] to pass rapidly to another theater, and not cause the state of Tamaulipas more harm than the absolutely indispensable commotion." By mid-March Díaz was less sanguine; to the major Porfirian leader in Jalisco he wrote that "Governor Canales presents himself well to us, if one looks at his offers. . . . With him or without him I will operate against Matamoros." Other Porfirian leaders complained that Canales's hesitations prejudiced their operations, and Díaz pleaded for immediate action, saying "Your silence is hurting me."[54]

It is difficult to conclude anything other than that Canales was an opportunist and perhaps was awaiting a respectable show of force

53. Díaz to Fidencio Hernández, 23 March 1876, ibid., p. 105; Santos de la Garza Gutiérrez to Díaz, 26 April 1876, ibid., p. 252; Aurelio Melgarlejo to Díaz, 21 December 1876, ibid., 15:107–10.

54. Díez Gutiérrez to Díaz, 29 February 1876, ibid., 11:332; Díaz to Canales, 23 February 1876, ibid., p. 320; Díaz to Donato Guerra, 18 March 1876, ibid., 12:84; Miguel de la Peña to Díaz, 10 March 1876, ibid., p. 59; Ignacio Martínez to Díaz, 28 March 1876, ibid., p. 123; Díaz to Servando Canales, 9 April 1876, ibid., p. 173.

from the Porfirian armies before committing himself; nevertheless, his arguments were good—that he had first to win reelection to the governorship in the pending campaign, that he had few resources, and that Díaz's campaign against Matamoros would result in a governmental reinforcement of Tampico, which would inconvenience his own supply route from that port.[55] Furthermore, the rebels gained at least two advantages by Canales's apparent loyalty to the government. First, the congress of the Tamaulipas government gave Canales extraordinary powers "to attend to the conservation of the public peace" and to sustain "the legitimate authorities and the institutions of the nation," powers which Canales then monopolized but did not use to send troops against the "armed parties pertaining to other places," as a substitute governor would have done (and later did) had Canales openly declared for Porfirio Díaz.[56] Second, assuming the posture of a loyal governor, Canales received government intelligence which he passed along to General Díaz.[57] Finally, Canales did pronounce at a moment when Díaz needed additional forces and the prestige of new adherents.

Further west of Cuéllar, Martínez, and Canales, Porfirian Col. Hipólito Charles was operating near Saltillo, capital city of the north-central state of Coahuila. He had 600 men in mid-April and soon received a contingent from Naranjo. During the first week of April he engaged Colonel Ordóñez in Montemorelos, Nuevo León.[58]

Most of these forces were small, some too small to act effectively, some only potential forces until the commander firmly committed himself or until he found necessary war materials. Nevertheless, they existed and were effective in dividing the government forces and even in discrediting the government. An interesting letter from President

55. Carlos Díez Gutiérrez to Díaz, 29 February 1876, ibid., 11:332.

56. (Servando Canales) to the inhabitants of Tamaulipas, 18 March 1876, ibid., 12:165; government of the state of Tamaulipas, Section 1ª, Circular Nº 7, 11 March 1876, ibid., p. 164; Ceballos is alone among historians to suggest that Canales's "complicity" with Díaz enabled the latter's success on 2 April: *Aurora y ocaso*, 2:444; now having the correspondence between Canales and Díaz, and reducing "complicity" to "witholding state aid from Matamoros," there still remains evidence of great positive assistance to the *Tuxtepecanos*.

57. Santos de la Garza Gutiérrez to Díaz, 11 April 1876, APD, 12:184.

58. Treviño to Díaz, 16 March 1876, ibid., p. 73; Charles to Díaz, 5 April 1876, ibid., p. 150.

Lerdo to the governor of San Luis Potosí written in mid-March indicated the government's dilemma. Referring to rebel activity in Tula, San Luis Potosí, the president advised the governor that Colonel Ramírez was ordered to look into the matter, but "it seems that he has not had occasion to tend to it." And concerning the rebel force "that might be in Valle del Maíz," state of Tamaulipas, Lerdo had consulted General Escobedo about the possibility of sending a force in that direction "if thought opportune, according to circumstances."[59] The government was apparently too busy to attend to Tula and Valle del Maíz.

Another example of the governmental embarrassment follows: in the city of Mier on the northern frontier, the municipal government advised Díaz that the city preferred its tranquillity to joining the rebellion and informed him that it would accept the leadership of the state authorities, who were loyal to the national government. Twelve days later, however, after municipal, state, and national governments had demonstrated their inability to protect the city from marauders, citizens let Díaz know that they would deliver the city to any force that would maintain order.[60]

The Lerdo government was in fact harassed and discredited by extended rebel activity. The rebels were investing towns to collect men, arms, contributions, and supplies. They were engaging in skirmishes for any advantage that might turn up, for the purpose of demonstrating their existence, and forcing the government to reinforce every unit and every post. They were not concentrating at Matamoros, for then Ordóñez and even Fuero from Monterrey could have marched to the aid of Matamoros.

Those pockets of rebel activity and areas affected by rebellious activity are isolated examples of situations across the length and breadth not only of the northeast but of the entire nation. The view that Díaz crossed the frontier with 40 men, and that those men, or the 400 he was able to concentrate at Matamoros, represented the Porfirian forces in the north leaves a faulty impression that few people rebelled against Lerdo in early 1876, and tends to reduce the personal capacity and influence of Porfirio Díaz. It also tends to cast into the

59. Lerdo to Pascual M. Hernández, 14 March 1876, CPD, 1:344.
60. *Ayuntamiento* of Mier to Díaz, 8 April 1876, APD, 12:162–63; Pedro González to Díaz, 20 April 1876, ibid., p. 221.

shadows the larger strategy of the insurrection and results in a misappraisal of the importance of the northeastern campaign within the national movement of Tuxtepec.

Five conclusions can be drawn from the foregoing. First, leaders for the northeastern campaign of Tuxtepec were recruited almost entirely among men who were not part of the Lerdo administration. Although the incumbent governors and military leaders with troops and supplies at their command were invited to join the rebellion, generally they did not. Leaders came from the opposition to local regimes who raised forces where they had personalist following.

Second, the raising of both leaders and troops for the rebellion was greatly embarrassed and delayed by the difficulty of acquiring financial resources for arms and supplies. There seems no justification, however, to imply that a correlation existed between that difficulty and the degree of sympathy or antipathy toward the rebellion, for the government forces experienced the same difficulty in acquiring resources.

Third, the strategy of the investiture of Matamoros was not a concentration of Porfirian forces at that port city but rather the strategy of the guerrilla war: many uprisings were prepared at many points for the military purpose of preventing a concentration of governmental forces upon the whole of the insurgent army and for the political objective of causing widespread belief that the insurrection was popular and national. Moreover, an additional reason for spreading out rather than concentrating forces was the logistical tactic of absorbing manpower, supplies, and financial sources throughout the northeast in order to deprive the government of those resources.

Four, that strategy was successful, if we may judge by the extent of the uprisings which, although small and sometimes short-lived, did in fact isolate Matamoros from reinforcement from elsewhere in the northeast. The investiture was accomplished as much by the absence of aid to the governmental garrison as by the political intrigues of *Tuxtepecanos* with persons of command within the city.

Five, the investiture of Matamoros was a part of the insurrectionary strategy, not the object of that strategy. Occupying Matamoros was useful to the *Tuxtepecanos* for its psychological value upon the whole country; it was useful for the customshouse as a collecting ground for financial contributions and for purposes of recruiting. Its place within the overall strategy should have been that of a great supply source for all the other forces in the northeast. Although it did serve that function, the degree of the accomplishment must have been disappointing to the *Tuxtepecanos*: never were resources sufficient in the northeast for a major campaign there in 1876.

The implications of that poverty in the northeast of Mexico upon a constantly changing *Tuxtepecano* strategy will be demonstrated in chapter 9, while the continued importance of extended guerrilla warfare will be demonstrated in chapter 10.

Chapter 9
The Meaning of Icamole

In the northwestern part of the state of Nuevo León on 20 May 1876 an encounter was fought known to history as the battle of Icamole. The histories now in print are unsatisfactory for the battle itself and wholly inadequate for the campaign of which the battle forms a part. It has been assumed that Díaz's plans are known and that those plans failed: Díaz planned to raise an army in Matamoros and march triumphantly across the central plateau, capturing the cities of Monterrey, Saltillo, San Luis Potosí, and the capital. Díaz lost the battle of Icamole northwest of Monterrey, however, and therefore abandoned the north, the northern campaign, and the northern strategy. This has been the major interpretation of those events. The problem is essentially that it employs a static view of the northeastern campaign.

The purpose of this chapter is to relate the *Tuxtepecano* northeastern campaign to the overall strategy of the insurrection of Tuxtepec and to place into that structure the battle known as Icamole. It will be shown that Díaz's plans for the northeast conformed to a grand national strategy that included alternatives at each shift of circumstances, and that the northern campaign was a dynamic one which changed in objectives as the conditions changed. Finally, it will be shown that the campaign essentially succeeded.

In the days following the battle of Icamole, the newspapers of the capital printed releases as quickly as reports arrived from the field, the progovernment press printing the governmental statements and the opposition press doubting and arguing.[1] The government claimed a great victory and prophesied an early end to the rebellion. This seemed a realistic appraisal in the capital, based as much on news that Gen. Mariano Escobedo had recaptured Matamoros for the government on 19 May as on reports of the defeat of Díaz, Gerónimo Treviño, Franscisco Naranjo, Hipólito Charles, and Juan C. Vara at

---

1. *Diario Oficial,* 21 May–9 June 1876; several are reprinted in APD, 12:7–17; the battle of the press is described in Cosío Villegas, *República restaurada,* pp. 874–75.

Icamole on 20 May. Furthermore, Díaz was not again seen in the north.

Finally, on 9 June the *Diario Oficial* published in full the long-awaited official report of the battle from General Fuero, the commanding general of the governmental forces at Icamole.[2] The Fuero Report claimed that the government forces numbered 1,040 and that the forces led by "don Porfirio Díaz, Naranjo, Charles and Vara . . . numbered more than 1,500 men." The rebel forces, it said, occupied "a military position truly advantageous." Nevertheless, after an hour and a half of fighting, the enemy "retreated in disorder and suffered . . . a complete defeat and dispersion. . . ." The report admitted a governmental loss of two officers and 65 soldiers dead, one officer and 24 soldiers wounded, and a body of unnumbered men captured, "the major part of whom were recovered after the defeat" of the rebels. The rebel dead and wounded were not reported, but the names of 55 men with grades of corporal through commander, captured by the governmental force, were included. Furthermore, the rebel force lost to the governmental force some 250 arms, 25,000 rounds of ammunition, and 258 horses.

Very early in the press commentaries Díaz was given the sobriquets "Cry-baby of Icamole," based on the rumor that he cried before his officers after the defeat, and "Run-away of Icamole," for having fled instead of mustering for another battle. Díaz had dispersed his forces and crossed the Texas border alone.

With the appearance of volume twelve of the Díaz archive in 1949, edited by Alberto María Carreño, a new interpretation has become possible. The correspondence published there demonstrates that before the battle of Icamole the rebels of central and southern Mexico insisted that Díaz should place himself at their head, that the battle of Icamole had not influenced Díaz to leave the northern theater, and that Díaz had decided to leave the north even before the battle. Although Carreño does not draw those conclusions, such conclusions are possible.

Carreño's contribution to the knowledge of the "battle of Icamole" is that the combat did not take place at Icamole, and, more important, that it was not fought between General Fuero and his fellow officers

2. *Diario Oficial*, 9 June 1876; the Fuero report is reprinted in Cosmes, *Historia general de Méjico*, 22:792, and in APD, 12:9–17.

and troops on the one side, and Generals Díaz, Treviño, Naranjo, Charles, and Vara with their respective officers and troops on the other. General Fuero met the column led by Francisco Naranjo at a place called Puerto del Indio. Generals Díaz, Treviño, and Charles, with the forces at their commands, were not present. They were at the *hacienda* of "Hicamole," about two miles distant from Puerto del Indio when the encounter took place.

The evidence for this startling discovery is a document published by Carreño, written by Treviño to Díaz on the day of the battle, including a description of the encounter by Naranjo for his immediate superior officer, Treviño. The document describes the entire engagement, and it mentions no persons or units not under the sole and immediate command of Naranjo. Had Treviño been present and Díaz absent, Treviño, as the leading commander, would have made the report. Had Díaz been present the report would have been superfluous: there was no one to whom Díaz was then reporting. Concluding the letter is Treviño's important explanation to General Díaz why Naranjo had found himself alone: "If General Naranjo was not opportunely aided by the bulk of the column it was because he [Naranjo] did not have orders [from Treviño] to engage in a decisive battle, but rather simply to make a reconnaissance and to skirmish with the enemy."[3] Icamole, then, was an isolated encounter involving a Porfirian subaltern who had been ordered not to engage in full battle.

There are two reasons why all historians have regularly thought that Díaz was present and in command at the battle of Icamole. First, the Fuero Report, which claimed a victory over Díaz personally, was made public and was widely known before Díaz was in a position to rectify the error. Secondly, Díaz never denied his presence at Icamole. His opportunities to do so were many.[4] Even in a copy of his official

3. Treviño to Díaz, 20 May 1876, APD, 12:331; the document is in AGNL, *ramo militar, caja N, expediente Naranjo*.

4. Díaz might have denied in the several histories of the period and in biographies of himself that were presented to him for revision before publication. Bancroft's biography was one. Cosío Villegas ("Lerdo," p. 186) says that a Spanish translation of Bancroft's biography of Díaz "was submitted for the approbation of Porfirio Díaz, who sent a list of corrections," now preserved in the Bancroft Library. Fortunato Hernández's *Un pueblo, un siglo y un hombre* (Mexico: Imprenta de Ignacio Escalante, 1909), dedicated to Díaz, was another. Carleton Beals described Hernández as a "paid eulogist," author of a

service record corrected in his own handwriting, listing the military actions in which he participated, appears "the battle of Icamole, Porfirio Díaz commanding, 20 May 1876, against General Carlos Fuero."[5] The simple explanations why Díaz allowed a defeat to be recorded against his name for a battle at which he was not commanding, or even present, are that he would not have been believed and after 1876 he was not interested in giving lessons in successful insurrection.

Appraisal of the battle at Puerto del Indio will pivot around why Díaz was at Icamole on 20 May. Was he not intending to attack Monterrey? Why was Díaz at Icamole rather than commanding all his forces at Puerto del Indio? Implicit in every printed account is that the Porfirian strategy was to arm the rebel forces with the wealth of Matamoros and then to converge upon Monterrey, followed by Saltillo, San Luis Potosí, and finally the capital. Not only was such a strategy an apparently obvious one, but Díaz in 1876 was telling many people that after acquiring materials of war in Matamoros he planned to "commence a serious campaign against the garrisons of Monterrey, Saltillo, San Luis and the capital." Later historians have taken him at his word, but probably Díaz planted false information to lead the government astray.[6] The government believed that the Porfirian strategy was the central plateau march. In April the garrisons of those cities were reinforced.[7] Escobedo telegraphed Servando Canales, governor of Tamaulipas, as early as 11 April that Díaz was ready to march "from Matamoros against Monterrey with 1,500 men."[8] As late

book "among those sent around the world in all languages to shape foreign opinion of Díaz and Mexico": *Porfirio Díaz*, p. 272.

5. This document belongs to Señora Marie Thérèse Gatouillat de Díaz Raigosa, the widow of General Díaz's grandson, who kindly allowed me to study it.

6. Evidence for this view is proffered in appendix 12.

7. *Diario Oficial*, 6 May 1876.

8. The telegram was immediately sent to Díaz: Santos de la Garza y Gutiérrez to Díaz, 11 April 1876, APD, 12:184–85. Meanwhile, the government forces burlesqued the Porfirian strategy: "Everyone . . . now contemplates Porfirio Díaz, General Treviño, and the other prominent chiefs of the revolution, pouring over these states and sweeping away with their victorious phalanges the 'insignificant' federal units which garrison the plazas of Monterrey, Saltillo, Zacatecas, and San Luis Potosí." *Porvenir de Catorce*

as 7 May Escobedo telegraphed a message to the minister of war that Díaz planned to occupy Monterrey in three days.[9]

The central plateau strategy was not a viable or realistic plan. Díaz wanted to occupy Monterrey, but did not plan to fight for it, and did not consider it as a step in the central strategy. Furthermore, Díaz had abandoned hope of occupying Monterrey by the time of the encounter at Puerto del Indio; indeed, he bypassed Monterrey in his march from Matamoros to Icamole. A consideration of nineteenth-century insurrectionary patterns, of which it is assumed here that Díaz was a master, will confirm this.

There were two phases of the successful nineteenth-century insurrection. First was the propagandistic appeal to the local leaders for supporting the pronouncement and its accompanying plan. During this phase the rebels did not want to meet governmental forces. They wanted to spread the conflagration to all parts of the country and discredit the government merely by continuing to exist in defiance. Military activity generally consisted of guerrilla warfare, the function of which was to demonstrate that the government could not crush the movement. This success was then used in appealing for further support as evidence that the government was less popular than the challengers.

Another recognizable phenomenon ran concurrently with the former. The longer the rebels continued their defiance and the more widespread became the insurrection, the more restrictive became governmental policy. The Lerdo government in 1876 declared military law in state after state, decreed forced loans, recruited by levy, and finally resorted to censorship of the press. One is reminded of Edmund Burke's observation that when subjects are rebels by principle, kings become tyrants by policy. With each step, the rebels turned the governmental restrictions into propaganda. Successful nineteenth-century insurrections in Mexico always had effective propaganda organizations that dwelt on the theme of tyranny.

"Existence in defiance" was an effective insurrectionary tactic in the nineteenth century and during the initial years of the twentieth cen-

---

(Tamaulipas), 26 April 1876, taken from *Boletín de la 3ª División* (of General Escobedo) and reprinted in *Diario Oficial*, 6 May 1876.

9. Escobedo to Ignacio Mejía, 7 May 1876, reprinted in *Diario Oficial*, 10 May 1876.

tury, because the national treasury could never afford to finance military action against prolonged resistance. When the treasury was unable to meet the ordinary expenses of the government, such as pensions and payroll, it suffered even greater loss of prestige and support. This was certainly the case in the rebellion of Tuxtepec, and the inability to pay for further supplies, not to mention meeting the military payroll, was one of the reasons why Lerdo did not attempt to raise another army later in 1876 after General Alatorre lost the Second Division at Tecoac on 16 November.

Ultimately, the successful insurrection would need to occupy a state capital in order to establish a state government that could divert finances and state militias to the movement. State capitals, however, were garrisoned. Furthermore, when governmental forces were in adjacent areas, garrisoned cities formed the block upon which rebel forces could be crushed. During the first phase of the insurrection, therefore, the rebels made great attempts to wean governors of the states and units of the garrisons from their loyalty to the government. This was what Díaz was trying to accomplish in Brownsville and Matamoros.

When the rebels controlled a state capital and a state government, the second stage of the successful insurrection began. It then became necessary to concentrate the rebel forces of the area in order to protect that city from approaching federal forces. The rebels might elect to meet those forces in the city they held or to use that city as a base of operations and march elsewhere to meet the federal forces. Nevertheless, a "showdown" battle had to take place before the rebels could march upon the capital. Late in the second phase the successful, mineteenth-century insurrection experienced the "bandwagon effect," as local leaders and even national figures read the writing on the wall and clamored to join the winners. In the Insurrection of Tuxtepec Oaxaca became the rebel base, the "bandwagon effect" began in early November, and the "showdown battle" took place at Tecoac on 16 November. All of this was far from the northeast and long after April.

The overall national strategy of the rebellion of Tuxtepec can be reconstructed. Probably the areas of greatest expectations, around which a strategy had been formed, were those of Puebla in the southeast and Jalisco-Durango in the west. Rebellions were to develop simultaneously, capturing the state governments and creating concentrations of forces sufficient to meet federal divisions. The northern strategy was that Matamoros was to serve as the arsenal and depot of the north, supplying several armies that would harass the major northern cities, isolate them from intercommunication, and occupy them if possible. If the federal units would react first to the rebellious southeastern nucleus and then to the western nucleus, the northern rebels would have time to establish state governments which could support armies to march to the aid of the rebellions further south. Final confrontations with the major governmental armies could be envisioned near the center of the republic.

No one recorded the overall strategy of the Insurrection of Tuxtepec, but this sketch conforms to the abilities of the avowed *Porfiristas,* to the lessons of La Noria, to the opportunities presented by the circumstances of 1876, and to geography. This was probably the primary Porfirian national strategy.

On the other hand, if the government were to react to the northern rebellion with a major campaign drawn from the south, then Díaz would shift to a secondary northern strategy, which would be to constitute the north into a widespread decentralized guerrilla war to hold down as many governmental forces as possible.

The first task for the *Tuxtepecanos* in 1876 was to raise as many rebellions as possible. Hermenegildo Carrillo was to pronounce in Puebla and Donato Guerra in Durango. Gen. Luis Mier y Terán was to rebel in Veracruz, and Justo Benítez would organize people, propaganda, and finances in Oaxaca and Mexico City. Guerra could be counted upon to use his influence with chiefs in the northwest. It was hoped that he could influence Gen. Sóstenes Rocha, the most audacious and feared general in Mexico and a political enemy of Lerdo since his exile to Celaya in 1875, to effect the defection of the key garrison of San Luis Potosí. Gen. Vicente Riva Palacio was to raise the rebellion in Morelos to the south of the capital. Michoacán was already in a rebellion, not of *Porfirista* inspiration, but nevertheless absorbing governmental energies. Meanwhile, a well-developed *Porfirista* party existed in the national capital composed of politicians, journalists, and lawyers. The insurrectionary "directory" in Mexico City, identified by the *Porfirista* journalist Ireneo Paz, consisted of Gen. Pedro Ogazón, Ignacio Vallarta, and Protasio Tagle, all of whom

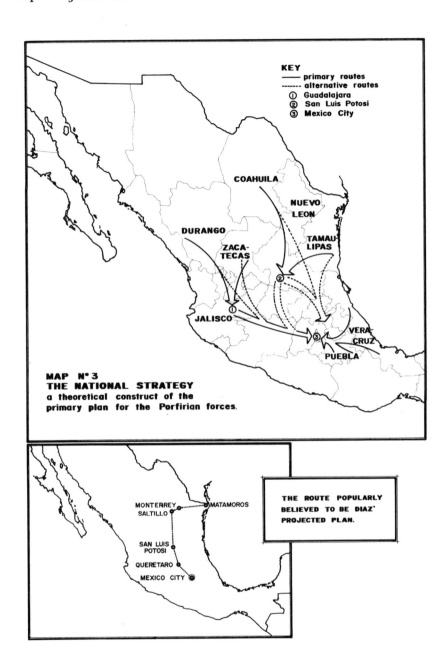

KEY
—— primary routes
------- alternative routes
① Guadalajara
② San Luis Potosi
③ Mexico City

COAHUILA

NUEVO LEON

DURANGO

TAMAU-LIPAS

ZACA-TECAS

JALISCO

VERA-CRUZ

PUEBLA

MAP N° 3
THE NATIONAL STRATEGY
a theoretical construct of the
primary plan for the Porfirian forces.

MONTERREY   MATAMOROS
SALTILLO

SAN LUIS POTOSI

QUERETARO

MEXICO CITY

THE ROUTE POPULARLY
BELIEVED TO BE DIAZ'
PROJECTED PLAN.

figured in Díaz's first cabinet. Early in the year *Porfirista* generals left Mexico City by assignment to areas where they enjoyed personalist followings—Juan N. Mirafuentes, Vicente Riva Palacio, Hermenegildo Carrillo, Feliciano Chavarría, José Cosío Pontones, Aureliano Rivera, Isidro Montiel, Antonio Rodríguez Bocardo, "and many others."[10] Generals Manuel González and Francisco Z. Mena accompanied Díaz to Brownsville to raise the north. The first stage of the national strategy was to arrange insurrections across the nation.

For the primary national strategy, there were surprises in store for the planners. Carrillo, Guerra, and Rocha all failed in their missions.[11] A dozen of the minor diversionary rebellions did break out, but none, not even that of González, Mena, and Díaz, sufficed to gain a state capital. Nevertheless, by curious circumstances, Oaxaca again became the rebel base in 1876, as it had been in 1871 when Félix Díaz, then governor of Oaxaca, pronounced against President Benito Juárez. Rebel forces concentrated in the southeast and confronted federal forces at the battle of Jazmín in Oaxaca and at Epatlán in Puebla. But the federal force was not annihilated in the southeastern campaign, and the *Tuxtepecanos* divided again and returned to an earlier stage of conflict.

Briefly, the events in the southeast were these: On 10 January one unknown Colonel Sarmiento pronounced for Díaz in Ojitlán, district of Tuxtepec in the state of Oaxaca, and proceeded to march his small force of national guardsmen into the state of Veracruz. The attempt was a failure, as had been the planned uprising of Hermenegildo Carrillo in Puebla. At that time, however, a purely local uprising in the Sierra of Oaxaca against the municipal chief in Ixtlán escalated into a rebellion against the state governor, José Esperón, who had sent militia units into Ixtlán. The *caudillo* of the Sierra, Fidencio Hernández, who had fought with General Alatorre for Juárez in 1872 against Díaz, now in 1876 accepted the Plan of Tuxtepec on 25 January and occupied the city of Oaxaca two days later. In one week he had escalated his quarrel with a local official to a direct challenge to the president of the nation. Naming Francisco Meijueiro as governor,

10. Paz, *Algunas campañas,* 3:359.
11. Although Donato Guerra thought the Rocha adhesion was secure (Guerra to Díaz, 10 February 1876, APD, 11:310), his alliance with *Porfirismo* was tenuous.

Hernández took the field against the government general of the Second Division, Ignacio Alatorre.[12]

In the battle of Jazmín on 17 February General Alatorre was thrown back with a loss of one-half of his army, but with a smaller loss in absolute numbers than that suffered by the rebels. Battles at San Cristóbal and at the convent of Yanhuitlán between Fidencio Hernández and Diódoro Corella, newly sent out to reinforce Alatorre, alternated with negotiations between Alatorre and the rebels. The Oaxacan rebels sought the defection of Alatorre. Refusing that, Alatorre offered to present a bargain to the government whereby Esperón would be removed from the governorship of Oaxaca in exchange for a rebel rejection of the Plan of Tuxtepec and recognition of the federal authorities. The negotiations broke down. The government seems to have wanted Alatorre to defeat the numerically superior rebel force and to impose Esperón upon the state. It may be, however, that Hernández refused to withdraw his support from the *Tuxtepecano* rebellion.[13] Whatever happened there, the government ordered a termination of the Oaxacan campaign in order to confront new developments in Puebla and Veracruz. Alatorre withdrew the

12. Iturribarría, *Oaxaca,* 4:150–63; Cosío Villegas, *República restaurada,* pp. 809, 829–31.

13. The point is moot. Compare Iturribarría, *Oaxaca,* 4:164–71, and Cosío Villegas, *República restaurada,* pp. 838–39. Iturribarría ponders the possibility of a party connection between Ignacio Mejía and Fidencio Hernández whereby Alatorre might be persuaded to support Mejía for the presidency in 1876 against Lerdo. The theory fits well with Mejía's use of federal forces in Oaxaca, which seemed to favor Hernández rather than the *Lerdista* Esperón. Cosío Villegas rejects this and (on the possibly biased authority of the anti-*Lerdista* paper *El Siglo XIX*) blames the collapse of the negotiations upon Hernández, who, Cosío maintains, insisted upon honoring the pledge to *Porfirismo.* Appearances and contemporary Porfirian propaganda favor Iturribarría, but evidence is lacking. A *Porfirista* participant later wrote that Alatorre retired from San Yanhuitlán because his relief, Corella, was beaten en route by another Porfirian army in Suchulahuaca: Celestino Pérez to anonymous, a 46-page unused manuscript about the Tuxtepecan campaigns in Oaxaca, which forms an appendix in Anonymous, "Génesis de la revolución tuxtepecano en el estado de Puebla, memorias, apuntes y recuerdos de un testigo presencial, 8 de febrero a 16 de noviembre de 1876," a 214-page heretofore unknown manuscript placed by this author in the Centro de Estudios Históricos, Universidad Veracruzana, Jalapa, Veracruz.

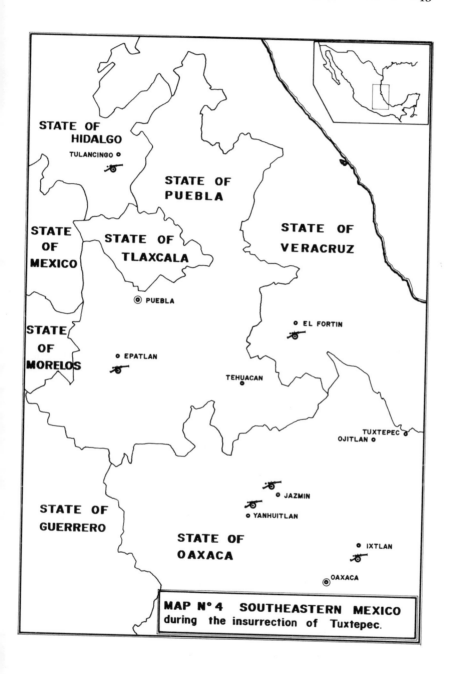

MAP N° 4   SOUTHEASTERN MEXICO
during the insurrection of Tuxtepec.

Second Division from Oaxaca on 27 March. The multiple points of rebellion that characterized the Insurrection of Tuxtepec assured the continuation of the Oaxacan base for *Porfirismo*.

The new developments which required Alatorre to retire from Oaxaca were the insurrections of Luis Mier y Terán in Veracruz and José María Couttolenc on the plains of Puebla. Mier y Terán was a professed *Porfirista* of many years, whereas General Couttolenc had been a *Juarista hacendado* whose rebellion in 1876 began as a local quarrel with the governor of Puebla, Ignacio Romero Vargas. Couttolenc led the ceremony of pronouncement at his mill in Tecamachalco on 8 February with words recorded by a participant and later anonymous memoirist:

> The proprietors of *haciendas* and small properties view with utmost disgust the new taxes and exaggerated gabelle, which day by day the state government augments against landholders. . . . It is necessary . . . to prepare to defend our interests. . . .

Antonio Gamboa, long-time *Porfirista* and then political chief and military commander of Tepexi, turned over the town to the Tuxtepec cause, and Col. Marcos Bravos, chief of the Line of Southern Puebla, placed his unit at the command of Couttolenc. Recruitment in Puebla was rapid, and battles commenced with a rebel victory at Santiagotzingo on 4 March. Within ten days defections took place in the battalion stationed in Puebla. Several battles occurred in March and April, and on 24 March the rebels occupied Tehuacán, headquarters of the federal Second Division, while Alatorre was negotiating with Fidencio Hernández in San Yanhuitlán. The anonymous memoirist claims that the Puebla rebels captured sufficient munitions in Tehuacán to last them for the rest of the insurrection.[14]

The rebel forces of Puebla, as well as those of General Mier y Terán in Veracruz, increased in size and importance during March and April and united with those of Oaxaca under the leadership of Fidencio Hernández. They met the division of Alatorre at San Juan Epatlán

14. Anonymous, "Génesis," p. 4–33; the citation is on p. 8. The author worked as a spy and agent for Couttolenc and later for Díaz. His episodes in arranging defections in the federal army and state militia are particularly revealing and are the only cases known to this author of federal and state soldiers defecting to Díaz before November, except at Matamoros.

on 28 May. Almost four thousand men fought on each side of that conflict. After eight hours of battle both sides retired with terrible losses. Diódoro Corella, the general second in command for the government, shortly died of wounds suffered there, and Gen. Luis Mier y Terán from the rebel forces was taken prisoner.[15] The battle represented attrition on both sides within the civil war of 1876 and helped assure that the war would be long. The immediate effect was the division of the rebel forces. Within the framework of insurrectionary patterns established here, the battle of Epatlán threw the rebellion back into the first phase of insurrection, even as it assured that Alatorre could not divest the rebellion of its base in Oaxaca.

Of the many battles of central Mexico the newspapers of the day and the historical sources mention an encounter at Tulancingo in the state of Hidalgo in June, while Díaz was en route to the south to take command. After the battle of Epatlán and the return to smaller tactical movements in the south, another concentration of rebel forces began to assemble in northern Puebla, Tlaxcala, and Hidalgo. Gen. Miguel Negrete, Rafael Cravioto, and Juan Crisótomo Bonilla had pronounced for the Plan of Tuxtepec and were developing significant armies. Generals Couttolenc and Hernández joined them, all under the command of the *caudillo* of the Sierra of Puebla, Gen. Juan N. Méndez, whom Díaz had recently named supreme commander of the eastern *Tuxtepecano* armies. The concentration is significant in that although the rebel forces reached 4,000 men, they were incapable of taking a position at Tulancingo held by 400 state militiamen. Celestino Pérez, later a correspondent with the anonymous memoirist, was present there. He wrote that negotiations took place at Tulancingo for the surrender of the government garrison and that the rebel army retreated after several hours without fighting and without his ever being informed of the cause. He mentions a meeting of thirteen rebel generals there.[16] The problem was apparently one of leadership, as it

15. The battle is described by the anonymous memoirist, "Génesis," pp. 58–82 ("after eight hours of battle no leaves were left on the trees"), and by Pérez for the Oaxacan rebels in "appendix," ibid., pp. 179–88.

16. Pérez, appendix, "Génesis," pp. 190–93. See also Iturribarría, *Oaxaca*, 4:177–80; Cosío Villegas, *República restaurada*, pp. 839–47. Dispersal followed; some units separated at Tulancingo and Couttolenc's forces dispersed a few days later in Jalapa, Veracruz, because, according to the anonymous

had been in the north during the insurrection of La Noria: that group of self-made men could not subordinate their wills to a single purpose. Many of those troops became the nucleus of the army which Díaz led to Tecoac five months later.

The northern campaign did not enter the second phase. Díaz probably planned to pronounce in the north simultaneously with his coreligionists in the southeast, or soon after. That he could not pronounce before 20 March indicates the extent of his failure. Matamoros fell to the *Tuxtepecanos* on 2 April, but thereafter the northern rebel army developed slowly and never reached sufficient proportions for a successful connection with the southern or western rebels. Matamoros had been important but could give Díaz no more strength after mid-April. Díaz left Matamoros on 25 April with 1,500 men—unready to meet governmental forces. He controlled no state capital and too few soldiers to invite a confrontation with a major federal force. He needed either the adherence of Governor Canales of Tamaulipas, an alliance which would have dictated a connection with the southern armies through Hidalgo, or a defection in Monterrey for a connection with the western rebellion. By late April, however, two conditions had developed that forced Díaz to take action. First, the southern campaign had reached the second phase, while the northern campaign was still in the first phase. The situation in the south was rapidly disintegrating into an anarchic series of local rebellions.

The second factor forcing Díaz's hand was the approach of federal forces. Should Lerdo and his minister of war, Gen. Ignacio Mejía, have decided to place the major part of their resources at the disposition of the federal generals operating in the southeast, then Díaz would have had more time to raise a northern army. They decided, however, to operate initially against the northern rebels. Withdrawing forces from Michoacán, which presented continuous hostility and depredations without directly threatening the government—since that

---

memoirist, of demoralization in the rebel forces due to ignorance about the location of Porfirio Díaz and rumors of his capture or death: "Génesis," pp. 95–112. Fidencio Hernández left Jalapa with 1,500 men and a great deal of armament only to lose everything a few days later to General Sánchez Rivera in an ambush near Fortín, Veracruz. The "battle" of El Fortín is described by Pérez, appendix, "Génesis," pp. 205–12.

Catholic rebellion had not succeeded in attracting national support—Lerdo sent three separate columns to the north in early April under the command of Gen. Mariano Escobedo. Díaz knew of that governmental decision before he left Matamoros on 25 April.

For these two reasons, the inability to raise a great army in the north and the government decision to operate first in the north, both of which were known to Díaz before 25 April, it may be concluded that it was not the battle of Icamole that destroyed the northern strategy or influenced Díaz to divide his forces and join the rebels of the south.

Indeed, Díaz may have judged the primary national strategy a failure even earlier. His confidential replies to friends, who were urging him to give personal leadership to the growing southern rebellion, indicate that in mid-March he was planning to turn the north into a grand diversionary activity. In early March, Protasio Tagle, identified by Paz as a member of the "revolutionary directory," counseled Díaz to go south: "You are needed here immediately; the situation [in the south] could not be better. Do not lose a moment. If you were in Oaxaca now, all would have been won."[17] Díaz answered a similar exhortation this way:

> The indications you make to me about the importance of my presence in Oaxaca or in Jalisco satisfy me little, first because were I to do so, the attention of the government would reconcentrate at the place where I would be. . . . [And second,] if I were not here, the frontier would remain indefinitely passive. What is needed is that the attention of the government be divided as much as possible.[18]

Two days before Díaz pronounced on 20 March he wrote to Donato Guerra that "before a week is out I will have given the government much to do, calling upon myself a great part of its attention." The diversionary aspect of the northern strategy was his concern: "At least this will leave our friends, who are operating in distinct points now in battle, a little less harried."[19] Díaz apparently saw the role of the north at that time as a grand attraction to draw off federal forces from the south and west. Only a few days later he began releasing

17. Tagle to Díaz, 9 March 1876, APD, 12:48.
18. Díaz to "El Gordo," 19 March 1876, ibid., p. 90.
19. Díaz to Guerra, 18 March 1876, ibid., p. 84.

indiscrete notices of his plan to march a large army from the north to the capital of the nation.

Díaz's plan was therefore to place in operation the secondary northern strategy. He would continue to raise as many points of rebellion, to make as much noise, draw to him as many federal soldiers as possible, and then leave the north to direct activities in another theater. In late April that theater might have been either in his home region of Oaxaca or in the Jalisco–Zacatecas–Durango region where Donato Guerra and Pedro Galván were operating. There was also an outside chance for the defection of Monterrey.

Díaz's tactics in late April would depend upon Escobedo, and it was not immediately clear from Matamoros what Escobedo would do. The worst contingency for Díaz would have been that Escobedo would garrison Monterrey, turning it into the customshouse and isolating Díaz in Matamoros. Thus Díaz divided his force into columns and marched out of Matamoros towards Monterrey. Escobedo might have elected to await Díaz at Monterrey.[20] But dissension reigned within the federal officer corps of Monterrey: it was best that they be sent campaigning. Lerdo was in need of an early triumph in the north in order to concentrate a final blow upon the southern rebels before the summer election. Escobedo, therefore, marched out to meet Díaz.

That Díaz did not want to meet the entire federal force in battle is as clear in the record of those events as it is in the above theory. It was Naranjo's opinion on 26 April that Díaz should attack Monterrey immediately. General González expected battle and victory. From Matamoros to Díaz, then in march, he wrote on 1 May, "If you triumph in Nuevo León . . . 400 men will suffice for me . . . in the district of the North." On 3 May Naranjo reported that he had information that Escobedo was about ready to leave Monterrey with 3,000 men who could not resist a *Tuxtepecano* attack for half an hour.[21] These were not, however, Díaz's opinions.

In the town of Mier on the Rio Grande Díaz held a council of war on 1 and 2 May. There he told his subordinates that there would be a

20. The American consul in Matamoros reported to Washington that "everyone understood" that Escobedo's plan was to await Díaz's attack in Monterrey: McCornack, "Frontera texana," p. 397.

21. Naranjo to Díaz, 26 April 1876, APD, 12:256; González to Díaz, 1 May 1876, ibid., p. 271; Naranjo to Díaz, 3 May 1876, ibid., p. 280.

change of strategy. It is not clear from the Díaz papers exactly what the new strategy would be. Díaz wrote to Treviño on 3 May that he was en route to Terán, some fifty-five miles southeast of Monterrey and so situated as to give Díaz alternatives: he could flee south, retreat to Matamoros, or threaten Monterrey. His letter to Treviño indicates that the direction of Escobedo's advance would determine his choice.[22]

Gen. Mariano Escobedo left Monterrey with between 2,500 and 3,000 men on 3 May, leaving about 1,500 men in that city under the command of Carlos Fuero. Escobedo marched northeast through Cerralvo to Mier on the Rio Grande, and thence downstream toward Matamoros. Generals Martínez and Quiroga with 900 cavalry had driven Treviño and Naranjo from Cerralvo on 4 May. Meanwhile, Díaz had not gone south to China and Terán, but rather at Tecometes (4 May) he turned east and retreated to Mojarras (6 May) and Charco Escondido, in the state of Tamaulipas (8 May), on the road to Matamoros. Soon Naranjo and Treviño were also moving east along the river bank toward Matamoros. And as Escobedo occupied Mier on 10 May, Díaz's artillery and infantry entered Matamoros.[23]

The new plan contained the possibility of a defensive battle at Matamoros—but Díaz would not be there. Matamoros was a good defensive position if Escobedo did not come in full force, and the march there was shorter for the Porfirian units than for Escobedo, who would tire his soldiers and lengthen his supply line. It would also be a long way from the southern and western rebellions. General Naranjo wrote on 7 May that captured mail indicated that Escobedo knew of the retreat to Matamoros and was marching on. Indeed, Escobedo telegraphed the minister of war on 7 May that, "This morning . . . I received notice from my scouts that they have withdrawn all their trains by the same road which they came from Matamoros." Naranjo was enthusiastic for a full confrontation at Matamoros, adding that "we need not only to throw Escobedo back; we need to destroy him. . . ." Toledo on the same day wrote that Matamoros is "where [Escobedo] will lose everything." Only on 6 May did General González learn of the new strategy. In his letter to Díaz of 7 May he

22. Díaz to Treviño, 3 May 1876, ibid., p. 278.
23. Escobedo to Ignacio Mejía, 7 May 1876, in *Diario Oficial*, 10 May 1876; Escobedo to Ignacio Mejía, 10 May 1876, in ibid., 15 May 1876.

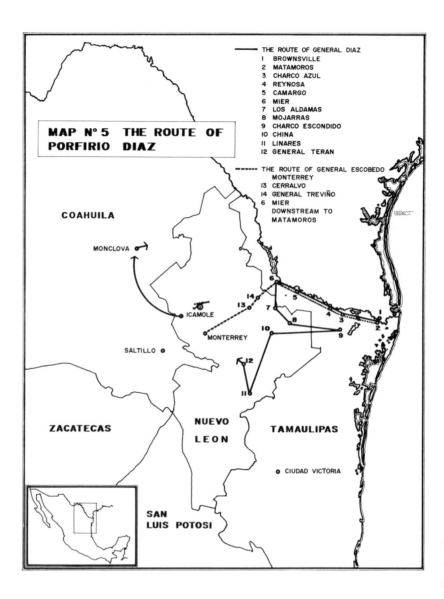

MAP N° 5 THE ROUTE OF
PORFIRIO DIAZ

THE ROUTE OF GENERAL DIAZ
1 BROWNSVILLE
2 MATAMOROS
3 CHARCO AZUL
4 REYNOSA
5 CAMARGO
6 MIER
7 LOS ALDAMAS
8 MOJARRAS
9 CHARCO ESCONDIDO
10 CHINA
11 LINARES
12 GENERAL TERAN

THE ROUTE OF GENERAL ESCOBEDO
MONTERREY
13 CERRALVO
14 GENERAL TREVIÑO
6 MIER
DOWNSTREAM TO
MATAMOROS

COAHUILA

MONCLOVA

ICAMOLE

MONTERREY

SALTILLO

ZACATECAS

NUEVO
LEON

TAMAULIPAS

CIUDAD VICTORIA

SAN
LUIS POTOSI

informed his chief that "this morning at six o'clock repairs on the fortification [of Matamoros] began."[24] Had Díaz decided earlier upon the defense, González would have been ordered to fortify earlier. And had Díaz merely decided to lure Escobedo away from Monterrey before dividing his forces again, he need not have spent precious time and resources fortifying—a job which proceeded at crash pace until at least 16 May.

One imagines that it was adversity, not strategy, that dictated the decision to retreat to Matamoros. The Porfirian forces in late April and early May experienced great depletion due to desertion. As early as 20 April Carlos Fuero telegraphed the minister of war that the soldiers at Matamoros enlisted by Díaz on 2 April were deserting and uniting with the government officer Lieutenant Colonel Arroyo at Mier, who at that time had 200 men. On 10 May *El Federalista* carried a letter written from Matamoros that claimed that Díaz's army was reduced by desertion to 800 by the time it had marched to Camargo and that at Mier "150 men pronounced against him or dispersed, crossing the river at El Almo, near Rome, Texas." An American observer of the maneuvers also recorded great desertion because of "thirst and lack of provisions," and related this to Díaz's decision to retreat. Similar desertions had taken place earlier in Matamoros. González wrote on 1 May that "the national guardsmen, who in great number crossed the river in order not to march, are returning to their homes and very few remain in Brownsville."[25] Similar desertions occurred days later: reports to Washington indicated that "hundreds" of Mexicans crossed the river upon the approach of Escobedo, because González was trying to obligate all able-bodied men to defend the city.[26] These few observations clearly establish the prevalence of desertion, and may have influenced Díaz to decide against his earlier plan.

24. Escobedo to Mejía, 7 May 1876, in ibid., 11 May 1876; Naranjo to Díaz, 7 May 1876, APD, 12:302–3; Jesús Toledo to Díaz, 7 May 1876, ibid., p. 303; González to Díaz, 7 May 1876, ibid., p. 301.

25. Fuero to Ignacio Mejía, 20 April 1876, *Diario Oficial*, 3 May 1876; *El Federalista*, 10 May 1876; reprinted in Ceballos, *Aurora y ocaso*, 2:500–501; McCornack, *"Frontera tejana,"* p. 397; González to Díaz, 1 May 1876, APD, 12:270.

26. McCornack, *"Frontera tejana,"* p. 398.

Díaz's plan was not to orchestrate a pitched confrontation with Escobedo at Matamoros. He did not personally return to that city. A report to Washington stated that General Revueltas, ordered ahead by Escobedo, gained the city by forced marches before Díaz could arrive there.[27] Díaz, however, had already given orders incompatible with a full confrontation at Matamoros. On 6 May Colonel Cuéllar, *Porfirista*, left Matamoros with 100 men and 25 mules to meet Díaz at Charco Escondido. On the same day Díaz ordered Colonel Amador south to China and Linares, the route Díaz himself took a week later. On 8 May Díaz sent Colonel Haro with 300 men to join Gen. Ignacio Martínez and aid Carlos Díez Gutiérrez in harassing San Luis Potosí.[28] A few days later Díaz himself marched south with Treviño, Naranjo, Charles, and Vera. The movements of dispersal prove that Díaz's secondary strategy was not to confront federal forces.

General González remained in Matamoros continuing the fortifications. As late as 14 May, four days before Escobedo's vanguard entered Matamoros, González wrote to Díaz that he commanded only 500 men. "According to your authorization," he said "[I have] these alternatives: either to divide the force into guerrilla bands or defend myself in the city. I choose the second." González made clear his motives: for guerrilla warfare he needed horses but had only 100, and for withstanding a siege "I judge that the national guard will be more useful defending their homes."[29] Four days later González also abandoned the city.

The alternatives given to González were probably contingent upon the nature of Escobedo's advance. If Escobedo were to divide his forces as Díaz had divided his, then González could have elected the defense. If Escobedo were to advance in full force upon Matamoros, however, then González should move all the forces at his command south into the Huasteca. Perhaps we may read into Díaz's earlier appointment his expectation of this development: on 24 April Díaz had named General González "Commander in Charge of . . . opening the campaign into the interior." Escobedo did order Colonel Ordóñez to pursue Díaz, but he continued to advance upon Matamoros in near

27. Ibid.
28. González to Díaz, 6 May 1876, APD, 12:298; Díaz to José María Amador, 6 May 1876, CPD, 1:128; Díaz to Juan de Haro, 8 May 1876, APD, 12:304; Díaz to Martínez, 8 May 1876, ibid., p. 308.
29. González to Díaz, 14 May 1876, CPD, 1:21.

full strength, occupying the city on 19 May.[30] Furthermore, González did open the campaign into the interior, with consequences of the highest importance: The reunion of González and Díaz six months later on the field of Tecoac carried Díaz to the National Palace.

As Díaz abandoned the vicinity of Matamoros for the second time he again had alternatives. General Escobedo thought Díaz's objective was to occupy Ciudad Victoria, capital of Tamaulipas, and sent orders to Governor Canales to impede the rebel advance. Díaz, however, turned toward the central plateau. He would have wanted to occupy Monterrey for the military stores, the financial resources, the opportunity to recruit, and the important psychological effect that insurrections need for their success. But with Gen. Carlos Fuero in that city, newly reinforced, neither siege nor assault was possible. Díaz's first objective, therefore, was to occupy Monterrey by the politics of defection.

As Díaz left Matamoros he had been in contact with Gen. Julián Quiroga in the Monterrey garrison for over a month. In late March General Díaz sent an authorization to General Quiroga to organize forces in Nuevo León for the *Tuxtepecanos*. The letter is similar to others sent to military officers in the attempt to recruit leaders.[31] Quiroga, however, had been commissioned by Lerdo to recruit a government force for the pacification of the frontier and personally disliked Naranjo and Treviño. Nevertheless, seemingly tempted to join the rebels, Quiroga maintained relations with Díaz through a Porfirian partisan for the next several weeks. The agent was Quiroga's long-time personal friend, Plácido Vega, who reported to Díaz on 29 March that Quiroga, although leading government troops at the time, was pursuing a policy favorable to the rebels, which "I hope will even improve." Vega, calling himself "Pedro Soto" and referring to Quiroga as "Sr. Quia," said that he believed Quiroga would ultimately choose for the rebels. In the meantime, however, Naranjo and Treviño should not interfere. Naranjo and Treviño had less patience, warning Díaz in April that Quiroga was not to be trusted.[32]

30. Díaz to González, 24 April 1876, ibid., p. 450; Ceballos, *Aurora y ocaso,* 2:498; McCornack, *"Frontera tejana,"* p. 400.
31. Díaz to Quiroga, 20 March 1876, APD, 12:94.
32. Plácido Vega to Díaz, 29 March 1876, ibid., p. 126, and 21 April 1876, ibid., p. 228; Vega to Díaz, 29 March 1876, ibid., p. 126; Vega to Díaz, 18 Jan 1876, ibid., 11:297; "Pedro Soto" to Díaz, 4 April 1876, ibid., 12:141–42.

Díaz maintained the contact, nevertheless, and the dissension among the officers of the Monterrey garrison looked promising. "Generals Ordóñez and Aguilar will seek their passports," wrote a Porfirian agent in Monterrey to Díaz on 2 May, "and come over to the *Porfiristas* if ordered to serve under Quiroga." Jesús Toledo had the information differently: "they are in complete anarchy," he wrote to Díaz about Escobedo's staff, "with Quiroga, Ordóñez, and Aguilar united against the rest of them. I think it convenient to send . . . [an offer] to Quiroga." Treviño sent an agent to Quiroga on 3 May, and told Díaz, "I have Quiroga at a distance of nine leagues, but he will do nothing against us as long as I am negotiating with him."[33] No further communication exists relating to the affair which must have been uppermost in Díaz's mind as he marched west. For some reason Escobedo did not take Quiroga with him to Matamoros, and Quiroga served with distinction under Gen. Carlos Fuero at Puerto del Indio on 20 May.

Although the defection of Monterrey would have been Díaz's first choice among the possibilities in mid-May 1876, he did not march toward Monterrey without alternatives. His second choice would have been to by-pass that city, leaving Treviño's forces in the area to harass the government garrisons and communication lines, while taking a body of men into Durango or Zacatecas. There he might have joined Donato Guerra or Pedro Galván, encouraging insurrectionary activity in Durango, Zacatecas, Jalisco, and Guanajuato, coordinating with the forces of Puebla, Oaxaca, and Veracruz for a pincer movement upon the national capital. The logic of the combination was much more promising than the advance against the garrisoned, plateau cities of Monterrey, Saltillo, and San Luis Potosí, because in the west the population was more dense, the resources more available, and the rugged terrain more suitable for insurrectionary operations.

Donato Guerra had been an inner member of the *Porfirista* circle for years. He and Díaz were the last to seek amnesty in 1872 from

---

There is hope in Treviño's letter of 5 April, but none a week later: Treviño to Díaz, 5 April 1876, ibid., p. 148, and 12 April 1876, ibid., p. 186. Naranjo speaks to Díaz of Quiroga's perfidy on 17 April, ibid., p. 215.

33. Juan Vargas Durán to Díaz, 2 May 1876, ibid., p. 274; Toledo to Díaz, 3 May 1876, ibid., p. 279; Treviño to Díaz, 3 May 1876, ibid., pp. 277–78; Naranjo was less optimistic: Naranjo to Díaz, 4 May 1876, ibid., p. 290.

Lerdo. They corresponded regularly during the lean years between 1872 and 1876; both were involved in agriculture, politics, and conspiracy. Guerra was one of the movers of the Insurrection of Tuxtepec and was certainly expected to raise the rebellion in the west-central states, where he had wide influence. He spoke in his letters of his activities in Durango, Zacatecas, Aguascalientes, Guanajuato, and Jalisco, and of the northwestern states of Sinaloa and Chihuahua. Díaz named Guerra the second in command of the rebellion in case of his own incapacitation. Díaz was never wont to put his confidential thoughts on paper, so that the following sentiment is as revealing of his relationship with Guerra as it is of his future politics:

> It is of the highest importance that you leave . . . the places you occupy . . . in absolutely friendly hands and place forces with persons of known confidence, for [when] the moment of the reconstruction [begins] we are going to have difficulty, which we will dominate only by imposing our will. For your part, assume command of as many troops as are organized under your influence or which exist within reach, without delegating [commands to other persons] for some principle of modesty or abnegation, which later we will have to regret.[34]

One might assume that had Guerra not been killed later in the year, he would have played a role close to Díaz in the years to follow.

It is difficult to know what happened in the west-central states. No historian has adequately reconstructed those events, and the contemporary newspapers were purposely misleading.[35] It is even more difficult to know what Díaz *thought* was happening there; and ultimately, Díaz's plans in mid-May were based upon what he thought. Díaz was receiving news by agents, newspapers, and correspondence. Of the first two we know nothing; of the last we cannot know if we have everything. If the extant letters are representative of Díaz's knowledge, he had reason to be confident that the west-central region would play its role well. Donato Guerra pronounced in Lagos, Jalisco, in early February and attracted others to do the same. With 300 cavalry he marched to Guadalajara, capital of Jalisco, to place himself

34. Díaz to Donato Guerra, 18 March 1876, ibid., pp. 84–85.

35. Of news releases in general, one distraught observer remarked that "nothing can be confirmed; it is a dreadful rumor mill, and one needs to doubt everything." P. de León to Díaz, 19 March 1876, ibid., p. 91.

at the head of forces already gathered against the *Lerdista* governor, José Ceballos. In February he wrote Díaz that all was ready in Durango, Zacatecas, and Aguascalientes and that his arrangements in Guanajuato "very soon will render their results."[36] Within days he occupied the city of Aguascalientes with 800 men and marched on to Zacatecas. Within the month he had beaten the government general, Angel Martínez. "Guerra is now in a position to organize," wrote a *Porfirista* to Díaz. "Within a few days he will be able to take the offensive."[37] In early March it was reported that Guerra commanded 1,000 men. Even the encounter, which the capital press claimed was a great government victory over Guerra, was reported to Díaz this way:

> In reference to the defeat of Guerra and *don* Rosendo Márquez, it had not the dimensions which M[anuel Sánchez] Rivera [the government general] gives out and I dare to assure you that they are the lies of a traitor who . . . wants to accredit himself with the government.[38]

Indeed, in early March Guerra was reported by Tagle to be en route to Durango, where he had promised to seize the capital, and by another observer to be in Jalisco "organizing without resistance." Meanwhile, another trusted Porfirian general, Pedro Galván, had pronounced in Jalisco, occupying Tequila on 14 February and Ameca two days later.[39] Tagle reported to Díaz that Galván and Florentino Cuervo commanded 2,000 men in early March. Within days Guerra and Galván were said to have united.[40] Here was the making of a significant army. At the same time Porfirio Díaz could hardly count upon 200 men. Nothing more appears in the Díaz papers about Donato Guerra or Pedro Galván until the report in September that

36. J. N. (?) to Díaz, 10 February 1876, ibid., 11:308; Guerra to Díaz, 10 February 1876, ibid., p. 310.

37. Anon. to Díaz, 14 February 1876, ibid., p. 313; Francisco M. Prida (?) to Díaz, 25 February 1876, ibid., p. 323.

38. Ignacio Martínez (?) to Díaz, 4 March 1876, ibid., 12:36; Anon. to Díaz, 8 March 1876, ibid., p. 43.

39. Anon. to Treviño, 10 March 1876, ibid., p. 54; Pérez Verdía, *Jalisco*, 3:521.

40. Protasio Tagle to Díaz, 9 March 1876, APD, 12:48; "El Gordo" (?) to Díaz, n.d. (early March 1876), ibid., p. 89.

Guerra had been defeated by Colonel Cristerna near Culiacán, in the state of Sinaloa.[41]

Perhaps Díaz learned by word of mouth while crossing the central plateau in mid-May that Guerra had divided his forces, that Rosendo Márquez and Pedro Galván had been beaten separately and captured, and that Guerra was defeated in late April at Tamazula by Gen. Angel Martínez, obliging Guerra to retreat into Colima, then into Tepic, and finally into Sinaloa. The *Diario Oficial* during the month of May reported one government victory after another against a score of rebel groups in the west-central states, including the capture and death of several leaders.[42] As Díaz was crossing the plateau toward Monterrey, there existed few prospects of successful rebellion in Durango, Jalisco, or Zacatecas.

The third alternative Díaz had in mid-May as he left Tamaulipas for the second time, if the first two choices failed, was to divide his forces for guerrilla activity in the north and return alone to his native state to take command of the developed forces there. So superior was the second alternative, however, that it might be presumed that had the defection of Monterrey materialized, it would then have been combined with the western strategy. Nevertheless, the first two alternatives dissolved in conditions adverse to the *Tuxtepecanos*.

One more alternative awaited decision. Treviño and Naranjo would move with Díaz until they had passed Monterrey. If Fuero did not make a sally to cut off the *Tuxtepecano* passage, Naranjo and Treviño would remain there, and Díaz and Charles could move south to Saltillo. If Fuero were to give chase, then they could move north toward Monclova. The pass through the mountains west of Monterrey, which opens onto the road to both Saltillo and Monclova, is through the district of García, northwest of Monterrey, in which is located the *hacienda* of "Hicamole." Fuero gave chase. It would not do to lead Fuero's column behind them into the area where Charles and Vara were already assigned to operate. The object was to lead Fuero as far

41. Francisco C. Arce to anon., 4 September 1876, ibid., 13:47.

42. Cosío Villegas, *República restaurada*, p. 882; Pérez Verdía, *Jalisco*, 3:522–24; *Diario Oficial*, 3–20 May 1876. Guerra's peregrination was one of steady attrition until he wandered almost alone into Chihuahua in September, where he was arrested and shot.

north as he would go, away from the north-central plateau. Díaz would then divide the forces into four separate armies to conduct guerrilla operations, while he would leave the region to go to the southeast, which in late May was the only area where armies stood ready for a commander. This was why Díaz was in Icamole. Meanwhile, confrontation combat was to be avoided; Fuero would not be fought. Naranjo was ordered only to reconnoiter and skirmish. Unfortunately for Díaz's reputation and the historical record, the division of that little army and Díaz's separation from it were preceded by an encounter at Puerto del Indio.

Concluding remarks for this chapter are brief, for the importance of the foregoing lies in the overall patterns which the detail proves but clutters. The object of presenting detail has been to demonstrate that the few facts usually emphasized must have a logic within the larger pattern, not a life of their own. The problem with the material now in print is that the few well-known facts have been used to create structures that are incompatible with the less-known detail. Exemplifying this is the oft-declared Porfirian attempt to march down the central plateau, capturing cities along the way. The near-universal observation has been that the plan failed. Thus the conclusion is drawn, in the face of the collapse of the Lerdo government, that Lerdo somehow bungled his advantage or that someone else pulled Díaz's chestnuts from the fire.

The Insurrection of Tuxtepec followed the patterns of successful nineteenth-century rebellion: a state government was secured as a base of operation, numerous local rebellions were promoted to divert and divide governmental energies, and concentrations of rebel forces formed to meet and defeat the governmental forces. The northern campaign was originally designed to mobilize the forces of the north while the government was occupied elsewhere, in order to combine with rebel armies further south that had successfully established a base of operations. The northern army, however, did not develop as large or as rapidly as was hoped, and it early became the primary object of governmental counterattack.

Nevertheless, the primary national strategy was essentially followed. Two results flowed from the Porfirian northern campaign that are fundamental to successful rebellions. First, it did in fact absorb significant governmental energies, drawing them away from the primary base of operations, whence would come the rebel confrontation army. That is, it drew the largest government army, that of Gen. Mariano Escobedo, into the far north, while the army which toppled the government was free to develop and deploy in the south. Second, a force did in fact march out of the north, augment in passing, and unite with the army of the rebel base to destroy the government army: the army of Gen. Manuel González left Matamoros in May, pushed along the ridge of the Huastecan mountain range, traversed the state of Hidalgo, and united in Puebla with the force that Porfirio Díaz forged in Oaxaca—united with it upon the field even as Díaz was engaged in the "showdown" battle of Tecoac.

Three factors have distracted the eye from the above pattern: the fact that the rebel base at Oaxaca was not part of a Porfirian plan; the fact that Díaz led a small force across the north which ended in dispersal rather than lead the army that began in the north and emerged upon the field of Tecoac; and the fact that the numerous small uprisings, although essential and basic to successful insurrection, generally won only limited and temporary military advantage before being overpowered.

To bring this discussion full circle, a parting remark is offered about Icamole. The meaning of that encounter which emerges from this discussion is the same as that of several score other encounters during the insurrection: it was a skirmish of a small military unit engaging a sally from a government garrison in typical guerrilla circumstances. It was "hit-and-run" activity that governments everywhere claim as victories over rebel fighters and which have as their collective effect the weakening of the government in its will, its resources, and its prestige. Had Gen. Porfirio Díaz not been nearby, the "battle of Icamole" would be known no better, nor have more significance attached to it, than the 17 March encounter at Lampazos, or that of 4 May in Cerralvo, or those of a hundred other places during the civil war of 1876.

Chapter 10
The War of *Guerrilleros*

Widespread guerrilla warfare was a necessary ingredient of successful nineteenth-century insurrection. Its function was to defy the government and to diffuse governmental reaction, forcing the federal army to garrison every city and town and to pursue every band of rebels, even as the *guerrilleros* continually threatened concentrations in new combinations. At the same time, the rebel guerrilla bands recruited, collected subscriptions, obtained armament, interrupted communications, and absorbed manpower and resources, which then became unavailable to the government. By dominating the hinterland of important cities the guerrilla rebels isolated those cities, disrupted normal patterns of commerce and economic life, interfered with the taxation base upon which the government operated, and forced the regime to exhaust its energies and resources in pursuit, while the guerrilla bands generally avoided combat.

The *Tuxtepecanos* maintained this type of guerrilla warfare. Even in the northeast, after the time, according to the historical sources, that Lerdo's armies had pacified the region, guerrilla activity was significant and essential to the *Tuxtepecano* victory.

Although patterns of warfare existed in all parts of the country, the area chosen for this study is principally the Huasteca-Tampico region. The Huasteca is a region in southern Tamaulipas, eastern San Luis Potosí, and northern Veracruz. Tampico is the port city which supplied that area and through which the products of the region reached world markets.

Ten days after Porfirio Díaz pronounced at Palo Blanco on 20 March, and a month before Díaz ordered Manuel González to "open the campaign into the interior"—whence González marched through the Huasteca—the United States consul at Tampico requested an American gunboat "on account of the insurrectionary condition of this part of the country and the suspension of telegraph and mail communication. . . ." The consul wrote to the commanding officer of the U.S. Naval Forces at New Orleans that "the various towns and cities near this port are in revolution. . . . No mails [have been] received from Mexico City in the present month. . . . The troops of this garrison are reduced to 300 men, most of those pressed men, and it is feared that this city will fall at any moment."[1]

Five days later the consul reported that "various bands of revolutionaries infest this state . . . distributed through the country and are more or less united in the same cause, and all are revolutionists." He added that his consular agent in Tuxpan, some 120 miles to the south, informed him that Temapache and Papantla were "pronounced and in full blast of revolution." The consul named "two desperate officers" by name, Emilio Parra and Braulio Vargas, who had a "band of from two to 300 armed men" between Tampico and Ciudad Victoria. Emilio Parra and Braulio Vargas were experienced rebels, having participated in an insurrection against Gov. Juan José de la Garza in 1867–68. They evaded Generals Sóstenes Rocha, Diódoro Corella, and Mariano Escobedo, who commanded 2,000 men between Tampico and the Huasteca in a five-month campaign that ended only by a written treaty with the government of Juárez. The consul sought the protection of a United States gunboat.[2]

On 12 April Col. Gregorio Soto occupied Alamitos with about 150 soldiers, taking possession of a nearby *hacienda*. According to the overseer, Blas Robredo, they remained ten days, subsisting upon the eighty square-mile estate, appropriating corn, beans, sugar, cattle, sheep, and 100 saddle-broken horses. Robredo was carried off with Soto's force through Bananaco, Aldama, San José, and Soto de Marina. In the latter place they imposed a forced loan and demanded horses, corn, cattle, and money from Martín de León, an American citizen. Arriving at Victoria, Robredo was released; he made his way to Tampico, reported his experiences to the American consul, and informed officials in Tampico that there was general insurrection in the state capital.[3]

In mid-April the consul reported that rebels were active in all parts of the state and recorded the first connection with "the Díaz party," which, he said, would attack Tampico in two columns, one by land from Ciudad Victoria and another by sea from Matamoros. The city

1. U.S. Consul Edmund Johnson to W. Hunter, second assistant secretary of state, 30 March 1876, *Despatches from Tampico*, 108.

2. Saldívar, *Tamaulipas*, p. 249; López Gutiérrez, *Mariano Escobedo*, pp. 426–28; Johnson to Hunter, 4 April 1876, *Despatches from Tampico*, 111.

3. Johnson to Hunter, 11 May 1876, ibid.

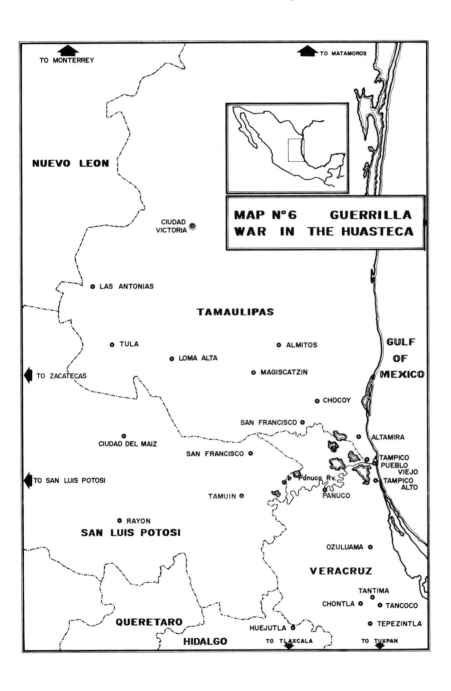

TO MONTERREY

TO MATAMOROS

NUEVO LEON

CIUDAD VICTORIA

**MAP N° 6   GUERRILLA
WAR   IN   THE HUASTECA**

○ LAS ANTONIAS

TAMAULIPAS

○ TULA

○ ALMITOS

GULF

○ LOMA ALTA

OF

TO ZACATECAS

○ MAGISCATZIN

MEXICO

○ CHOCOY

SAN FRANCISCO ○

○
CIUDAD DEL MAIZ

ALTAMIRA

SAN FRANCISCO ○

TAMPICO
PUEBLO
VIEJO

TO SAN LUIS POTOSI

Pánuco Rv.

TAMPICO
ALTO

TAMUIN ○

PANUCO

○ RAYON

SAN LUIS POTOSI

OZULUAMA ○

VERACRUZ

TANTIMA
○

CHONTLA ○   ○ TANCOCO

QUERETARO

HUEJUTLA ○

○ TEPEZINTLA

HIDALGO

TO TLAXCALA

TO TUXPAN

was in terror, and the municipal officials had ordered all male citizens between sixteen and fifty years of age to report to Gen. Jesús Flores for the defense of the city. Fortifications were being strengthened, new earthworks thrown up, and "the work is going on night and day." The consul again asked for a gunboat.[4]

By mid-April Porfirio Díaz may have known that Gen. Jesús Alonso Flores would not deliver the garrison and port of Tampico to the *Tuxtepecanos*, for Díaz wrote to Gov. Servando Canales in Ciudad Victoria that he was "persuaded that you can make yourself master of Tampico, as I have in Matamoros, with a little activity and absolute decision." The consul at Tampico agreed on both counts, that the insurrectionists could assault the city at will and that Flores was loyal to the government. However, the garrison at Tampico at the time of the capture of Matamoros "has been reduced to 300 soldiers, most of them *rancheros*, men serried and by force compelled to serve in the rank and file, and against their will; and if a fight comes, [they] would be as apt to join the enemy as to fight by compulsion."[5]

From Matamoros in the second half of April Díaz authorized several men to operate in the Huasteca. Capt. Simón Castillo was to undertake a mission in southern Tamaulipas, where he later joined the forces of General Jesús Toledo and Canales. Carlos Díez Gutiérrez was to lead the military operations in San Luis Potosí, with authority to draw forces from Veracruz, always respecting "the dispositions dictated by the governor of said state"—General and rebel-Governor Luis Mier y Terán. Col. Juan Haro was ordered to lead the rebel activities in the Veracruz Huasteca and to coordinate his activities with those of Díez Gutiérrez and Ignacio Martínez.[6] Juan Haro was from Pueblo Viejo, a town of some 2,000 persons about two miles from Tampico. He had been the political chief of Tampico in 1867 to whom Juárez gave military command when Gen. Ascención Gómez refused to lead his forces to Querétaro for the final battle against Maximilian. Escobedo then replaced him with Colonel López

4. Johnson to Hunter, 14 April 1876, ibid., 116.

5. Díaz to Canales, 15 April 1876, APD, 12:208; Johnson to Hunter, 4 April 1876, *Despatches from Tampico*, 111.

6. Díaz to "war section," 20 April 1876, APD, 1:448; Díaz to Díez Gutiérrez, 16 April 1876, CPD, 1:460; Díaz to Haro, 19 April 1876, ibid., p. 461. Notice should be made of this dispersal of forces on the eve of what has been called a concentration of all forces upon Monterrey.

in the 1867 military reorganization. In 1875, as president of the *ayuntamiento* of Tampico, Haro complained of General Flores's lack of support to the *ayuntamiento* when opposition political bands terrorized the city during an election. The American consul at Tampico identified him to the State Department as "one of the most popular military men of the state," saying that he "can raise more fighting material than any other two." The consul reported that Haro had left Pueblo Viejo about 1 April with an armed force to fortify himself in the mountains near Alamitos.[7] Haro, however, had been with Díaz at Matamoros.

Meanwhile the American consul at Tampico reported that construction of the fortifications was proceeding and that the merchants had formed a company of armed police for self-protection, as all order had vanished. He reported that the American Colonization Company's *hacienda*, formed within the year, "was raided on upward of ninety horses, many cattle [and] corn; all things necessary for a little army was taken away." The president of the company protested and sought United States aid. The consul had no hope for protection from Mexican officials, "for they have all they can do to keep anything but order." He asked for an American gunboat. In early May the consul reported that "the state of the country is seriously worse." Fortifications continued in Tampico but "were no more than rifle pits . . . untenable and capable of little resistance." He had information that General Mier y Terán "with a force of 12,000 men left Jalapa with the intent to capture Tuxpan, then proceed to this Port, with a view to form a junction with the troops of General Díaz."[8]

Before Gen. Mariano Escobedo left Matamoros he placed the frontier under martial law. The powers devolved upon General Revueltas, who remained there for the rest of the year. Governor Canales vigorously contested the right of and need for martial law but may have been angry that the respective powers were not conferred upon him. The national government probably did not trust Canales, perhaps questioning his ability as well as his loyalty. Certainly Canales and Escobedo shared a mutual antipathy: Canales had emerged from the

7. Saldívar, *Tamaulipas*, p. 245; Desiderio Pavón to Juárez, 7 October 1867, *Epistolario*, 1st ed., p. 412; Haro to Johnson, 16 June 1875, *Despatches from Tampico*, roll 6, no number; Johnson to Hunter, 4 April 1876, ibid., 111.

8. Johnson to Hunter, 28 April 1876, ibid., 117; Johnson to Hunter, 11 May 1876, ibid., 118.

Republican Resistance to the French regime with the greatest military reputation in Tamaulipas, principally because of his leadership at the battle of Santa Gertrudis. Canales then refused to recognize three of the first four governors of the state, José María Carvajal and Santiago Tapia, both named by Juárez, and Juan José de la Garza. Canales in 1866 beseiged Carvajal in Matamoros and occupied the city with Pedro Hinojosa, even as Juárez was setting aside Carvajal in favor of Tapia. Tapia led a campaign to dislodge Canales from Matamoros but died of cholera during the siege. Escobedo took over the task, only to be "joined" by Canales in protest against an American intervention. The next rebellion, against Governor Garza in 1867–68, was led principally by Generals Ascensión Gómez and Manuel Cuesta, the two major heroes of the liberation of Tampico from the French, and Canales. Escobedo again led the government's forces. Cuesta was shot by his own men who were trying to submit to the government, but Canales emerged unscathed, negotiating a peace with Gen. Sóstenes Rocha by which Canales recognized Garza as governor and became military commander of the state forces. When the state legislature retired Garza and exiled him from the state, Canales won the gubernatorial election. By then he had hedged against Juárez's disfavor by defeating Pedro Martínez in the rebellion of San Luis Potosí, but his relations with Escobedo were always strained, and the resultant feud between them in the spring of 1876 bore bitter fruit for the government by summer.[9]

By June it was still difficult to determine Canales's position. Four days after the battle of Icamole, Gen. Carlos Fuero reported that the rebels were scattered and that Canales was pursuing them. Yet a Porfirian supporter in Anhelo thought General Treviño was approaching Monterrey from the west, while Servando Canales, "with a considerable force," was marching from the east. The consul at Tampico reported that it was believed at the port that Canales had pronounced for Díaz on 5 May and "will attack this city with a force estimated from 1,500 to 2,000."[10]

9. Saldívar, *Tamaulipas*, pp. 239–43; Rocha to Juárez, 15 October 1869, DDC, 13:1010–11. José María Iglesias later wrote that Canales was in open battle with the federal government for several months following the declaration of martial law: *Cuestión presidencial*, p. 35.

10. Fuero to Mejía, 24 May 1876, APD, 12:9; Macario Treviño to Hipólito

In early June Adm. William E. LeRoy, commanding the American ships *Hartford, Swatara,* and *Marion,* visited Tampico. His ships drew too much water to cross the sandbar beyond the bay and so lay twelve to fifteen miles from Tampico. Since Flores would not permit LeRoy to land troops, the ships withdrew. Communications with the interior remained cut off, but Flores had formed a well-disciplined force of about 1,000 men. The consul thought that "in case of attack the place will be hotly defended." He reported that Toledo, Haro, and Manuel González had joined forces at Concepción with 1,200 well-armed men and eight pieces of artillery. They were awaiting Miguel Pérez who, it was said, had occupied Ozuluama, fifty miles south of Tampico, with an estimated 150 to 200 men and was expected to occupy Pueblo Viejo the following day. The consul had news from an American steamer that Tuxpan was under rebel seige. Included with his report were the applications for United States protection from the consul of the German Empire, the consul of Italy, the vice-consul of Spain, the French consular agent, and various citizens of the United States.[11]

In early July Secretary of War Ignacio Mejía ordered 640 men out of Tampico to be sent to Gen. Ignacio Alatorre in San Andrés, southern Veracruz, not because the government was optimistic about the military situation in Tamaulipas, but rather because it was sorely pressed everywhere. That action must have greatly disturbed General Flores in Tampico, for three days earlier Gen. Servando Canales finally pronounced with 1,000 men for the *Tuxtepecanos.* He issued paper money to the extent of 50,000 pesos and authorized local commanders to use the national guard units and raise loans and recruits "in order to sustain the integrity and honor of Tamaulipas, threatened by the national government." According to the United States consul at Tampico, Canales "has marched with his forces on Tampico, demanding forced loans and subsisting on the country."[12]

Charles, 26 May 1876, ibid., p. 9; Johnson to Hunter, 11 May 1876, *Despatches from Tampico,* 118.

11. Johnson to Hunter, 9 June 1876, ibid., 119.

12. Mejía to Ignacio Alatorre, 2 July 1876, APD, 13:18; Circular in AGNL, *Ramo Militar, expediente* Escobedo, 1 July 1876; Canales to president of the *ayuntamiento* of Mier, ibid.; Canales's pronouncement is cited in full in Ceballos, *Aurora y ocaso,* 2:565–67; decree of 15 July 1876 in *Despatches from Tampico,* 130; Johnson to G. C. Wiltze, 19 July 1876, CPD, 1:209.

Tampico had doubtless become a rebel objective. Besides the Canales threat from the northwest, the consul reported that General Toledo and Colonel Haro with 1,200 men and six pieces of artillery had occupied Ozuluama south of Tampico, causing the government commander, Col. Julián Herrera, to retreat to Pueblo Viejo. On 21 July Toledo and Haro occupied Pueblo Viejo after a thirteen-hour cannonade that obliged Colonel Herrera to retreat to Tampico. The consul also reported that to the north Gen. Juan N. Cortina had occupied San Fernando near Soto la Marina with a force of 800 men; although this information, said the consul, "is generally believed here, I do not credit it." He did credit the rumor that to the west in Maíz Gen. Pedro Martínez of the government forces, with between 800 and 1,200 men, had pronounced for the *Tuxtepecanos*, because General Escobedo had recalled his command. "It is highly probable that he has taken that step." The consul was truly apprehensive: "In fact the whole country appears to be in a great state of alarm; commerce is completely paralyzed, and murder and robbery, we can say, is the order of the day." To Captain Wiltze, whose steamboat *Shawmut* the consul wanted to see in Tampico "to give confidence of protection to American citizens," he wrote, "Thus you may see that the combination of the rebels may be said to form a complete chain by land with a considerable force to attack Tampico. . . . I consider the situation very critical, and general alarm is felt by all classes."[13]

The consul was wrong on two counts. Cortina had joined the contest not at Tampico but at Matamoros and remained there until the end of the campaigns of the northeast. Juan Nepomuceno Cortina from Camargo, Tamaulipas, was a powerful frontier *caudillo* with a long military record. He had fought against General Taylor in 1847, against the conservatives in the Three Years' War, against the French at Puebla on 5 May 1862 and again at the siege of Puebla in 1863, and had participated at both the siege of Querétaro and the siege of Mexico in 1867. Throughout the Restored Republic he was accused by Americans of being the leading bandit and cattle-rustler in southern Texas. American authorities continually sought his extradition,

13. Johnson to Hunter, 21 July 1876, *Despatches from Tampico*, 124; Johnson to John W. Foster, 19 July 1876, CPD, 1:211, Johnson to G. C. Wiltze, 19 July 1876, ibid., doc. 209.

even as Canales in Victoria wanted him removed from frontier politics. But he had served Juárez well, fighting for the government in the
San Luis Potosí rebellion and in the rebellion of La Noria. Lerdo,
however, had given in to pressures, particularly American pressures,
to arrest him in 1875. Escaping his captors in Mexico City in May
1876, Cortina pronounced for the Plan of Tuxtepec from Atzcapot-
zalco.[14]

The United States consul was also mistaken in his belief that Pedro
Martínez had joined the *Tuxtepecanos*. Indeed, Martínez, a relative of
Mariano Escobedo, had been approached by a Porfirian agent early in
the year, but he could not be persuaded to abandon the government.
Pedro Martínez had judged poorly: he had fought against Juárez in
the San Luis Potosí rebellion and lost, and for Lerdo in 1876. It seems
that Escobedo had suggested Martínez as commander for the government forces at Monterrey. Generals Condey, Flores, Revueltos,
Palacios, and Quiroga, however, opposed the selection. Apparently
Martínez remained in the vicinity of Maíz, state of San Luis Potosí,
and the city of Tula in southwestern Tamaulipas, commanding units
for the government until late October.[15]

Nevertheless, the consul's instincts were correct: the pace of the
rebel campaign was mounting. Rebels in Tansayuquita and Tancas-
neque, two small villages on the headwaters of the Tamesí River,
pronounced for Díaz in mid-July; rebels in Pánuco pronounced on 19
July. In Altamira, a town of 2,000 inhabitants twenty miles distant
from Tampico, rebels pronounced on 20 July. And rebels in
Huejutla, Tantoyuca, Ozuluama, Tamtina, and Pueblo Viejo all pronounced in the week preceeding 21 July. The Tampico sandbar,
commanding the mouth of the Pánuco River and the city of Tampico,
fell to the insurgents on that latter day. The consul saw that "the
forces from the interior are drawing an entire circle by land of

14. Cortina to Díaz, 12 December 1876, APD, 14:278–79; Baltazar Fuentes
to Díaz, 14 December 1876, ibid., pp. 312–13. Cortina may have placed himself briefly at the orders of Iglesias, but he presently returned to the Porfirian
ranks: B. Arriaga to Díaz, 1 January 1876 (*sic*, 1877), ibid., 11:285; political
declaration signed by Marcos Morales, 4 January 1877, ibid., 16:38–39.

15. Martínez to Díaz, 4 March 1876, ibid., 12:36; Lerdo to Flores, 29 October 1876, ibid., 13:147; Ramón Ramírez to Díaz, 18 December 1876, ibid.,
15:39.

superior forces, well-armed and officered, subsisting upon a rich country and shutting off all supplies."[16]

For the next month the rebels at Pueblo Viejo and the Tampico garrison exchanged fire across the river. No shipping was conducted, communications were cut, and Tampico was isolated. General Flores ordered a forced loan, fixed at 4,000 dollars per week, from the merchants of Tampico to sustain the garrison. The consul reported that "the money of the merchants is exhausted by the long strain of insurrection in the State. No products can be received or sent to the interior, and hundreds of thousands of dollars of valuable goods are lying in Store houses, on which the Government has received the duties; in some cases foreign credits are due, but Merchants cannot pay because they have no sales." The agent of an American company feared that the rebel bombardment of Tampico would fire his warehouses, containing 142 tons of coal and 20,000 feet of white pine boards. The consul sought permission from General Flores to cross the river in the consular boat to confer with Toledo for the safety of foreign property.[17]

On 20 August General Canales, then in command of the entire operation against Tampico, held a council of war in Ciudad Victoria with Generals Toledo and Díez Gutiérrez. Orders went out to Col. Francisco Almaguey to join forces with Toledo at Magiscatzin in order to campaign against Tampico on the side of Altamira, the largest city north of Tampico and only some twenty miles distant. A week later they joined forces. Toledo ordered Colonel Almaguey to situate 150 men at Altamira and 70 or 80 at Rayón. He was further ordered "in both places to be careful to prevent all classes of supplies and merchandise from passing into Tampico."[18] The success of the latter was the type of activity that had caused the consul to report that commerce was paralyzed. Such stoppage reduced places like Tampico to government liabilities, because without the movement of taxable

16. Johnson to Hunter, 21 July 1876, *Despatches from Tampico*, 124.

17. Johnson to Hunter, 10 August 1876, ibid., 125. Permission was granted, but the consul registered an official complaint when government shots crossed his bow: "I was surprised and astounded at so grievous an outrage to my flag, and beg that you will give me some explanation of it, that will be satisfactory to my government."

18. Canales to Almaguey, 21 August 1876, APD, 13:62–63; Toledo to Alamaguey, 28 August 1876, ibid., p. 62.

commerce the port and garrison were neither adding to government revenues nor even self-sustaining. Nevertheless, government occupation of the port city had to be maintained in order that it might not support the rebel cause. Tampico was clearly a strategic liability. Guerrilla warfare in the Tampico area was doubtless straining government resources. *Tuxtepecano* rebels in August collected by forced loans in the cities and towns of Chontla, Tantima, Amatlán, Tancoco, Ozuluama, and Pueblo Viejo the considerable sum of 11,800 pesos. At the same time a government partisan, the ex-governor Deciderio Pavón and *hacendado* on the Pánuco River, wrote to President Lerdo that "here in Tampico there are no funds for the garrison, and commerce is paralyzed."[19]

The Mexican gunboat *Independencia* finally anchored off the Tampico bar. The commander came ashore, counseled with Flores and Herrera, and decided to attack the rebels in Pueblo Viejo. The gunboat set up a cannonade during the night of 21–22 August, and Herrera led a force across the river under the cover of darkness. The rebels withdrew; they had occupied Pueblo Viejo one month. Deciderio Pavón ventured that the rebels were so impotent that they might "have been destroyed before they had occupied [Pueblo Viejo] if this garrison had been reinforced by Julián Herrera with some hundred men."[20] That may have been the case, but more likely the guerrilla force would have melted into the countryside earlier, without presenting battle, to appear elsewhere. The point is that even without battles and without taking Tampico, the Porfirian forces in the northeast were causing the government to overstrain its reserves and overextend its manpower. Meanwhile, the rebel forces were disrupting commerce, absorbing available resources, and generally discrediting the Lerdo government. The United States vice-consul reported the military success to the State Department, but added that the rebels were regrouping and acting "in combination to attack this city. The danger is imminent and general alarm is felt by all classes." He asked for a gunboat.[21]

19. Accounting signed by Jesús Toledo and Ignacio Sánchez, 31 August 1876, ibid., pp. 37–38; Pavón to Lerdo, 13 September 1876, ibid., p. 57; Luis N. de la Lastra to Hunter, 22 September 1876, *Despatches from Tampico*, 130.
20. Pavón to Lerdo, 13 September 1876, APD, 13:57.
21. Lastra to Hunter, 28 August 1876, *Despatches from Tampico*, 128.

The numerous guerrilla forces in rebellion in various areas did divide the government's attention and strain its resources. General Flores in mid-September asked that the government steamship *Independencia* not be removed from Tampico Bay. The government granted his request but was forced to deny a similar appeal from Guillermo Palomino, who led the government forces in Mérida, Yucatán, because "General Flores has been unable to free the one [steamship] at Tampico and the other one is insufficient for everything that incessantly threatens in Veracruz and along the coast."[22] Rebel activity in one area aided that in another.

In regions adjacent to the Huasteca the same conditions prevailed. Further north at Matamoros the government general, Ignacio Revueltas, was distressed. In early September he asked for replacements; he thought it "easier to do" because Escobedo since 31 August had replaced Gen. Ignacio Mejía in the ministry of war and was "knowledgeable about the necessity of concluding this campaign quickly." The rebel force on the border was impotent, he wrote, not only lacking boldness to attack the city but withdrawing a distance because of government persecution.[23] What Revueltas failed to comprehend was that the rebels could withdraw and wait; government commanders commonly ascribe lack of valor or lack of strength to *guerrilleros* who do not stand their ground in open battle, and therefore predict imminent rebel collapse. Nevertheless, the government garrison needed replacements—presumably because of desertions.

The main problem at Matamoros during the summer of 1876 was financial. So low were the reserves for the garrison and so poor the government credit that Revueltas authorized a loan of 30,000 pesos at 55 percent discount, having to choose, he said, "between the loss of this amount or the city." The government inspector (*visitador*) approved of the disadvantageous loan, but the administrator of the customshouse at Matamoros, although he signed the declaration, had private thoughts. Writing to President Lerdo in person by way of New Orleans ("that being the only safe route" because the rebels held the hinterland) he claimed that he opposed the usurious loan but that

22. Flores to Lerdo, 11 September 1876, APD, 13:53; Lerdo to Palomino, 8 October 1876, ibid., p. 56.
23. Revueltas to Lerdo, 11 September 1876, ibid., pp. 53–54.

Generals Revueltas and Bernabé de la Barra had obliged him to yield to it. The customshouse was already overdrawn, he said, owing payments since the previous July on earlier loans made at 30 and 40 percent. "Within twenty days, thirty at the most," he predicted, "we will be in a worse situation, because money will not be available at any price." The administrator also ventured an opinion about the military situation: although the position was not grave, he stated, there was no communication with the outside except by way of the United States, for "the telegraph is interrupted from here to Monterrey, . . . [and] it can be said that we are besieged." President Lerdo's answer must have been small comfort to the conscientious administrator. "Do what you can," he said, in effect. "I would send something from Veracruz if I had it." All late summer and fall Generals Cortina and Plácido Vega clung to the edges of Matamoros. Revueltas wrote for more arms.[24]

The same financial crisis and rebel harassment affected other northern cities. After the battle of Icamole General Fuero sent a series of orders to all *Alcaldes Primeros* of the counties (*municipios*) of Nuevo León to impose extraordinary taxes on personal properties valued at greater than 5,000 pesos, to organize county militias "for the defense of the counties and persecution of the rebels," to send a list of names to the state government of all the men of each county that had joined the rebels, and to remit a list of all men who had hidden in order to avoid serving in the county militias; he also included an order setting forth the conditions for pardoning rebels, designed as a pacification tactic. Soon thereafter, Fuero named military commanders to organize and lead those militia with authority superior to that of the local officials for recruiting, levying forced loans, and commandeering horses, arms, and supplies.[25]

The hardships encountered by those men are recorded in the correspondence between them and the office of the secretary of gov-

24. Copy of declaration, 18 September 1876, CPD, 1:184; Ignacio Revueltas to Lerdo, 20 September 1876, APD, 13:69–70; Eugenio Chavero to Lerdo, 21 September 1876, and answer, 20 October 1876, CPD, 1:185; Paz, *Algunas campañas*, 3:426; Escobedo to Revueltas, 11 October 1876, *Archivo de la Dependencia de Asuntos Terminados de la Secretaría de la Presidencia*, letterbooks of Mariano Escobedo (hereafter ASP), 3:270.

25. AGNL, *Ramo Circulares 1876; Alcalde Primero* Fernando Hinojosa to *Secretario de Gobierno*, AGNL, *Ramo Alcaldes Primeros, China*, 31 May 1876; *Secretario de Gobierno* to Hermenegildo Frías, AGNL *Ramo Militar, expediente Frías*, 22 July 1876.

ernment in Monterrey. One commander in Mier complained that the telegraph was interrupted and that he had no person of confidence to carry extraordinary correspondence and no funds to repair the deficiencies. One English merchant complained that goods moved into Monterrey only after paying duties to both rebel forces and the *Lerdista* government. Conditions worsened as fall approached. Rebels were reported everywhere. Commander Berlanga in Montemorelos confessed he could no longer carry out his orders because of lack of funds; he could not collect taxes; no one was left to conscript "because they are so demoralized . . . that they are not even to be found." He expected his reduced force to be overcome by a surprise attack and asked for a month's leave to attend his private business that had been sacked by rebels. His request was denied.[26]

From Monterrey Gov. Narciso Dávila wrote a desperate letter in late September to the national government. Escobedo promised to do what he could "to attend to the necessities of the forces which conduct the campaigning in your zone . . ." and to remit funds to General Fuero "as soon as possible." He said, however,

> I hope you will take into account the circumstances under which I have taken this ministry, the most complete bankruptcy, the warehouse exhausted, without a single weapon, not even a uniform for the troops.

"With the defeat of Naranjo," said Escobedo, "the frontier should be safer." Nevertheless, five days later Treviño occupied Ciudad Cadereyta Jiménez, a few miles southeast of Monterrey.[27]

In Coahuila one military commander wrote to Escobedo that he could not post more communications; "the people with money sympathize with the rebellion," and the rest hid from the government recruiters. "This jurisdiction cannot comply with your orders." He asked to be replaced. The wealthy *hacendado* Evaristo Madero sought

26. Antonio González y Evia to Escobedo, AGNL, *Ramo Militar, expediente Escobedo*, 15 June 1876; William L. Purcell to John O'Sullivan, 26 July 1876, *Frontier Mexico, 1875–1894, Letters of William L. Purcell*, ed. Antia Purcell (San Antonio, Tex.: Naylor Co., 1963), p. 15; Berlanga to *Gobernador y Comandante Militar*, AGNL, *Ramo Militar, expediente Berlanga*, 26 November 1876.

27. Escobedo to Dávila, 13 October 1876, ASP, 3:32; Paz, *Algunas campañas*, 3:426–27; Berlanga to *Secretario de Gobierno*, AGNL, *Ramo Militar, expediente Berlanga*, 19 October 1876.

Escobedo's intervention with the treasury so that he might be excused from his taxes, inasmuch as the rebel activity was damaging his operations and he was contributing to the government's efforts against local rebel bands. Escobedo promised to make "the necessary recommendations . . . in conformity with your desires," for he was willing to do everything possible "for the good of the frontier" and "in favor of my friends . . . hoping to conclude the pacification of those *pueblos*." An English merchant in Saltillo wrote to a family member not to come to Mexico, for commercial houses were collapsing, stores were closed, no goods had entered from Matamoros since March, mail deliveries were precarious, and business had not been so bad for many years.[28]

In San Luis Potosí the state government was so pressed for money that it mortgaged the machinery in the government mint, and Escobedo urged Angel Martínez, the government general, to use his "proverbial energy and wisdom wherever necessary, for our enemies do not cease to work in every manner to frustrate the results of our operations," using whatever methods come to hand, "however depraved." Gov. Pascual Hernández in late September objected to the government's use of the state militia of San Luis Potosí. He wanted all state forces to be recalled from the Huasteca, because they were needed against rebel activity near the state capital.[29]

In Durango the *Lerdista* military commander was urged to be severe with the "thieves and sackers," and the government general in Zacatecas, who feared that the rebel Trinidad García de la Cadena would attack the city, was told to organize as many citizens as possible for the defense.[30]

Urgent requests from governmental commanders throughout the north streamed into the ministry of war for finances and supplies. Lieutenant Colonel Ramírez informed the ministry that "there are no resources" in Tula, and that "the treasury in San Luis Potosí is

28. Saltillo (?) to Escobedo, AGNL, *Ramo Militar, expediente Escobedo,* 16 June 1876; Escobedo to Madero, 13 October 1876, ASP, 3:32; Purcell to Charles Bagness, 16 September 1876, *Frontier Mexico,* p. 17; Purcell to John O'Sullivan, 6 October 1876, ibid., p. 18.

29. Escobedo to Cástulo Camacho, 23 October 1876, ASP, 3:160; Escobedo to Angle Martínez, 13 October 1876, ibid., p. 32; Escobedo to Pascual Hernández, 14 October 1876, ibid., p. 49.

30. Escobedo to Florentino Carillo, 16 October 1876, ibid., p. 70; Escobedo to Mariana Cobrera, 29 October 1876, ibid. p. 246.

empty." Narciso Dávila in Monterrey wrote that "the garrison lacks all resources, for which reason General Guerra . . . has been commissioned to impose a loan of 15,000 [pesos]." The answer read: "Received, and offer a discount. . . ." Col. Jacinto Ordóñez from San Luis asked "for even three days of rations for the troops," and General Condey in the same city reported "that there were not any types of arms left in the depot for the cavalry when I took command."[31] The implications are clear that the government did not have sufficient finances to supply as many troops as were needed and that provisions given to one commander meant that another went without.

Due to the lack of roads and bridges in the hinterland around Tampico, the Pánuco River served to carry the livestock and agricultural products of the area between the Huasteca and the coast to the port city of Tampico. For one month in the summer of 1876 the forces under Generals Toledo and Haro commanded that commercial artery from their base at the city of Pánuco, some five leagues from the mouth of the river. There, according to the *hacendado* Deciderio Pavón, they lived by forced loans and "ruined" the *haciendas,* taking the horses and cattle, even the furniture in the houses, burning those belonging to government supporters, and forcing local inhabitants to supply them with fodder and corn. Desirous of immediate action and blaming General Flores for losses to himself, Pavón wrote to President Lerdo that

> in vain has the Government made the sacrifice to send the gunboat *Independencia* to this port, because they have not known how to use it at Pánuco to destroy the force of Toledo and Haro. . . .

"That boat can navigate as far as Pánuco without any inconvenience," wrote the *hacendado,* "and it is certain that the enemy could make no resistance." Probably in order to explain his lack of aggressiveness against the rebels along the river, General Flores answered that send-

31. Francisco Ramírez to Escobedo, 4 September 1876, ADN, 481.4:9223:9, and 10 September 1876, ibid., p. 3; Narciso Davila to Escobedo, 6 September 1876, ibid., p. 10; Jacinto Ordóñez to Escobedo, 7 September 1876, ibid., p. 12; and Ambrosio Condey to Escobedo, 8 September 1876, ibid., p. 16; others, ibid., pp. 24–36.

ing the *Independencia* upstream to Pánuco would leave the bay area without gunboat protection for four days. He was merely awaiting the opportunity, he said.[32]

In the second week of September the government forces at Tampico scored some successes. Guerrilla soldiers under the commands of Castillo and Almaguey—the latter recently named by Jesús Toledo as "General of Division and Chief of the Line of Operations of Altamira"—occupied the city of Altamira and levied forced loans.[33] A battle took place there on 12 September in which troops loyal to the government captured twenty-four *Tuxtepecanos*.[34] Four days later, at the insistence of the commercial elements and the *hacendados* of the Pánuco area, and after the removal of the threat from Altamira, Flores sent the *Independencia* upstream. On 16 September a cannonade from the steamship drove Toledo and Haro from Pánuco, causing them to abandon their wagon train and escape by wading across river. "Had we had a platoon of infantry, all of them would have been taken prisoners," wrote one government partisan.[35] But they did not have a platoon of infantry, the Pánuco was unable to support government troops when they arrived, and Toledo and Haro escaped. The government effort was too little and too late; there was too much to do in too many places.

Finally in late September government reinforcements landed at Tampico from Veracruz aboard the steamship *Libertad* and were placed under the command of Col. Julián Herrera. Accompanying the troops was an order from the minister of war to Flores to give Herrera 100 men and sufficient money to open the campaign in the Tampico-Huasteca area. General Sánchez Rivera was to proceed north from the state of Mexico to join him. Unfortunately, Flores and Herrera did not cooperate. Flores refused to provide the men and resources, telling Herrera he had insufficient men for the garrison of

32. Pavón to Lerdo, 13 September 1876, APD, 13:58; Flores to Lerdo, 11 September 1876, ibid., p. 53.

33. Toledo to Francisco Almaguey, 4 September 1876, ibid., pp. 62–63; Pavón to Lerdo, 13 September 1876, ibid., pp. 57–58.

34. After Díaz occupied the capital, a spokesman among the rebel prisoners sought transportation for them from a military prison in Veracruz to their homes in Tamaulipas: Emiliano de la Garza to Díaz, 27 November 1876, ADN, 481.4:8637:6.

35. Miguel González to Lerdo, 25 September 1876, CPD, 1:183.

Tampico. Herrera was free, however, to raise what money he could. Flores explained to the government that he would have remained with only 180 effective soldiers had he complied with orders, but Herrera on the day of his departure counted 614 effectives. Flores's zealous enemy, Deciderio Pavón, who wanted government protection of *haciendas* in the countryside, wrote to Lerdo that "there are 700 men [in Tampico], a gunboat worth 2,000 men, and no . . . enemy!"[36] Herrera raised 5,000 pesos in Tampico and departed for the campaign with 300 infantry.

Miguel González, a merchant in Tampico, aided the provisioning of the force and predicted to the government that "Herrera will find no enemy to combat from Pueblo Viejo to Huejutla." Only a small force was in Temapache, he said, and Tuxpan was nearly cleared. Toledo and Haro were reported in Tamuín, about forty miles from Tampico, while Cristóforo Redondo, one of Toledo's officers, was taking his men south toward Tantima to attack Dominquillo in Tepezintla. Almaguey had scattered his force and was in Presas. Canales, further inland, was imposing a contribution of 1,200 head of cattle on Horcacitas, Escandón, and Presas.[37]

When government forces arrived, the rebels had vanished, and the area could provide few provisions for the *Lerdista* troops. Such is the nature of guerrilla warfare: the rebel forces are wherever the army is not, and they pick the countryside clean of resources that are needed by the government.

Within a week of leaving Tampico and having found no enemy, Herrera wrote that he knew nothing of the federal force commanded by Sánchez Rivera, the general who had been ordered north from the state of Mexico. Herrera was equally uncertain about rebel movements, writing that Redondo and Leonardo Díaz commanded 300 men, "who might be found probably in Chicontepec, if they have not holed up in Temapache, or perhaps taken the route to Papantla." Soon Herrera was complaining to the government that Flores "manifests to me that he cannot send me anything," suggesting that Herre-

36. Herrera to Lerdo, 24 September 1876, APD, 13:74–75; Flores to Lerdo, 3 October 1876, ibid., p. 106; Pavón to Lerdo, 1 October 1876, ibid., pp. 97–98. Pavón hinted that Flores was opposed to the changes in Lerdo's cabinet and publicly predicted disaster with Escobedo at the war desk.
37. Miguel González to Lerdo, 25 September 1876, CPD, 1:182–83.

ra secure what he needed "as if offices were here capable of providing resources and capital. . . ." The suggestion was impossible because the rebels "have already sacked these towns." Escobedo answered for Lerdo, promising that orders would be sent to the customshouse at Tampico to remit funds to Herrera. A few days later, however, Escobedo appealed to the Tampico merchant, Miguel González, to raise the funds for Herrera which the government could not send.[38]

The rebel movements had become obscure. Rumor had it that Generals Carlos Díez Gutiérrez and Ignacio Martínez had occupied Tula as government troops evacuated the city to campaign in San Luis Potosí. Toledo and Haro were reported to have collected 25,000 pesos where they had passed, and arrived in Chocoy on 2 October, "supposedly on the way to Victoria."[39] On the following day, however, they were reported in Loma Alta and Concepción, Tamaulipas, united with Castillo, Almaguey, Capistran, and Villaverde, the latter two bringing arms from the frontier. Indeed, Flores wrote that Haro and Toledo were approaching Altamira with 500 men in order to attack Tampico, which would be vulnerable due to Herrera's having left the city to campaign in the Veracruz-Huasteca, "where for the present there is no major enemy force." That Flores could not be more explicit was due, he said, to Herrera's refusal to inform him of the enemy movements. The United States vice-consul agreed; Haro and Toledo, he had heard, were marching to Tampico, which "will again be besieged by the end of the month." Shortly thereafter, Toledo and Haro were reported countermarching against Tula.[40] This report turned out to be accurate. In short, no one could be sure where the rebel forces were located or where they were going.

38. Herrera to Lerdo, 30 September 1876, and answer, 10 October 1876, APD, 13:95–96; Herrera to Lerdo, 5 October 1876, ibid., p. 120; Escobedo to Herrera, 23 October 1876, ASP, 3:150, and 2 November 1876, ibid., p. 305; Escobedo to González, 2 November 1876, ibid.

39. Flores to Lerdo, 3 October 1876, APD, 13:106; Flores to Herrera, 3 October 1876, ibid., p. 108; Pavón to Lerdo, 1 October 1876, ibid., p. 97; Miguel González to Lerdo, 3 October 1876, CPD, 1:181.

40. Flores to Herrera, 3 October 1876, APD, 13:108–9; Flores to Lerdo, 3 October 1876, ibid., p. 106; Lastra to Hunter, 13 October 1876, *Despatches from Tampico*, 135; Flores to Lerdo, 14 October 1876, and answer, 29 October 1876, APD, 13:146.

In October the United States vice-consul in Tampico reported that "this place is still in a precarious condition." The authorities were without means for supporting the garrison, making disadvantageous loans from merchants at heavy discounts, and a second federal emergency tax was being collected. The garrison was reduced to 500 men owing to desertion, and the general fear was that in case of rebel attack "the lower class [is] ready to join the invading party merely for the chance of plundering the wealthy of any nationality." He requested an American gunboat.[41]

Rebel control of the state government of Tamaulipas was a positive danger to the Lerdo government. Lerdo therefore named José Martínez, a local landowner, to occupy the governorship in Ciudad Victoria. Lerdo nevertheless informed Flores that he should retain all authority in Tampico and environs ". . . because of the difficulty of communications to the center of the state"—meaning that the port, as well as the state capital, were isolated by rebel-controlled hinterland.[42] Martínez rallied the propertied classes in Victoria, but before he could organize a defence the *guerrillero* Col. Eugenio Loperena with 600 men attacked the capital city. Martínez fled to La Presa, where he was beaten by a brigade led by Gen. Ascensión Gómez on 30 October at the battle of the *hacienda* of La Mesa. Gómez sent an officer to capture Martínez, who murdered Martínez instead, and the officer looted Santa Engracia, Martínez's private porperty. The vice-consul at Tampico reported that the rebels then sacked Victoria, and that Gómez had allowed his soldiers "to commit all the crimes of which his hordes are capable."[43]

The obscurity of the rebel movements added to the government's

41. Lastra to Hunter, 13 October 1876, *Despatches from Tampico*, 135.

42. Lerdo to Flores, 29 October 1876, APD, 13:147.

43. Saldívar, *Tamaulipas*, pp. 252–53; Flores to Lerdo, 14 October 1876, and answer 29 October 1876, APD, 13:146; Ramón Ramírez to Díaz, 18 December 1876, APD, 15:38–41; Z. Martínez to Díaz, 28 November 1876, APD, 14:69–70; Lastra to Dept. of State, 8 November 1876, *Despatches from Tampico*, 137. Mariano Escobedo wrote to his friend the Mexican consul in Hamburg on 29 October that "the revolution is over" in the north and the zone pacified (Escobedo to Pedro Landázuri, ASP, 3:243–45) but two days earlier notified José Martínez that he was rushing Col. Pedro García to Ciudad Victoria to organize the forces for a campaign in that state (Escobedo to Martínez, ASP, 3:209).

having to answer multiple and urgent calls. Herrera occupied Temapeche, reporting a victory, after rebel forces led by Pedro Hinojosa had evacuated that town. General Rivera had counter-marched from Tulancingo to Huachinango to halt Manuel González, who escaped pursuit and continued his route to his destination at Tecoac.[44] The government sent reinforcements to Pedro Martínez at Tula,[45] but they arrived too late. He evacuated his position in the third week of October and the rebels, reported everywhere and found nowhere, made a significant concentration: Canales, Toledo, and Haro occupied Tula unopposed on 24 October, while Colonel Herrera was seeking an enemy, General Flores was pinned down in Tampico, and Gómez was occupying Ciudad Victoria.

The vice-consul at Tampico reported: "I can say that with the exception of Matamoros and this Port . . . the whole state of Tamaulipas is under the unquestioned control of the Revolution." He reported that a third federal emergency tax had been levied and that Flores had decreed an early collection of the state tax for the first third of 1877. He feared for Tampico, which "will have to share the sad fate of Tula and Victoria, Sack and Plunder." He urgently requested that an American gunboat be sent immediately to Tampico.[46]

Those rebel movements were important for what soon transpired. From the rebel base in Tula, San Luis Potosí was exposed. The appraisal of both government and rebel leaders was that Canales would march with his estimated 3,000 men from Tula against San Luis Potosí. Gen. Trinidad García de la Cadena, the most important *Porfirista* leader in the northwest after the death of Donato Guerra, had beaten a government unit in Santa Clara, Zacatecas, on 29 September and had captured and shot the government commander, Col. Jacinto Ordóñez. In early November García de la Cadena wrote to General Díaz that he thought "positively to occupy Zacatecas within a month, because as weak as is San Luis, it cannot send aid [to Zacatecas], if General Canales approaches it [San Luis], as I suppose he will."

44. Lerdo to Herrera, undated answer to Herrera's letter of 5 October 1876, APD, 13:121; Justino Fernández to Lerdo, 5 October 1876, ibid., p. 117.

45. Flores to Lerdo, 14 October 1876, and answer, 29 October 1876, ibid., pp. 146–47; Escobedo to Pedro Martínez, 23 October 1876, ASP, 3:148.

46. Lastra to Hunter, 3 November 1876, *Despatches from Tampico*, 136; 8 November 1876, ibid., p. 137.

Indeed, in the next few days García de la Cadena did occupy
Zacatecas, while to the south in the same week Porfirian forces occupied Tlaxcala, assuring that the government could not aid San Luis
from that direction.[47]
    Meanwhile, José María Iglesias had pronounced against Lerdo in
Guanajuato on 28 October. A partisan wrote him in November that
San Luis was divided in a factional dispute between General Condey
and the governor, Pascual Hernández. The informant presumed that
from Tula Canales would attack the city, which was garrisoned, he
said, by only 800 soldiers. Pedro Martínez, he reported, was ordered
to stop Canales's advance with 1,000 men. Indeed, Gen. Pedro Martínez then had 2,000 men, the government reinforcements having
arrived, and Martínez occupied Mier y Noriega on 15 November.
Martínez's 2,000 men were insufficient, however. At the *hacienda* of
Las Antonias near Mier y Noriega on 18 November General Martínez
suffered a heavy defeat, losing his baggage, artillery, and some 700
men taken prisoner at the hands of Servando Canales, Ignacio Martínez, Eugenio Loperena, Díez Gutiérrez, and Julio Hernández.[48] The
rebel forces had, after all, made a significant concentration and had
fought an important battle. Two days earlier, General Díaz and Gen.
Manuel González had beaten Gen. Ignacio Alatorre at Tecoac.

    Historians have regularly made the connection between the events
at Tecoac and Mexico City. But they have failed to mention the battle
of Las Antonias, the fall of Mier y Noriega and Ciudad Victoria, the
open road to San Luis Potosí, the isolation of Matamoros and Tampico, the threatened positions of Monterrey and Saltillo, and the desperate situation of a score of other points across the country with
conditions similar to, and interrelated with, those of the northeast.
    The rest was anticlimactic. In the final week of November Generals

47. Escobedo to Ignacio Alatorre, 3 October 1876, APD, 13:105; García de la
Cadena to Díaz, 9 November 1876, ibid., p. 189; José O. Herrera to Díaz, 13
November 1876, ibid., p. 213; Ignacio Alatorre to Escobedo, 8 November
1876, ibid., p. 187.
    48. Mendoza to (José María Iglesias?), 13 November 1876, ibid., pp. 206–8;
Ceballos, *Aurora y ocaso*, 2:743; Canales to Díaz, 27 November 1876, APD,
14:55; Hernández to Díaz, 4 December 1876, ibid., p. 184. Loperena died in
the battle of Las Antonias.

Canales, Toledo, Cuéllar, and Julio Hernández occupied the area north of San Luis, and Díez Gutiérrez that to the east. On 2 December the *Lerdista* generals in San Luis wrote to General Díaz that they accepted the Plan of Tuxtepec and would deliver the garrison and city to Generals Ignacio Martínez and Servando Canales. On the same day Generals Hipólito Charles and Gerónimo Treviño occupied Saltillo, capital of Coahuila.[49] Hostilities in Tampico terminated through negotiations whereby Flores kept his rank and post, and the loans made to him by the port merchants were assumed by the government.[50] By 22 December Treviño, as Porfirian governor of Nuevo León, occupied the long-desired state capital, Monterrey, after General Fuero had abandoned it to carry on the battle against the *Tuxtepecanos* in Durango under the banner of José María Iglesias.[51] From Monterrey Treviño sent troops to occupy Piedras Negras and Laredo and then pursued General Fuero into Durango, where the latter capitulated to Díaz in January.[52] On the frontier Baltazar Fuentes and Gen. Juan Cortina occupied Camargo, incorporating those of the 300 defenders who cared to join their force and dismissing the others. By mid-December they were operating against Matamoros. Before the month was out General Revueltas was in contact with Treviño to recognize the government of Porfirio Díaz.[53]

49. Benigno Arriaga to Díaz, 27 November 1876, ibid., p. 50; Canales to Díaz, 24 November 1876, ibid., pp. 12–13; Andrés Martínez to Díaz, 2 December 1876, ibid., pp. 151–52; Charles to Díaz, 3 December 1876, ibid., 15:169–70.

50. Aurelio Melgarejo to Díaz, 21 December 1876 (not 1875; Carreño errs), ibid., 11:280–83; 15:107–10; see also the interesting communications concerning who should command at Tampico; ibid., 15:228, 230, 258–60, 338–39, and reports of further forced loans in Tampico in December, *Despatches from Tampico*, 139; for Flores's decree of adhesion see ibid., 143.

51. Naranjo to Díaz, 22 December 1876, APD, 15:120; Angel Cancino to Luis Curiel, 20 November 1876, ibid., 14:109; Fuero turned over the command of Monterrey to General Miguel Palacios on 7 November 1876, AGNL, *Ramo Militar, expediente Escobedo.*

52. Gerónimo Treviño to Díaz, 5 January 1877, APD, 16:61; Benigno Arriaga to Díaz, 15 January 1877, ibid., p. 190; Genaro Raigosa to Díaz, 17 January 1877, ibid., p. 239.

53. Baltazar Fuentes to Díaz, 14 December 1876, ibid., 14:312–13; Benigno Arriaga to Díaz, 27 December 1876, ibid., 15:209, 216; Díaz to J(uan) N. Méndez, 28 December 1876, ibid., p. 283.

The *Tuxtepecanos* controlled the northeast as soon they controlled the rest of the country. Indeed, forces from the northeast, led or sent by Canales, Toledo, Ignacio Martínez, Treviño, Charles, and Díez Gutiérrez, aided the occupation and pacification of the central states of Durango, Zacatecas, Querétaro, and Guanajuato during December and January.[54] From the rebel point of view, the guerrilla warfare in the northeast had played its role well.

Two conclusions can be drawn from the events related here. First, significant guerrilla warfare existed in the northeast after Díaz left that area to campaign in the southeast. That guerrilla warfare isolated important cities from intercommunication and attracted significant governmental manpower and resources from the area where Díaz was raising the forces that destroyed the government army at Tecoac.

The second conclusion is offered in order to relate the importance of these events to the overall structure established in the preceding chapter, where it was maintained that alternate reactions were implicit within the national *Tuxtepecano* strategy. Let it be supposed that the government had decided not to protect the various northern cities but to allow their temporary collapse and occupation by rebel forces in order to place all governmental resources in the southeast, planning to destroy Díaz and thereafter to reoccupy and pacify the north. Then the *Tuxtepecanos* could have established governments in the northern states with ease and developed significant armies with the resources of those rebel governments in order to march south for yet different concentrations. This hypothetical situation lends further credence to the contention supported in both chapter 9 and here: The rebellion in the northeast was an integral part of the national strategy of Tuxtepec, and the role it played as a strong diversionary operation contributed to the *Tuxtepecano* concentration in the south and the confrontation against the government forces of Lerdo de Tejada.

Finally, it has been seen how after the collapse of *Lerdismo* the Porfirian armies of the northeast were available to proceed against *Iglesismo*. That was yet another and unforseen contribution of the northeast to the Insurrection of Tuxtepec. The rise of *Iglesismo* in the central and western states of Mexico as an alternative to *Lerdismo* and to *Porfirismo* is the subject to which we now turn.

54. Numerous letters in ibid., 15 and 16 describe these movements.

Chapter 11
The Challenge of *Iglesismo*

Porfirismo was not the only anti-*Lerdista* movement in 1876. That year provided the unusual spectacle of a three-cornered civil war, since the "Revolution of Salamanca" of José María Iglesias competed with the "Revolution of Tuxtepec" of Porfirio Díaz for the anti-Lerdo forces. In other words, President Lerdo in 1876 confronted two rebellions—not to mention the Catholic *Cristero* rebellion in Michoacán—rather than one.

José María Iglesias had been active in public life for three decades before he strove for the presidency of Mexico. He entered politics in 1846 as a councilman of the municipal government of Mexico City. He opposed the Treaty of Guadalupe Hildalgo of 1848, and later as editor of *El Siglo XIX* he opposed the dictatorship of Santa Anna. After the triumph of the "Revolution of Ayutla" Iglesias held an official post in the treasury department, enforcing the *Ley Lerdo* of 1856 for the disamortization of ecclesiastical property. Successively thereafter Iglesias headed the ministry of justice and the ministry of treasury. He served on the Supreme Court when Benito Juárez was Court president. During the Three Years' War Iglesias defended the liberal cause in the press and rejoined the liberal government between 1860 and 1863. With Juárez during the Republican Resistance to the French Intervention, Iglesias served first as minister of treasury and then as minister of justice. During the Juárez administration Iglesias acted variously as congressman, tax assessor for the Federal District (*administrador de rentas*), minister of government (*gobernación*), and minister of justice. In 1873 Iglesias became president of the Supreme Court.[1]

The period of the Iglesias Court was important for the events of 1876. The president of the Court was an elected official and was the vice-president in the line of presidential succession. In 1873 a case appeared before the Court which became famous as the *Amparo de Morelos*. The plaintiffs, a group of *hacendados* in Morelos, sought an *amparo*, or stay of execution, against a state law imposing taxes on

1. José María Iglesias, *Autobiografía* (Mexico: Antigua Imprenta de E. Murguía, 1893), pp. 1–51.

certain lands. They argued that the legislature which passed the law was illegal because its *quorum* included a person who had been elected to the position while occupying the office of political chief—a circumstance prohibited by the state constitution. They further argued that the governor who promulgated the law was incompetent to do so because he occupied his office in contravention to the state constitutional prohibition against gubernatorial reelection. Although the appropriate electoral colleges had declared the legislator and the governor elected, the majority of the Court led by Iglesias granted the *amparo*. The legal doctrine which emerged from the case became known from Iglesias's majority opinion as "incompetence of origin." In 1874 the Court granted an *amparo* against a decree of the governor of Puebla on the same legal argument.[2]

The Iglesias doctrine, fully developed in his legal brief, entitled "Constitutional Study of the Jurisdiction of the Court of Justice" (*Estudio constitucional sobre facultades de la corte de justicia*), caused a great constitutional and political debate in the Mexican political classes. The constitutional question revolved around whether a court judgment upon the legality of an election, over and against the resolution of an electoral college, threatened the sovereignty of the states. The political question threatened to shake the very foundations of the presidential-gubernatorial control of elections. Some congressmen gave serious consideration to a plan for indicting Iglesias and the six justices who voted with him before a national grand jury, but the plan was rejected in favor of congressional legislation: the law of 19 May 1875 prohibited the federal courts from ruling against the resolutions of an electoral college.[3]

Iglesias believed the law was unconstitutional. He argued that judicial protection of the people from illegal and fraudulent acts of the political institutions—in this case the electoral colleges—was within the court's constitutional jurisdiction, which could not be limited by legislative act. He resigned from the Court in protest, but Lerdo persuaded him to remain on the Court to avoid "the confusion inevitably provocated" by the scramble to occupy the vacancy, with the understanding that Iglesias would protest against the law from the bench.

2. Iglesias, *Cuestión presidencial*, pp. 5–10; Cosío Villegas, *El porfiriato*, 1:16–17.
3. Dublán and Lozano, *Legislación Mexicana*, 12:727.

Iglesias acquiesced, issued a vigorous protest, and continued to issue *amparos* based upon the doctrine of "incompetence of origin" without Congress or the president taking action to apply the sanctions of the law of 19 May.[4]

There is no doubt that Iglesias understood the political impact of his doctrine. He later claimed that he only intended to save republican government from legislative incursions upon judicial authority to interpret the constitution and to insist that electoral colleges did not have the power to legalize patently illegal elections.[5] Nevertheless, everyone understood that the *Iglesista* doctrine was immediately applicable to the *Lerdista* incumbents, such as Governor Leyva of Morelos and Governor Romero Vargas of Puebla. Iglesias wrote into his earlier "Constitutional Study" that in the absence of the electoral colleges, of the state governments, and of Congress to insist upon legal elections, then the Court would find juridical authority to do so. "The entire country knows upon whom they may rely in a question of the greatest importance"; thus Iglesias served notice in 1874 that if Lerdo's reelection involved electoral fraud, Iglesias would not hesitate to invoke his doctrine, even against the highest electoral college in the land, Congress in its function of counting the presidential votes.

This was Iglesias's panacea to forestall revolutions, for the judicial *amparo* against decrees of fraudulently elected officials was, in Iglesias's seldom-read words, "the safety valve that [would] impede the establishment of the political machine," which Iglesias believed was the origin of insurrections in the Restored Republic.[6] Lerdo well understood the threat to the presidential political machine. Iglesias and Lerdo knew they were traveling a collision course, with the impact due in 1876.[7]

How much further political implication existed in the *Iglesismo* of 1874–75 is impossible to ascertain. Iglesias did construct a party in 1876 designed to carry him to the presidency and did attract men to his banner who apparently believed that a new power party was in the making. Iglesias later claimed that his attempt to resign from the

4. Iglesias, *Cuestión presidencial,* pp. 10–19; Cosío Villegas, *El porfiriato,* 1:18–23, 32–38.
5. Iglesias, *Cuestión presidencial,* pp. 18–19.
6. *Estudio constitucional,* cited in Cosío Villegas, "Iglesias," p. 27.
7. Cosío Villegas agrees, *El porfiriato,* 1:16–18.

Court proved his lack of personal ambitions.[8] Daniel Cosío Villegas argues that had Iglesias resigned in protest against the government in 1875, he would immediately have become the presidential candidate of all the opposition, including the Porfirian opposition, in time for the presidential elections in 1876.[9] That would explain Lerdo's vehement attempts to convince Iglesias to remain on the Court, which otherwise, as events transpired, appears as Lerdo's mistake. Frank Knapp sneers that any man who had to write as much as Iglesias wrote to deny his ambition must surely have had a lot of it on his conscience.[10] Nevertheless, Iglesias's later argument appears realistic, that he had "almost complete certainty of being the successor of Sr. Lerdo in the natural order of things." He would be vice-president until his term ran out in 1879 and be the most eligible candidate in 1880 by "only feigning ignorance of the assaults upon the institutions."[11] Almost all historians have handled Iglesias as the ultimate legalist and uncompromising idealist. Even the most sustained diatribe against him in print is based on his having weakened Lerdo and thereby left the door open to Porfirio Díaz.[12]

The historical question, nevertheless, is not whether Iglesias was constructing a party to seize power from the *Lerdistas*. Before 1876 both Lerdo and Iglesias knew they were adversaries. Certainly Iglesias directly challenged *Lerdismo*. It is equally certain that after Lerdo's reelection was assured, Iglesias could only break the impasse by becoming president, a move which required armed insurrection. Not even that presidential ambition at all cost, however, threatens Iglesias's reputation as idealist, for the liberal idealism of the day imagined no other solution but changes in governmental personnel. Unfortunately, idealists who clung to the practices of free elections merely lost elections to men who were willing to use the methods that worked, and thereby lost their opportunity to influence further events. The historical question, therefore, is whether Iglesias, turning to rebellion to save the nation from machine politics, after it became clear that the doctrine of "incompetence of origin" could not break

8. Iglesias, *Cuestión presidencial*, p. 17.
9. Cosío Villegas, *El porfiriato*, 1:37–38.
10. Knapp, *Lerdo*, p. 238.
11. Iglesias, *Cuestión presidential*, p. 77.
12. Ceballos, *Aurora y ocaso*, 2:686–703.

that machine, possessed a realistic solution to the problems of the Restored Republic. He did not: the real problems of the Restored Republic were outside the realm of liberal solutions.

Historical judgments about the rightousness of the three contending factions in 1876 reflect the judgments of the day. *Lerdistas* in 1876 charged that both Díaz and Iglesias were rebels against the legal government. The partisans and later sympathizers of Iglesias have believed that Lerdo and Díaz were equally outside and abusive of constitutional law in order to obtain presidential power, Díaz by military force and Lerdo by fraudulent election. They considered *Iglesismo* as the only legal path back to constitutionalism, and many supposed that the *Porfiristas* would join Iglesias to give legality to their rebellion. *Porfiristas* held that Lerdo and Iglesias were machine politicians, the equally corrupt, sinister heirs of *Juarismo*. They considered Iglesias an opportunist who joined the rebellion against Lerdo after Díaz had created an army and when Iglesias stood to become president. Certainly Iglesias had not challenged the electoral results of 1871.[13] A contemporary of the events of 1876 wrote six years later that "there was no other way [than war]: the interests of the three parties were irreconcilable."[14]

The most important single variation from those three partisan positions is the historical judgment that Iglesias at least meant well and was personally honest but misguided. Porfirian historians early assumed this position, which was consistent with the political tendency of Porfirian conciliation.[15] They would never say the same about Lerdo, who had to remain a tyrant as justification for the rebellion.[16]

13. This statement of partisan rightousness emerges from a reading of factional newspapers from 1876. Secondary books usually reflect one position or another.

14. Altamirano, *Política de México*, p. 194.

15. Iglesias won his final struggle—the struggle for his historical reputation—for everyone reviewing the events of 1876 uses his book, *La cuestión presidencial en 1876*, and several closely parallel his autobiographical justification; see for example, Rafael Zayas Enríquez, *Porfirio Díaz*, p. 120; Justo Sierra, *Political Evolution*, pp. 356–57; and García Naranjo, *Porfirio Díaz*, p. 196. Zayas Enríquez was *Porfirista* in 1876, Justo Sierra was *Iglesista;* García Naranjo, a generation younger, was anti-*Porfirista* until *Porfirismo* came under extreme attack and later became anti-*Maderista* and *Huertista*.

16. Cosío Villegas, "Lerdo," p. 172 ff.

It will never be known to what degree the elections of June and July 1876 were fraudulent. Lerdo certainly had been honing his political machine to guarantee his reelection. Frank Knapp wrote that "of fraud, force, and violence there was probably neither more nor less than had been an integral part of previous elections."[17] Knapp rather attacked Iglesias, who "had suddenly become hypersensitive to matters with which he had long been familiar and acquiesced in."[18] That must have made both *Lerdistas* and *Porfiristas* suspicious of Iglesias's indignation. Iglesias, seeking support from people who had immediately witnessed that election, wrote in his pronouncement that "it is a fact which everyone recognizes that in more than 100 districts [of 227] there were no elections."

> Moreover, in various [districts] fraud was committed with so little ability . . . that in some places the electoral colleges did not contain a legal *quorum*, while in others the electors reached a number incompatible with [legal] prescriptions. . . . As in one case so in the other, the respective votes ought not be computed, given their patent nullity.

Iglesias then dealt with a third irregularity, that of canceling elections in areas in a "state of siege" due to rebel activity and of holding elections under military guidance. The state of siege was declared, he maintained, not for military necessity, but rather for the political ends of obtaining electoral results favorable to the administration in hostile areas. The fourth irregularity was open fraud in those areas controlled by the administration. From this Iglesias concluded "that in the months of June and July 1876 there were no elections for the president of the Republic."[19]

Certainly no elections had taken place in areas where Porfirian rebels dominated. The governor of Morelos wrote that "due to the existence of various bands of insurgents, the elections did not take place." The governor of Guanajuato merely reported that the electoral colleges of his seventh and eighth districts did not meet. The governor of Veracruz reported that the elections had not been held in

17. Knapp, *Lerdo,* p. 245.
18. Ibid., p. 238.
19. Iglesias, *"Manifiesto a la nación"* in *Cuestión presidencial,* pp. 22, 365–66, 367.

the district of Tuxpan "because the counties which ought to have concurred in them are in rebellion against the Supreme Government." Gen. José Ceballos, military governor of Jalisco and Lerdo's man in western Mexico, telegraphed Mexico City that Lerdo "was elected by unanimous vote of the colleges" and that the districts of Tepic, then under military rule, and of the state of Colima "gave the same vote."[20]

Iglesias claimed that once he became aware of the irregularities and fraudulent practices involved he determined to oppose the results. If Congress had first declared the winners of the elections of justices of the Supreme Court for the seats that would become vacant in 1876, Iglesias planned to align sufficient support on the Court to refuse admission of the new members on the grounds that the elections had not been properly conducted.[21] Such a course would have provided a minor governmental crisis and served notice to Congress that a major crisis would result should they declare Lerdo reelected. If Congress declared the elections void, Iglesias would become provisional president on 1 December. He could then have overseen new and legal elections, as he promised to do in his "plan of government":

Not one soldier, not a cent from the federal treasury will be employed to falsify the vote of the electors. The parties which form will work with ample liberty for the triumph of their respective candidates [and] the victory will go to those who verifiably have the greatest popularity.

He might have worked the formula of no-reelection into the constitution as he promised, and he might have commenced constitutional amendment procedures for mandatory executive enforcement of *amparos*.[22]

20. Governor of Morelos to Minister of *Gobernación,* 10 July 1876, *Archivo General de la Nación* (AGN), Mexico City, *Ramo de Gobernación, legajo* 579, *carpeta* 2, *documento* 28; Governor of Guanajuato to Minister of *Gobernación,* 15 July 1876, ibid., 579:2:30; Governor of Veracruz to Minister of *Gobernación,* 28 June 1876, ibid., doc. 37; Governor of Jalisco to Minister of *Gobernación,* 10 July 1876, ibid., doc. 27.

21. Iglesias, *Cuestión presidencial,* pp. 31–32.

22. "*Programa de gobierno del presidente interino constitucional de la república mexicana,*" reprinted in ibid., pp. 413–18.

Iglesias's attempt to head off the reelection by his court strategy did not work. Congress delayed its declaration until 26 October, and at that time did not first declare the winners of the elections for justices. By then Iglesias was no longer on the bench, and the majority of the remaining justices rejected the resolution that he had left with his partisans, two of whom were then arrested by the Lerdo government.[23]

Iglesias's congressional strategy also failed, for he lacked the support of the necessary majority of congressmen. He later claimed that a delegation of antireelectionist congressmen sought him out, saying they would oppose a congressional declaration of reelection. What they wanted is now uncertain. Ignacio Altamirano, a contemporary of those events, later wrote that congressional *Lerdistas*, who had been slighted by Lerdo's policy of governing with the *Juaristas*, promised Iglesias that they would delcare the elections void "to the end that he would assume the presidency in conformity to the law, *if he consented to govern with them.*"[24] The congressional delay of the declaration, however, gave Lerdo time to shuffle his political stock: On 31 August Lerdo asked for the resignation of his entire cabinet and gave the ministerial portfolios to men from the *Lerdista* party.[25] Altamirano believed the events were interconnected, that Lerdo changed the cabinet to win the electoral declaration from a disaffected Congress.[26] It might be, however, that the discontented *Lerdistas* sounded out Iglesias, became convinced that he was sincere in his opposition to the machine politics by which so many of them held office, and therefore accepted the reelection of Lerdo upon the condition of revamping the cabinet.

They may even have threatened Lerdo with the specter of *Iglesismo* to win the cabinet change. At any rate, Lerdo acceded to the demand of his party to substitute his ministers after resisting it for four years, and Congress declared him president. Some congressmen thereafter

23. Ceballos, *Aurora y ocaso,* 2:696–97.

24. Iglesias, *Cuestión presidencial,* pp. 136–37; Altamirano, *Política de México,* p. 199; italics added.

25. Mariano Escobedo in war, Romero Rubio to foreign affairs, Antonio Tagle to development *(fomento),* and Juan José Baz in *gobernación.*

26. Altamirano, *Política de México,* pp. 199; Knapp *(Lerdo,* pp. 246–47) and Cosío Villegas ("Lerdo," p. 189) agree.

left Mexico City to follow the standard of *Iglesismo*. Conspicuous among them were Francisco Gómez del Palacio and Joaquín Alcalde, who had led the anti-*Lerdista* opposition in Congress and had even voted against the congressional resolution in 1873 by which Iglesias became president of the Supreme Court.[27]

The politics of 1876 became more complex in the fall. Iglesias became uneasy with the congressional delay of the electoral declaration. Fearing arrest for his deepening conspiracy, he disappeared from the Court on 1 October. The *Tuxtepecanos* were not yet beaten and had promised to expel everyone from office who had served the Lerdo administration.[28] Lerdo was losing prestige, as the cries against that particular election were melting into the cries against reelection. Congress was sharing Lerdo's mounting unpopularity by delaying its duty to declare the election results. Men in public life—above all the governors—had to begin to make personal decisions.

Iglesias augmented the governmental crisis by his activities in October. In Guanajuato on 28 October, timed to coincide with the congressional proclamation of Lerdo's reelection, Iglesias published his "Manifesto of Salamanca." The manifesto proclaimed that the congressional declaration constituted a coup d'état against the institutions and that all federal powers had ceased to be legitimate. According to the manifesto, the congressmen who had voted for the reelection resolution, Lerdo, and all those individuals throughout the republic who had been accomplices in the electoral frauds had forfeited their legal standing. Presidential powers, therefore, devolved upon the vice-president as interim executive, who was of course, himself.[29] Thereupon, Iglesias called upon the nation to sustain the constitution and the "Government of Legitimacy," as he thereafter called the group he assembled around him.

Iglesismo was not an empty threat to the Lerdo administration. Some politicians in office who opposed Lerdo on any of a dozen issues were

27. Ordaz, *Cuestión*, p. 58. Iglesias listed the names of forty-eight persons, almost all of them outstanding liberals and reformers, who supported him: *Cuestión presidencial*, p. 79.

28. Plan of Tuxtepec, Article three, APD, 12:99.

29. Iglesias, *Cuestión presidencial*, pp. 60–84; the "Manifesto of Salamanca" or *Manifiesto a la nación del presidente de la corte de justicia*, 28 October 1876, is reprinted in *Cuestión presidencial*, pp. 364–76, and in Ceballos, *Aurora y ocaso*, 2:940–50.

gratified to see anti-*Lerdista* leadership in the Supreme Court and in someone as respected as Iglesias. Some of those men doubted that Lerdo could sustain his government and greatly preferred *Iglesismo* over *Porfirismo*. Some congressmen and bureaucrats at state and national levels, as well as some governors, fit into those circumstances.

Florencio Antillón, *Lerdista* governor of Guanajuato, embraced Iglesias. During the summer of 1876 he had conferred with his friends and decided that if Lerdo demanded troops or money from Guanajuato, or if he declared a "state of siege" and replaced the governor, they would withdraw recognition from him and immediately recognize Iglesias as interim president. They had decided to raise 3,000 troops and seek as commander Sóstenes Rocha or one of the officers in San Luis Potosí or Zacatecas. Antillón's motive, according to one informant, was that he did not wish to lose the governorship and that the others had financial interests which would be vulnerable to exactions during a state of siege. At least one other of the group, Francisco del Río, had a long-vested interest as a member of the state legislature. The reported group thinking was that they would remain in power if Lerdo remained in power, which was only a "degree less than impossible," and would lose their positions if Díaz should win, "which is more probable." Therefore, they should rebel.[30] The arrangement was made between Iglesias and Antillón by the end of September, and Guanajuato became first Iglesias's sanctuary and then the seat of his government. If the above informant was correct concerning Antillón's motive, then he and his friends opposed Lerdo because they thought Lerdo would lose, and they could not join Díaz and keep their positions. They were thus willing to support Iglesias to save themselves from Díaz.

A second group of men attracted to *Iglesismo* were the legalists in and out of office who opposed *Lerdista* reelection and *Porfirista* rebellion. Lawyers everywhere could identify with Iglesias not because the doctrine of "incompetence of origin" was irrefutable but because it was plausible and, since it had been enunciated by the president of the Court, respectable. Lawyers who aspired to offices that were closed by incumbents could oppose Lerdo and reelection because the Supreme Court did. Probably most men believed that "incompetence of origin"

30. Juan de la Peña to Lerdo, 1 October 1876, APD, 13:99–101.

was essentially a constitutional cover-up for political opposition: "incompetence of origin" in 1876 was anti-*Lerdismo*. Nevertheless, sincere idealists and anti-reelectionists, as well as those who accepted the ᵀglesias doctrine, could also belong to this group.[31]

A third group attracted to *Iglesismo* was the military. The republican army emerging from the fall of Maximilian's empire was liberal, supporting liberal institutions during the Restored Republic. It was proud of its "professionalism," a term used to mean that it was obedient to the government and not insurrectionist. The most widely held value in the military was that rebellion was treasonous. Few officers in the regular army joined Díaz before the battle of Tecoac, but many of them were disgusted with the reelection and therefore became interested in *Iglesismo*. Politics was important also. Ignacio Mejía, the bureaucratic politician general and titular head of the *Juaristas*, had been replaced by Mariano Escobedo in the ministry of war. If Díaz were defeated, it could be expected that Escobedo would make changes in top commands. Should Díaz win, the Porfirian generals would occupy the top commands. Those generals who knew by experience the relentlessness of the *Tuxtepecano* rebellion and began to doubt Lerdo's ability to crush it could find legal reasons for supporting *Iglesismo*.

Gen. Felipe Berriozábal was such a man. Hero of the Reform and the Republican Resistance to the Intervention, Berriozábal had been *Orteguista* in 1866–67. Rehabilitated, he sat in Congress between 1871 and 1875. Berriozábal was reinstated in the army in 1875, serving in headquarters in the state of Mexico without a personal command in 1876.[32] He joined Iglesias in Toluca, accompanied him to Guanajuato, and became the minister of war in the "Government of Legality."[33] During the fall of 1876 he sent invitations to the governors and to officers of the army, urging them to second the "movement of Guanajuato."[34]

31. Justo Sierra, Guillermo Prieto, Francisco Cosmes, Francisco Sosa, and Francisco Gómez y Palacio, among others, were of this group.

32. ADN, 10:3:1–29, 54–55, 63.

33. Iglesias, *Cuestión presidencial*, pp. 42–43, 55, 113.

34. Joaquín Martínez to Manuel González, 12 November 1876, APD, 13:201–2. After the collapse of *Iglesismo* Berriozábal was arrested and ordered to Mexico City. There he wrote to the Díaz government the following

Particularly among the military, the idea spread that *Iglesismo* would not be legal until the completion of Lerdo's term on 1 December. The logic was that the reelection was void because of the fraud, as Iglesias had declared; therefore, no allegiance was owed to Lerdo after the expiration of his legal term of office on 30 November. *Iglesismo* was mere rebellion, however, until 1 December. Men who believed this were called "Decembrists." The Porfirian press worked to make *Iglesismo* and *Decembrismo* synonymous, for provisional loyalty to Lerdo was half-hearted loyalty, and suspended loyalty to Iglesias was unfulfilled potential. Iglesias was against *Decembrismo* and argued to anyone who would listen that Lerdo had broken the bonds of legality and therefore had forfeited his authority to the vice-president when Congress declared his reelection. His government was constitutionally legal, he affirmed, not on 1 December, but on 26 October.[35]

Working against the logic of *Decembrismo*, Iglesias appealed to officers of the army. Concurrence of opinion in 1876 was that Mexico's greatest living general was Sóstenes Rocha. Hero of the Republican Resistance to the French Intervention, he had caught Mexico's imagination during the rebellion of San Luis Potosí-Zacatecas in 1869–70 by his smashing victory against the rebels at Lo de Ovejo, and again during the rebellion of La Noria in 1871–72 by overwhelming the rebels at Tampico, slaughtering with fearful bloodshed the insurgents at the Ciudadela in Mexico City, and breaking the offensive tide with the terrible battle of La Bufa in Zacatecas. In 1875, however, Rocha

---

(the military honor associated with constitutionalism is evident): "As a soldier and a man of public affairs, repeatedly I insisted upon protecting and having protected the political constitution of the nation. Loyal to my insistence, I supported the President of the Supreme Court of Justice who by the express precepts of the same constitution is the only man called to cover the vacancy which is created by the absence of the Constitutional President. As a liberal of profound conviction I have always combated for that same constitution, which has been my only banner. Therefore, my conscience is tranquil and I believe I have complied with my duty": Berriozábal to Pedro Ogazón, minister of war, February 1877, ADN, 11:1–29, 46. Berriozábal thereafter made a rapid return to public life: Cosío Villegas, *El porfiriato*, 1:286.

35. "In case Congress had expedited a decree declaring Lerdo monarch of Mexico and had he sanctioned it, to no one would it have occurred to sustain that he should continue as legitimate president until November 30, 1876" (*Cuestión presidencial*, p. 73).

was involved in an attempted insurrection against Lerdo and was skillfully isolated, arrested, and then mysteriously demoted to an unimportant post at Celaya, Guanajuato.[36] Foe of Díaz since La Noria, mistrusted by Lerdo, Rocha was sought out by Iglesias.

Through mutual friends, Rocha and Iglesias reached an accord. It was agreed that Rocha should await the congressional declaration of the reelection, in order, according to Iglesias, "to give a constitutional character to a movement which would have been a simple military uprising without this previous requisite." Then Rocha was to appear before all or part of the First Division of Mexico City which he had previously commanded, capture the city for the "Government of Legality," and arrest Lerdo and the persons responsible for the declaration of the reelection. Lerdo learned of the proposed coup d'état, and Rocha was "sent to Europe to study military science."[37] In retrospect Iglesias judged that

> if the frustrated combination had been carried out, the constitutionalist cause [*Iglesismo*] would have counted on the capital of the Republic, a city of immense importance in every sense. Once secured, it would not have later fallen to the *Porfiristas*, and the course of events would necessarily have been entirely different.[38]

After Rocha, Iglesias judged that Gen. Ignacio Alatorre, general of the Second Division, which stood between Díaz and the capital, was one of the most important men in Mexico for his cause. On behalf of Iglesias, León Guzmán visited Alatorre in the latter's headquarters after an unsuccessful visit to Díaz's camp. Alatorre indicated his willingness to join Iglesias on 1 December but wanted first to defeat Díaz. José de Jesús López, partisan of Iglesias and the Puebla judge who had granted the *amparo* against the governor of Puebla in 1874, also visited Alatorre. The general indicated to him that Lerdo could not be saved and would probably step down after the congressional declaration of his reelection had saved his *amour propre*. According to

36. Cosío Villegas, *República restaurada*, pp. 780–88.
37. Iglesias, *Cuestión presidencial*, p. 42; Rocha's service record: ADN, 148:11:111: 1–178:55.
38. Iglesias, *Cuestión presidencial*, p. 118.

Iglesias, Alatorre told López that he would serve Lerdo until 30 November and, if Lerdo refused to step down, would join Iglesias.[39]

After Congress declared the reelection of Lerdo, Judge López took the resolution with a written protest of the antireelection congressmen to Alatorre, and Congressmen Alcalde and Nicoli went to Alatorre's camp at Tepeaca on 29 October to urge again the union with Iglesias. Alatorre told them he would limit his actions to trying to persuade Lerdo to renounce the reelection. If unsuccessful, he would resign from his command but would not pronounce against Lerdo with his division. Alatorre claimed he sent a letter to Lerdo to that effect on 30 October with Congressman Manuel Aspe, seeking separation if Lerdo refused to renounce the reelection. During the first week of November Lerdo and Escobedo called Alatorre to Mexico for a briefing and sent him back to his post.[40]

Iglesias later wrote that Alatorre's hesitancy at that time left open three disadvantageous alternatives: Alatorre could lose to Díaz and thereafter be of no use to Iglesias; he could defeat Díaz and thus strengthen Lerdo; or he could be replaced by another federal officer.[41] Iglesias was looking for explanation but appears a poor analyst here. Had Alatorre expressed his open adherence to Iglesias on the eve of battle with Díaz, the three-way rivalry would have become immensely more complicated. The urge to unite the two anti-*Lerdista* forces in both Alatorre's camp and Díaz's camp in order to avoid combat would have become formidable. It is questionable that Díaz could have stemmed the tide; Alatorre could not have, as indicated by the 4 November defection of General Tolentino from Alatorre's *Lerdista* camp to the Porfirian camp of Manuel González. Alatorre would have been swept aside, either by those who sought union with the *Tuxtepecanos* or by the still-loyal *Lerdistas* in his camp. Lerdo would have tried to remove Alatorre, or, failing that, Escobedo would have worked his will upon others of Alatorre's officers. Certainly no more supplies would have been sent from Mexico to the Second Division. *Iglesismo* was only as healthy before Tecoac as was

39. Ibid., pp. 43, 119.

40. Ignacio Alatorre, "*Una exposición de las operaciones militares practicadas en la última campaña por la división que fue a sus órdenes,*" *El Siglo XIX*, 12 October 1877, reprinted in Iglesias, *Cuestión presidencial,* pp. 165–73.

41. Iglesias, *Cuestión presidencial,* p. 120.

Alatorre's Second Division. Dividing the Second Division before defeating Díaz would have been disastrous for *Iglesismo.* Alatorre was right; however, Díaz crushed the Second Division a few days later at Tecoac.[42]

Another important general whom Iglesias sought out was Ignacio Mejía. His known ability as a combination maker and political dealer among Mexican generals made him enormously valuable. Mejía had opposed Díaz from the ministry of war for years, was widely believed to be seeking the presidency against Lerdo in the early months of the year, and in August had been dismissed from Lerdo's cabinet. He seemed ideal for *Iglesismo.* To mutual friends who sought out Mejía for Iglesias, however, the general was wont to say, "When the time comes I shall comply with my duty." Iglesias pondered whether the time was 1 December and whether he could then count on Mejía. When the time came, however, Mejía's duty proved to be self-exile.[43]

Gov. and Gen. Servando Canales of Tamaulipas was another apparently natural ally for *Iglesismo,* inasmuch as he opposed Lerdo's reelection and the "state of siege" imposed by Escobedo, and was himself seeking reelection in 1876. According to Iglesias, Canales sought out the president of the Court through Congressman Santos Garza Gutiérrez before those two citizens of Tamaulipas became *Porfiristas.* Iglesias thereafter supposed he could count upon Canales, but he acted too late: Canales pronounced for the Plan of Tuxtepec in mid-year and remained loyal to the end.[44]

42. Knapp argues that Alatorre sought the presidency for himself: *Lerdo,* pp. 250–51.

43. Iglesias, *Cuestión presidencial,* pp. 39–40. A *Porfirista* reported to Díaz in December that an officer in Saltillo was trying to win adherents to *Iglesismo,* armed with a letter from Mejía for that purpose: Santos de la Garza y Gutiérrez to Díaz, 13 December 1876, APD, 14:297–98; Altamirano held it as certain that Mejía influenced the army to join Iglesias: *Política de México,* p. 200. Mejía lived in Cuba and Europe until his return to Mexico in 1884, and, although he lived until 1906, he never again played a public role.

44. Iglesias, *Cuestión presidencial,* pp. 35–37. Canales's pronouncement gives as motives the declaration of the "state of siege" in Tamaulipas and Lerdo's disrespect for states' rights: Ceballos, *Aurora y ocaso,* 1:565–67. Between the three parties in 1876 Canales chose correctly from the point of view of longevity: he was later strong enough to override Díaz's constitutional amendment for no reelection of governors, dying in office in 1881. Thus Canales was one of the most successful *caudillos* of the second half of the nineteenth century.

Iglesismo, nevertheless, was not an empty threat. Even as the Porfirian troops were concentrating in Puebla to confront Alatorre, *Iglesismo* was gaining strength north and west of the national capital. Governor and General Antillón placed the forces of the state of Guanajuato in the service of Iglesismo on 30 October. General Franco of those forces occupied Querétaro City on 2 November, dislodging *Lerdista* General Loera. The congress of the state of Querétaro on 4 November recognized the government of Iglesias, and its resources thereafter flowed toward Guanajuato.[45] On 12 November the military commander of San Luis Potosí, Gen. Manuel Sánchez Rivera, put himself and the forces at his command "on the side of the venerable representative of the law, Citizen José María Iglesias."[46] *Lerdista* forces under General Vélez returned to Querétaro on 13 November as Franco was withdrawn for the *Iglesista* siege of Lagos, an important garrison still *Lerdista* in the state of Jalisco. Also on 13 November General Pérez Castro, commander at Lagos since his expulsion of Donato Guerra in February, accepted *Iglesismo* and placed 1,100 troops at Iglesias's disposition.[47]

More pronouncements were made for the "Government of Legality" after the battle of Tecoac and the flight of Lerdo from the capital. The state of Aguascalientes pronounced on 20 November. On the following day García de la Cadena pronounced with the forces of Zacatecas. On 23 November Col. Juan Malda in Piedad, Michoacán, pronounced with his brigade of 1,000 men. On 26 November the important federal garrison of 3,000 men at San Luis Potosí recognized the government of Iglesias. On the following day Gen. José Ceballos, commander of the Fourth Division in Guadalajara, did the same. Ceballos then began using his influence upon commanders and *caciques* in Tepic, who also joined the *Iglesista* cause. On 28 November the authorities of the state of Morelos followed suit, as did those of Colima on 30 November.[48]

45. Iglesias, *Cuestión presidencial,* pp. 132–33, 145.
46. The proclamation is reprinted in Ceballos, *Aurora y ocaso,* 2:715.
47. Iglesias, *Cuestión presidencial,* pp. 148–49.
48. Ibid., pp. 191, 200, 243, 288; Angel Cancino to Luis Curiel, 30 November 1876, APD, 14:108–9; Pérez Verdía, *Jalisco,* 3:532–33; José Ceballos to Domingo Nava, 5 December 1876, CPD, 1:176–78; Francisco G. Cortes to Díaz, 2 December 1876, APD, 14:147–48; Angel Cancino to Luis Curiel, 30 November 1876, ibid., pp. 108–9.

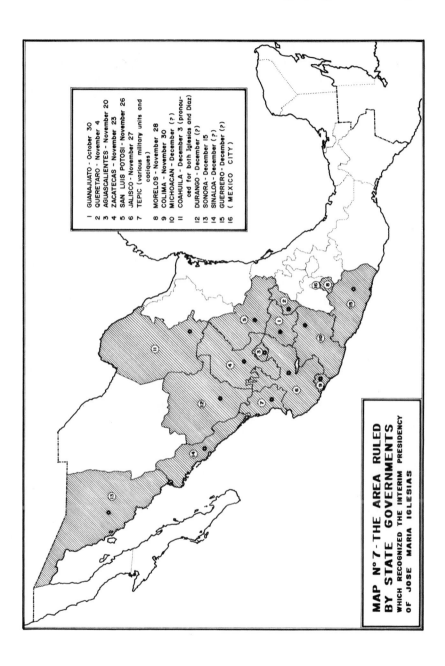

MAP N° 7 - THE AREA RULED
BY STATE GOVERNMENTS
WHICH RECOGNIZED THE INTERIM PRESIDENCY
OF JOSE MARIA IGLESIAS

1 GUANAJUATO - October 30
2 QUERETARO - November 4
3 AGUASCALIENTES - November 20
4 ZACATECAS - November 23
5 SAN LUIS POTOSI - November 26
6 JALISCO - November 27
7 TEPIC (various military units and
     caciques)
8 MORELOS - November 28
9 COLIMA - November 30
10 MICHOACAN - December (?)
11 COAHUILA - December 3 (pronoun-
     ced for both Iglesias and Diaz)
12 DURANGO - December (?)
13 SONORA - December 15
14 SINALOA - December (?)
15 GUERRERO - December (?)
16 (MEXICO CITY)

In December, as Díaz began mounting his campaign against *Iglesismo, Decembrismo* came of age. On 1 December Gen. Francisco Olivares of Morelia, having served as Lerdo's escort through the state of Michoacán until 30 November, pledged his allegiance to the government in Guanajuato, taking a full brigade to the cause. When Antillón, raised to division commander by Iglesias, occupied Morelia, capital city of Michoacán, and placed Luis Couto in the governorship, that state signed an act of adhesion to the Iglesias government. Then on 6 December Col. Epifanio Reyes pronounced at Pátzcuaro, Michocán, at the head of 500 men. From the Sierra Gorda, formidable mountain fortress in the states of Querétaro and Guanajuato, Gen. Rafael Olvera, long time *cacique* of many isolated towns and villages, pronounced for Iglesias. On 3 December Gen. Hipólito Charles, whom Díaz named governor and military commander of the state of Coahuila, recognized Iglesias, after having occupied Saltillo, the capital of Coahuila, on 2 December. In Durango with part of the federal Third Division, Gen. Carlos Fuero, *Lerdista* general at Icamole in May, pronounced for Iglesias. Gen. Vicente Mariscal, governor and military commander of the state of Sonora, recognized Iglesias on 15 December. General and Governor of Sinaloa Francisco O. Arce did the same and began collecting all the units of the line, state, and federal forces. Authorities of the state of Guerrero followed suit, as did the Pacific Squadron under the command of Capt. Luis Valle, giving to Iglesias all of the Pacific ports.[49]

Not all the *Iglesista* pronouncements were useful for the immediate task at hand, which was to confront the approaching Porfirian army. Nevertheless, Iglesias had three divisions, one led by General Antillón, being the forces of Guanajuato, a column of Colonel Reyes, and the troops from Lagos; the Fourth Federal Division of General Ceballos; and the division of General Echeagary (who had been commander of the penitentiary at Salamanca from which Iglesias pronounced) with the forces of Querétaro, the brigade of Colonel Malda, the section of General Olivares, a squadron commanded by Colonel Villaseñor, and the garrison of San Luis Potosí. In terms of territory over which

49. Iglesias, *Cuestión presidencial*, pp. 198–99, 222–23, 228, 232; Charles to Díaz, 3 December 1876, APD, 14:169–70; Vicente Mariscal, Circular, 15 December 1876, APD, 14:335 (Mariscal had earlier declared that *Iglesismo* was a "national scandal": Mariscal, Circular, 25 November 1876, ibid., pp. 26–27); J. M. Ferreira to Díaz, 15 December 1876, ibid., pp. 332–33.

Iglesista commanders held jurisdiction, more than half of the nation supported the "Government of Legality."

Various authors have explored the impact of *Iglesismo* upon *Lerdismo*. Their arguments are summarized easily. First, the division in the *Lerdista* camp with the rise of *Iglesismo* augmented the chance that Díaz would be the ultimate victor, making it necessary that every politician reconsider his plans. Thus *Iglesismo* undermined what *Lerdista* solidarity had existed. Alternately, some *Lerdistas* became imbued with Iglesias's legality, with the same results: *Lerdista* solidarity dissolved. Second, when Iglesias pronounced in Guanajuato on 28 October, Lerdo was obliged to send against Iglesias the forces that Alatorre needed against Díaz in mid-November. Third, the two anti-Lerdo movements could possibly unite, making *Lerdismo* even less viable.[50] These arguments are so convincing that no exceptions to them are made here.

The reason usually proffered for the failure of Iglesias is defection to Díaz.[51] While this explanation is true, it is inadequate, for it does not explain why such defection occurred. Several historians propose that Iglesias lost because of tactics: he should have remained in Mexico City and opposed the election from the Court. Although suffering prison at Lerdo's hands, he would have gained a prestige which the *Porfiristas* would have found difficult to overcome when they occupied the capital. Sufficient numbers of the *Tuxtepecanos* would have insisted upon the constitutional procedure that Iglesias would have been elevated to the presidency.[52] The argument assumes that without an *Iglesista* government in Guanajuato and its army in Querétaro, Díaz nevertheless could have destroyed the Second Division and occupied the capital. If so, then *Iglesismo* as it developed did not have an effect on *Lerdismo*.[53]

50. Cosío Villegas, *República restaurada,* pp. 827–28, 906; Iturribarría, *Oaxaca,* 4:207; Knapp, *Lerdo,* p. 235; Sierra, *Political evolution,* p. 357.

51. Zayas Enríquez, *Porfirio Díaz,* pp. 121; García Naranjo, *Porfirio Díaz,* p. 199; García Granados, *Historia de México,* 1:113; Mariano Cuevas, *Historia de la nación mexicana,* 3d ed. (Mexico: Editorial Porrúa, 1967), p. 1026.

52. Zayas Enríquez, *Porfirio Díaz,* pp. 120–21; García Granados, *Historia de México,* 1:109; Iturribarría, *Oaxaca,* 4:215–16.

53. This might be argued at length to show that either one group or the other is wrong, either those who believe that *Iglesismo* destroyed *Lerdismo* or those who argue that Iglesias ought to have stayed firm in Mexico. In fact,

Iglesias did not plan to be saved from prison by Díaz. When Iglesias pronounced, it was not at all certain that Díaz could survive a conflict with Alatorre's division in Puebla. It will be shown in chapter 12 that Iglesias behaved as though he believed that Alatorre would beat Díaz and then support him.

Other historians have invoked Iglesias's doctrine of "incompetence of origin" as his mistake, arguing either that the doctrine was patently absurd,[54] and thus attracted no followers,[55] or that by the doctrine itself only the Court could declare an election illegal, not the president of the Court;[56] that by his own doctrine he was legal only on 1 December, not 26 October;[57] and that at any rate the people wanted real change, not judical reforms.[58] These and other arguments are used by those who claim Iglesias was, like Díaz, a simple rebel.[59] The Manifesto of Salamanca, however, makes clear that Iglesias was not using the doctrine or declaring the election illegal as chief justice. "Only the people" could do so. He was merely calling upon fellow citizens to refuse the imposition of a president by way of fraudulent elections and was announcing that in his capacity as vice-president he was establishing a provisional government in the absence of a legal one and calling upon the people to sustain it.[60] How he could separate the offices he did not explain. Nevertheless, it was not his office, but the people's "right of revolution" that formed the base of his "legality." At any rate, the argument that he attracted no followers because his

---

García Granados argued both ways. I favor the former, but no evidence can be adduced for a hypothetical case.

54. Iturribarría, *Oaxaca*, 4:217; García Granados, *Historia de México*, 1:106, 113; García Naranjo, *Porfirio Díaz*, p. 196.

55. García Naranjo, *Porfirio Díaz*, p. 197.

56. Ordaz, *Cuestión*, p. 35; Iturribarría, *Oaxaca*, 4:215; García Naranjo, *Porfirio Díaz*, p. 196.

57. García Naranjo, *Porfirio Díaz*, p. 196; García Granados, *Historia de México*, 1:104, 107.

58. José C. Valadés, *El porfirismo, historia de un régimen, el nacimiento, 1876–1884* (Mexico: Antigua Librería Robredo, de José Porrúa e hijos, 1941), p. 17; García Granados, *Historia de México*, 1:111.

59. Iturribarría, *Oaxaca*, 4:216; Ordaz, *Cuestión*, pp. 31–32; García Naranjo, *Porfirio Díaz*, p. 196; Zayas Enríquez, *Porfirio Díaz*, p. 121; García Granados, *Historia de México*, 1:103, 110.

60. Iglesias, *"Manifiesto,"* 28 October 1876, in *Cuestión presidencial*, pp. 372–76.

position was illogical is specious. As has been seen, Iglesias had at least as many followers by 15 December as Díaz had had on 15 November.

Early in his opposition to Lerdo, Iglesias might better have turned opposition politician than have combined constitutionalism with rebellion. Iglesias was certainly in rebellion the moment he withdrew recognition from the executive branch of government and from those congressmen who voted for the declaration of reelection, for no constitutional provision allowed withdrawal of recognition. Iglesias's answer was that Lerdo and those congressmen were committing an illegal act. Lerdo and Díaz were "revolutionaries," according to Iglesias, not himself.

Nevertheless, all phases of *Iglesismo* failed. "Incompetence of origin" was not a realistic solution to party machines and executive centralism. The *amparo* only gave relief to the individual plaintiff from the effects of the governmental action from which he sought protection. It did not strike down the law and certainly did not remove the official from office. Lerdo and his entire executive party ignored the Court, and Lerdo's machine successfully secured his reelection and the congressional declaration.

Iglesias's other plans also failed. His attempt to undermine the election returns from the Court and occupy the presidential chair by default failed because *Lerdista* congressional leaders refused to give Iglesias the opportunity to deny admission of the new justices to the Court. The congressional conspiracy fell also. Lerdo had opposition in Congress, but it was not composed of sufficient numbers of men who wanted to change the system. The congressional delay of the election proclamation gave Lerdo time to destroy the *Iglesista* military conspiracy and to defuse his congressional opposition by altering his cabinet. *Decembrismo* undermined Iglesias's opportunity to develop an army until he faced Díaz rather than Lerdo.

The most important point worth making about the *Iglesista* attempt to curb *Lerdismo* is this: not even a successful *Iglesista* rebellion—one that carried Iglesias to the presidency—could have curbed political machines, power monopolization, and presidential centralism. The present examination of Mexican politics suggests that if Iglesias had captured the presidency and overseen an honest and open election, the local elections would have been dominated by governors, who would have established local monopolistic machines. Without a nationwide alliance of governors, the local opposition to gubernatorial monopoly of power would have plunged the nation into prolonged strife. That strife would have continued until some strongman again created a national, all-embracing alliance for the monopolization of power. Without the necessary economic solution and a powerful institution, not yet developed in Mexico today, to guarantee that local elites could not monopolize whatever economic growth that could be generated, then local rivalry against regional dictatorship could only be reined in by total executive dominance. Furthermore, it is not certain that Mexico could have suffered another period of strife without internal dissolution or foreign intervention. Iglesias may have been sincere in his publicly proclaimed aims, but he became another in the series of men in Mexican independent history to be broken by the realities of Mexican politics.

Chapter 12
The Politics of Victory

Several historians have made judgments about the effects that the three contending parties of 1876 had upon each other. Zayas Enríquez typifies a common appraisal by laying the *Porfirista* victory to "the stupidity of the government, the skepticism of Lerdo, and the lack of confidence of the army, rather than to the political and military skill of General Díaz and the efforts of his followers." *Iglesismo* in such accounts was ineffectual, "without strength nor prestige to conquer power, but enough to mortally wound . . ." Lerdo. In the same vein but with a slight twist in the implications, Knapp wrote that "with a motley of professional military discontents [Díaz] won the revolution through opportunism, the strange operation of events, and military might. . . ."[1] If "opportunism" is used not as a moral perjorative, but as a synonym for "tactical flexibility," then the term aptly describes *Porfirismo* in 1876. "The strange operation of events" refers to the rise of *Iglesismo*, which was not an ineffectual force; it had wide appeal among practical men, especially after the fall of Lerdo. Knapp, however, arranges his materials for that year in such a way as to show that

> Lerdo's government, down to the outbreak of Iglesias' plot, seemed stable and capable of crushing the Díaz uprising, but the new explosion cleft the government supporters and its military power, setting in motion a chain of disastrous defection which made Díaz' victory possible. . . . If any one man directly erected the dictatorship of Porfirio Díaz, it was José María Iglesias.[2]

The difference of opinion concerns the stability and capacity of Lerdo's government. Beyond that it seems possible to lay aside the indig-

1. Zayas Enríquez, *Porfirio Díaz*, p. 123; García Naranjo, *Porfirio Díaz*, p. 197; Knapp, *Lerdo*, pp. 237–38.
2. Knapp, *Lerdo* p. 239; also: "The undeniable result of Iglesias' revolt was that it gave the mortal blow to Lerdo's government" (ibid., p. 249). For concurring opinions see Paz, *Algunas campañas*, 3:422; Salvador Quevedo y Zubieta, *El General Gonzalez y su gobierno en México: anticipo a la historia*, 2 vols. (Mexico: Establecimiento Tipográfico de Patoni 4, 1884), 1:53; Ceballos, *Aurora y ocaso*, 2:701–3; Sierra, *Political Evolution*, p. 357.

nation: Lerdo had no better claim to the presidency after the mid-year elections than anyone else. The Mexican presidency thereafter belonged to the shrewdest politician with the greatest military support. The *Porfiristas* and *Iglesistas* were equally anxious for that prize. The object of this chapter is to describe the relations between *Porfirismo* and *Iglesismo* and to explain why *Porfirismo* won.

The *Porfiristas* and *Iglesistas* began their curious relationship by written invitation—the Plan of Tuxtepec as reformed at Palo Blanco. The plan pronounced by Sarmiento on 10 January 1876 had been hastily concocted and had not been approved in advance by the man whom it designated general-in-chief of the army.[3] Indeed, Díaz was then in Brownsville, Texas, and on 21 March in Palo Blanco, Tamaulipas, Díaz published a reform of the original plan. The principal difference between the two documents was in article six, which described the procedure for the selection of the provisional president after the overthrow of President Lerdo. The original plan called for the governors of the various states who adhered to the plan to select a provisional president, who would hold an election for the constitutional president. The Reform of Palo Blanco offered the provisional presidency to the next in line of succession, the president of the Supreme Court, José María Iglesias.[4]

Díaz probably had two motives for inviting Iglesias to join him. First, he would have been under considerable pressure to adopt legal formulas: the adhesion of Iglesias lent an apparent constitutionality to the movement, for withdrawal of recognition from Lerdo for uncon-

3. Ireneo Paz claimed he wrote the Plan of Tuxtepec under conditions of stress: ". . . that grotesque figure was the political plan which was proclaimed in Tuxtepec, and which fortunately was later reformed in Palo Blanco": *Algunas campañas*, 3:354–55; compare Cosío Villegas, *República restaurada*, pp. 797–98.

4. The Plan of Tuxtepec and the Reform of Palo Blanco are reproduced in APD, 12:96–100, and in Miguel León-Portillo, et al., *Historia documental de México*, 2 vols. (Mexico: Universidad Nacional Autónoma de México, 1964), 2:358–67. The Plan of Tuxtepec is reproduced and discussed in Ceballos, *Aurora y ocaso*, 2:430ff., and the Reform of Palo Blanco in ibid., pp. 898–901; both plans are reproduced *in toto* and discussed in López-Portillo, *Porfirio Díaz*, pp. 103ff. They are discussed in Cosío Villegas, *República restaurada*, pp. 796ff.; Bancroft, *Vida de Porfirio Díaz*, pp. 497ff.; Knapp, *Lerdo*, pp. 236ff.; Quevedo y Zubieta, *El Caudillo*, pp. 230–36; Cosmes, *Historia general de Méjico*, 22:759–63.

stitutional behavior logically should have transferred executive power to the constitutionally prescribed next-of-succession. Second, any political and military support that Iglesias commanded would be added to the Porfirian movement and subtracted from the Lerdo government.[5]

Nevertheless, Díaz did not want Iglesias to assume the command of the movement, and certainly did not want him to control the interim government after the fall of Lerdo. In case Iglesias were to accept, and probably calculated to make him decline, while still attempting to satisfy the antireelectionists and constitutionalists, Díaz wrote modifications into article six. Iglesias had to accept within one month after the plan appeared in the capital city press and then would only have "administrative functions" pending new elections. If Iglesias refused or remained silent, then all power (*"el carácter de jefe del Ejecutivo"*) would fall to Porfirio Díaz.[6] Iglesias refused. He had another plan by which he might become president without joining Porfirio Díaz.

Iglesias's attitudes toward *Porfirismo* and toward Díaz during the tense summer of 1876 are not on record. By September, however, three developments induced Iglesias to seek out Díaz. First, Congress convened after its summer recess without making the customary election-year declaration of the winner. A long delay would upset Iglesias's schedule for his proposed maneuver against Lerdo's reelection. Second, the insurrection of the capital city garrison was in jeopardy of being exposed and nullified. Third, Díaz had successfully united with his southern army, had control of the state of Oaxaca, and had taken the field. Iglesias was in danger of being left out of the great events of the year. Moreover, that *Porfirismo* and *Iglesismo* should gravitate toward one another was natural; both were anti-Lerdo. Díaz could profit by Lerdo's having to establish another front, and Iglesias needed Díaz's army. Subordinates in both movements wanted union; if the leaders did not, each could imagine he could use the other.

5. Quevedo y Zubieta (*El Caudillo*, p. 236), López-Portillo (*Porfirio Díaz*, pp. 111–12), and Cosío Villegas (*República restaurada*, p. 816) use parts of these two arguments.

6. This point has not been commented upon by the various authors who have discussed the significance of the Reform of Palo Blanco; see appendix 13.

They could work out temporary terms, and each could imagine he could ultimately rid himself of the other.

Through intermediaries Iglesias contacted Díaz. Essentially Iglesias offered to clothe the *Tuxtepecanos* in legality. In Iglesias's words, Díaz was invited "to enter the constitutional path, leaving to one side the exaggerations and unsustainable points of his revolutionary plan." Iglesias thought, he said in retrospect, that Díaz would not refuse if he were sincere that his "principal objective was to assure the liberty of popular suffrage which had been audaciously attacked by the reelection of *señor* Lerdo. . . ."[7] Perhaps Iglesias wanted Díaz's armed organization for his own purpose. The communication, however, should be seen as a first offer; the negotiations were on.

Díaz's answer of 16 October sought to undermine the distinction Iglesias had made that the former was a rebel and the latter the soul of legality. Iglesias, according to Díaz, had lost his legality upon his flight from the Court, without having joined the popular insurrection at the time of the *Tuxtepecano* proclamation at Palo Blanco. Nevertheless, the *Tuxtepecanos* would recognize Iglesias as provisional president if Iglesias acted upon the following basis: Iglesias should accept the Plan of Tuxtepec reformed at Palo Blanco, with an explanation of why he had not done so within the period stipulated in the plan; he should not modify the *Tuxtepecano* program and should promise to choose his ministers from the ranks of the revolution; he should swear not to accept any person employed in the Lerdo regime for any level of the interim government or the military, except persons who had pronounced for the insurrection and had brought necessary resources to the movement; and Iglesias should recognize all the acts of the revolution.[8] In essence, Díaz asked Iglesias for a complete and total capitulation. Iglesias would be provisional president in exchange for turning over his entire movement to the *Tuxtepecanos* to operate through a ministry loyal not to Iglesias, but to Díaz. These were, however, Díaz's first demands—presumably negotiable.

7. Iglesias, *Cuestión presidencial,* pp. 46–47.
8. *Manifiesto del presidente interino constitucional de la república, sobre las negotiaciones seguidas con el Sr. D. Porfirio Díaz,* 1 December 1876, reprinted in Iglesias, *Cuestión presidencial,* pp. 379–80, and discussed in ibid., pp. 126–27. Cosío Villegas, *El porfiriato,* 1:57, cites the original letter: Díaz to Joaquín Ruíz, 15 [*sic*] October 1876, *Archivo del Sr. D. Fernando Iglesias Calderón* AGN.

Iglesias answered Díaz from Salamanca, Guanajuato, on 30 October two days after he had published his proclamation against the elections and against Lerdo. Iglesias found the *Tuxtepecano* conditons "inadmissible." Díaz's first condition was inadmissible because it would convert Iglesias to the status of a common rebel. The second would deprive him of all initiative and freedom of action in his own government. The third would leave him "limited to authorizing with my name that which others might will." The fourth he could not accept because he was ignorant of the various acts of the revolution. "It is impossible for me to cede in points of such vital importance," he wrote. "If the revolution does not wish to cede its exigency, it has its natural representatives who will do what seems best to them."[9]

It may be asked why Iglesias took such an adamant stand. The Porfirian demands were exacting, but they formed an offer. Iglesias answered strongly in the negative without proposing alternatives. Iglesias was not a novice in politics; to get something he had to give something. That he gave nothing indicates that on 30 October he needed nothing Díaz could offer, or that he could obtain more of what he wanted by giving nothing to Díaz. Iglesias had pronounced two days earlier. He had a collection of promises in his portfolio from persons who could not have seconded a plan which Iglesias had not yet pronounced. At that time, 30 October, in a firm refusal to Porfirio Díaz, Iglesias would show the nation, and particularly the elements he was trying to attract, and most particularly Gen. Ignacio Alatorre of the Second Division, who wanted to destroy *Porfirismo* before joining Iglesismo, that he would not succumb to demands set by Díaz.

An exchange of communications between Iglesias and Díaz of greater transcendency took place in November. In his camp at Acatlán on 7 November, Díaz signed a "convention" with Joaquín Alcalde, who claimed to represent Iglesias. The Convention required Díaz to recognize the interim presidency of Iglesias. The two leaders would then dispose of Lerdo's government and establish a coalition government to oversee new elections.[10]

Díaz probably accepted the Convention of Acatlán because it was good public relations to appear conciliatory with other anti-*Lerdista*

9. Iglesias, *Cuestión presidencial*, pp. 378–81.
10. The negotiations surrounding the "Convention of Acatlán" are discussed in appendix 14.

forces. Some of his own followers wanted the union, as they had at
Palo Blanco. And, if Iglesias were to refuse the pact, the opprobrium
for continued war would fall upon Iglesias. Furthermore, military
action in the *Iglesista* camp may have appeared to merit attention. The
cavalry section of Antillón's division under General Franco occupied
Querétaro on 2 November, obliging the *Lerdista* General Loera to
evacuate that city. The legislature of Querétaro on 4 November recognized the Iglesias government, which thereby attained an advanced
position on Mexico City.[11]

Díaz had yet another reason for conducting negotiations. Alcalde
rode to Acatlán ten days before Díaz rode to Tecoac. Díaz had been in
Oaxaca for three months, raising and equipping an army. Although
guerrilla movements had broken out all over the nation, the *Tuxtepecanos* only controlled the government of Oaxaca. Tamaulipas and
Zacatecas were anomalies, dominated by *caudillos* in search of their
own interests. Iglesias controlled two states, Guanajuato and Querétaro, and it was widely believed that the federal army was Decembrist,
awaiting 1 December to render their allegiance to the government at
Guanajuato. The strongest federal army stood between Díaz and the
capital, led by a man Díaz thought was loyal to Iglesias. Díaz's entire
career stood in the balance and was contingent upon the destruction
of or alliance with the Second Division of Gen. Ignacio Alatorre.

Alatorre, a known Decembrist, wanted to crush Díaz before joining
Iglesias. A clause referring to Alatorre appears in the Porfirian version of the Convention of Acatlán which is omitted from the Iglesias
version.[12] Article ten refers to the eastern and central states, which by

11. Iglesias, *Cuestión presidencial*, p. 145. It is not certain that these *Iglesista*
movements of the first week of November were known to Díaz at the time of
the Covention of Acatlán; thus they may not have influenced his decision.

12. Protasio Tagle, newly appointed minister of *gobernación* in the *Tuxtepecano* government, published the Porfirian version of the negotiations of 29
November: *Circular expedida por el C. Licenciado Protasio P. Tagle, ministro de
gobernación en que se dan a conocer las negociaciones entabladas con el C. Lic. José
María Iglesias para dar término a la guerra civil, y que fueron rotas por su parte*
(Mexico: Imprenta del Gobierno, 1876); the *Iglesista* version was published on
1 December as *Manifiesto del presidente interino constitucional de la república, sobre
las negociaciones seguidas con el Sr. D. Porfirio Díaz*, reprinted in Iglesias, *Cuestión
presidencial*, pp. 378–94. Both documents were designed to win public support
by attempting to prove that the rival faction was guilty of breaking relations
between the anti-Lerdo forces and therefore responsible for the civil war.

the Convention would fall under Porfirian control, ". . . and . . . which will be joined almost certainly by the Second Division which Alatorre commands. . . ." Iglesias made no comment on that, but certainly Díaz meant that Iglesias should order Alatorre to surrender control of Puebla to the *Porfiristas*. Two days before Díaz sat down with Alcalde, General Tolentino deserted from the Second Division with 1,000 soldiers, pronounced for Díaz, and joined the forces of Manuel González. Perhaps others would do so if Díaz openly joined Iglesias. Gen. Jesús Alonso of the Second Division sat on the sidelines with 1,000 men on the day of battle, allowing González to gain entrance to the field and turn the tide. Alonso then pronounced for Iglesias *and* Díaz. How many others of the Second Division were discouraged at Tecoac, thinking that *Porfirismo* and *Iglesismo* were allied and that two weeks later they would be *Iglesistas*, cannot be known. It perhaps had something to do with the outcome of the battle. If so, Díaz had prepared the terrain at Acatlán.

Iglesias received Alcalde's copy of the Convention of Acatlán on 16 November and wrote a temporizing answer the following day. He instructed Alcalde to inform Díaz of those parts he accepted and those which should be renegotiated. Although Iglesias's concrete objections to individual articles of the Convention were entirely phrased in the guise of constitutional argumentation, they are uniformly concerned with power. He agreed that the interim government should accept the revolutionary debts of the *Tuxtepecanos*, although they had no basis in constitutional law, but when he was asked to turn over control of the army to Porfirio Díaz and to surrender a section of the country to the Porfirian party, the suggestions stuck in his throat—and he thrust forward constitutional objections.[13]

Iglesias's objections to Díaz's conditions for union ultimately caused the collapse of *Iglesismo*. That seems to argue that he preferred defeat to unprincipled compromise. Iglesias wrote for posterity that his "triumph would have been immediate" if he had accepted "certain

13. Only Cosío Villegas among historians has examined Iglesias's objections to the Convention of Acatlán. He finds them evidence of Iglesias's "genuine desire to come to an understanding with Díaz" and says that the answers to articles 5, 6, and 10 "could not have been more just and prudent." *El porfiriato*, pp. 60, 63. A different appraisal of Iglesias's criticisms of the Convention of Acatlán is proffered in appendix 14.

exigencies." He insisted, however, that his aspiration was not victory but rather the fulfillment of his duty, "although he was completely certain of an unfavorable result."[14] He wrote that passage in 1877, when the only cause he could still win was the salvaging of his reputation. In 1876, while insisting that his objections—particularly that he could not accept Díaz into the ministry—were to guarantee a free election, he accepted Antillón in Guanajuato, Ceballos in Jalisco, Arce in Sonora, and Alvarez in Guerrero, all *Lerdistas* who had recognized Iglesias and would be conducting those elections.

Possibly Iglesias imagined that his answer of 17 November would restrain Díaz for a while longer. Perhaps in the interim 1 December would come; Alatorre would march on the capital and invite Iglesias to assume his place in the national palace. Then he could deal with Díaz as the new conditions might warrant. Telegraphic communications between Puebla and Querétaro passed through Mexico City, which was controlled at that time by *Lerdistas.* Unfortunately for Iglesias, as he wrote his temporizing letter of 17 November he had not heard that on the preceding day Alatorre's Second Division had been destroyed at Tecoac.

The communications between Díaz and Iglesias demonstrate two things. First, the antagonists were not merely a general and a constitutional lawyer but two politicians establishing their bases of power. Iglesias's minister of treasury, Emilio Velasco, who joined his cabinet in order to unite the two movements, told Joaquín Ruiz to emphasize in his negotiations with General Díaz that the *Porfiristas* could not succeed alone and that the anti-Lerdo forces should unite behind Iglesias.[15]

Second, and more important for the immediate dynamics of their relationship, Díaz could claim that from 10 October to 7 November he and Iglesias were negotiating, and from 7 November until 23 November, when he claimed to have received Iglesias's rejection of the Convention of Acatlán, they were allies and partners. On the other hand, Iglesias could claim that they were negotiating only until 30 October, at which time Iglesias had refused further dealings; then they were negotiating on a different basis from 16 November, when he received Díaz's "proposals" made at Acatlán, to some such time as

14. Iglesias, *Cuestión presidencial,* p. 319.

15. Velasco to Ruíz, AFIC, 16 November 1876, cited by Cosío Villegas, *El porfiriato,* 1:64.

Díaz would indicate his willingness to accept the 17 November modifications or arrange with Iglesias an acceptable compromise. Moreover, due to the poor state of cummunications during November, assumptions were sometimes made upon incorrect information. Civil war was in the offing.

The Tagle *Circular* of 29 November and the Iglesias *Manifiesto* of 1 December were obviously political documents, designed to win public support in the approaching civil war by blaming the other party for the broken negotiations. Tagle for the *Porfiristas* argued that the Iglesias letter of 17 November, received by the *Porfiristas* when they occupied Mexico City on 23 November, only then gave them notice that Iglesias had not accepted the pact of Acatlán.[16] Treachery, Tagle claimed, had been discovered after the battle of Tecoac in a letter from the Iglesias government found in the baggage of Alatorre. That letter, dated 1 November, invited Alatorre to pronounce for the "government of legality" and, depending upon the reactions of the *Tuxtepecanos,* to treat them as rebels or allies. Tagle used the letter as evidence of Iglesias's simultaneously negotiating with both sides. The argument was fraudulent, for the *Porfiristas* believed as late as 7 November, as evidenced by the Convention of Acatlán, that Alatorre was *Iglesista.* On the other hand, from an *Iglesista* point of view, on 1 November no negotiations existed between *Iglesistas* and *Porfiristas,* and Alatorre was being instructed to accept the *Tuxtepecanos* as allies if they were in agreement.

The *Iglesistas* argued that the first act of bad faith occurred in Puebla after the battle of Tecoac. There on 18 November at the home of Gen. Jesús Alonso a group of ex-*Lerdista* federal and state officers met. Alonso was the general of the Second Divison posted by Alatorre to prevent the entrance of General González to the field of Tecoac. The group, presided over by José de Jesús López, either believed that an accord existed between Díaz and Iglesias or was attempting to force one.[17] They decided to recognize Iglesias as president and Díaz as chief of the "Constitutional Forces."[18] Díaz reacted by dividing

16. Without citing his source, Cosío Villegas claims that the *Porfiristas* read Iglesias's response somewhat earlier, because Justo Benítez purloined Alcalde's mail: *El porfiriato,* 1:69.

17. Iglesias only mentions the former: *Cuestión presidencial,* p. 203.

18. Signed by Alonso and 161 others and sent to Iglesias and Díaz, APD, 13:236–37.

Alonso's forces among his own various units, leaving him without a command. Iglesias claimed that Díaz at that time allowed the impression to stand that Díaz recognized the government in Guanajuato, but that he then isolated and discarded all *Iglesista* officers of Puebla, and those of the capital a few days later.[19]

Confusion and opportunism reigned in the political class. The development of the negotiations, the difficult communications, and the rapidly changing political-military combinations due to the battle of Tecoac on 16 November, Lerdo's flight on 20 November, and the Porfirian occupation of the capital on 23 November, resulted in a plethora of pronouncements and alliances which changed from area to area and day to day partly because of real confusion and partly because of opportunism. Ireneo Paz described the situation on the Matamoros-Brownsville frontier in the following manner:

> The greatest vacillations began to reign in the revolutionary party [*Porfiristas*], from which many deserted, believing that the most certain and natural party—the one most dedicated to constitutional order—was that of Iglesias. . . . During those days many who served the government [*Lerdistas*], seeing an opportunity . . . [to abandon Lerdo] became *Iglesistas*. And many *Porfiristas,* whose only interest was to be on the side which obtained the victory, also went with that party [the *Iglesistas*].[20]

The situation in Zacatecas was more complicated, but it indicated the same blend of confusion and opportunism. From Fresnillo, Zacatecas, Gen. Trinidad García de la Cadena wrote Díaz on 9 November that Iglesias's pronouncement offered new combinations. The general pledged his personal loyalty to Díaz and claimed that he did not know if an agreement between the forces of Tuxtepec and Salamanca had been concluded. Nevertheless, "whatever turn the events take" he foresaw an advantage for the *Porfiristas:*

> If Iglesias accepts the Plan of Tuxtepec . . . and guarantees free suffrage, the ultimate result will be in your favor. This means that

19. Iglesias, *Cuestión presidencial,* p. 204; Iturribarría does not accept the motive that Iglesias attributed to Díaz but implies that Díaz did not respect Alonso for having betrayed his trust by standing on the sidelines of the battlefield to join the victors: *Oaxaca,* 4:209–10.

20. Paz, *Algunas campañas,* 3:421–22.

we ought not to reject the contact with the new standard; and this is how I propose to work.[21]

Lerdo had declared a state of siege in Zacatecas on 13 September, and the *Lerdista* Gen. Angel Martínez had evicted antireelectionist Governor Agustín López de Nava from office. General García occupied the state capital on 2 October, abandoned it to Martínez a week later, and fought Martínez on 3 November at the battle of Herradura. On 21 November he pronounced for Iglesias. In the interim, López de Nava resumed the governorship of Zacatecas, proclaiming recognition of the Iglesias government on 22 November. García then reoccupied the capital city, evicting López de Nava once again.[22] The issue between López de Nava and García de la Cadena, at least from García's point of view, was the personal one of controlling the state in the period following the civil war. García had been a *caudillo* governor of Zacatecas after the French Intervention, had joined the Porfirian opposition party in Congress, and had led an armed rebellion against Juárez in the 1869–70 insurrection of San Luis-Zacatecas and again in the 1871–72 insurrection of La Noria. Accepting amnesty after each failure, García de la Cadena lost his position of power as well as his personal fortune. It appears that he meant to repair both adversities by his efforts in 1876. Joining Iglesias during the highwater of *Iglesismo,* he abandoned him as the tide ebbed. Having settled who was to govern Zacatecas, García on 16 December proclaimed that

> two people of high position, promising to realize the same political ideas, are separated in the means of establishing the constitutional order. . . . Considering the [*Iglesista*] cause lost, the State of Zacatecas . . . declares for the Plan of Tuxtepec reformed in Palo Blanco. . . .[23]

General García de la Cadena may have been consistently loyal to Díaz, as implied in his letter of 9 November, or he may have merely settled upon a plan to join the winners. On the other hand, he may have harbored the belief widely held in the country that the two anti-*Lerdista* movements were allied, or he could have been trying to

21. García de la Cadena to Díaz, 9 November 1876, APD 13:189–90.
22. Dublán and Lozano, *Legislación mexicana,* 25:461; Cosío Villegas, *República restaurada,* p. 885; Iglesias, *Cuestión presidencial,* pp. 151, 192–95, 243.
23. García de la Cadena to Díaz, 16 December 1876, APD, 15:59–60.

unite them. The point is that the situation in late 1876 lent itself to dual adhesions and switching of allegiances.[24]

If some men opportunistically supported both anti-Lerdo forces, others were honestly confused. The *Porfirista* Gen. Joaquín Martínez wrote to Manuel González in mid-November that "the news has circulated through these parts that General Porfirio Díaz accepts the political plan of Guanajuato. I am hoping it will please you to communicate with me on this particular in order to form operations [with *Iglesista* forces] . . . to cooperate in the fighting against *Lerdista* forces."[25] On the same day, the Porfirian commander of Oaxaca, Francisco Meijueiro, asked Díaz to confirm a telegraphic message which he had received stating that, ". . . General Díaz recognizes Iglesias who in turn recognizes the General." Indignant, the commander asked, "What is this mutual recognition between you and *señor* Iglesias? Not having the slightest indication of this matter from you, I beg of you please to communicate what you have done on this particular."[26] In Silao, Guanajuato, a *Porfirista* wrote to Díaz that "many friends of this city, as also in Guanajuato City, León, Irapuato and other places, are asking me to find out if indeed you are or are not in agreement with the Provisional Government."[27]

Another *Porfirista* in Guanajuato asked Díaz if he and his friends were directed to join Iglesias.[28] The municipal government of Cholula, state of Puebla, congratulated Díaz for his victory at Tecoac. The *Cholutecans* expected Díaz to bring about a happy ending "by establishing in the capital of the Republic the Government of Legitimacy which resides today in the heroic state of Guanajuato." On 23 November, the day General Díaz occupied Mexico City, the city of Tepic pronounced, "recognizing José María Iglesias as Interim President and you [Porfirio Díaz] as General in Chief of the Army."[29]

24. García remained at the head of the Zacatecas government until elevated to the Díaz cabinet as minister of treasury. Despoiled of that position, he ran for president in 1880 on a socialist ticket. Rebelling against the governor of Zactecas in 1886, he was caught and shot on 1 November 1886: Valadés, *Porfirismo, nacimiento,* pp. 43, 46, 223, 399.

25. Mariínez to González, 12 November 1876, APD, 13:201–2.

26. Meijueiro to Díaz, 12 November 1876, ibid., 204–5.

27. José O. Herrera to Díaz, 13 November 1876, ibid., p. 212.

28. Nicolás de la Peña to Díaz, 15 November 1876, ibid., pp. 224–26.

29. *Ayuntamiento de Cholula* to Díaz, 20 November 1876, ibid., p. 256; Domingo Nava to Díaz, 28 November 1876, ibid., 14:59.

Servando Canales and his followers, then campaigning in Nuevo León, confessed to Díaz that they were "ignorant here about what exists between you and *señor* Iglesias," who "writes me insisting that he is in charge of the Presidency of the Republic with your approval, and orders me to support him with my forces." Canales wanted to be informed "on this particular" in order "to normalize my operations." The case may be an isolated one in which Iglesias was claiming the alliance, but apparently he played upon a widespread rumor in order to obtain an advantage. Certainly he could not have believed that by the Convention of Acatlán he and Díaz were allies who merely had yet to work out the details. Of equal interest is the answer from Díaz: ". . . the Revolution has nothing in common with *Decembrismo* and as a consequence no understanding exists between *señor* Iglesias and me."[30]

To a similar question from Matehuala, San Luis Potosí, Díaz sketched these words upon the letter: ". . . in no way am I in accord, nor could I be, with *señor* Iglesias, inasmuch as the Plan of Tuxtepec and *Decembrismo* are so different and dissimilar."[31]

So the word went out. At the port city of Guaymas, General Vicente Mariscal, Porfirian governor and military commander of the state of Sonora, publicly condemned *Iglesismo* as ". . . an unheard of scandal . . . , contrary to public sentiment . . . , against the legitimate government of the nation, which will cause all good citizens to come to the defense of liberty." Mariscal had previously pronounced for Iglesias and Díaz.[32] In Maravatío, Michoacán, Joaquín Yáñez, whom Iglesias promoted to general, had recognized Iglesias as president and Díaz as general-in-chief. During the first week of December he learned of his error, denounced Iglesias, and sought orders from Díaz. Gen. Domingo Nava in Tepic discovered his error on 8 December and properly repronounced. Authorities in Morelia, capital of Michoacán, who had earlier recognized both Iglesias and Díaz, claimed to have learned that they were not of the same movement only by 10 December. General Condey, who had worked for Iglesias and Díaz at

30. Canales to Díaz, 24 November 1876, and undated answer, ibid., pp. 12–13.

31. Z. Martínez to Díaz, 24 November 1876, and undated answer, ibid., pp. 13–14.

32. Vicente Mariscal, Circular to the citizens of Sonora, 25 November 1876, ibid., pp. 26–27.

San Luis Potosí, was only informed of his error in time to write Díaz to that effect on 20 December.[33] One detects a good deal of opportunism in some of the denials, but confusion also reigned for a time.

Two things can be deduced from this correspondence. First, ironically, even as *Iglesistas* and *Porfiristas* were fighting in some places, representatives of those two anti-Lerdo forces were in other places cooperating. Second and more important, some *Iglesistas* and some *Porfiristas* recognized that the confusion was advantageous to them. If the struggle could be suspended between *Tuxtepecanos* and the "Government of Legitimacy," it sapped the strength and confidence of *Lerdismo*. Lerdo would seem to be facing an overwhelming combination, and the "bandwagon" effect of flight from the collapsing government at Mexico could be induced. After occupying the city of Mexico, Díaz clarified his relations with Iglesias to his most trusted lieutenants.[34]

After Díaz occupied the capital city, his relationship with Iglesias was essentially belligerent; they were at war. But as before, Díaz preferred to win political battles that would avoid military encounters. José Valadés's assertion that the Porfirian campaign against Iglesias from 28 November to 9 January was a "triumphal march" from Mexico City to Guadalajara[35] applied only to his military success. The war was fought politically, and an evaluation of why Díaz won must be made with politics in view. Díaz had already won three of the political battles—Tecoac, Lerdo's flight, and the occupation of the capital.

The battle of Tecoac was fought between *Lerdistas* and *Tuxtepecanos* in name only. The army facing Díaz at Tecoac was a Decembrist army,

33. V. Moreno to Díaz, 5 December 1876, ibid., 197; Domingo Nava to Díaz, 8 December 1876, ibid., pp. 236–37; Pedro Ogazón to Díaz, 20 December 1876, ibid., 15:67; Ambrosio P. Condey to Díaz, 20 December 1876, ibid., 15:84.

34. It was Díaz's habit at that time to place a brief note on each piece of correspondence as an indication to his secretary how the letter should be answered. It cannot be known that no note meant no answer, but two things are clear: the clarification note does appear on correspondence after Díaz occupied the capital; and continual requests from the same persons earlier in November indicate that they were not receiving answers.

35. Valadés, *Porfirismo, nacimiento,* p. 20.

loyal to Lerdo for two more weeks before recognizing Iglesias.[36] Because of Díaz's victory, *Porfirismo* became a stronger political attraction for fleeing *Lerdistas* and public support than *Iglesismo*.

Lerdo's flight on 20 November was the second Porfirian political victory over Iglesias: it opened the eyes of all those who previously had refused to see. A few individuals still refused and labored for another two years to reinstall Lerdo. Those people who had to make realistic decisions, that is, the politically conscious people who intended to remain viable, had to recognize the anti-Lerdo forces. While many *Lerdistas* preferred Iglesias because of the legal and civilian tone of *Iglesismo,* others considered that the most important factor was to be with the winners. This became for some a flight to Díaz, for others a flight to Iglesias and then to Díaz. Still other men in those days of late November and early December tried to ride two horses, Tuxtepec and Salamanca. They chose as individuals, and many of them chose more than once. Nevertheless, in the ebb and flow, the volume of movement was consistently toward Díaz.

The Porfirian occupation of the capital on 23 November was the third political victory over *Iglesismo*. Control of the capital had always bestowed a large measure of legitimacy upon its holder. It seemed to give Díaz the right to describe the nature of the relationship between his movement and that of Salamanca. He set out the terms of negotiation. When they were rejected, he seemed to enjoy the right to call Iglesias a rebel. Furthermore, the resources of the capital included military units. One Porfirian partisan wrote three days after Tecoac that the capital city garrison was composed of less than 800 raw recruits with no will to fight. He thought the garrison officers were *Iglesistas* and that Iglesias planned to send a force upon the city immediately, and he hoped Díaz would arrive first. An *Iglesista* in mid-November wrote to Iglesias on behalf of himself and friends that "the desire we have is that you occupy the capital first." Another partisan in the capital informed Iglesias on 20 November that the lower house of Congress would meet that morning to accept Lerdo's resignation and to name Iglesias interim president. He urged Iglesias to occupy the capital immediately and "in order to sustain your independence . . . you will need your own [military] force." A Porfirian partisan in

36. Knapp believes Alatorre sought the presidency for himself: *Lerdo,* p. 251.

the capital wrote Díaz on 16 November that, according to his information, the officers of the garrison had signed a pact to recognize Iglesias on 1 December, "and it is my judgment that when the time comes they will unite with the closest forces. I still believe it is a question of who arrives in Mexico first."[37]

That was also Iglesias's appraisal years later. "It can be said with certainty," he wrote, "that he who possessed Mexico would be the arbiter of the situation. . . . The delivery of Mexico [to Díaz] with its entire garrison was doubtlessly . . . the cause of the collapse of the Government of Legality."[38] Men who had been sympathetic to *Iglesismo* but who fully intended to join the winning party had then to reconsider their plans. Many still became *Iglesistas;* many others were neutralized, preferring to await an *Iglesista* victory before committing themselves. Some became outright *Porfiristas* at that time. On balance, the shifting was again in Díaz's favor.

That was the immediate effect. The garrison in Orizaba, Veracruz, recognized Díaz on 24 November:

> Because the recent political events have terminated the duties which as a soldier I had to sustain—the government of *señor* Sabastián Lerdo de Tejada in his legal period—I have convoked today in council the generals, chiefs and officials who are my subordinates, and making known to them the present political situation of the country . . . [we recognize] the Plan of Tuxtepec and the government which should emanate from it.[39]

So also was the effect in the important port city of Veracruz, where, upon learning that Díaz had occupied the capital, the garrison formally recognized the "Government of Tuxtepec."[40]

Even at that point *Iglesismo* was a viable force, and Díaz was caught between two influences. On the one hand were the intransigent *Tuxtepecanos* who were urging Díaz on to total victory. Their influence cannot be measured, and they left few documents. They were, how-

---

37. A. Alvarez to Díaz, 19 November 1876, APD, 13:245–48; Mendoza to Iglesias, 12 November 1876, ibid., pp. 206–8; Yáñez to Díaz, 20 November 1876, cited by Cosío Villegas, *El porfiriato,* 1:67; Julio Falcón to Díaz, 16 November 1876, APD, 13:227–28.

38. Iglesias, *Cuestión presidencial,* pp. 190–91.

39. Juan López to Díaz, 24 November 1876, APD, 14:14–15.

40. J. A. Ruíz, 25 November 1876, ibid., pp. 27–28.

ever, the men closest to Díaz. Certainly Tagle and Benítez were of this group; one detects it in the Tagle *Circular* and in the Benítez negotiations with Iglesias, considered below. Other second-rank *Tuxtepecanos* were also intractable. Miguel de la Peña had urged a hard-line, total victory as early as Palo Blanco. As recently as 13 November Julio Falcón had written Díaz from the capital that "I cannot conceive how we can come to an understanding with Iglesias, and I fear any arrangement; popular parties are always lost through diplomacy."[41] In the field a Porfirian general reported that "the Decembrists and reelectionists in these parts have wanted to join our ranks, but not even through the force of circumstances has it seemed to me convenient to receive them."[42] Perhaps Díaz was not as intransigent as his general, but his own sentiments must have tended in the same direction in late November of 1876.

On the other hand were those whose greatest desire was to avert further civil strife and to make any political accord that would bring peace to Mexico. Certainly most Mexicans were of this group. They were the moderates, the war-weary, and those who could accommodate themselves best in a compromise solution. Díaz could not afford to alienate that group entirely. The majority of such men would be attracted to *Iglesismo*. Conversely, *Iglesismo*—basically moderate and pacifist—appealed to men who were least inclined to fight for it.

How completely Díaz had control of the Tuxtepec movement is not certain, but he chose the hard line and utilized the conciliators to undermine Iglesias. Once in power he slowly adopted a policy of conciliation, ridding himself of men like Tagle and Benítez, accommodating old *Lerdistas* like Manuel Rubio Romero and old *Iglesistas* like Felipe Berriozábal. As he occupied the capital, however, he let the conciliatory Justice Ezequiel Montes believe that he would recognize Iglesias but that he had to work carefully in order not to break with the hard-line *Tuxtepecanos*. He encouraged Montes to communicate with Berriozábal and dissuade him from marching on Mexico City, for it would result in civil war and encourage the *Lerdistas*. Montes sent the warning to Berriozábal, who showed it to Iglesias. Berriozábal implored Montes to ". . . use your influence with Díaz . . ." to arrange peace between the two governments. Montes gave the letter to Díaz,

41. Falcón to Díaz, 13 November 1876, ibid., 13:208–9.
42. Rafael Cravioto to Díaz, 26 November 1876, ibid., 14:39.

with the recommendation that Díaz recognize Iglesias as provisional president.[43] Díaz thus knew of the desire of the leaders of *Iglesismo* to conciliate their differences with the *Tuxtepecanos*.

Once in the capital Díaz allowed conciliators to arrange a personal meeting with Iglesias. Then pleading overwork, Díaz cancelled the arrangement and substituted a telegraphic negotiation to take place on 27 November. Meanwhile, Díaz published the decree that all persons who had held government positions during the Lerdo administration were released from service. That intransigent position would have made the telegraphic negotiations with Iglesias exceedingly difficult; nevertheless, Iglesias accepted.[44] But again Díaz found himself too busy and sent Justo Benítez to the telegraph office in his stead. Benítez then made no reference to the pending negotiations of Acatlán and essentially gave Iglesias an ultimatum. The interchange speaks for itself:

> Benítez: My Dear Sir: By commission of General Díaz I am at your disposal to transmit immediately whatever it is your convenience to tell him.
>
> Iglesias: My Dear Sir: Please manifest to me what you have to say in the name of General Díaz about the explanation and modifications which I made to the convention of Acatlán.
>
> Benítez: *Señor* Iglesias: The indispensable condition for any arrangement must be the Plan of Tuxtepec reformed in Palo Blanco as a genuine expression of the national will. Do you accept?
>
> Iglesias: *Señor* Justo Benítez: I do not accept, I cannot, nor ought I to accept the base which you specify as indeclinable. I will reject everything which is apart from the Constitution of 1857, for I am the representative of legality.
>
> Benítez: *Señor* D. J. M. Iglesias: I regret the disagreement between you and the nation, which stands armed precisely to defend the Constitution of 1857, particularly after ten months of war and bloody battles. General Díaz cannot abandon the

43. Montes to Berriozábal, 24 November 1876, ibid., pp. 10–12; Berriozábal to Montes, 29 November 1876, ibid., pp 88–89; Montes to Díaz, 2 December 1876, ibid., pp. 150–51.

44. Iglesias, *Cuestión presidencial,* pp. 207, 387; Decree no. 7503, 25 November 1876, reprinted in APD, 14:16; Francisco Gómez del Palacio and Joaquín M. Alcalde to Díaz, 26 November 1876, ibid., p. 38.

banner he has raised without jeopardizing the sacrifices which the fall of the falsifiers of the suffrage has cost.[45]

Díaz was the aggressor, but Iglesias may have had his own reasons to terminate the conference: *Decembrismo* was only four days away. Furthermore, intransigence was part of the Mexican tradition. Juárez had stood firm in Veracruz during the Three Years' War against Félix Zuloaga and Miguel Miramón, and again in the north against the interventionists. Iglesias may have considered himself a new Juárez against an insurrectionist party. Soon he would have an army but Díaz immediately took the next intransigent step by assuming executive power on 28 November.[46]

Both men withdrew to muster their forces to decide by armed conflict. Each sought to blame the other for the failure of the negotiations by publication of the *Circular* on the part of the *Tuxtepecanos,* and the *Manifiesto* on the part of the "Government of Legality."

On the next day Díaz seized another political advantage by naming Gen. Juan N. Méndez as provisional president, ostensibly to dedicate himself to the "pacification of the country." He declared Iglesias a rebel against the government of Mexico. The belief that Díaz would win the elections held by an *Iglesista* provisional government had been widespread. The conciliators had held out that argument to Díaz as one of the advantages, besides constitutional legality, that he could reap by recognizing Iglesias as provisional president. Many Mexicans must have then thought it useless to fight to make Iglesias provisional president, knowing that Díaz would become constitutional president following either Méndez or Iglesias. That attitude helped Díaz and hurt Iglesias.

As Díaz marched toward Guanajuato the dramatic days of *Decembrismo* commenced: multiple pronouncements for Iglesias threatened to reunite much of *Lerdismo* and *Iglesismo,* but under Iglesias.

Iglesias apparently wanted to lead a crusade against reelectionism and militarism. His natural allies, however, were reelectionists and, of necessity, militarists. Díaz played upon those contradictions to the disadvantage of Iglesias. He sent out letters to his supporters in *Iglesista* territory, urging them to propagandize for the Plan of Tux-

45. Tagle, *Circular,* pp. 26–27.
46. Decree no. 7504, 28 November 1876, reprinted in APD, 14:56–57.

tepec, to negotiate with *Iglesista* officers to defect, and to launch new *pronunciamientos* around which latent support could rally. Pedro Delgado, *Porfirista* since the beginning of the year, was asked to utlilize the press of Guadalajara in favor of the *Tuxtepecanos*. Cirilio Ramírez and Sabino de la Vega were working for public opinion in the cause of *Porfirismo* in Querétaro and relaying military information to Díaz. Díaz's agent in Zacatecas was Juan de D. Villalón, sent there to coordinate with Gen. Trinidad García de la Cadena. Protasio Tagle recommended one Fermín Ramos as a Porfirian agent in Salamanca and Guanajuato City. Another agent was sent to deal with General Ceballos.[47]

The Porfirian government prepared propaganda in large quantities for distribution in enemy territory, among *Tuxtepecano* armies, and in the areas left in their rear. In mid-December Díaz asked the Méndez government to send more copies of the Tagle *Circular*.[48] The Porfirian government sent a printed letter to a wide range of selected individuals, explaining why and how they could help to restore peace in the nation.[49] A thousand copies of a Mexico City newspaper article, thought by *Tuxtepecanos* to be favorable to their cause, were sent to Díaz for his use.[50] To a group of citizens in Querétaro representing "commerce, industry, the propertied class and the laboring class" who wished to meet with Díaz in the cause of peace, he answered that he would be pleased to speak with them "about the interesting proposal for which you have been commissioned."[51]

In another way Díaz took advantage of the politics of *Iglesismo*. As the established politicians joined Iglesias, their local rivals became

47. Díaz to Pedro Delgado, 26 November 1876, ibid., p. 249; Delgado compiled and reported favorable results: Delgado to Díaz, 10 December 1876, ibid., p. 249; Cirilo Ramírez to Díaz, 30 November 1876, ibid., p. 111; Juan de D. Villalón to Diaz, 3 December 1876, ibid., p. 60; Protasio Tagle to Díaz, 14 December 1876, ibid., p. 299; Jesús Altamirano to Díaz, 16 December 1876, ibid., 15:11.

48. Díaz to Pedro Ogazón, 13 December 1876, ibid., 14:290.

49. Circular, early December 1876, ibid., pp. 116–17; Juan Ortiz Careaga in Guadalajara may have been the recipient of one of them; his reaction was favorable to the *Tuxtepecanos:* Ortiz Careaga to Díaz, 10 December 1876, ibid., pp. 249–51.

50. Vicente Riva Palacios to Díaz, 13 December 1876, ibid., p. 298.

51. Anon. to Díaz, 19 December 1876, and answer, ibid., 15:54.

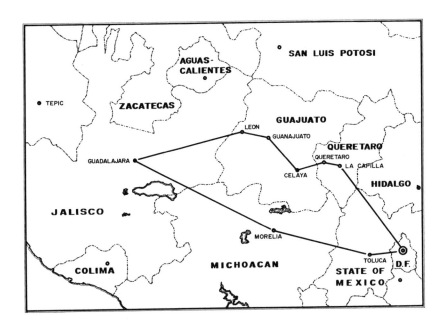

MAP N° 8   THE ROUTE OF PORFIRIO
DIAZ in the *iglesista* campaign.
(◎ MEXICO CITY)

attracted to *Porfirismo*. The politically conscious merchants, teachers, and small businessmen, whether they sympathized with Iglesias because they believed him sincere or with Díaz because he offered them change, were not likely to be activists. With the fall of Lerdo, governors and legislators joined Iglesias. A *Tuxtepecano* in Mexico City wrote to Díaz after the battle of Tecoac that ". . . a great number of congressmen and senators who voted for the extraordinary faculties and the reelection are planning to name a commission of five persons to go to Guanajuato to offer the destinies of the country in the name of both chambers to Iglesias."[52] Well they might: Díaz had promised to sweep out the city halls, the courthouses, the statehouses, and the legislative chambers. The proclamation of 25 November appealed to local rivals of such men.

Juan Ortiz Careaga in Guadalajara believed that the governors "who have arranged their own elections once, twice or more, who falsify the suffrage and who have at hand the means to do so, will not cooperate with a reform against their interests and their ambitions." He guessed that even if Iglesias wanted to join Díaz, "the legislators would not let him, because they are the tools of the governors and the introduction of reforms is not convenient to them."[53]

José O. Herrera, a *Porfirista* in Silao, Guanajuato, expressed his jacobin fear of governors and distrust of centralism: "Our work will be abortive if this centralization of power is not stopped whereby the governors name the authorities in the villages." He suggested that Díaz issue a decree for annual elections of village officials.[54]

For men who thought like Ortiz Careaga and Herrera, *Iglesismo* offered nothing, whereas article seven of the Plan of Tuxtepec assured a constitutional amendment guaranteeing the independence of the municipalities. The spirit of decentralization and freedom from the governors was more apparent in *Porfirismo* than in *Iglesismo*.

The district of Tepic had recently been under the domination of José Ceballos. Díaz offered an alternative to those who felt that they had suffered sufficiently from Ceballos. A prominent *Porfirista* there wrote to Díaz:

52. A. Alvarez to Díaz, 19 November 1876, ibid., 13:245–48.
53. Ortiz Careaga to Díaz, 25 November 1876, ibid., 14:18.
54. Herrera to Díaz, 13 November 1876, ibid., 13:212–14.

You know it is not convenient for us to put ourselves under Ceballos, because he had been one of the principal *Lerdistas,* besides, he was highly indignant that we had thrown off his yoke earlier, so that he would cause us as many evils as possible. . . . I send this, looking for your protection for these towns from the malevolent influence of Ceballos. . . . Send me your orders.[55]

Gen. Florencio Antillón, in turn a *Juarista* and a *Lerdista* since the French Intervention, held dominion over the state of Guanajuato that his enemies considered total. Indicative of both hatred for Antillón and hope that Díaz represented a new order is the following passage from a letter of a citizen of León, Guanajuato:

Antillón, Rosado and another mulitude of tyrants, . . . who form the same *Lerdista* clique, are so cynical and unashamed that by the force of their chicanery they are on top of the situation again, even though they crudely oppress the people with scandalous executions, the levy, forced loans, persecutions and unheard-of extortions.

The letter writer also seemed piqued that "they have recently received honors and military promotions which the generosity of *señor* Iglesias has given them without merit of any nature."[56] Civic indignation, party factionalism, and personal ambition combined to make that person in León a *Porfirista* in 1876.

The representative of the "Liberal Circle" of Guanajuato City wrote to Díaz that the "program of *señor* Iglesias does not concern more than the [prohibition of] reelection of the President of the Republic and omits, seemingly by intent, the no-reelection of the Governors." That was an omission which "for those of us who live in the states is of vital importance . . . since we see that the Antillón dynasty . . . now counts twelve years in power. . . ." The "Liberal Circle of Guanajuato" was fighting Antillón and recognized the Plan of Tuxtepec.[57]

55. Domingo Nava to Díaz, 8 December 1876, ibid., 14:236–37. That Domingo Nava became a much feared *cacique* in Tepic does not alter the argument that local groups saw in Díaz in 1876 an ally against overbearing state political machines. In December 1879 Domingo Nava fell victim to the *ley fuga*—he was shot "while trying to escape" from Díaz's rural police: Valadés, *Porfirismo, nacimiento,* p. 130.

56. Manuel Pacheco to Díaz, 28 November 1876, APD, 14:63–65.

57. Nicolás de la Peña to Díaz, 15 November 1876, ibid., 13:224–26.

In Guerrero the old *Lerdista* party machine was controlled by Gov. Diego Alvarez, who recognized Iglesias. A *Porfirista* commander there reported that "although don Diego [Alvarez] and the state legislature pronounced for the so-called government of *señor* Iglesias on the 28th, the villagers have enthusiastically adopted the Plan of Tuxtepec."[58]

Francisco Arce, as governor and leader of the incumbents in Sinaloa, recognized Iglesias after the fall of Lerdo. A local *Porfirista* officer wrote to Díaz in mid-December that "they recognize Iglesias, but the state of siege, the extraordinary faculties, the suspension of guarantees continue . . . in order that no newspapers are published which would inform the state that these men propose nothing other than saving their positions and operating for their own accounts." The correspondent believed that Arce recognized Iglesias because he "feeds on the hope that someone needs him in order that he can prolong his hold on this state. . . ."[59]

The importance of local and partisan discontent with the prospect of continued *Lerdismo* by way of *Iglesismo* is not possible to assess definitively. It doubtless aided Díaz to some degree. The belief was widespread that Díaz represented change and that *Iglesismo,* legal or not, meant a continuation in office of those who had made office a career. The decree of 25 November, barring *Lerdistas* from office, was for many Mexicans worth fighting for. *Iglesismo* attracted the governors and forced many local rival groups toward *Porfirismo.*

In another way Díaz's politics aided his military campaign. Even as he was marching into *Iglesista* country, the conciliators were trying to unite the two movements and end the war.[60] Díaz recognized the political importance of appearing conciliatory—such was the nature of the Tagle *Circular* which even then he was distributing. Moreover, given the nature of *Iglesismo*—legalist and moderate—pending negotiations would have the effect of neutralizing *Iglesista* activities. When Joaquín Ruiz, president of the "Liberal Circle of Puebla," a

58. Vicente Jiménez to Díaz, 3 December 1876, ibid., 14:173–74.

59. J. M. Ferreira to Díaz, 15 December 1876, ibid., pp. 332–33.

60. Letters from San Luis Potosí and Puebla appeal to Díaz and Iglesias to settle their differences: M. Rivera to Díaz, 6 December 1876, ibid., pp. 211–13; Jesús Sáenz to Díaz, 8 December 1876, ibid., pp. 232–34. Sáenz blames the intransigent position on Justo Benítez, whom he begs Díaz to remove.

group working for conciliation, telegraphed both leaders on 14 December that he would mediate between them, Díaz replied that he was no longer his own agent, being only a general under orders from the Méndez government to conduct the campaign into Guanajuato.[61] Nevertheless, wishing to do everything possible for the cause of peace, he said, he would transmit Ruiz's offer to Iglesias, who could arrange with Ruiz a place for an interview, "without forgetting that I am in march," he added.[62] Díaz could negotiate and advance at the same time.

The telegraph lines between Celaya, temporary seat of the nomadic *Iglesista* government, and Puebla passed through Díaz's camp as well as through Mexico City. Díaz sent the Ruiz proposal to Iglesias, who answered affirmatively on the same day and set the meeting for Sunday, 17 December, in San Juan del Río, state of Querétaro. Receiving no answer from Ruiz, Iglesias sent another, more urgent message on 17 December, again through Díaz and again without answer from Ruiz. Iglesias cited in his book a pamphlet written by Ruiz in 1877 in which Ruiz said he never received those telegrams. Iglesias claimed to believe that Díaz transmitted the telegrams but that the intransigent *Tuxtepecanos* in Mexico City intercepted them.[63] Be that as it may, Iglesias waited and Díaz advanced.

Benigno Arriaga, who had been representing the *Tuxtepecano* movement in San Luis Potosí, opened a new path to negotiation. Arriaga vistied Díaz's camp in San Juan del Río and arranged a meeting between the two leaders for 21 December at the *Hacienda de La Capilla* near Querétaro.[64] During the intervening three days Díaz struck into *Iglesista* territory and occupied the city of Querétaro.

Iglesias and Díaz met on schedule, with Iglesias doing all the travel-

61. Joaquín Ruiz to Díaz and Iglesias, 14 December 1876, ibid., p. 304; Iglesias, *Cuestión presidencial*, p. 396.

62. Díaz to Méndez, 14 December 1876, APD, 14:304.

63. Iglesias to Díaz, 14 December 1876, ibid., p. 304; Díaz to Iglesias, 15 December 1876, ibid., p. 305; Iglesias to Ruíz, 17 December 1876, ibid., 15:18; Iglesias to Díaz and Díaz to Iglesias, 17 December 1876, ibid., p. 29; Iglesias, *Cuestión presidentcial*, pp. 253–55, 397–99.

64. Arriaga to Iglesias, 18 December 1876, APD, 15:45; Iglesias to Arriaga, 19 December 1876, ibid., 57; Arriaga to Iglesias, 20 December 1876, ibid., p. 63; Iglesias to Díaz and Díaz to Iglesias, 20 December 1876, ibid., p. 63; Iglesias, *Cuestión presidencial*, pp. 399–400.

ing and making all the concessions in decorum. Iglesias made the only record of the meeting.[65] According to him, he fully explained to Díaz his constitutional view and how it followed that he was the representative of legality, all of which moved Nemesio García Naranjo later to write, "What ironies has our history! One revolutionary giving lessons in constitutional law to another revolutionary!"[66]

Iglesias's version of the interview at *La Capilla* began with the points upon which he and Díaz agreed. They concurred, he said, upon no-reelection (presidential and gubernatorial?), freedom of suffrage, and the punishment of those found guilty of "assaults upon the institutions" occasioned by the election of 1876. Taking the Tagle *Circular* instead of the Convention of Acatlán as his point of departure, Iglesias noted that they had only two points of discord. The first was the manner of restoring the Congress, whether by entirely new elections, as Díaz sought, or by recognizing a rump congress composed of those who had not supported the reelection, as Iglesias had recommended in his *Manifiesto*. The second point concerned when the interim government would call elections. The *Porfiristas*, who had specified one month in the Plan of Tuxtepec, had accused Iglesias in the Tagle *Circular* of wishing to establish an unlimited dictatorship. Iglesias at *La Capilla* was willing to cede on that point. He only insisted, he said, upon the recognition of his legality.[67]

According to Iglesias, Díaz answered simply that those points were no longer important. The constitutional path that he had first wanted to take had failed, and he had decided to accept the revolutionary route. His principal object in conceding the interview of that day, in Iglesias's words, ". . . was as a friend to proffer [to Iglesias] a way to escape from a desperate situation. . . ."[68] The conference was over. Díaz did not add that further motives for accepting the conference were to conciliate the conciliators and to neutralize the *Iglesistas* for

65. José María Iglesias, "*Manifiesto del presidente interino constitucional de la república sobre las nuevas negociaciones seguidas con el señor don Porfirio Díaz y los últimos acontecimientos*," 2 January 1877, in Iglesias, *Cuestión presidencial*, pp. 395–408, and discussed pp. 251–56.

66. García Naranjo, *Porfirio Díaz*, p. 198.

67. Iglesias, *Cuestión presidencial*, pp. 402–3.

68. Ibid.

another week while the Porfirian army moved deeper into *Iglesista* territory.

Even as Díaz's political acts aided his military campaign, so his campaign aided his politics. Having secured the eastern and northeastern regions, and having occupied the capital city, Díaz ordered the resources of those areas into the *Iglesista* territories of the west. He claimed to have 16,000 troops involved in the campaign and was receiving 10,000 pesos per day for its pay and maintenance.[69] On 16 December Iglesias abandoned Querétaro, where his government had been located since 20 November. His cavalry retreated to Celaya, and 1,000 men under the command of General Olvera moved into the mountains.[70] Díaz occupied the city without firing a shot. While a score of his military units moved forward with minor encounters reported daily, Díaz advanced to Celaya and on to Guadalajara. Simultaneously, *Porfirista* forces occupied and pacified the states of Michoacán, Morelos, and Guerrero.[71]

Defection was another aspect of the *Iglesista* debacle. A fatal flaw of *Iglesismo* was the promise to trim the military establishment. Some *Lerdista* officers pledged to Iglesias would surely be purged following an *Iglesista* victory. Many of them would be purged by Díaz if they fought for Iglesias and Díaz won. But they would be incorporated into the *Tuxtepecano* army if they joined Díaz. They simply had no long-term interest in *Iglesismo.* Moreover, the *Iglesista* forces were suffering a deprivation of pay and provisions. These factors, in addition to the low morale in the *Iglesista* forces for a cause that promised to secure the positions of the old *Lerdistas,* the hope for a final accord between Iglesias and Díaz, the Porfirian agents working on individual *Iglesista* officers, and the approach of an army of 16,000 well-supplied men, all combined to induce a first defection.[72]

69. Díaz to García de al Cadena, undated answer to telegram of 16 December 1876, APD, 15:60; Justo Benítez to Díaz and answer, 16 December 1876, ibid., p. 17.

70. Miguel Equiluz to Díaz, 17 December 1876, ibid., p. 22.

71. Numerous communications indicate the movements and supply of those Porfirian forces in December: ibid., 14 and 15.

72. Where and when the first defection occurred is uncertain. Iglesias reported that Diego Guerra was the first on 14 December, followed by Generals García de la Cadena, Condey, and Olvera: *Cuestión presidential,* pp. 240–45;

Defection started. On 1 December the officers of the garrison at Quiroga, Michoacán, decamped to Díaz with their forces. Between 5 and 10 December Col. Joaquín Yáñez in Maravatío, Gen. Domingo Nava in Tepic, and the authorities of Morelia, Michoacán, abandoned Iglesias. Col. Diego Guerra proffered his allegiance to the *Tuxtepecanos* on 14 December in San Juan del Río, Querétaro, with 500 dragoons.[73] Accepted with grace into the *Tuxtepecano* army and immediately supplied, they served as models for the next defection.

The next defections were the militia of Michoacán and General García de la Cadena with the forces of the state of Zacatecas. On 20 December Rafael Olvera of the Sierra of Querétaro with 400 men, and Gen. Ambrosio Condey in San Luis Potosí with the entire garrison of 3,000 men pronounced for the Plan of Tuxtepec. On the same day or the next, the garrison at San Miguel de Allende, state of Querétaro, forsook *Iglesismo* with 1,000 men and joined Díaz.[74]

The isolated incident became a trickle, then a general tendency, and finally a torrent. The *Tuxtepecanos* publicized each defection, thereby encouraging another. Iglesias's minister of war, in a telegram to his cabinet colleague Gómez del Palacio at month's end, affirmed that in only fifteen days *Iglesismo* had lost 9,000 soldiers and the control of Aguascalientes, Coahuila, Nuevo León, Querétaro, San Luis Potosí, and Zacatecas.[75] During those same days the preparations for the conference at *La Capilla* were made; successful Porfirian political warfare ultimately made military encounters unnecessary. The

---

this seems to be the source of Cosío Villegas (*Repúblic restaurada*, p. 922) and Iturribarría (*Oaxaca*, 4:215), who also mention only those four.

73. Díaz to Pedro Ogazón, 16 December 1876, APD, 15:10; V. Moreno to Díaz, 5 December 1876, ibid., p. 197; Nava to Díaz, 8 December 1876, ibid., 14:236–37; Ogazón to Díaz 20 December 1876, ibid., 15:67; Guerra to Díaz, and Díaz to Guerra, 14 December 1876, ibid., 14:299.

74. Juan N. Méndez to Díaz, 18 December 1876, ibid., 15:50; García de la Cadena to Díaz, and answer (". . . and I salute you because I hope you will be followed by other chiefs who have recognized Iglesias. . . ."), 16 December 1876, ibid., pp. 59–60; Rafael Olvera to Díaz, 30 December 1876, CPD, 1:195; Fidencio Hernández to the governors of Oaxaca, Puebla, and Veracruz, 20 December 1876, APD, 15:72; Díaz to Méndez, 20 December 1876, APD, 15:72–73; Adolfo I. Alegría to Alfonso Labat, 21 December 1876, APD, 15:95.

75. Cosío Villegas, *República restaurada*, p. 924.

negotiations, the military advances, and the defections interlocked and escalated together toward a total *Porfirista* victory.

Díaz never saw fit to publish his version of the conference at *La Capilla;* it sufficed that he won the campaign and the country. Díaz wired Joaquín Ruiz, who was in Mexico City awaiting instructions for his immediate departure to the conference, that "yesterday I spoke with *señor* Iglesias without result because events had arrived at such a point that agreement was no longer possible. . . ." To General José Couttolenc he wrote, "As for Iglesias, he resolved to retire to private life and desist in his pretentions." A Porfirian officer wired a friend in Mexico, "Iglesias was broken in the conference."[76]

It was not the literal truth that Iglesias had "resolved to retire to private life and to desist in his pretentions." He returned to Celaya and continued to command his army, to raise money, and to retreat. There were two small battles, two more manifestos to the nation, more appointments to his cabinet, more scattered adhesions to his cause, but many more defections and retreats. The cause was lost: Iglesias had never siezed that single symbolic victory around which his potential allies could rally. Díaz had seized the initiative at Tecoac and had kept it. Iglesias retreated into foreign exile and obscurity.[77]

Iglesismo was potentially strong, composed of military officers, some of whom commanded armies, and politicians who controlled the resources of their offices. It also attracted many anti-*Lerdistas,* including idealists who deplored the insurrectionism of *Porfirismo.* Nevertheless, it failed.

Before the fall of Lerdo, *Porfirismo* and *Iglesismo* had two things in common, their anti-*Lerdismo* and their exclusive desire for power. The former tended to bring them together, and the latter made their union impossible.

Many sympathizers and followers of the two anti-*Lerdista*

76. Ruíz to Díaz, and answer, 22 December 1876, APD, 15:113; Díaz to Couttolenc, 25 December 1876, ibid., p. 78; Adolfo I. Alegría to Alfonso Labat, 21 December 1876, ibid., p. 95.

77. Through 109 pages of his book, Iglesias described the events of his last efforts to sustain his government and, failing that, his dignity: *Cuestión presidencial,* pp. 256–364.

movements desired to unite, first to overthrow Lerdo and then to avoid a continuation of the civil war. After the fall of Lerdo most Mexicans wanted the union, and many of them claimed to see no difference between the two antireelectionist movements. Furthermore, the two leaders had something to gain by the union. Díaz might have conciliated his own constitutionalists and attracted others, and the *Iglesistas* might have limited the extent of the purge of the personnel of government that the *Porfiristas* promised.

Dividing the movements were the leaders' exclusive desire for power. Even as Díaz invited Iglesias to join the insurrection by the Reform of Palo Blanco, probably to satisfy the constitutionalists, he placed significant limitations upon the interim presidency. Later, by his letter of 16 October, Díaz insisted that Iglesias could join only after subordinating himself to the leaders and the program of Tuxtepec.

Iglesias was equally exclusivist. His offer to Díaz in September demanded the complete subordination of *Porfirismo* to his own movement. Díaz, apparently wanting the union on the eve of the battle of Tecoac, offered to recognize Iglesias as interim president in the Convention of Acatlán. Iglesias thought Alatorre would destroy the *Porfirista* army and join Iglesias. Thus Iglesias was intransigent at that time and categorically refused the principal items of the Convention of Acatlán. After Tecoac and the occupation of Mexico City, the *Porfiristas* did not need Iglesias and dealt harshly with Iglesias in the telegraphic exchange. Nevertheless, it is not unreasonable to believe that Iglesias's staunch refusal on 27 November was equally calculated: he expected his stock to rise appreciably on 1 December.

For a time in November there was considerable confusion about whether the two anti-*Lerdista* movements were united, and the leadership of both movements found that confusion useful. Until the fall of Lerdo the possible union of the antireelectionist movements doubtless weakened the government. Once having occupied the capital, Díaz did not need Iglesias and let it be known that the two antireelectionist movements were not allied. After learning of the defeat of Alatorre, Iglesias had reason to let it stand that the two movements were allied and took the position, after rejecting the essence of the Convention of Acatlán, that negotiations were still in progress.

Díaz led a large army into his adversary's territory. The campaign turned out to be "a triumphal march," but Díaz's total effort and tremendous expenditure demonstrated that he had respected the strength of his enemy.

Several factors combined to assure a total Porfirian victory. Although Decemberism was a potential *Iglesista* boon, it occurred too late: Díaz occupied the capital city and organized a de facto government before 1 December. And although Iglesias attracted large parts of the military, the professional soldiers had no long-run security interests in *Iglesismo:* they could avoid a purge only by adopting the *Tuxtepecano* cause and making it win. That was the basis of the military defection. Furthermore, although the established governors were overwhelmingly *Iglesistas,* the *Tuxtepecano* politicians skillfully mobilized local discontent and local rivalries against those *Iglesista* governors. Also, the *Tuxtepecanos* adroitly used negotiations after the battle of Tecoac as mere tacitcs to neutralize the moderates and conciliators in both camps. That Díaz was not truly negotiating is demonstrated by his progressively tougher stand in each negotiation.

While Díaz was advancing into *Iglesista* country, the *Tuxtepecano* armies of the northeast and southeast were occupying the state capitals everywhere. The skill with which Díaz and a few determined *Porfiristas* managed the political and military operations turned the campaign against *Iglesismo* into a "triumphal march."

The *Porfiristas* gained power, which they then had only to consolidate. Much of the consolidation was partially assured as militant *Tuxtepecanos* occupied the governorships. An all-embracing political alliance was in the making. As Juárez had built before and after 1867, so Díaz built in 1876 and thereafter a national political machine for the monopolization of power.

Chapter 13
Conclusions and Epilogue

The monopoly of government for class interest has dominated Mexican history, and ideological justification has supported privileged power to provide political stability and continuity. The Hapsburg system of government was laid out in the sixteenth century, even as the various regions of Spain were being brought under monarchical and centralized control. Spaniards of the sixteenth century who effected the conquest of Mexico were not primarily officers of the crown but adventurers who sought the aristocratic status of feudal lords. The king's interest lay in replacing such independent figures with royal servants, whose motive for accepting appointments in the New World was membership in a privileged governing class that did not share its power with the governed and the opportunity to return to Spain with wealth. The justification for such monopolized governance lay in the king's right to appoint his representatives to govern lands which he personally owned, the supposed superiority of persons born in Spain, their higher loyalty to the crown, and the spreading of a superior culture. As a class the Spanish administrators in the New World were men who were accustomed to privilege, wealth, and power or who aspired to become accustomed to them.

The attractiveness of imperial salaries was not what induced individual Spaniards to seek appointments in the Americas; no imperial taxation system anywhere in western civilization could pay the cost of an extended system of crown administrators. Men accepted public office or bought public office for self-aggrandizement; almost universally they sacked their offices of all they could or all they dared. That Hapsburg tradition of a privileged governing class extending loyalty to an executive figure and to a system in exchange for the opportunity to seek private advantage became deeply implanted in Mexico. Never uprooted, it has influenced every government to this day.

The same factors prevailed during the Bourbon period of Mexican history, but a new justification for monopolizing governmental power within a privileged elite was added. The declared intention of government was to promote rational policies for imperial economic growth and prosperity. Benefits were to flow to wider sectors of the population. The servants of the crown were to be more highly trained for efficient and uniform administration, lessening the role of aristocracy and clergy in government. These new enlightened precepts augmented divine right to justify the privileges of the governing elite. This governmental tradition also became firmly rooted in Mexico, and the promotion of prosperity still justifies the monopoly of power within the circle of privileged elites.

The wars of independence introduced yet another governmental tradition. Republicanism flowed to New Spain by way of freemasonry, British commerce, French and Anglo-American example, and even by way of Spain. Republicanism became associated with the forces that rebelled against the ruling Spanish class after 1810, but by 1815 the republican armed forces were defeated. New Spain might have established the kind of governmental alliance of monarchy, aristocracy, and church that developed in Europe after the fall of Napoleon. The Spanish Empire, however, underwent a liberal revolution in 1820, and a liberal Congress adopted laws that upset the interests of established elite groups. Conservative groups in New Spain stood aghast that a decade of fighting in the name of monarchy and empire should result in anticlerical liberalism. Thus the conservative privileged groups, particularly the church and the new military class, joined the forces for independence and carried New Spain out of the Spanish Empire. After the short-lived Mexican empire of Agustín de Iturbide, republicanism was adopted by default. Thereafter, the conservative classes learned to maintain their privileges by controlling the republican institutions. Elite republicanism, a third governmental tradition to develop in Mexico, allowed privileged groups to monopolize power and rule for themselves in the name of the nation. This tradition also is presently very much alive in Mexico.

Even as the wars for independence popularized republicanism and returned the clergy to politics, it introduced militant *caudillismo* to politics and allowed political roles to *hacendados* who had previously enjoyed only social and economic power. The new power elite in the early republic was therefore composed of church, military, *caudillos*, and *hacendados,* influenced to a degree by the foreign commercial class that entered Mexico to replace the privileged and monopolistic

Spanish merchants. That combination might have successfully established stable government but for a number of factors. First, the economy could satisfy neither high consumption patterns for the elite groups nor basic necessities for the masses. Fiscal policy could not meet the demands of government. Traditional centralism, supported by the church, was not in the interest of the regionally oriented *hacendados* and *caudillos*. And the military devoured the lion's share of revenues. Militarism in politics, introduced by the wars, resulted in endemic *pronunciamientos,* coups d'états, and civil wars. Caste wars and foreign wars were both effects and further causes of governmental instability.

The injection of liberalism into Mexican society was not a stabilizing influence. Nineteenth-century liberalism was not only a political philosophy of republicanism but a package including democratic social values, economic free enterprise, a legal bundle of civil rights to protect individualism, and a group consciousness of nationalism. Major groups within Mexican society, however, did not support the liberal institutions. Aristocratic *hacendados* did not support the democratic social values, the church condemned popular sovereignty and opposed the local power implied in federalism, the military resisted civilian control, and the *caudillos* overrode the republican process with regional dictatorships. Nor did foreigners from the liberal nations support liberal institutions in Mexico, being more interested in law-and-order regimes and profits. All of the elite groups sought to protect their interests by manipulating the republican political institutions. Those dominant groups violated the civil rights of opponents and used nationalistic rhetoric as well as the liberals used it to support or oppose any given government. Free enterprise economics was no match for the onerous conditions of economic stagnation. The dominant elite groups were able to pursue their own vested interests, condoned by liberalism, through the exploitation of the lower classes.

Three elements of liberalism were desperately needed—democratic social values, guaranteed civil rights, and popular participation in strong local government. But no Mexican traditions supported them. The surest way to thwart the development of such traditions was to allow political and economic power to combine and concentrate, and nothing exists in liberalism to prevent that development. Mexico needed institutional protection and encouragement of individual and collective attempts to keep and use the fruits of labor. It needed guarantees against brute-force monopolization of opportunity. It needed a distribution of the means of independent production and enforced limits on concentrations of wealth. It needed an absolute separation between public office and private enterprise. Liberalism did not contain these solutions.

Besides the inadequacies of the liberal model to solve the problems, the working alliance supporting liberalism guaranteed a course of action by which the problems were avoided. Liberals were correct that the conservatives offered no solution. The conservatives looked to the Bourbon tradition of governmental promotion and centralism. Lacking a monarch, conservatives supported strong executives who tried to undermine regionalism. That drove aristocratic *hacendados* and dictatorial *caudillos* into a working alliance with liberals, all of whom had interests in preserving local and regional autonomy. Thus the constructive parts of the liberal promise were ignored in a struggle with the conservatives. Mexican liberalism largely became anticlericalism, to the point that the church and its conservative military support were blamed for every malady that Mexico suffered. Liberal historians have subsequently repeated the charges, as though the liberals held the correct solution to Mexico's ills in the first decades of independence.

The liberals seized power with the Reform in the mid-nineteenth century. Liberalism, however, was not enthroned. The insurrection of Ayutla of 1854–55 was not precisely a liberal victory but rather the defeat of Santa Anna by an alliance of his enemies. The Three Years' War of 1858–60 between the liberals and the conservatives was not decisive, as demonstrated by the conservatives' ability to acquire foreign allies and sustain five years of fighting from 1862 to 1867. The Republican Resistance to the French Intervention and to the Maximilian Empire was successful not primarily because of an agreement among Mexicans for a liberal state but rather because the Juárez government skillfully converted the war from a liberal-conservative contest to a nationalistic expulsion of a foreign invasion.

The reformers as a class had not been the major power-wielders in the period prior to the Reform, although many of them had held political office. They were the professional and commercial men, a potential bourgeoisie who could benefit by a strong voice in government, as had the bourgeoisie of Europe and Anglo-America who earlier had fought the privileged orders for power. Once in power— uncontested power after the collapse of the Maximilian Empire—the Mexican ruling class did not need liberalism. They did not need to continue to cultivate the support of the masses or to keep open the channels to the political arena, any more than French liberals needed to consult the peasantry, or British and American liberals need to consult the industrial workers. They could wield power for their own interests in the name of the entire nation, within an ideology that supported institutions that they controlled.

By 1867 Mexican liberalism had three factors working for it: a liberal constitution which had become the banner for nationalism and independence, a foreign policy based on isolation from the great monarchies of Europe and an uneasy friendship with liberal United States, and a victorious government that had paid years of lip-service to liberalism. Working against liberalism were all the contradictions between that ideology and the real conditions of Mexico, as described in the first chapter, and all of Mexico's historical traditions—the Hapsburg tradition, the Bourbon tradition, and the tradition of elite republicanism. Not even the Juárez government between 1858 and 1867 had been able to implement liberalism in practice. During the Restored Republic more powerful forces were working against the successful application of liberalism than were working for it.

Benito Juárez has been elevated to a position of greatness in Mexico. He died, however, during a devastating civil war that was fought against his continuing in office and his abuse of republican ideals. It is not Juárez's fault that he is applauded as the great republican but rather the fault of later politicians who have wanted to bathe in the same reputation. Nevertheless, greatness may be ascribed to Juárez. He correctly comprehended that a return to colonialism was not in the interest of his country. He must be honored for his correct appraisal that Mexicans could successfully resist and repel the French occupation in the 1860s and for his leadership in the task. Furthermore, Juárez was an extremely resourceful politician: after some forty presidents were broken by Mexican politics, Juárez seized the reins and held on for fourteen turbulent years.

Juárez recognized that he had to govern by two lights—the accepted ideology of liberalism and the demands of the real conditions of Mexico. The historical moment of the early 1860s demanded that he advocate the liberal model in order to avert the then-present danger of being absorbed into the French Empire. He recognized that liberalism was not the correct prescription for Mexico; he overrode its application for fourteen years. The suspicion is great that had he applied its political dictums, his administration would have been as short as that of Francisco I. Madero, the only Mexican president who did try to apply them.

The major governmental concept of the Reform was to limit executive power by decentralizing it and dividing it among the three branches of national government and between the national and state governments. Juárez and Lerdo were centralists, believing that the real conditions of Mexico demanded centralism. Competitive power centers in Mexican history have always resulted in civil war; power centers in the provinces have led to secessionist movements, and the absence of unity has encouraged foreign powers to threaten Mexican independence. In an age of nationalism—another trait of liberalism that has caused more grief than benefits to humanity—Mexico surely could not have maintained its independent existence as a collection of caudillistic satrapies. Had the republic failed to maintain its unity or its independence in the 1860s or in the 1870s, what judgment would history make upon Juárez and Lerdo? They became centralists to avert what they believed would be the consequences of an alternate policy.

Given the monopolization of local power and opportunity, to govern Mexico has been to govern centrally, and centralism has demanded political machines. The struggle between centralism and federalism, recorded in one form or another for nearly all periods of Mexican history, including the Restored Republic, was in practice the struggle between executive control or caudillistic control of the various regions of Mexico. Centralist control required alliances with governors—even *caudillo* governors. *Caudillos* and governors were invited to accept presidential leadership and to receive in return the support of presidential power for their continuance or the furtherance of monopolistic control of their regions. Those who did not cooperate were replaced. Such is the nature of a political machine, the object of which is to control the personnel of government at all levels.

In practice, governors could not invariably control all personnel of government within a state. They could not, for example, invariably name congressmen to the national legislature. From place to place, other individuals or entrenched interests influenced the selections, including political chiefs, military chiefs, rival *caudillos, hacendados,* clergymen, and agents from other factions. Any of those figures might prevail in a given area to thwart the republican electoral laws of the land, and any of them might work at cross purposes with the governor. Furthermore, the constitutional republican format did operate to some degree. Nevertheless, gubernatorial selection of congressmen "to be elected," generally by the selection of local political chiefs, was the usual result of gubernatorial control of the political process in the states. When all of this took place within an alliance with the president, with or without his orders, then a political machine, not the liberal republican model, was in operation.

Machine politics became common practice during the Juárez administration. Juárez did not invent it, perhaps did not even desire it, but as has been seen, he helped advance it in state after state. Lerdo continued and abetted the process.

In the absence of popular participation in public administration, those machines were necessary. In one case study after another this work has demonstrated that the alternative to the presidential party, and the extension of it, was warfare. Moreover, machine politics caused alienation that ultimately caused warfare. Some forty insurrections, catalogued in appendix 1, harassed the government of Juárez and Lerdo. A dilemma existed in the Mexican political tradition by which machines were necessary to avoid warfare at the same time that they contributed to alienation and warfare.

One of the several aspects of the dilemma has been seen in electoral practices. Machine politics in republics is based upon the ability of incumbents to control elections. The attempts to control elections through fraud and violence have been demonstrated throughout this study. The best assurance against electoral fraud was mass voting, but the masses were not voting. If the people did not vote, then elections would be decided elsewhere. If elections were decided other than at the polls, however, people would not go to the polls, and elections were thus easier to control by those who would do so. Mexico has never overcome this aspect of the dilemma.

The Porfirian interpretation of the politics of the Restored Republic was simply that the replacement of independent governors by men loyal to the president and the retention of incumbents of the president's faction through dishonest elections constituted centralist tyranny. The opposition to Juárez and Lerdo contended that political incumbents retained possession of political office through fraudulent electoral practices and were in league with the national executive toward that end. Furthermore, the *Porfiristas* contended that, because elections were fraudulent, the only means of changing policy was to capture the reins of power by armed force. The justification for armed force was always to restore liberty and to save the constitutional institutions from the tyranny of public officials. Díaz probably accepted this rationale in 1867; whether he accepted it in 1876 is moot. The record shows that Díaz thereafter became the master politician of gubernatorial alliances and parliamentary majorities, and various sources record the level of electoral violence which sustained that monopoly of power. That may have come as a surprise to the many men who witnessed Díaz's poor leadership of his congressional party during the Restored Republic, particularly during the period of the *liga,* which potentially controlled a majority. An opposition party in Mexico, however, is harder to direct than an incumbent machine, which operates on self-interest.

Political instability, men thought, was the cause of the overwhelming economic stagnation, and the liberal model called for political stability in order to attract private investment. It is incredible in hindsight that so simplistic a model was adopted for economic development. If they erred toward simplicity in political economy, however, some men understood that political stability was proportional to the all-inclusiveness of the alliance of political authorities. Such all-inclusiveness or monopolization of power, however, generated its own violent reaction among those who shouted tyranny. In turn, opposition violence signaled the need for the incumbent faction to increase its control in order to establish the political stability which was the original object. In this manner, further alienation was assured and revolts multiplied.

Juárez, Lerdo, and Díaz were all astute politicians; their utterances of the liberal doctrines have never been surpassed. But they knew how Mexico was to be governed. Díaz, as an opposition leader, could be more idealistic and less responsible than Juárez for the consequences of his demands for republican practices. He was also younger than Juárez, less patient, and less practiced in real Mexican politics. He had fewer favors to bestow and dealt with a more popular and more militant element than did Juárez. As the loser during the Restored Republic, Díaz was more indignant and belligerent. Of the three men, Lerdo was the least idealistic leader and the most overt assailant against the republican forms of government. He recognized earlier than the others that the institutions had to be manipulated from above. As a minister in Juárez's cabinet his intrigues were more Machiavellian and closeted; as president, however, his intrusions were open. Juárez and Díaz coveted public approval. Lerdo did not seem to care.

Once in office Díaz sought Juárez's reputation and largely used Juárez's methods. By disenfranchizing all *Lerdistas* he quickly had a party in office that thereafter sought its own advantage. Díaz was thereby able to saddle Mexico with his chosen successor, Manuel González, who was more like Lerdo in his disregard for republican institutions and public opinion. He operated more aggressively and openly than the other three to break all rival factions. Díaz returned to power in 1884, and after a four year tune-up the *Porfirista* machine ran on the momentum of personal interest of subordinates. Díaz seems not to have needed to interfere with his own elections thereafter, although he did intervene on behalf of chosen partisans for the rest of the *Porfiriato*. By 1900 elections were more a mockery than they had been in 1867.

The longevity of Díaz's political career, from 1877 to 1911, was doubtlessly the result of his powerful political machine. Ironically, Porfirio Díaz, who fought the Lerdo machine as he had fought the Juárez machine, carried through the same practices until his own machine was the most totally monopolistic political party ever fashioned in independent Mexico. The rigidity of his machine, however, resulting in the monopolization of careers, the blockage of social mobility, and a concentration of wealth greater than had ever been witnessed in Mexico, caused the most complete political alienation, followed by the most devastating upheaval in Mexican history—the Mexican Revolution.

If the machine politics of the Restored Republic resulted in insurrections, then the more complete machine politics of the *Porfiriato* ought to have resulted in yet more insurrections. Other developments, however, were taking place. The military reforms of the *Porfiriato*, the building of railroads which carried federal forces rapidly to areas of rebellion, the effects of the political policy of conciliation, the workings of a rural police and a system of political police, and the gradual disappearance of a free press made insurrection an increasingly less viable weapon against machine politics. Furthermore, Díaz did not attempt an immediate reelection after his first term as president. The reelections of 1867, 1871, and 1876 had caused great opposition. Díaz stepped down to Gen. Manuel González in 1880 and appeared to be recalled by acclaim in 1884 after González's administration was tainted by scandal. Nevertheless, there were numerous insurrections during the first Díaz administration and the administration of Manuel González. Their suppression helped to make insurrection, as a method of changing personnel and policy of government, less attractive. The *Pax Porfiriana* was based upon a successful continuation of the machine politics of the Restored Republic, made more efficient by new administrative and technological innovations. Alienation existed during the *Porfiriato*, but its manifestations were suppressed—until 1910.

It is frequently said that Díaz sacrificed republicanism to financial stability and economic growth. This examination of machine politics in Mexico suggests that there was in the Restored Republic little real republicanism to sacrifice. Yet Díaz did turn out to be the great liberal. During his presidency, Mexico reaped the results that liberalism has to bestow on the nonindustrial world: the concentration of capital goods and inequities of wealth. The opulent few were allowed to dominate republican institutions, override civil rights, warp democratic values, and utilize nationalist rhetoric to camouflage the alliance that prevailed between the national elite and a foreign elite. Mexico became a bonanza for foreign capitalists, who, in supporting the Porfirian system, helped the Díaz government to monopolize power to a degree that Juárez and Lerdo may not have dreamed of. This is the pattern that characterizes the *Porfiriato*, and its political underpinnings are found in the Restored Republic.

Mexico has always been a class society. The traditional attitudes about the natural and inevitable relations between classes in class societies are overwhelming forces against liberalism in the countries outside of the North-Atlantic community. Local and national elites in those countries can readily use republican insititutions to support their own interests. They adopt liberal economic models to entice foreign investing elites to establish trade patterns that make both elite groups wealthy. The foreign elites may pay adequate wages and salaries to their own workers in the capital-financial countries, but the elites of the raw-material nations do not. Justified by their class attitudes, they use their wealth to create elite lifestyles and to control republican institutions. With political and economic power they move out the raw materials to the benefit of the industrial countries and their own monopolistic elitism. This is the truth that unifies Porfirian history, which liberal historians have always narrated as the "progress" of Porfirian peace and the oppression of Porfirian dictatorship—the "good" results and the "bad" results of Porfirian development. The two aspects were one; they inevitably developed together.

Liberals have never understood how liberalism in the raw-material producing nations evolves into dictatorship. Those dictatorships merely worsen, and the shame of the industrial countries deepens when the governments of the industrial nations support the elites of the nonindustrial nations with diplomatic and military aid. Such aid always promotes "progress" and the further monopolization of power and wealth by elite classes in the raw-material nations. Justified in the twentieth century to avert the threat of "communism," the process continues until the allies of the industrial nations are almost universally dictatorships.

Bravo Ugarte says that all Mexican governments between 1867 and 1910 were dictatorships. If dictatorship is defined as executive centralism based on political machines wherein electoral violence for the control of governmental offices is ordered or condoned, then the statement is true. Bravo Ugarte also claims that of those dictatorships only the Porfirian dictatorship was progressive.[1] That is true also, from a positivist point of view, whereby progress is measured by gross national product, monetary stability, industrial growth, and such indices.

The Revolution of 1910 did not terminate the patterns that have been explained here. The Madero movement turned out Díaz and the *científicos;* the Constitutionalist Forces of Venustiano Carranza and

1. Bravo Ugarte, *Historia de México, 3:347.*

others destroyed the Porfirian federal army; Carranza then purged the Porfirian bureaucracy. But the old governmental traditions lived on. Carranza tried to organize an electoral victory through alliances with governors for the 1920 elections and reaped an insurrection like Tuxtepec. The successful insurrectionists of Agua Prieta of 1920 promulgated accurate charges against "imposition of official candidates." The victorious general, Alvaro Obregón, set about establishing a machine not different in any important aspect from those established by Juárez and Lerdo. Mexico in 1920 was a collection of regions dominated by armed *caudillos,* much as it had been in 1867. Obregón had to deal with those *caudillos* as Juárez had done earlier, by forming alliances and trying to replace independent *caudillo* governors with men loyal to the presidential party. In the process he reaped a series of rebellions; his La Noria was the de la Huerta rebellion. The only difference between them was that Juárez in 1871 arranged his own reelection and Obregón in 1923—whose reelection was prohibited by constitutional law due to Madero's popular cry of 1910, "Effective Suffrage and No-Reelection"—was preparing the "official imposition" of his chosen successor. Plutarco Elías Calles was imposed on Mexico as Díaz had imposed González in 1880. De la Huerta's "Plan of Veracruz" contained the accusation that Obregón was violating popular suffrage and using official violence to arrange a presidential election. The charge was true, and the resulting civil war lasted a full year.

President Calles, like President González before him, arranged a constitutional amendment to interpret no-reelection to mean no immediate reelection, and used his presidential alliance—his political machine—to arrange the reelection of Obregón. After the reelection of 1928, however, Obregón was assassinated. Then Calles converted the alliance of *caudillos* into a political party, the PNR, and the political machine became regulated. Even as Juárez and Lerdo replaced independent *caudillos* with loyal machine politicians, so Obregón, Calles, and successors gradually replaced the revolutionary *caudillos* with loyal machine politicians, and the PNR became a party of executive centralism.

The basic difference between the developments of 1867–1911 and those of 1920–40 was that a slightly variant model was used. Liberalism by 1910 was discredited because the alliance between government and business for economic growth had created intolerable social inequities. The liberal promises of democratic social values and civil rights had been mauled by that alliance. The revolutionary model, outlined in the Constitution of 1917, showed its distrust of liberalism by limiting property rights and establishing governmental protection for workers. Nevertheless, it proclaimed federalism, division of powers, popular sovereignty, and republican institutions. The new model was to be populist government for popular benefits. But Mexican reality, if the people are to be ignored, in order to contain the manifestations of alienation and to maintain the privileged elites in alliance demands centralism. Populists after 1917, like liberals after 1857, could applaud presidential wreckage of regional caudillistic dictatorship, which advanced centralism. Interestingly, even as liberalism found its advocate in Francisco Madero, populism found its champion in Lázaro Cárdenas. They were both ineffectual in Mexican political development: executive centralism for elite governance and elite benefits won out.

The latest development in Mexican political history is also a repetition. As positivism in the *Porfiriato* adjusted the liberal model to allow the alliance between business and government for economic growth without regard to social consequences, so also after 1940 the populist model was adjusted in the same way for the same ends. The executive centralism of Lázaro Cárdenas, wielded for popular benefits, was thereafter geared for popular sacrifice. The justification in both cases has been that the entire nation will one day benefit. And so the Mexican nation is again harnessed to a monolithic political machine—the PRI, Juárez's great-grandchild—by which the elite dominate republican institutions, maintain alliances with the elites of the industrial nations, and export Mexico's natural resources for the revenues to maintain the machine. The elites again monopolize both the wealth and the power, while the masses endure poverty and nonparticipation.

Populist leadership has occasionally tried to modify this reality in the direction of greater popular benefits. After Cárdenas, President López Mateos (1958–64) and President Luis Echeverría Alvarez (1970–76) made serious attempts, but the elites have been too strong. Mexico's social programs are financed with residual funds after the elites collect the top portions and the pockets of an enormously corrupt bureaucracy are filled.

So Mexico still writhes within the three great governmental traditions of its history. The Hapsburg tradition of privileged families, monopolizing the great economic and political power and supported by corrupt bureaucracies, the Bourbon tradition of state promotion of economic growth through "enlightened despotism," and elite republicanism devoid of real democratic values—these have remained the constant forces in Mexican history, the combined traditions first made viable by political machines in the days of Benito Juárez, evolving into *Porfirismo,* which is again the dominant force in Mexico today. No *Porfirista* need feel estranged in contemporary Mexico, although revolutionaries might have to rethink their case.

Appendix 1

Frequency of Insurrections during the Restored Republic

The frequency of insurrection during the Restored Republic is a measure of the size of the problem. In 1867 Jesús Betangos, León Ugalde, and Ascensión Gómez rebelled in Picachos, Hidalgo; Vicente Jiménez led a long and vexing rebellion in Guerrero; General Urrutia rebelled in Jalisco; Manuel M. Cuesta, Braulio Vargas, and Servando Canales led a rebellion against the governor of Tamaulipas; Miguel Negrete rebelled in the Sierra de Puebla, and Marcelino Villafeña and others in Yucatán.

In 1868 José María Gálvez and Carlos Sotomayor led separate rebellions in the state of Mexico; Angel Martínez, Adolfo Palacios, Jesús Toledo, and Jorge García Granados rebelled in Sinaloa; Paulino Noriega raised insurrections in Hidalgo; as did Felipe Mendoza in Perote, Veracruz; Aureliano Rivera and Sostenes Escandón in Cuautitlán, state of Mexico; Jesús Chávez López in the states of Mexico, Puebla, and Tlaxcala; Honorato Domínguez in Huatuxco, Veracruz; and Juan Francisco Lucas in Zacapoaxtla, Puebla.

In 1869 generals Miguel Negrete and Julio Bolaños, in Zoquitlan, Puebla; Desiderio Díaz in Tlacotalpan, Veracruz; Francisco Aguirre and Pedro Martínez in San Luis Potosí; Narciso Arcevedo in Padilla, Tamaulipas; Pedro Hinojosa in Camargo; Trinidad García de la Cadena in Zacatecas; Jesús Toledo in Aguascalientes—all rebelled against the government.

In 1870 Rosario Aragón, Eduardo Arce, and Feliciano Chavarría led a rebellion in Morelos; Francisco Cortés Castillo in Orizaba, Veracruz; Amado Antonio Guadarrama in Jalisco, and Plácido Vega in Sinaloa.

In 1871 Cristobal Andrade, Márquez, and Parra rebelled in Sinaloa; and later in the year in the insurrection of La Noria, Porfirio and Felix Díaz rose up in Oaxaca, Gen. Miguel Negrete and Aureliano Rivera in the state of Mexico, Agustín García in Michoacán, Hermenegildo Carrillo in northern Veracruz, Frederico Labastida in

Jalisco, Juan N. Cortina in Camargo, Juan N. Méndez in the Sierra de Puebla, Trinidad García de la Cadena again in Zacatecas, and Jesús Leyva in Guaymas, Sonora. The rebellion of La Noria was a veritable civil war, lasting until late 1872.

The following year Manuel Lozada led an invasion into Jalisco and Sinaloa from Tepic which required a major federal campaign to contain and crush.

The Cristero rebellion lasted more than two years in western Mexico between 1874 and 1876. Three of the leaders were Ignacio Ochoa, Eulogio Cárdenas, and Francisco Gutiérrez.

The rebellion of Tuxtepec extended throughout the year of 1876, involving widespread guerrilla war and major campaigns. The José María Iglesias rebellion lasted from October 1876 to January 1877, attracting fully half of the governors of the nation to its banner. Details of several of the insurrections are discussed in the various chapters. Some of them were not serious as events transpired, but all of them had to be dealt with. Several were significant; those were troubled times.

Appendix 2
Orteguismo

As *Orteguismo* receded from view it left many of his followers in precarious positions. Some of them left public life, some found ways back to Juárez's favor, others attached themselves to the governmental pretensions of José María Iglesias in 1876 after minor roles during the Restored Republic, and still others after 1867 joined the Porfirian opposition. Two or three careers from each of the four groups follow.

Miguel Ruiz, minister of justice for President Ignacio Comonfort in 1857, had accompanied Juárez to Veracruz, where he was responsible for writing three of the later famous laws of the Reform—the nationalization of ecclesiastical property, the ex-claustration of religious orders, and the civil registry of matrimony. During the Intervention Juárez named Ruiz as governor of Tamaulipas where he supported the Ortega claims to the presidency. Arrested and eventually absolved, Ruiz retired to private life, dying in 1871 at the age of forty-nine.

José María Patoni was a liberal governor of Durango during the Republican Resistance. Arrested with González Ortega in 1867, Patoni suffered the same period of imprisonment as Ortega. Upon his release in 1868 Patoni proceeded to his home in Durango where Gen. Benigno Canto, an active federal officer at the time and an elected congressman, arrested and executed him without trial. Canto's grand jury trial was a *cause célèbre* in 1868 because he had "confessed to superior orders" during the pretrial investigation, but at this trial he rested his case on the argument that Potoni was about to launch an insurrection. The grand jury found him guilty, and he died in prison before the Supreme Court sentenced him.[1] Ruiz and Patoni would likely have played important political roles during the Restored Republic had they not supported Ortega.

Some other *Orteguistas* were able to rehabilitate themselves and find places with Juárez and Lerdo. Gaspar Sánchez Ochoa fought with

1. Benigno Canto had the right to a congressional grand jury trial because he was a member of Congress after the 1867 elections. The proceedings of his trial are in Tovar, *Cuarto congreso,* vol. 1.

Comomfort in the Rebellion of Ayutla, with Gen. Ignacio de la Llave during the Three Years' War, and with González Ortega at Puebla in 1863. Sent to the United States to secure a loan, he joined Ortega. Upon the fall of the empire he established himself in San Luis Potosí and won a seat in Congress. The government declared him subject to trial and the *Juarista* Congress rejected his credentials.[2] Nevertheless, Sánchez Ochoa was rehabilitated and restored to the army in 1871 in time to fight against the *Porfirista* rebels of La Noria.

Another military officer to return to Juárez's ranks after espousing *Orteguismo* was José Montesinos. He joined the liberals in 1862 after a career with the conservatives in the insurrection of Ayutla and the Three Years' War. He fought with Ortega at Puebla in 1863 and was taken to France as a prisoner of war. Arriving at Matamoros in June 1866, Montesinos became involved in the *Orteguista* movement. The charges against him were apparently dropped, for he participated in the siege of Querétaro and thereafter remained in the active army, defending the government in the San Luis Potosí-Zacatecas rebellion of 1869–70 and again in the rebellion of La Noria.

Another case more spectacular because of his closeness to political events was that of Juan José Baz. A long-time liberal, Baz was associated in 1846 with the second administration of Valentín Gómez Farías. During the Three Years' War Baz published the liberal newspaper *La Bandera Roja* and raised funds for the republican government in New York during the French Intervention. In New York Baz became involved with *Orteguismo,* after which he made a circuitous return to governmental confidence. A letter of his to Ortega, urging him not to press his claim to the presidency because of considerations for unity against the French, was included in a pamphlet published at Juárez's orders to demonstrate the widespread acceptance of his extension of his presidential tenure the preceding November. When Baz returned to Mexico he joined Díaz, who named him "political chief of Mexico City" during the siege of Mexico in 1867 after Juárez had explicitly ordered Díaz not to name a "governor of the Federal

2. Tamayo, *Juárez,* 13:94–95; DDC, 13:107–17; Zamacona, Prieto, and Montes spoke for allowing Sánchez Ochoa to take his seat, but he was rejected by a vote of seventy-nine to thirty-two: Tovar, *Cuarto congreso,* vol. 1., 26 February 1868. *Porfiristas* were outraged; see Juan Torres to Díaz, 29 December 1867, APD, 5:404.

District." Thereafter Baz worked loyally for Juárez and later became a *Lerdista* in the national congress. In 1876 he joined Lerdo's cabinet as secretary of *gobernación* in time to fall with Lerdo.

Still other men, separated from Juárez by *Orteguismo,* never again became close to him and attempted to return to closer executive confidence in 1876 by way of *Iglesismo.* Of several men in that category the most outstanding were Guillermo Prieto and Felipe Berriozábal.

Felipe Berriozábal had an impressive career before his involvement with González Ortega. A veteran of the war against the United States, he was named military commander for the district of Toluca when the Three Years' War commenced, rising to brigadier general under Gen. Santos Degollado. In 1859 Berriozábal was divisional general, governor, and military commander of the states of Mexico and Guanajuato. He fought at Puebla in the battle of 5 May 1862 and again there in the siege of 1863. He escaped his French captors, and Juárez named him minister of war. Leaving the cabinet, he held several important commissions: governor and military commander of Veracruz, commander of the Fourth Division, governor of Michoacán, military commander of the northern district of Tamaulipas and chief of the line of Rio Bravo with command of the forces of Coahuila, Nuevo León, and Tamaulipas.[3] Berriozábal could have anticipated an important role in the Restored Republic. In Matamoros, however, in 1866 and 1867 Berriozábal joined the cause of González Ortega. As *Orteguismo* receded, Berriozábal was retained as a federal military officer but without command. He sat in Congress from September 1868 to September 1869 and again after September 1873, but during the four intervening years he was assigned to a post in Toluca without soldiers at his command. In 1876 he joined the *Iglesista* revolutionary government, acting as secretary of war against Lerdo's reelection and Díaz's insurrectionary movement of Tuxtepec. Only later did he join Díaz.

Other *Orteguistas* were totally alienated from Juárez and thereafter drifted to Porfirio Díaz. Some important ones were Servando Canales, Miguel Negrete, Manuel M. de Zamacona, Epitacio Huerta, Rafael de Zayas Enríquez, and Joaquín Villalobos.

Gen. Servando Canales, liberal warrior of the Three Years' War and of the French Intervention, seized Matamoros, Tamaulipas, for

3. Eugenia W. de Meyer, *La figura prócer de Felipe Berriozábal* (Mexico: Secretería de Educación Pública, 1966), pp. 14–48.

Ortega in 1866. Routed by a temporary seizure of the town by United States troops, he nevertheless captured the governorship of Tamaulipas in 1867. Juárez praised him for his military actions against Pedro Martínez and the latter's remnants from the 1869–70 rebellion of San Luis Potosí-Zacatecas, but did not like or trust him. He supported Díaz's electoral campaign of 1871 without involving himself in the following warfare. Lerdo tried in 1875 to replace him. Still governor in 1876, Canales waited until mid-year to commit himself to the Porfirian rebellion, saving himself from the gubernatorial changes of that year when the *Porfiristas* took power. Canales thereafter defied the Tuxtepec principle of no-reelection in 1880 and died in office in 1881. Canales was thus one of the most successful *caudillos* of his age; generally picking the winning side in every contest, he was so entrenched in his local position that his support of Ortega in 1866 did not shake him loose from power. Canales was first a *Canalista* and only secondly a *Porfirista,* but he became *Porfirista* in the absence of Ortega.[4]

Another *Orteguista* between 1865 and 1869 who became a *Porfirista* was Gen. Miguel Negrete. Negrete had fought in the war against the United States, with the liberals against Santa Anna, with the conservatives in the Three Years' War, and with the liberals against the French. A hero of the battle of Puebla on 5 May 1862, he became minister of war in 1864 in Juárez's cabinet. Leaving the cabinet in 1865 to support Ortega, he divided himself irreparably from Juárez and Lerdo. He supported Maximilian in 1867 and then offered his undeniably popular support to Díaz for the elections of that same year but was rebuffed. He rebelled for Ortega in 1868 and for Santa Anna in 1869, the latter time capturing the city of Puebla and holding the forts of Loreto and Guadalupe for a day. Captured and condemned to death, Ortega was pardoned, partly because of Díaz's intercession. Negrete thereafter campaigned for Díaz in the elections of 1871 and pronounced and fought for Díaz in the rebellions of La Noria and Tuxtepec.

A clearer case of a great liberal who broke relations with Juárez and became an influential and dedicated *Porfirista* was Manuel María de Zamacona. Like Negrete a native of Puebla, Zamacona was a literary

4. Canales's important role as a *Porfirista* rebel is traced in chapter 10.

man and politician rather than a soldier. Zamacona served in Juárez's cabinet in 1861 as minister of foreign relations. Perhaps his struggle with the first-term congressman Sebastián Lerdo de Tejada over the Zamacona-Wyke treaty with Britain, followed by Zamacona's resignation from the ministry, was sufficient for him thereafter to oppose the Juárez-Lerdo government. Zamacona's belief in parliamentary control of the ministry also separated them. Zamacona more than any other person opposed the governmental persecution of González Ortega. Using first his editorial position on the newspaper *El Globo* and then his congressional seat during the Juárez and Lerdo administrations, he maintained that the constitution had been violated and that Ortega's civil rights had been abused. In 1867 Zamacona led the newspaper promotion of the Porfirian presidential candidacy, led much of the Porfirian congressional opposition, and after 1876 occupied several positions of importance in the government of Porfirio Díaz.

The following conclusion seems appropriate: Although the Ortega case was not the primary cause of the liberal division of 1867 and although support of Ortega in 1865 did not invarably result in perpetual ostracism from a public life during the administrations of Juárez and Lerdo, the episode shook the political classes. Some men were appalled by Juárez's extension of power. The incarceration of Ortega during the elections of 1867 seemed to others that continuation in power rather than the pursuit of justice was Juárez's prime motivation. The issue helped divide the liberal faction in 1867, and some men who might have supported Jesús González Ortega, or who might have supported Juárez if the *Orteguista* affair had never arisen, turned to Porfirio Díaz.

Appendix 3
Porfirio Díaz's Resignation in 1867

So frequently has Díaz's resignation been cited as an issue between Díaz and Juárez that it should be analyzed. There may have been some substance to the issue; the two men did become political opponents shortly thereafter. Nevertheless, the innocent view may be the correct one: Díaz was tired and harried. He was sincere that constitutional law should be restored at the earliest moment, and his resignation would serve as an example to other generals. He would have wanted his resignation on record before his extended command was whittled away in the natural course of events. His resignation, therefore, would save his future pride and would scuttle fears of his personal ambition. We may assume that Juárez understood these motives: his deep understanding of men and their motives is surely one of the qualities upon which his greatness is based.[1] In this case Juárez was not irritated; he simply overlooked the resignation, desiring that Díaz gather his strength and make a further sacrifice for the nation.

On the other hand, Díaz's resignation may have been carefully calculated. A close reading of his resignation indicates that he was surrendering the command of eastern and southern Mexico, not the military command of the operations against Mexico City.[2] If he anticipated the military reorganization, he might have tried to head off the possibility of being relegated to a provincial post by occupying the command in Mexico City. There he could hope to influence the Juárez government, remain in close contact with political events, or launch a political career with greater ease than elsewhere. If this was his plan, Juárez parried it by overlooking the resignation and, only twelve days after occupying the capital, ordered the military reorganization which shifted Díaz to Tehuacán, Puebla. In this case,

1. Puig Casauranc demonstrates Juárez's understanding of men with Juárez's correspondence, *Archivo privado*, 1:12–16.
2. Díaz, *Memorias*, 2:190.
3. Ibid., p. 173.

Juárez may have been suspicious of Díaz's motive, and Díaz may have been angered by the refusal.

Although the second interpretation is possible, there are reasons to prefer the first. Díaz ran the risk with his resignation that Juárez might simply have accepted it, leaving Díaz without any command. If Juárez harbored a suspicion that Díaz had political ambitions, he would have taken that step, because a disloyal or ambitious general with troops was more dangerous than one retired, as the González Ortega case demonstrated and as the Díaz case eventually showed. Furthermore, if Díaz had politics in mind in mid-July, he most certainly would have filled the governorships of the east and south with partisans before resigning. If fact, he called his brother Félix from the military command of Oaxaca to aid him in the siege of Mexico and replaced him with the loyal *Juarista,* Miguel Castro.[3] Finally, if Díaz planned a political career that challenged that of Juárez, of which the resignation was a part, then the resignation cannot be cited as the cause of Díaz's opposition.

This analysis leaves two further alternatives. First, Díaz's motives were innocent, but Juárez suspected personal ambition and thus relegated Díaz to the provinces, which then irritated Díaz when he recognized Juárez's suspicions. Second, Díaz planned a political career that would not challenge Juárez and then interpreted Juárez's response as a means of keeping him out of politics, which irritated Díaz. He then entered politics in opposition to Juárez. These are possible.

Appendix 4
León Guzmán and the *Convocatoria*

Cosío Villegas writes that Governor Guzmán's refusal to publish the *convocatoria* "was a case of rebellion, the first ostensible rebellion presented to the government; a rebellion, furthermore, abusive of the interpretation of the *convocatoria*, because Guzmán spoke of the reforms as though they would be enacted by way of the popular vote, when in reality, [the *convocatoria*] only said that [the popular vote would] authorize congress to initiate them."[1] There is error here. Congress already had authorization to initiate amendments, those or any other. The public, according to article 9 of the *convocatoria*, ". . . will express . . . its will in respect to whether the next Congress of the Union, without necessity of observing the requirements established in article 127 of the Federal Constitution, can reform it or amend it. . . ."[2] Article 127 established that constitutional amendments would be ratified by a majority of the state legislatures before having the effect of law. Clearly, the popular vote in 1867 would not allow Congress merely to initiate but to enact, by bypassing the state legislatures, where Juárez could expect to find great opposition to his desire of increasing executive power.

The legal issue was whether the special powers which Congress bestowed upon Juárez in 1863 and which he unilaterally extended in 1865 allowed him to convoke the people to bypass the state legislatures in the amendment process. León Guzmán was not a rude soldier, although he rose to the rank of general during the Intervention. He was an illustrious member of the Constitutional Convention of 1857 and a learned jurist. Guzmán's pamphlet on the unconstitutionality of the *convocatoria* is an erudite statement. The interpretation that Juárez was acting unconstitutionally is stronger than that León Guzmán was a rebel.

1. Cosío Villegas, *República restaurada*, p. 166.
2. *Convocatoria*, article nine, 14 August 1867, DDC, 12:325–32.

Appendix 5
Appraisals of Historical Accounts of Elections in the Restored Republic

The early chapters describe and document the ways in which the Mexican political system operated. Documents were preferred over the historical judgments of secondary sources. Herein is a discussion of the judgments of eight Mexican authors and three American authors who have discussed the political life of the Restored Republic. Some tendencies exist of great interest.

During the first presidential administration of Porfirio Díaz in the late 1870s, Justo Sierra used the newspaper *La Libertad* as a forum for his argument that the Constitution of 1857 was not based upon Mexican realities and consequently needed reform. Specifically, an imbalance of power existed in the constitution between the legislature and the executive in favor of the former and between state security and individual liberties in favor of the latter. Because the Constituent Congress of 1856–57, in reaction to the dictatorship of Santa Anna, had written numerous guarantees of personal liberties into the constitution, the government was unable to govern without resort to article 29, the constitutional procedure to invest the executive with extraordinary faculties. "In a country such as ours, in which crisis is a normal state," wrote Sierra, the executive was forced to govern continually with the extraordinary faculties.[1]

Ignacio Altamirano, outstanding man of letters during the Restored Republic, observed that "in the exercise of the Executive function [Juárez] introduced practices and precedents that have paralyzed or denaturalized the democratic process. He established the system of coalition with the governors of the states for the imposition of official candidates. . . ."[2] Referring to the election of 1871, Altamirano wrote that it was "the power of the government and not the public will which

1. Cosío Villegas, *La constitución de 1857*, pp. 18–40.
2. Altamirano, *Historia y política*, pp. 179–80.

decided the election, with official pressure and with a thousand elements which [the president] commands in order to influence the suffrage."[3]

Ireneo Paz, journalist and perpetual revolutionary of the period, commenced his memoirs with these lines:

> The party of Juárez' opposition was formidable, and existed principally because that functionary had armed himself with power without allowing other aspirants to gain office.[4]

> Sr. Juárez . . . began to prostitute the electoral right, having himself been elected twice by violence and intrigue. [Opposition candidates] found the terrain occupied by official elements which in each election became increasingly dominant, and consequently more hated.[5]

> I saw by personal experience that the rights and guarantees of men were passed over because every office-holder did with his enemies what he wished; . . . I observed that the electoral right was charged to authorities who consigned the votes; . . . I saw that state sovereignty existed in name only, and was delivered over to the military at whatever moment without consideration. . . .[6]

Ireneo Paz was justifying his own revolutionary role, but his recollections add to our understanding of the beliefs by which some men were acting and supply another participant's view of the relationship between politics and rebellion.

José María Iglesias, long a part of the established authority of the Restored Republic, wrote that

> as a general rule the irregularities or vices of the elections depend upon the lack of popularity of the person who is to be elevated to power. When popular enthusiasm is declared in a frank and unequivocal manner in favor of a certain candidate, there is no need to resort to illicit means in order to obtain a triumph already assured by a true prestige.[7]

3. Ibid., p. 167.
4. Ireneo Paz, *Algunas campañas: memorias*, 2d ed., 3 vols. (Mexico: Imprenta y Litografía de Ireneo Paz, 1884–85), 1:5.
5. Ibid., p. 7.
6. Ibid., p. 8.
7. Iglesias, *Cuestión presidencial*, p. 63; the *Iglesista* rebellion is discussed in chapters 11 and 12.

The corollary is that, if the candidate to be elevated to power did not have "popular enthusiasm" and "true prestige," then electoral irregularities and vices were necessary. Again, Iglesias was a rebel at the time of issuing the statement, but he enjoys a reputation for honor and veracity far above that of, for example, Ireneo Paz in Mexican history.

Francisco Cosmes, young journalist during the latter part of the Restored Republic and *Iglesista* in 1876, a quarter of a century later wrote a history of that decade in four large volumes, in which appears the following observation:

> The natural apathy of the Mexican people makes them indifferent and disdainful of the electoral act. This indifference reaches such a degree that even partisans, who find themselves in defense of their cause, abstain from voting in the electoral booths, because they have little faith in the efficacy of suffrage.[8]

Cosmes wrote that the elections of 1869 "were the first ones in Mexico that gave place to the scandal of military force intervening in a direct way. Complaints and protests came from all parts of the country of violence used by the administration to control the suffrage."[9] Cosmes characterized those elections of 1869 in this manner:

> opposition electors reduced to prison on futile pretexts on the eve of the [secondary] elections; polling places assaulted by the police; presidents and secretaries [of polling *mesas*] taken to jail; false credentials in the urns in substitution for the legitimate ones; in a word, as many frauds and violences as is possible to imagine by a tyrannical government. . . .[10]

In reference to the elections of 1871 Cosmes wrote that "those who know Mexican politics . . . know well how decisive was the influence of the national government . . . in the victory of Juárez."[11] Díaz had little hope of winning those elections, according to Cosmes, "knowing that the governmental pressure would incline the electoral balance in favor of the reelection."[12] Cosmes editorialzed that it was as illegal and violent to employ arms to force the popular vote as it was to appeal to

8. Cosmes, *Historia general de Méjico*, 22:746–47.
9. Ibid., p. 749.
10. Ibid., p. 755.
11. Ibid., p. 7.
12. Ibid., p. 9.

arms to overthrow a government established by popular vote. Such "revolution" by the government was the cause of revolution against the government.[13]

In 1906 Ricardo García Granados argued that the national executive dominated through control of elections. Such official influence on the elections was inevitable, however, for if the president did not do so, the governors would, and if not they, the church would do so, and public liberties would cease.[14] García argued further that because of the transcendent powers of the legislature, the executive had either to commit suicide or to influence the elections in order to construct an executive party in the legislature.[15] He also held that centralism and militarism had been destroyed by the liberal victory in 1867 and that the liberal chieftains in each region established local power akin to that of feudalism.

> They governed arbitrarily . . . [and] did not grant more power to the national government than the latter was capable of forcing them to recognize.

The result was a continual struggle between the state governments and the national government. The people, he maintained, were simple spectators or inoffensive victims, "and it is false when it is assured that in those times real popular elections took place." Politics became a web of intrigues and conspiracies with continual armed insurrection as a result.[16]

Perhaps the most famous critic of the Mexican political system is Emilio Rabasa, among whose works was *La organización política de México*, written in 1912. Rabasa was primarily writing a brief against universal manhood suffrage, which had been incorporated into the Constitution of 1857 and the electoral law of 12 February 1857. The public, he said, was so unused to and incapable of suffrage that governmental influence upon elections was necessary in order to acquire a semblance of respect for the law. Furthermore, the imbalance between executive and legislative powers made it necessary for the president to constitute a dictatorship and to govern dictatorially. Elections played no real part in the succession to office:

13. Ibid., 20:752.
14. García Grandos, *La constitución de 1857*, p. 125.
15. Ibid., p. 45.
16. Ibid., p. 123.

In the succession to power the people do not express their will to elect a new president, but rather depose the one who governs; and they express it by raising up arms and battling him. Once the victory is won the election is unnecessary because there is no candidate other than the chief of the subversive movement. . . .[17]

Fraudulent elections were intimately related to insurrections: "The prospect of the Republic presents itself in this simple but difficult dilemma: either elections or revolutions."[18]

In 1923 García Granados's *Historia de México* appeared with a thesis worthy of note: The idealistic makers of the Constitution of 1857 had assumed a homogeneous nation, which did not exist. Thus the creation of equal and universal male suffrage placed elections in the hands of the established authorities, since the opposition to any incumbent could never move the ignorant masses, who by custom obeyed orders of the established authorites.

Juárez and Lerdo knew this perfectly and therefore imposed governors upon the states who were political allies rather than those who were popular, so that they would not establish popular roots and follow independent policies.[19]

Juárez and Lerdo employed federal forces to undermine the sovereignty of the states rather than to defend the citizens against local tyranny of state authorities. Furthermore, according to García Granados, Juárez and Lerdo were dedicated to a policy of indefinite rule, which alienated all those men who aspired to political careers. Since the methods of remaining in power were considered tyrannical, those who aspired to political office turned to rebellion. "These were, in my judgment, the principal causes of the repeated revolutions."[20]

Even as this school of thought about the nature of politics in the Restored Republic was running its course, another school developed. The authors of the second school also commence with Justo Sierra, this time the Sierra of the late *Porfiriato*. Sierra's influential works, brought together as *The Political Evolution of the Mexican People*, ap-

17. Rabas, *La organización política*, p. 134.
18. Ibid., p. 135.
19. Ricardo García Granados, *Historia de México desde la restauración de la república en 1867, hasta la caída de Huerta*, 2d ed., 2 vols. in one (Mexico: Editorial Jus, 1956), 1:59.
20. Ibid., p. 60.

peared in the first years of the twentieth century. The interpretive structure is principally found in the title word *evolution*.[21] The great influence of the work lies in the interpretation that the divisions of the Mexican past, the many tragedies, and the colossal failures all had a meaning within an evolutionary development which finally produced a successful, progressive, national identity. In that process the program of Benito Juárez looms impressive and important, so fully that Juárez became subject of a separate biography by Sierra.[22] The Juárez reputation, indeed the Juárez cult, largely derives from the works of Justo Sierra. A second concept in Sierra's work is *mestizaje*, also an evolutionary concept so loved by his generation—the mixture of the Indian and the Spaniard in the formation of the Mexican people.[23] It is for the great unifying interpretations and their satisfying effects upon Mexican intellectuals, not for the accuracy and detailed account of the Restored Republic, for which men have turned again and again to Justo Sierra.

Sierra taught that upon the collapse of the Maximilian empire Mexico found her national soul. The influence on Mexican politics of the religious-aristrocratic view of Mexico faded from view, replaced by the triumphant liberal view and the national policies of the liberal party represented by Benito Juárez. Juárez recognized the need for unity, economic progress, and national strength. To effect those needs,

> to make the desideratum a reality, Juárez and his ministers followed the only feasible plan, that of strengthening the power of the central governmenl at all costs within the bounds of constitutional procedures. . . . The central power must be strengthened because it was responsible for peace and order throughout the country and would have to furnish the leadership and the means to transform the country's economic life.[24]

21. Sierra, *Political Evolution*.

22. Justo Sierra, *Juárez, su tiempo y su obra* (Mexico: Universidad Nacional Autónoma de México, 1948).

23. Both these concepts are found in *México a través de los siglos*, ed. Vicente Riva Palacios, upon which Sierra heavily relied and which Sierra improved. It terminates in 1867, where this study commences, and thus is not dealt with here.

24. Sierra, *Political Evolution*, p. 344.

This is a more positive view of the same thing that other historians were saying, that Juárez had to step into politics and build a personal following, which he then set up in office in return for political support. The task facing Juárez was staggering, according to Sierra, and not the work of a day, but Juárez laid firm foundations. He needed an army of steel, but one purged of the old-style political generals. He needed a new financial underpinning and a constitutional bolstering of the executive branch in the face of a "neurotic despotism" embodied in the chamber of deputies. The evil cancer of insurrectionism, however, reminiscent of the days of Santa Anna, threatened to cripple the program. Bold blows were dealt to the rebels, and the people, hoping for lasting peace, became ever more confident in their government.[25]

The Juárez program of unity and progress demanded continuity; and continuity in 1871 required reelection. That in itself implied civil war, for the opposition always claimed that the government arranged its own reelection, and it was never possible for a government to prove otherwise. Porfirio Díaz, focus of the opposition that was jealous and suspicious of ministerial determination and concentration, led the rebellion. The government successfully repressed the rebellion, and the Juárez program was progressing admirably when death cut him down.[26]

The Sierra interpretation of politics in the Restored Republic is clearly subordinate to the overall interpretation of Mexican evolutionary development. It has been accepted and perpetuated by later historians, it is thought here, because of the attraction of the greater interpretation.

Daniel Cosío Villegas, the contemporary historian most thoroughly steeped in the four decades following the collapse of the Maximilian empire, joins a long line of intellectuals who pondered the evolution from the democratic-republican objectives of the Constitution of 1857 to the dictatorship of Porfirio Díaz. Unlike his predecessors, Cosío Villegas rejects the notion that elections before the administrations of Porfirio Díaz were fraudulent. He traces the Comonfort election of

25. Ibid., pp. 348–49.
26. Ibid., pp. 349–52.

1857, the Juárez elections of 1861, 1867, and 1871, the Lerdo elections of 1872 and 1876, and the two elections of 1877 and 1880 conducted by Porfirio Díaz. He concludes that the official returns in each case did reflect the contemporary popularity of the candidates. Rather than estimating the popularity of the candidates by the election results, however, he finds the results accurate because he estimates that the candidates were as popular as the results indeed showed. The argument, according to Cosío, is "not less convincing [and] has to weigh more than the unfounded affirmation of Rabasa of the illegality of all Mexican elections."[27]

A contradiction exists here for the historian of the Restored Republic. It was the conventional wisdom of opposition accounts that governmental politics caused insurrections. Later Mexican authors, particularly Daniel Cosío Villegas, have insisted that the ambitions of militarists, the short-sightedness of opposition journalists, and the interests of shallow politicians caused instability which led to war and dictatorship. One check upon this contradiction is provided by a small number of modern American historians who have recently written directly from documentation about politics during the decade in question. Three of them are worthy of note, Ralph Roeder, Frank Knapp, and Walter V. Scholes. Their works are considered here for the evidence they independently uncovered and, surprisingly, for the different assumptions about the relation between the political process and the rise of the opposition.

Roeder argues that federalism in Mexico following the collapse of the Empire was an anachronism; the war had created a national feeling, and the nation required a corresponding strengthening of the national government. Juárez needed more constitutional powers but was unmercifully attacked by a jealous congressional opposition, which had of necessity played a minor role during the war against the French.[28] The congressional opposition seized upon all executive attempts to enlarge its constitutional authority as proof of dictatorial tendencies. A leader for the opposition to pit against Juárez was difficult to find, but they turned to the military and adopted Porfirio Díaz, who had an enviable war record and a personal following com-

27. Cosío Villegas, *La constitución de 1857*, pp. 129–38.
28. Ralph Roeder, *Juárez and His Mexico*, 2 vols. (New York: Viking Press, 1947), 2:682–83.

posed of army veterans cast upon the impoverished countryside without means of employment.[29] The congressional opposition to Juárez raised up Díaz for the presidential election of 1867 and then claimed governmental manipulation of the election when Juárez won. Roeder ponders that

> such charges were impossible to prove or refute. They were the concomitant of every election in Mexico and the inevitable result of the right of universal suffrage bestowed on a people unprepared to exercise it responsibly. The mass basis of democracy in an electorate which in its overwhelming majority was illiterate, inert, and pliable to all the processes of the political machine, was necessarily a fiction: the reality was supplied by the process of natural selection provided by indirect elections. Droves of illiterate but schooled voters, herded to the polls and handed a prepared ballot by the local bosses and ward-heelers, created the college of electors with whom the actual decision lay and who were subject, in turn, to all the deals, the inducements, the pressures prevalent in more advanced stages of democracy. . . . The machinery invited at every stage, from the raw material to the finished product, manipulation and abuse, which the government was in the best position to exercise, although it held no monopoly of the controls, which were freely used against it.[30]

Roeder calmly describes the bitter air surrounding the election of 1871 as Juárez sought yet another term:

> Politics, in the narrow professional sense, bore the same relations to reality as sport to war, a harmless outlet for the combative instincts, a sham battle fought with conventional sound and fury, which none of the players, for all the zeal they put into it, took seriously. The objurgations of the Opposition were the hackneyed cant of partisan controversy, the objections to his re-election so flimsy that no one but their authors mistook them for genuine arguments.[31]

In this way Roeder recognizes a serious problem and sympathetically dispatches it in favor of Juárez. The charges of the opposition are merely academic and based upon jealousy.

29. Ibid., p. 684.
30. Ibid., pp. 685–86.
31. Ibid., p. 718.

Juárez won a plurality in that election and was declared president by Congress, while the opposition, "definitely defeated by the elections, branded them a scandalous farce and a cynical formality." Díaz, "affected by the volatile gases that rose from the press," rebelled against the election results, but was not followed, for he "mistook the grumbling of the ignorant and the habit of the people of blaming their ills on the government for a mandate to rebel. . . ." "Thus, though with specious complaints and fallacious arguments, the Opposition succeeded at last in creating a real crisis in 1871."[32] Roeder thus diminishes the veracity of the opposition within the government and of Díaz's personal role within the opposition.

The second account in English to note is that of Frank A. Knapp.[33] Whereas others have regularly damned Lerdo for a variety of sins, Knapp so closely identifies with Lerdo that the protagonist's adversaries become enemies of the biographer. Porfirio Díaz is singled out as the perpetrator of violence and a man without principle. In 1871 "Díaz dropped the mask of Cincinnatus" to rebel against the election results by the plan of La Noria.[34] Knapp cites Edward L. Plumb, former United States charge to Mexico, who "accurately described the Plan of La Noria as 'absurd.' "[35] One of Díaz's specific accusations in the *Plan de la Noria*, we will recall, was governmental manipulation of elections.

Concerning the insurrection of Tuxtepec in 1876 by which Lerdo was overthrown Knapp writes that

> when Díaz began "pronouncing" against Lerdo, none with any degree of enlightenment should have been deceived that he was other than a typical barracks leader, without the slightest variation in the usual Mexican motif. Hence, it can be asserted that the men who backed Don Porfirio were composed of the "outs" of the

32. Ibid., pp. 718–21.

33. Daniel Cosío Villegas began an article with the observation that "excepting the North American historian, Frank A. Knapp, no one has seriously studied Sebastián Lerdo de Tejada." ("*Sebastián Lerdo de Tejada, mártir de la república restaurada,*" *Historia Mexicana* 17, no. 2 [October–December 1967]: 169–99.) Since the statement overlooks other studies, the meaning must be that Cosío Villegas prefers the Knapp interpretation.

34. Knapp, *Lerdo*, p. 157.

35. Ibid., note.

political milieu, who hoped for tangible reward: but of principle they knew not the definition.[36]

Again, fraudulent elections were specifically cited in the Plan of Tuxtepec as the motive for that rebellion.

This appraisal of Díaz as an unprincipled, ambitious general is not uncommon, and it is not the particular purpose here to claim the contrary. Porfirio Díaz was a single man. He came to power because he forged a following of men with certain grievances. What is of immediate interest is how Knapp recognized those grievances as real without admitting the connection between them and the armed insurrections of the period. Knapp writes amazingly perceptive and coherent history, but his attachment to Lerdo obstructs logical conclusions. Note his excellent reporting in the following paragraphs.

In the elections for the president of the Supreme Court in 1867 no one received a clear majority, thus throwing the selection to Congress, where Lerdo was favored over Díaz by seventeen state delegations to six. This was obtained "thanks less to his popularity than to the unity of the Juarist party. . . . The decision, coming from a congress which Juárez and Lerdo manipulated, indicated that the Indian President clearly preferred Lerdo as his successor."[37] In reference to the struggle between *Lerdistas* and *Juaristas* in 1870 and 1871 to seat rival slates in the municipal government of Mexico City Knapp says that "Juárez handled [the affair] so as to make clear that he intended to cling to the presidency and to use his decisive political influence toward that end by uprooting all political opposition."[38]

Knapp recognized that Juárez's minister of war, Gen. Ignacio Mejía, illegally used the army in the election process. Following a citation from Mejía indicating Mejía's intention to do so against Lerdo in 1871, Knapp concedes that

Mejía's pregnant remark—that it would be "very difficult for him [Lerdo] to compete"—was not only a veiled commentary on official interference in elections but an accurate forecast of the re-

36. Ibid., p. 236.
37. Ibid., p. 129.
38. Ibid., p. 149.

sults: Mejía would be manipulating the units of the federal army on polling day in behalf of the reelection of Juárez.[39]

Again, in reference to the presidential elections of 1871, Knapp writes that

> the Juarists counted on the larger portion of the bureacracy in federal and state offices in addition to the federal army, always a major and usually a decisive factor in the final result, through direct interference in the balloting and by enforcing the loyalty of the state governors.[40]

In that year *Lerdistas* and *Porfiristas* worked a congressional alliance to thwart Juárez's reelection; however, according to Knapp,

> all the fruits of victory which the [*Lerdo-Porfirista*] League produced were sterile, for Juárez had the funds and machinery of government to expend on his reelection, resources which far outweighed in practical value the legislative maneuvers of the League.[41]

In an excellent paragraph upon the subservience of Congress during the Lerdo administrative Knapp notes that

> throughout his years in office Lerdo kept a firm grip on congress, converting it into a servile tool of his will. The solid majority which he controlled in the legislature was not a reflection of his "popular support," but represented his control over the state governors, who returned cooperative deputies to the national capital, and also the efficacy of the federal army in swaying elections in his favor.[42]

The essence of the matter is shown in this argument: Knapp faults Juárez's decision to seek reelection in 1871

> but not because of the methods he used to realize that end. Lerdo and Díaz and their respective followers had no grounds for complaint upon that score, both using the governmental resources to perpetuate themselves in the presidency when the opportunity arrived.[43]

39. Ibid., p. 151.
40. Ibid., p. 155.
41. Ibid., p. 186.
42. Ibid., p. 158.
43. Ibid.

The argument is sophistry, particularly since Knapp admits that Juárez's electoral violence "partially justified the revolutionary program of the Porfirists."[44] Juárez's electoral violence did justify the insurrection of 1871, from the point of view of the men who suffered by that violence. Lerdo's fraudulent means in 1876 justified another insurrection. Díaz's fraudulent means in 1892 or in 1910 justified Flores Magon and Francisco Madero. The point to make is precisely the one Knapp refuses: Grounds existed for complaint, and armed insurrection did follow fraudulent elections. Nevertheless, Knapp concludes that the *Porfiristas,* and particularly Porfirio Díaz, were men of bastard ambition and little principle, without substantive charges in their complaints.

Walter V. Scholes also finds evidence of electoral fraud, but concedes more substance to the opposition complaints. Referring to the congressional elections of 1869 he writes that "the government intervened very actively . . . and armed force played a role in the balloting of San Luis Potosí, Puebla, and Jalisco. Even in Mexico City . . . polling places were taken over by the police, and ballot boxes were stuffed."[45]

Nevertheless, Scholes does not lay the blame for the 1869 insurrection in San Luis Potosí and Zacatecas to fraudulent electoral practice. He singles out the *convocatoria* of 1867, the administrative policy of reserving appointive positions for unconditional supporters, and the demobilization of the army into a depressed economy. The first and third cause took place in 1867, the revolt in 1869. The immediate political events of 1869 in San Luis Potosí are discussed in chapter 4.

Scholes's best and most complete political analysis concerns the presidential election of 1871.[46] He discusses the composition, programs, and records of the three contending parties, the *Juaristas, Lerdistas,* and *Porfiristas.* Then, well taken, Scholes acknowledges that

> the programs and the record were merely window dressing. The opposition parties recognized the hard political fact that the administration's control of federal funds and the army gave it a stranglehold on success. . . .[47]

44. Ibid.
45. Scholes, *Mexican Politics,* p. 132.
46. Ibid., chap. 7, and his article "*El Mensajero* and the Election of 1871 in Mexico," *Americas* 5 no. 1 (July 1948): 61–67.
47. Scholes, *Mexican Politics,* p. 152.

This recognition led to the *Lerdista-Porfirista* bloc in the Fifth Congress, as well as to the *Lerdista-Juarista* struggle over the control of the municipal government of Mexico City and the struggle for the governorship of Jalisco. Omitted are those of Guerrero, San Luis Potosí, Morelos, and Puebla. Scholes records the breakdown of the opposition bloc and the split in the *Porfirista* party but fails to trace the connection between them.[48] Scholes alone recognizes the substantive complaints in Díaz's 1871 pronouncement of La Noria, but he does not describe the *Juarista* election irregularities. All in all, it is the best account of that tremendous year of 1871.

The most admirable characteristic of Scholes's work, which in this dimension makes it superior to the other two works in English, is the nonpartisan stance. Through it, Scholes helps us break away from the Sierra–Cosío Villegas–Roeder school toward an understanding of how the political system operated.

The conclusion of this short survey of literature, only in reference to the relationship between the political process and insurrections, is that the accounts are less accurate as the authors separate in time from the events, but that the authors who describe the period are generally more accurate than the biographers.

48. This is discussed in chapter 6.

Appendix 6
Description of Roll-Call Votes on Political Issues

The issues selected for the eight roll-call votes, which are used to establish party affiliation in chapter 5, are described below.

Roll-call vote 1. Session of 8 October 1869. The issue here was whether a congressman could question a minister who had been summoned by Congress to make a report. Congressman Herrera had been denied the floor a few days earlier on the grounds that there was no motion on the floor to discuss. In this session he argued that the presiding officer could so deny the floor. Joaquín Baranda and Nicolás Lemus argued against the position. Deputy Montiel was acting president, and Macín was acting secretary. A roll-call vote was taken on whether the presiding officers could deny the floor to a deputy who wished to interrogate a minister. Since congressmen used the tactic to embarrass the administration, an affirmative vote is here considered pro-administration. The proposition failed, seventy to sixty-six.[1]

Roll-call vote 2. Session of 12 October 1869. The credentials committee had earlier been instructed to bring to the floor a resolution of non-admittance for any person elected as congressman who had served the empire in any position during the French Intervention. Many cases had come to a vote in the Fifth Congress, with a tendency toward leniency so as to avoid the necessity of holding new elections. The credential of Juan José Baz is interesting because of his known friendship with Sebastián Lerdo de Tejada, who in 1876 called Baz to the ministry of *gobernación*. The resolution not to seat Baz was defeated seventy to fifty-three, and Baz was admitted. A negative vote is here considered pro-administration.[2]

Roll-call vote 3. Session of 6 December 1869. The Executive had initiated a four-point bill to raise taxes. The standing committee on *hacienda* reported out a resolution to set aside the third and fourth

1. *Diario de los debates, quinto congreso,* 1:130–32.
2. Ibid., pp. 169–70.

points. Castañeda, a *Juarista* congressman, spoke for the committee. He said that the committee recognized the need for higher revenue but did not recommend this particular bill, adding that the committee would soon report out a substitute. Such a rei ort usually satisfied Congress. Observing that Congress would accept the committee report, Mendiolea took the opportunity to associate the vote with a stinging censure of the administration. He blamed the administration for the financial deficit, noting that the executive office had been paid in full, while pensions to widows and orphans had not. He revealed the case of a banker whose tax had been lowered from 20,000 to 3,000 pesos, adding that "it is a great government which strangles the poor [through higher taxation] and enriches the rich." He suggested a half-dozen ways by which expenditures could be cut, starting with Juárez's table.

Matías Romero, minister of *hacienda,* took the floor to destroy Mendiolea's tactic. After he noted that Mendiolea's speech had been indecorous and disrespectful, made of such grave charges that he ought either to present them to a grand jury or keep silent, Romero talked earnestly about the dangers to the peace induced by short pay to soldiers. He then explained the reasoning of the executive bill but stressed that the executive was not insistent upon this particular bill. In an attempt to disassociate the executive from the vote to send the financial problem back to committee, Romero said that the president was quite satisfied that the committee would be considering alternatives. Time ran out before the vote was taken, and the sessions closed.

The next day, Lerdo de Tejada, minister of foreign relations, addressed Congress on the foreign debt. His information was only tangential to the issue before Congress, and quite obviously his real task was to calm the passions of the previous day. When he finished, the secretary of Congress read a message from Romero, asking permission to withdraw the administration bill. At that point Ezequiel Montes, constitutional lawyer and exponent of the ministerial interpretation of congressional-executive relations, became indignant. Whereas the executive had the right to initiate a bill, he said, the withdrawal of a bill required a resolution, which was considered to be a matter of internal congressional ordering. "Since when does it fall to the executive to propose what pertains to the internal deliberations of the chamber?" Montes must have spoken loudly and in anger, for there was commotion in the galleries, and the president of the Congress closed the session. Then commotion broke out on the floor, and the session was opened again but with threats to close it if order did not prevail. Montes continued, turning the attack upon the whole cabinet. Whereas the executive would like Congress to vote for the retirement of the bill, Montes said, "some congressmen present think they should retire the members of the cabinet." Lerdo then maintained that an executive consultation of Congress could not be construed as executive pressure on Congress. Castañeda insisted that the committee report was not designed as a censure of the cabinet. The secretary then stated the matter upon which the final vote was taken: "Would the chamber permit the executive to withdraw its initiative?" After further interchange, an affirmative vote was taken, ninety-eight to forty-seven. The administration was spared a vote that would have been picked up by the opposition press as a censure. An affirmative vote for allowing the executive to withdraw the bill is here considered pro-administration.[3]

Roll-call vote 4. Session of 11 January 1870. In 1869 a rebellion erupted in San Luis Potosí that quickly spread to other states. The situation became critical for the administration, which sought extraordinary faculties in the ministries of war and finance. Congress always considered itself the jealous guardian of individual guarantees and of financial expenditures, and therefore debated long upon this surrender of congressional authority to the executive. An additional factor weighing upon the deputies was the widely expressed assumption that the rebels at San Luis Potosí were inspired by Díaz. Because of the general opinion of the day that insurrectionary activity had to be crushed at all costs to avoid a return to pre-Reform militarism and instability, the bill passed readily, but only after a sizable group used parliamentary methods of delay. One method of delay was the attempt to refuse to allow a resolution for the suspension of procedures, by which passage of the bill would be expedited. Congressman Pablo Herrera, whose voting record demonstrates a pro-administration proclivity, sought the suspension. Avila, whose record demonstrates anti-administration sentiments, spoke against the suspension. The suspension was allowed by a vote of 104 to 50, and the bill became law

3. Ibid., pp. 573–78.

four days later. An affirmative vote for the suspension of procedures is here considered pro-administration.[4]

Roll-call vote 5. Session of 15 January 1870. As Congress was about to adjourn its first period in January 1870, a bill was proposed to cover routine matters during the recess. Article four would allow the executive to appoint a deputy to an office in the executive branch without need to seek special permission from Congress, as was stipulated by law. Congressman Montes accused the committee of the bill's origin of being more ministerial than the ministry, "since it wishes to concede a congressional faculty which the executive had not sought." Congressman Cañedo of the committee stated that the faculty had been sought in a committee meeting with a cabinet minister. Article four was passed into law by a roll-call vote of seventy-one to forty-three. An affirmative vote is here considered pro-administration.[5]

Roll-call vote 6. Session of 7 April 1870. The period of the Restored Republic was greatly troubled by kidnappers and highwaymen. There were honest differences of opinion about whether the individual guarantees of the law were too generous for the needs of pacification. The executive generally held that law-enforcement officials needed more authority to perform their functions, while others argued that the problem lay in the lack of economic opportunity and imaginative leadership to create more favorable conditions of employment. The question was a natural one for party strife, for it could be boiled down to authoritarianism versus freedom and prosperity, or security of life and property versus licentiousness and insurrectionary militarism. Furthermore, opposition groups claimed to fear that suspension of guarantees for kidnappers and highwaymen would be used fraudulently for political reasons in some areas, if opposition politicians could be shot as highwaymen without due process. In April 1870 the issue arose in Congress as the executive sought a suspension of guarantees for one year for kidnappers and highwaymen. The bill passed after considerable debate ninety-four to thirty-one. An affirmative vote is here considered pro-administration.[6]

Roll-call vote 7. Session of 6 May 1870. The insurrection of San Luis Potosí-Zacatecas in 1869 constituted a major threat to the Juárez pro-

4. Ibid., p. 849.
5. Ibid., pp. 874–75.
6. Ibid., 2:71.

gram of internal peace. Not only did federal military units join the rebels, but the insurrection involved officials of state. When Trinidad García de la Cadena, rebel governor of Zacatecas, was captured in battle, letters were found in his baggage which compromised his relative, Trinidad García, an anti-administration congressman. In the congressional session of 18 April 1870 a resolution passed to convene the Congress as a grand jury to hear evidence against Trinidad García. It may be safely presumed that the administration wanted the grand jury to find an indictment justified, for the case would serve well as a precedent against extreme use of congressional immunity, would tend to discredit congressional opposition, would bring into the net of proscribed rebels an avowed *Porfirista,* and would remove an opposition congressman from the voting rolls. (See García's consistent anti-administration voting record in the sample cases.) García was defended by Rafael Martínez de la Torre, but the resolution ("there is sufficient evidence to proceed against the deputy Trinidad García") passed by a vote of sixty-nine to sixty-five.[7] An affirmative vote is here considered pro-adminstration.

Roll-call vote 8. Session of 16 May 1870. On 4 April the Standing Committee on Budgeting reported out a resolution to disapprove the administration's accounting of income and expenditures for the 1868–69 fiscal year. There was a good deal of opposition to the resolution, as is testified by reactions to Congressman Avila's consistent attempts to bring the resolution to debate.[8] At one point Guillermo Prieto argued against debating the resolution on the grounds that it had no practical results and that "it has no other objective than fixing ministerial responsibility" for fiscal deficits.[9] On the day of the final vote Congressman Lemus spoke "of the possibility of giving a vote of censure to the ministers," saying that "they are not infallible and therefore their acts may be reproached one time."[10] Clearly, many congressmen considered the resolution a vote of censure upon the administration. The resolution failed of passage by a vote of eighty-three to fifty-five. A negative vote is here considered pro-administration.

7. Ibid., pp. 280–306.
8. Ibid., 29 April 1870, pp. 240–41; 2 May 1870, p. 261; 7 May 1870, p. 309.
9. Ibid., p. 261.
10. Ibid., p. 309.

Appendix 7

Roll-Call Voting Records on Selected Issues in the Fifth Congress

Columns one through eight of the following charts record the votes of every congressman on the political test cases. Columns A through J are the votes on the ten issues of federal intervention. Columns A–D refer to Querétaro; E–G to Jalisco; H to San Luis Potosí; and I–J to Guerrero. An "o" signifies a pro-administration vote, and an "x" an anti-administration vote. Blanks are abstentions or absences.

	1	2	3	4	5	6	7	8	A	B	C	D	E	F	G	H	I	J
1 Acosta, Juan B.	o	o	o	o	o	o	o	o	o	o	o	o		o	o	o	o	o
2 Aguirre de la Barrera	o	o	o			o	x	x		x	x		x	o	o	o	x	x
3 Alcala y Alcala, J. A.	o	o	o			o	o	o	o	x	o		x			o	x	x
4 Alcalde, Joaquín			x	x		o	x						x	x	x	o	x	x
5 Alcocer				x	x	o	x	x	x	x			x	x	x	o		
6 Alfardo, Jesús	x		x	x	x	x	x	o	x	x	x	x	x	o	o	o	o	o
7 Alva	o		o				o	o	x	x			o	o		o	o	o
8 Alvirez, Luis			o	o	x	o	o	o							o	o	x	x
9 Alvirez, Manuel			o	o	x	o	o	o		o			x	x	x	o	x	x
10 Ampudia, Enrique			o	o	o	o	o	o		o			o	o	o	o	x	x
11 Ancona, Eligio	o	o	o	o	o	o	o	o	o	o	o		x	x	x	o	x	o
12 Andrade, Fernando				o			o	o		x			o	o	o		o	o
13 Andrade, Francisco					o	o												
14 Andrade, Carlos	o		o				o	o		o	x	o	o	o	o	o	o	o
15 Arcaute	o	x	x	x	x	x	x	x	x	x	x	x	x	x	x		x	
16 Arevalo	x	o			x	o	x	o	x	x	x	x	x	o	o			o
17 Avila, Eleuterio	x	x	x	x	x	x	x	x	x	x	x	x	x	x	x	x	x	x
18 Avendano, Juan														o	o		o	o
19 Aviles														o	o			
20 Baez	x		x	x			x		o	o			x	x	x			
21 Balda																	o	o
22 Baranda, Joaquín	x	o	o	x				o	x	x	x	x	x	x	x			

	1	2	3	4	5	6	7	8	A	B	C	D	E	F	G	H	I	J
23 Baranda, Pedro	o	o	o	o	o	o	o		x	x	x	x	x	x	x		o	o
24 Barreiro, Eugenio	o	o	o	x	o	o	o	o		x	x	x		x		x	o	o
25 Baz, Juan José						o	o	o		x			x	x	x	x	o	o
26 Baz, Valente		o				o	o	o					x	x	x		o	o
27 Benítez, Justo					x	x	x	x					x	x	x	o	x	x
28 Berdusco	o	x	o	o	o	o	o	o	o	o	o	o	o	o	o	o	o	o
29 Bohorques	x	o	x	o	o				o	o	o	o	o	o	x	o	o	x
30 Calderón, Florentino P.	o		o	o	o	o	o			x	x	x	x	x	o			o
31 Calvillo	o	o	o	o	o	o	o	o		x	x		x	x	x	x		
32 Camara, M. J.	o	o	o	o			o	o		o	o		x	x	x	o	o	o
33 Canalizo	o		o	o	o													
34 Canseco, Crisóforo	o	o	o	o	o	o	x	o	o	o	o	o	x	o	o	o	x	x
35 Canedo	o	x	o	o	o	o	o	o	x	o	o	o	o	o	o		x	x
36 Carballar	x	x	o	o	x	o	o			x		x					x	x
37 Carballo Ortegat, Albino	o	o	x	x	x	x	x	x	o	o	x	o	x	o	x		x	x
38 Carbó, Juan	x		o	o	x	x	x	x	x		o	o	o	x	x	o	x	x
39 Carrión, Francisco	x	o	x	o	x	x	x	x	o		x	x	x	o	o		x	x
40 Castañeda, Agustín	o	o	o	o	o	o	o	o	o	x	o	x	o	o		o	o	o
41 Castañeda, Eduardo	x	x	o		x	x	x	x	x	x	x	x	x	o	x	o	o	x
42 Castañeda, Jesús	x	x	o		o	o	o	x	x	x	x	x	o	o		o	o	o
43 Castellanos, Miguel			o		o	o	o			x		x	o	o	o	o	x	o
44 Castro, José	o	o	o	x	o	o	x	o		o	o	o	o	o	o	o	o	o

	1	2	3	4	5	6	7	8	A	B	C	D	E	F	G	H	I	J
45 Cejudo	x	x	x	x	x	x	x	x		x	x	x	x	x	x	x	o	o
46 Celaya, J. M.	x	x							x	x	o	x	x	x	x	x	o	o
47 Centeno									x							o		
48 Clavería	x	o	o	o	o	o	o	o	x	o	x	x	x	x	x	o	o	o
49 Condés de la Torre, J.	o	o	o	o		o	o	o	x		o	x			x		o	
50 Contreras, Juan	x	x	x	x			o		x	x	x			o	x	x		o
51 Contreras, Manuel	o	o	o	o			x	o	o	o	o	o	o	o	o		x	x
52 Cortés																	x	x
53 Dávila, Gregorio			o	o		o	o	o				o		o	o		x	x
54 Díaz, Porfirio													x	x		o	x	x
55 Díaz, García	x	x				o			o	x								
56 Díaz de Leon, Jesús	x	o	x	o		o	x	o	x	x	x	x	x	o	o	o	x	x
57 Díez Gutiérrez, Carlos	x	x	o	x		o	x	x	x	x	x	x	x	x	x	x	x	x
58 Dondé, Rafael	x	o	o	o		o	o	o	o	o			o	o	o	o		
59 Doria, Juan C.																		
60 Domínquez, Rafael							o		o						o		o	o
61 Echeverría	o	x	o	o	o	o			x	x	x	x	o	o		o	x	x
62 Elizaga, Lorenzo	x	o	o	o		o		o	x	x	x	x	x	o	o	o	o	o
63 Elizondo	o	o	o	o	x	x	o	o	x	x	x	x	x	o	x	o	x	x
64 Elozúa	o	o	o	o		o		o	x		o	o	o			o	o	o
65 España y Reyes	x	x	o		o	o		o	x	x	x	o	o	o		o	o	o
66 Esparza	x	x	x	x	x	x	x	o	x	x		x	x	x	x	x	o	o

	1	2	3	4	5	6	7	8	A	B	C	D	E	F	G	H	I	J
67 Espinola, Victoriano	o	o	o	o	o	o	o		x	x			x	x	x	o	x	x
68 Espinoza, Francisco	o	o		o	o	o	o		x		x	x	o	o		o	x	x
69 Fernández, Agustín	x	x	o	o	o	x	o		o	x	o	o	o	o		o	x	x
70 Fernández, José			x					o		o	x					x	x	o
71 Fernández, Justino	x		o	o	o	o	o				o			x		o	o	o
72 Fernández, Ramón	x	x	x	x	o	x	x	x	x	x	x	x	x	x		x	x	x
73 Flores	x	x	o	o	x	x	x	o	o		o	x	x	o	x		o	o
74 Galván, F. M.	x	x	x	x	x	x			o		x	x	x	x	x	x	x	x
75 Gaona, Leonides R.	o		o	o	x	x	o	o	o			o	o		o			o
76 García, Alejandro				o	o	o	o	o			x	x	o			o	o	x
77 García, Trinidad	x	x	x	x	x	o	o	o	x	x		o	x	x	x		x	o
78 García Brito, Juan	x	o	o	o	o	o	o	o	o	x	x	x	x	x	o	x	o	x
79 García Guerra	o		x	o	x				x	x		x		x		x	x	o
80 García López	x	x	o	o			o	o										o
81 García Ramírez, Luis																		
82 Garza y Garza, Pedro D.	o	o	x	x	x		x	x	x	x	x	x	x	x	x	x	x	x
83 Garrido, Alejandro	o	o	o	o	o	o		o	o		o		o	o	o		o	o
84 Gil																	o	
85 Gochicoa, Francisco P.	x	x	x		x	x		x	x	x	x	x		o		o	x	x
86 Gómez, Luis	x	o							x	x	x							o
87 González, Francisco W.	o	o	o	o	o	o	o	o	o	x	o	o	x	o	o	o	o	x
88 González y Fernández	o	o		o	o	o	x	o	x	x	x		x	x		o	o	o

		1	2	3	4	5	6	7	8	A	B	C	D	E	F	G	H	I	J
89	González Gutiérrez				o	o				o			o		o	x	o	x	x
90	Gordillo Reynoso						o	o										o	o
91	Goytia, Manuel E.	o	o	o						o	o	o	o		x				
92	Guerrero Moctezuma											o							
93	Gutiérrez, L.	x		o							x		o	o					
94	Guzmán, Ramón	x	x	o	o	o	o	o	x	x	o	o	o	o	o	o	x	x	x
95	Hermosillo	x	x	x	x	x	o	x	x	x	x	o	x	x	x	x	o	x	x
96	Herrera, Hipólito	o	o	o	o	o	o	x	o	x	x	o		o	o	x	o	o	o
97	Herrera, Pablo	x		x	x	x	x			x	x				x	x		x	x
98	Herrera, Rafael		o		o	o	o		o	o				o	o	o		o	o
99	Híjar y Haro, Ramón							x										o	o	o
100	Ibarguen, Pedro	x	x	o	o	o	o	x	o	x	x	o	o				o	o	o
101	Inda, Manuel				o	o	o	o	o									o	o
102	Islas, Gabriel M.	x	o	x	x	x	o	x	o	x	x	o	x	x	x	x	x	o	x
103	Islas, Lauro	x	x	x	x	x	o	x	x	x	x	x	o	x	x	o	o	o	x
104	Landazuri, P.	x	o	o	o	o	o	o	o	o	o	o	o	o	o	x	x	x	x
105	Lebrija, Vicente	x	o	x	o	o	x	x	x	x	x			x	x			x	x
106	Lemus, Nicolás	x	o	x	o	o	o	o	x	x		x	x	o	o	o	o	x	x
107	León Armas			o	o	o	o						x					x	x
108	Lerdo de Tejada, Fco.	x	x	o	o	o	o	o	o	o	o	o	o	o	o	o	o	x	x
109	Lobato, José G.	x	x	o	o	x	o	o	o	o	x	o	o	o	o	o	o	x	x
110	López, Jesús Fructuoso		o	o	o	o	o	o	x	x	x							x	x

	1	2	3	4	5	6	7	8	A	B	C	D	E	F	G	H	I	J
111 López, José F.	O												O	O	x			O
112 López de Nava, Agustín	O	x	O	O	O	O		O	x	x	x	x					O	O
113 Lozano, José María	O	x	O	O	O				x	x	x	x	O	O	O	O	x	x
114 Macin, Fco. Delfín	x	O	O	O	O	O	O		x	x	x	x			O	O	x	x
115 Mancera, Gabriel	x					O		x	x		x	x	x	x	x	x	O	O
116 Mancilla, Antonio	x			O				O		x	x	x	x	x			O	O
117 Márquez			x						O	x		x	x	x	x	O		
118 Mártinez de la Concha								O	x	x	x	x	x	x	x		O	O
119 Martínez Negrete, J. M.	x	x	x	x			x	O	O	O				x			x	x
120 Martínez de la Torre	O		O	x							x		x	O		O		
121 Martínez Vaca	O	O	O	O	O	O	O	O	x	x	O	O	O	O	O			O
122 Mejía	O	O			O				x		O							
123 Mejía, Enrique A.				O	O								O	O	O		O	O
124 Mejía, Francisco				x	x	x	x						x		x		O	O
125 Mena, Francisco	O		x	x	x	O	x		x	x	x	x	x				x	x
126 Méndez Salcedo	x	x	x	x	x	x	O	O	O	x		O	x			O	x	x
127 Mendiolea, Manuel	x	x	x	x	x	x	x	O		O	x	x	x	x	x		x	x
128 Menocal, Francisco	O	x	O	O	O	O	O	x	x	x			x	O	O	O	x	x
129 Merino, Justo			x	x	O	x	x	x			O		O	x	x	x	x	x
130 Millan	O		O	O	O	O	x	O	x	x			x	O		O		
131 Molina, O.			x	x	x	O	O	O					O				x	
132 Montes, Ezequiel	O	O	x	O	x	O	x	x	x	x	x	x	x	x	x	x	x	x

	1	2	3	4	5	6	7	8	A	B	C	D	E	F	G	H	I	J
133 Montiel, Isidro A.	o	o	o	o	o	x	o	x	o	x	o	o	x	o	o		x	x
134 Morales, Antonio		o		o			o	o		x	o		x			o		x
135 Morales Puente, Manuel	o	o						o								o		
136 Moreno, Espiridión	x			x		o			x				x	o	x		x	x
137 Múgica y Osorio, Juan	x	o	o	o	x	o	x	x	x	x	x	x	x	o	x	o	o	o
138 Muñoz, José Eligio	o	o	x	x	x	x	x	x	x	x	x	x	x	x	x	x	x	x
139 Muñoz Silva	x	x	x	x	x	x	x	x	o	o			x	x	x	x	x	x
140 Muro, Manuel	o					o			o									
141 Núñez, Lázaro	x	o	x		x	o	x	x	x	x	x	x		o	x	o	o	o
142 Necoechea																		
143 Obregón	x	o	o	o	o	o	o	o	x	x	o	x		o	o	o	o	o
144 Ogarrio	x	o	o	x	x	o	x	x	x	x	x	x	x	x	x		x	x
145 Ojeda	o	o	o	x	x	x	o	x						x	x		x	x
146 Ordórica			x				x	x					x	x	o		x	x
147 Orozco, Ricardo	x	x	x	x	x	o	x	o		x	x	x		o	o	x	x	x
148 Ortega	x	o		o		o	o	o			o	x	o	o	x	o	o	o
149 Ortiz de Montellano	x	x	x		x	x	x	x		x	o	x	o	o	o	o	o	o
150 Patino				o	o	o	x	x										
151 Peniche, Manuel	o	o	o	o	o	o	o	o	o	o	o		o	o	o		x	x
152 Peón Contreras, Juan	x	o	o	o	o	o	o	o	o	x				x				
153 Perales, Antonio		o	o	o	o	o	o	o				o	o	o	o	o		
154 Pérez, Joaquín Oton	x	x	o	o	o	o	o				o		o	o	o	o	x	x

		1	2	3	4	5	6	7	8	A	B	C	D	E	F	G	H	I	J
155	Pérez Jardón, Gregorio	x	o	o	o	o	o			x				o	o		o	o	o
156	Prieto, Guillermo		o	o	x		o	o	o		o			x	x		o	o	o
157	Prieto, José		o		o					o	o		o	o	o	o		x	x
158	Puig y Sevilla																	x	x
159	Quintanar	x	x	x	x	x	x	x	x	x		x	x	x	x	x		x	x
160	Quiñones, Toribio			x		x		x	x				x	x	x	x	x	o	o
161	Ramos, Onofre	o	o	o	o	o	o	o	o	x	x	x	x	o	o	o	o	o	o
162	Ramos, Santiago	x	x	x			o	x	x	x		x	x	x	x	x	x	o	o
163	Ramírez, Ricardo				o		o	o	o					o	o		o	o	o
164	Revilla			o	x					x	o	o							o
165	Rincón, Manuel E.	x	o	x	x	x	x	x	o	x	x	x	x	x	x	x	x	o	o
166	Rios						o							o	o	o	o		
167	Rivas, Carlos	o	o				o			x				o	o	o		x	x
168	Rivas Góngora, Luis					x													
169	Rivas, Luis													x				o	o
170	Rivas Palacio																		
171	Robert, Cipriano	o	o	o	o	o	o	o	x	x				o	o		o	x	x
172	Rodríquez, Ramón	o	o	o	o	o	o	o	o			o	o					o	o
173	Rodríquez de la Vega	o	x	o	o	o	o	o	o	o		o	o	o	o	o	o	x	x
174	Rojas, J. Luis	o	o	o	o		x	x	o	x	x			o	o	x		o	o
175	Rojas, J. Manuel			x	x					x				o	o	x			o
176	Rojo, Manuel	o	o	x			o				x						o	o	o

		1	2	3	4	5	6	7	8	A	B	C	D	E	F	G	H	I	J
177	Rojo, Mariano	o	o				o	o	o	o	o	o		o	x	o	o	o	o
178	Romero, José	o	o	o	o	o	o	o	o	o	x	o	o	o	o	o	o	o	o
179	Romero Rubio, Manuel	x	x	o	o	o	x	x	x					x	o	x		x	x
180	Rosas, Gregorio						x	x	x				o	x	x	x		x	x
181	Saavedra, Manuel	x									x								o
182	Salas			o							x								
183	Sánchez, Atilano			x	x	x	x	x	x	o	o	x	x	x	x	x	x	x	x
184	Sánchez, Eulalio	o	x		o	o	o	o	o	x	x	x	x		x	x	o	o	o
185	Sánchez Azcona, Juan	x		x	x	o	o	o	o	x	x	x	x	x	x	o	o	o	o
186	Sánchez Solís			o	o		o	o						o	o				
187	Sandoval	x		x	o	o	x	x	x		x	x	x		o	x		o	o
188	Sanromán			x	x			o	x			x	x					x	x
189	Santacilia, Pedro	o	o	o	o	o	o	o	o	o	o	o	x	o	o		o	o	o
190	Serrano, F.			x	x			x			x	x							
191	Soto, Francisco	o	x	o	o	o	o			o	o	o			o				
192	Soto, Manuel Fernando	o	o		o	o	o	o	o	x	o	o	o	o	x	x		o	o
193	Suárez del Real		o	o	o	o	o	x	x	o	x	o	o	x	o	o	x	x	x
194	Tagle	o		x	x	o	o	x		o	x		x	x	x	x	x	x	x
195	Talancón	x	x	x	x		o	x	x		o		o	o		x	o	x	x
196	Talavera	o	o	o	o	o				o	o	o	o	x	x	x	x	o	o
197	Tapia, A.	o	o	x	x					o			x	x	x	o	o	o	o
198	Tellaeche	x	o	x	x					o	x		x	x	o	o	o	x	x

	1	2	3	4	5	6	7	8	A	B	C	D	E	F	G	H	I	J
199 Torre, León Alejo	o	o	o	o	o			o	x	x	o	o	o	o	o		o	o
200 Treviño, Cayetano E.	x	o	o	o	o		o	x	o	x	o	x	o	o			x	x
201 Unda, Juan Santos		o	o			o	o	o	o		x		x	x			o	o
202 Urbina, Juan				x	o	o	x	o			x	x	x	x	x	o	o	o
203 Urquidi		o	o		o	x	o	x					x	x	x		x	o
204 Vallarta, Ignacio Luis	o	o	o	o	x	o	o	o	x		o	x	o	o		x		
205 Valle, Guillermo										x		o				o	o	o
206 Vega, Joaquín			o	o	o			o				x						
207 Velarde																o		
208 Velasco, Emilio	x	o	o	o	o	o	o	o	o	o	o	o	o	o	o	o	x	x
209 Vigil, José María	o	x	o	o		o	o	o	o		o	o	o	o	o	o	x	x
210 Villada, José Vicente	x	x	x	x	o	o	x	x		o	o	o	x	o	o	o	x	x
211 Zamacona, M. M. de	x	x	x	o	x	x	x	o		x	o	x	o	x	x	x	x	x
212 Zamora, B. Vicente	x	x	o	o	x	x			x	o	o	x	o	o	o	o	x	x
213 Zárate, Julio	x	x				o	o		o		o	o	x	o	o	o	x	x
214 Zarco, Francisco	o		x					o	o	o	o	o	o	x				
215 Zayas, Juan	x					o		o	x	x	o	x		o	o	x	x	x
216 Zenteno			o				o	o			x	o	x	o				
217 Zerega, Francisco	o	o	o	o	o	o	o	o	x	x	o		o	x	o		o	o
218 Zetina, Manuel	x	x	o	o	o	o	x	x	o			o			o		o	o
219 Zurita	o	o	o	o	o	o	x	x					x	x		x	o	o

Appendix 8
Scores for All Congressmen

The following charts indicate the scores of each congressman in this manner:

column 1—the "test score"

column 2—the "federal score"

column 3—the "improved federal score"

column 4—the "improved federal score" after the elimination of the Guerrero vote from the known *Lerdistas*.

Three stars indicate that insufficient votes were cast to calculate the score. The criterion for calculation was five votes cast for the eight "test cases," five votes for the ten "federal cases," or four votes if they were consistently pro- or anti-administration.

	Congressmen	1	2	3	4
1	Acosta, Juan B.	100	100	100	100
2	Aguirre de la Barrera	***	38	42	56
3	Alcala y Alcala, J. A.	83	50	56	56
4	Alcalde, Joaquín	20	***	50	***
5	Alcocer	***	***	50	50
6	Alfaro, Jesús	0	0	0	0
7	Alva	100	75	75	75
8	Alvirez, Luis	83	50	56	56
9	Alvirez, Manuel	80	***	***	***
10	Ampudia, Enrique	100	71	75	100
11	Ancona, Eligio	100	44	50	67
12	Andrade, Fernando	***	83	67	67
13	Andrade, Francisco	***	***	***	***
14	Andrade, Carlos	100	89	92	92
15	Arcaute	14	0	0	0
16	Arevalo	***	38	56	56
17	Avila, Eleuterio	0	0	0	0

	Congressmen	1	2	3	4
18	Avendano, Juan	***	100	100	100
19	Aviles	***	***	***	***
20	Baez	0	40	50	50
21	Balda	***	100	100	100
22	Baranda, Joaquín	60	0	0	0
23	Baranda, Pedro	100	22	33	33
24	Barreiro, Eugenio	86	29	25	25
25	Baz, Juan José	***	33	25	25
26	Baz, Valente	100	40	50	50
27	Benítez, Justo	0	0	0	0
28	Berdusco	86	100	100	100
29	Bohorques	80	78	67	67
30	Calderón, Florentino P.	100	71	78	78
31	Calvillo	100	38	50	50
32	Camara, M. J.	100	50	50	50
33	Canalizo	***	***	***	***
34	Canseco, Crisóforo	88	40	33	33
35	Canedo	88	80	75	100
36	Carballar	50	0	0	0
37	Carballo Ortegat, Albino	33	0	0	0
38	Carbó, Juan	17	67	63	63
39	Carrión, Francisco	14	0	0	0
40	Castañeda, Agustín	100	89	92	89
41	Castañeda, Eduardo	29	38	50	50
42	Castañeda, Jesús	43	33	42	42
43	Castellanos, Miguel	100	71	75	75
44	Castro, José	75	100	100	100
45	Cejudo	0	22	25	25
46	Celaya, J. M.	***	60	67	67
47	Centeno	***	***	***	***
48	Clavería	88	25	42	42
49	Condés de la Torre, J.	100	60	67	67
50	Contreras, Juan	20	***	***	***
51	Contreras, Manuel	80	67	58	58
52	Cortés	***	60	50	50
53	Dávila, Gregorio	100	71	75	100

Congressmen	1	2	3	4
54 Díaz, Porfirio	***	***	***	***
55 Díaz, Garcia	***	***	***	***
56 Díaz de León, Jesús	***	50	50	67
57 Díez Gutiérrez, Carlos	0	0	0	0
58 Dondé, Rafael	88	100	100	100
59 Doria, Juan C.	***	***	***	***
60 Domínquez, Rafael	***	100	100	100
61 Echeverría	83	14	33	33
62 Elizaga, Lorenzo	***	67	75	75
63 Elizondo	75	20	33	33
64 Elozúa	100	71	83	83
65 España y Reyes	67	67	81	81
66 Esparza	20	13	25	25
67 Espinola, Victoriano	100	13	25	33
68 Espinoza, Francisco	100	38	50	67
69 Fernández, Agustín	57	67	69	92
70 Fernández, José	***	60	50	50
71 Fernández, Justino	86	40	50	67
72 Fernández, Ramón	0	29	25	25
73 Flores	33	25	25	25
74 Galván, F. M.	13	33	33	33
75 Gaona, Leonides R.	***	***	100	100
76 García, Alejandro	100	86	75	75
77 García, Trinidad	17	0	0	0
78 García Brito, Juan	88	50	56	56
79 García Guerra	***	11	8	8
80 García López	60	***	***	***
81 García Ramírez, Luis	***	***	***	***
82 Garza y Garza, Pedro D.	29	0	0	0
83 Garrido, Alejandro	100	100	100	100
84 Gil	***	***	***	***
85 Gochicoa, Francisco P.	0	38	50	67
86 Gómez, Luis	***	***	50	50
87 González, Francisco W.	100	67	61	81
88 González y Fernández	80	38	50	50
89 González Gutiérrez	80	40	50	50

Congressmen		1	2	3	4
90	Gordillo Reynoso	***	***	***	***
91	Goytia, Manuel E.	100	86	67	67
92	Guerrero Moctezuma	***	***	***	***
93	Gutiérrez, L.	***	***	***	***
94	Guzmán, Ramón	57	75	67	100
95	Hermosillo	13	11	8	8
96	Herrera, Hipólito	86	50	56	56
97	Herrera, Pablo	0	0	0	0
98	Herrera, Rafael	80	100	100	100
99	Hijar y Haro, Ramón	***	***	100	100
100	Ibarguen, Pedro	57	67	75	75
101	Inda, Manuel	100	***	100	100
102	Islas, Gabriel M.	50	43	44	44
103	Islas, Lauro	14	11	25	25
104	Landazuri, P.	63	80	75	75
105	Lebrija, Vicente	17	0	0	0
106	Lemus, Nicolás	57	33	50	67
107	León Armas	80	50	50	67
108	Lerdo de Tejada, Fco.	71	71	75	75
109	Lobato, José G.	63	70	69	69
110	López, Jesús Fructuoso	100	20	33	50
111	López, José F.	***	***	34	34
112	López de Nava, Agustín	86	33	50	50
113	Lozano, José María	80	44	50	67
114	Macín, Fco. Delfín	86	14	33	50
115	Mancera, Gabriel	***	22	25	25
116	Mancilla, Antonio	***	33	33	33
117	Márquez	***	29	44	44
118	Martínez de la Concha	***	25	33	33
119	Martínez Negrete, J. M.	17	33	33	33
120	Martínez de la Torre	***	***	67	67
121	Martínez Vaca	100	75	83	83
122	Mejía	***	***	***	***
123	Mejía, Enrique A.	***	100	100	100
124	Mejía, Francisco	0	***	50	50
125	Mena, Francisco	20	0	0	0

	Congressmen	1	2	3	4
126	Méndez Salcedo	50	43	42	42
127	Mendiolea, Manuel	14	13	11	11
128	Menocal, Francisco	67	50	50	67
129	Merino, Justo	0	14	25	25
130	Millan	86	60	67	67
131	Molina, O.	***	***	***	***
132	Montes, Ezequiel	38	0	0	0
133	Montiel, Isidro A.	75	56	47	71
134	Morales, Antonio	***	***	50	50
135	Morales Puente, Manuel	***	***	50	50
136	Moreno, Espiridión	***	20	17	17
137	Múgica y Osorio, Juan	50	40	58	58
138	Muñoz, José Eligio	25	0	0	0
139	Muñoz, Silva	0	25	25	25
140	Muro, Manuel	***	***	50	***
141	Núñez, Lázaro	29	44	63	50
142	Necoechea	***	***	***	***
143	Obregón	100	100	100	100
144	Ogarrio	33	17	11	11
145	Ojeda	57	0	0	0
146	Ordórica	***	0	0	0
147	Orozco, Ricardo	33	29	50	50
148	Ortega	***	71	67	67
149	Ortiz de Montellano	17	78	83	83
150	Patino	***	***	***	***
151	Peniche, Manuel	100	71	67	100
152	Peón Contreras, Juan	***	***	25	25
153	Perales, Antonio	100	100	100	100
154	Pérez, Joaquín Oton	71	67	67	100
155	Pérez Jardón, Gregorio	80	83	75	75
156	Prieto, Guillermo	83	67	75	75
157	Prieto, José	***	75	67	100
158	Puig y Sevilla	***	***	***	***
159	Quintanar	0	0	0	0
160	Quiñones, Toribio	0	29	25	25
161	Ramos, Onofre	100	60	75	75

Congressmen		1	2	3	4
162	Ramos, Santiago	17	22	25	25
163	Ramírez, Ricardo	100	100	100	100
164	Revilla	***	80	84	84
165	Rincón, Manuel E.	14	20	25	25
166	Rios	***	100	100	100
167	Rivas, Carlos	***	50	33	33
168	Rivas Góngora, Luis	***	***	***	***
169	Rivas, Luis	***	***	50	50
170	Rivas Palacio	***	***	***	***
171	Robert, Cipriano	***	50	50	50
172	Rodríquez, Ramón	100	***	100	100
173	Rodríquez de la Vega	86	78	75	75
174	Rojas, J. Luis	71	63	67	67
175	Rojas, J. Manuel	***	60	56	56
176	Rojo, Manuel	60	***	67	67
177	Rojo, Mariano	***	***	50	50
178	Romero, José	100	100	100	100
179	Romero Rubio, Manuel	67	70	69	92
180	Rosas, Gregorio	***	0	0	0
181	Saavedra, Manuel	***	***	***	***
182	Salas	***	***	***	***
183	Sánchez, Atilano	0	25	25	25
184	Sánchez, Eulalio	86	50	67	67
185	Sánchez Azcona, Juan	***	30	50	50
186	Sánchez Solís	***	100	100	100
187	Sandoval	17	43	50	50
188	Sanromán	***	***	0	0
189	Santacilia, Pedro	100	89	94	94
190	Serrano, E.	***	***	50	50
191	Soto, Francisco	***	***	***	***
192	Soto, Manuel Fernando	100	57	56	56
193	Suárez del Real	80	67	58	88
194	Tagle	40	0	0	0
195	Talancón	0	38	25	25
196	Talavera	100	89	88	88
197	Tapia, A.	***	33	33	33

	Congressmen	1	2	3	4
198	Tellaeche	***	60	67	67
199	Torre, León Alejo	100	75	83	83
200	Treviño, Cayetano E.	67	43	44	67
201	Unda, Juan Santos	100	50	50	50
202	Urbina, Juan	60	60	67	67
203	Urquidi	60	17	17	17
204	Vallarta, Ignacio Luis	***	33	33	33
205	Valle, Guillermo	100	63	75	75
206	Vega, Joaquín	***	***	***	***
207	Velarde	***	***	50	50
208	Velasco, Emilio	88	78	75	100
209	Vigil, José María	***	78	75	100
210	Villada, José Vicente	43	78	75	75
211	Zamacona, M. M. de	14	0	0	0
212	Zamora, B. Vicente	40	30	38	38
213	Zárate, Julio	57	78	75	100
214	Zarco, Francisco	***	100	***	***
215	Zayas, Juan	67	50	42	63
216	Zenteno	***	29	17	17
217	Zerega, Francisco	100	71	67	67
218	Zetina, Manuel	50	88	92	92
219	Zurita	71	40	33	33

Appendix 9
Statistical Analysis of Congressional Voting

The records of the Fifth Congress established a precedent for format which continued for many years. Among the changes from the records of the Fourth Congress was the inclusion of the names of the congressmen who voted for and against a measure whenever a roll-call vote (*votación nominal*) was sought by a majority of the congressmen present. The record of roll-call votes allows one to correlate the voting record of individual congressmen in the attempt to judge the degree of factionalism in Congress.

In an attempt to determine factional alliance eight "test cases" are chosen from the first eight months of the Fifth Congress. All the cases are chosen as political issues upon which factional loyalty to the president or a sense of opposition might be measured. The eight test cases were chosen from a larger number after subjecting them to a statistical analysis of variation.[1] The test cases are described in appendix 6, and the roll-call voting on them is recorded in the first eight columns of the charts in appendix 7. Throughout, an "o" signifies a pro-administration vote, and an "x" signifies an anti-administration vote. From this information a score may be assigned to each congressman, indicating the percentage of his pro-administration votes cast on the eight test cases. These test scores are recorded in column one of the charts in appendix 8.

It is an arbitrary operation to assign score ranges for identifying party affiliation. The chart below indicates the problems inherent in the attempt. The figures in column one indicate the number of congressmen who would be tabulated as pro-administration voters, anti-administration voters, and independents if it could be assumed that scores between thirty-four and sixty-six determined an independent,

1. The probability for rejecting the hypothesis that all test cases measured the same quality (factionalism in Congress) among the pro-administration party was .05 and for the anti-administration party .001. Formulas and probability charts from Franklin A. Graybill, *An Introduction to Linear Statistical Models* (New York: McGraw-Hill, 1961).

with lower scores indicating opposition, and higher ones identifying pro-administration congressmen. Column two records the percentage of the total congressmen in each of the three groups. In similar manner columns three and five record the numbers of each group, using limits of thirty and seventy, and twenty and eighty, respectively, for dividing the range of scores into the three groups. Columns four and six are the percentages in each case.[2]

TABLE 1

Congressional Factions in Absolute Numbers and Percentages According to Test Scores

	1	2	3	4	5	6
Range limits	34–67	%	30–70	%	20–80	%
Pro-administration	79	54	74	51	67	46
Independent	23	16	32	22	43	30
Anti-administration	43	30	39	27	35	24
Total	145	100	145	100	145	100

Considerable variation appears in the numbers of factional congressmen simply by varying the criteria for factional voting a few percentile points. *Juaristas* controlled between 46 and 54 percent of the chamber, the opposition controlled between 24 and 30 percent of the chamber, and independents were perhaps as few as 16 percent or as numerous as 30 percent. Clearly, establishing absolute limits for score ranges in order to distinguish factional alliances cannot be done.

Although we cannot define the factions with certainty, it remains clear that a significant number of congressmen maintained a voting pattern that negates a hypothesis that the voting proceeded on the merits of the issue. That is, the voting patterns, when graphed on a simple "yes-no" basis, conform closely to a normal distribution curve, but when charted as pro-administration or anti-administration votes, the pattern polarizes, indicating that many congressmen held a political position vis-a-vis the executive.

Important votes on the issue of using federal power to resolve problems in the states, discussed in chapter 5, were recorded in col-

2. The table omits seventy-four congressmen who had insufficient votes to calculate a "test score," using the criterion for inclusion the casting of five votes or a 100 percent record on four votes.

umns A through J of appendix 7. The ten roll-call votes came from the cases of Querétaro (columns A–D), Jalisco (columns E–G), San Luis Potosí (column H) and Guerrero (columns I and J). Similar to the test score for each congressman, a so-called federal score has been calculated, based on the percentage of votes cast in favor of the presidential alliances with governors and state factions. The federal scores are recorded in column two of the charts in appendix 8.

With this information we may return to the original hypothesis of chapter 5, that congressmen voted on the issue of federal intervention in state politics according to the political realities of factional interest. This hypothesis is supported if a positive correlation exists between the two sets of scores.

The Pearson Product Moment Correlation is a measure of such correlations. Ranging between -1 and $+1$ (the former indicating a perfect negative correlation and the later the reverse), the Pearson Correlation should be near zero if federal voting were totally unrelated to the test scores. Using all the cases of congressmen where data is available on both scores, the coefficient is found to be 0.63. The level of significance of the coefficient is .001, meaning that the chances that the results are in error are one out of one thousand.[3]

The correlation is again demonstrated in the graph below, which summarizes a scattergram of the 137 pairs of scores. The test scores are ranged from zero to 100 on the vertical axis and the federal scores on the horizontal axis. The graph is further divided at the points of 33 and 67, roughly marking off the pro-administration congressmen, the independents, and the opposition, as measured by the test scores. The number in each cell is the number of congressmen who voted within the score ranges indicated on both axes.

One notices the increase in the number of cases in the administration row of cells from nine through twenty-eight to thirty-nine—indicating the heavy concentration on the right sides of the graph, which

3. The formula for the Pearson Product Moment Correlation is

$$\frac{[n \cdot \Sigma (x_1 \cdot x_2)] \cdot [(\Sigma x_1) \cdot (\Sigma x_2)]}{\sqrt{[(n \cdot \Sigma x_1^2) - (\Sigma x_1)^2] \cdot [n \cdot \Sigma x_2^2) - (\Sigma x_2)^2]}}; \quad n = 137.$$ A chart for

the level of significance is found in Robert K. Young and Donald J. Veldman, *Introductory Statistics for the Behavioral Sciences*, 2d ed. (New York: Rinehart and Winston, 1972), p. 542. Further calculations are made below to improve the measure of the data, which raises the correlation coefficient to .63 and finally to .67.

corresponds to the support of the administration on the federal issues. Similarly, the number of cases in the bottom row of cells, representing the opposition, decreases from thirty-two through seven to
two, indicating again a correlation of opposition between the two sets
of issues. Indeed, one notices that, although the opposition in the
Juárez Congresses always claimed that the administration lined up
votes (for important issues, one presumes), the opposition had a more
tightly correlated voting pattern than did the administration on these
issues.

GRAPH 1

Correlation of Test Scores and Federal Scores by Sectors

Administration faction	9	28	39
Independents	8	4	8
Opposition	32	7	2

This manner of viewing the voting results lends itself to the "chi
square (χ^2) test." The graph is repeated below, wherein the "O" in
each cell repeats the number of cases observed and the "E" tells the
number of cases expected if no association exists.[4]

The value of χ^2 is then found to be 51.8, which is significant at the
.01 level.[5] This means that the chances that the conclusion is in error
are less than one out of one hundred.

GRAPH 2

Correlation of Test Scores and Federal Scores by Sectors Using the χ^2 Test

				Cases Observed
Administration faction	cell 1 O = 9 E = 27	cell 2 O = 28 E = 22	cell 3 O = 39 E = 27	76

4. The formula is $E = \dfrac{\Sigma R \cdot \Sigma C}{n}$, wherein R = row, C = column, and
n = the number of pairs of scores (n = 137).

5. The formula is $\chi^2 = \Sigma \dfrac{(O-E)^2}{E}$; a chart for levels of significance is
found in Young and Veldman, *Introductory Statistics*, p. 544.

				Cases Observed
Independent	cell 4 O = 8 E = 7	cell 5 O = 4 E = 6	cell 6 O = 8 E = 7	20
Opposition	cell 7 O = 32 E = 7	cell 8 O = 7 E = 12	cell 9 O = 2 E = 15	41
Cases observed	49	39	49	137

Key: O = cases observed; E = cases expected by chance. Notice the four corner cells, which are significant: cell numbers 1 and 9 have greatly fewer observed cases than expected by chance, and numbers 3 and 7 have greatly more observed cases than expected by chance.

Conclusions for this discussion are simple and clear. First, the *Juaristas* did not have an automatic majority. Second, the opposition was apparently too large to support the contention that Juárez had an effective political machine by 1869, when the Fifth Congress was elected. Third, the size of the independent group explains the dramatic constitutional debates for which the Congresses of the Restored Republic were famous, debates which would not have been necessary had either the *Juaristas* or the opposition controlled a majority.

Fourth, the hypothesis is statistically acceptable—a significant tendency existed in the Fifth Congress for congressmen to cast their ballots on the issue of whether to use federal forces in state political disputes according to which political faction on the national level would benefit from federal intervention.

The federal scores can be improved by changing their weights from equality among the ten votes to equality among the four state situations. Thus, one, two, or three votes on the Jalisco issue is worth one through four votes on the Querétaro issue, and equal to the single vote on San Luis Potosí, as well as either or both votes on the Guerrero issue. New calculations were made using these criteria for an "improved federal score," which is recorded for each congressman in column three of the charts in appendix 8.

Again using the Pearson Correlation, the following coefficients are recorded in table 2.

TABLE 2
Correlation on the Whole Congress

	Federal Score	Improved Federal Score
Test Score	.63	.64

One final calculation is here offered. The historian using statistical methods must not place the methods above his historical knowledge. We know that as long as Sebastián Lerdo de Tejada was secretary of *gobernación,* he used his office to establish in Congress a group of congressmen loyal to him. Lerdo broke relations with Juárez in January 1871 to campaign against Juárez for the presidency, and *Lerdista* congressmen formed a coalition, then known as the *liga* or the *unión,* with the *Porfiristas* and together voted against the *Juaristas.* For a few weeks in the spring and summer of 1871 the *liga* was able to outvote the *Juaristas.*

One of the state issues recorded in this study came to a vote in Congress after the *liga* was performing. Indeed, the *Porfirista* and *Lerdista* congressmen agreed to exchange votes, whereby *Porfiristas* would vote to install the *Lerdista ayuntamiento* in the municipal government of Mexico City against the *Juarista ayuntamiento,* in return for *Lerdista* votes on the Guerrero issue, which would have favored the Catalán-Jiménez government against the *Juarista* Arce government in time for the 1871 presidential elections.[6]

In the preceding calculations, *Juaristas* and *Lerdistas* have been added together, for indeed *Lerdistas* were part of the Juárez alliance. The "Guerrero business" came to a vote in April 1871, and most *Lerdistas* complied with the *liga* agreement. A Porfirian congressmen later wrote to Díaz that eight *Lerdistas* has broken their pledge, but he did not name them.

Inasmuch as the *liga* in Congress was an arrangement to vote according to factional interest, a new correlation is here calculated, having omitted the Guerrero votes from the records of known *Lerdistas.* The following thirty-five congressmen are identified as *Lerdistas* according to the sources of the information cited.

6. See chapter 5.

T A B L E 3
Lerdistas in the Fifth Congress

1	2	3	4	5
Aguirre de la Barrera	Lázaro Núñez[8]	Jesús Castañeda	José María Lozano[10]	Eligio Ancona
Joaquín Alcalde		Emilio Velasco		Cañedo
Enrique Ampudia		José María Vigil[9]		Gregorio Dávila
Jesús Díaz de León				Francisco Espinoza
Rafael Dondé				Augustín Fernández
Victoriano Espínola				Justino Fernández
Francisco P. Gochicoa				Francisco W. González
Ramón Guzmán				León Armas
Nicolás Lemus				Manuel Peniche
Jesús F. López				José Prieto
Francisco Delfín Macín				Suárez del Real[11]
Francisco Menocal				
Isidor A. Montiel				
Manuel Muro				
Joaquín Oton Pérez				
Manuel Romero Rubio				
Cayetano E. Treviño				
Julio Zárate				
Juan Zayas[7]				

[7]Source: Alberto María Carreño, *Archivo General Porfirio Díaz, memorias y documentos*, 30 vols. (Mexico: Editorial Elede, 1946–61), 10:330–33.
[8]Source: ibid., 9:159–60.
[9]Source: Knapp, *Lerdo*, p. 153.
[10]Source: Tamayo, *Juárez*, 14:710.
[11]These congressmen are identified as *Lerdistas* in another study of the *liga* prepared by the author.

By withdrawing the Guerrero votes (variables I and J in the data charts in appendix 8), the coefficient on the Pearson Correlation between the test scores and the improved federal *Juarista*–minus–*Lerdista* scores is 0.67, well above the 0.001 level of significance for 141 pairs of data, meaning that the chances of error in the conclusion are less than one out of one thousand.

Appendix 10
The *Porfiristas* Accept Lerdo's Amnesty

Most of the rebels of La Noria rushed to accept Lerdo's amnesty. Some could accept it in a sense of victory: they had fought Juárez's reelection, and Juárez was no longer president. Others could accept an escape from a poorly led insurrection without defeat, punishment, or accusation of disloyalty. Others were encouraged to accept amnesty as the prospects diminished for a total victory because of the loss of Juárez as the enemy and the defection of fellow insurrectionists who had already accepted the amnesty. Two major rebel leaders had already indicated to the government their willingness to negotiate, Treviño after his victory at Topochico against Diódoro Corella, and Pedro Martínez, whose earlier antagonism against Treviño had grown.[1] Miguel Negrete and Luis Mier y Terán accepted the amnesty on 1 August, Pedro Martínez on 2 August, Pepe Cosío Pontones, Aureliano Rivera, and Jesús Betazos soon after. A host of others followed, Méndez, Carrillo, and Lucas in the Sierra de Puebla, Márquez in the west, Vicente Jiménez in Guerrero. Treviño sought amnesty on 29 August. Donato Guerra successfully negotiated with the government in September; the Sinaloa rebels who still held Mazatlán accepted amnesty in early October; and Díaz was forced to concede also, doing so only one day before the electoral colleges met on 27 October 1872.[2] The amnesty did contribute to the early pacification of the nation. By the time Díaz accepted, he had no other choice, because he had no allies.[3]

1. Cosío Villegas, *La Noria,* pp. 258–59.
2. A list of rebels who early accepted amnesty appears in *Monitor Republicano,* 7 August 1872; see also Bulnes, *Rectificaciones,* p. 226, and Riva Palacio, *Lerdo,* pp. 65, 81.
3. Díaz tried to negotiate his amnesty; it is discussed in Bancroft, *History of Mexico,* 6:392–96.

Appendix 11
The Assault on Matamoros

Porfirio Díaz's assault on Matamoros on 2 April 1876, carried out on the ninth anniversary of his assualt on Puebla in 1867, has not been handled well in printed works. Díaz's admirers have turned it into a heroic military feat, while his detractors have stressed the elements of treason which were also involved. No agreement has existed in the sources about the numbers involved on either side.

Hubert Howe Bancroft wrote a decade later that "the 40 men who followed General Díaz [over the border] soon expanded to 400 and more, and with those he marched against Matamoros, key to the North east."[1] That is probably the most accurate figure in print. It compares almost exactly with the total number of recruits described in chapter 8. In addition, Díaz wrote to Donato Guerra that "after overcoming very serious difficulties, I have been able to put into action in front of Matamoros 400 very well-armed cavalry. . . ."[2]

The government forces at Matamoros are placed at 2,000 by García Granados, Quevedo y Zubieta, and López-Portillo.[3] Cosío Villegas, using the Brownsville *News* as a source, reports that 600 men of the national guard at Matamoros joined Díaz after the fall of that city, and that, according to a Mexico City newspaper, Díaz took 550 federal soldiers as prisoners.[4] These figures imply that there were 1,150 defenders. Bancroft says that Díaz took 700 prisoners.[5] But since there were few casualties on either side,[6] and only a small squadron accompanied General Bernabé de La Barra in his flight,[7] the resultant figure is only slightly over 700. *El Federalista*, a Matamoros newspaper, placed the final defenders at Casa Mata, exclusive of federal cavalry

1. Bancroft, *Vida de Porfirio Díaz, reseña histórica y social del pasado y presente de México.* (San Francisco: The History Co., 1887), p. 500.

2. Díaz to Guerra, 18 March 1876, APD, 12:83–84.

3. Quevedo y Zubieta, *El Caudillo*, p. 236; López-Portillo, *Porfirio Díaz*, p. 113; García Granados, *Historia de México*, 2:139.

4. Cosío Villegas, *República restaurada*, pp. 869–70.

5. Bancroft, *Vida de Porfirio Díaz*, p. 501.

6. Díaz to Fidencio Hernádez, 7 April 1876, APD, 12:160.

7. Cosío Villegas, *República restaurada*, p. 870.

and all the national guard, at 500, assuring its readers that those forces were seriously outnumbered by the attackers.[8]

Consistently overlooked by historians is the figure reported by General La Barra himself, the lowest on record: Matamoros, he said after the battle, had 500 defenders.[9] A general who had lost a battle had motive for understating his support; however, there is reason to believe him. A Lieutenant Johnson of the United States Navy and commander of the *USS Rio Grande,* then docked at Matamoros, thought Díaz's forces were between four and five hundred, "insufficiently armed and without much organization," and added that, although small, the force was not smaller than that which the government had organized to resist the attack.[10] Furthermore, Díaz wrote to Protasio Tagle one month before the assault that there were 450 *Lerdistas* in Matamoros.[11] By then, Lieutenant Colonel Arroyo had already arrived with 149 infantry and 38 cavalry.[12] On 13 March González wrote to Díaz that Col. Manuel Parrat entered Matamoros with 150 men. But these were doubtless the same forces, returning from a sally, that had arrived from Camargo on 3 March and had therefore been included in the earlier counts, for a few days past mid-March Díaz wrote to General Naranjo that he was, "about in equilibrium with the enemy."[13] If no other major change occurred during the next two weeks, which appears to be a correct conclusion,

8. Cited in Ceballos, *Aurora y Ocaso,* 2:442.

9. As early as 2 January, General La Barra, then administrative head of the Matamoros customhouse, had recommended to President Lerdo that Matamoros be reinforced: Ignacio Mejía to Carlos Fuero, 2 January 1876, ADN, 481.4:9224:2; La Barra was raised to commanding officer of the garrison in March due to complaints about Gen. José Cristo's judgment: Carlos Fuero to Ignacio Mejía, 3 March 1876, ibid., C–42:111:60; the La Barra report was written the day after the assault in Brownsville to his commanding general, Carlos Fuero, in Monterrey. No one reconstructing the events of 2 April has used the report, possibly because of the belief that La Barra was blaming others for his mistakes. It is printed in full in Ceballos, *Aurora y ocaso,* 2:902–5.

10. Cited in McCornack, *"Frontera tejana,"* p. 394.

11. Díaz to Tagle, 7 March 1876, APD, 12:38.

12. Cristo to Ignacio Mejía, 11 January 1876, ADN, 481.4:9224:19.

13. Manuel Gonzánez to Díaz, 13 March 1876, APD, 12:63; Carlos Fuero to Mejía, 3 March 1876, ADN, C–42.D:111:60. Undated answer to letter of Francisco Naranjo to Díaz, 16 March 1875, APD, 12:73.

then La Barra's figure is the best: only some 500 men were defending Matamoros.

If Bancroft's account is the most accurate in reference to statistics, it is deficient in the basic tactics of the assault. Here is his description:

> The smallness of the force which yet lacked organization animated the garrison cavalry to effect a sally. . . . The old revolutionary ardor seized the general, who led the counter attack with such vigor that the enemy column pulled back and then fled toward the gates of the city. The attackers followed closely, gaining the drawbridge before it could be raised.[14]

We are assured by González a month later, as he was fortifying Matamoros against an attack of the government forces, that on one side of town "there is no wall nor ditch for a distance of a little more than a thousand meters."[15] Why Díaz entered the front gate of the city becomes apparent later, rather than in Bancroft's account. He proceeds:

> The pace of the charge was slowed by the sheer mass of fugitives fleeing toward the plaza but caught in the narrow streets. This loss of time enabled the surpris d and desperate commander [of the government forces, Gen. Bernabé de La Barra] to seek his salvation on the other side of the river in territory belonging to the United States. He had remained long enough to see his cavalry surrender. The infantry maintained itself a short time longer in the fort, but then followed the example of the others [in surrendering].[16]

That Díaz had a "fifth column" in that town was well known shortly after Matamoros fell to the *Tuxtepecanos,* and it has been recorded by most historians since then. Porfirio Díaz certainly has not lacked admirers among historians; however, none of them has chosen to deal with this colorful episode, leaving it to Díaz's detractors, who have accepted the maxim that no respectable general steals a victory without proper announcement and full frontal attack. Notice the tone of López-Portillo:

14. Bancroft, *Vida de Porfirio Díaz,* p. 500.
15. Manuel González to Díaz, 14 May 1876, CPD, 1:21.
16. Bancroft, *Vida de Porfirio Díaz,* p. 500.

The history written during the autocratic regime of Porfirio Díaz, claims that he, at the head of 500 improvised soldiers, without artillery, without money, and with but a few poor weapons, attacked at full charge and took the city of Matamoros, defended by 2,000 men, well supplied with cannons and with abundant provisions of war. A second prodigy! Another miracle! In sum, a new Second of April! But the truth is that he took the city by the defection of the garrison officers, Toledo, Ramírez Torrón, and Villarreal. . . .[17]

Carleton Beals wrote that in Brownsville Díaz was "buying arms, directing the frontier chieftains, and getting together a band of ruffians," but that he

was having much trouble arranging the betrayal of Matamoros. Toledo [an officer in Matamoros] wrote him March 9, predicting his fall "into the abyss." The revolution was "nothing but bastard ambitions . . . degenerate filibusterism," defending no political idea except Porfirio's own "rise to power." Díaz wished "thousands of men to die" merely that he might "for a little while occupy the gilded presidential seat." Matamoros would never aid him in such a "crime. . . ." Díaz begged Toledo for a personal interview to correct his "lamentable error," and whether eloquence, promises, bribery or all three turned the scales, Toledo was won over.[18]

López-Portillo and Beals have their basic data but have misinterpreted them. The Toledo and Díaz letters from which Beals quoted were published in Mexican newspapers of the day.[19] Not available to Beals, and not used correctly by Carreño or his users, was the correspondence between Toledo and Díaz before Toledo's damning letter was published on 9 March. Carreño, referring to it, wrote:

. . . General Toledo . . . demonstrated scruples about uniting . . . with the rebel, perhaps supposing that by having established himself in Brownsville, [Díaz] was going to receive some aid from the United States. General Díaz asked him to come talk with him and

17. López-Portillo, *Porfirio Díaz*, p. 113.
18. Beals, *Porfirio Díaz*, pp. 201–2. Ellipsis in the original.
19. Ceballos, *Aurora y ocaso*, 2:438; reproduced, 895–98; also see Jesús Toledo to Díaz, (no day) March 1876, APD, 12:23–25; Díaz to Toledo, 9 March 1876, APD, 12:48.

see that all his fears were unfounded. Surely he [Díaz] convinced him [Toledo], because [the latter] shortly joined [Díaz] and together they initiated the campaign against Matamoros.[20]

Carreño is not convincing. Cosío Villegas deserves closer attention: "One of the 'businesses,' " he wrote, taking the word from some Díaz correspondence to supporters, "which detained Díaz in Brownsville so long and which could not be confided to anyone, was to secure the defection of the defenders of Matamoros." By the end of February the affair "was well advanced"; "General Díaz should never have doubted a certain one of the defenders who was considered willing to run his luck." He was referring to Toledo. Cosío points out, however, that Toledo's forces were but a few armed guards. To have control of the federal troops or of the state militia (national guard), Díaz had first to win over the main officers. Díaz thus set Toledo to work on Colonel Parrat. After the occupation of the city Díaz would see to Parrat's "well-merited rise."[21] All of this needed Toledo's care, arranged at night in successive personal rendezvous at the water's edge. More important than Parrat was La Barra, commanding general at Matamoros in early March. For this Toledo gained La Barra's confidence by repeated assurances of loyalty, which won for Toledo the rank of general and command of the national guard. Toledo went even further by publishing the denunciation of 9 March, which was applauded in Mexico City as a noble deed. Díaz answered rapidly, publishing his letter proposing an interview.[22]

The implication in Cosío's account is that the Toledo letter of 9 March, which denounced the Porfirian movement as filibusterism, was written after Toledo and Díaz were in agreement. Supporting this conclusion are four other pieces of correspondence between Jesús Toledo and Porfirio Díaz in the Díaz papers; there were more letters, referred to by those extant. Besides the letters, there was verbal communication during nocturnal meetings on the banks of the Rio Grande. The correspondence and meetings, all but one prior to the published one of 9 March, indicate that Toledo and Díaz came to an

20. APD, 4:20.
21. Cosío Villegas, *República restaurada*, p. 866; Díaz to Toledo, 3 March 1876, APD, 12:33.
22. Citations and paraphrasing from Cosío Villegas, *República restaurada*, pp. 866–68.

agreement. The 9 March letter almost assuredly does not represent a breakdown in the previous relationship, for Díaz in his answering letter suggests a personal meeting in order to convince Toledo of his errors, a meeting which would have been superfluous in view of the previous meetings. Indeed, the probable object of publicly suggesting such a meeting was to allay suspicions of earlier meetings. To voice the same arguments used by the partisans of the government so that Toledo would more thoroughly win the confidence of the government—and the command of government forces—seems to have been the object of the Toledo letter.

This conclusion seems to be what Cosío implies. Then, however, Cosío errs:

> Porfirio, interviewed by Toledo, lost confidence in him since his conduct seemed suspicious; therefore, in order to affirm his adhesion, perhaps it would be best to write a compromising letter which would fall into the hands of General La Barra.

It would appear that General Díaz was not above blackmail in order to gain adherents to his small cadre. Cosío's implication is that this is what happened, for

> the cooperation of the national guard of Matamoros in effect secured the success of the capture of that city—a capture, however, which was not precisely a battle.[23]

This interpretation, that General Díaz was suspicious of Toledo's loyalty, rests upon the incorrect reading of two other letters in the APD, an unsigned note written in Matamoros dated 29 February and the letter dated 23 March suggesting that a "compromising letter" be allowed to fall into the hands of General La Barra to force Toledo to take his stand with the *Porfiristas*. Carreño says that the handwriting of the note appears to be that of Gerónimo Treviño.[24] Cosío Villegas, correct in writing that Treviño was never in Matamoros during the Rebellion of Tuxtepec, holds that the author of the note was "very probably Jesús Toledo."[25] About that Cosío is again correct.[26] The important points are as follows:

23. Ibid., p. 869.
24. APD, 11:334.
25. Cosío Villegas, *República restaurada*, p. 866.
26. Not merely "very probable," but *certain*, for it fits absolutely into the context of the other letters which are signed and dated. See below.

2: I cannot explain why General Díaz lacks confidence in my adhesion to his person when he has so many proofs of my loyalty and abnegation.

3: If I have manifested my desires to him to wait, it has only been because I do not know the elements he has on hand; mine in this city, without the order of a certain person, are naught. This person has to resolve in three or four more days, as the general [Díaz] knows.

4: I am sure that the resolution of this person will be favorable, because of recent news I have.

7: General Díaz should never lack confidence in a friend such as I. . . .[27]

Obviously, doubt existed in the relationship between Díaz and Toledo; but the doubt was Toledo's, not Díaz's. Overlooked by Cosío was Díaz's answer to the note, dated 2 March. Point by point the note is answered:

2: You are right. A lack of confidence between us would have no explanation, inasmuch as we are working toward the same ends, excepting that we are using different means. . . .

The leader of men is speaking: "You are right, but you must do things the way I tell you." The note continues:

3: I have not told you of the internal elements because I have never found you completely resolved to emancipate yourself from the person mentioned. I know that if you were aware of them you would be decidely with me, judging the question exclusively from practicality; but I also know that if a previous commitment ties you to that person, you will resent me and for that reason I have not been very explicit; please pardon me, but occupy for a moment my place, and I know that you will do the right thing.

"You could know the secrets, too; I have not wanted to try your loyalties; you would do the same as I," the salesman says.

4: I do not understand upon what you base your hope that that "person" will resolve in *pro*.

Carreño writes that *"persona"* is Justo Benítez, which is erroneous. *"Persona"* is General La Barra.

27. (Toledo) to Díaz, 29 February 1876, APD, 11:334–35 (numbered in the original).

7: Excuse me again, you have my good faith [*mi apretón de mano*] and I reproduce my number two.[28]

That task done for a temperamental follower, Díaz could sit back and await the windfall. But even before Toledo was given his answers he wrote Díaz on 1 March, "I accept your way if it is best and shortest; your judging it so is sufficient for me." Of the other persons Toledo wanted involved he wrote, "I see your reasons for reserve and I respect them, but I am able to assure you upon my word that I have no loyalty other than to you."[29] Díaz had his man; now an apparent concession could be made so that his follower could keep his self-respect and carry no grudges:

I see success assured with my identification with you and the two persons you refer to and . . . now my reserve has no object. . . .[30]

If there was a breakdown of confidence between Díaz and Toledo, it was repaired before the 9 March letter, and long before the mention of a "compromising letter" on 23 March.

The compromising letter to be directed into La Barra's hands is the second letter, which seems to have led Cosío Villegas to his conclusions.[31] Carreño assigns the letter to Porfirio Díaz but admits his doubt with a question mark after the signature. It was supposedly written to Servando Canales in Ciudad Victoria. Letter writing in the nineteenth century can cause difficulties, for the practice varied from person to person regarding the position of the names of the recipient and sender on the page. Either one or the other's name and address might be placed at the end of the letter. Furthermore, because correspondence in that time of warfare was carried by runners, who could inform the recipient of the sender's identity and who could be captured, the signature was frequently omitted. Handwriting is not always a clue; both Porfirio Díaz and Servando Canales had secretaries. Internal logic argues, however, that the letter did not originate with Díaz. The sender, besides declaring that "the conduct of Toledo has been and is very suspicious," regrets that the receiver has recently moved. Díaz had crossed the international frontier three days earlier;

28. (Díaz to Toledo), 2 March 1876, ibid., 12:27–28.
29. Toledo to Díaz, 1 March 1876, ibid., p. 25.
30. Díaz to Toledo, 3 March 1876, ibid., p. 32.
31. (Servando Canales to Díaz), 23 March 1876, ibid., pp. 106–7.

Canales had been in Ciudad Victoria for some time. Furthermore, the letter suggests a plan whereby Amador and Loperena would join La Barra in Matamoros in a Trojan horse operation; then the receiver would retire his forces to Mier, a city some 120 miles from Matamoros, in order to draw off La Barra's loyal soldiers, leaving the city, garrisoned by Porfirian sympathizers, open for a sudden appearance by the rebel forces. General Díaz was in such a position to withdraw; Canales had not yet pronounced nor entered military activity. Moreover, General Díaz was not suggesting strategy in those days; he was the object of suggested strategy. The conclusion must be that Díaz was the receiver, not the sender. Díaz did not write the sentiments on 23 March harboring suspicions of Jesús Toledo, who was already well within the Porfirian ranks; the suggestion of using blackmail was not Díaz's; and the pressing business detaining Díaz in Brownsville after the first week of March was not the defection of Matamoros, which was already arranged. It was probably finances and armament.

Nevertheless, the letter is an interesting one, for it presents a plan similar to that which was used. When Díaz appeared before Matamoros on 2 April, the cavalry unit which left the city in a sally against the invaders was led by Porfirian partisans. That unit was not sent reeling back into the city in full retreat, as Bancroft describes, to surrender in the city square. It *joined* Díaz, tipping the numerical scales in Díaz's favor, and attacked the city with him.[32]

Furthermore, the Canales letter reveals that Toledo was not the only individual in Matamoros who was working with the *Porfiristas*. This has been uncertain history. López-Portillo names Ramíerz Torrón and Villarreal, as well as Toledo, as those whose "infidelity" enabled Porfirio Díaz to capture Matamoros.[33] Of persons by the names of Ramírez and Villarreal, common enough in Spanish, the Díaz papers are so replete that guessing which ones were sought by the *Porfiristas* for their aid is sheer speculation. For example, one municipal official (*alférez*) in Matamoros by the name of Anatasio Ramírez was being hunted by Porfirian officials after the capture of the city as late as 26 April, while one Luis Ramíerz of the government forces in Matamoros, according to information that Peña had a week

32. This was stated quite clearly by General de la Barra in his official report: Ceballos, *Aurora y ocaso*, 2:902–5.

33. López-Portillo, *Porfirio Díaz*, p. 113.

before the city was assaulted, was "suggested for [and] wants to speak with Loperena."[34]

The most important Villarreal was one Sebastián of that surname, who on 2 April was an official of the national guard of Matamoros—the unit which defected.[35] Quevedo y Zubieta, in describing the battle, mentions that the "national guard, some captained by General Toledo, others by Colonels Cristo and Villarreal, remained inactive."[36] If López-Portillo assumed, however, that Villarreal had taken his unit to the enemy on the evidence that that unit did indeed defect, he is in error. In early March Sebastián Villarreal was in Texas, pursued by forces of the United States for recruiting for the *Tuxtepecanos* in that country against the recognized government of Mexico.[37] With thirty-five men he joined Manuel González on 11 March.[38] In all probability, inasmuch as Díaz led the forces that General Gonzáles had collected, Sebastián Villarreal fought with Díaz in the capture of Matamoros, but not from the inside. Being a native of that region and having demonstrated his ability, he was probably appointed to his position within the national guard of Matamoros on that same day, but after the battle.[39] If this was the Villarreal López-Portillo meant, he did well to omit the given name, for another Villarreal was playing a vital and heretofore unknown role in the conspiracy preceding 2 April.

Elena Villarreal de Ferrer, a woman living in Brownsville, was attracted to the Porfirian cause in January 1876 by Miguel de la Peña.

34. Manuel Gonzánez to Díaz, 26 April 1876, APD, 12:257; Miguel de la Peña to Díaz, 26 March 1876, ibid., p. 119. (No Ramírez Torrón appears in the Díaz papers.)

35. Budget of the National Guard of Matamoros signed by Sebastián Villarreal, 2 April 1876; ibid., p. 129.

36. Quevedo y Zubieta, *El Caudillo*, p. 237.

37. Sebastián Villarreal to Díaz, 11 March 1876, APD, 12:60.

38. Manuel González to Díaz, 11 March 1876, ibid., p. 60.

39. Seemingly conclusive evidence that Sebastián Villarreal joined Díaz as soon as the latter entered Mexican territory is his name affixed to the Reform of Palo Blanco, declared by Díaz in a location of that name near Matamoros on 21 March—but not so. Cosío Villegas, using a document from the APD (Miguel de la Peña to Porfirio Díaz, 27 March 1876, APD, 12:121), successfully demonstrates that Miguel de la Peña, whose name also appears on the Plan, was not present and even objected to that revision of the Plan de Tuxtepec: *República restaurada*, p. 817.

The first of her several services was conducting correspondence clandestinely between Brownsville and Matamoros, delivering it to the home of one Francisco Bucher twice a day between January and March. By her testimony, written years later to President Porfirio Díaz, she was denounced to General La Barra, Colonel Cristo, and Colonel Parrat, who ordered her apprehension "at all costs." Those three officers, with all the resources at their command, were unable to seize her, however, and she continued her mission "until leaving it finished." Her success might well have been due to some high-placed protection. According to her testimony, one unnamed federalist officer in Matamoros, who regularly employed spies to follow her and know the location of her mother's home in Matamoros where she spent the nights, but who was "in favor of señor General Díaz" and "was in accord with us," helped her to escape to Brownsville, probably when he could no longer protect her.[40] Did one of those three officers knowingly appoint a Porfirian partisan to her case? Might it have been Colonel Parrat?

The loyalty of the other two officers, La Barra and Cristo, has never been questioned and is affirmed by letters in the Díaz papers.[41] José Bravo Ugarto writes that only La Barra and Cristo remained loyal; no one else is mentioned.[42] Cosío Villegas records that Díaz tried to suborn Colonel Parrat through Toledo but is certain only of Toledo as one who aided Díaz.[43] Indeed Cosío states that after the cavalry joined Díaz and he had entered the city

> Colonels Cristo and Parrat hardly fought half an hour; then they learned of the defection and the withdrawal of their superior. By nine o'clock in the morning, Porfirio, at the head of his forces, paraded victoriously through the central streets of Matamoros.[44]

It would seem that Parrat had decided for the government.

That must have been a disappointment for the *Porfiristas*, for they

40. Elena Villarreal Viuda de Ferrer to Porfirio Díaz, n.d., CPD, 40:863.

41. Letters found on the following pages of APD, 12 invariably refer to Colonel Cristo or General La Barra as enemies of the Porfirian cause: 65, 68, 84, 85, 106, 107, 119, 134, 137, 260, 270, 271, 301.

42. José Bravo Ugarte, *Historia de México*, 2d ed. rev., 4 vols. (Mexico: Editorial Jus, 1944), 3:364.

43. Cosío Villegas, *República restaurada*, p. 867.

44. Ibid., p. 870.

had not spared effort to win his allegiance. Miguel de la Peña, after he had occupied Reynosa, wrote to Díaz on 2 March that "the luggage of the officers here is to be given to Parrat and his officers if they second our plan, and if not, [it will be given] to my soldiers as booty."[45]

On the following day Díaz urged Toledo to advise him if Fuentes and Parrat "accept and are as resolved as yourself."[46] General González wrote on 13 March in reference to a skirmish with Parrat that

> it would be convenient for you to put pressure on the com-
> promised ones [of the enemy forces] telling them that if Parrat
> escaped yesterday from a positive disaster, it was for complying
> with your orders not to attack him and to remain on the defense,
> but they ought to respond quickly to our friendly action because
> he was really in our hands.[47]

Parrat, however, remained loyal to the government, serving between June and November of 1876 in the Veracruz-Puebla theater until he joined the *Tuxtepecanos* with Gen. Jesús Alonso on 19 November, three days after the battle of Tecoac and four days before the *Porfiristas* occupied the national capital.[48]

Of other persons aiding Díaz in Matamoros there is more certainty. In a letter Díaz wrote on 19 March to one "B.F." in Matamoros, assuredly Baltazar Fuentes, the municipal president, Díaz went straight to the point:

> Between the two means you proposed to our friend Loperena in
> yesterday's conversation, that of leaving with all the armed
> soldiers that can be gathered, for being more practicable than the
> movement in the city with the conditions which you want, the
> latter would be indubitably better, given the possibility.[49]

The alternatives are suggestive even to one who had not attended "yesterday's conversation," but not absolutely certain. The certainty is

45. Peña to Díaz, 3 March 1876, APD, 12:29.
46. Díaz to Toledo, 3 March 1876, ibid., p. 32.
47. Manuel González to Díaz, 13 March 1876, ibid., p 63.
48. Jesús Alonso and 161 others: manifesto, 19 November 1876; ibid., 13:236–37. Parrat was placed under Alonso's command in the week before the battle of Tecoac: Manuel Parrat to Doroteo León, 13 November 1876, ibid., p. 205.
49. Díaz to Baltazar Fuentes Farías, 19 March 1876, ibid., 12:90.

that the nocturnal meetings were group affairs, involving at least two and maybe more officers from Matamoros. It would seem that Col. Eugenio Loperena, mentioned so frequently in these intrigues, was the Porfirian agent on the river bank.

Giving still more certainty to the belief that Fuentes was part of the subversion of Matamoros are these lines from the letter quoted above, indicating the confidence Díaz had in him:

> It remains firm, then, that they will leave protected, with myself careful of the day and hour of the event in order to execute a movement which will give confidence to the garrison and turn rapidly to the inside of the walls at the opportune moment. . . . Knowing everything and how it will work, I will prepare myself in advance and will have everything ready.[50]

Again the personal correspondence of Díaz adds overdue credibility to General de La Barra's official report, which explicitly blames Fuentes for the defection of the cavalry which made the sally from Matamoros on 2 April.[51] From this correspondence, it is not unreasonable to conclude that Elena Villarreal's high-placed protection was probably the municipal president, Baltazar Fuentes.

Another *Porfirista* in Matamoros was ex-Colonel Mariano Aguirre de Venero, a municipal official who was using his influence to promote the Tamaulipas gubernatorial campaign of the pro-Díaz incumbent, Servando Canales, against the avowed *Lerdista,* Gen. Rómulo Corella.[52]. Whatever were his services to the cause, he won his reward two days after the fall of the city when Díaz named him postmaster of Matamoros.[53]

After those events of 1876 were long over, Quevedo y Zubieta wrote that Díaz's "excursions were frequent to that city; one night he attended a dance held there in his honor. These comings and goings across the Rio Grande occasioned risks. One Luna was sent out from Mexico with orders to assassinate him. That was not so easy in Matamoros, surrounded as was the *caudillo* with friends, who increased in numbers every day."[54]

50. Ibid.
51. Ceballos, *Aurora y ocaso,* 2:904.
52. Aguirre de Venero to Díaz, 14 January 1876, APD, 11:290–91.
53. Díaz to Aguirre de Venero, 4 April 1876, ibid., 12:140.
54. Quevedo y Zubieta, *El Caudillo,* p. 234.

But Quevedo y Zubieta was wrong. There had been no such excursions into Matamoros. That Porfirian author was wise enough to know there was no battle at Matamoros, but he preferred popular acclamation over political conspiracy as his interpretative framework. Matamoros was not so friendly that Díaz could enter when he pleased. The line from Quavedo y Zubieta, "surrounded as was the *caudillo* with friends" in Matamoros, takes on an interesting additional meaning unsuspected, or unrecorded, by that *Porfirista* historian.

Appendix 12
Porfirio Díaz and the Plateau Strategy

General Díaz's earliest statements in Matamoros are not explicit with reference to the direction of his pending movements. Within five days of capturing Matamoros, Díaz wrote to the leading *Tuxtepecano* general of his home state of Oaxaca that he had occupied Matamoros "with a few losses on my side and few of the enemy. Then I organized a column of 2,500 to 3,000 men, my own and those I conquered, which I will march into the center of the country."[1] Barring fear of intercepted mail, Díaz might have been more frank with a militant partisan who had need to know Díaz's plans. On 11 April Díaz wrote to one Emiliano Martínez in New Orleans the same information; again he omitted the precise direction of the intended march, giving the letter a cautious note.[2]

Then on 14 April Díaz wrote to one Romero Ancona not only that he would march inland but that he would join the forces in Nuevo León, "thus opening a formal campaign upon the cities occupied by the enemy between here and the capital."[3] Whatever degree of confidence may have existed, risk of interception was also present.

By the latter part of April the earlier caution had been discarded. On 20 April one Antonio Guerra in Matamoros wrote to General Díaz objecting to the terms of payment offered to his place of business for mules and horses delivered to the Porfirian forces. Díaz ordered the treasury to pay Guerra in four monthly installments from the income of the customshouse in Laredo "after the occupation of Monterrey."[4] One would like to know if the merchant had been given the information about Monterrey. Meanwhile, a businessman in Monterrey sought by mail a certificate from Díaz that would protect his goods in shipment from other *Porfiristas*. Díaz answered him on 22 April that protection from *Porfiristas* was never necessary, but that anyway, "in

1. Díaz to Fidencio Hernández, 7 April 1876, APD, 12:160.
2. Díaz to Martínez, 11 April 1876, ibid., pp. 183–84.
3. Díaz to Ancona, 14 April 1876, ibid., pp. 202–3.
4. Guerra to Díaz and answer, 20 April 1876, ibid., pp. 223–24.

order to set you at ease . . . within a few brief days I will commence my march toward your city, and . . . my presence there is the best guarantee which I can offer you that your business and person will be respected."[5] A near certain way to make the government aware of his plans was to reveal them to disgruntled merchants.

The same information was imparted to friends and agents. Díaz wrote to his confidential agent, Plácido Vega, on 22 April that "within two days at the latest I will commence the march upon Monterrey."[6] To a friend in Veracruz a week later Díaz wrote that he had left Matamoros "with 2,000 men and I am marching on Monterrey."[7] That was written the day before Díaz changed his entire campaign plan.

Did Díaz plan to march on Monterrey? Puzzling is the case of Lieutenant Governor Antoine of Louisiana, to whom a letter which appears in the Carreño publication of the Díaz papers dated 11 April is addressed. In that letter Díaz stated that he took Matamoros "on the 2nd of this month. . . ." and that

> within a few brief days I will begin my march to the interior of the country with a column of approximately 3,000 men, joining soon the forces of Generals Treviño and Naranjo of Nuevo León, in the number of 1,000 men. Then I will be in a position to commence a serious campaign against the garrisons of Monterrey, Saltillo, San Luis and the Capital.[8]

Francisco Cosmes cites a letter that Díaz wrote from Matamoros which Cosmes says circulated in the Mexican press in May and which carried the date 11 May. That letter was also directed to Antoine. Carrying almost the same information, the letters nevertheless employ different words and phraseology. Furthermore, Díaz's troops are adjusted to 800, as Escobedo would have known on 11 May. The message is the same: Díaz would unite with Treviño and Naranjo, thus having "sufficient force to open a true campaign and advance against Monterrey, Saltillo, San Luis, and finally against the capital."[9]

5. Díaz to Estanislao Hernández, 22 April 1876, ibid., p. 240.
6. Díaz to Vega, 22 April 1876, ibid., p. 239.
7. Díaz to Donaciano Lara, 30 April 1876, ibid., pp. 262–63.
8. Díaz to C. Antoine, Esq., 11 April 1876, ibid., p. 185.
9. Cosmes, *Historia general de Méjico*, 22:779–80.

It is possible that the first letter was sent with an honest reflection of Díaz's expectations and that the 11 May letter was the same one, updated by press editors for news value and printed after having been translated into English and back again. The numbers may have been edited by government newspapermen in order to give the impression to capital city readers that Díaz's recruiting had not been successful. In that case, however, they uncannily chose the right figure. A better explanation is that Díaz wrote both letters, at least the second one designed to fall into government hands. The letters tell too much; the central plateau strategy seems to have been a hoax to mislead the government.

Appendix 13
The Reform of Palo Blanco

Interpretations of the motives for the Reform of Palo Blanco are numerous. Bancroft maintains that the reform represents an abnegation on the part of Díaz, who would have become constitutional president by the first plan because he could have unseated the governors who refused to accept the plan before the elections. Díaz preferred to support the constitution, says Bancroft, by offering the provisional presidency to Iglesias.[1] This argument overlooks the later refusal of Díaz to give the position to Iglesias and Díaz's frank adhesion to a revolutionary course in order to purge the bureaucracy before applying the constitution.

Quevedo y Zubieta maintained that between the publication of the Plan of Tuxtepec and the Reform of Palo Blanco Iglesias had broken from Lerdo and that Díaz did not want his revolution against Lerdo to raise Iglesias to the presidency, as his insurrection of 1871 against Juárez had raised Lerdo to the presidency. Therefore, the Palo Blanco reform was designed to undercut Iglesias.[2] Besides the objection that it was the death of Juárez, not the insurrection of La Noria, which elevated Lerdo to the presidency, one wonders how the offer to make Iglesias the provisional president undercut him. Quevedo's explanation was that it was not in doubt that Iglesias would refuse the offer and that thereafter Iglesias would be "implicitly eliminated" from the provisional presidency.[3] That would have been a good guess, but Díaz apparently was not certain, for he wrote into article six a cumbersome disabling clause in case Iglesias might accept.

López-Portillo suggested that the Reform of Palo Blanco was designed to win the support of Iglesias by making him think the revolution would make him president.[4] This argument rests upon the assumption opposite to that of the former argument, that Iglesias would accept the invitation; nevertheless, the same objection obtains, that Díaz did not want to make Iglesias provisional president, for then

1. Bancroft, *Vida de Porfirio Díaz*, p. 499.
2. Quevedo y Zubieta, *El caudillo*, pp. 235–36.
3. Ibid., p. 236.
4. López-Portillo, *Porfirio Díaz*, pp. 111–12.

Iglesias would control the machinery for the election of constitutional president.

Another interpretation is that the offer was made to force Lerdo's reaction, not Iglesias's reaction. Lerdo could be expected to take all the political advantage available in the situation. It was not certain in March that Lerdo would seek reelection. He was mysterious. He could yet have arranged the mid-year elections for Iglesias in order to deny the antireelection issue to the insurgents. The Porfirian offer to Iglesias was to make irreparable the break between Lerdo and Iglesias.[5] The argument is good, excepting two factors. First, it overlooks the "Spirit of '76"—the suspicions and hostility between Lerdo and Iglesias. Second, it assumes that Lerdo only had Iglesias available as his successor in order to deflate the rebellion. In fact, he might have offered the name of any of a dozen other men.[6]

Cosío Villegas has added to the discussion his opinion that the reform of article six was designed to attract Iglesias to the movement to disqualify him from the elections for constitutional president and thus assure the electoral victory for Díaz. Díaz, however, later turned down Iglesias's collaboration when the same electoral advantage was to be gained and nevertheless won the constitutional presidency by the mere expediency of naming a partisan to the provisional presidency and then offering himself as candidate for constitutional president.

According to Cosío Villegas, Díaz was trying not only to outmaneuver Iglesias but also to outmaneuver his followers. This observation is important, for it recognizes that the *Tuxtepecano* movement was a heterogeneous force. The evidence, however, is erroneous. Cosío has revealed that an earlier reform to the Plan of Tuxtepec was initiated at Reynosa on 2 March. Although a copy of the "Plan of Reynosa" has not come to light, Cosío assumes that the Reynosa reform offered the presidency to Iglesias without specifying what would happen if Iglesias were to refuse to associate himself with the *Tuxtepecanos,* and that without consulting the signers of the Reynosa document Díaz added the concept in the Reform of Palo Blanco that, were Iglesias

5. This is a composite interpretation, drawn by extension and implications.
6. Cosío Villegas argues that Lerdo had no one to propose other than Iglesias: "Lerdo," p. 172; however, candidates have frequently been "manufactured" between nomination and election in many countries.

not to join the movement within thirty days, the executive power would revert to the leader of the revolutionary movement. Thus, Cosío concludes, at Palo Blanco Díaz co-opted the provisional presidency for himself.[7] In this way Díaz thwarted the desires of his followers who at Reynosa saddled him with Iglesias.

Cosío's interpretation is based upon a letter published by Carreño, in which Peña stated that he had seen published in *Progreso*, a newspaper in Brownsville, "a new plan dated the 21st in Palo Blanco, which I consider apocryphal, since my name appears on it, when I have not signed any other than that of Reynosa, which differs substantially."[8]

Two difficulties exist for this interpretation. First, article six of the Reform of Palo Blanco did not extend the provisional presidency to Díaz in the event of Iglesias's refusal. Clearly article six offers Iglesias the "executive power without attributions other than the administrative . . . until elections take place. . . ." The alternative in the event of Iglesias's refusal is phrased in a separate sentence: "The silence or refusal of the functionary who conducts the Supreme Court will invest in the chief of the army the character of Executive Chief." Iglesias thus could be a mere executive administrator or could stand aside and watch Díaz assume total power, which, according to article three, would be without limitations imposed by any other governmental power named by Lerdo or brought to office by the election of 1875.

The second difficulty with the Cosío Villegas interpretation of the motives for inviting Iglesias to join the *Tuxtepecano* movement is that Cosío has misread the information available about the Reform of Reynosa. Peña was not pleased with the changes made at Palo Blanco to the Reform of Reynosa; that is certain. But he was not upset that the Palo Blanco reform invested more power in Porfirio Díaz. "The revolution," Peña explained in the same letter

> seems to me powerful in its means, but needs all the vigor of your intelligence as *caudillo,* and an unmovable base in order to triumph, and in order not to be a mere phase rendering a pacific and legal solution.[9]

7. Cosío Villegas, *República restaurada,* p. 818.
8. Miguel de la Peña to Díaz, 27 March 1876, APD, 12:121.
9. Ibid.

Peña obviously opposed the offer to Iglesias that was made at Palo Blanco, "of which I have heard."[10] Indeed, after hearing of Palo Blanco, Peña wrote his opinion quite clearly:

> The Revolution . . . ought not to obligate the Supreme Court of Justice of the Nation to violate the fundamental code and to convert itself into a revolutionary [force], thus breaking its [legal] titles and lowering its dignity.[11]

Peña thus opposed the offer to Iglesias on theoretical and political grounds. To avoid the theoretical evils of converting the court into a revolutionary force and to work revolutionary political changes rather than a mere "pacific and legal solution," Peña had another remedy: "The only prudent thing is for the revolution to hand over and deposit the supreme power to the person named by the nation."[12]

That is, all power to Porfirio Díaz! The conclusion to be drawn is that the Reform of Reynosa which Peña had signed did not offer a position to Iglesias and may even have given full power to Díaz. Díaz did not co-opt the provisional presidency at Palo Blanco. Indeed, at Palo Blanco, not Reynosa, the first gesture was made to Iglesias.

10. Peña to Díaz, 26 March 1876, ibid., p. 118.
11. Ibid.
12. Ibid.

Appendix 14
The Convention of Acatlán

Even as Iglesias was writing his manifesto concerning the negotiations between the two anti-*Lerdista* factions, Protasio Tagle, newly appointed to the *Tuxtepecano* cabinet as minister of *gobernación*, published a circular which proposed, as did that of Iglesias, that the nature of the negotiations be made known. No mention is made of the October correspondence in the Tagle *Circular*. Iglesias later wrote that his letter of 30 October reached Joaquín Ruiz for transmission to Díaz only on 21 November, two weeks after Joaquín M. Alcalde presented himself in Iglesias's name at Acatlán.[1]

At the Porfirian camp at Acatlán on 6 and 7 November Congressman Joaquín Alcalde held a convention in the name of Iglesias with the Porfirian Generals Díaz, José Couttolenc, Vicente Riva Palacios, and Francisco Mena. The Iglesias manifesto of 1 December says that Alcalde ". . . spontaneously directed himself to the camp of *señor* Díaz, animated by a patriotic desire to unite the forces of the common enemies of the coup d'état . . ." It would seem thus that Alcalde was a mediator at best, not Iglesias's representative. Iglesias admitted, however, that he had earlier given Alcalde "important confidential commissions" for the cause.[2] In the Tagle *Circular* of 29 November it is maintained, however, that Alcalde arrived

> competently commissioned and with the instructions necessary to unify the action of all those who were combating the Lerdo administration, and to solicit certain modifications and reforms in the Plan of Tuxtepec.[3]

At that time, according to Tagle, the Plan of Salamanca (published twelve days earlier) was not known to the *Tuxtepecanos*. Nevertheless, they certainly knew that Iglesias had pronounced.

In view of the circumstances of suspicion and rivalry, the Convention of Acatlán, in tone and in most of its provisions, is an amazingly conciliatory document.[4] By its terms Díaz and the *Tuxtepecanos* were to

1. Iglesias, *Cuestión presidencial*, p. 152.
2. Ibid., p. 381.
3. Tagle, *Circular*, p. 5.
4. The Convention of Acatlán is described with Iglesias's comments article

recognize Iglesias as provisional president. *Porfiristas* and *Iglesistas* were to unite their efforts to overturn Lerdo's administration and to cooperate in the new government. Ten terms were appended. Of them Iglesias accepted four without change: by article three liberty of suffrage would be guaranteed in the elections held by the provisional government; by article four, the interim executive would send an amendment to Congress prohibiting reelection of the president and governors; by article seven, the government would assume the debts of the *Tuxtepecanos* to a maximum of 80,000 pesos; and by article nine, the governors of Puebla and Morelos should be expelled from their offices.

Compromises were made on both sides in these articles. Iglesias's support was mainly from reelection governors, and he specified in his Plan of Government, published with his Manifesto of Salamanca, only that the national president should be ineligible for reelection. Including governors in the prohibition was a *Tuxtepecano* demand, as was also the governmental assumption of the revolutionary debt. On the other hand, the *Tuxtepecanos* were being moderate in limiting to the cases of Puebla and Morelos their demands for immediate dismissal of the governors. The whole nation knew that Iglesias had opposed the governors of Puebla and Morelos in the *amparo* cases. The *Tuxtepecanos* were fighting most governors and had made promises to and interim appointments to governorships for many of their followers.

Iglesias held reservations toward three other articles of the convention of Acatlán. Article one would withdraw recognition of the federal powers that had sustained the reelection. Article two promised new elections. Article eight would establish as policy that anyone who had held office during the Lerdo administration should be barred from the new administration. On each point Iglesias wanted to limit the application to individuals involved in the electoral frauds of 1876 and in the declaration of its legality. Iglesias had too many friends and supporters at all levels of the government—indeed the bureaucracy was the very core of *Iglesismo*—to sanction the thorough purge advocated by the *Tuxtepecanos*, while the rank and file of *Porfirismo* were office seekers.

---

by article in his letter to Díaz of 17 November in *Cuestión presidencial*, pp. 381–86, and is cited in full in Tagle, *Circular*, pp. 17–20, with Iglesias's answer, ibid., pp. 20–26.

Article six stated that Iglesias should choose men of the stature of Joaquín Ruiz and Francisco Gómez del Palacio for cabinet ministers. Iglesias pretended to be offended that the *Tuxtepecanos* thought it necessary to oblige him to promise to appoint honorable and capable men. In truth, the article was highly political and related to article five, discussed below.

Iglesias subjected two articles to strenuous criticism. Article ten proposed that in the east-central states under the control of the revolutionary army the military chiefs be appointed by the commander of the army until the governments of those states were reconstructed with persons who had not supported the reelection. In essence, Díaz intended to govern a large section of the country under military law until men of his party were securely in control of those states, making the eastern and central states of Mexico a bastion of his personal power.[5] Iglesias pointed out that the commander of the army in the constitutional order was the president, who would appoint military commanders as circumstances required, and that the people had constitutional procedures for filling governmental vacancies by themselves. Iglesias was legally correct; he wanted immediate return to constitutional procedure. Procedures favoring legalism, however, favored *Iglesistas* in 1876. Díaz wanted to insure his base of operations. A conflict of fundamental interest was involved.

The second area of conflict was embodied in article five. That article proposed to allot three of the ministers of the provisional government to the *Tuxtepecanos* and three to the *Iglesistas*, with the ministry of war forepromised to Porfirio Díaz. Such a compromise among politicians would seem to be inevitable. Iglesias observed, however, that the procedure attacked the constitutional prerogative of the president to name and remove at will all members of his cabinet. Leaving principle, he then promised to appoint both Ruiz and Gómez del Palacio. The phraseology, however, was unfortunate. It belied that lack of faith which causes compromises to fail—that lack of faith which divided *Iglesistas* from *Tuxtepecanos* in the first place. Iglesias fully meant by his promise to fill two of the three *Tuxtepacano* cabinet appointments with the two men whom both sides regarded as acceptable, Joaquín Ruiz and Francisco Gómez del Palacio, leaving Iglesias his

5. The Republican party in the United States in 1876 was abandoning the same policy with respect to the southern states.

own three choices. Article six, which Iglesias chose to consider offensive for personal reasons, contained the *Tuxtepecano* intention that Ruiz and Gómez del Palacio should figure into Iglesias's three appointments. Then from trickery Iglesias slipped to disaster; he would not accept Díaz into the ministry.

In the whole convention of Acatlán certainly the *sine qua non* from the *Tuxtepecano* point of view was that Díaz should occupy the ministry of war. Had Mexicans been Romans they would have established a *duumvir* in the first place. They had, however, to observe Mexican constitutionality in order to acquire some degree of legitimacy.

Iglesias advanced the argument that in his plan of government he had promised that the interim government would not sponsor an official candidate, and that he and his ministers had promised not to be candidates. He said, however,

> [it] being evident that General Díaz must figure as a candidate in the next elections, his entrance into the Ministry of War breaks the program in one of its essential points. Certain that I am that no one [in the government] would do anything [to insure] the triumph of his candidacy, it is nevertheless indubitable that the suspiciousness of the parties would consider that the liberty of the elections is restricted and that the government has proffered an official candidate.[6]

The real issue from the beginning was who would rule the provisional government. In the overthrow of Lerdo's government, the pacification of the country, and then new elections under some kind of interim administration, the army would govern. Both Iglesias and Díaz wanted control of that army. Iglesias skirted the real issue and chose to stress the promise that no minister would be a candidate. The issue was high politics; they would have to fight.

6. Tagle, *Circular*, pp. 23–24.

Appendix 15

Caciquismo in Mexico

Mexico needed and still needs strong local government with sufficient popular participation to destroy *caciquismo* and *caudillismo*, which have always implied elite monopolization of economic opportunity and exploitation of the weak. Mexicans know this. The following observation is taken from a 1975 popular magazine:

> It is a vicious circle: the authorities are elected every three years, and need to ingratiate themselves with the respective *cacique*, whose outrages and abuses must be endured.
> In this way the public official protects outlaws who in turn support the official against wind and tide.
> Nevertheless, from time to time the indigenous community rebels against the *cacique* and against the public official, and then more serious political conflicts pour forth, because the peasants seize the municipal buildings, which provokes the intervention of the public force, solicited by the public officials.
> The day the authorities issue from truly free popular elections there will be no fear of the *caciques*, because the popular support will give them an incontestable force.
> Here, then, is the first step: if the popular will is respected in the elections for the municipal presidents, they will have a working relationship with the people instead of with the *caciques*.[1]

1. *Impacto,* no. 1315 (14 May 1975), p. 18.

Bibliography

Unpublished Documents

Ann Arbor, Mich. Clements Library. The Porfirio Díaz Papers.

Cholula, Puebla. University of the Americas. Colección General Porfirio Díaz.

Mexico City. Archivo de Cancelados de la Secretaría de la Defensa Nacional.

———. Archivo de la Dependencia de Asuntos Terminados de la Secretaría de la Presidencia.

———. Archivo General de la Nacion. Archivo de Fernando Iglesias Calderón.

———. Archivo General de la Nación. Ramo de Gobernación.

———. Archivo Histórico de la Secretaría de la Defensa Nacional.

———. Gabinete de Manuscritos de la Biblioteca Nacional de México.

———. Museo Nacional de Antropología e Historia. Archivo del General Porfirio Díaz.

———. Museo Nacional de Antropología e Historia. Correspondencia del Archivo del Ejercito de Oriente. Archivo de Lic. Justo Benítez.

Monterrey, Nuevo León. Archivo General del Estado de Nuevo León. Sección Histórica.

U.S. Department of State. Despatches from United States Consuls in Monterrey, 1849–1906. Micro-copy no. M–165.

———. Despatches from United States Consuls in Tampico, 1824–1906. Micro-copy no. M–304.

Manuscripts

Cary, B. Dean. "The Role of the Satirical Press in the Downfall of Sebastián Lerdo de Tejada." Mimeographed. University of the Americas, Puebla, Mexico, 1969.

"Génesis de la revolución tuxtepecano en el estado de Puebla, memorias, apuntes y recuerdos de un testigo presencial, 8 de febrero a 16 de noviembre de 1876." (1909): Centro de Estudios Históricos, Universidad Veracruzana, Xalapa, Veracruz.

Gibbs, William E. "Spadework Diplomacy: United States—Mexican Relations during the Hayes Administration, 1877–1881." Ph.D. dissertation, Kent State University, 1973.

Miller, David Lynn. "Porfirio Díaz and the Army of the East." Ph.D. dissertation, University of Michigan, 1960.

Sinkin, Richard Nathan. "Modernization and Reform in Mexico, 1855–1876." Ph.D. dissertation, University of Michigan, 1971.

Webster, Michael G. "Texan Manifest Destiny and the Mexican Border Conflict, 1865–1880." Ph.D. dissertation, Indiana University, 1972.

———. "Texan Manifest Destiny and the Republic of the Sierra Madre: A Chronicle of an Expansionist Concept." Mimeographed. Paper delivered at the Western History Conference, Fort Worth, Texas, 1973.

Newspapers

El Ahuizote
La Conciencia Pública
El Correo de México
El Diario Oficial
El Globo
El Federalista
El Mensajero
El Monitor Republicano
La Orquesta
El Periódico Oficial del Estado de Nuevo León
El Universal
El Siglo XIX

Printed Sources

Acereto, Albino. *Historia política desde el descubrimiento européo hasta 1920.* Enciclopedia yucatanese, vol. 3. Mexico: Gobierno de Yucatán, 1944–47.

Altamirano, Ignacio M. *Biografía de Ignacio Ramírez.* Mexico: Secretaría de Fomento, 1889.

———. *Historia y política de México.* "El liberalismo mexicano en pensamiento y en acción." Mexico: Empresas Editoriales, 1958.

Anguiano, Angel. *Morelia en 1872: su historia, su topografía y su estadística.* Morelia: Imprenta de Octaviano Ortiz, 1873.

Arnade, Charles W. "The Porfirio Díaz Papers of the William Clements Library." *Hispanic American Historical Review* 33:324–25.

Bancroft, Herbert Howe. *History of Mexico.* 6 vols. San Francisco: History Co., 1885–88.

———. *Vida de Porfirio Díaz: reseña histórica y social del pasado y presente.* San Francisco: History Co., 1887.

Baz, Gustavo. *Vida de Benito Juárez.* 2d ed. Puebla: Editorial José M. Cajica Jr., 1972.

Bazant, Jan. *Alienation of Church Wealth in Mexico: Social and Economic Aspects of the Liberal Revolution, 1856–1875.* Edited and translated by Michael P. Costeloe. Cambridge: Cambridge University Press, 1971.

———. *Cinco haciendas mexicanas; tres siglos de vida rural en San Luis Potosí, 1600–1910.* Mexico: Colegio de México, 1975.

———. "Peones, arrendatarios y aparceros en México, 1851–1853." *Historia Mexicana* 23:330–57.

———. "Peones, arrendatarios y aparceros, 1868–1904." *Historia Mexicana* 24:94–121.

Beals, Carleton. *Porfirio Díaz, Dictator of Mexico.* Philadelphia: J. B. Lippincott Co., 1932.

Bravo Ugarte, José. *Historia de México.* 3 vols. Mexico: Jus, 1944.

———. *Historia sucinta de Michoacán.* 3 vols. Mexico: Jus, 1962–64.

Buelna, Eustaquio. *Apuntes para la historia de Sinaloa, 1821–1882.* Mexico: Departamento Editorial de la Secretaría de Educación, 1924.

Bulnes, Francisco. *Juárez y las revoluciones de Ayutla y de la reforma.* Mexico. 1904.

———. *Rectificaciones y aclaraciones a las memorias del general Porfirio Díaz.* Mexico: Biblioteca histórica de *El Universal,* 1922.

Cadenhead, Ivie E., Jr. "González Ortega and the Presidency of Mexico." *Hispanic American Historical Review* 32:331–46.

Callahan, James Morton. *American Foreign Policy in Mexican Relations.* 2d ed. New York: Cooper Square Publishers, 1967.

Carreño, Alberto María, ed. *Archivo del general Porfirio Díaz: memorias y documentos.* 30 vols. Mexico: Editorial Elede, 1947–61.

[Carrillo, Adolfo]. *Memorias inéditas de don Sebastián Lerdo de Tejada.* Puebla: Imprenta Guadalupana, n.d.

Cavazos Garza, Israel. *Mariano Escobedo: el glorioso soldado de la república.* Monterrey: Publicaciones del Gobierno del Estado, 1949.

Clendenen, Clarence C. *Blood on the Border: The United States Army and the Mexican Irregular.* New York: Macmillan Co., 1969.

Coatsworth, John H. "Railroads and the Concentration of Land Ownership in the Early Porfiriato." *Hispanic American Historical Review* 54:48–71.

Colección de artículos y documentos relativos a los atentados cometidos en Jalisco por D. Sebastián Lerdo de Tejada y D. José Ceballos desde junio de 1875 hasta 6 de enero de 1877. 2 vols. Guadalajara, 1877.

Cosío Villegas, Daniel. *Historia moderna de México, el porfiriato, vida política interior.* 2 vols. Mexico: Editorial Hermes, 1970–72.

———. *Historia moderna de México, la república restaurada, vida política.* Mexico: Editorial Hermes, 1959.

———. *Porfirio Díaz en la revuelta de la Noria.* Mexico: Editorial Hermes, 1953.

———. "Sebastián Lerdo de Tejada, mártir de la república restaurada." *Historia Mexicana* 17:170–96.

———. *The United States versus Porfirio Díaz.* Translated by Nettie Lee Benson. Lincoln: University of Nebraska Press, 1963.

Cosmes, Francisco. *Historia general de México: continuación a la de don Niceto de Zamacois, parte contemporánea, los últimos 33 años.* 4 vols. (19–22). Barcelona, 1900–1902.

Creelman, James. *Porfirio Díaz, Master of Mexico.* New York: Appleton, 1911.

Cuevas, Mariano. *Historia de la iglesia en México.* 4 vols. Mexico: Editorial Patria, 1921–26.

————. *Historia de la nación mexicana.* 3d ed. Mexico: Editorial Porrúa, 1967.

Díaz, Porfirio. *Memorias de Porfirio Díaz, 1830–1867.* 2d ed. 2 vols. in 1. Mexico: El Libro Francés, 1923.

Díaz y Díaz, Fernando. *Caudillos y Caciques.* Mexico: El Colegio de México. 1972.

Didapp, Juan Pedro. *Partidos políticos de México: la político del dinero y la política del patriotismo disputando la sucesión de la presidencia del país.* Mexico: Librería Española, 1903.

Domínguez Castilla, José M. *Ensayo Criticohistórico sobre la revolución de la Noria.* Mexico: Casa impresora el Cuadratín, 1934.

Dublán, Manuel, and Lozano, José María. *Legislación mexicana o colección completa de las disposiciones legislativas expedidas desde la independencia de la república.* 30 vols. Mexico: Imprenta del Comercio a cargo de Dublán y Lozano, Hijos, 1876–1899.

Foster, John W. *Diplomatic Memoirs.* 2 vols. Boston: Houghton Mifflin Co., 1909.

Frazier, Donald J. "La política de desamortización en las comunidades indígenas, 1856–1872." *Historia Mexicana* 21:615–52.

Fuentes Díaz, Vicente. *Los partidos políticos en México,* 2d ed. Mexico: Editorial Altiplano, 1969.

Fuentes Mares, José. "La convocatoria de 1867." *Historia Mexicana* 14:423–44.

Galaviz de Capdevielle, María. "Descripción y pacificación de la Sierra Gorda." *Estudios de Historia Novohispana* 4:113–49.

Galindo y Galindo, Miguel. *La gran década nacional: relación histórica de la guerra de reforma, intervención extranjera y gobierno del archiduque maximiliano, 1857–1867.* 3 vols. Mexico: Imprenta y Fototipía de la Secretaría de Fomento, 1904–1906.

García, Ruben. *El Antiporfirismo.* Mexico, 1935.

García Cantú, Gastón. *El pensamiento de la reacción mexicana: la historia documental, 1810–1962.* Mexico: Empresas Editoriales, 1965.

————. *El socialismo en México, siglo XIX.* Mexico: Ediciones Era, 1969.

García Granados, Ricardo. *La constitutión de 1857 y las leyes de reforma en México.* Mexico: Tipografía económica, 1906.

————. *Historia de México desde la restauración de la república en 1867 hasta la caída de Porfirio Díaz.* Reprint ed., 4 vols. in 1. Mexico: n.p., n.d.

García Naranjo, Nemesio. *Porfirio Díaz.* San Antonio, Tex.: Editorial Lozano, 1930.

Gibaja y Patrón, Antonio. *Comentario a las revoluciones sociales de México.* Mexico: Tipografía Universal, 1934.

González, Luis. *La economía mexicana en la época de Juárez.* Mexico: Secretaría de Industria y Comercio, 1972.

González Navarro, Moisés. *Historia moderna de México, el porfiriato, vida social.* Mexico: Editorial Hermes, 1957.

————. *Raza y tierra: la guerra de castas y el henequén.* Mexico: Colegio de México, 1970.

————. *Vallarta en la reforma.* Biblioteca del Estudiante Universitaro, no. 76. Mexico: Ediciones de la Universidad Nacional Autónoma de México, 1956.

————. "Venganza del sur." *Historia Mexicana* 21:677–92.

Gonzalez Ortega, José. *El golpe de estado de Juárez.* Mexico, 1941.

Gregg, Robert D. *The Influence of Border Troubles on Relations between the United States and Mexico, 1876–1910.* Baltimore: Johns Hopkins Press, 1937.

Guiral Moreno, Mario. *El Régimen porfirista en México: su apoteosis.* Mexico: Librería de Andrés Botas y Miguel, 1913.

Gutiérrez Santos, Daniel. *Historia militar de México, 1876–1914.* Mexico: Ediciones Ateneo, 1955.

Hamon, James L. and Niblo, Stephen R. *Precursores de la revolución agraria en México.* Mexico: SepSetentas, 1975.

Hart, John M. *Los anarquistas mexicanos, 1860–1900.* Mexico: SepSetentas, 1974.

————. "Miguel Negrete: la epopeya de un revolucionario." *Historia Mexicana* 24:70–93.

Hernández, Fortunato. *Un pueblo, un siglo y un hombre.* Mexico: Imprenta de Ignacio Escalante, 1909.

Horgan, Paul. *Great River: The Rio Grande in North American History.* 2 vols. New York: Rinehart and Co., 1954.

Iglesias, José María. *Autobiografía.* Mexico: Antigua Imprenta de E. Murguía, 1893.

————. *La cuestión presidencial en 1876.* Mexico: Tipografía Literaria de Filomena Mata, 1892.

Iturribarría, Jorge Fernando. *Historia de Oaxaca.* 4 vols. Oaxaca: Publicaciones del Gobierno del Estado de Oaxaca, 1956.

————. *Porfirio Díaz ante la historia.* Mexico: Carlos Villegas García, 1967.

Juárez, Benito. *Archivos privados de D. Benito Juárez y Pedro Santacilia.* Edited by José Manuel Puig Casauranc. Mexico: Publicaciones de la Secretaría de Educación Pública, 1928.

————. *Documentos, discursos y correspondencia.* Edited by Jorge L. Tamayo. 16 vols. Mexico: Secretaría del Patrimonio Nacional, 1964–72.

————. *Epistolario de Benito Juárez.* Edited by Jorge L. Tamayo. Mexico: Fondo de Cultura Económico, 1957, 1972.

Knapp, Frank Averill, Jr. "The Aprocryphal Memoirs of Sebastian Lerdo de Tejada." *Hispanic American Historical Review* 31:145–51.

————. *The Life of Sebastian Lerdo de Tejada: A Study in Influence and Obscurity.* Austin: University of Texas Press, 1951.

————. "Parliamentary Government and the Mexican Constitution of 1857: A Forgotten Phase of Mexican Political History." *Hispanic American Historical Review* 33:65–87.

————. "Two contemporary Historians: José María Iglesias and Herbert Howe Bancroft." *Pacific Historical Review* 20:25–29.

Knowlton, Robert J. *Church Property and the Mexican Reform, 1856–1910.* De-Kalb: Northern Illinois University Press, 1976.

León-Portilla, Miguel, et al. *Historia documental de México.* 2 vols. Mexico: Universidad Nacional Autónoma de México, 1964.

Lieuwen, Edwin. *Guerrilla Government in Mexico.* Albuquerque: University of New Mexico Press, 1967.

López Gutiérrez, Gustavo. *Escobedo: republicano demócrata benemérito de Chiapas, 1826–1902.* Mexico: Edición del Autor, 1968.

López-Portillo y Rojas, José. *Elevación y caída de Porfirio Díaz.* Mexico: Librería Española, 1920.

Loret de Mola, Carlos. *Manuel Cepeda Peraza, soldado y estadista de la república.* Mexico: Secretaría de Educación Pública, 1967.

Lozoya, Jorge Alberto. "Un guión para el estudio de los ejércitos mexicanos del siglo diecinueve." *Historia Mexicana* 17:553–63.

McCornack, Richard Blaine. "Porfirio Díaz en la frontera texana, 1875–1877." *Historia Mexicana* 5:373–410.

McLean, Malcolm Dallas. *Vida y obras de Guillermo Prieto.* Mexico: Fondo de Cultura Económico, 1960.

Mecham, Lloyd J. "The Jefe Político in Mexico." *Southwestern Social Science Quarterly* 13:333–52.

Mejía, Francisco. *Memorias de don Francisco Mejía.* Mexico: Secretaría de Hacienda y Crédito Público, 1958.

Mena Brito, Bernardino. *Reestructuración histórica de Yucatán.* 3 vols. Mexico: Editores Mexicanos Unidos, 1965–69.

Mexico. Cámara de Diputados. *Historia constitucional, 1847–1917.* Vol. 2 of *Derecho del pueblo mexicano: México a través de sus constituciones.* 8 vols. 1967.

Mexico. Congreso. *Diario de los debates, quinto congreso constitucional de la unión.* 4 vols. Mexico: Imprenta del Gobierno, 1871–73.

Mexico. Congreso. *Diario de los debates, sexto congreso constitucional de la unión.* 4 vols. Mexico: Imprenta del Gobierno, 1872–74.

Mexico. Diario Oficial. *Recopilación de leyes, decretos, y providencias de los poderes legislativo y ejecutivo de la unión formada por la redacción del Diario Oficial.* Vol. 10. Mexico: Imprenta del Gobierno, 1873.

Mexico. Secretaría de Relaciones Exteriores. *Correspondencia diplomática relativa a las invasiones del territorio mexicano por fuerzas de los Estados Unidos, 1873 a 1877.* Mexico: Imprenta Ignacio Cumplido, 1878.

Meyer, Eugenia W. de. *La figura prócer de Felipe Berriozábal.* Cuadernos de Lectura Popular: La Victoria de la República, Mexico: Secretaría de Educación Pública, 1966.

Meyer, Jean. *Problemas campesinos y revueltas agrarias, 1821–1910.* Mexico: SepSetentas, 1973.

Monterde, Francisco. *Ignacio Ramírez, el Nigromante.* Mexico, 1944.
Muro, Manuel. *Historia de San Luis Potosí.* 3 vols. San Luis Potosí: Imprenta de F. L. González, 1910.
Ochoa Campos, Moisés. *Historia del Estado de Guerrero.* Mexico: Porrúa Hnos., 1968.
Ordaz, Emilio. *La cuestión presidencial.* Mexico: Imprenta de Francisco Díaz de León, 1876.
Palavicini, Félix F. *México: historia de su evolución constructiva.* Mexico: Distribuidora Editorial, 1945.
Parades Colin, Joaquín. *Apuntes históricos de Tehuacán.* 2d ed. N.p., 1953.
Parkes, Henry Bamford. *A History of Mexico.* 3d rev. ed. Boston: Houghton Mifflin Co., 1970.
Paz, Ireneo. *Algunas campañas: memorias.* 2d ed. 3 vols. Mexico: Imprenta y Litografía de Ireneo Paz, 1884–85.
———. *México actual: galería de contemporáneos.* Mexico: Imprenta y Litografía de Ireneo Paz, 1898.
Pérez Verdía, Luis. *Historia particular del estado de Jalisco desde los primeros tiempos de que hay noticia hasta nuestros días.* 2d ed. 3 vols. Guadalajara: Gráfica Editorial, 1951–54.
Powell, T. G. *El liberalismo y el campesinado en el centro de México, 1850 a 1876.* Mexico: SepSetentas, 1974.
Prida, Ramón. *De la dictadura a la anarquía.* El Paso, Tex.: Imprenta de El Paso del Norte, 1914.
Prieto, Alejandro. *Historia, geografía y estadística del Estado de Tamaulipas.* Mexico: Tipografía Escalerillas Núm. 13, 1873.
Prieto, Guillermo. *Lecciones de historia patria escritas para los alumnos del Colegio Militar.* Mexico: Secretaría de Fomento, 1886.
Purcell, William L. *Frontier Mexico, 1875–1894: Letters of William L. Purcell.* San Antonio, Tex.: Naylor Co., 1963.
Quevedo y Zubieta, Salvador. *El caudillo, continuación de Porfirio Díaz, ensayo de psicología histórica.* Mexico: Librería de la viuda de C. Bouret, 1909.
———. *El general González y su gobierno en México.* 2 vols. Mexico: Establecimiento Tipográfico de Patoni, 1884–85.
Rabasa, Emilio. *La evolución histórica de México.* 2d ed. Mexico: Editorial Porrúa, 1956.
———. *La organización política de México: la constitución y la dictadura.* Madrid: Editorial América, 1912.
Rangel Frias, Raúl. *Gerónimo Treviño, héroes y epígonos.* Cuadernos de Lectura Popular: La Victoria de la República. Monterrey: Secretaría de Educación Pública, 1967.
Relyea, Pauline Safford. *Diplomatic Relations between the United States and Mexico under Porfirio Díaz, 1876–1910.* Northhampton, Mass.: Smith College Press, 1924.
Reyes, Bernardo. *El ejército mexicano: monografía histórica escrita en 1899 por el*

general don Bernardo Reyes para la obra México y su evolución social.
Mexico: J. Ballesca y Cía., 1901.

Reyes de la Maza, Luis. *El teatro en México con Lerdo y Díaz, 1873–1879.*
Mexico: Instituto de Investigaciones Estéticas, Universidad Nacional
Autónoma de México, 1963.

Rippy, Merril. "Theories of History: Twelve Mexicans." *The Americas*
17:223–40.

Riva Palacio, Vicente. *Historia de la administración de don Sebastián Lerdo de
Tejada.* Mexico: El Padre Cobos, 1875.

Roeder, Ralph. *Hacia el México moderno, Porfirio Díaz.* 2 vols. Mexico: Fondo de
Cultura Económico, 1973.

———. *Juárez and His Mexico.* 2 vols. New York: Viking Press, 1947.

Roel, Santiago. *Apuntes para la historia de Nuevo León.* 2 vols. Monterrey, 1938.

Rojas, Basilio. *Miahuatlán, un pueblo de México: monografía del distrito de
Miahuatlán, Estado de Oaxaca.* 3 vols. Mexico: Gráfica Cervantina,
1960–64.

Romero Vargas, Ignacio. *Manifestación que hace al Estado de Puebla el ciudadano
Ignacio Romero Vargas, diputado por el primer distrito de la capital, de los
hechos ocurridos con motivo de la elección de gobernador constitucional.* Puebla: Impreso por José María Osorio, 1868.

Saldivar, Gabriel. *Historia compendiada de Tamaulipas.* Mexico: Editorial Beatriz
de Silva, 1945.

Santibáñez, Manuel. *Reseña histórica del cuerpo de Ejército de Oriente.* 2 vols.
Mexico: Tipografía de la Oficina Impresora del Timbre, 1892–93.

Scholes, Walter V. "*El Mensajero* and the Election of 1871 in Mexico." *The
Americas* 5:61–67.

———. *Mexican Politics during the Juárez Regime, 1855–1872.* Columbia: University of Missouri Press, 1969.

Sierra, Justo. *Evolución política del pueblo mexicano.* Mexico: Fondo de Cultura
Económico, 1940.

———. *Juárez, su obra y su tiempo.* 2d ed. Mexico: Porrúa, 1971.

———. *Periodismo político.* Vol. 4 of *Obras completas del Maestro Justo Sierra.*
Edited by Agustín Yáñez. 14 vols. Mexico: Universidad Nacional Autónoma de México, 1948–50.

Tagle, Protasio Pérez. *Circular expedida por el licenciado Protasio P. Tagle, ministro de gobernación, en que se dan a conocer las negociaciones entabladas con el
C. licenciado José María Iglesias para dar termino a la guerra civil y que
fueron rotas por su parte.* Mexico: Imprenta del Gobierno, 1876.

Taracena, Angel. *Porfirio Díaz.* Figuras y Episodios de la Historia de México.
Mexico: Editorial Jus, 1960.

Torrea, Juan Manuel. *La vida de una institución gloriosa: el Colegio Militar,
1821–1930.* Mexico: Tallares Tipográficos Centenario, 1931.

Tovar, Pantaleón. *Historia parlamentaria del cuarto congreso constitucional.* 4 vols.
Mexico: Imprenta de Ignacio Cumplido, 1872–74.

Trens, Manuel B. *Historia de Veracruz.* 4 vols. Mexico: La Impresora, 1946–50.
Valadés, José C. *Breve historia del porfirismo.* Mexico: Editores Mexicanos Unidos, 1971.
————. *El pensamiento político de Benito Juárez.* Mexico: Editorial Porrúa, 1956.
————. *El porfirismo: historia de un régimen, el nacimiento, 1876–1884.* Mexico: Antigua Librería Robredo, de José Porrúa e hijos, 1941.
Vallarta, Ignacio L. *Votos del C. Ignacio L. Vallarta, presidente de la Suprema Corte de Justicia en los negocios mas notables resueltos por este tribunal.* 2 vols. Mexico: Imprenta de Francisco Díaz de León, 1879–81.
Vanderwood, Paul J. "Los rurales: producto de una necesidad social." *Historia Mexicana* 22:34–51.
Vasconcelos, José. *Breve historia de México.* Mexico: Botas, 1944.
Velasco Valdés, Miguel. *Historia del periodismo mexicano.* Mexico: Librería de Manuel Porrúa, 1955.
Velázquez, Primo Feliciano. *Historia de San Luis Potosí.* 4 vols. Mexico: Sociedad Mexicana de Geografía y Estadística, 1946–48.
Webb, Walter Prescott. *The Texas Rangers: A Century of Frontier Defense.* 2d ed. Austin: University of Texas Press, 1965.
Webster, Michael G. "Intrigue on the Rio Grande: The Rio Bravo Affair of 1875." *Southwestern Historical Quarterly* 74:149–64.
Wheat, Raymond C. *Francisco Zarco, el portavoz liberal de la reforma.* Translated by Antonio Castro Leal. Mexico: Editorial Porrúa, 1957.
Yáñez, Agustín. "Justo Sierra y el porfiriato." *Cuadros Americanos* 43:201–13.
Zarco, Francisco. *Textos políticos.* Mexico: Universidad Nacional Autónoma de México, 1957.
Zamacois, Niceto de. *Historia de México desde sus tiempos más remotos hasta nuestros días.* 18 vols. Mexico: F. J. Parres y Cía., 1876–82.
Zayas Enríquez, Rafael de. *Benito Juárez: su vida, su obra.* 2d ed. Mexico: SepSetentas, 1971.
————. *Los Estados Unidos Mexicanos: sus progresos en veinte años de pas, 1877–1897: estudio histórico y estadístico, fundado en los datos oficiales más recientes y completos.* New York: H. A. Rost Co., n.d.
————. *Porfirio Díaz.* New York: D. Appleton and Co., 1908.
Zorrilla, Luis G. *Historia de las relaciones entre México y los Estados Unidos de América, 1800–1958.* 2 vols. Mexico: Editorial Porrúa, 1965.

Index

DATE DUE